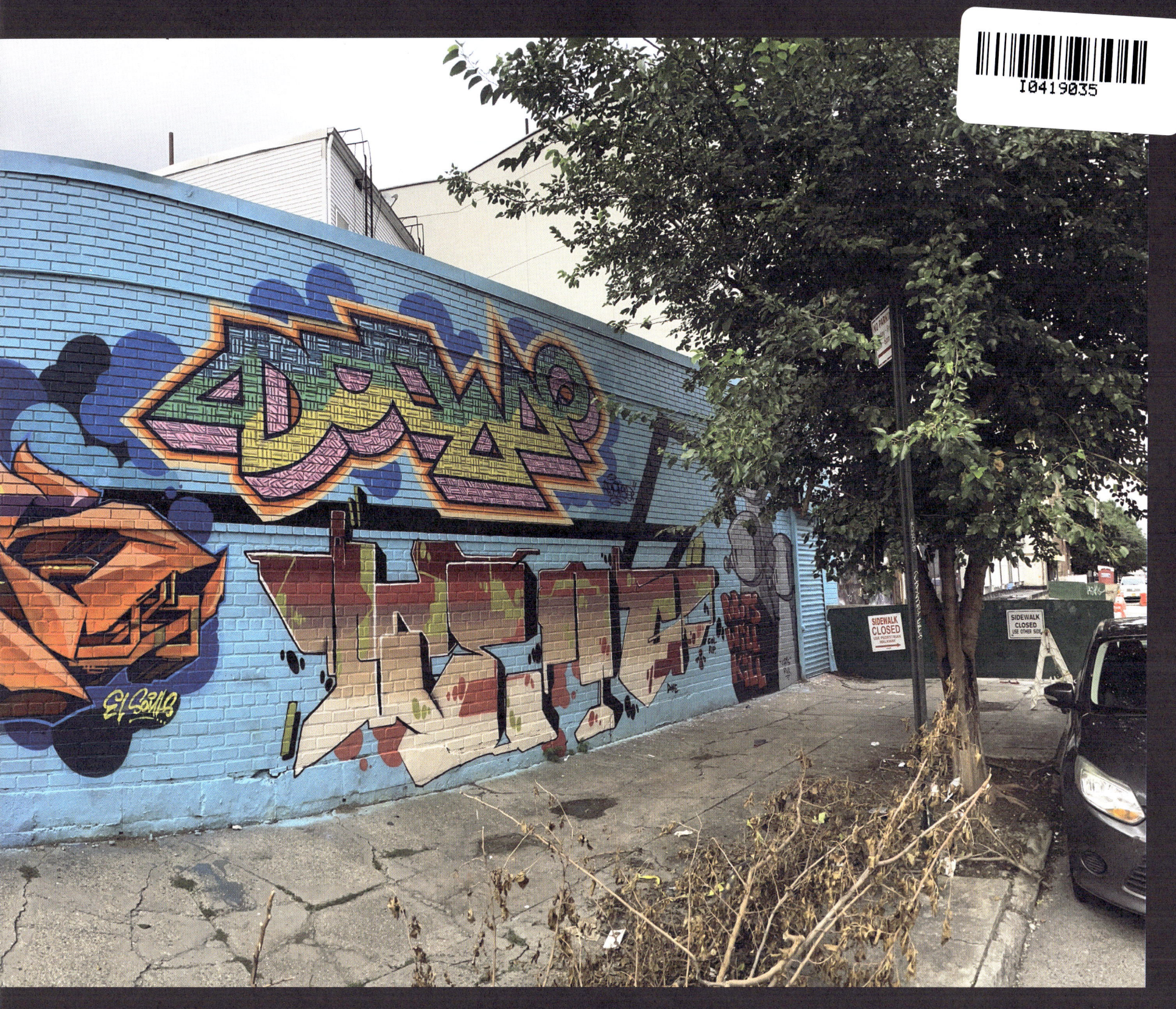

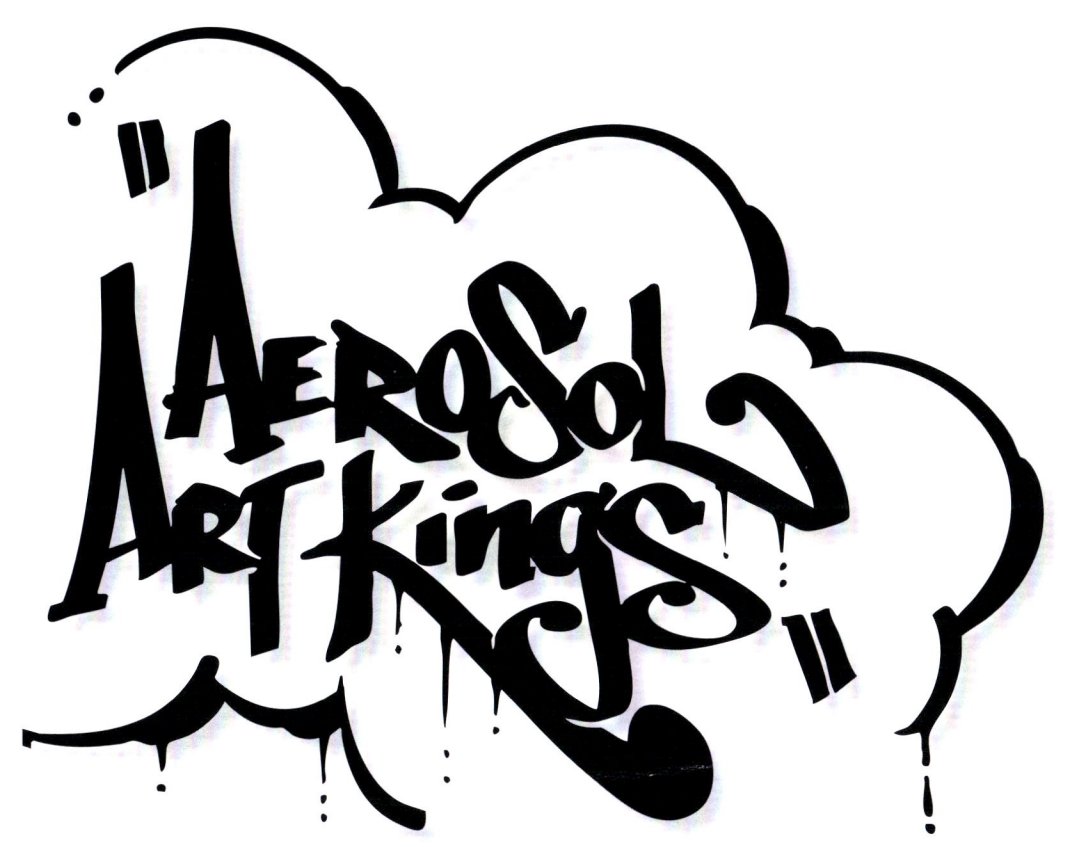

PHOTOGRAPHS OF STREET ART
IN NEW YORK CITY, 2018-2024

KURT BOONE

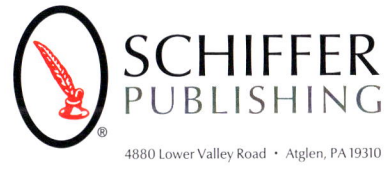

SCHIFFER
PUBLISHING

4880 Lower Valley Road • Atglen, PA 19310

Library of Congress Control Number: 2025930169

Designed by Jack Chappell

Type set in A Dripping Marker/Avenir/Micro Technic/Univers

ISBN: 978-0-7643-7027-4
ePub: 978-1-5073-0614-7
Printed in China
10 9 8 7 6 5 4 3 2 1

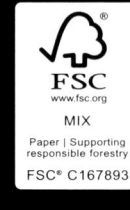

Published by Schiffer Publishing, Ltd.
4880 Lower Valley Road
Atglen, PA 19310
Phone: (610) 593-1777; Fax: (610) 593-2002
Email: info@schifferbooks.com
Web: www.schifferbooks.com

For our complete selection of fine books on this and related subjects, please visit our website at www.schifferbooks.com. You may also write for a free catalog.

Schiffer Publishing's titles are available at special discounts for bulk purchases for sales promotions or premiums. Special editions, including personalized covers, corporate imprints, and excerpts, can be created in large quantities for special needs. For more information contact the publisher.

TABLE OF CONTENTS

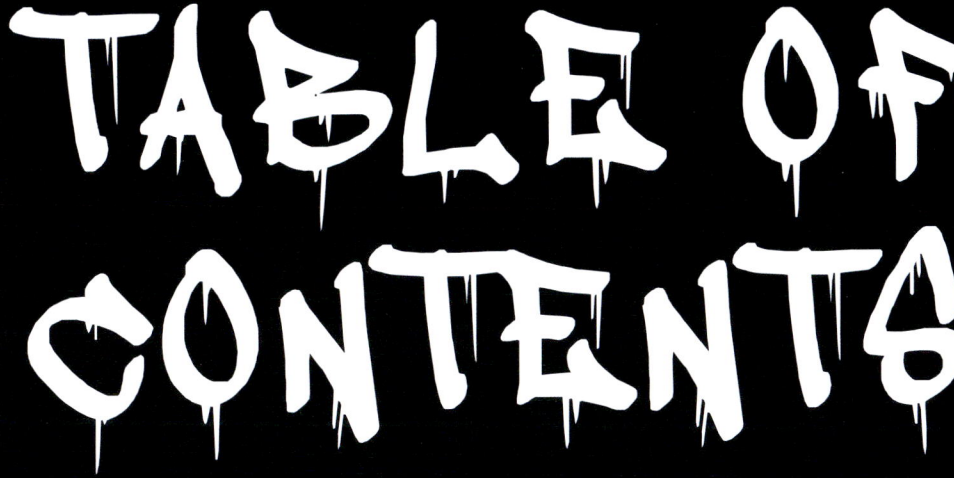

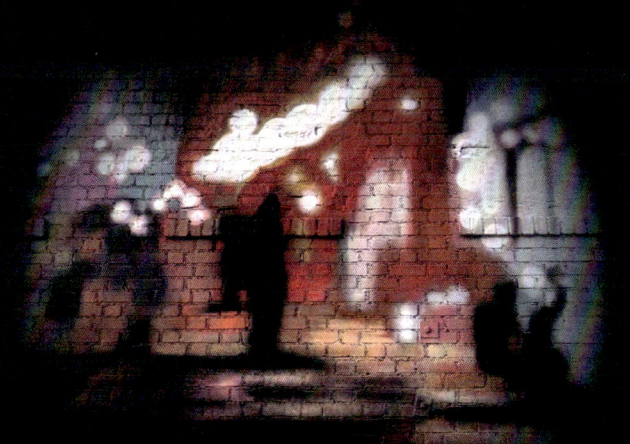

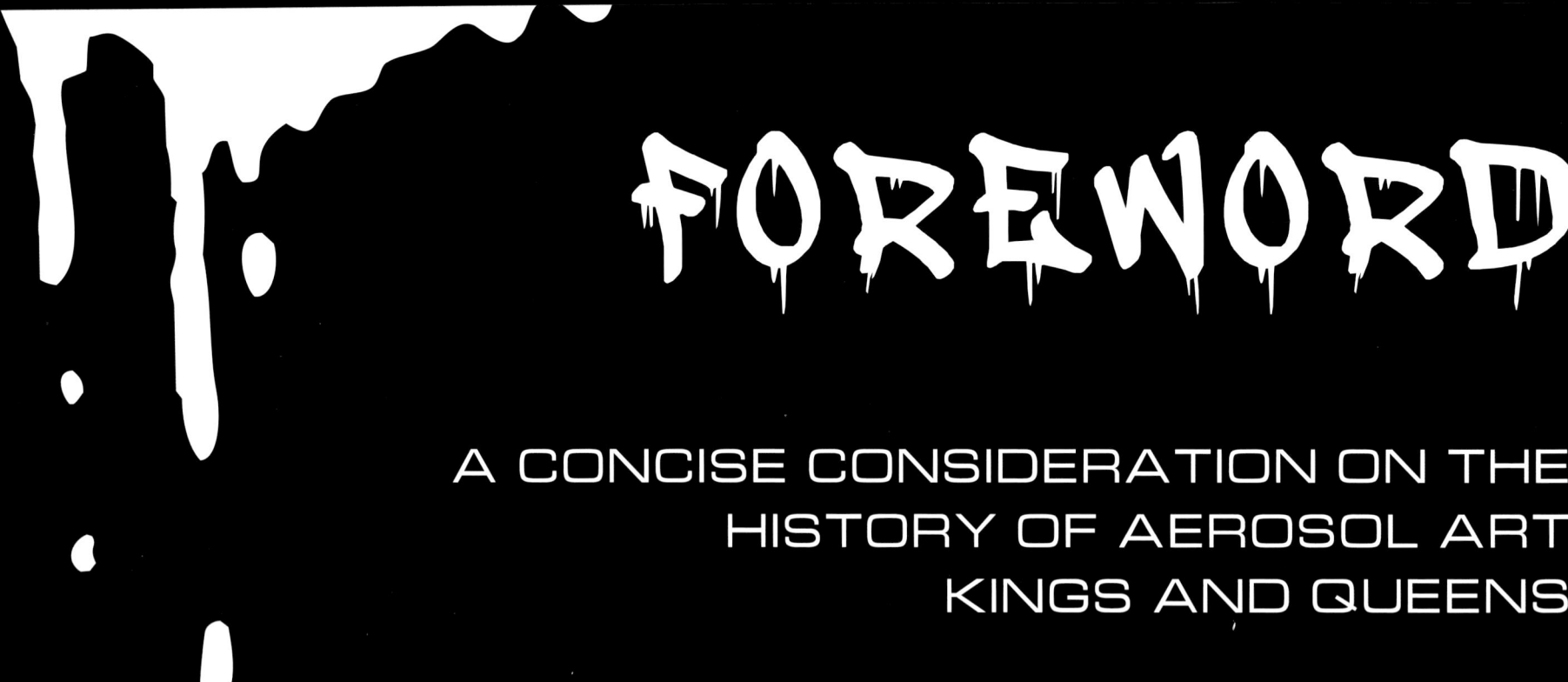

FOREWORD

A CONCISE CONSIDERATION ON THE HISTORY OF AEROSOL ART KINGS AND QUEENS

One may marvel at a mural or a masterpiece painted on the streets of their city, without knowing the history. However, the knowledge of history adds layers of nuance to a casual appreciation for the art form. The transformation of indiscreet tags into an international art movement is thanks largely to the aerosol cannister, better known as the spray can.

While who was "first" is a matter of contention, and many matters of the early days are a question of oral history, Philadelphia's CORNBREAD is often credited as the foremost for writing his name across the City of Brotherly Love in the late '60s with a spray can. Around the same time, Mike 171 and SJK 171 were scrawling their names across Washington Heights, as were other New York youths in Inwood and the South Bronx, not knowing the impact they would have. While the who, where, and when was first is debatable, New York's legacy reigns supreme over the culture.

Coming from humble working-class and impoverished backgrounds, these young writers used their names as a way of imprinting themselves on a world that would otherwise ignore them. When starting out, these writers were teenagers and kids, making do with markers and household items before they found the power of the can. Frequently they learned via informal mentorships, learning from an uncle or older

brother how to get their lettering right. As the phenomenon spread, it became necessary to elevate your game to have your name stand out, leading to more-creative elements being incorporated, such as arrows, stars, and other inscriptive aspects. But what really advanced the art was the adoption of spray paint.

Without the appropriation of the aerosol can into the arsenal of graffiti tools, the medium could never have evolved to its current level of complexity. Coming from lesser means, writers would often go about "racking" (stealing) spray cans from neighborhood hardware stores. Aerosol offered several advantages to writers—with a can, they could cover more space on a wall, allowing bigger tags and quicker drying than markers, and the illegal nature of the work meant the need to execute a mission fast, for which the ease of a can could allow one to get up and get out without a detection. It's for this reason that aerosol remains the dominant device for both graffiti and street art.

Necessity is said to be the mother of invention, but perhaps convenience is the father. A paint salesman, Ed Seymour, created the first spray can while working to cover a radiator in aluminum coating. For many of the same reasons that it was adopted by writers, the device was integrated into the autobody and home-furnishing industries for painting.

Utilizing these aerosol cannisters, writers would modify their cans to better suit their needs, experimenting with different caps to find which were best for crisp lines or thick fillers. Eventually, companies would start producing custom caps for artists. Early producers of aerosol paint included American companies such as Krylon & Rust-Oleum; however, they were hesitant to market directly toward artists due to the illicit nature of the craft and the social condemnation of the act.

By the '90s, though, European companies such as Molotow and Montana had gotten into aerosol paint and were selling high-quality equipment advertised directly toward artists. As competition developed in this growing market, a wider range of colors became available, as well as more options in terms of caps, allowing artists to flourish.

While paint is obviously a key part of the equation, the surface you paint on is just as important a component in the formula. Whether it's a wall, a fence, a roll-down gate, a plywood board, or a full-scale building, artists must approach the terrain with tact. Certain materials can soak up paint, or the surface can distort an image (the ridges of a roll-down are a well-known headache for aerosol creatives).

Over the past few decades, graffiti and its offspring, street art, have seen greater social acceptance; as such, the criminality has lessened (though graff writers will still find themselves in the crosshairs of the cops). Due in large part to the image-focused nature of social media platforms such as Instagram, it's easier now for artists to build a wide following and a successful career off their art, with major brands partnering with creatives, drawn in by the impressive imagery and allure of aerosol art, with the spark of rebellion it represents. Even more, the culture has developed into a thriving community, with international festivals and paint jams.

While the scene has gone international, New York remains at the heart of aerosol art culture. As such, Kurt's photos showcase the best of the best in the Big Apple, displaying the incredible depth of what one can do with spray paint. This book is split into four chapters: "Social Justice," "Style Writing," "Street Art," and "Murals," each demonstrating an assortment of art that a creative mind can concoct. Art, particularly ephemeral art, is almost impossible to neatly categorize, and these chapters blend and blur into one another like lines of paint dripping down a wall.

"Social Justice" focuses on art created during and inspired by the tumult of the pandemic and the subsequent racial strife. In the wake of George Floyd's murder, artists took to the streets to express their discontent with the status quo by painting on the plywood walls of boarded-up businesses, showing solidarity and social activism. Elsewhere, "Style Writing" emphasizes contemporary graffiti and the complexities of lettering, depicting the myriad ways a talented artist can work an aerosol can. "Street Art" centers on the more colorful and playful side of the medium, highlighting walls meant to radiate and shine cheerfully, whether seen in person or through a post. Meanwhile, "Murals" is aerosol art taken to its greatest heights, the composition of a dozen cans and creators to construct art in large scale. Magnified across whole buildings, murals are the peak of what one can do with a can.

Aerosol art, whether it's graffiti or street art, is a creative form unlike any other, and this essay only scratches the surface of the rich history the medium is made of. While writing may provide some insight, flip through this book to see for yourself—as they say, a picture is worth a thousand words.

—T. K. Mills

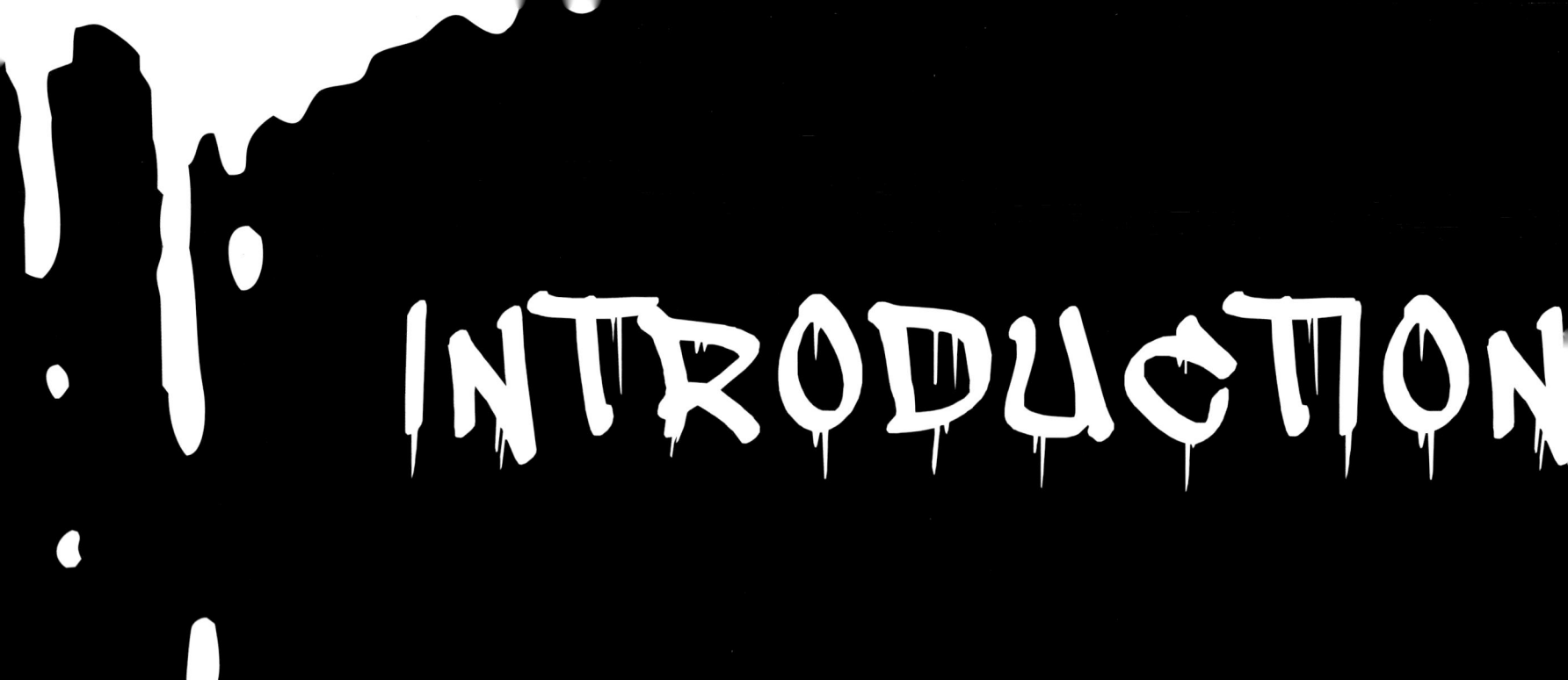

INTRODUCTION

have been traveling across the streets of New York City for the last six years photographing aerosol art wherever I saw it or, nowadays, at dedicated street and graffiti art festivals. I began with a lucky break in 2018 through curator and graffiti artist James Top, who gave me the opportunity to photograph the storied Graffiti Hall of Fame in Harlem. I watched some of the innovators of aerosol art such as Cope 2, Wane COD, Delta 2, and Skeme work on their art pieces. In 2019, I had the opportunity again to photograph the Graffiti Hall of Fame. Fascinated by street artists handling their spray paint cans to create their art, I would spend hours photographing as many different artists as possible, having three cameras at my disposal to get the best shot. My aim was to get a perfect photograph of the completed street art mural or style-writing masterpiece. After two years of photographing the Graffiti Hall of Fame, I decided to publish an artist book titled *Aerosol Art Culture: A Day at Graffiti Hall of Fame*.

In 2020, I found myself on the streets of Soho in Manhattan photographing murals and street art on plywood that was used to protect storefront windows. This was during the Black Lives Matter social justice movement to end police brutality in United States and to protest the tragic murder of George Floyd, a African American, by a Minneapolis police officer. I photographed over 400 social justice artworks in addition to some street art related to the COVID-19 pandemic. I knew the

street art I was photographing in this short time window, from the end of May to September, was historic. I asked one of my book designers, Josefina Modeste, to design me a catalog for 300 murals that I titled *Fresh Plywood NYC: Artists Rise Up in Age of Black Lives Matter* so the New York City community and the world could see what had happened in Soho. *Fresh Plywood NYC* would bring me many accolades from the New York City communities for my documentary photography, including an appearance on PBS Metro Focus.

While marketing *Fresh Plywood NYC* and photographing a mural project commission by New York Public Library with artists One Rad Latina and Soho Renaissance Factory, I met Daniel Sacks, a representative of Mana Public Arts. Mana Public Arts had an initiative to collect social justice murals on plywood boards that were all over Soho. Daniel invited me to take a tour of Mana Contemporary in Jersey City and subsequently the opportunity to photograph the Jersey City Mural Festival, an event that provided a platform for local and international muralists and street artists to showcase their artwork, as well as to support local businesses that had been adversely affected by the COVID-19 pandemic.

I spent many days photographing the Jersey City Mural Festival which had over seventy aerosol artists participating. I photographed the artists at work and the completed murals, though I went back weeks after the festival, multiple times, to photograph the completed murals to ge the best shots of the murals that I could. Seeing another opportunity to showcase my street art photography, I produced a catalog of Jersey City Mural Festival that was designed by Anthony Firetto. On the basis of the photographic work I did at Jersey City Mural Festival in 2021, I was invited by Mana Public Arts to photograph their Miami Mural Festival during Art Basel Week. The Miami Mural Festival gave me access to photographing top-tier aerosol artists from around the world.

In 2022, I started learning about more street and graffiti art festivals in New York City, and I continued to photograph street and graffiti art around the city wherever I saw it, using my iPhone camera most of the time. Though when I went to Graffiti Hall of Fame, Bed-Stuy Walls, Boone Avenue Walls, Welling Court Mural Project, or Bushwick Collective, I brought my Canon DLSR EOS Rebel 6 or 7 and a point-and-shoot camera. The aerosol art in this book is divided into the sections "Street Art," "Style Writing," "Murals," and "Social Justice." There are over 200 artworks from around the city on a myriad of surfaces by many different aerosol artists. The book also includes the name of each artist or artists who painted the artwork, whether it was style writing or a mural, and the location of the artwork in the city and an indication if the artwork was part of a New York City art festival production. Sometimes it's hard to read the artist's name in graffiti style writing, or a street art painting doesn't have a clear message but is beautifully done. I included it in the book because of its artistic merit, or the aerosol artist is re-nowned in the New York City Street art community. It is also very important to understand that street art is an ephemeral art form; most of the artwork photographed in this book is no longer there. The photograph becomes the permanent record of the artwork's existence.

A note about the title. There is some slang meaning, with the word "Kings" going back to 1970s graffiti culture. That meaning doesn't apply here and is not used today by most street artists. The "King" means that in the 1970s, a certain type of artist was known as a "King" because his name was painted on many MTA subway cars across all of New York City. Some artists at that time would even paint a crown by his name to signify he was a "King." The slang of graffiti culture is over fifty years old and, as mentioned, does not apply to the culture today per se and does not apply to the title *Aerosol Art Kings*. The word "Kings" in this context represents many artists, and the word "Aerosol" alludes to the artists' medium of spray paint. These artists primarily used spray paint to create their works of art on the streets, from fifty years ago, when the aerosol art culture began its development, to today. Not only are there hundreds or even thousands of artists creating public artwork with spray paint, but there are many manufacturers specializing in making cans of spray paint in a multitude of colors along with its accessories.

In the foreword, above, is a short essay by T. K. Mills, editor in chief of *Up Magazine*, on aerosol art movement and culture. I am still fascinated by spray paint art, and I hope you see what I see: that this wonderful art form began by youth in the late 1960s and '70s has grown to magnificent heights. *Aerosol Art Kings* is a contribution to the testament of this dynamic art form.

—Kurt Boone

STYLE WRITING

Style writing is the most popular form of graffiti and street art. It is often an entry point into the culture of aerosol art. It is the art of letter writing and the creation of names. Artists generally don't use their given name, but an alias. These groups of artists with aliases define themselves as writers. For early New York City writers from the late 1960s and early '70s such as Taki 183 and Mike 171, simply writing your name with markers on as many walls and surfaces, including subway cars around the city, was the thing to do. Later in the early days, instead of markers, aerosol paint was introduced into writing culture not long after. Early 1970s writers such as Staff 161, Phase 2, and Charmin 65 were spray-painting their names on New York City subway cars. By the late 1970s and early '80s, artists' style-writing groups, better known as crews, were formed. Some of the early crew names were the Ebony Dukes, Three Yard Boys, the Fabulous Five, IND's, Mad Transit Artists, and Rolling Thunder Writers. Style writers Futura, Lee Quinones, Crash, and Dondi would become world-renowned artists in later years. Today's style writing can be 40 to 50 feet high on a wall. In this chapter, you will see photos of works by many different artists. Each photo of the artwork is credited to the artist or the artist crew or both.

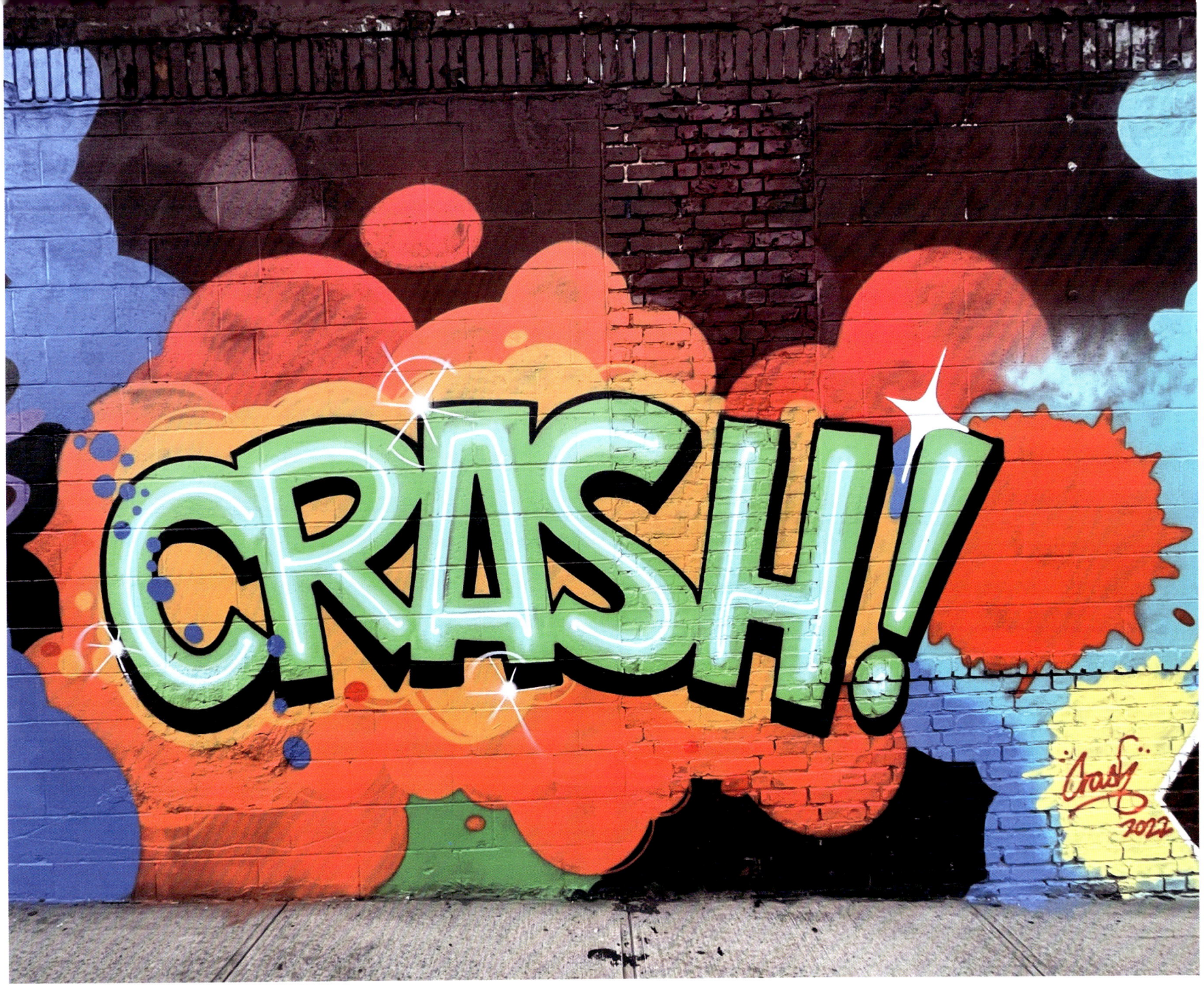

CRASH

A pioneering aerosol artist of the 1970s and '80s subway graffiti era. Now a muralist with an art studio practice, whose work has been exhibited around the world.
THE BRONX, PHOTOGRAPHED IN 2023

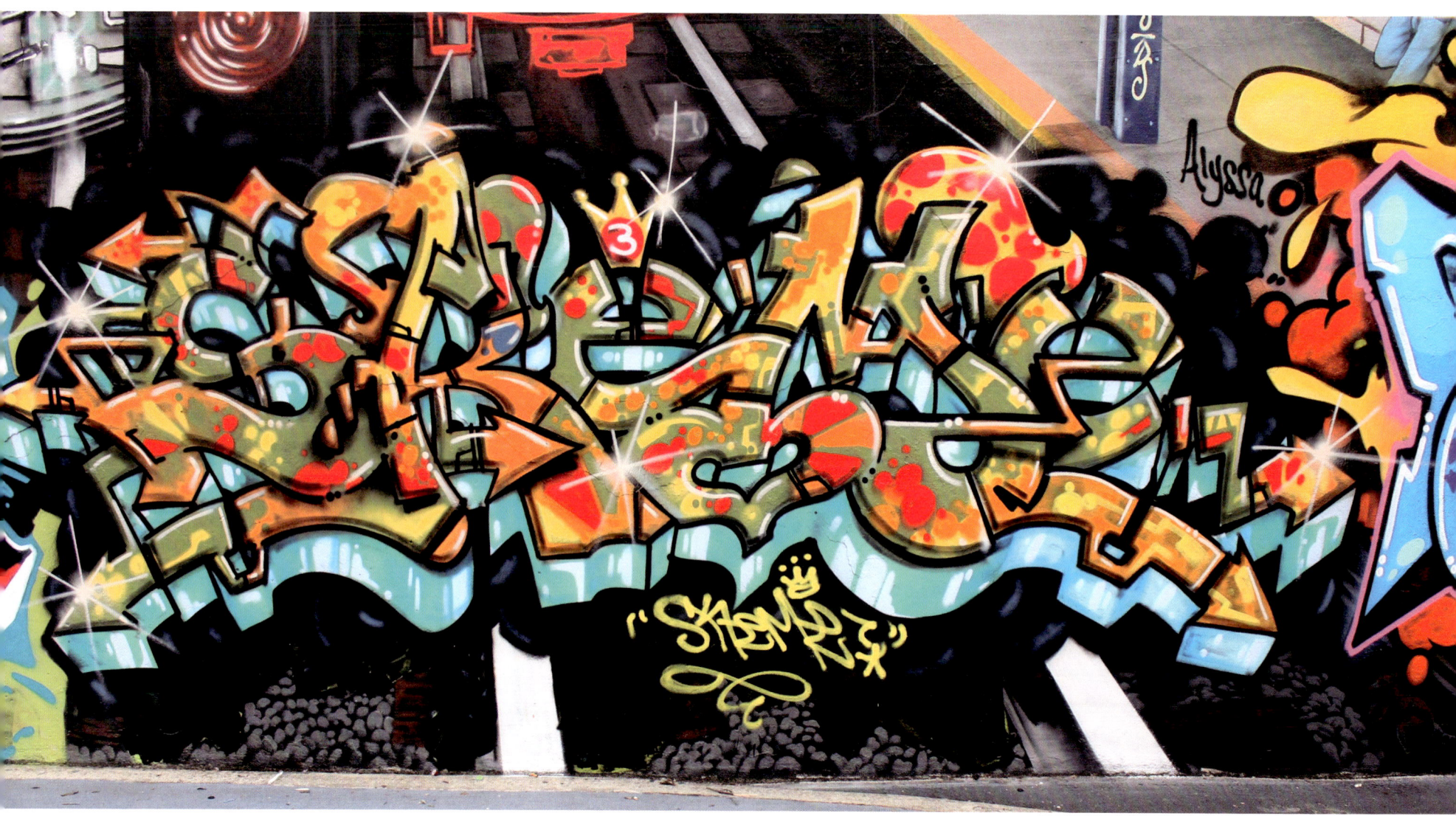

SKEME
Pioneer of aerosol art. One of the featured artists in the film *Style Wars*.
GRAFFITI HALL OF FAME, MANHATTAN, PHOTOGRAPHED IN 2018

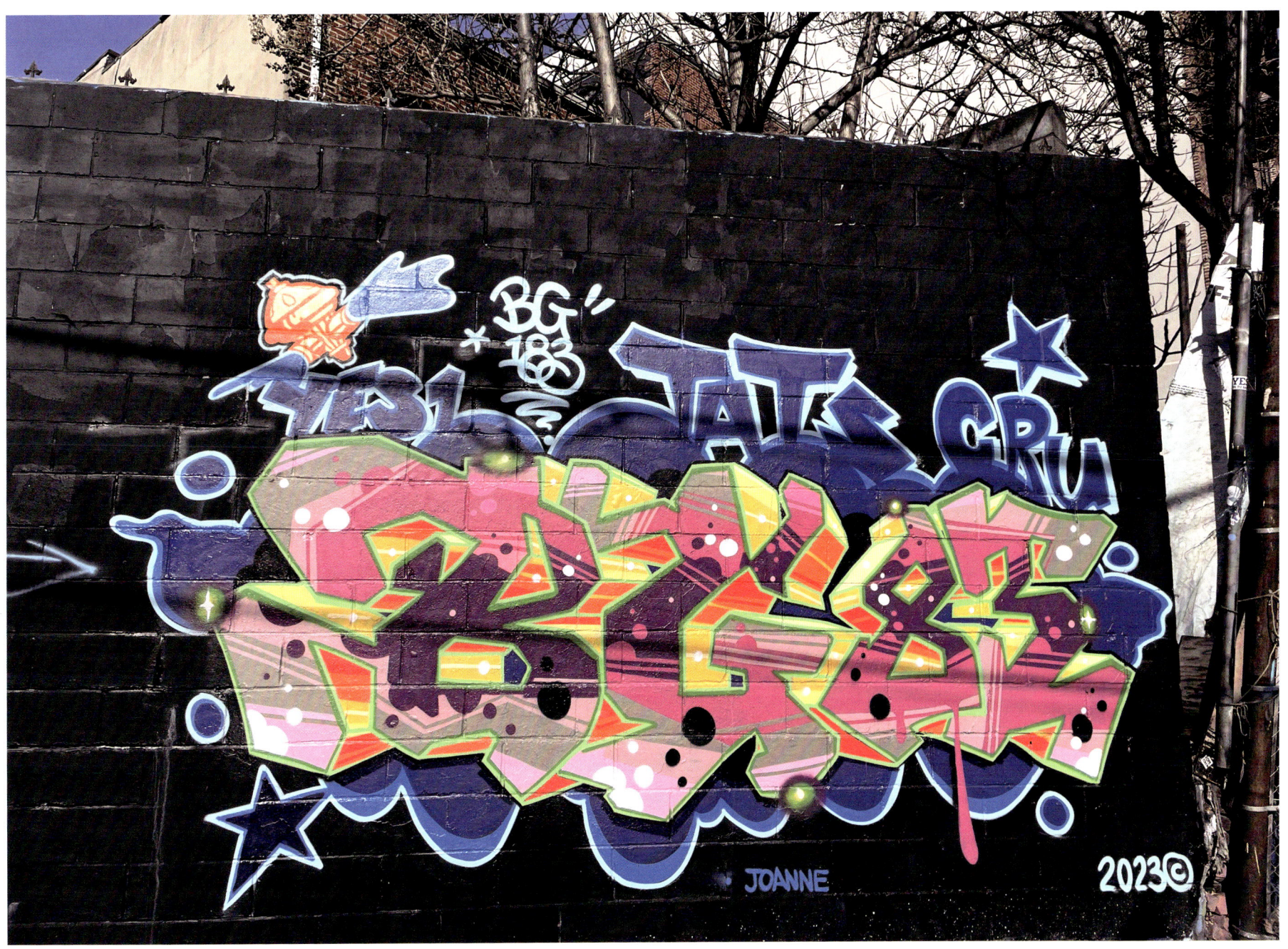

BG 183 TATS CRU

One of the founding members of Tats Cru and Mural Kings, and an innovative aerosol artist who has been among the leading artists in aerosol art culture since early 1980s.
WELLING COURT MURAL PROJECT, QUEENS, PHOTOGRAPHED IN 2024

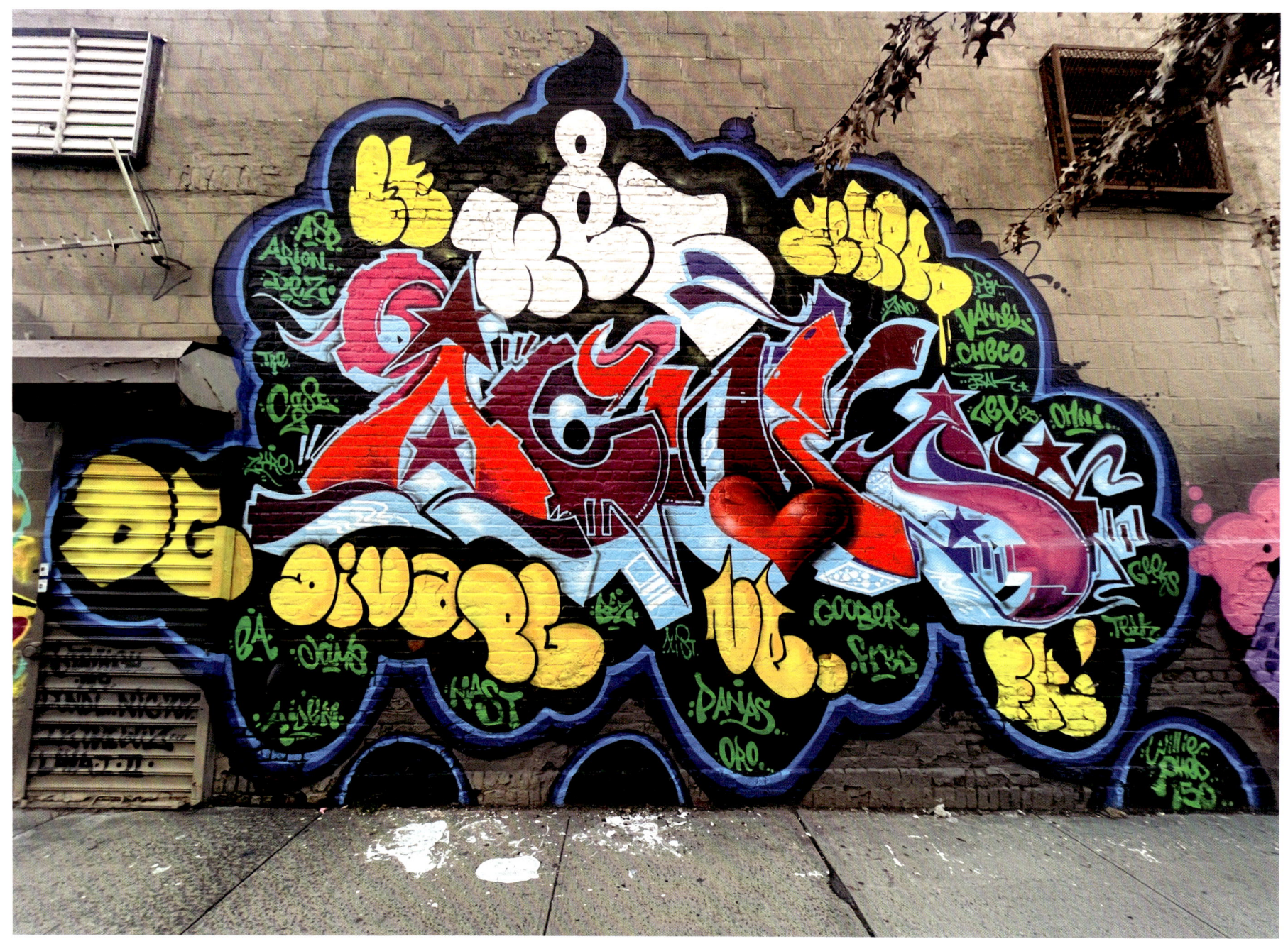

SPOT KMS CREW

Spot tribute wall to artists who have passed away.
BOONE AVENUE WALLS, THE BRONX, PHOTOGRAPHED IN 2022

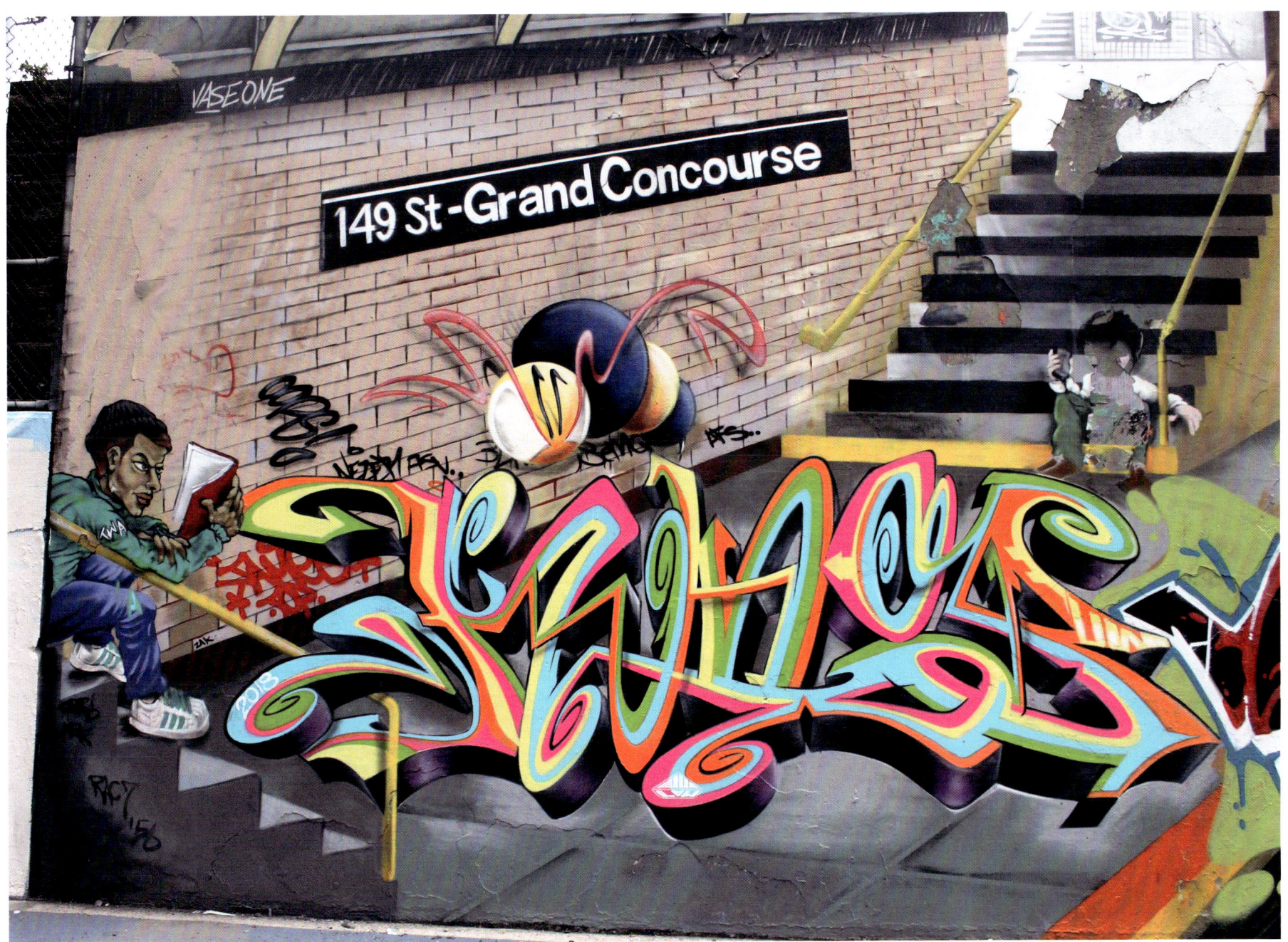

KING BEE UW

An in-demand aerosol artist since the 1980s, whose mural works can be seen across the city.
GRAFFITI HALL OF FAME, MANHATTAN, PHOTOGRAPHED IN 2018

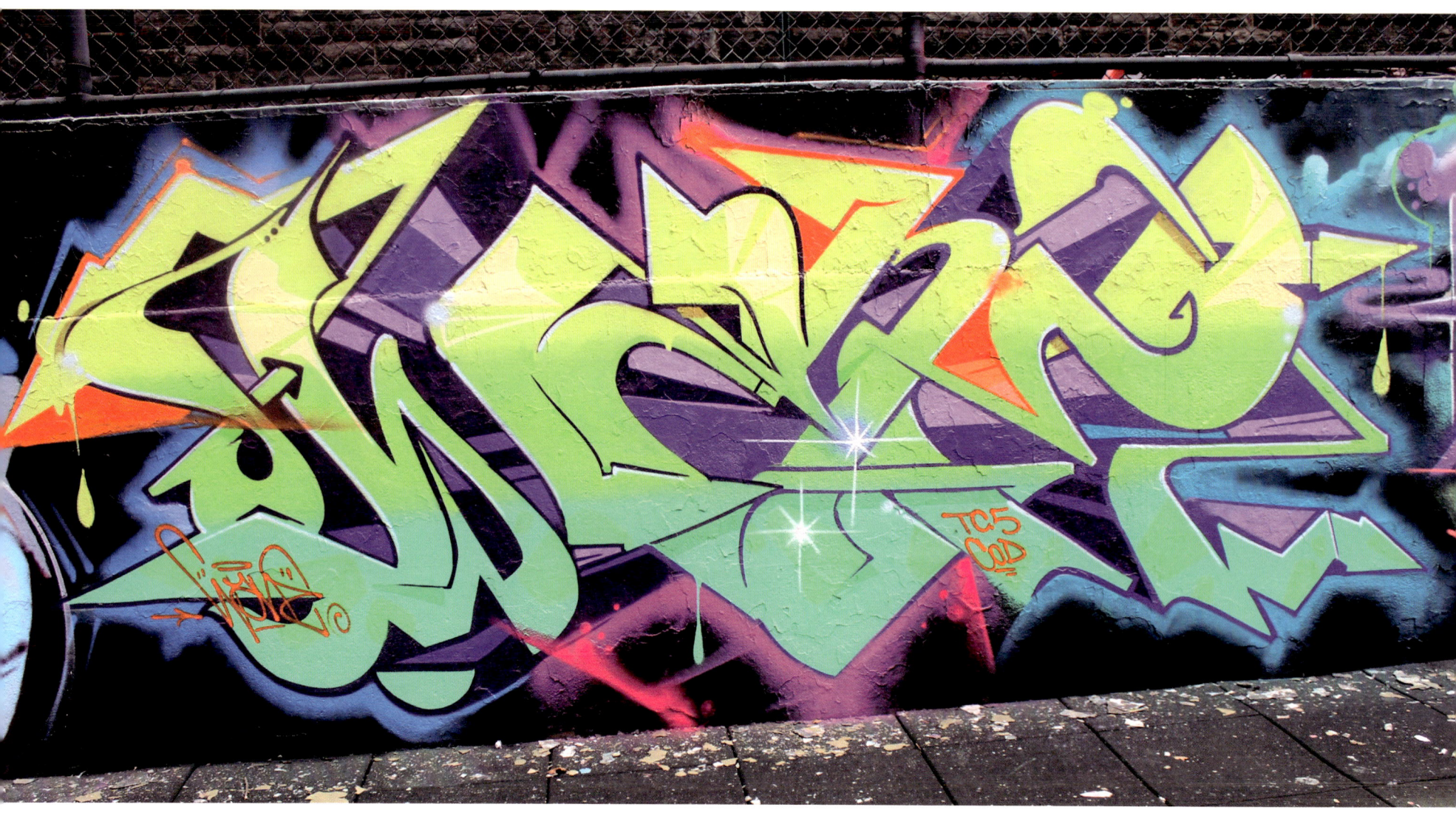

WANE COD
A well-known and internationally acclaimed aerosol artist, Wane Cod is also Montana Cans' sponsored artist.
GRAFFITI HALL OF FAME, MANHATTAN, PHOTOGRAPHED IN 2018

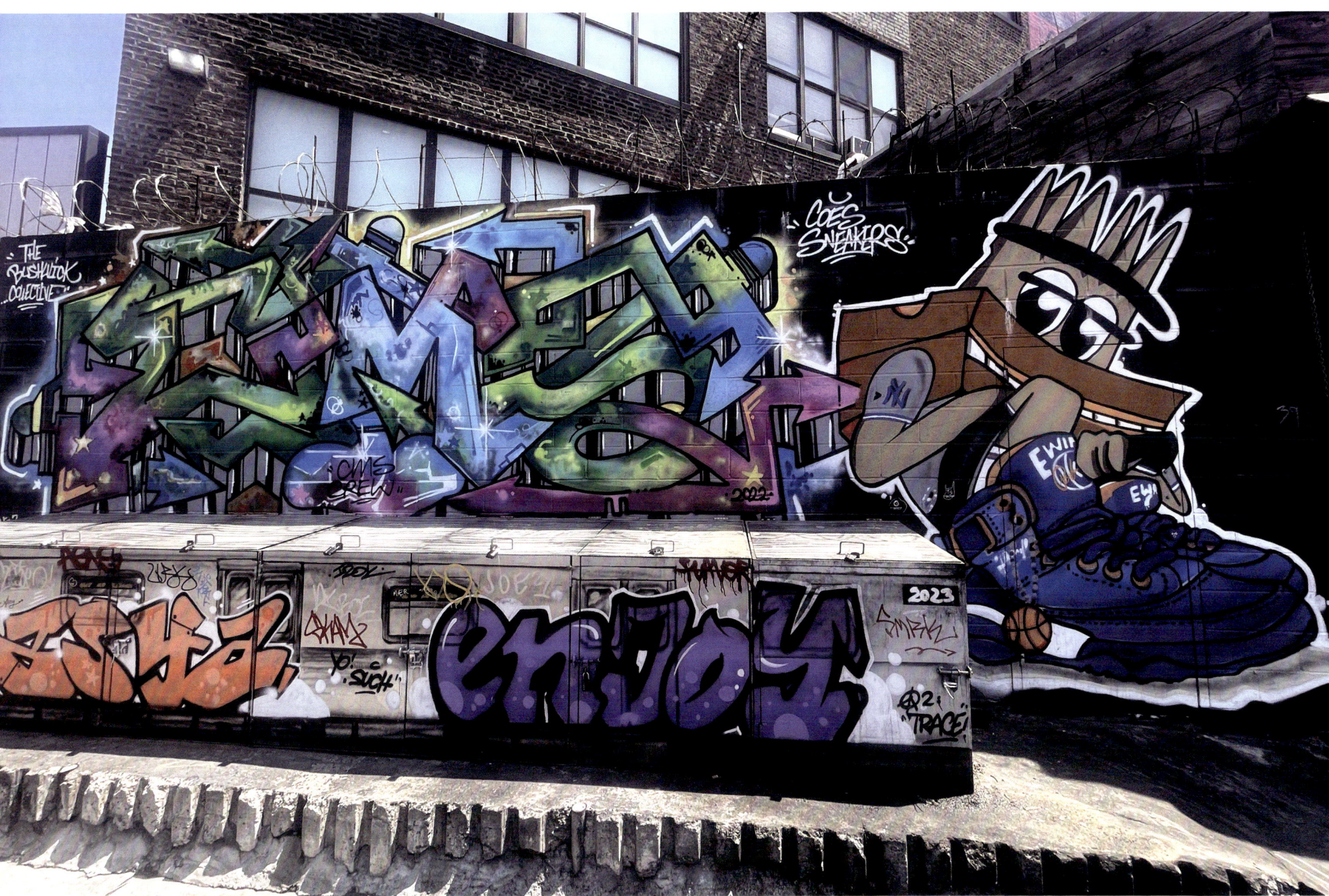

COES SNEAKERS

A great style-writing work of art with a character and sneakers. Coes Sneakers is known for his street art depicting sneaker culture.
BUSHWICK COLLECTIVE, BROOKLYN, PHOTOGRAPHED IN 2023

15

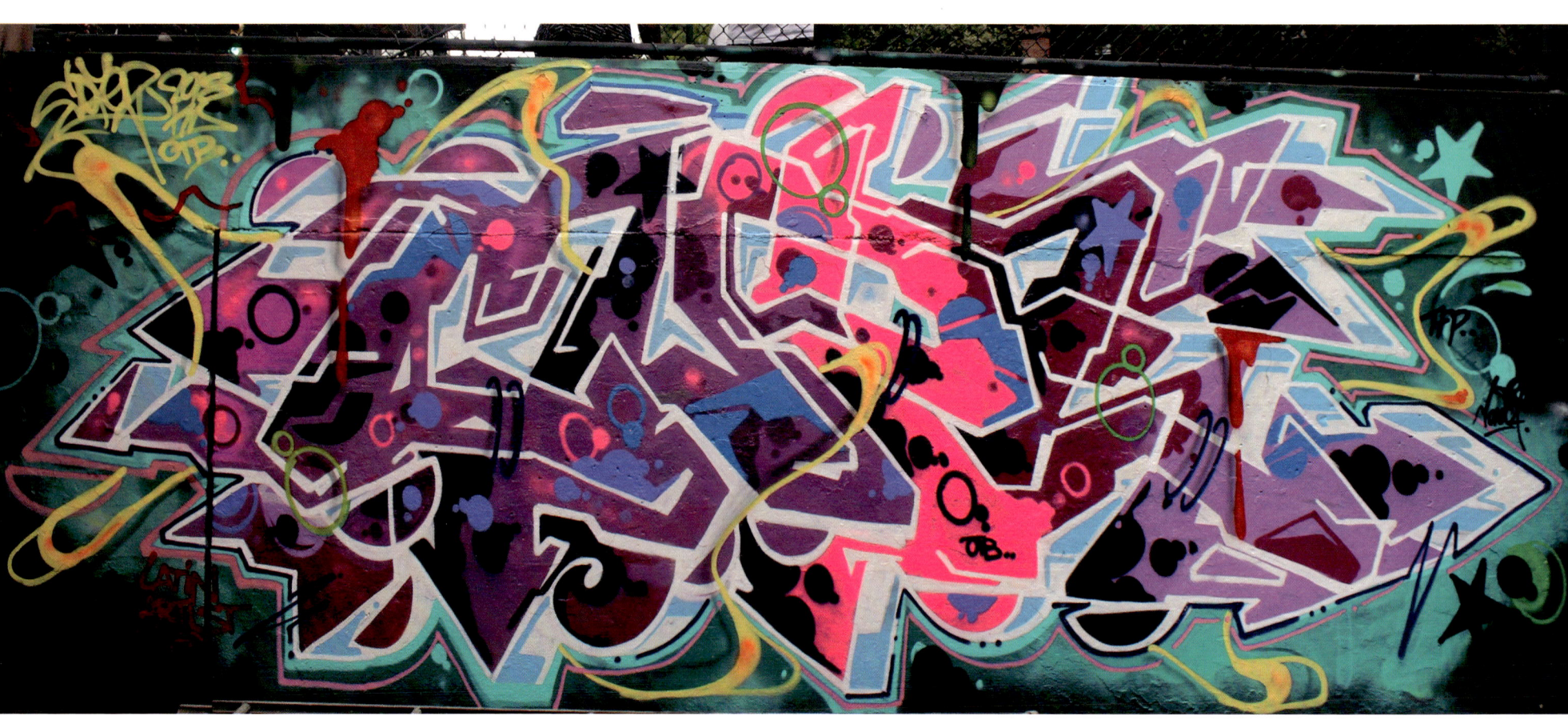

COPE 2

A world-famous aerosol artist from the Bronx, New York, whose monograph is published by Schiffer Books.
GRAFFITI HALL OF FAME, MANHATTAN, PHOTOGRAPHED IN 2018

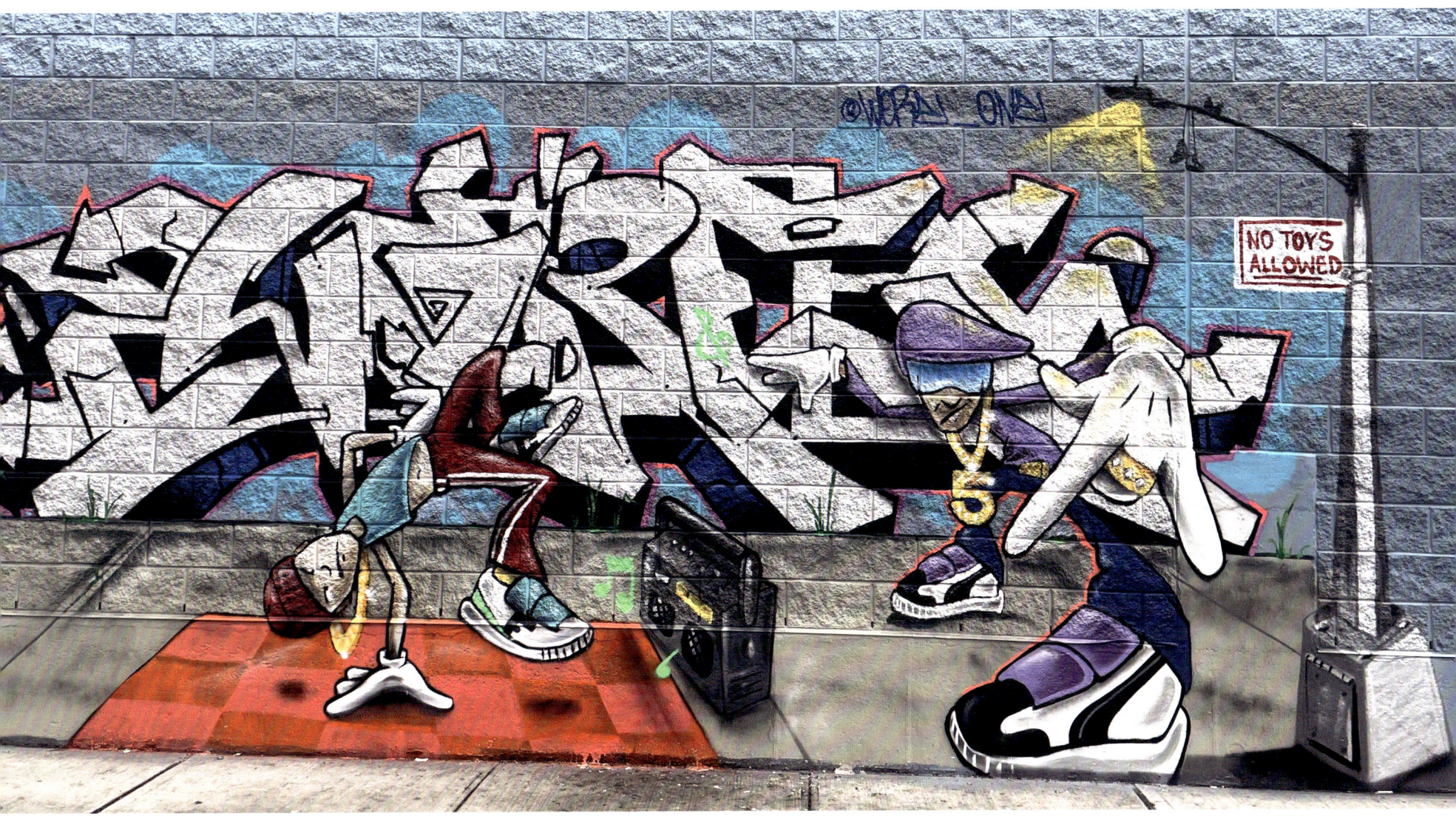

WORE ONE
BOONE AVENUE WALLS, THE BRONX, PHOTOGRAPHED IN 2023

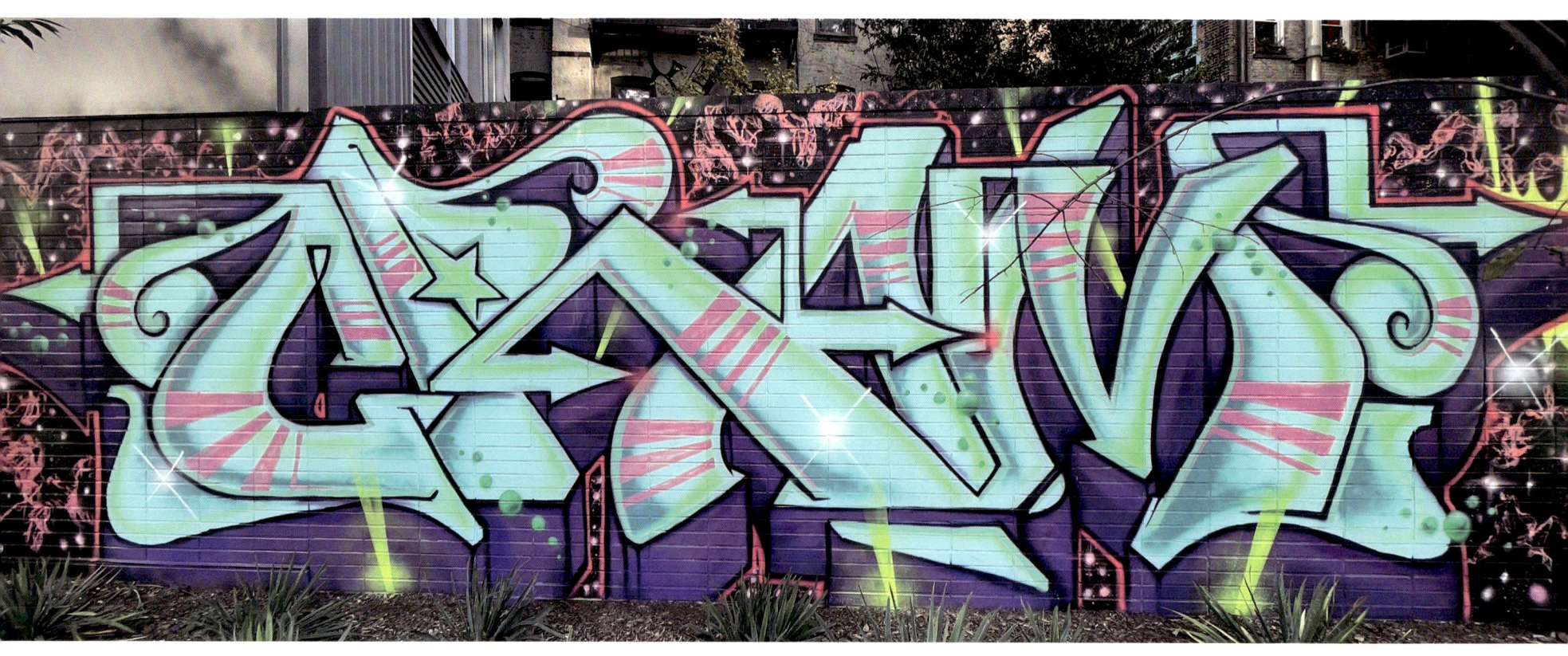

CRAM CONCEPTS

Cram Concepts displays his unique style of graffiti art at First Street Green Art Park.
FIRST STREET GREEN ART PARK, MANHATTAN, PHOTOGRAPHED IN 2023

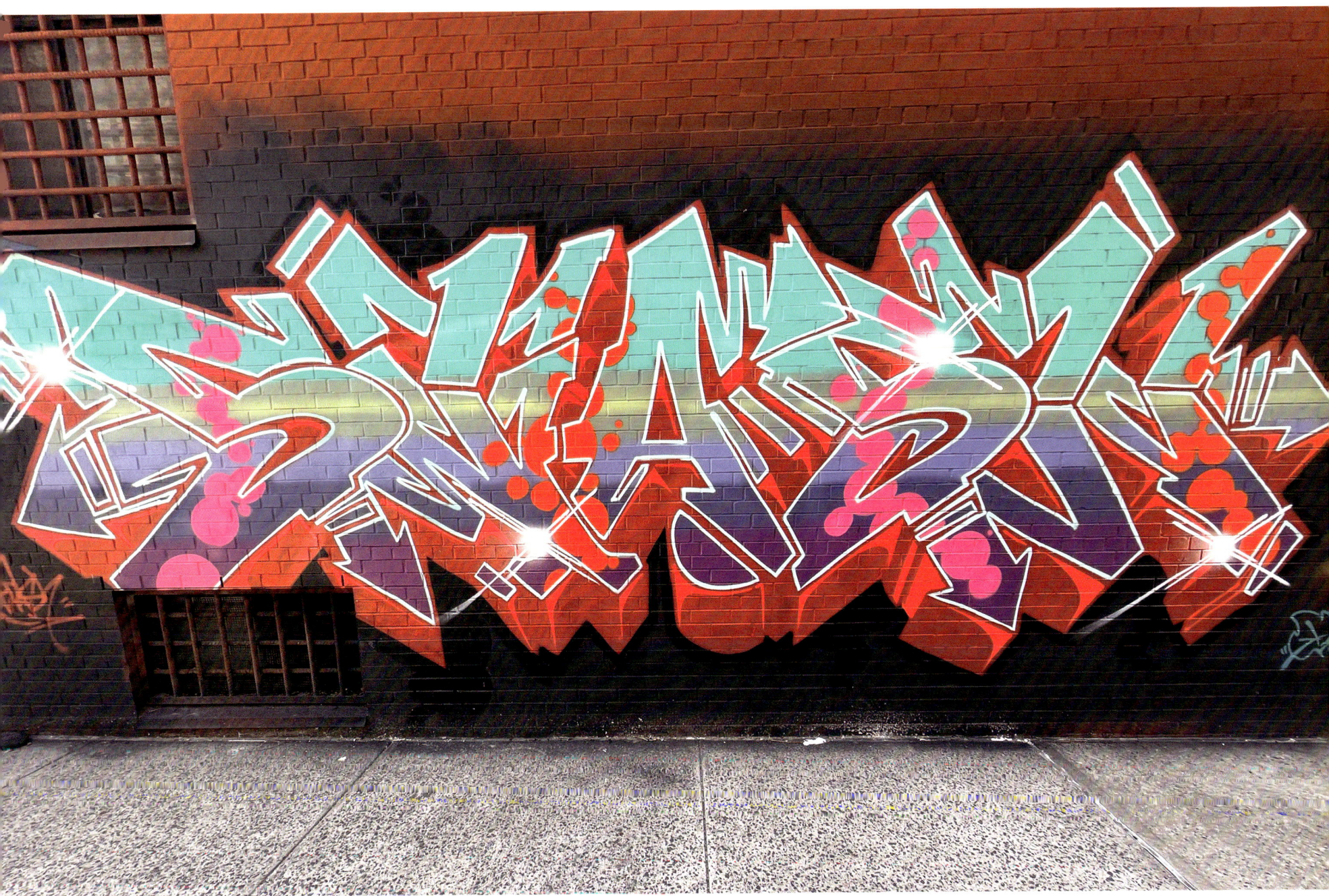

STASH

Stash is a well-known aerosol artist and entrepreneur. His art has led him to collaboration with Nike and other brands.

BOONE AVENUE WALLS, THE BRONX, PHOTOGRAPHED IN 2024

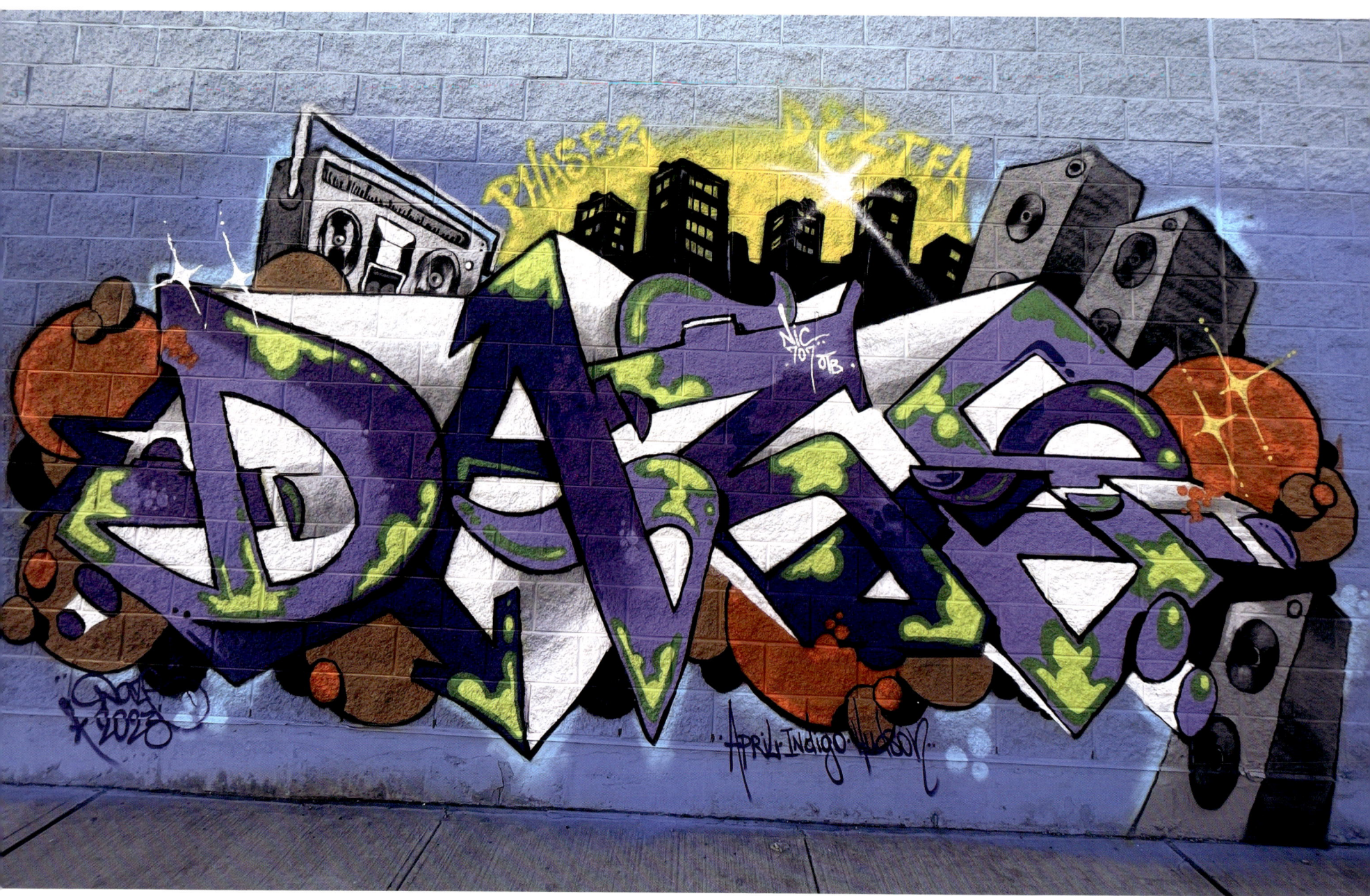

DAZE

Early pioneer of aerosol art from the 1970s NYC subway graffiti era whose monograph is published by Schiffer Books. He also has a studio practice.
BOONE AVENUE WALLS, THE BRONX, PHOTOGRAPHED IN 2023

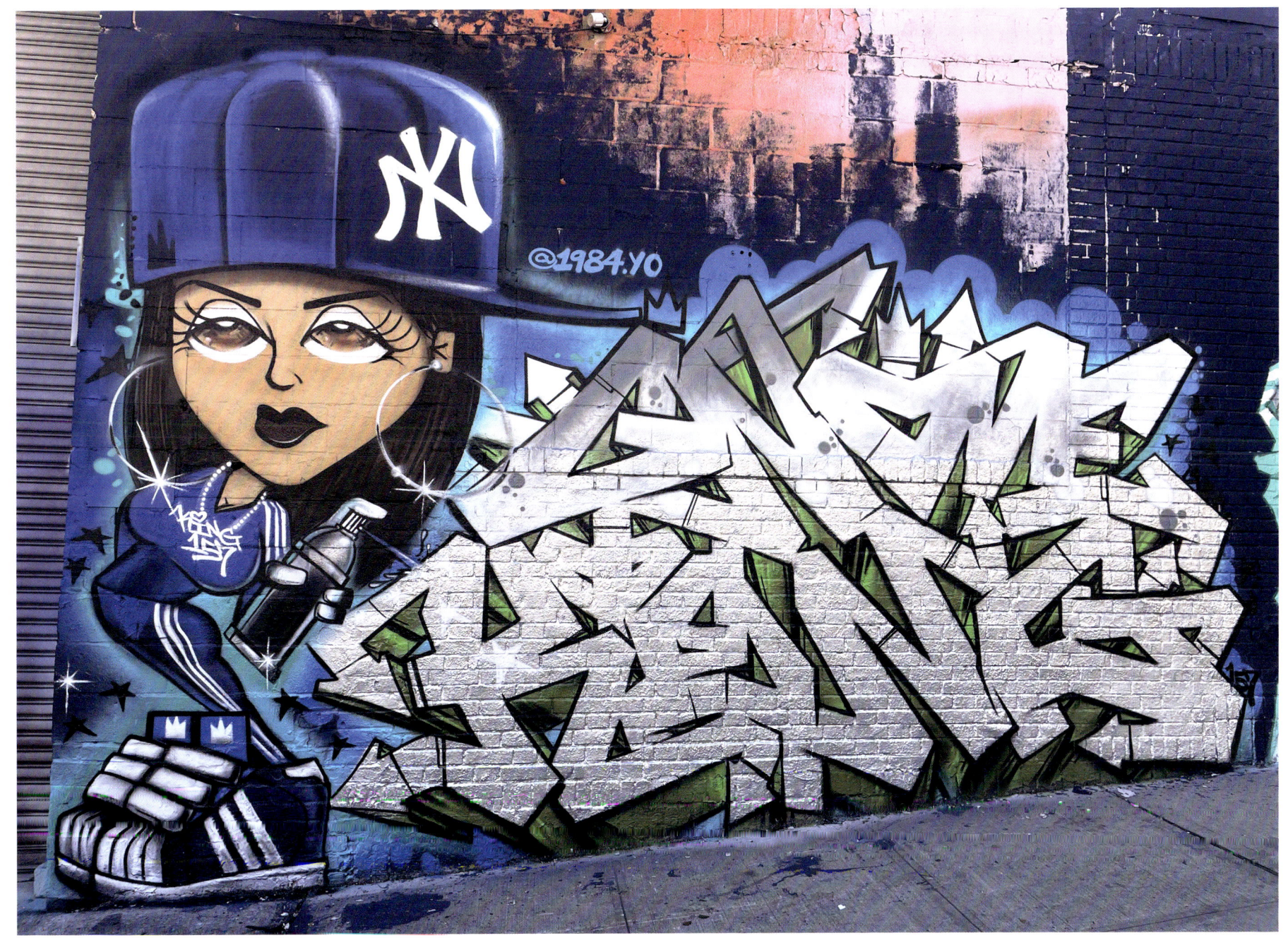

KING 157
BOONE AVENUE WALLS, THE BRONX, PHOTOGRAPHED IN 2023

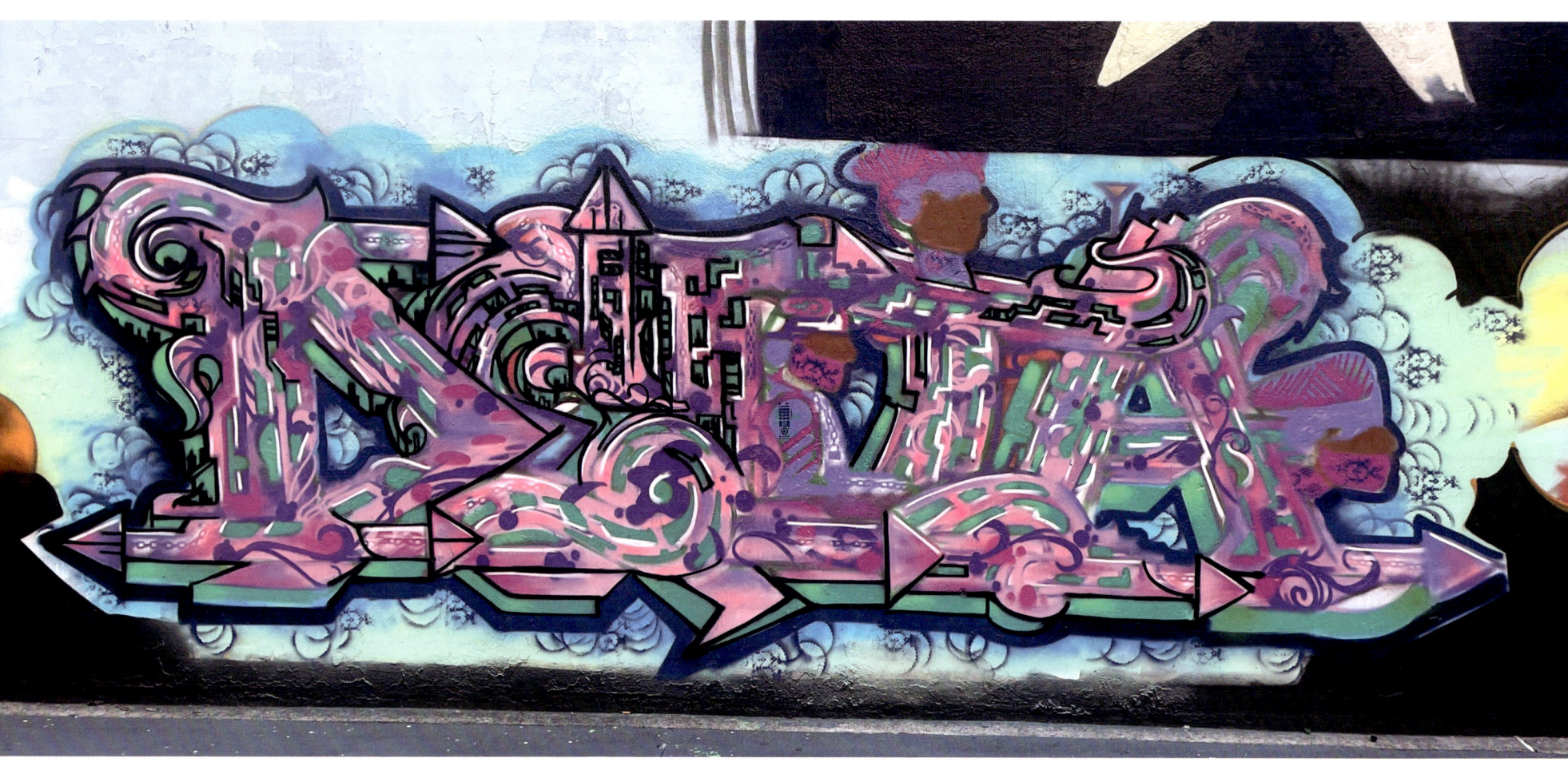

DELTA 2
A pioneer of aerosol art from the NYC subway graffiti era of the 1970s and '80s.
GRAFFITI HALL OF FAME, MANHATTAN, PHOTOGRAPHED IN 2023

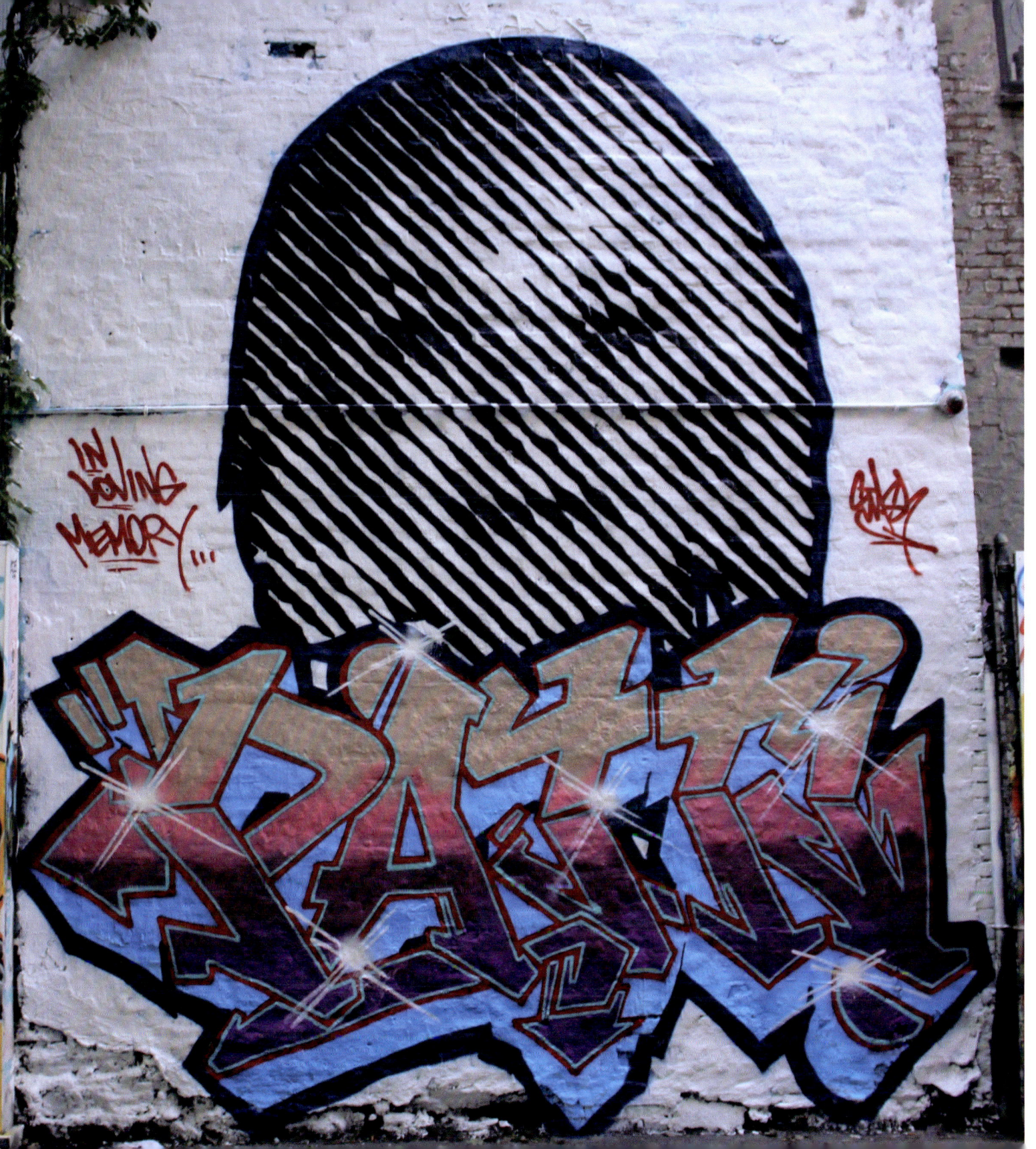

STASH
An aerosol artist and graphic designer whose work goes back to NYC subway graffiti of the 1980s and is known worldwide for his collaborations with Nike and other brands.
FIRST STREET GREEN ART PARK, PATTI ASTOR TRIBUTE, MANHATTAN, PHOTOGRAPHED IN 2024

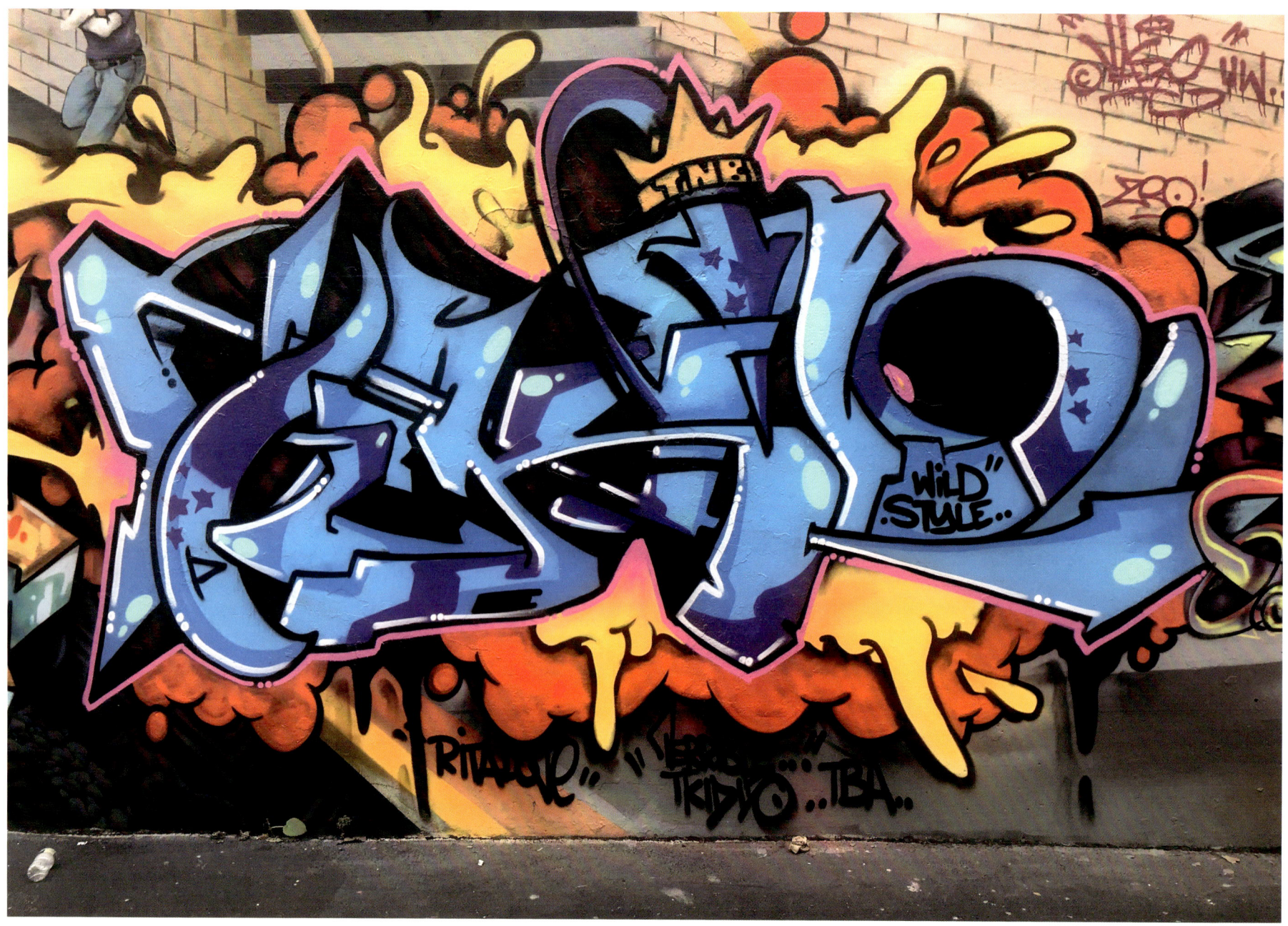

TKID 170

A pioneer of aerosol art from the subway graffiti era of the 1970s and '80s.

TKID was the subject of a feature-length documentary, *The Nasty Terrible T-Kid 170: Julius Cavero in 2014*, and a book of same name.

GRAFFITI HALL OF FAME, MANHATTAN, PHOTOGRAPHED IN 2018

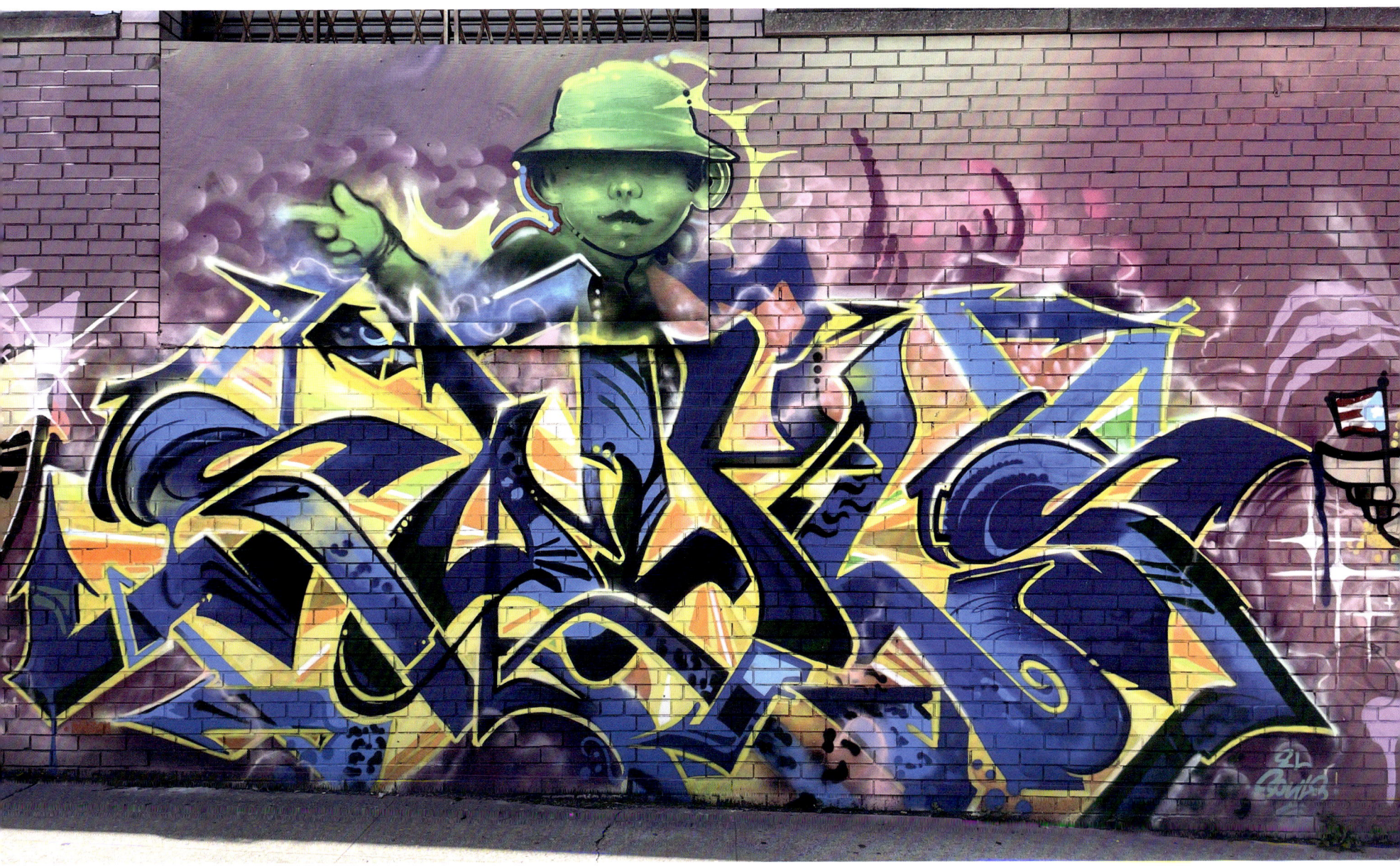

EL SOULS

El Souls is a member of Tats Cru. Many observers of street art look to him as an example of the next generation of acclaimed aerosol artists.

BOONE AVENUE WALLS, THE BRONX, PHOTOGRAPHED IN 2023

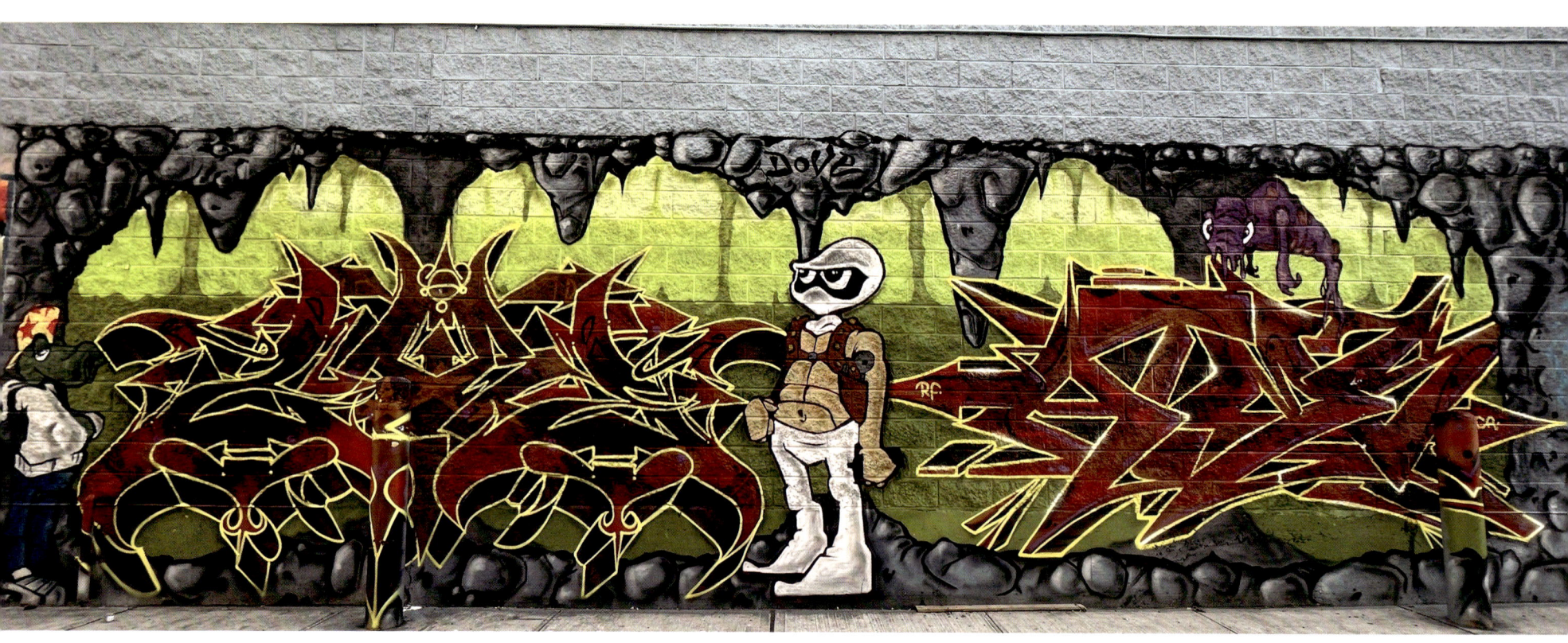

DOVE ROC, ZORE 64, ADAM FU

Pieces by Zore64 (*left*), Atom (*right*), and myself (Dove Roc) on the background and characters. Rocking some classic characters from *Cobalt 60* as well as Cheech Lizard.
BOONE AVENUE WALLS, THE BRONX, PHOTOGRAPHED IN 2024

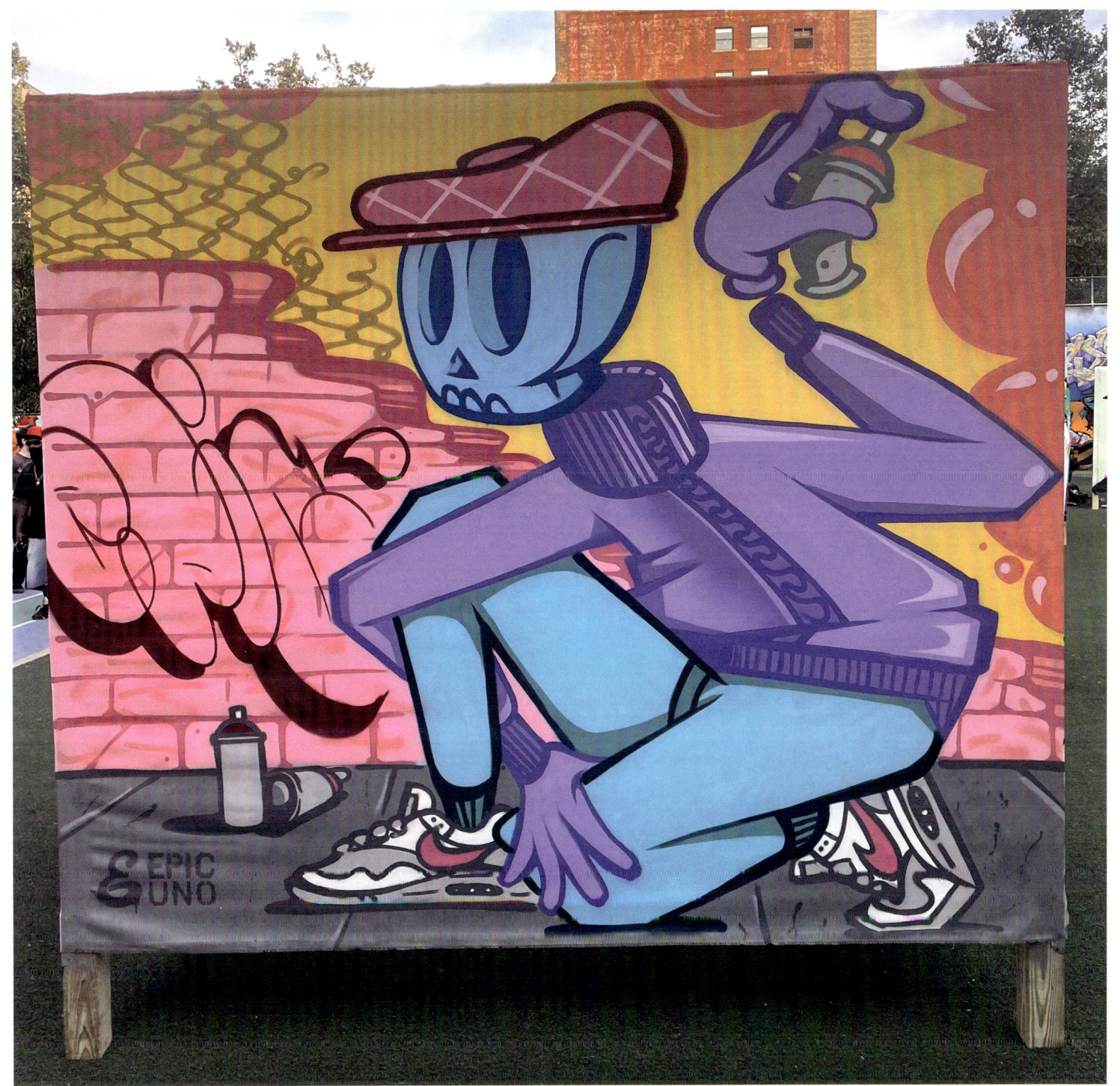

EPIC UNO
GRAFFITI HALL OF
FAME, MANHATTAN,
PHOTOGRAPHED IN
2023

**MIKE 171, SJK 171,
ALBERTUS JOSEPH,**
QUEENS,
PHOTOGRAPHED IN
2021

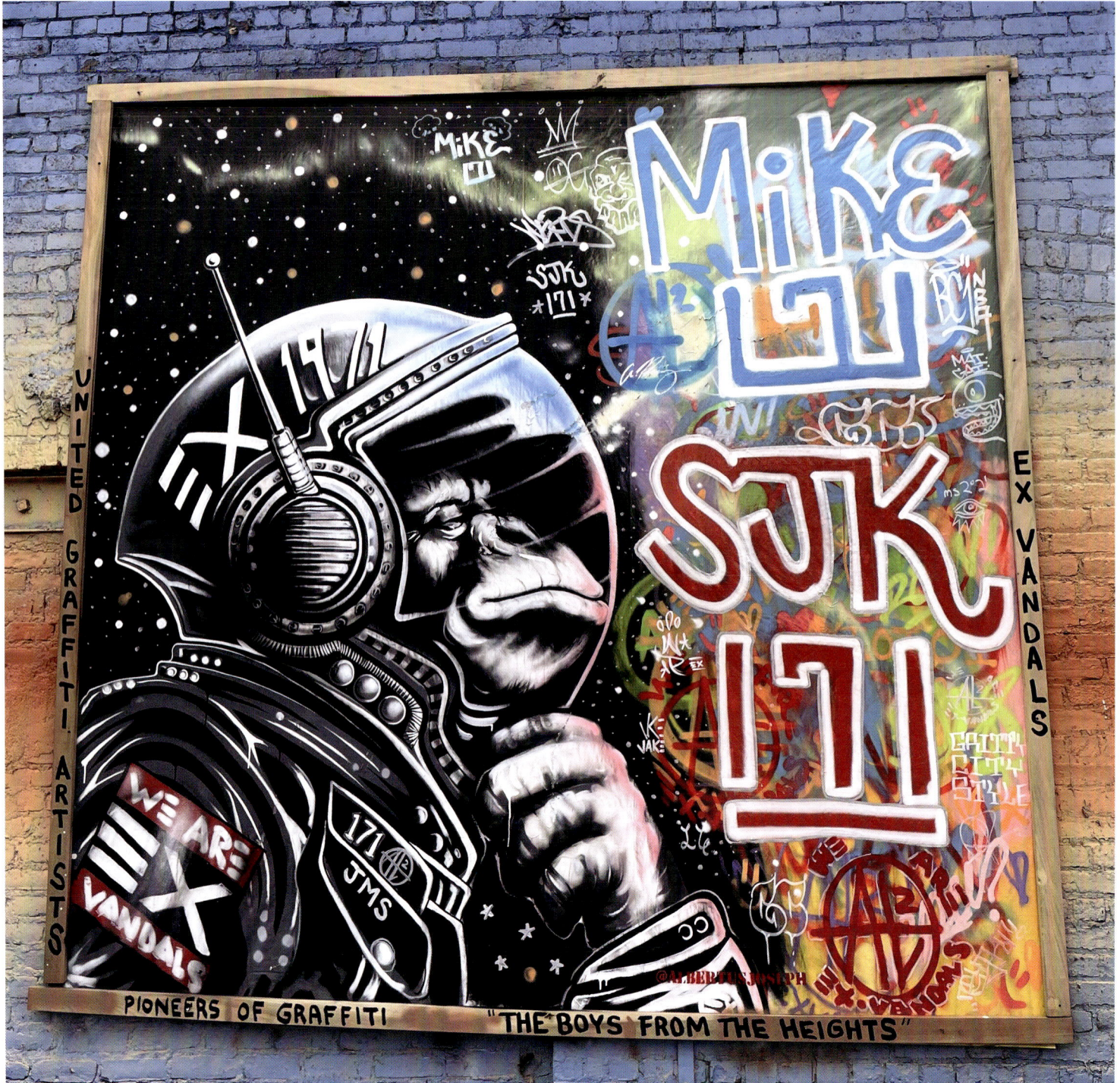

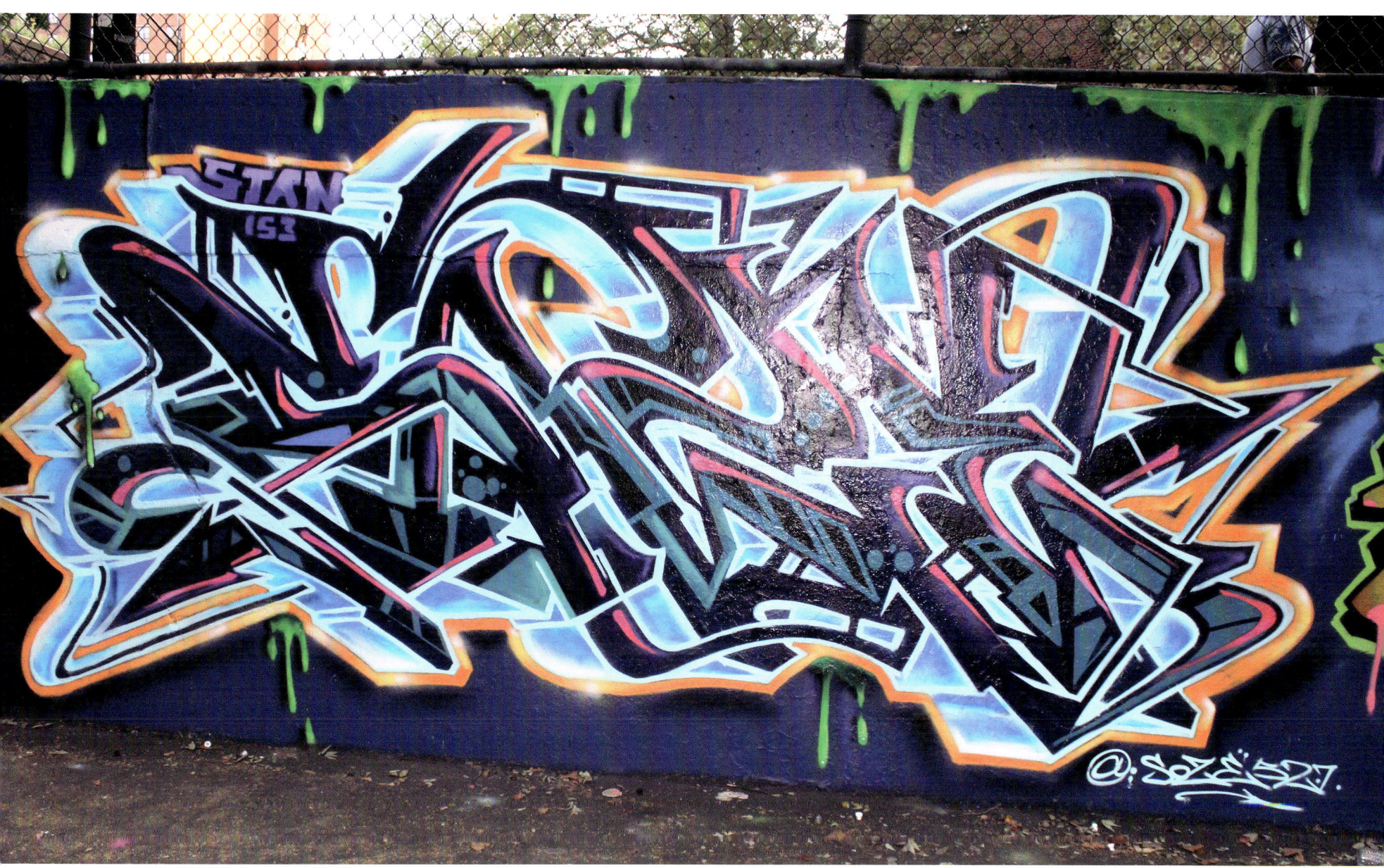

SOZE 527
GRAFFITI HALL OF FAME, MANHATTAN, PHOTOGRAPHED IN 2018

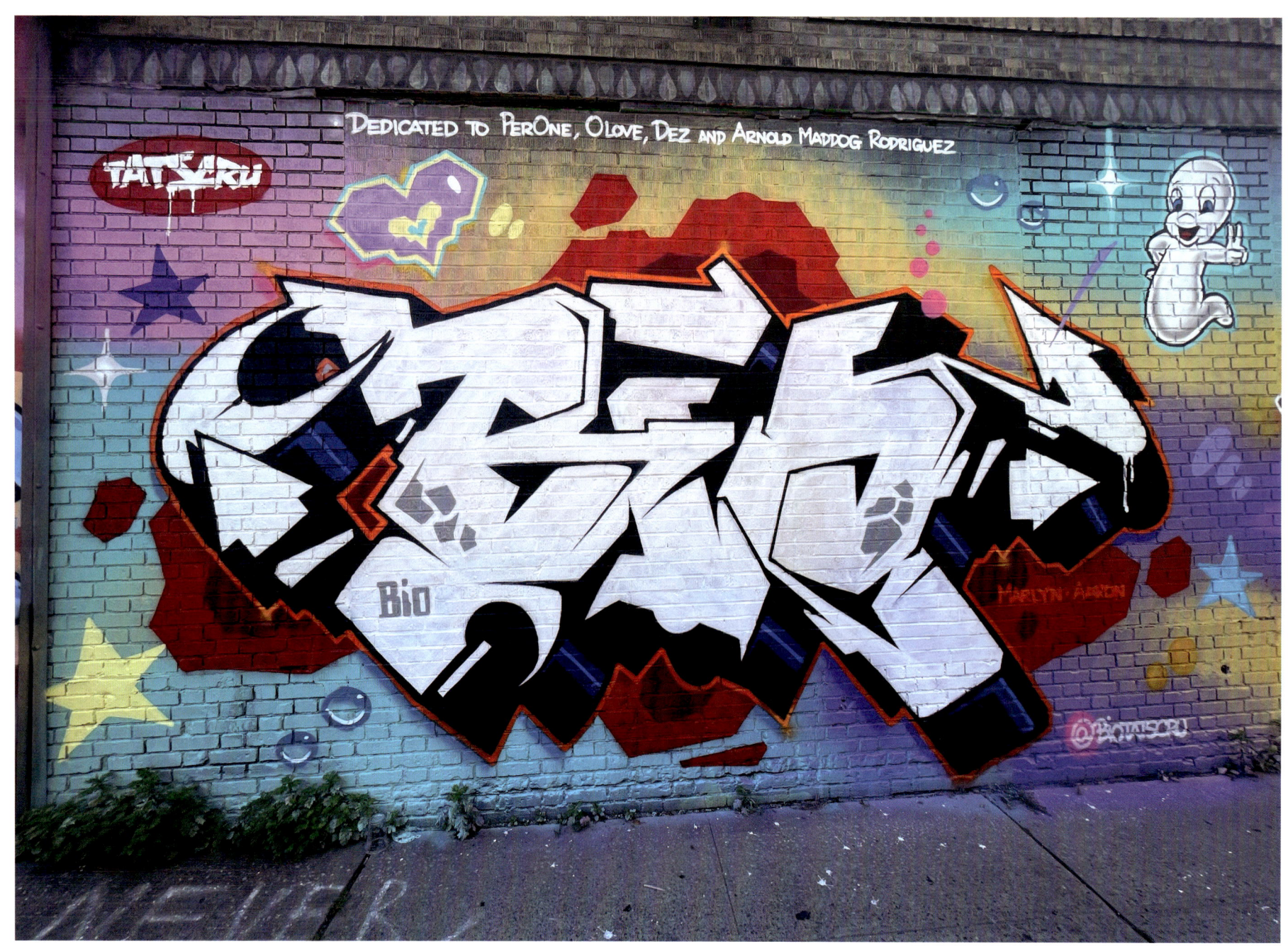

BIO TATS CRU

Bio is a founding member of Tats Cru.
BOONE AVENUE WALLS, THE BRONX, PHOTOGRAPHED IN 2023

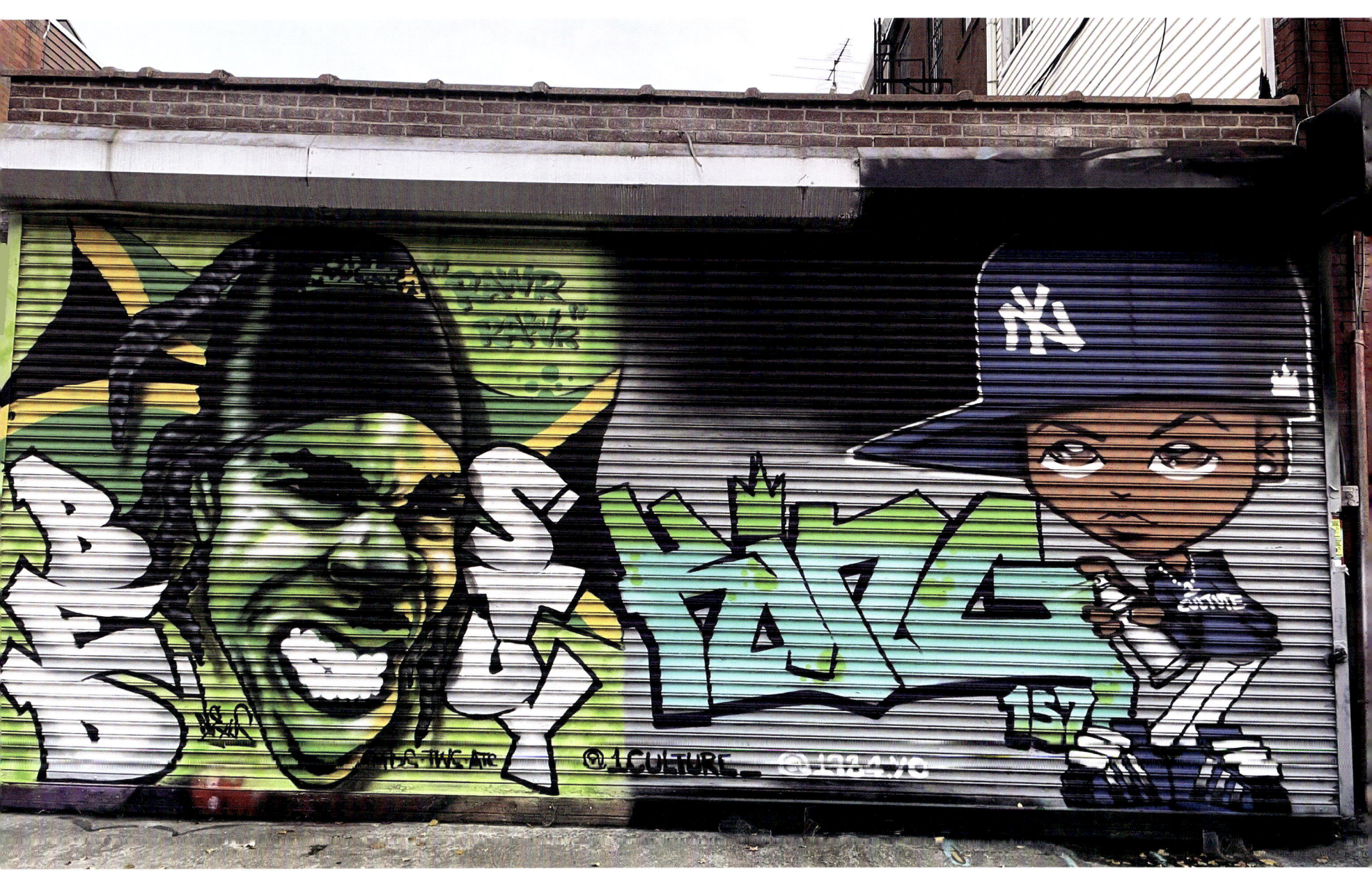

ROBERT NEXUS, KING 157
BED-STUY WALLS, BROOKLYN, PHOTOGRAPHED IN 2023

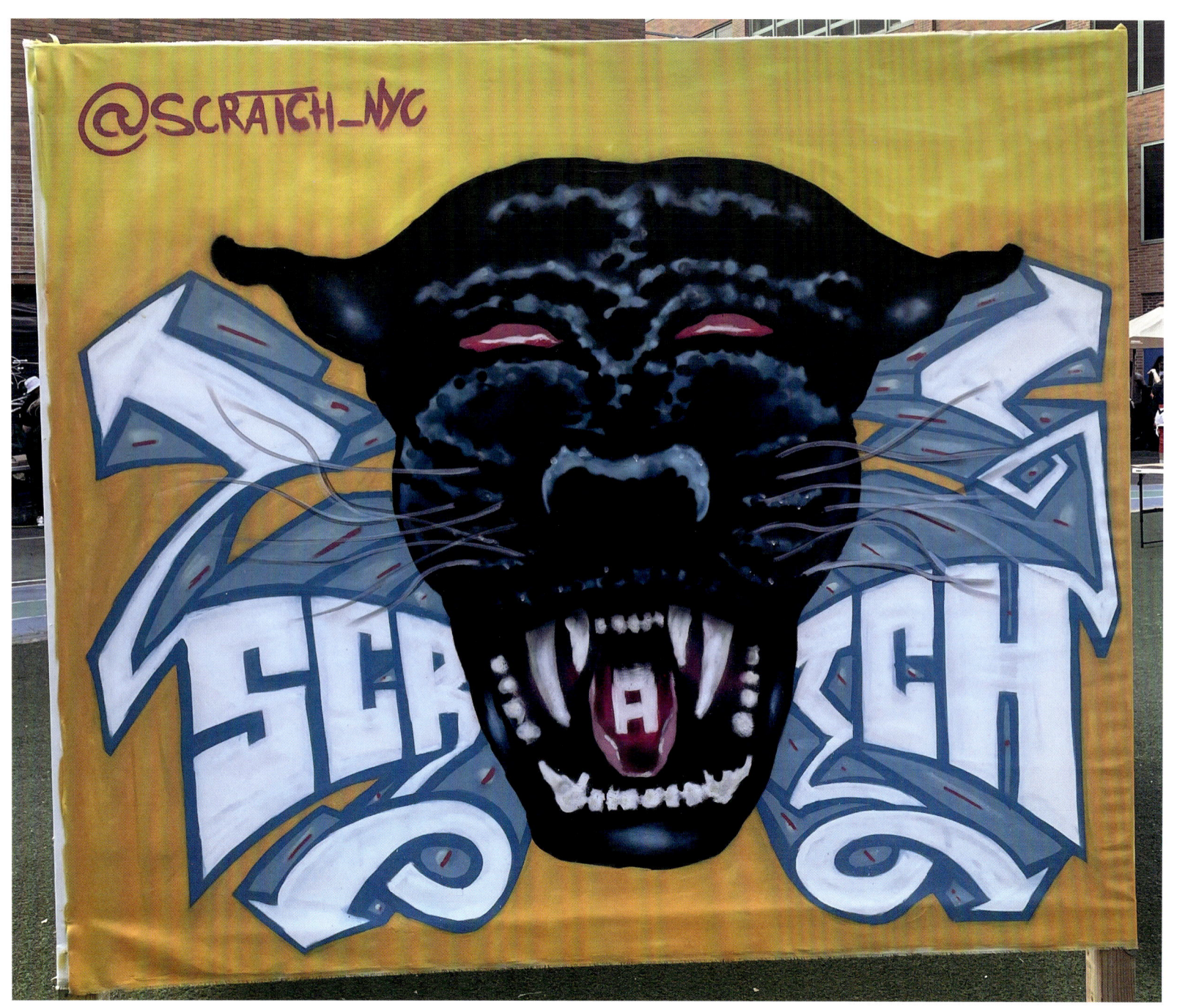

SCRATCH
GRAFFITI HALL OF FAME, MANHATTAN, PHOTOGRAPHED IN 2023

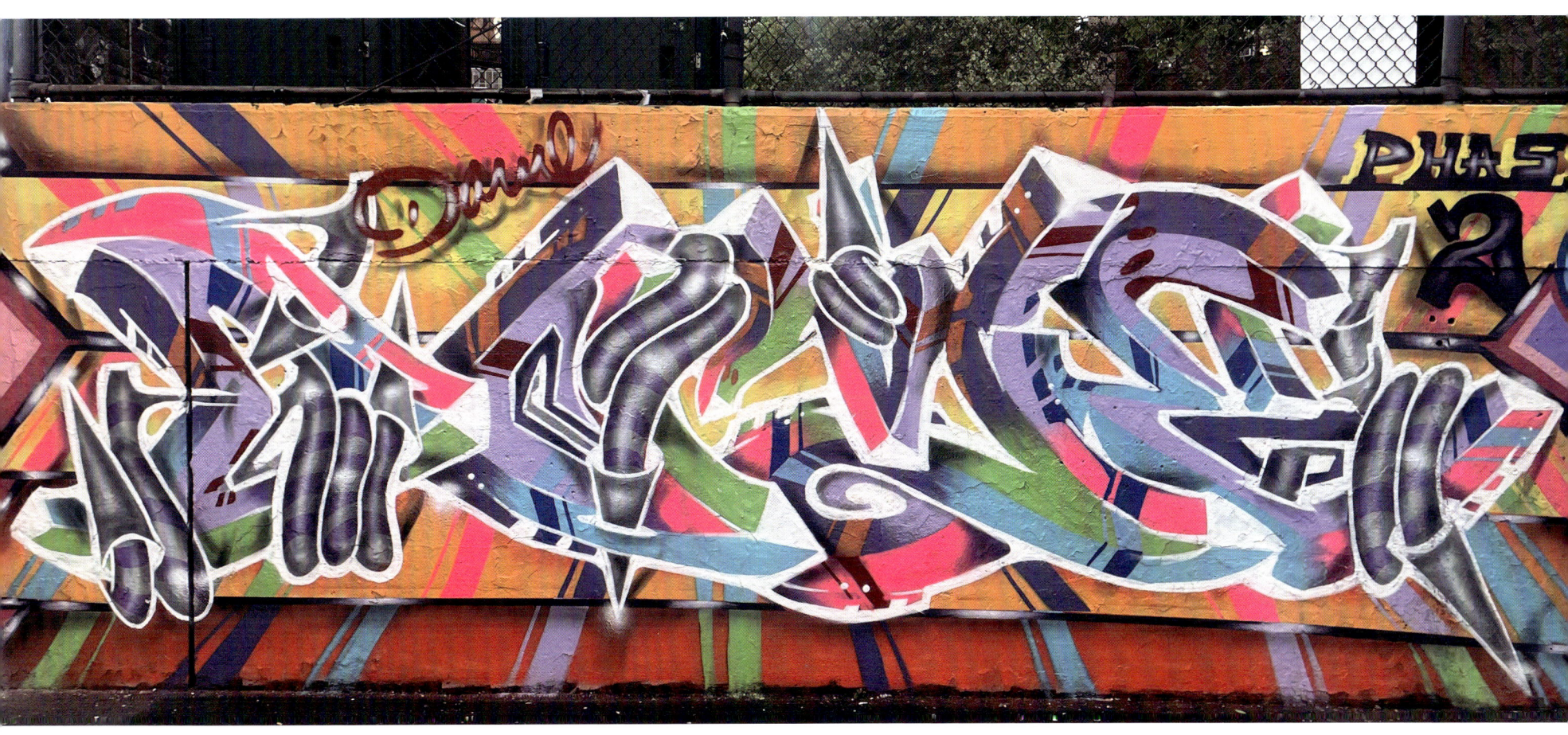

DOME NYC

Dome is a talented aerosol artist who got started in the late 1980s and was a friend of Phase 2, a pioneering aerosol artist.

GRAFFITI HALL OF FAME, MANHATTAN, PHOTOGRAPHED IN 2023

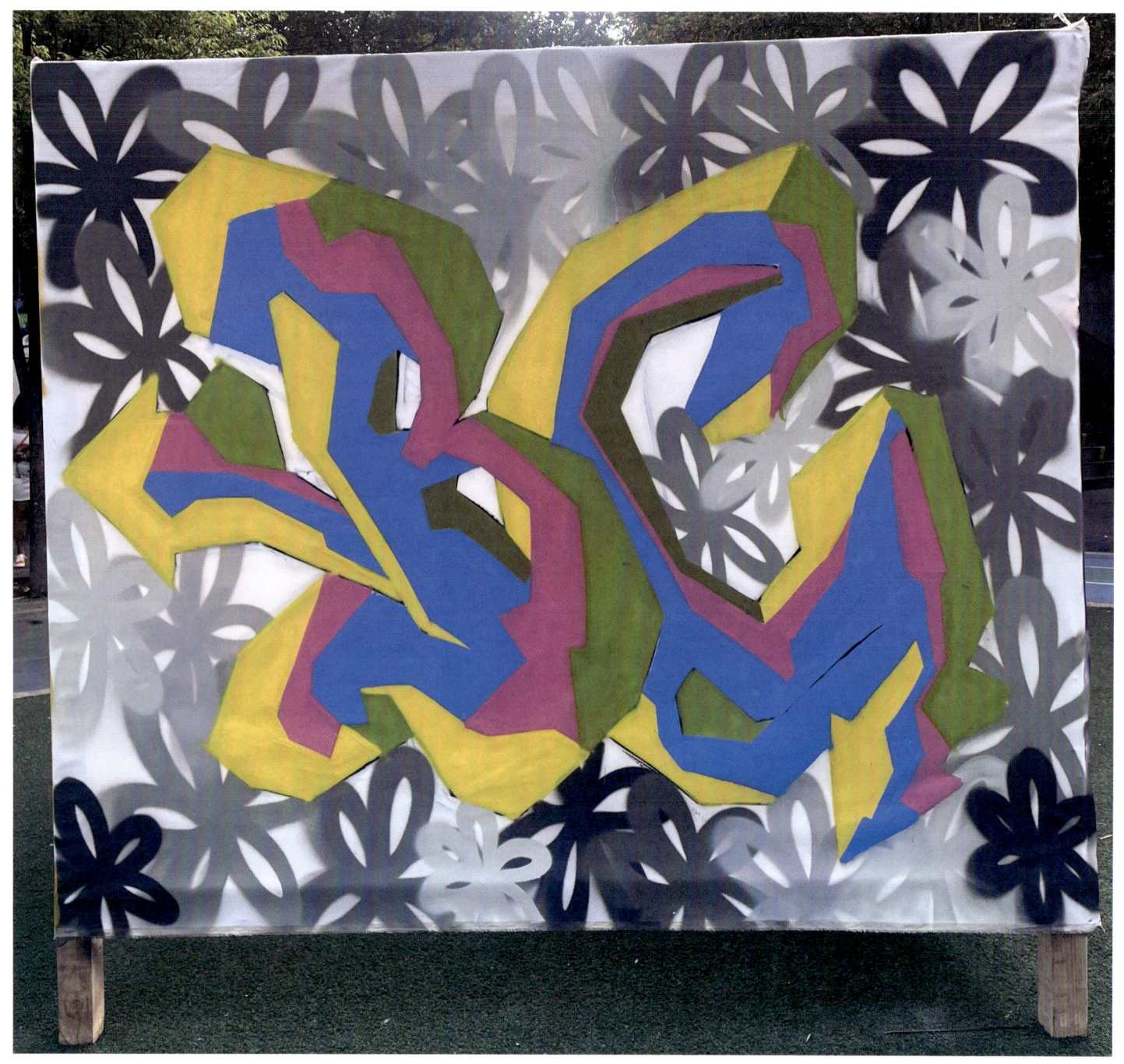

BC
GRAFFITI HALL OF FAME, MANHATTAN, PHOTOGRAPHED IN 2023

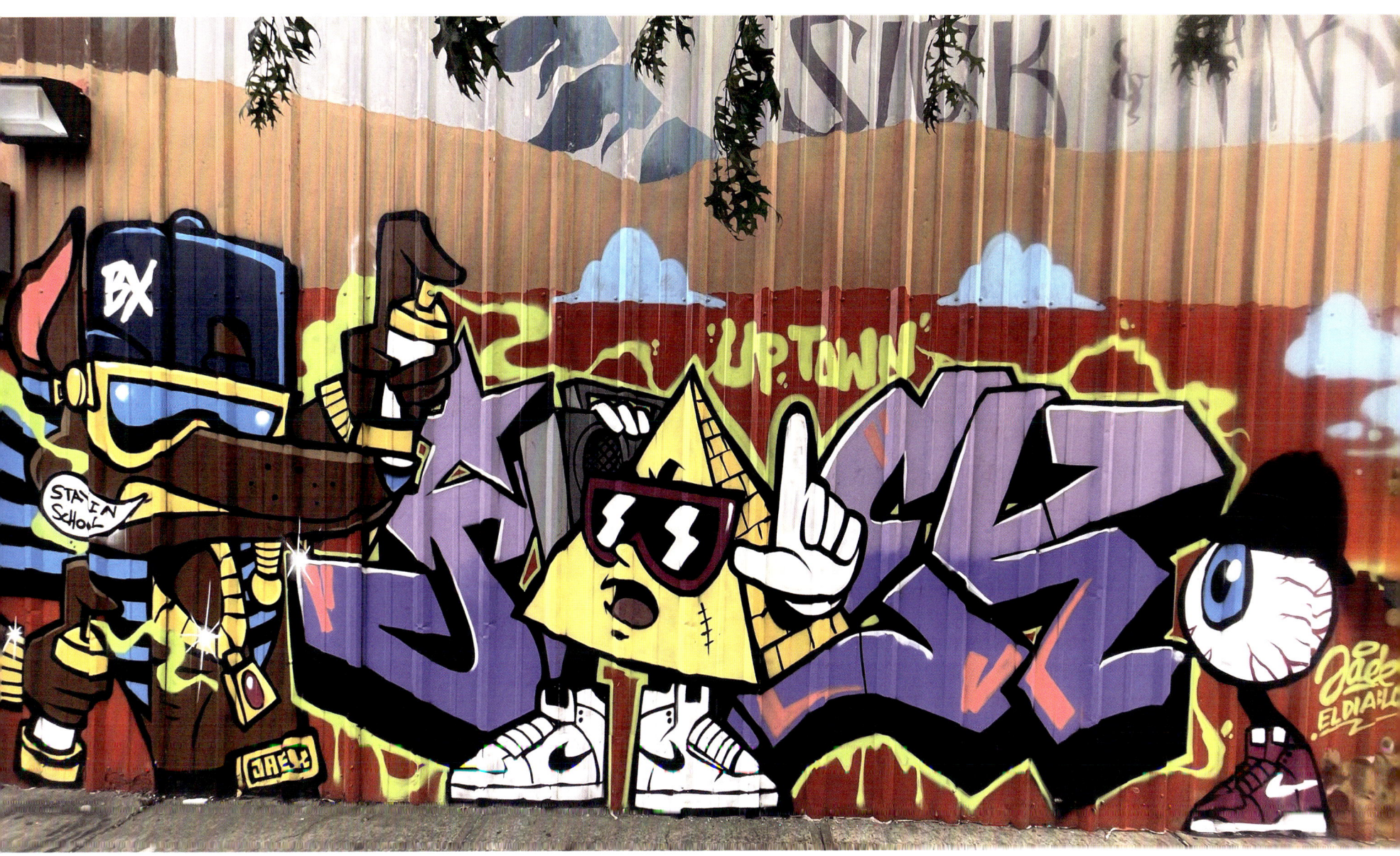

JAEK EL DIABLO
Jaek El Diablo is a native of France. He shows his unique style of lettering and characters at Boone Avenue Walls Art Festival in 2023.
BOONE AVENUE WALLS, THE BRONX, PHOTOGRAPHED IN 2023

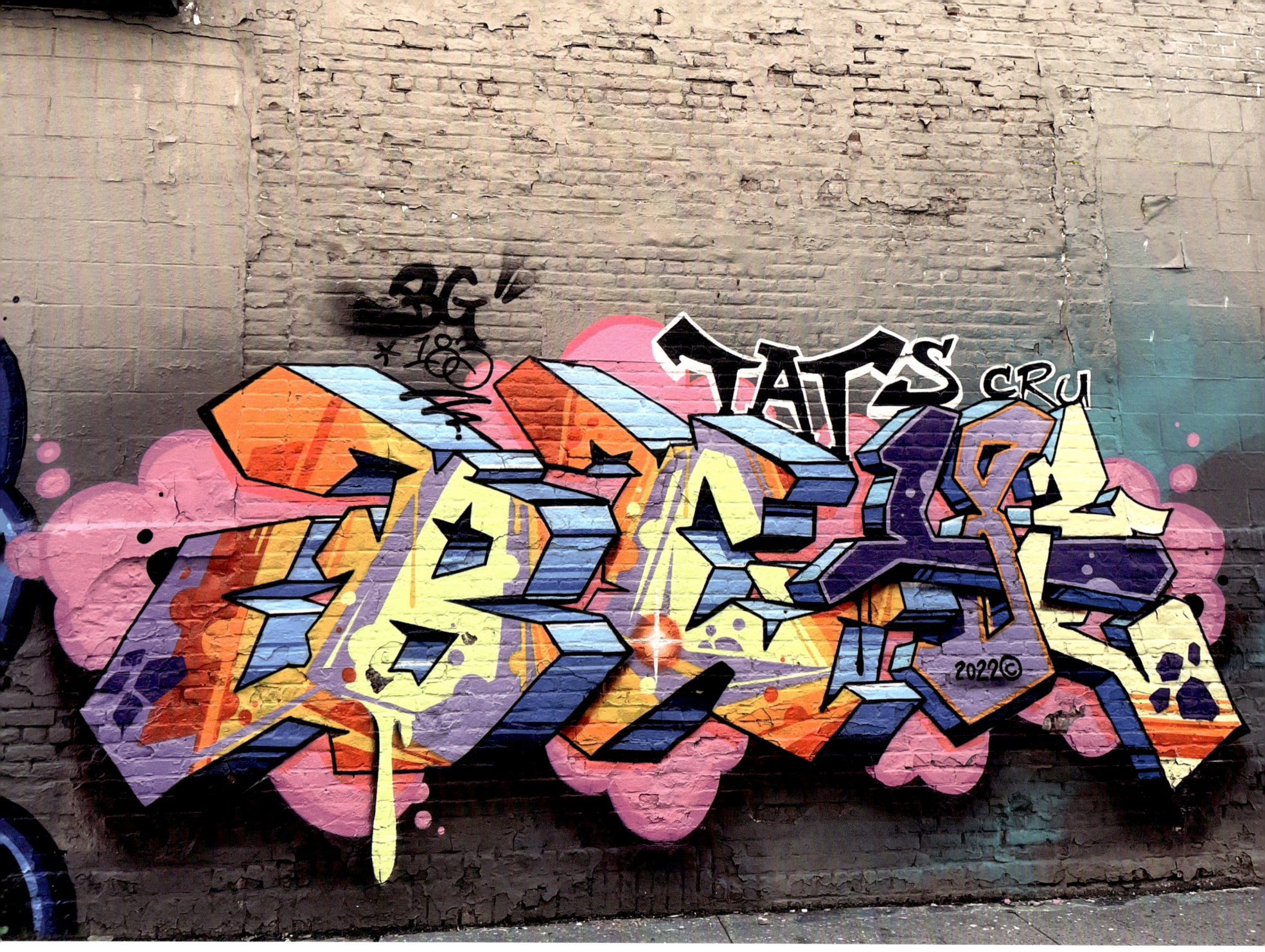

BG 183 TATS CRU
BOONE AVENUE WALLS, THE BRONX, PHOTOGRAPHED IN 2022

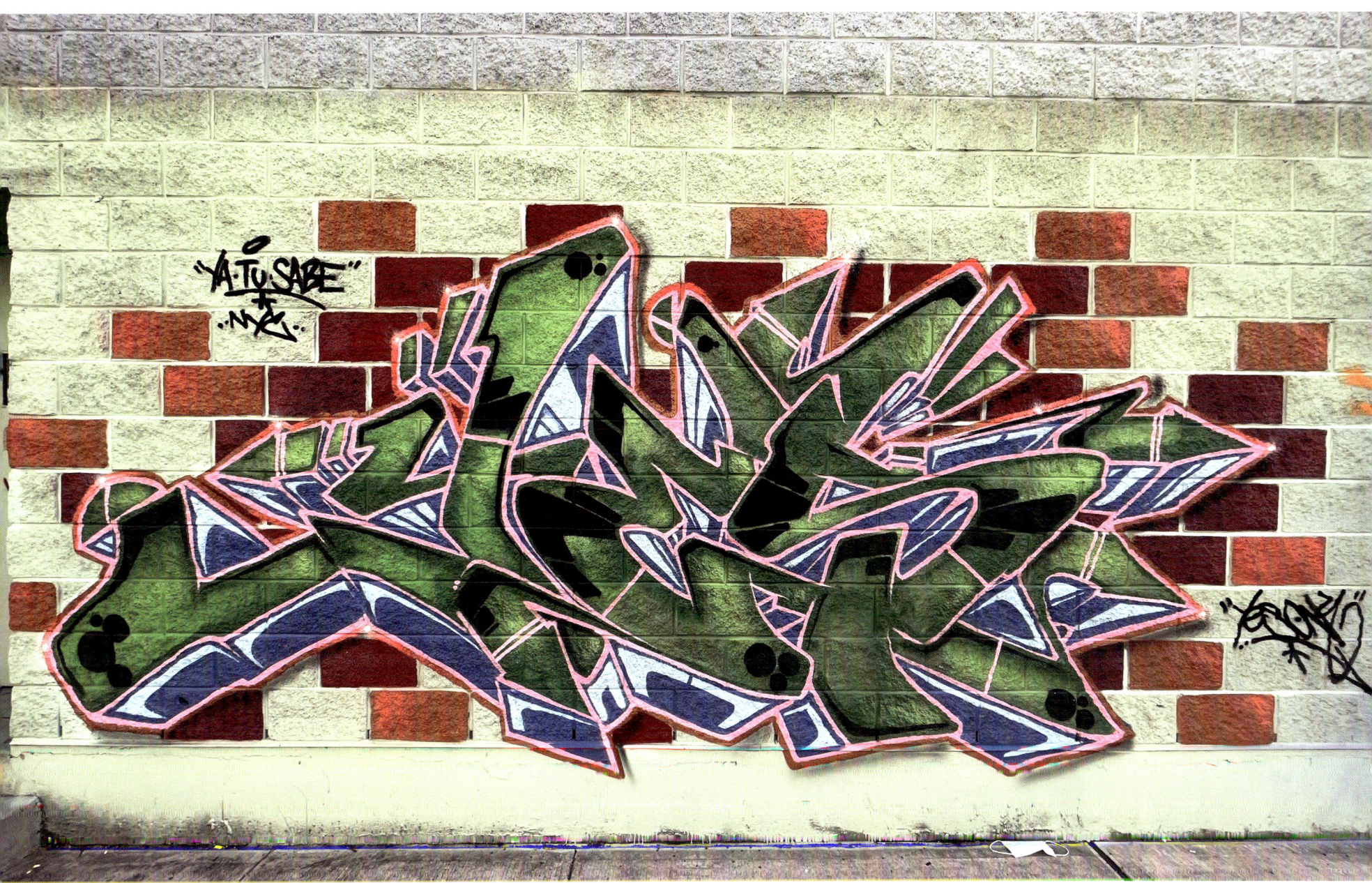

YES ONE
BOONE AVENUE WALLS, THE BRONX, PHOTOGRAPHED IN 2024

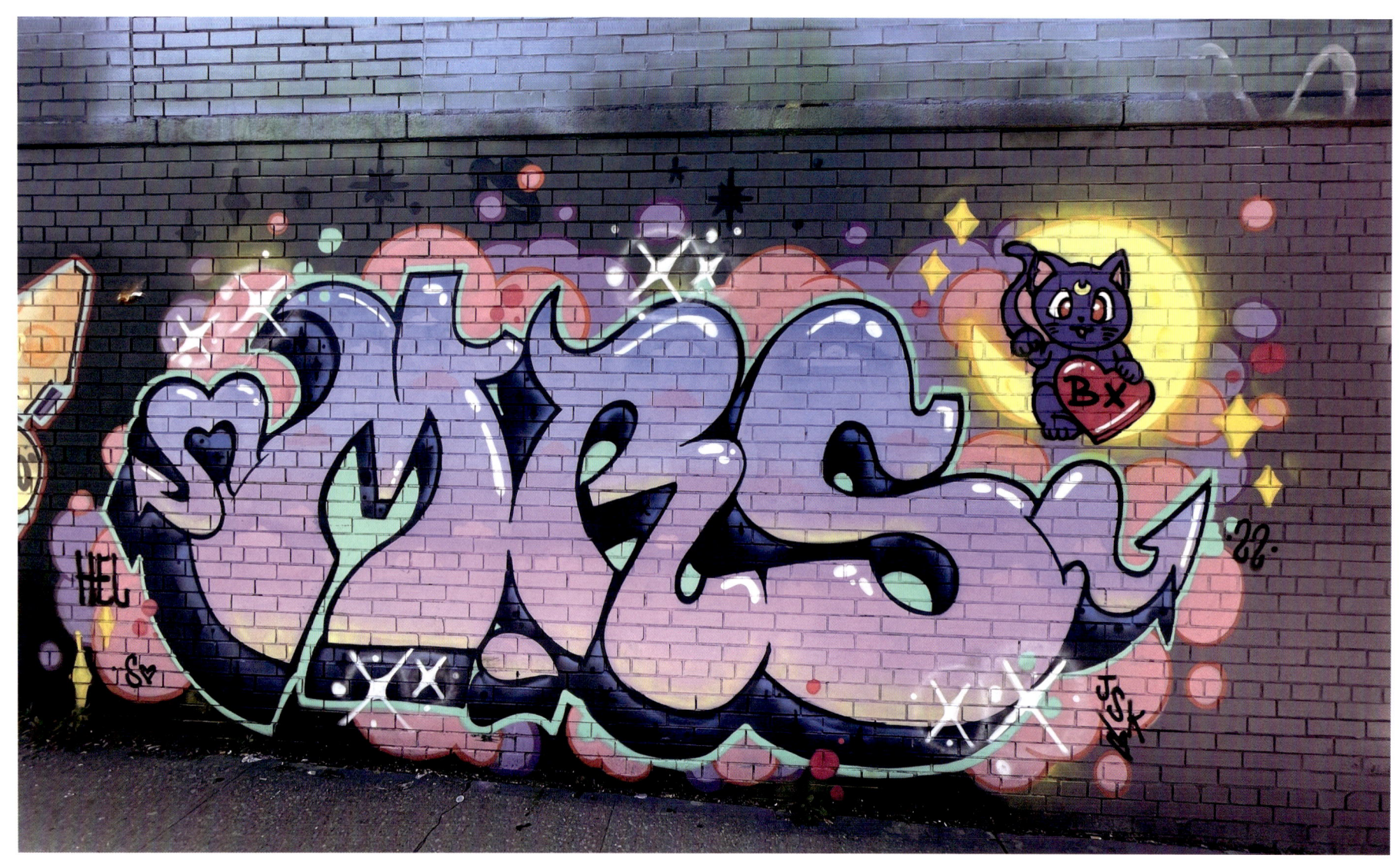

MRS BX
BOONE AVENUE WALLS, THE BRONX, PHOTOGRAPHED IN 2023

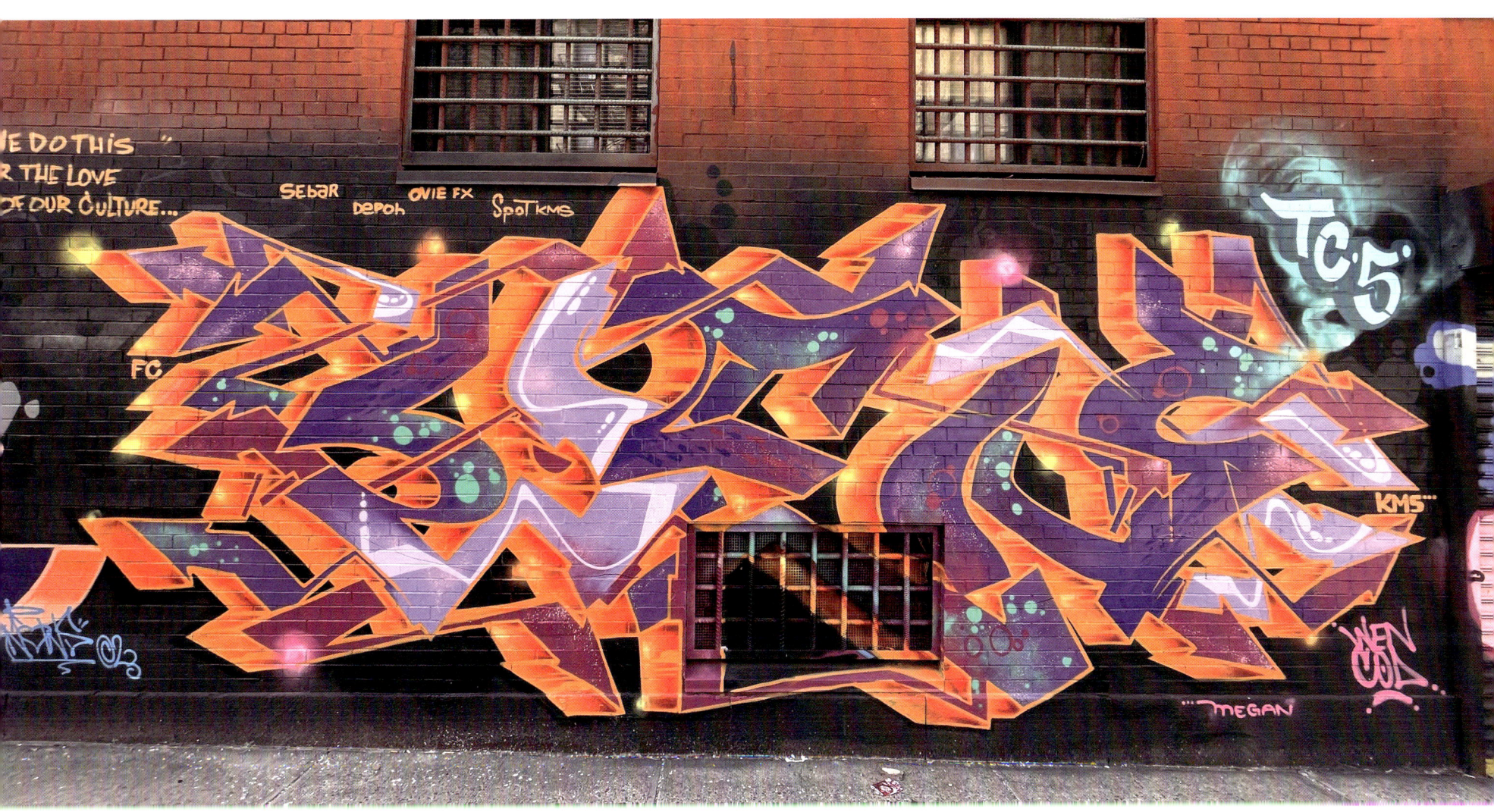

WEN COD
Curator of Boone Avenue Walls and aerosol artist since the 1980s.
BOONE AVENUE WALLS, THE BRONX, PHOTOGRAPHED IN 2024

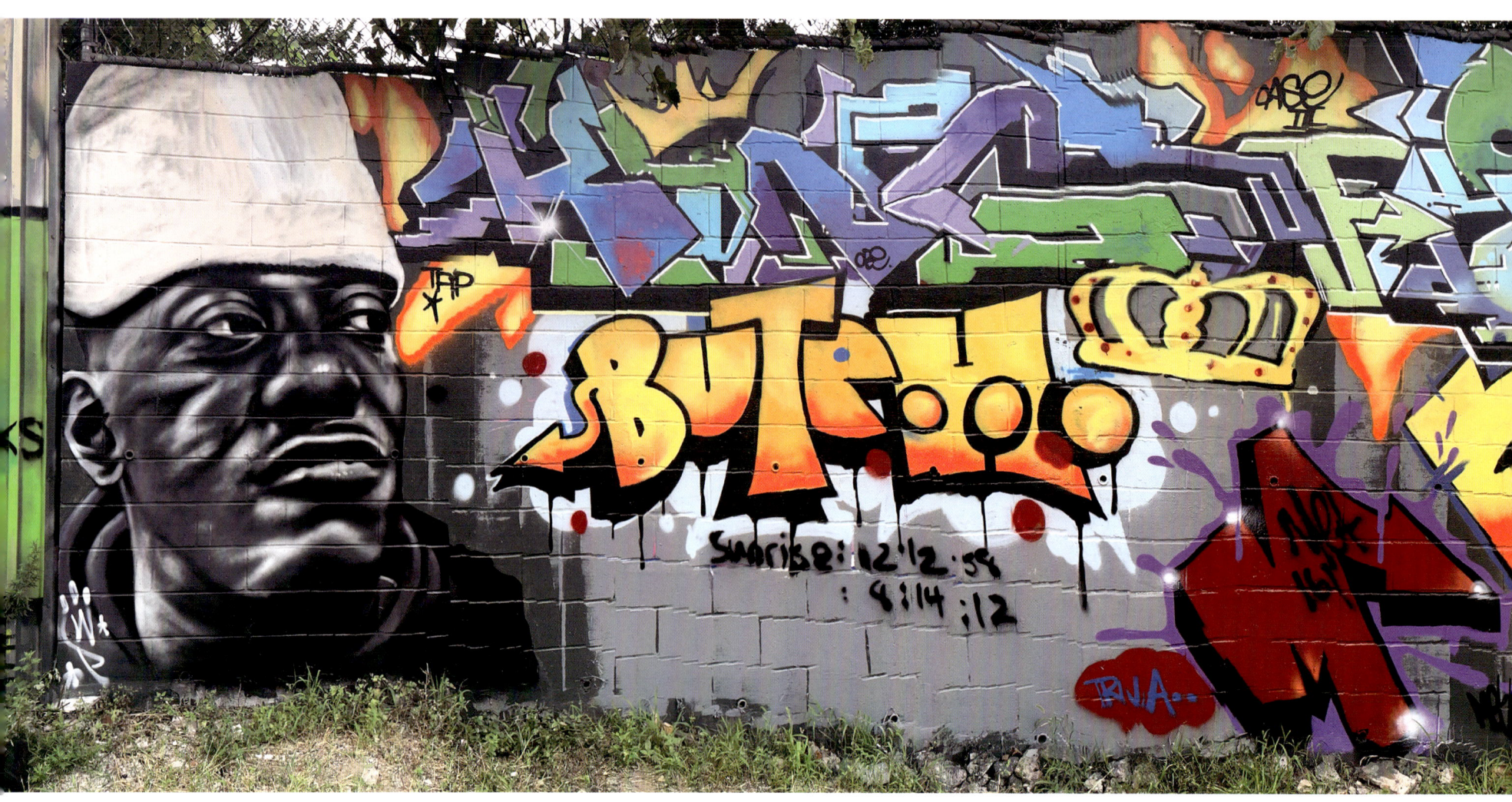

WILL POWER, BUTCH 2 TFP, BOT 707, OBE 1, AND DAC
Tenth-Anniversary Memorial Mural for legendary King of Style artist CASE 2 by Butch 2 TFP, Will Power, Bot 707, and Obe 1.
THE BRONX, PHOTOGRAPHED IN 2024

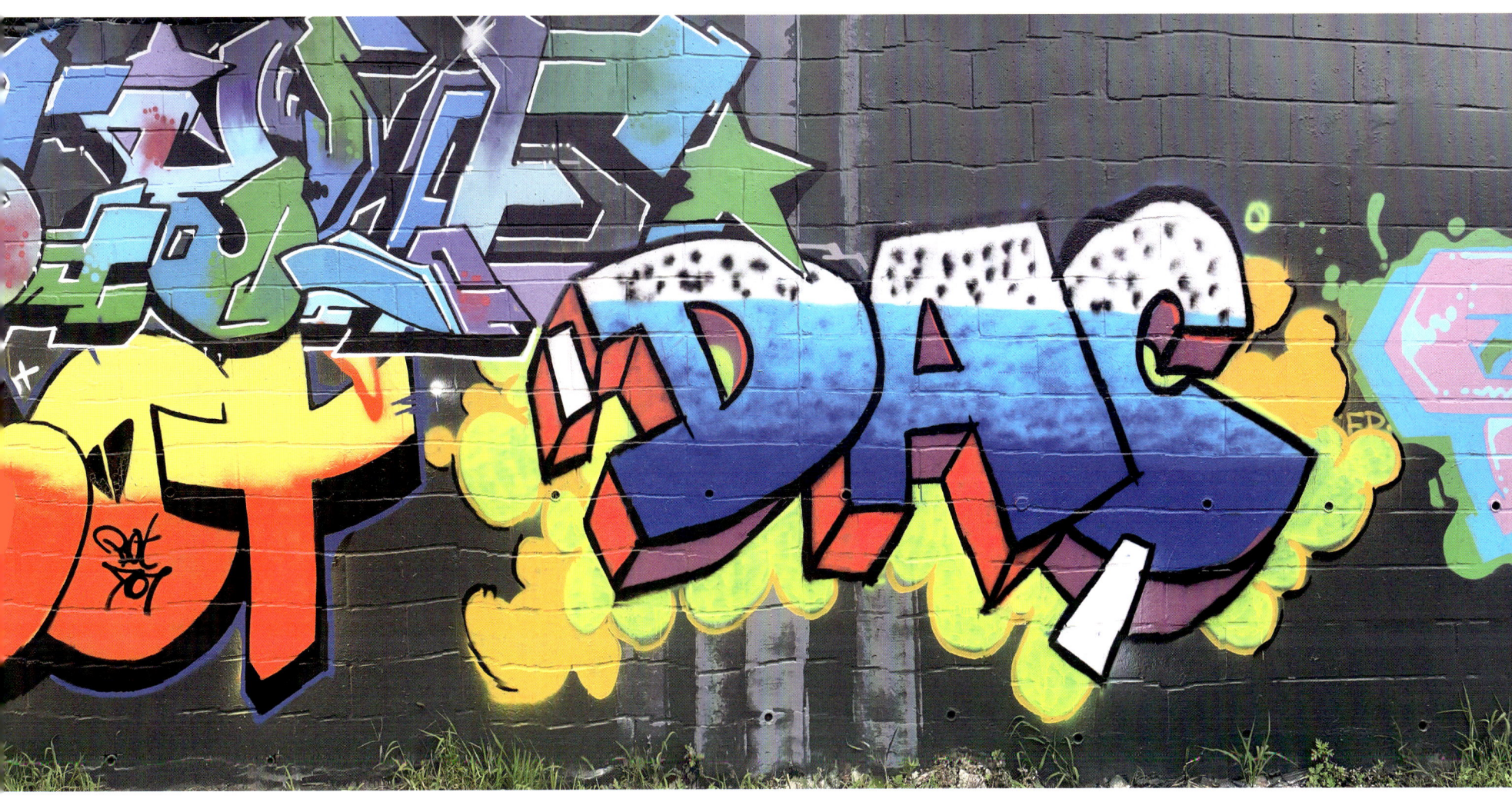

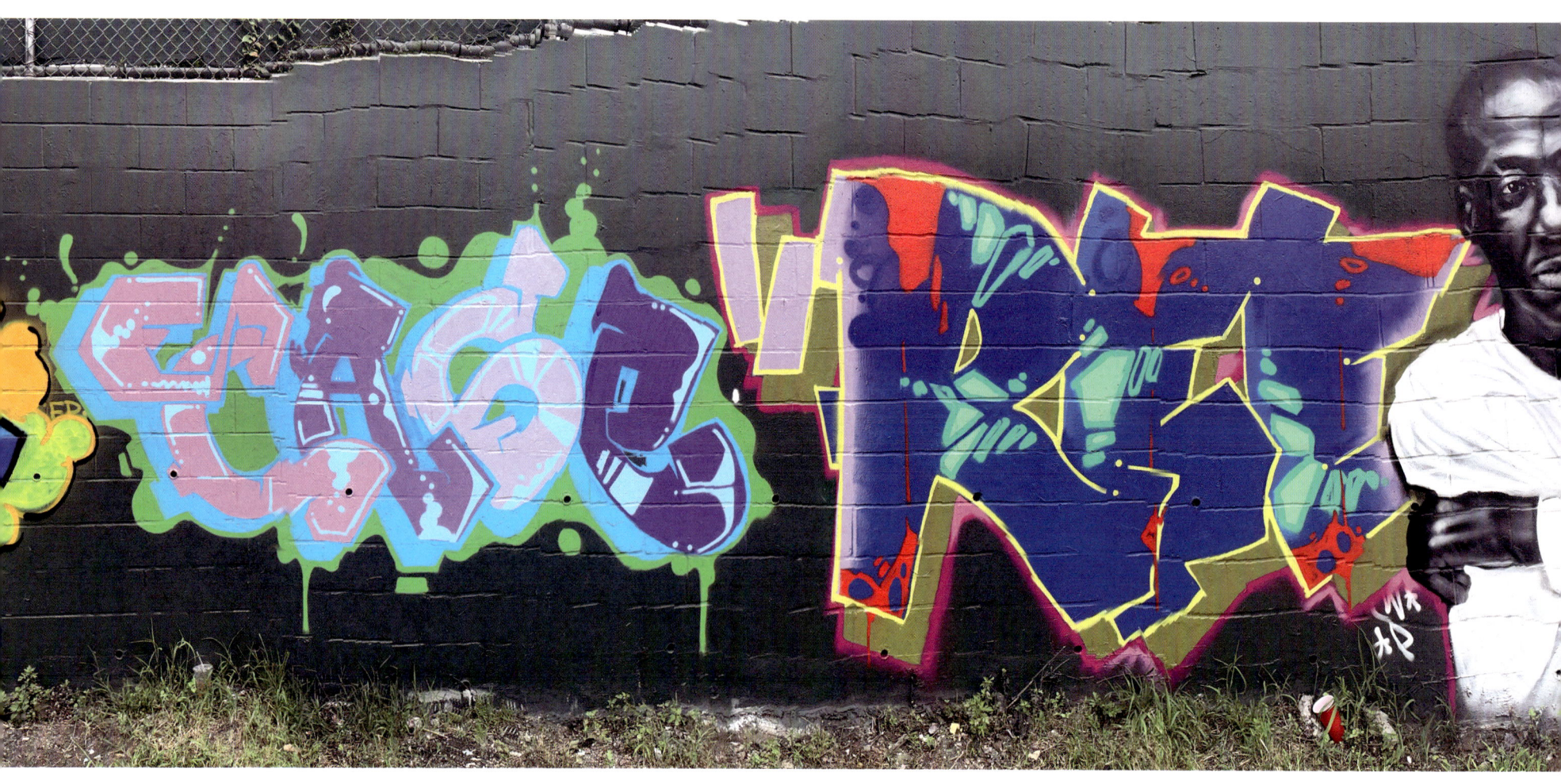

REE 2, WILL POWER, CHAIN 3

Tenth-Anniversary Memorial Mural #2 for legendary King of Style artist CASE 2 by REE 2, Will Power, and CHAIN 3.
THE BRONX, PHOTOGRAPHED IN 2021

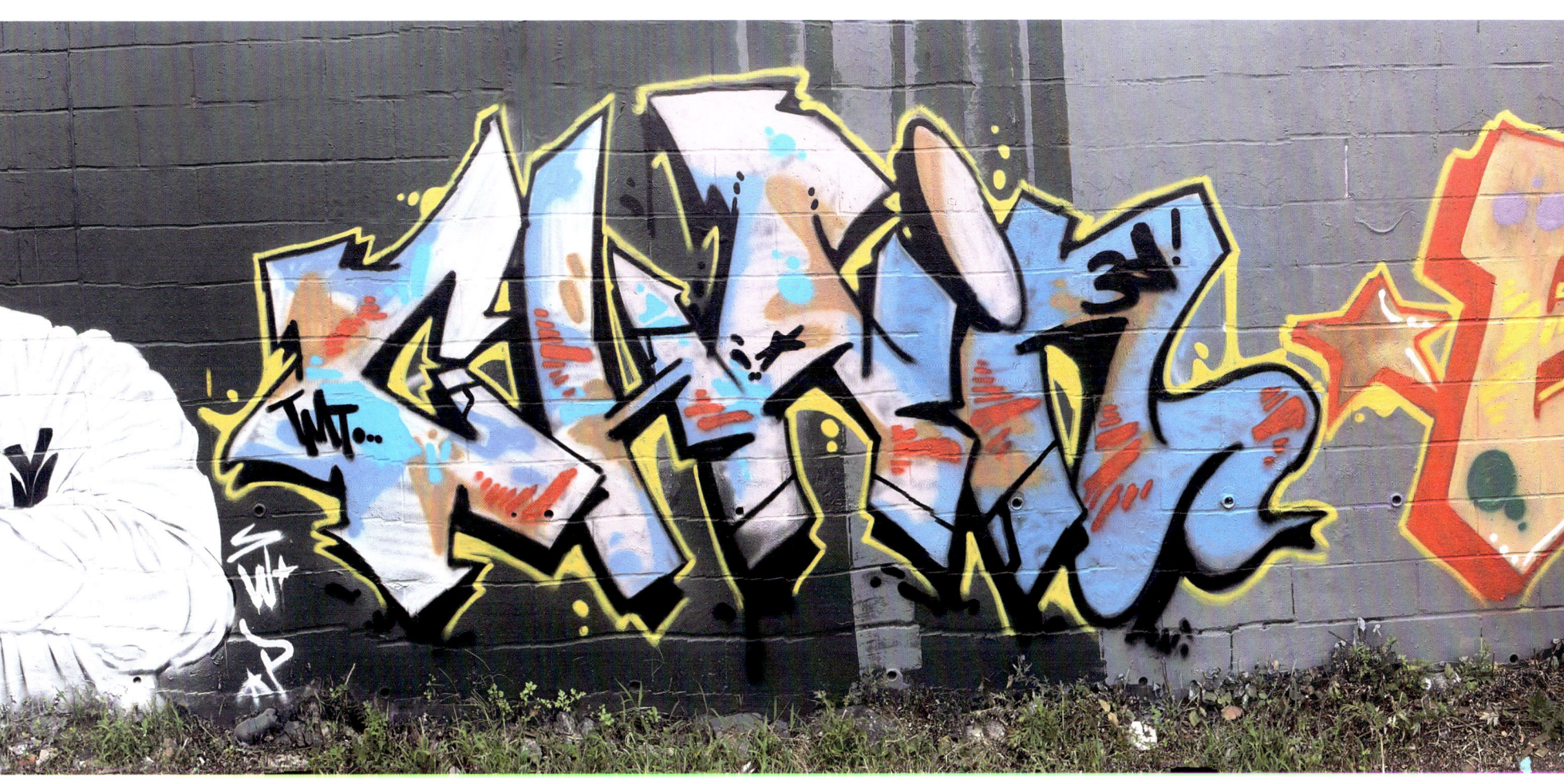

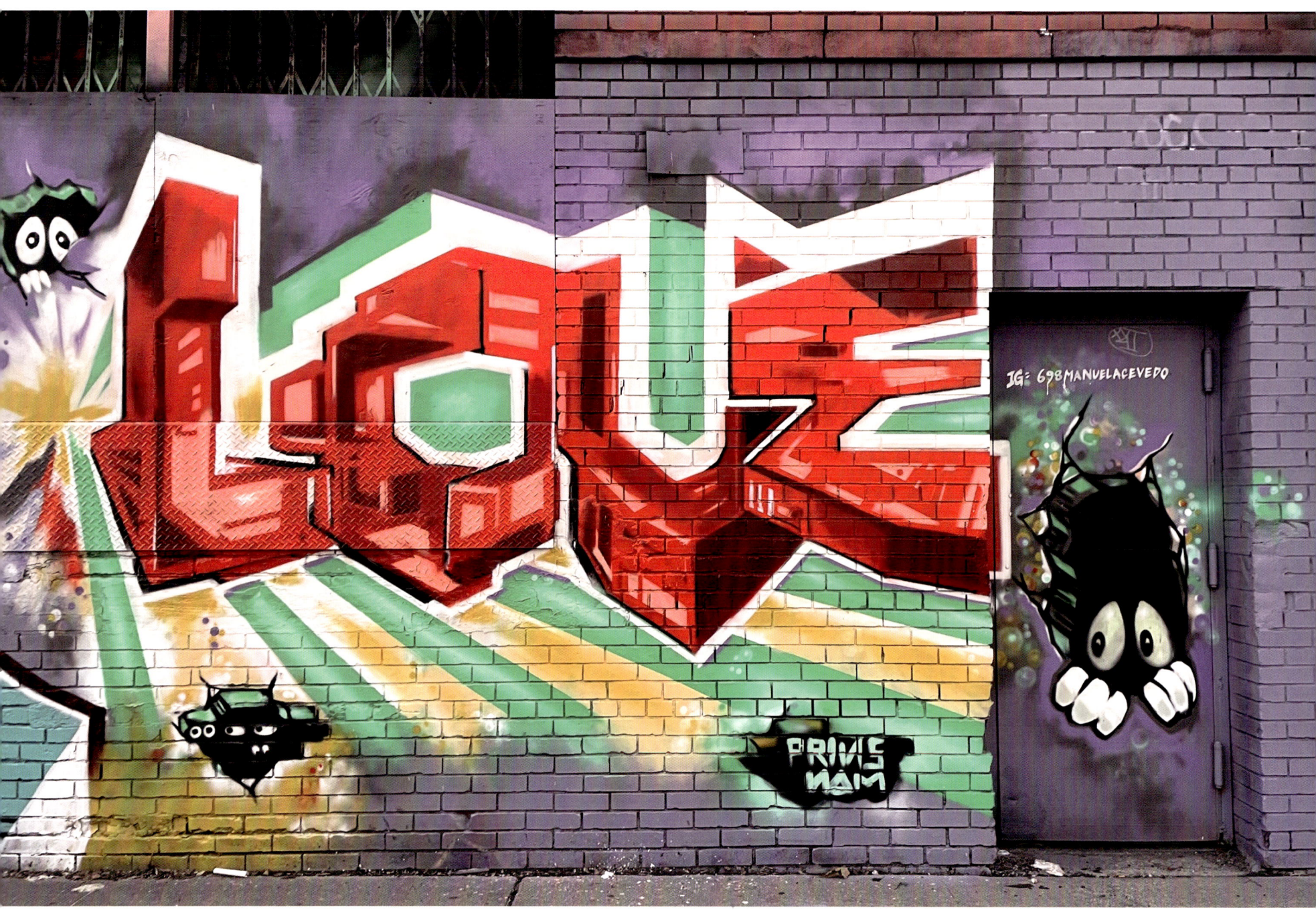

MANUEL ACEVEDO, PRINS
BOONE AVENUE WALLS, THE BRONX, PHOTOGRAPHED IN 2022

44

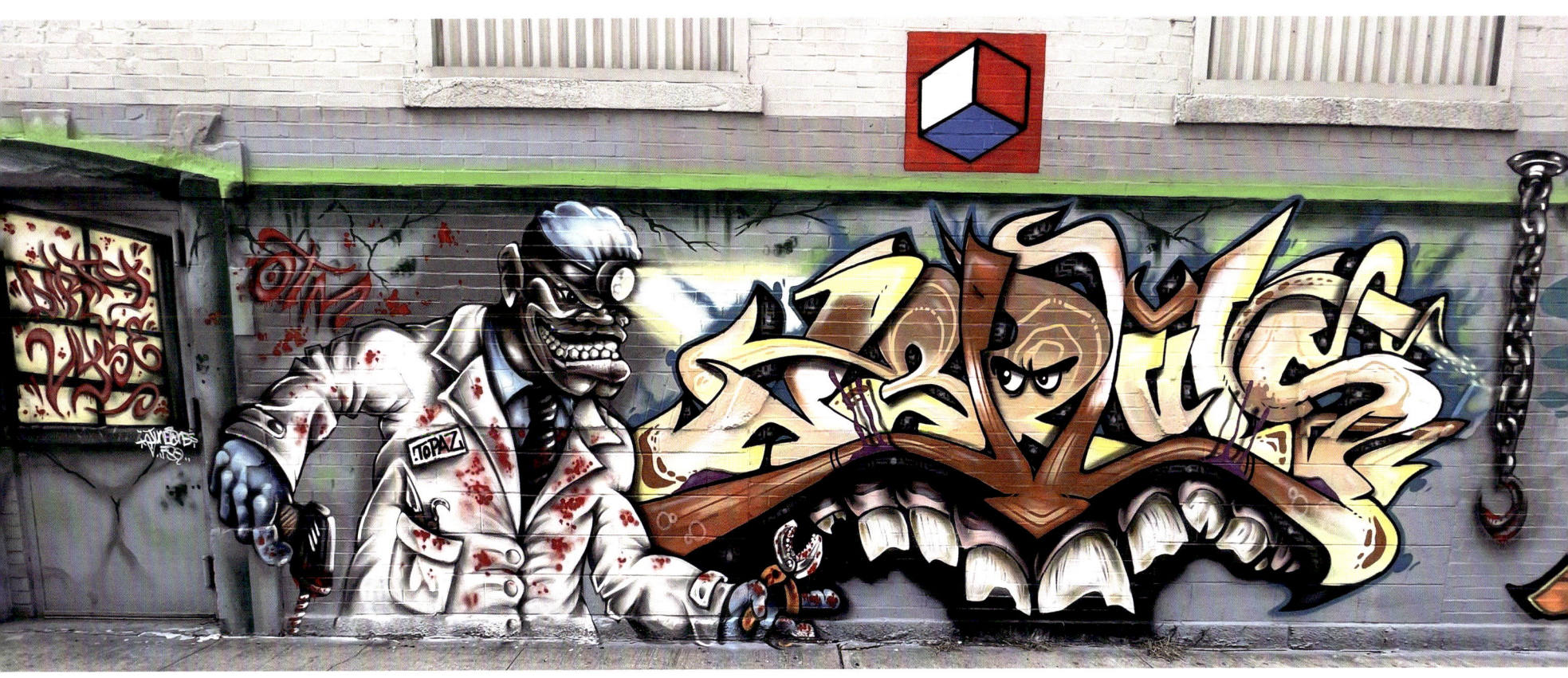

TOPAZ FTR, JERMS

Topaz and Jerms collaborated at Boone Avenue Walls to create this masterpiece of style writing.

BOONE AVENUE WALLS, THE BRONX, PHOTOGRAPHED IN 2024

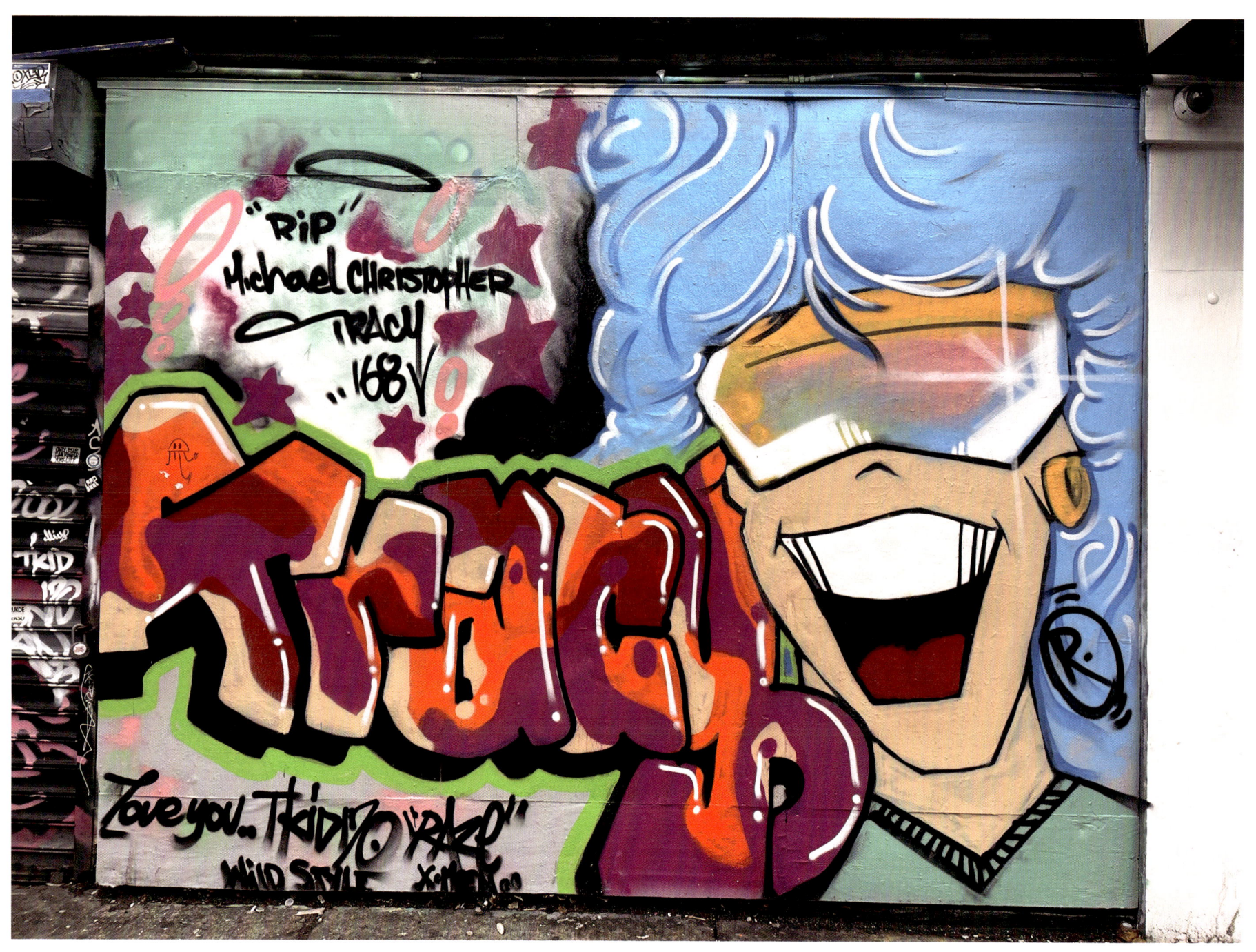

TKID 170
MANHATTAN, PHOTOGRAPHED IN 2024

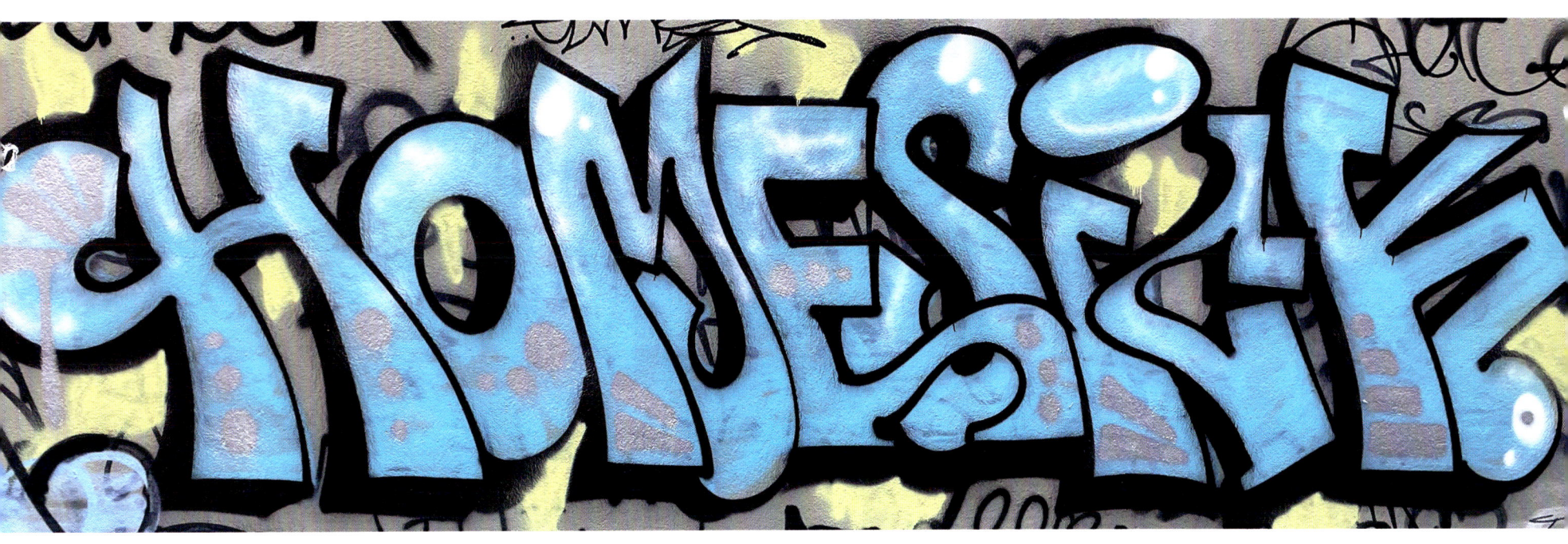

HOMESICK

One of the top young graffiti artists in New York City. You can see his tag on many buildings in Brooklyn, Manhattan, and other boroughs.
MANHATTAN, PHOTOGRAPHED IN 2024

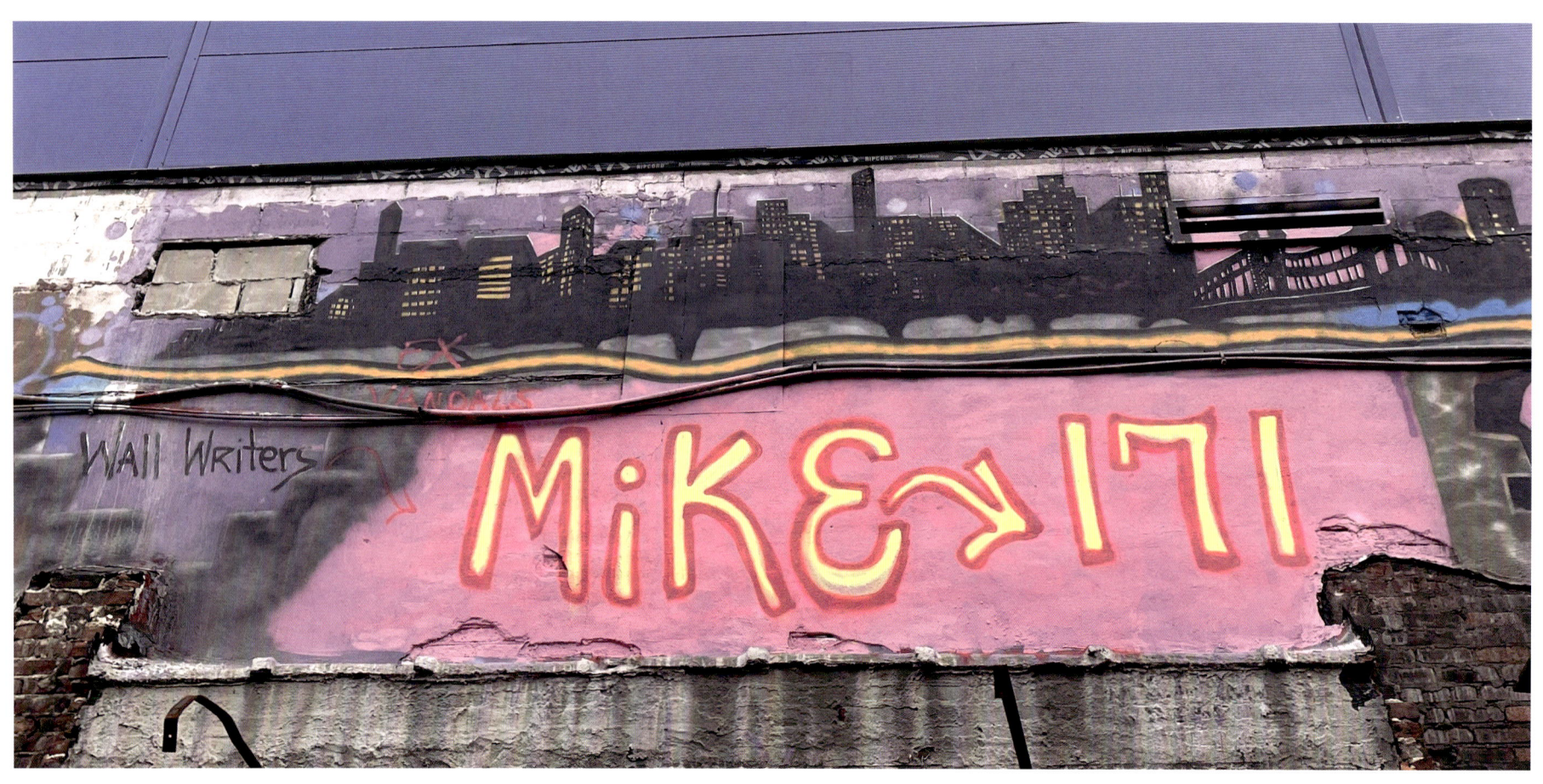

MIKE 171
ROOFTOP GRAFFITERIA, QUEENS, PHOTOGRAPHED IN 2023

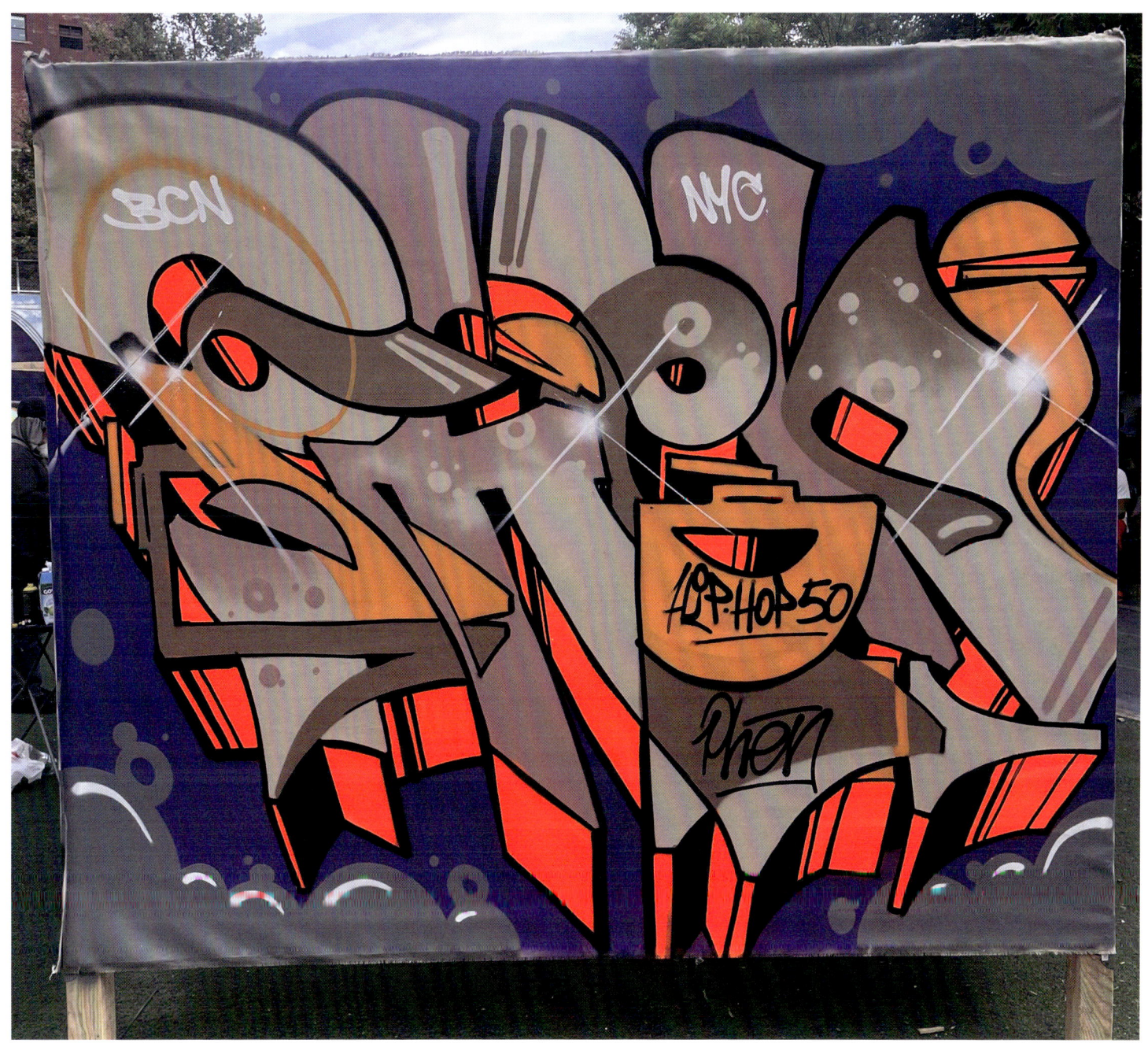

STEFANO PHEN

I selected Stefano Phen's great work to be in the book because of his unique style of letter writing.

GRAFFITI HALL OF FAME, MANHATTAN, PHOTOGRAPHED IN 2023

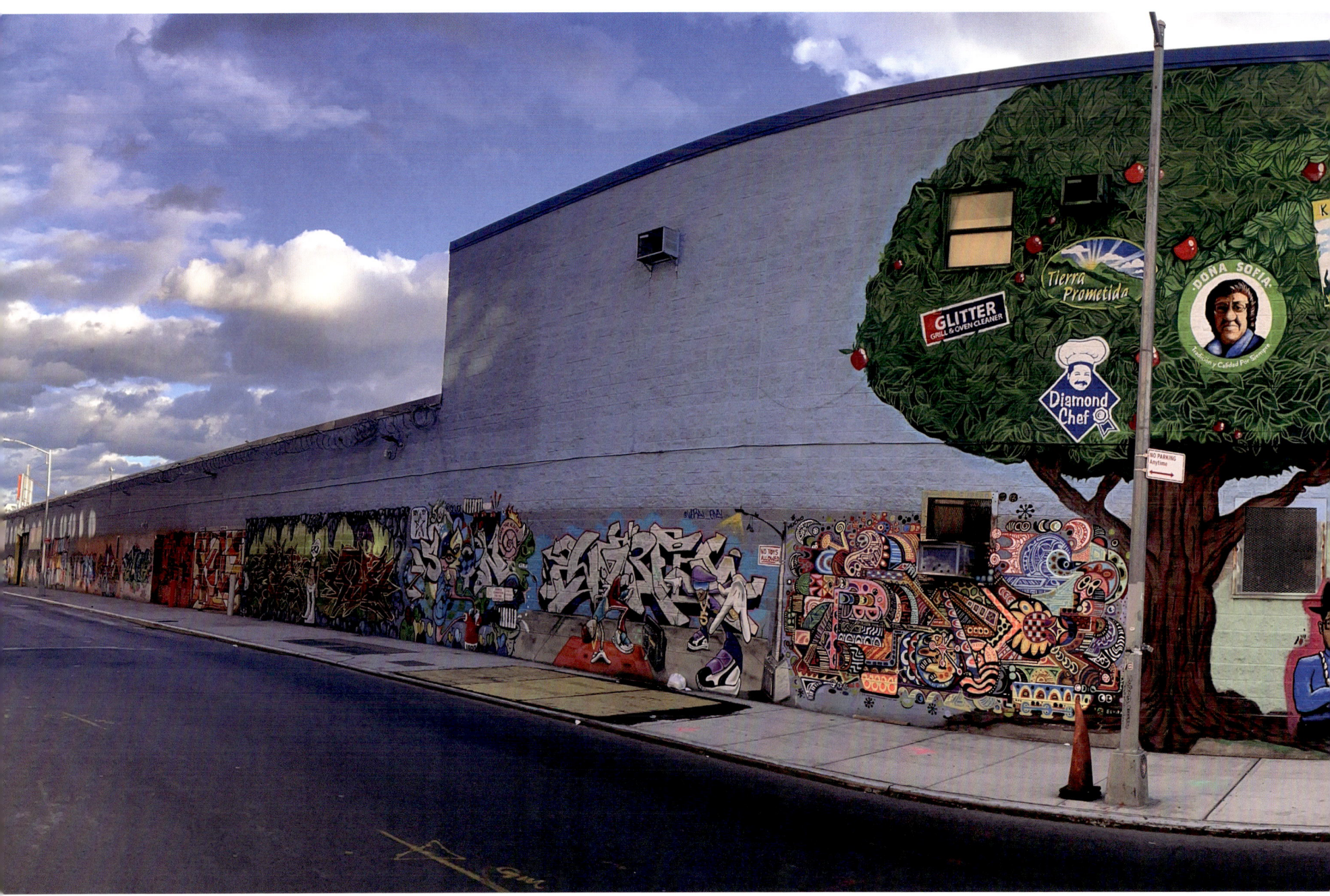

BOONE AVENUE WALLS ARTISTS
FoodFest Depot Wall in the Bronx. Curated by Boone Avenue Walls Foundation.
BOONE AVENUE WALLS, THE BRONX, PHOTOGRAPHED IN 2024

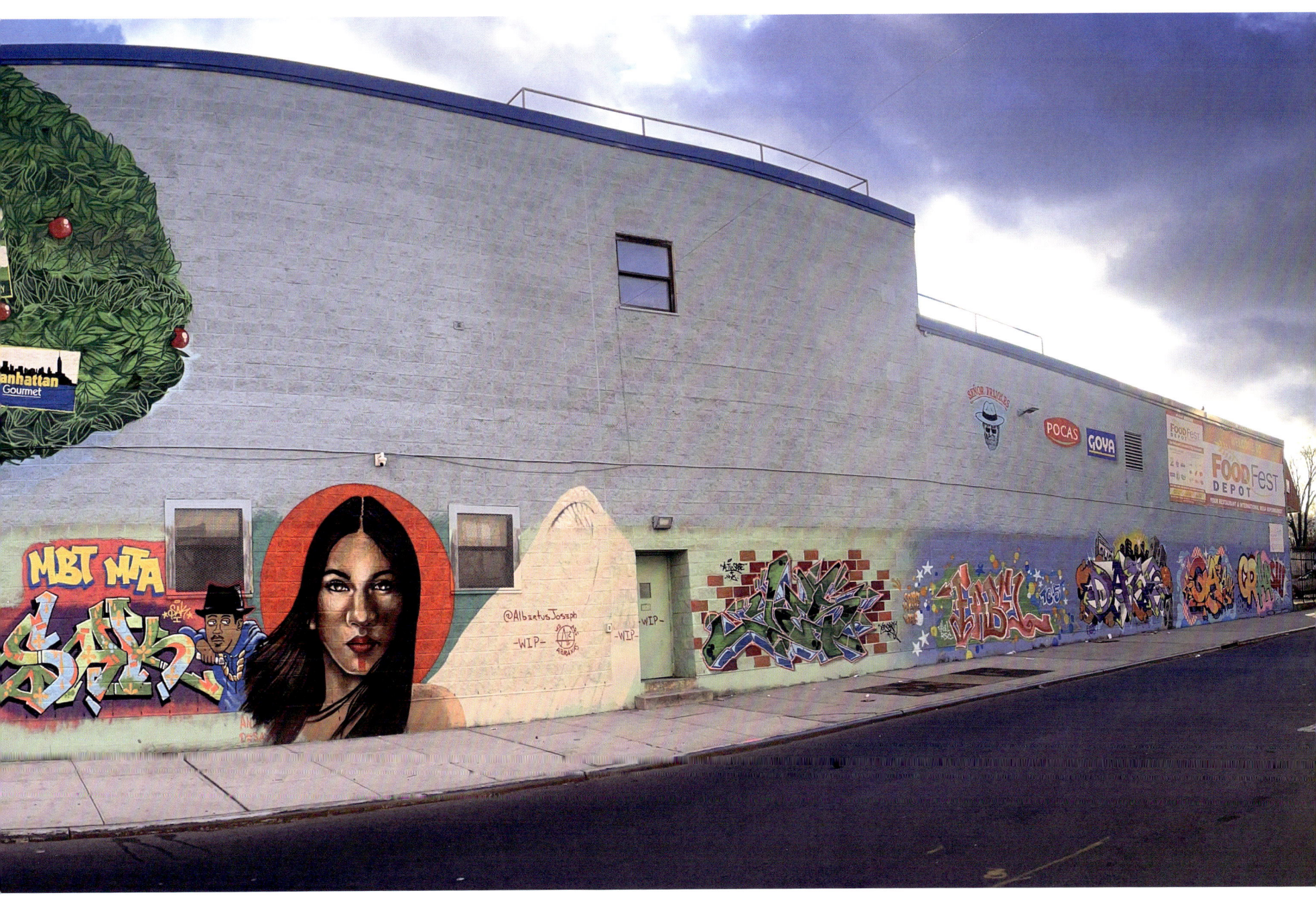

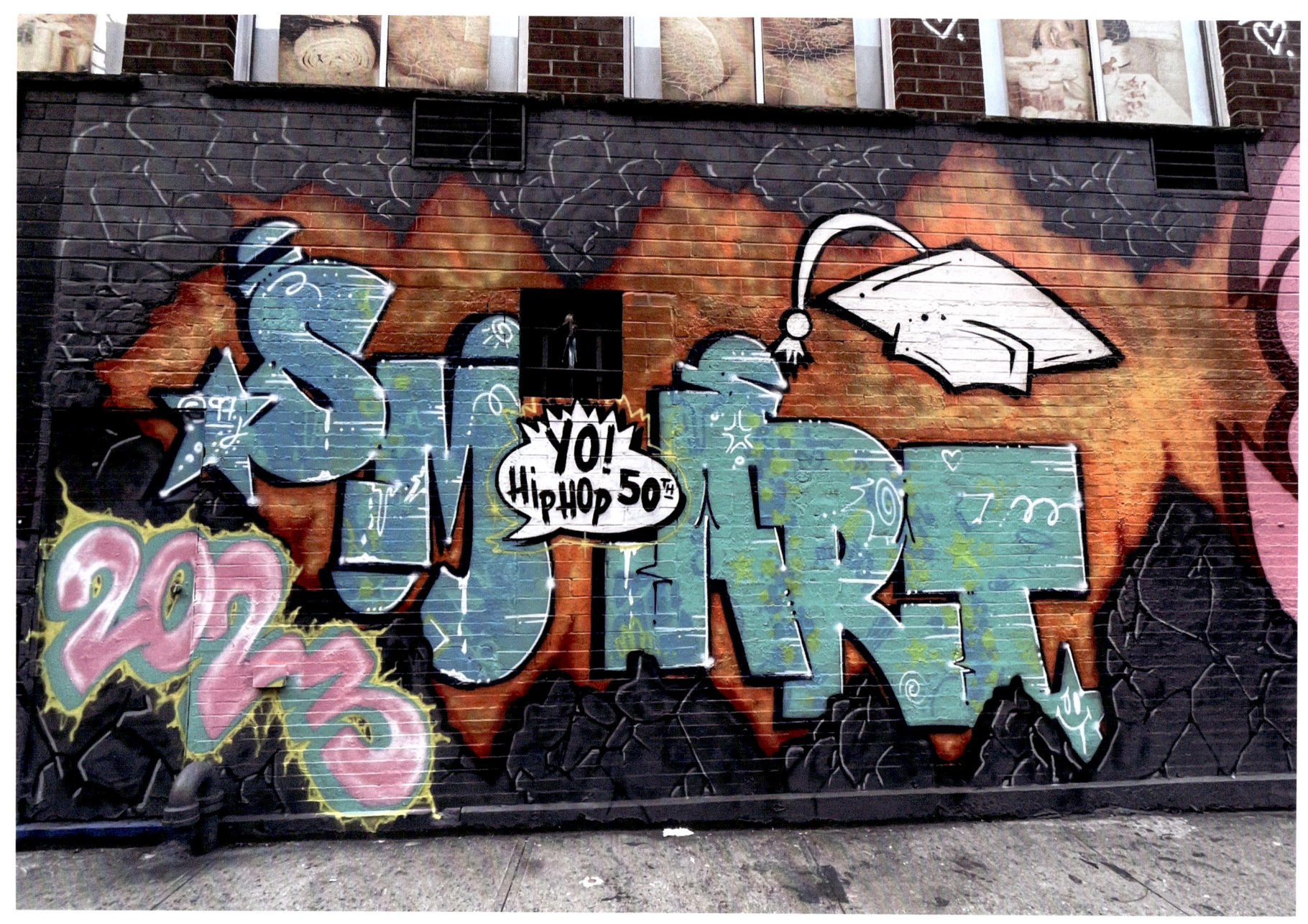

SMART RIS
MANHATTAN, PHOTOGRAPHED IN 2024

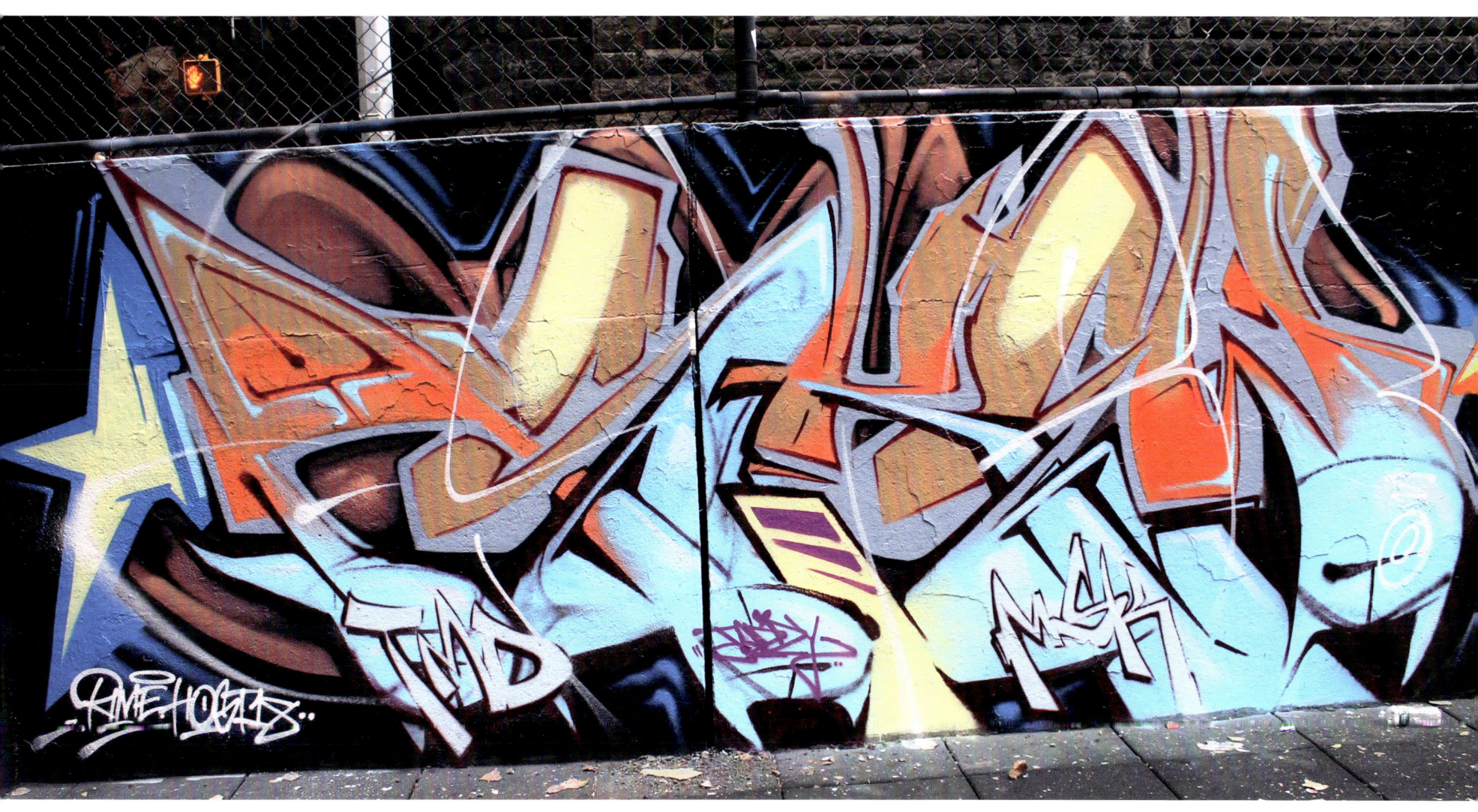

RIME MSK
GRAFFITI HALL OF FAME, MANHATTAN, PHOTOGRAPHED IN 2018

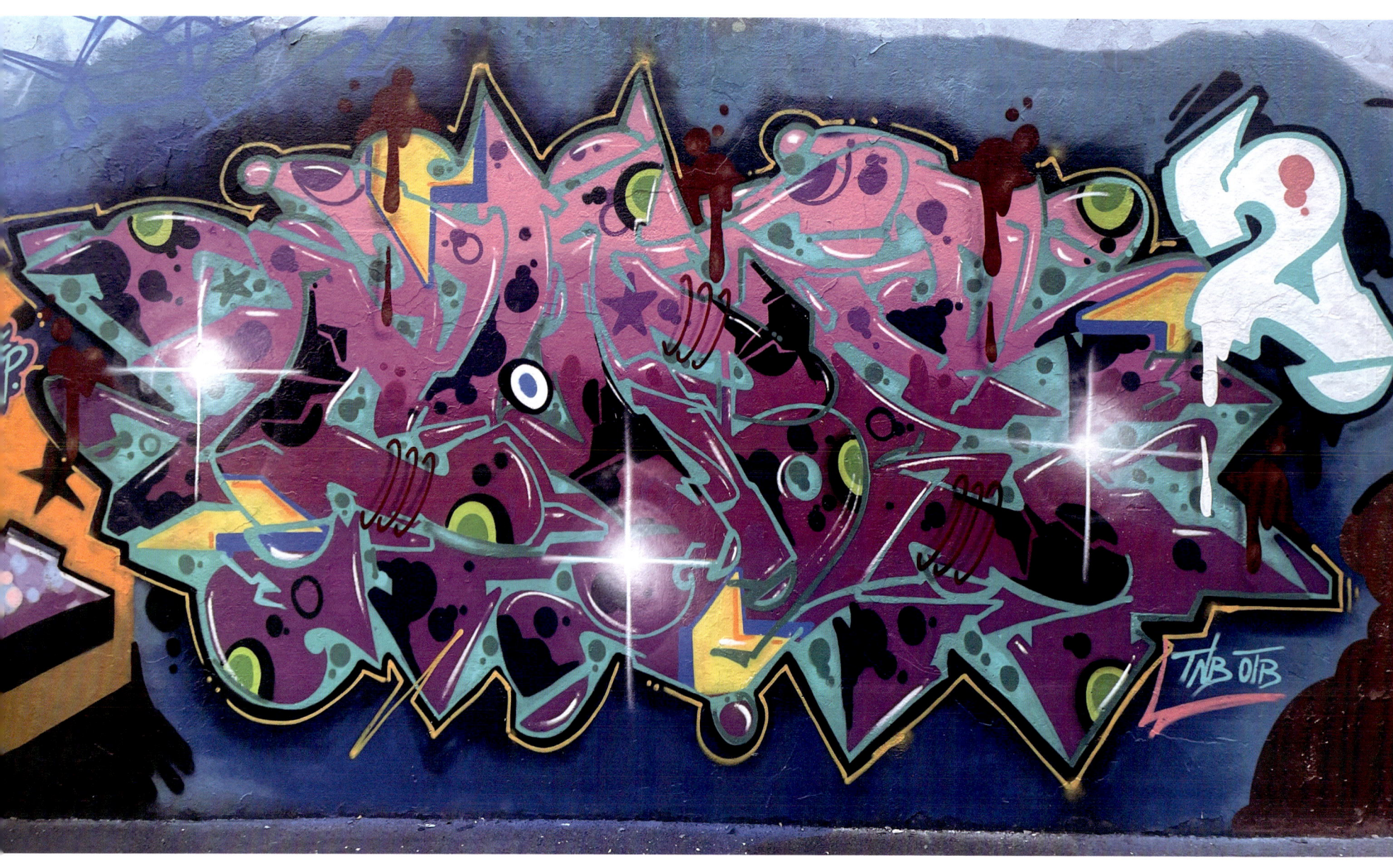

COPE 2
GRAFFITI HALL OF FAME, MANHATTAN, PHOTOGRAPHED IN 2023

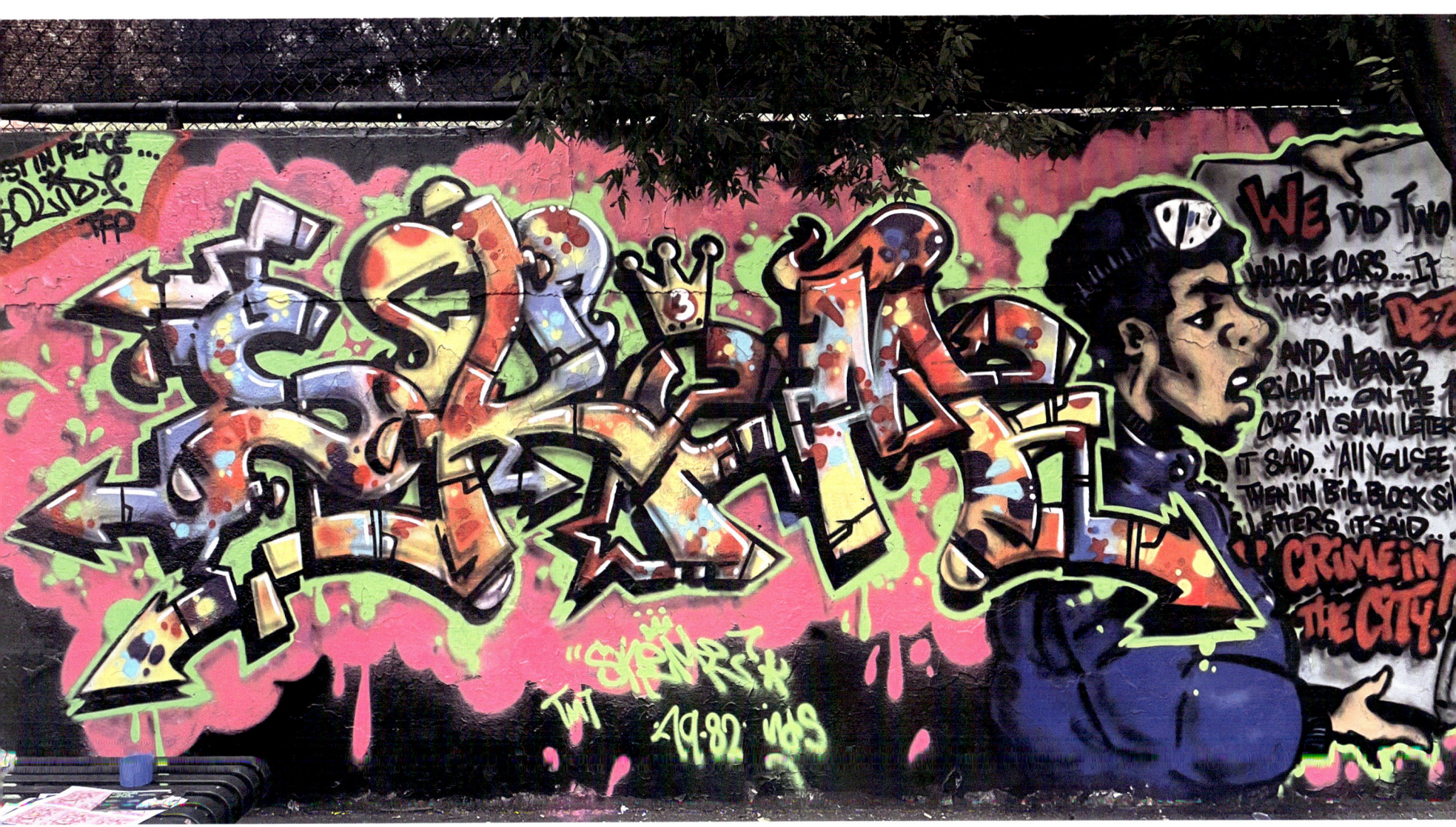

SKEME

Skeme was one of the stars in the movie *Style Wars*. He was a prolific subway writer in the 1970s and '80s.
GRAFFITI HALL OF FAME, MANHATTAN, PHOTOGRAPHED IN 2023

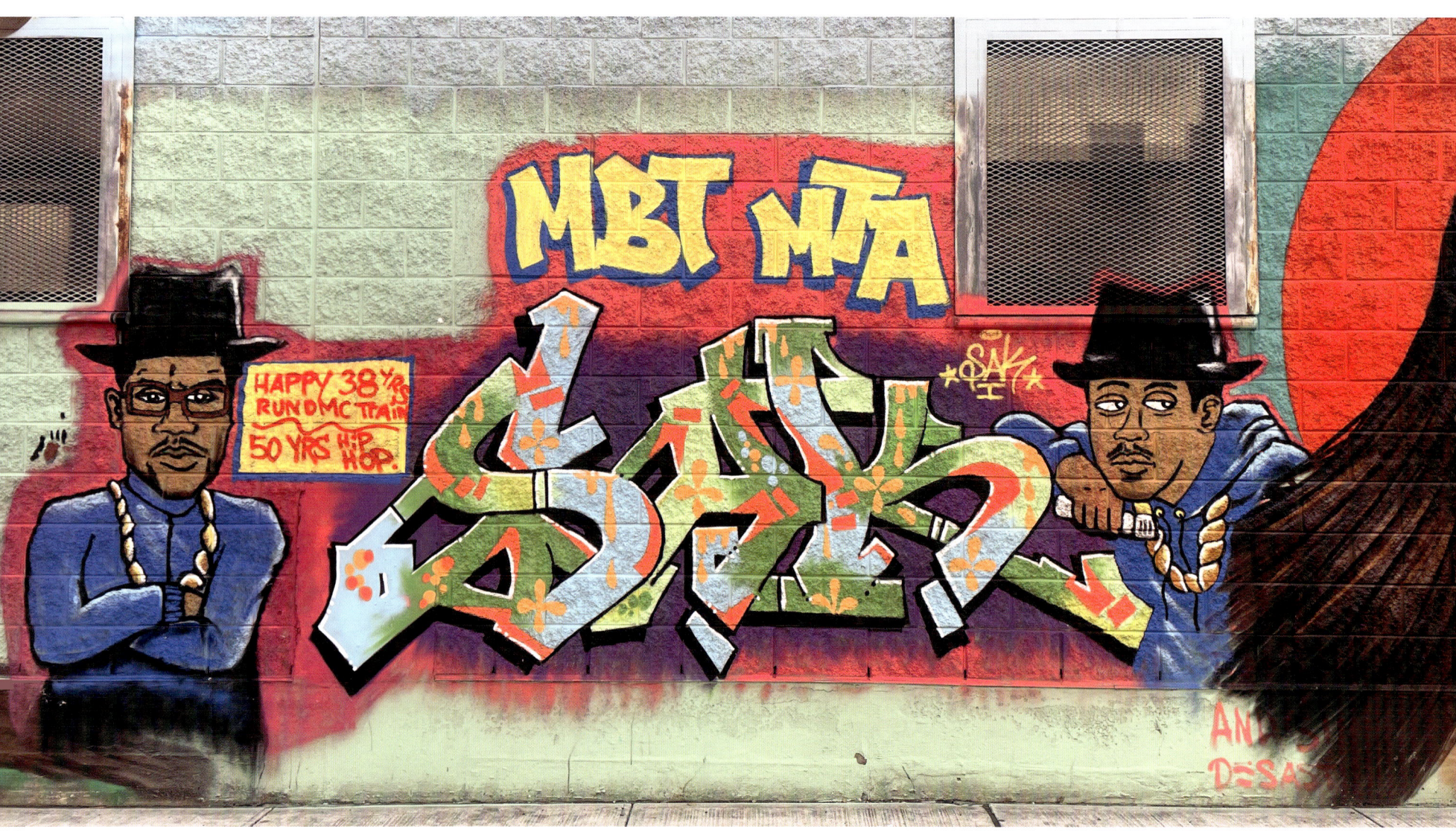

SAK

Sak was New York City subway writer starting in 1980s. He was a member of MBT Crew (Masters Burning Together).
BOONE AVENUE WALLS, THE BRONX PHOTOGRAPHED IN 2024

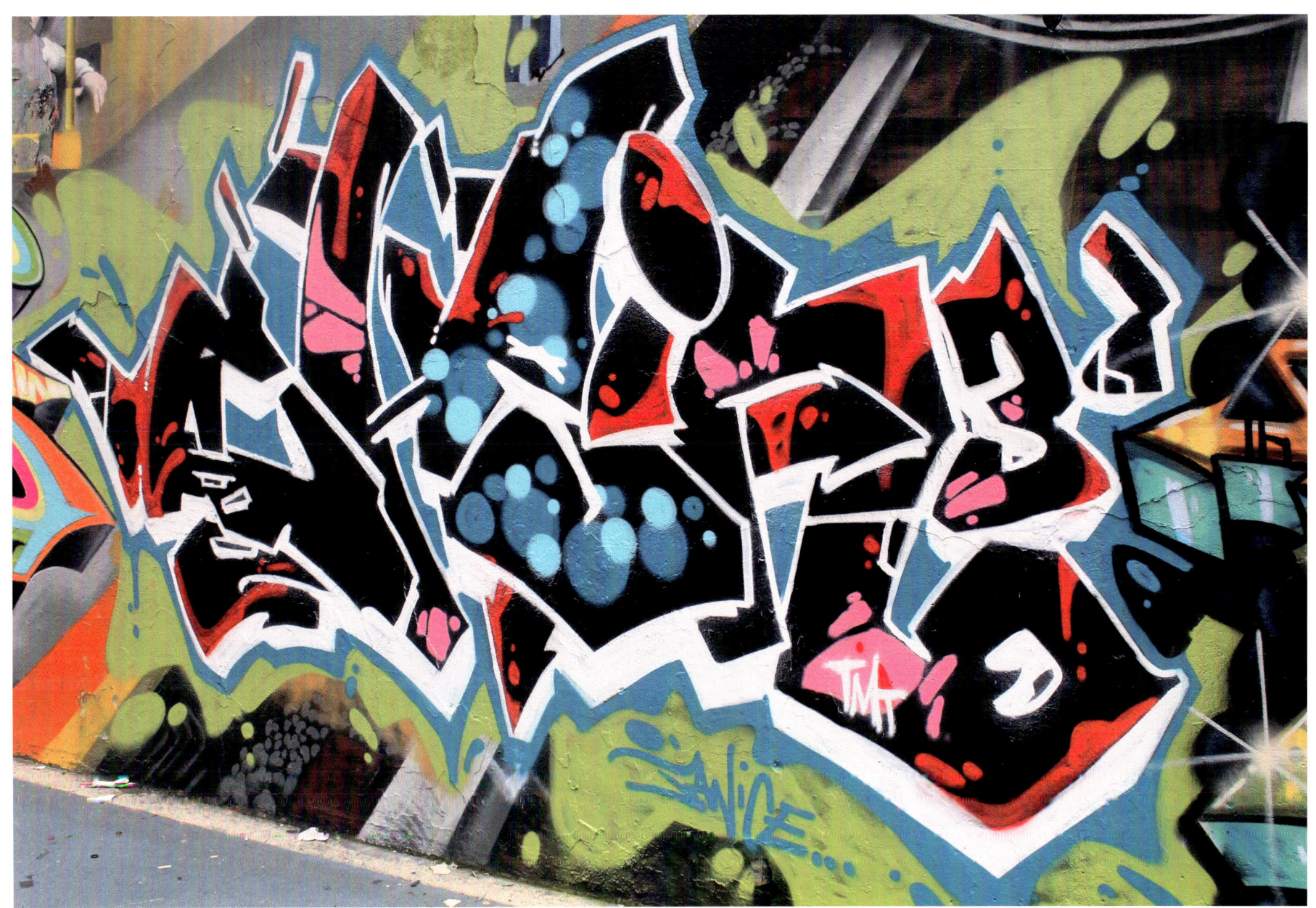

CHAIN 3

An early practitioner of aerosol art in the 1970s and '80s.
GRAFFITI HALL OF FAME, MANHATTAN, PHOTOGRAPHED IN 2018

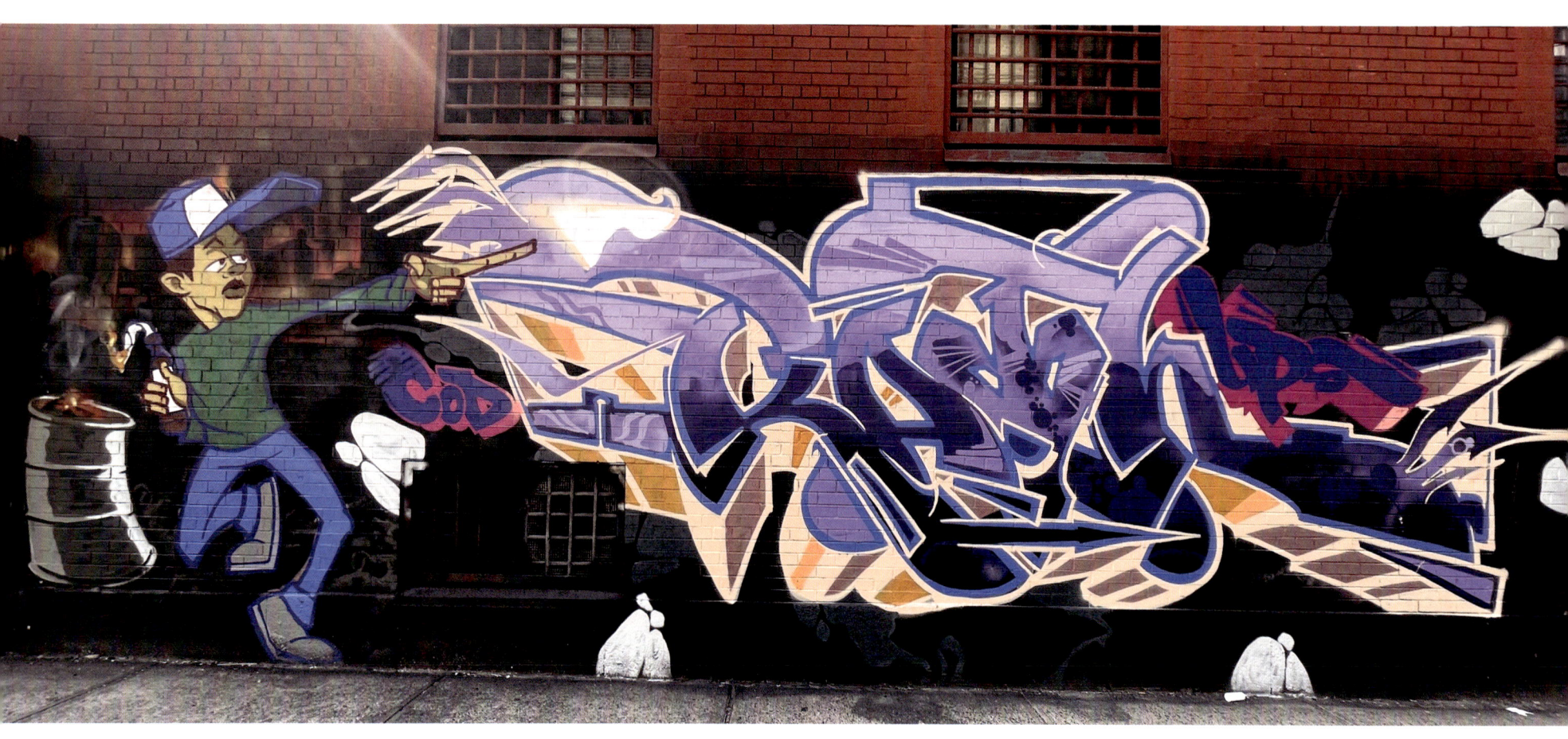

RATH COD

An early practitioner of aerosol art beginning in the 1980s.
BOONE AVENUE WALLS, THE BRONX NEW YORK, PHOTOGRAPH IN 2024

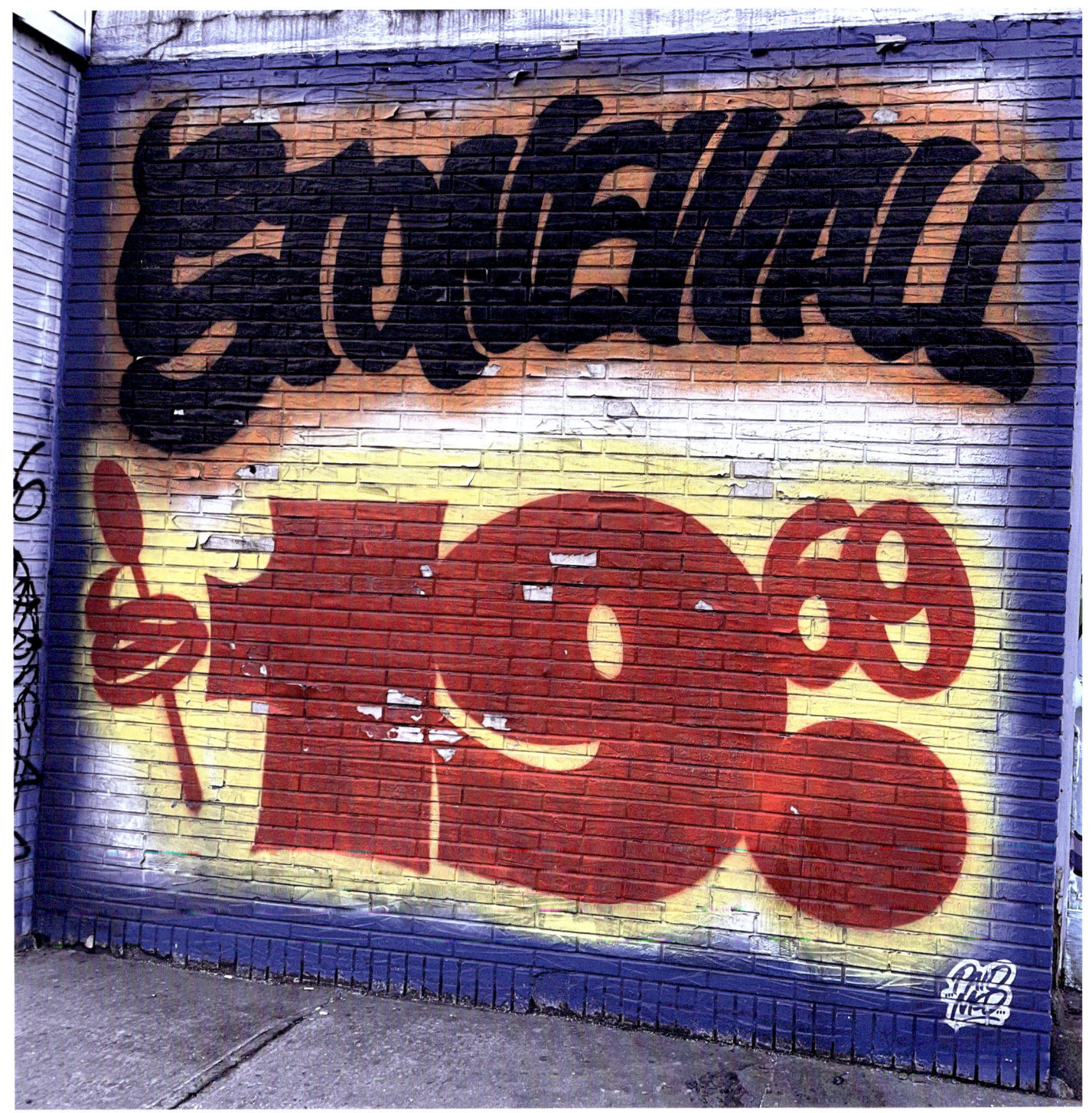

PETER PAID
An artist who uses the techniques of sign painting in his graffiti art. He began his art journey during the subway graffiti era of the 1980s.
BROOKLYN,
PHOTOGRAPHED IN 2024

DEGRUPO

DEGRUPO is a graffiti bomber and street artist. His name can be seen on buildings across New York City and other cities. His repelling graffiti stands out in New York City. Recently, he has exhibited his work in art exhibitions.
BROOKLYN, PHOTOGRAPHED IN 2024

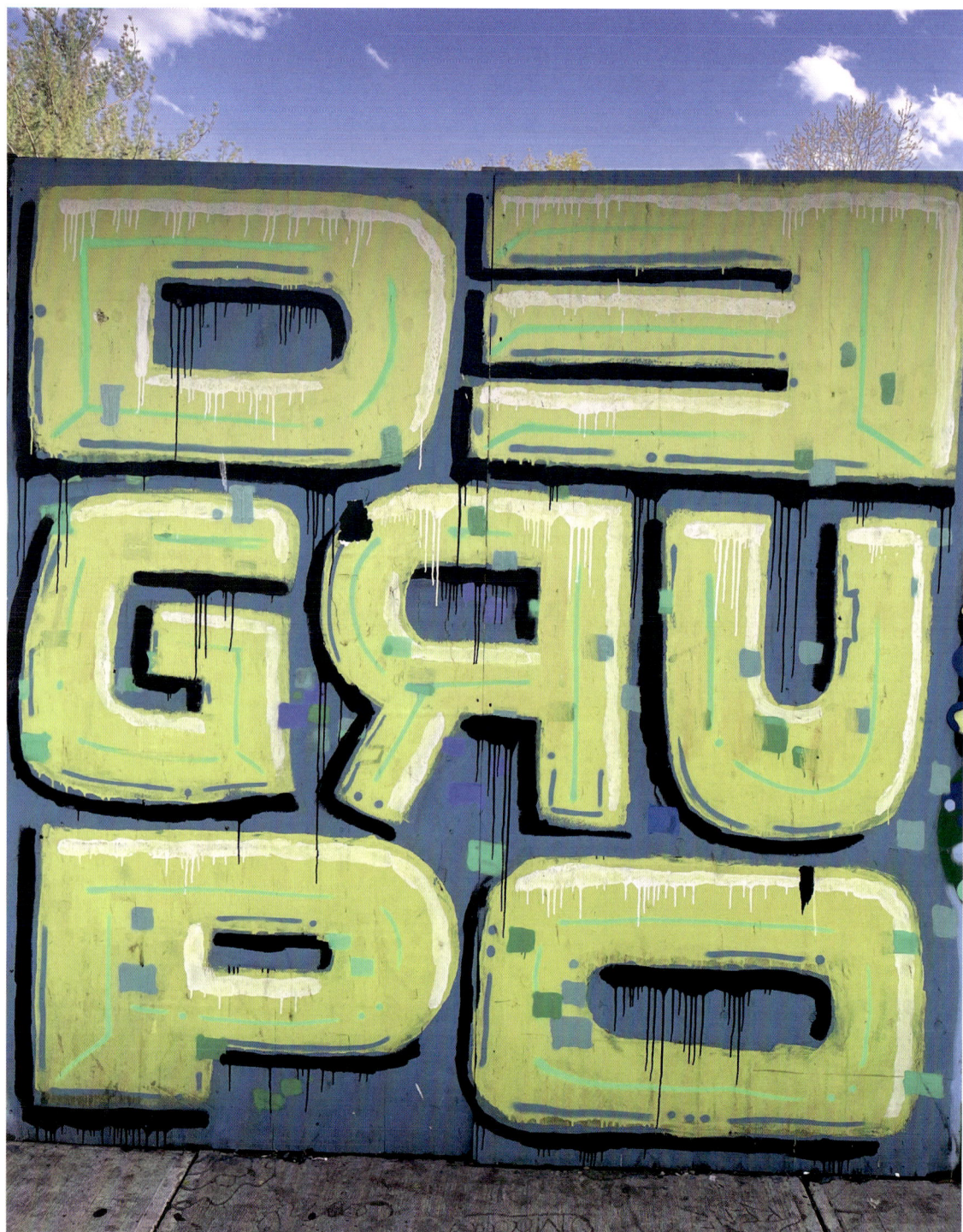

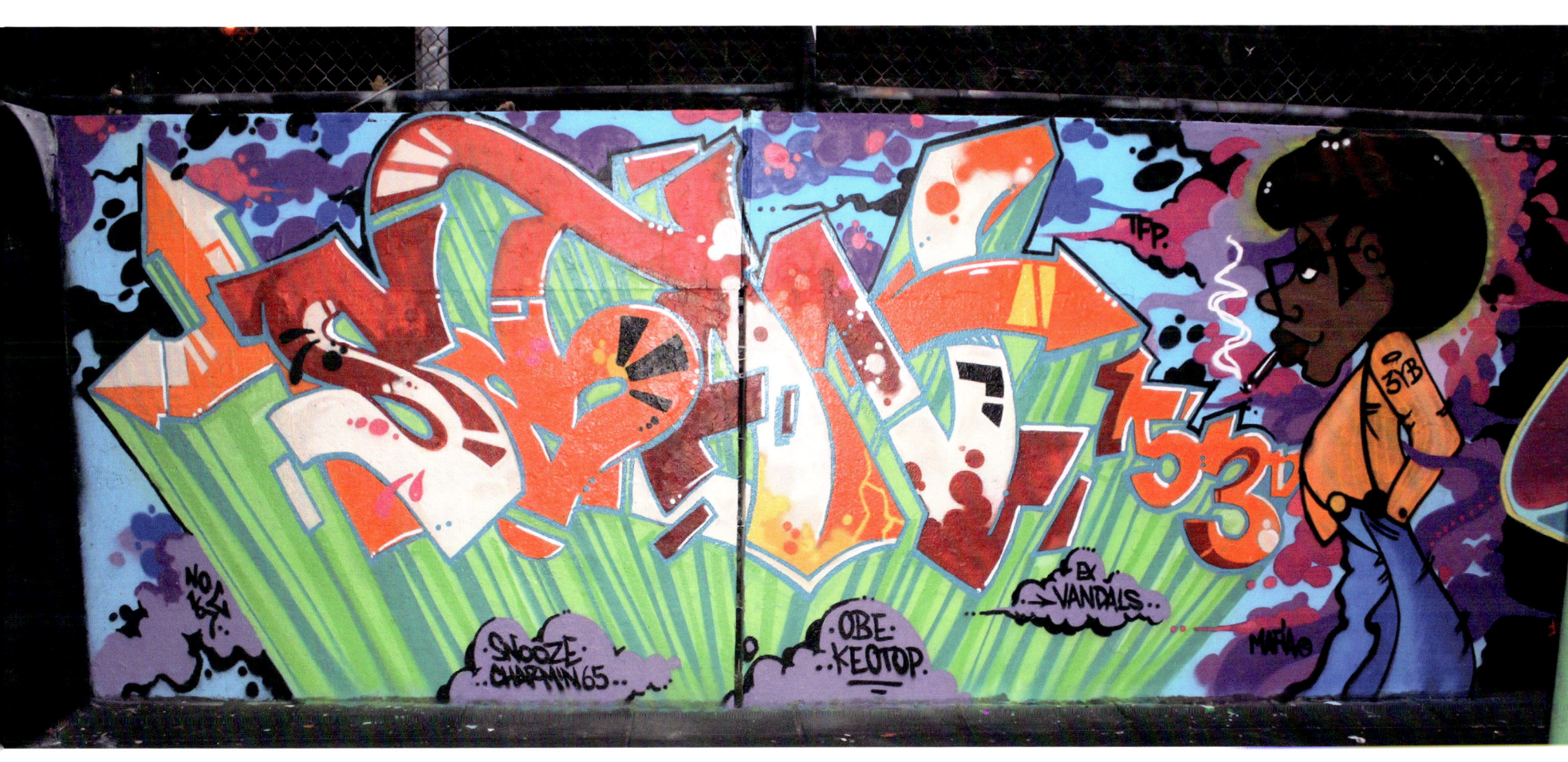

OBE, KEO
GRAFFITI HALL OF FAME, MANHATTAN, PHOTOGRAPHED IN 2019

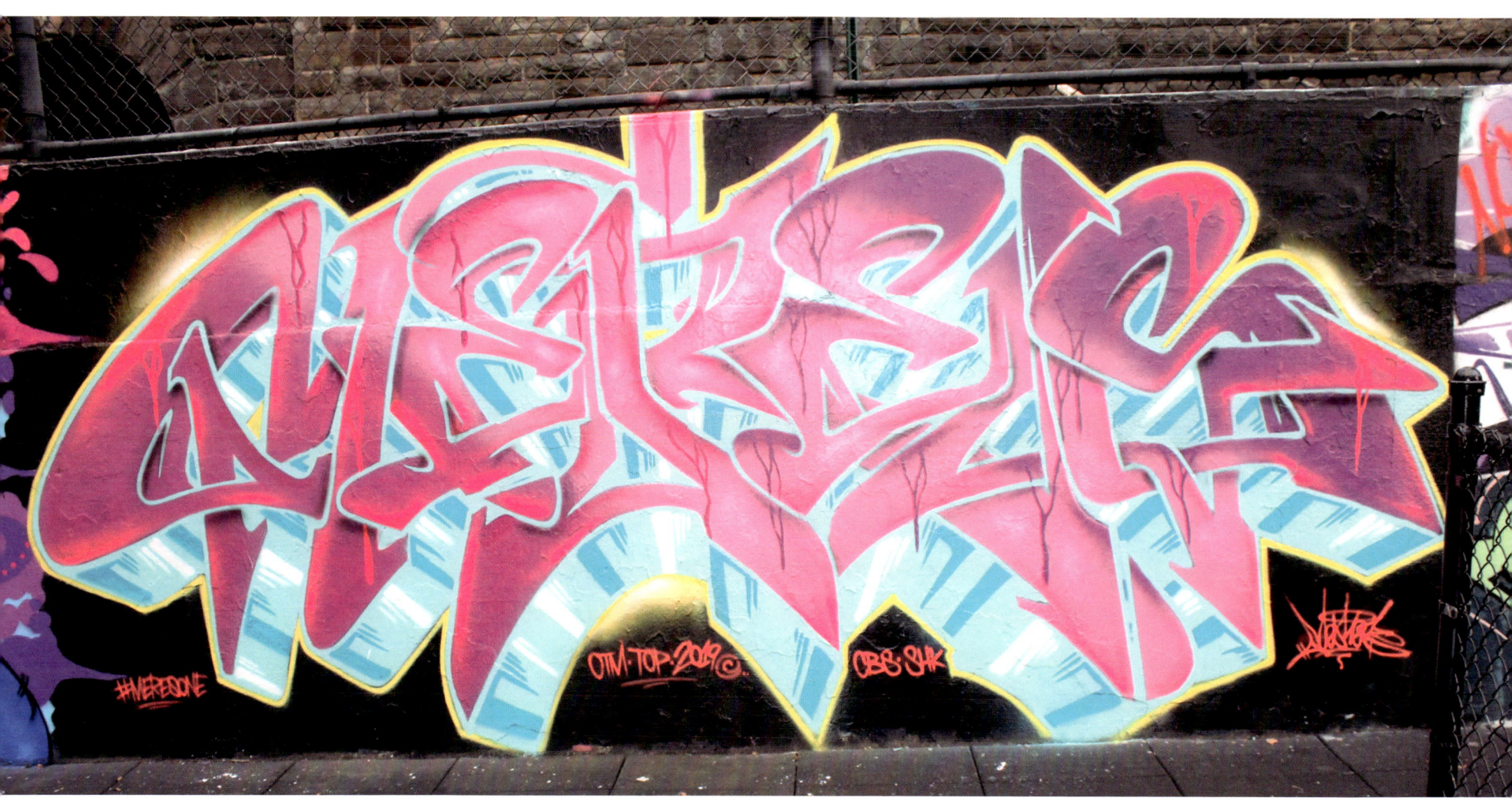

MERES ONE

A prolific aerosol artist who was curator of the 5 POINTZ Aerosol Art Center in Long Island City, Queens.

GRAFFITI HALL OF FAME, MANHATTAN, PHOTOGRAPHED IN 2019

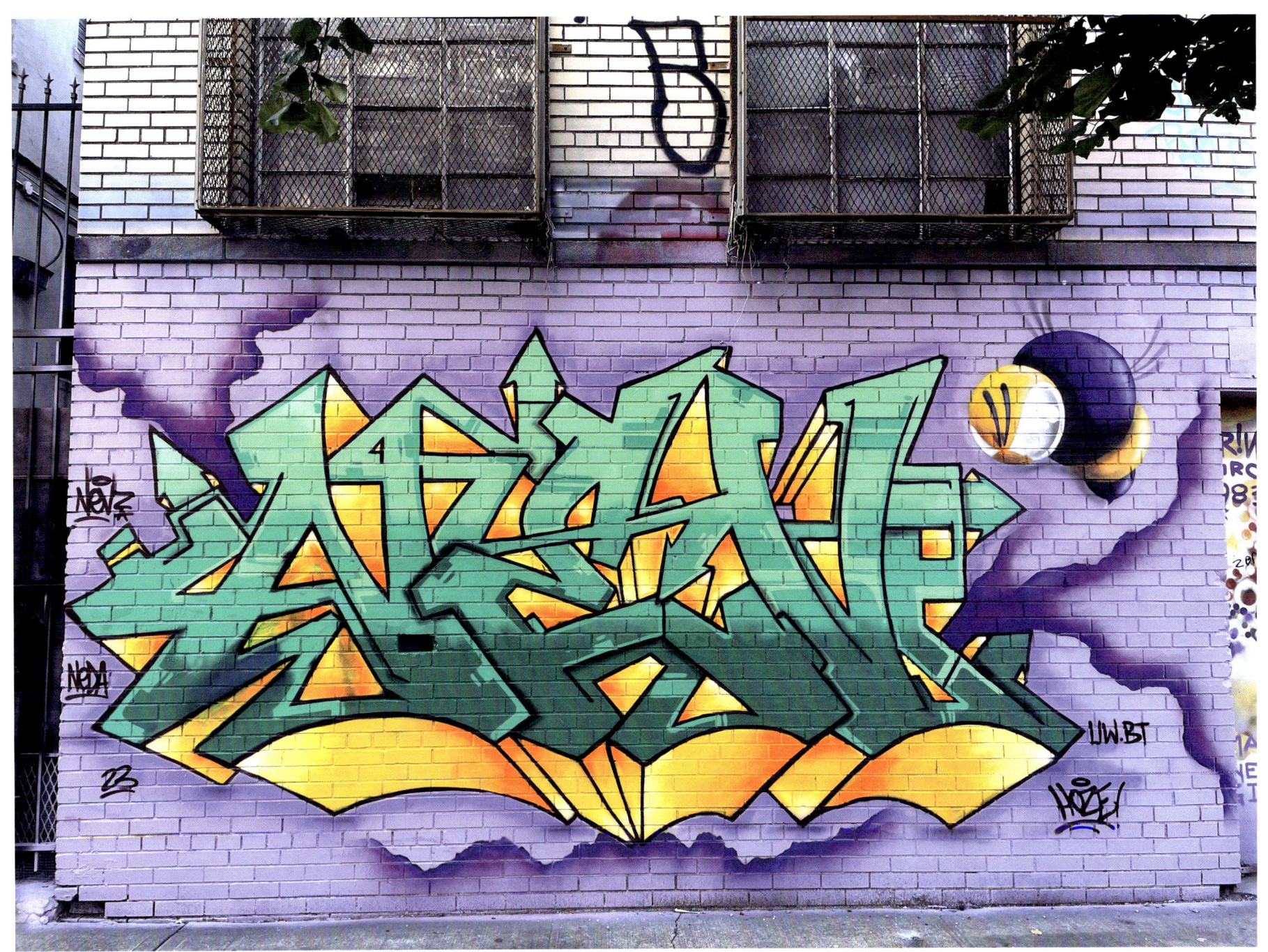

NEV, KING BEE UW
BOONE AVENUE WALLS, THE BRONX, PHOTOGRAPHED IN 2023

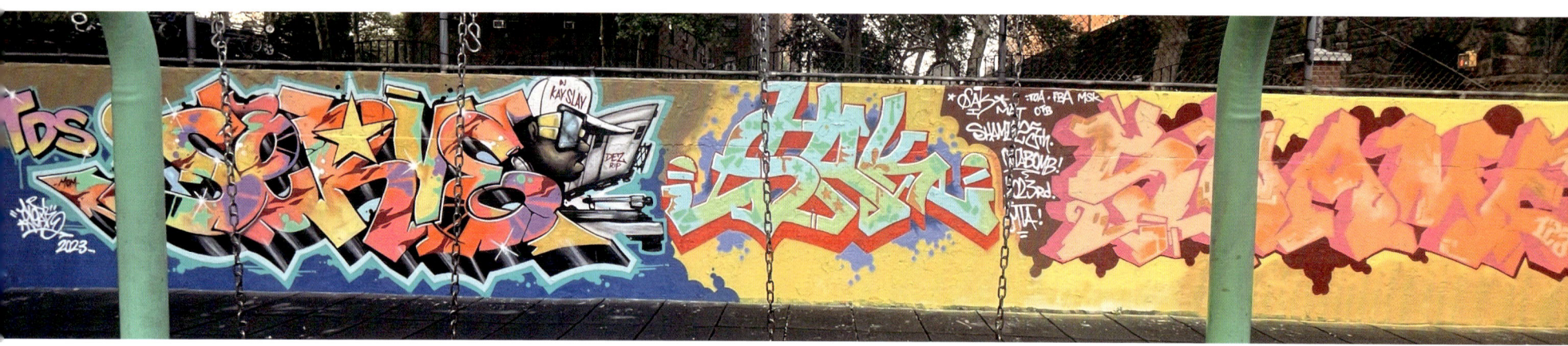

SERVE, SAK, SHAME 125

Tribute to Kay Slay wall at the Graffiti Hall of Fame.

GRAFFITI HALL OF FAME, MANHATTAN, PHOTOGRAPHED IN 2023

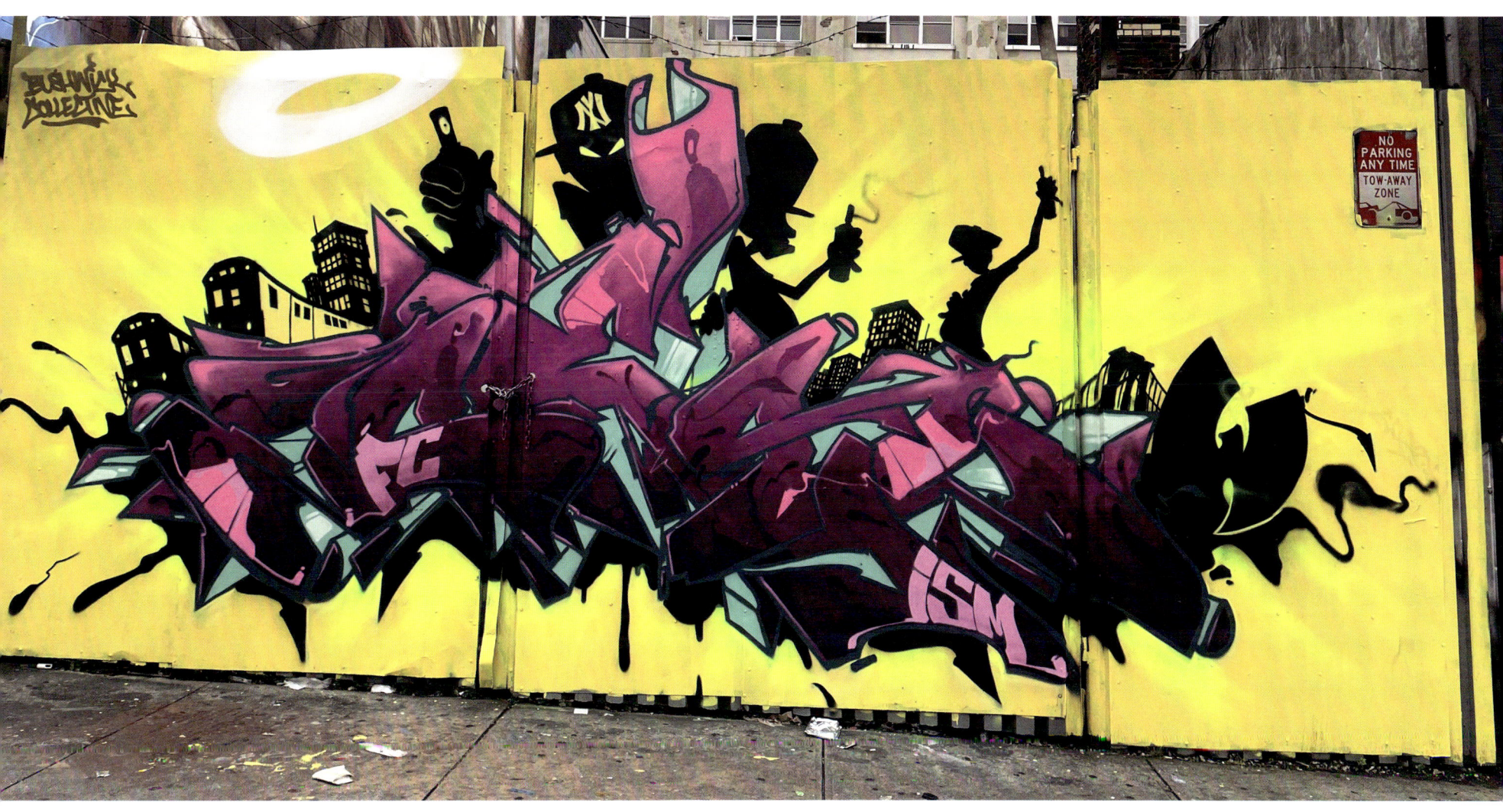

ROB CES PROVENZANO
CES is a leader of streamlined and aerodynamic WILDSTYLE lettering in the graffiti arts.
BUSHWICK COLLECTIVE, PHOTOGRAPHED IN 2024

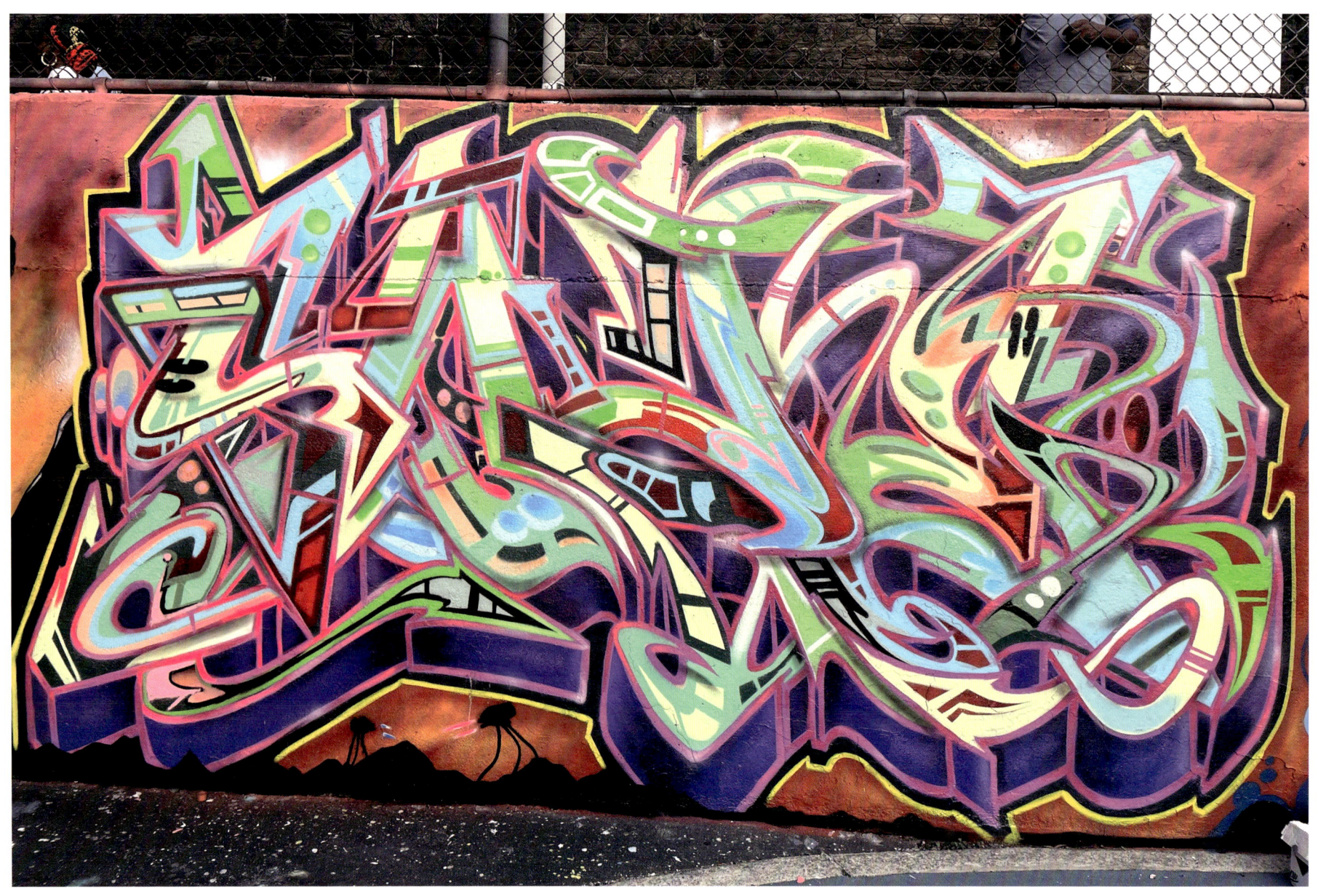

SOZE 527

Soze is a longtime aerosol artist. Here he displays his artistic skills with spray paint at the Graffiti Hall of Fame.
GRAFFITI HALL OF FAME, MANHATTAN, PHOTOGRAPHED IN 2023

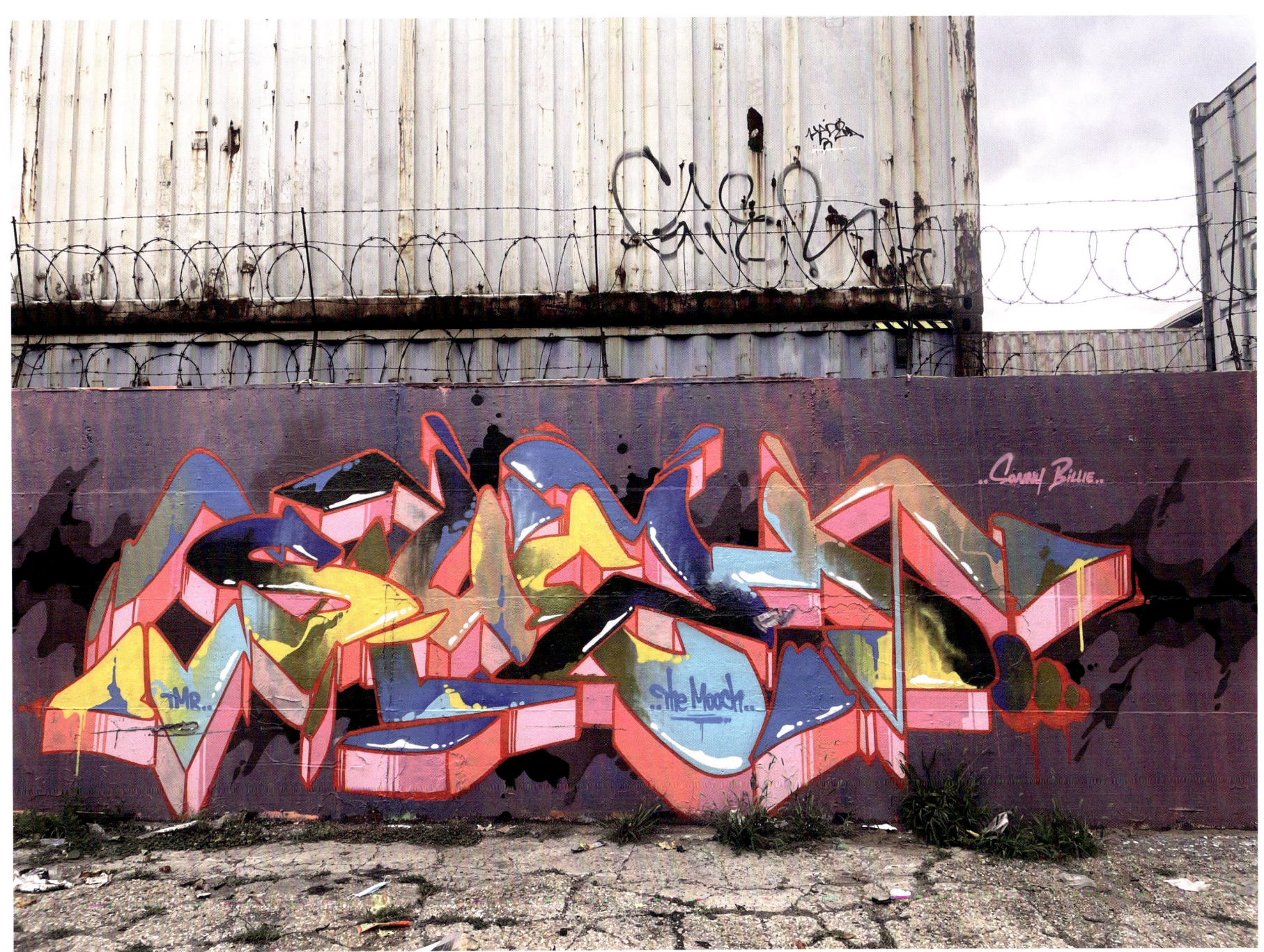

SUCH RIS
BROOKLYN, PHOTOGRAPHED IN 2024

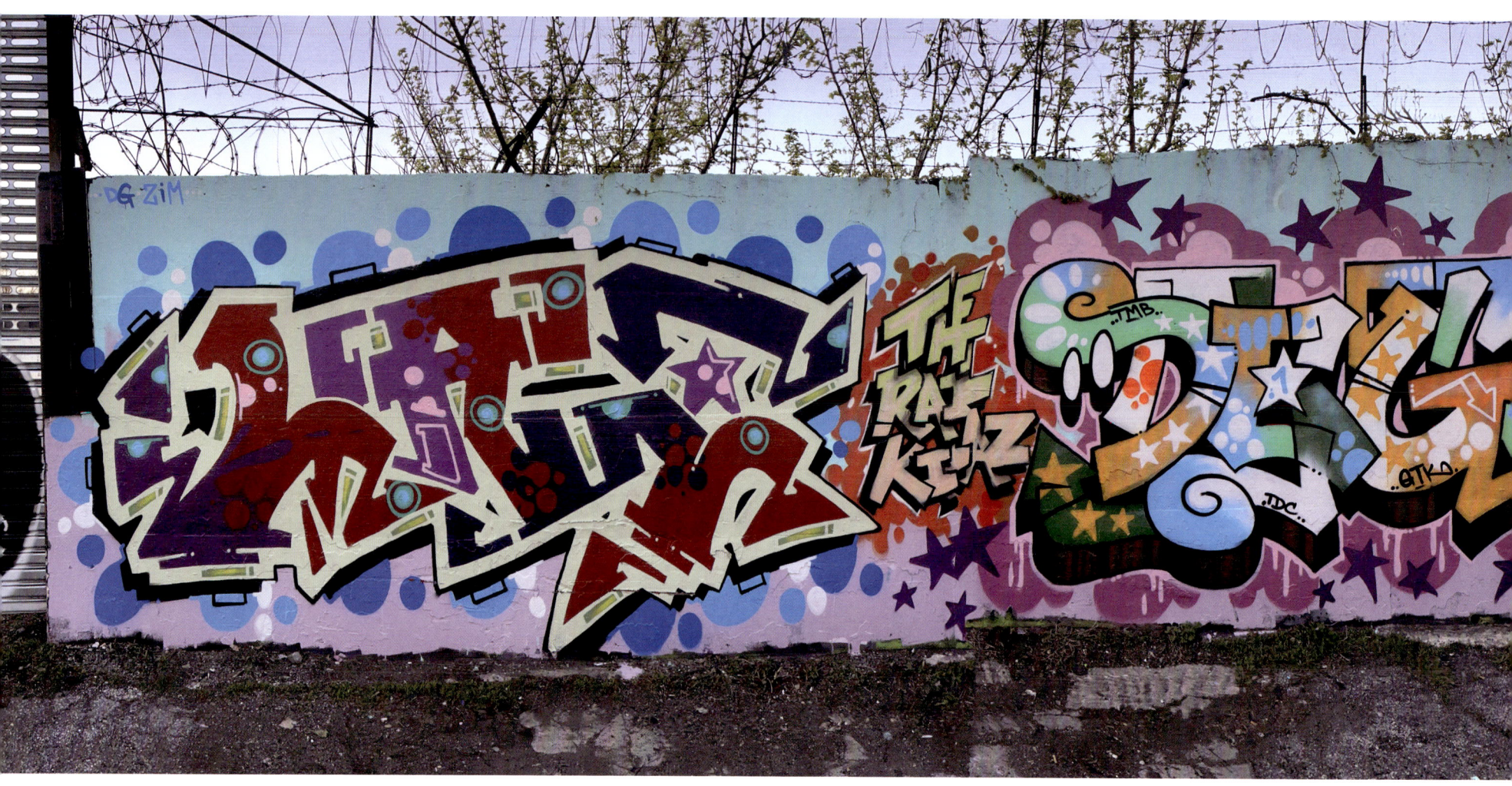

GOOD TIMES KREW
ZIM DG ONE ACNE MEMORIAL WALL, BROOKLYN, PHOTOGRAPHED IN 2024

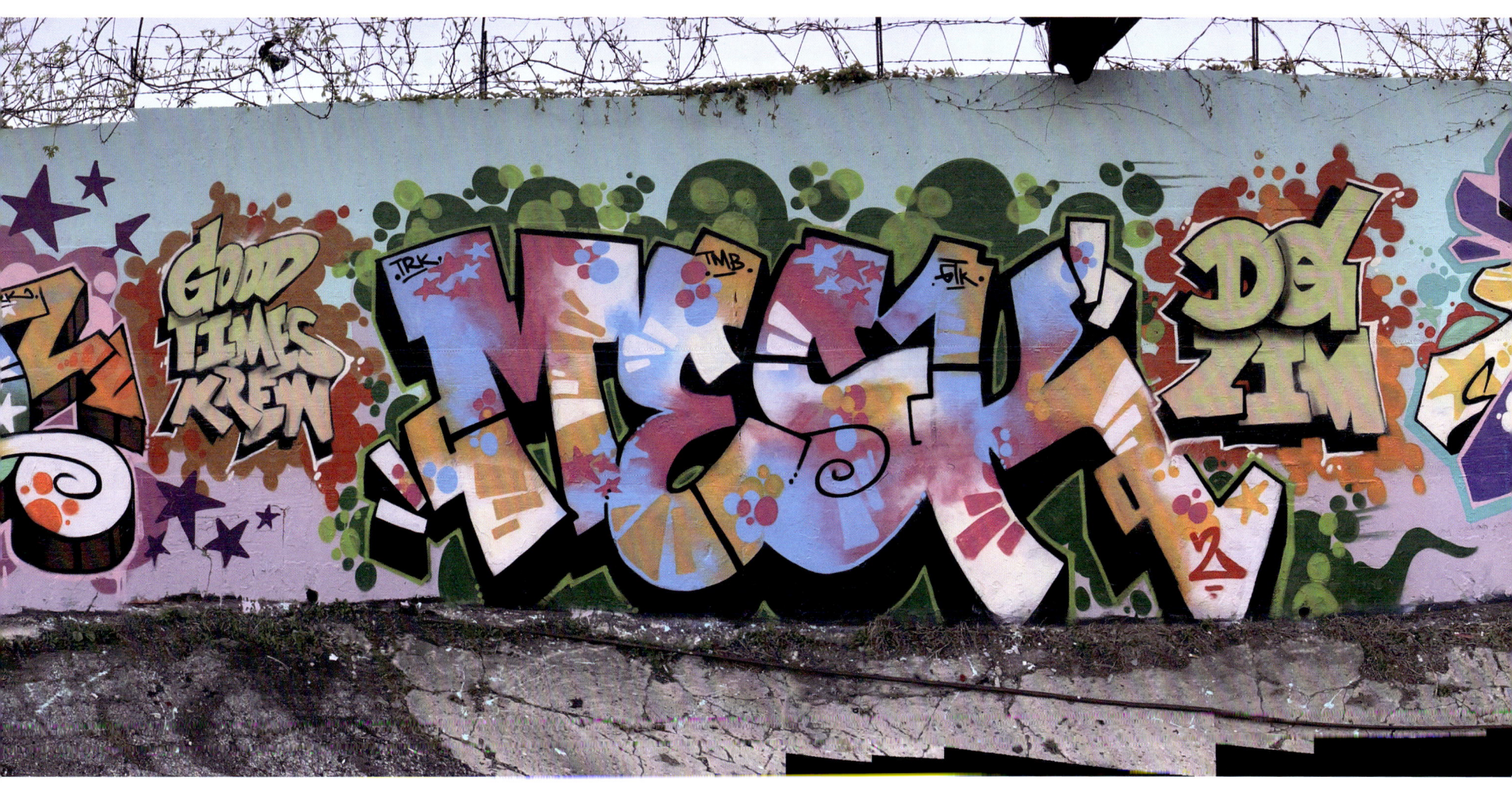

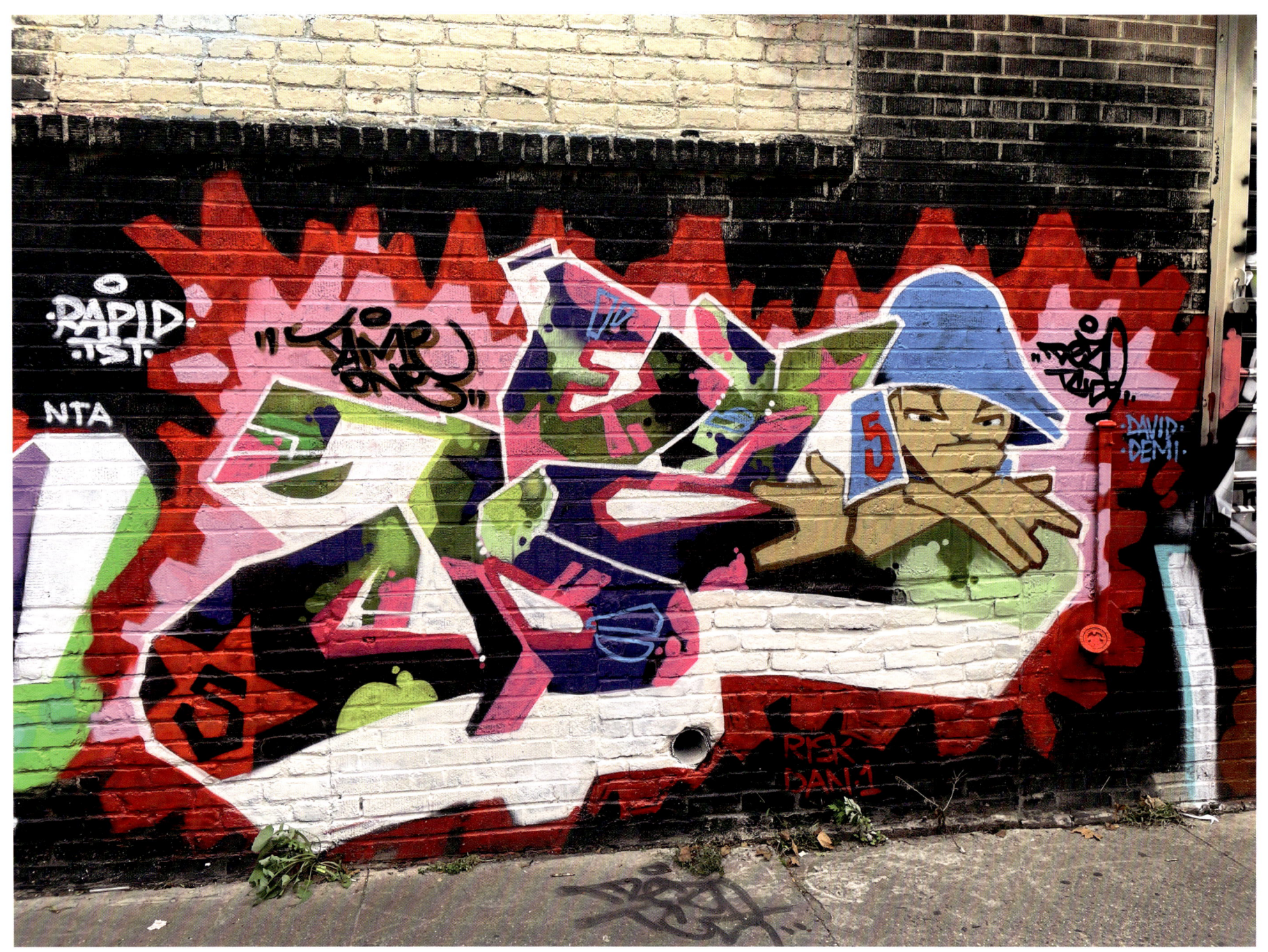

DEZO
BOONE AVENUE WALLS, THE BRONX, PHOTOGRAPHED IN 2023

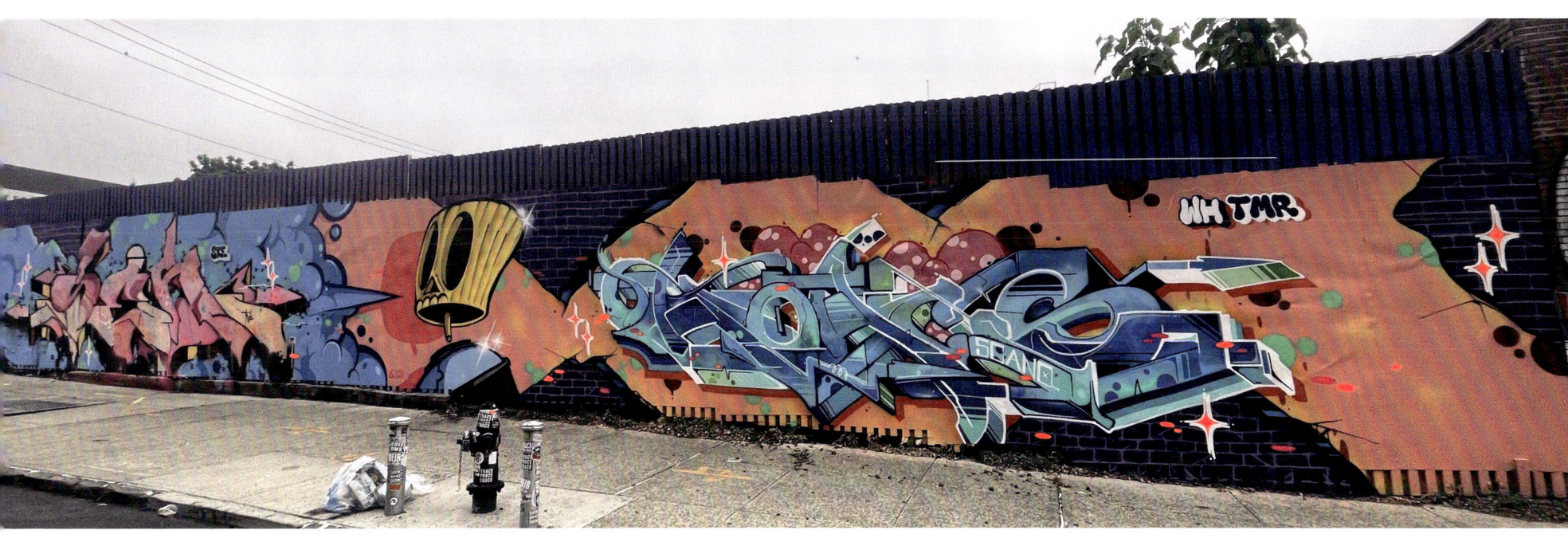

SEN2 FIGUEROA, HOACS, EPIC UNO
BUSHWICK COLLECTIVE, PHOTOGRAPHED IN 2024

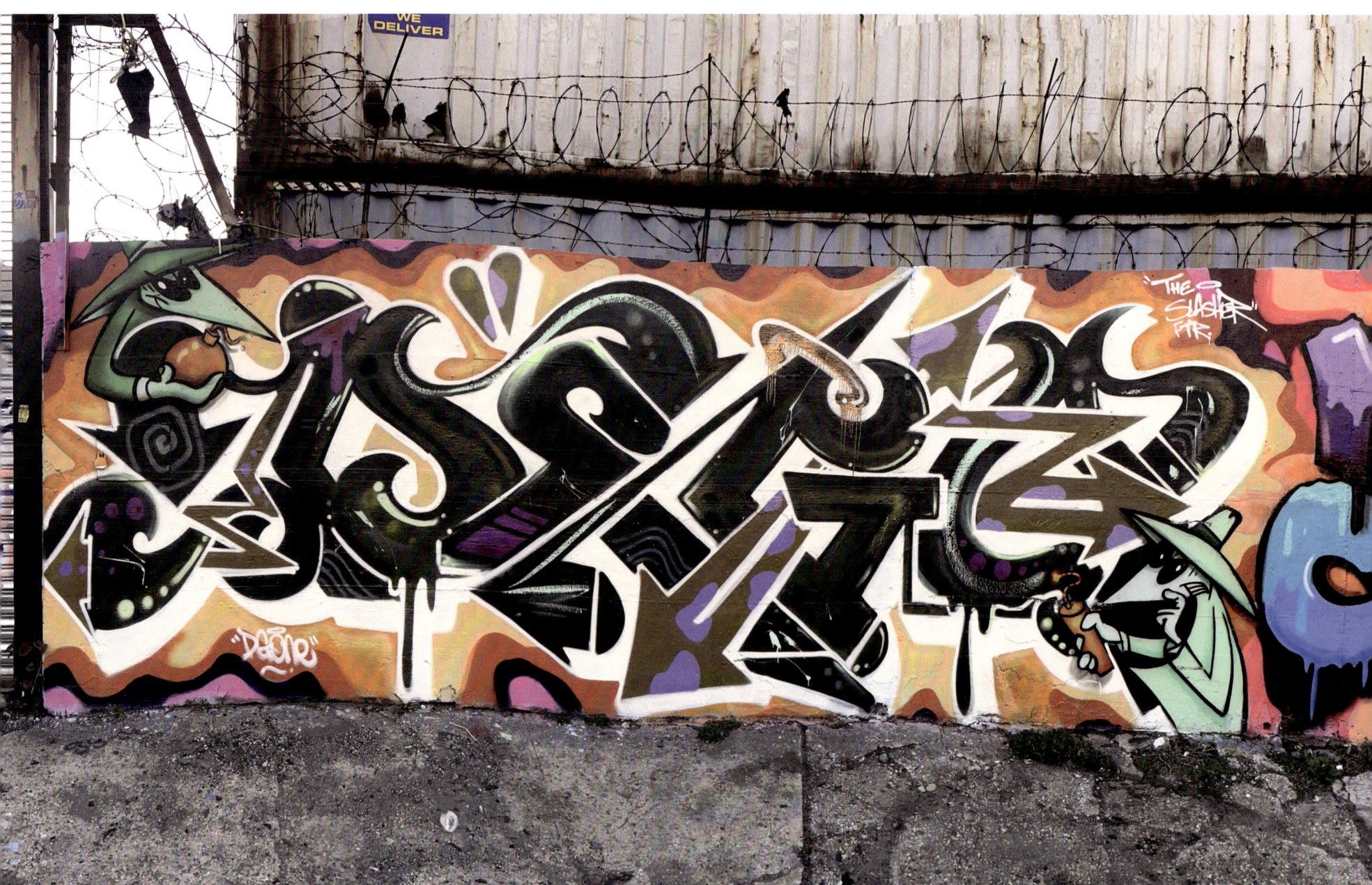

NWC CREW

DG ONE Memorial

BROOKLYN, PHOTOGRAPHED IN 2024

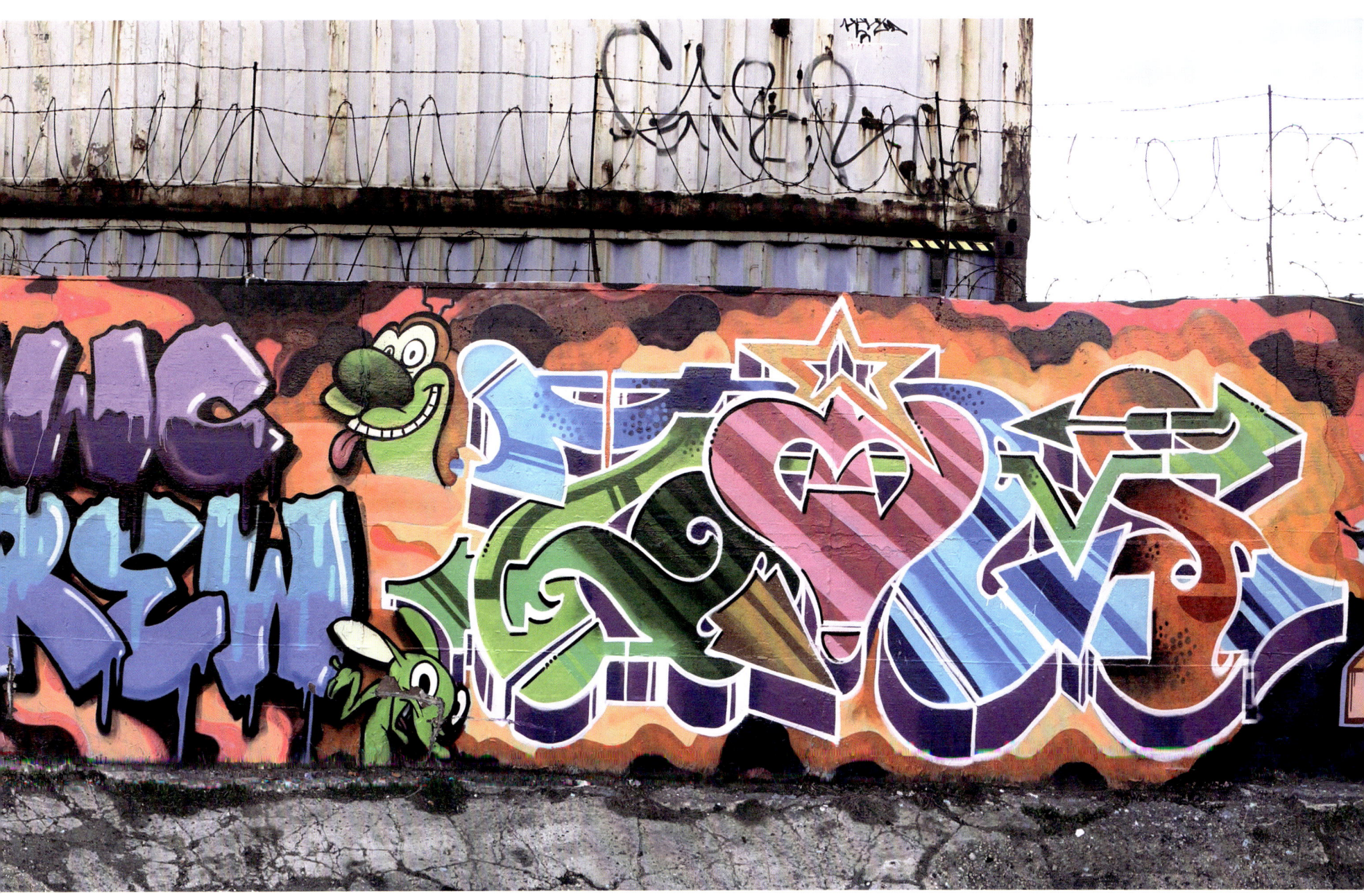

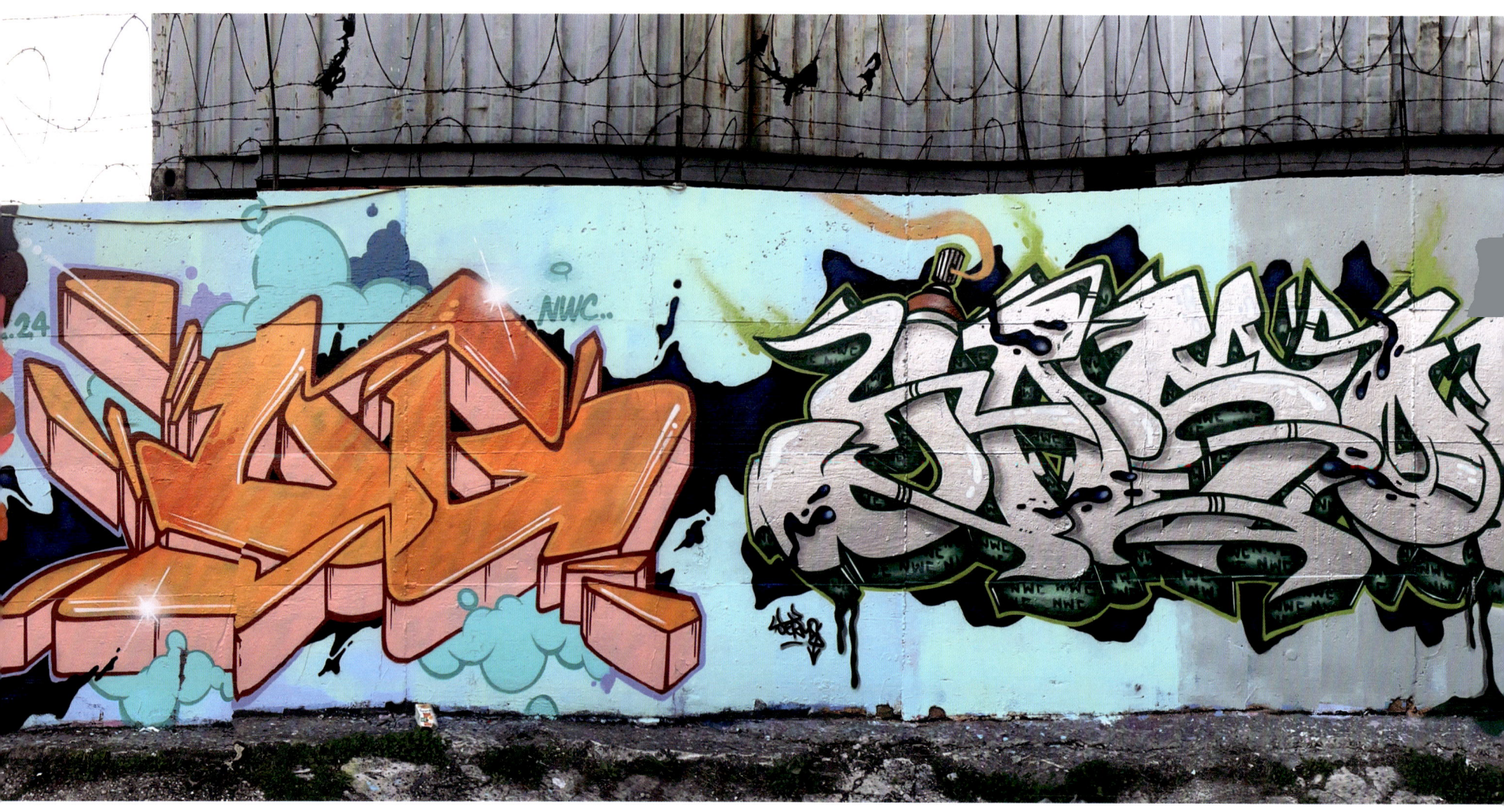

ZIM NWC
DG ONE Memorial
BROOKLYN, PHOTOGRAPHED IN 2024

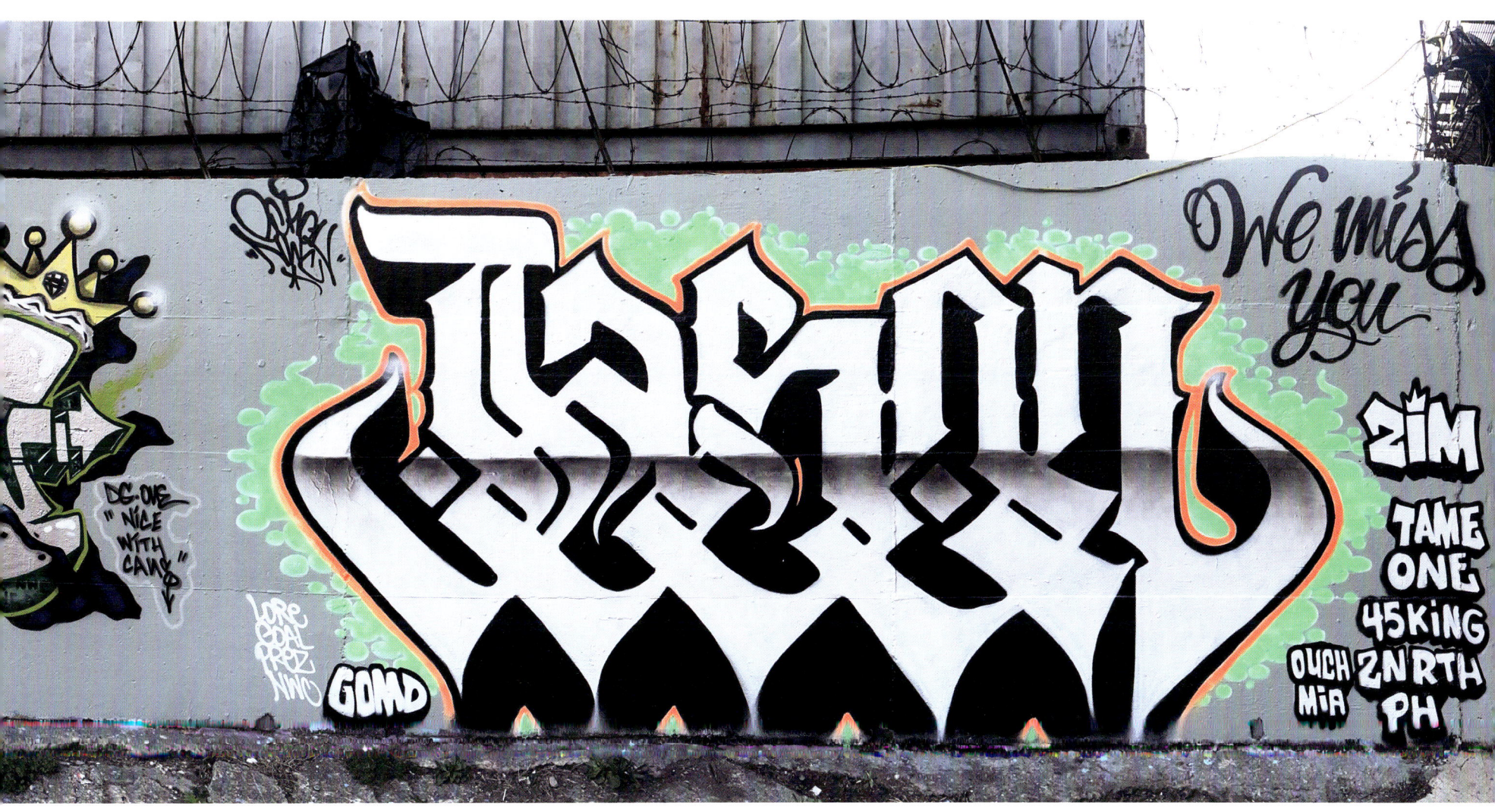

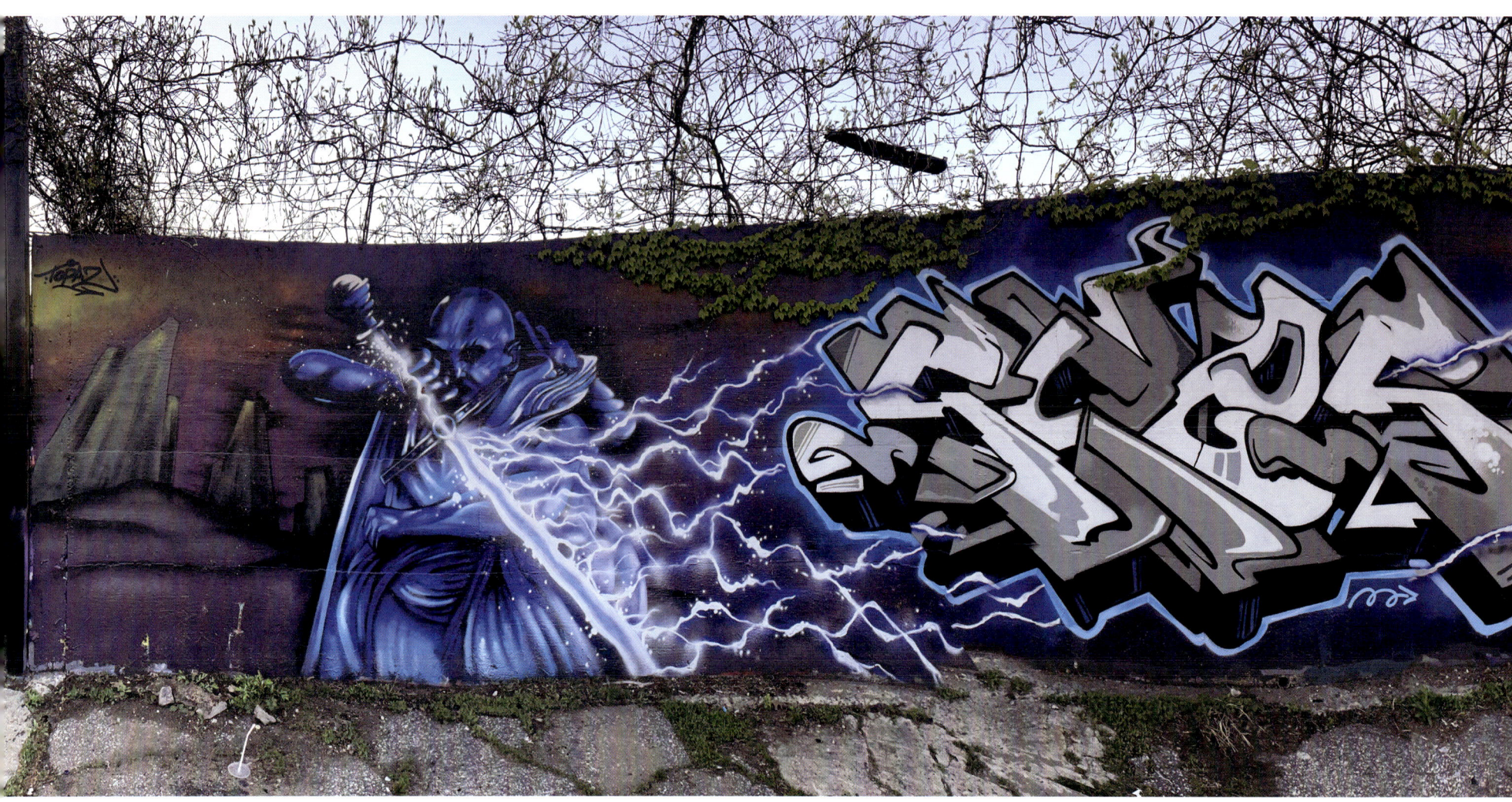

THE LASH ONE, TOPAZ
BROOKLYN, PHOTOGRAPHED IN 2024

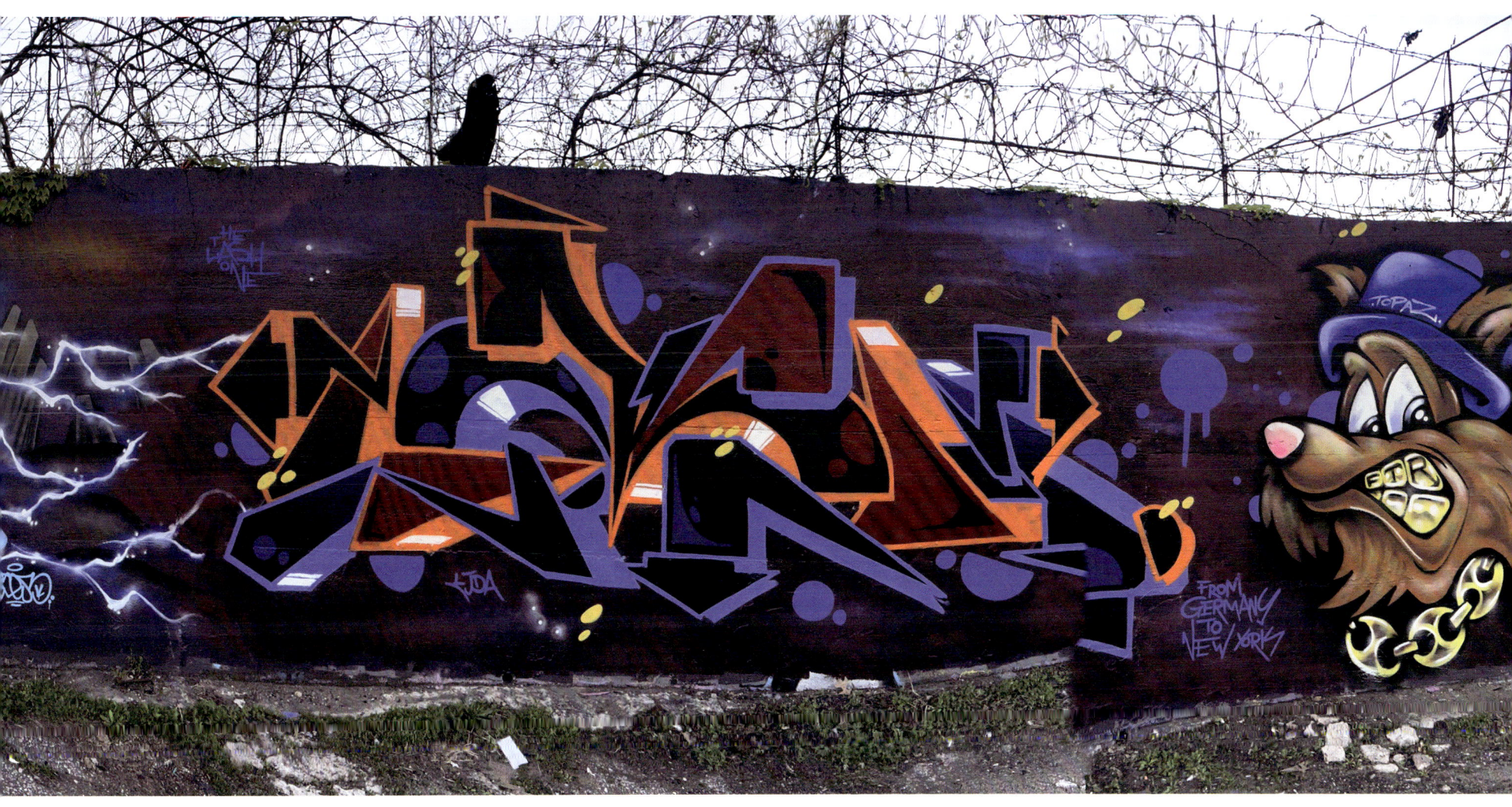

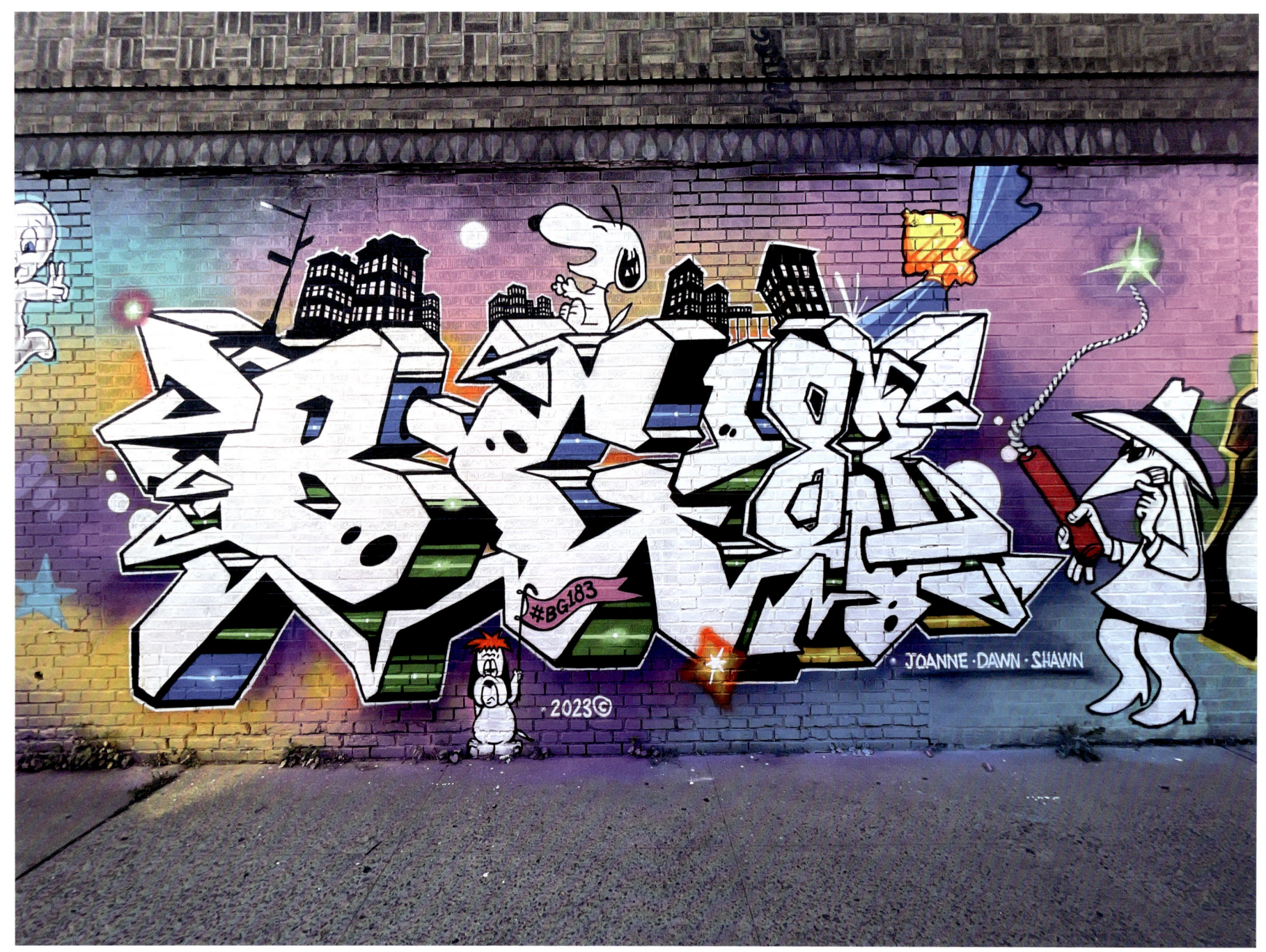

BG 183 TATS CRU
BOONE AVENUE WALLS, THE BRONX, PHOTOGRAPHED IN 2023

SOCIAL JUSTICE

I mention in my introduction that I photographed over 300 artworks on plywood in support of Black Lives Matter and justice for George Floyd, who was tragically murdered by a Minneapolis police officer in 2020. This chapter includes many of those pictures. The chapter also includes street art in support of women's rights, clean water, and combating climate change. With this kind of public art, aerosol artists address critical issues in New York City and the world at large. Around the time that Ruth Bader Ginsburg (RBG) passed away, artists

Lexi Bella and Bianca Romero painted her likeness in murals that represented the power that women hold in society at First Street Green Art Park in Manhattan, whereas V Ballentine and Espartaco Albornoz Abreau painted a Black Lives Matter mural in Park Slope, Brooklyn. The nature of street art is that it is ephemeral, since these three murals that I just mentioned are no longer there. The photographs become the primary source to remember and see these works of art.

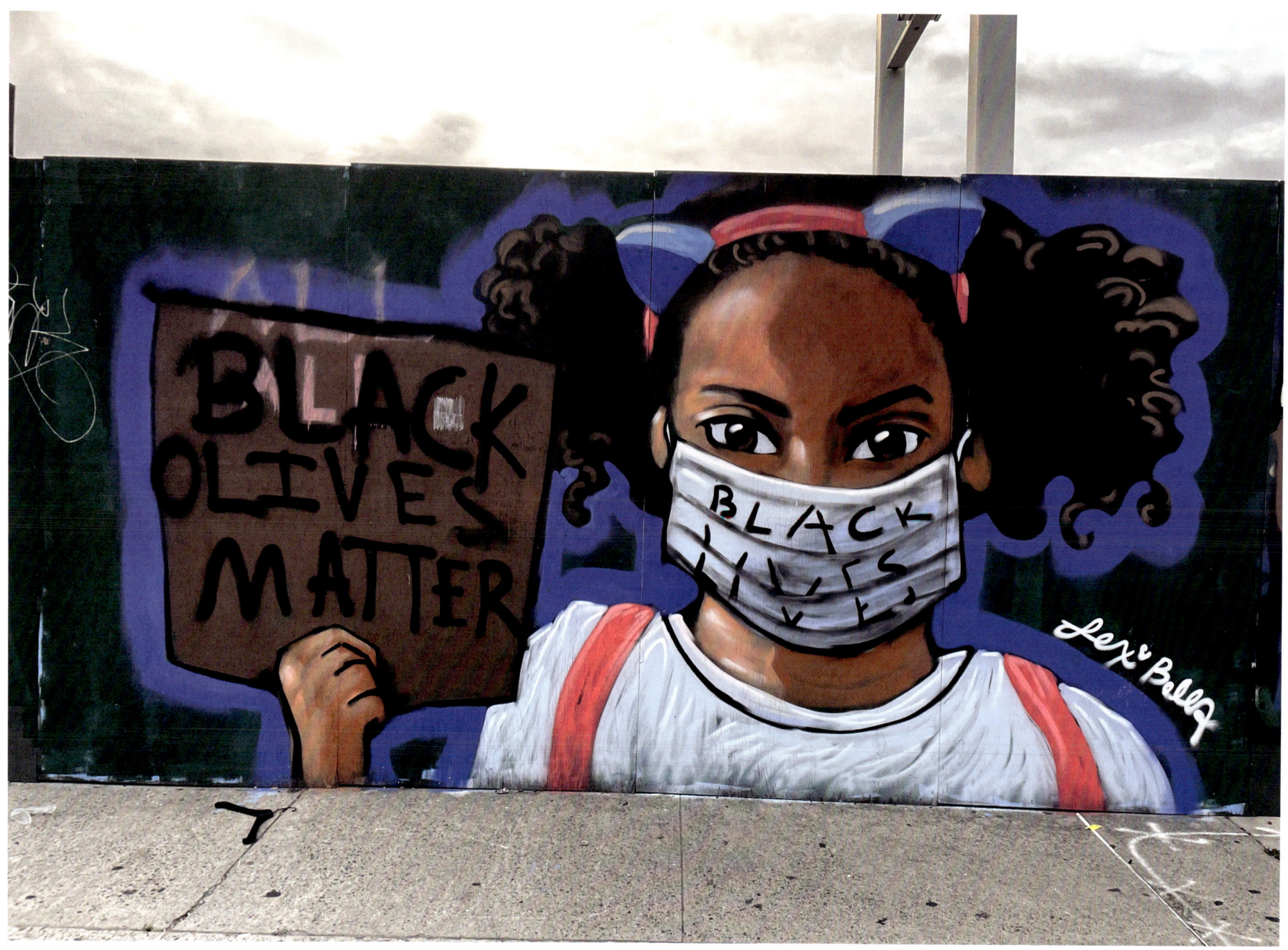

LEXI BELLA

This work is by talented street artist Lexi Bella, addressing Black Lives Matter and the COVID-19 pandemic. Her mural work can be seen around the city.
BROOKLYN, PHOTOGRAPHED IN 2021

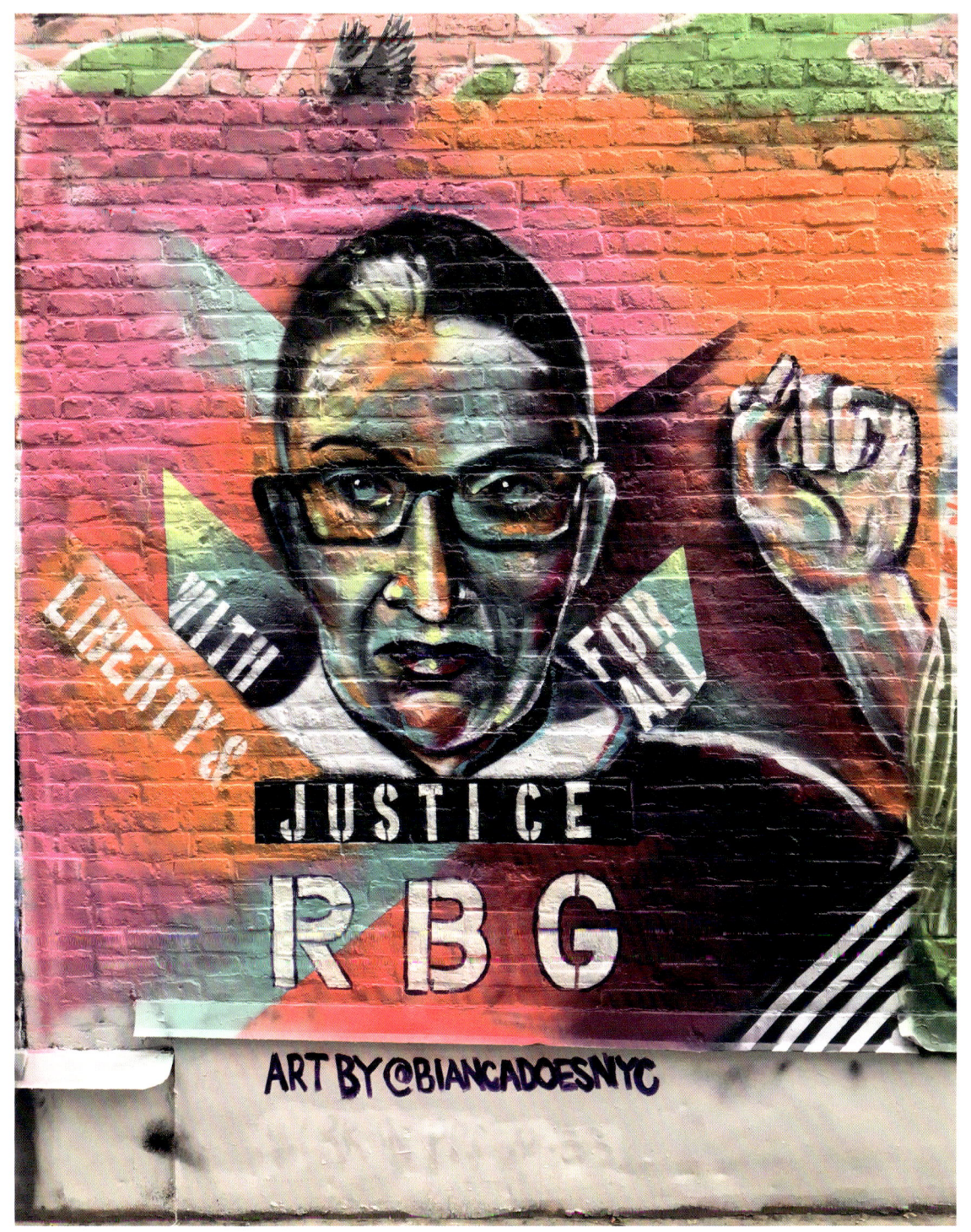

BIANCA ROMERO

Bianca is a talented muralist in New York City. You can often see her street art while traveling around the city. FIRST STREET GREEN ART PARK, MANHATTAN, PHOTOGRAPHED IN 2020

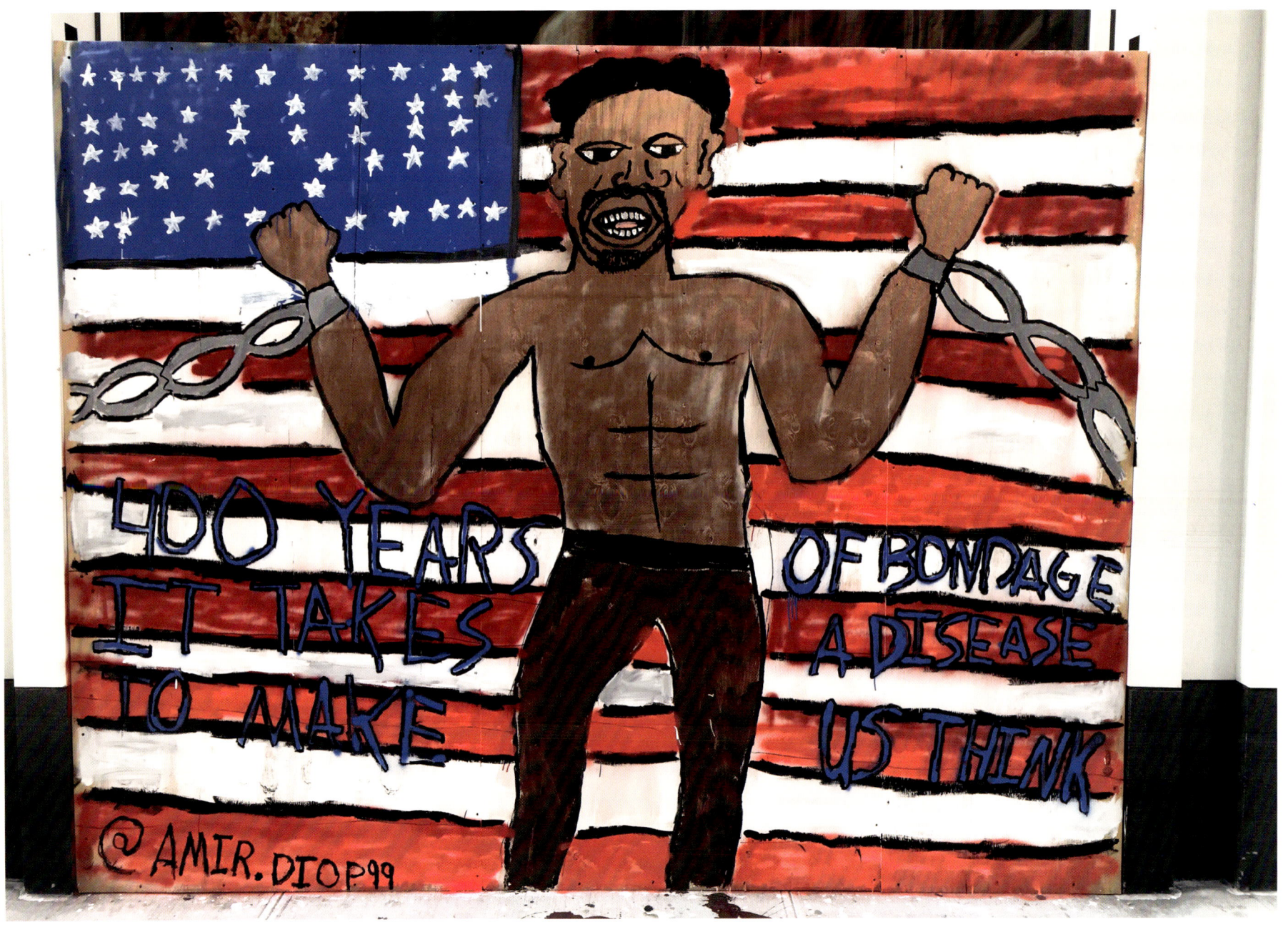

AMIR DIOP

Amir is a young artist whom I met in 2020 in Soho, when local artists painted social justice murals on boarded-up retail windows to protest police brutality. This artwork speaks to the suffering and bondage that African Americans face here in America.

MANHATTAN, PHOTOGRAPHED IN 2020

LOUIS MICHEL

This is a powerful work by Louis Michel addressing climate change.
FIRST STREET GREEN ART PARK, MANHATTAN, PHOTOGRAPHED IN 2023

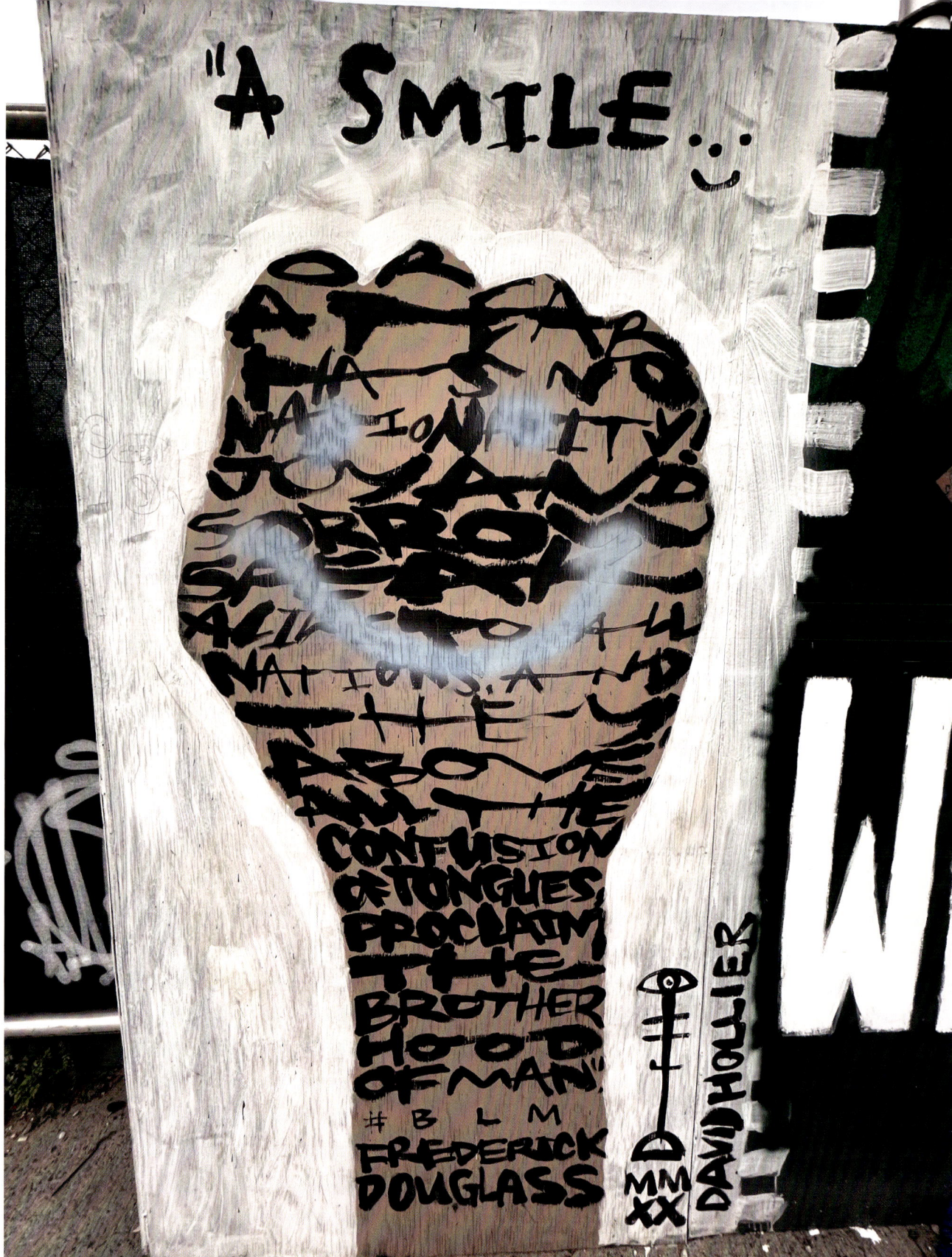

DAVID HOLLIER

This is a great artwork by David Hollier in support of Black Lives Matter.
BROOKLYN, PHOTOGRAPHED IN 2021

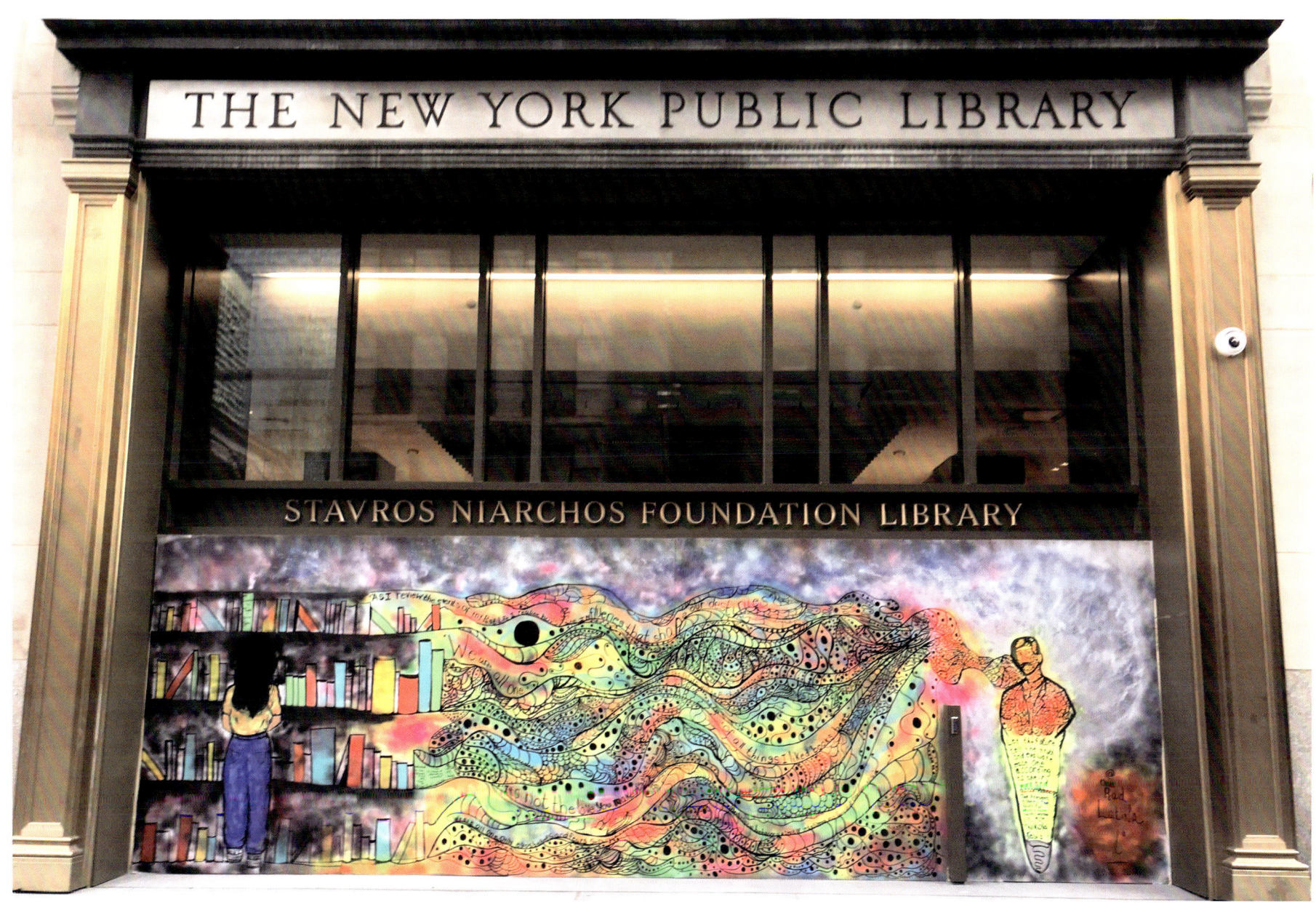

ONE RAD LATINA

One Rad Latina did this mural for the New York Public Library. One Rad Latina found refuge in the public library while growing up in New York City. *Commissioned by New York Public Library*
MANHATTAN, PHOTOGRAPHED IN 2020

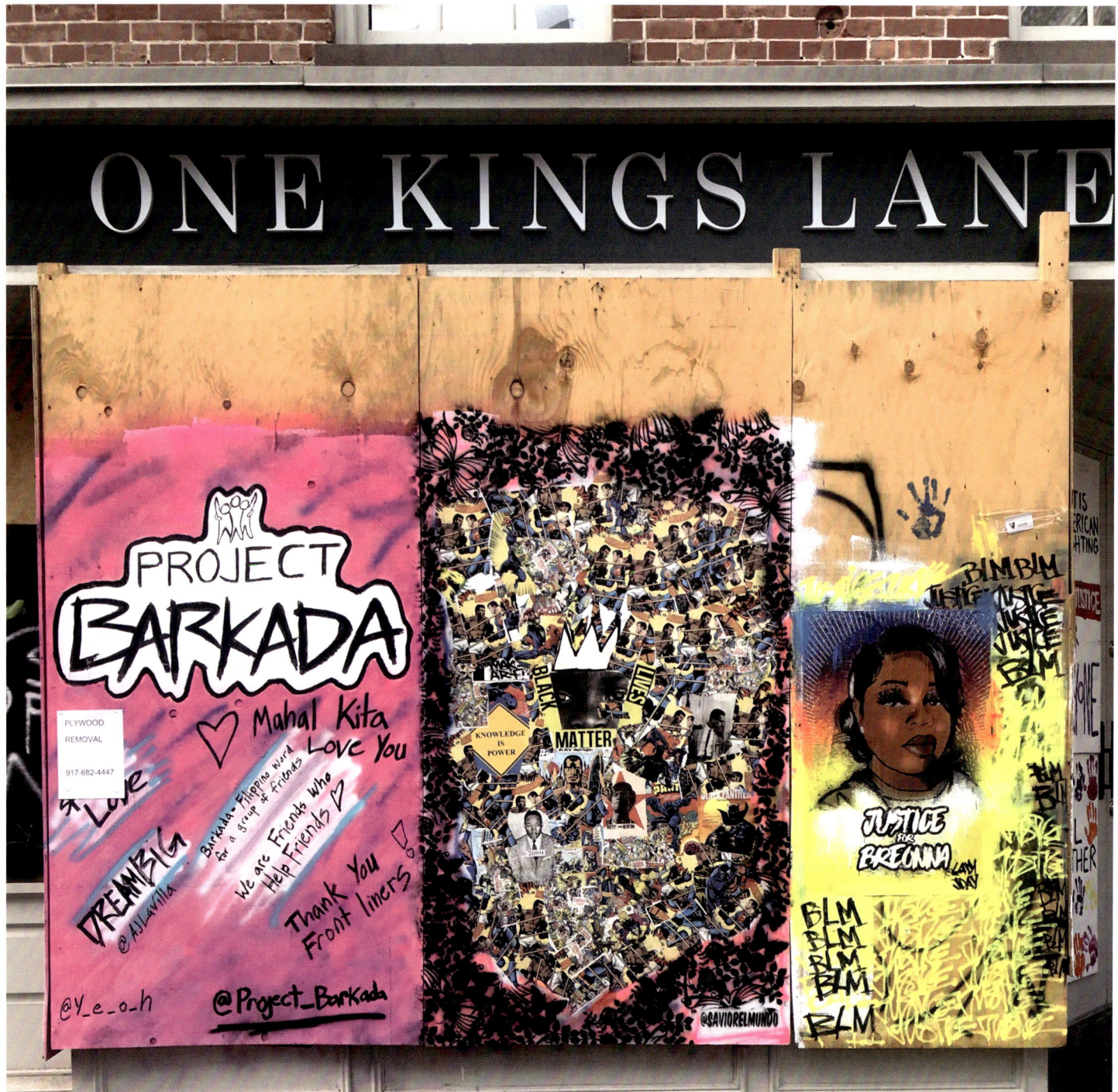

PROJECT BARKADA, SAVIOR EL MUNDO, LADY J DAY
Three different artists painted this mural in support of essential workers during the COVID-19 pandemic and the Black Lives Matter protests.
MANHATTAN,
PHOTOGRAPHED IN 2020

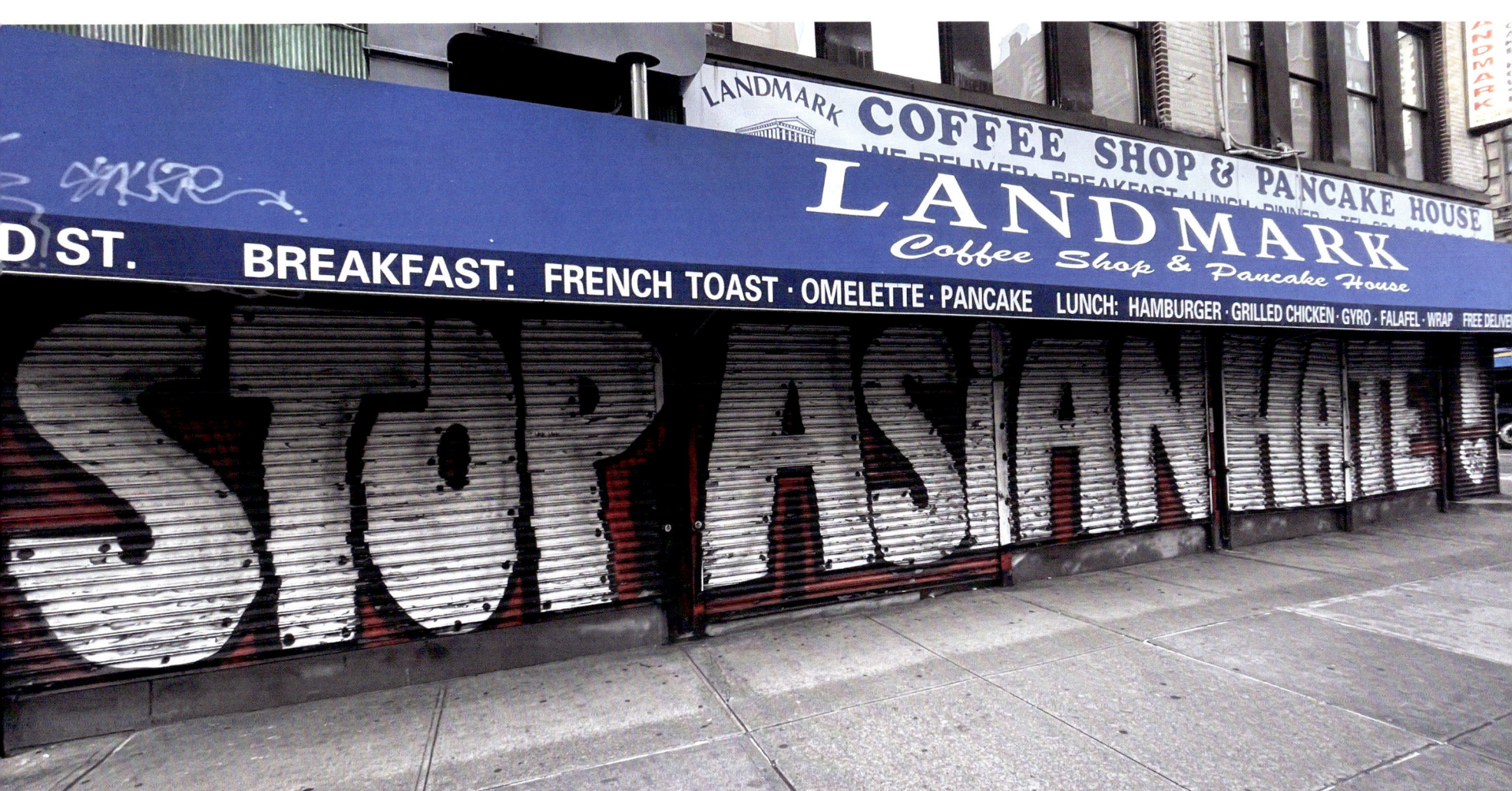

HEK TAD
This artwork is by well-known street artist Hek Tad, calling for a stop to Asian hate.
MANHATTAN, PHOTOGRAPHED IN 2023

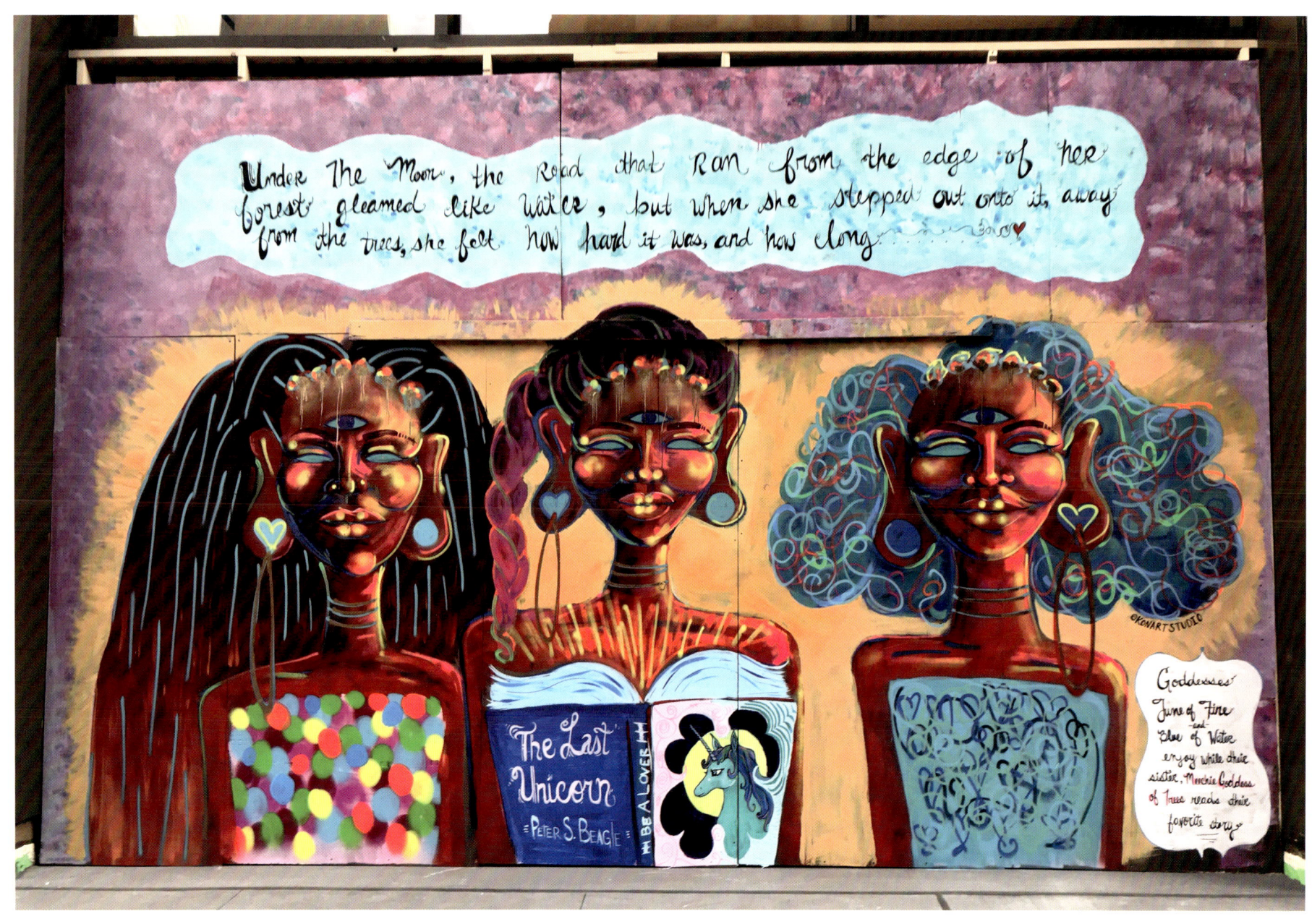

KONSTANCE PATTON

Talented street artist and Native American Konstance Patton painted a beautiful mural showing the rich beauty of her people's hair and faces.

Commissioned by New York Public Library

MANHATTAN, PHOTOGRAPHED IN 2020

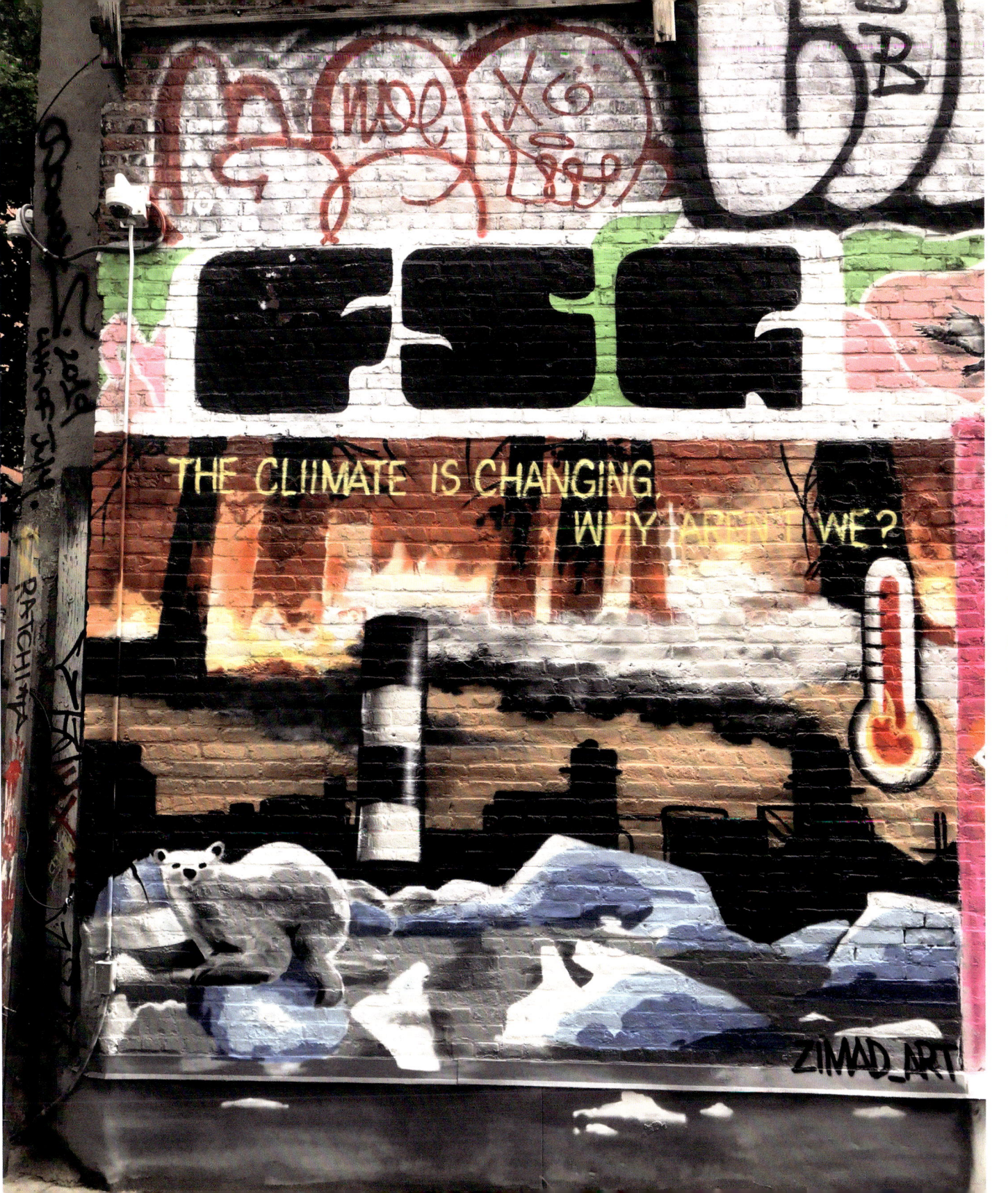

ZIMAD

Zimad Art painted a beautiful mural addressing climate change.
FIRST STREET GREEN ART PARK, MANHATTAN, PHOTOGRAPHED IN 2020

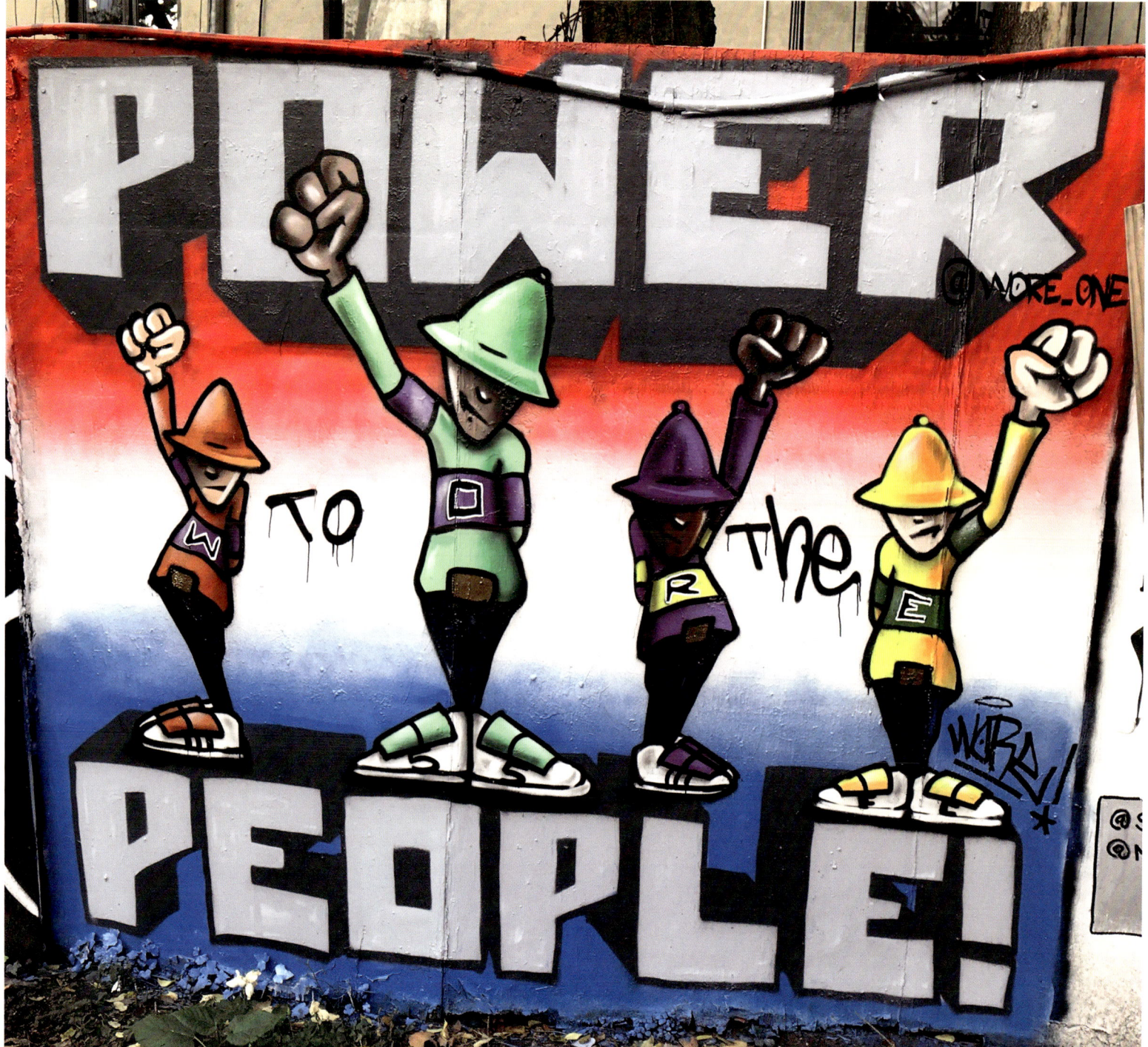

WORE ONE

Wore One is a respected and well-known aerosol artist in New York City. He painted power to people at First Street Green Art Park.
FIRST STREET GREEN ART PARK, MANHATTAN, PHOTOGRAPHED IN 2020

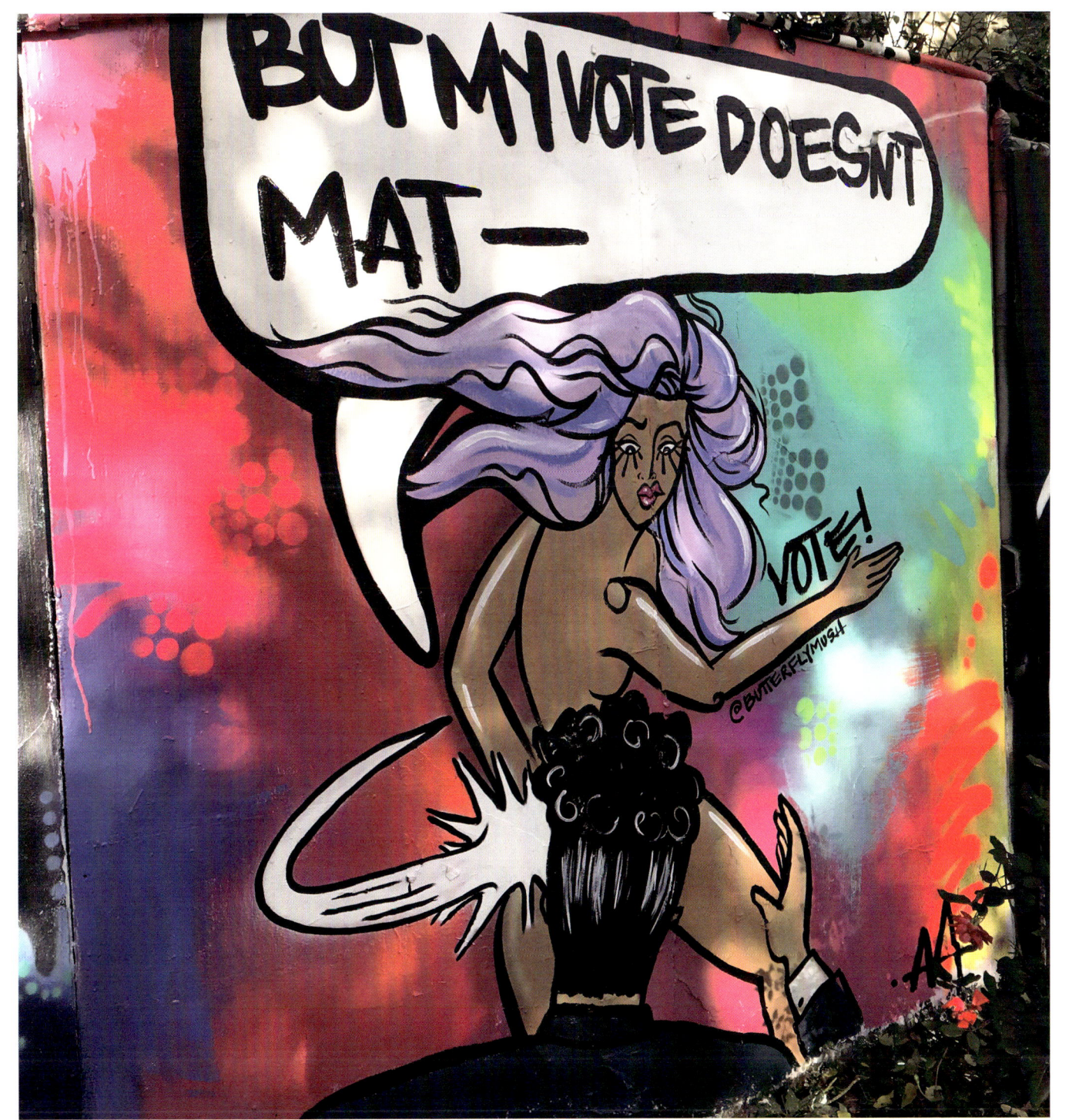

BUTTERFLY MUSH
FIRST STREET GREEN ART PARK,
MANHATTAN, PHOTOGRAPHED
IN 2020

AMIR DIOP
MANHATTAN, PHOTOGRAPHED IN 2020

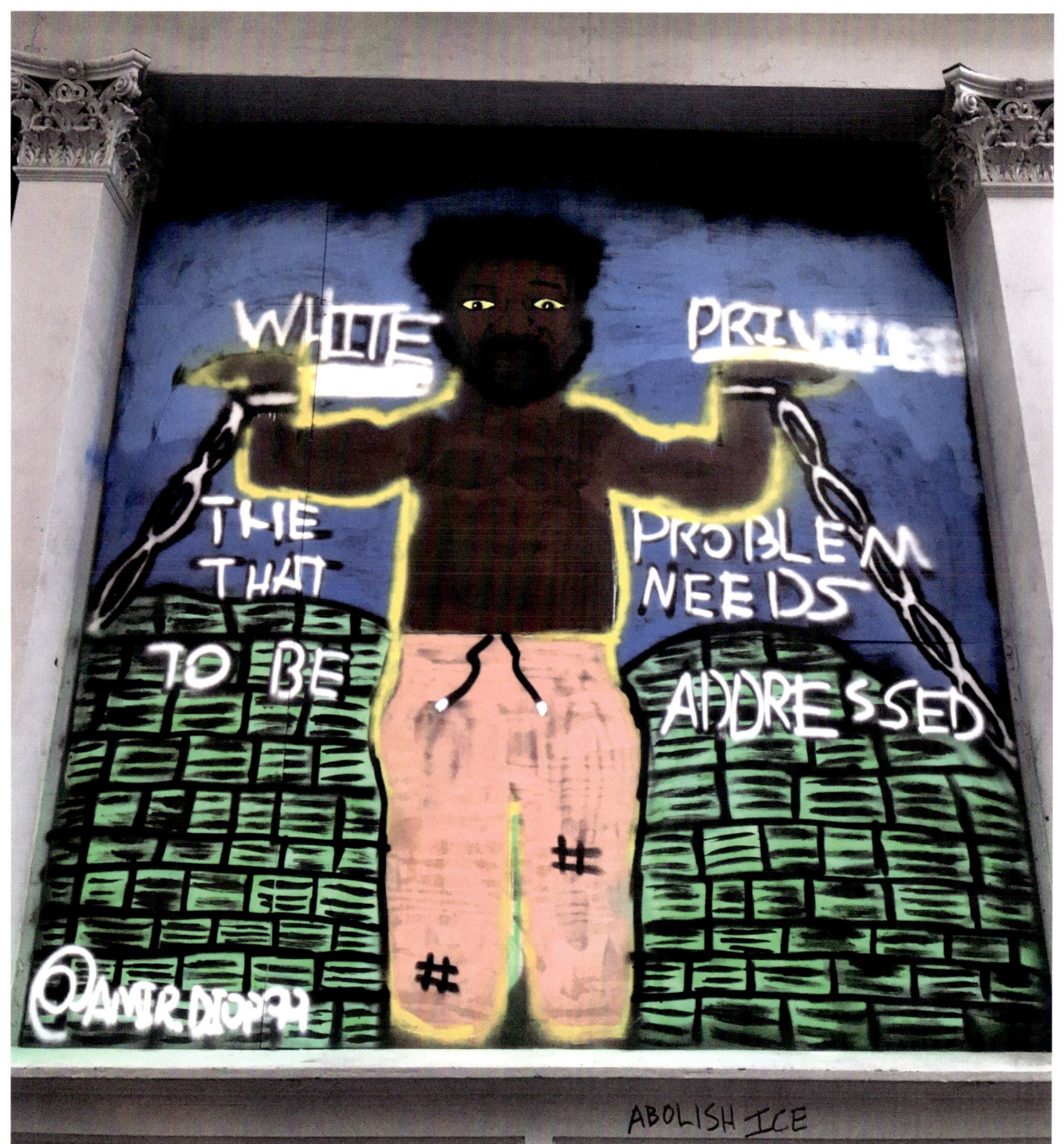

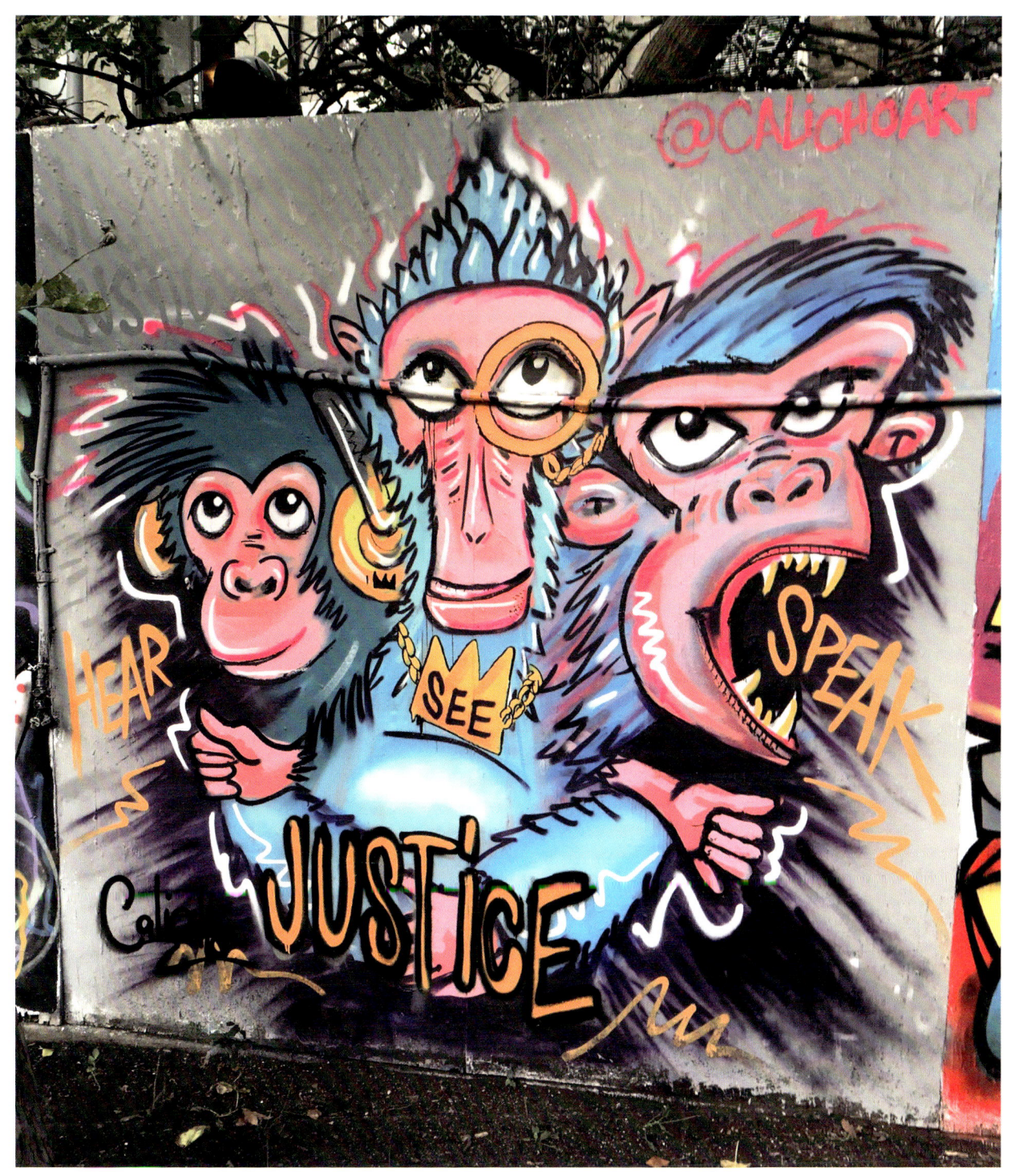

CALICHO ART

Colombian artist Calicho painted a colorful mural in support of freedom of speech in America.
FIRST STREET GREEN ART PARK, MANHATTAN, PHOTOGRAPHED IN 2020

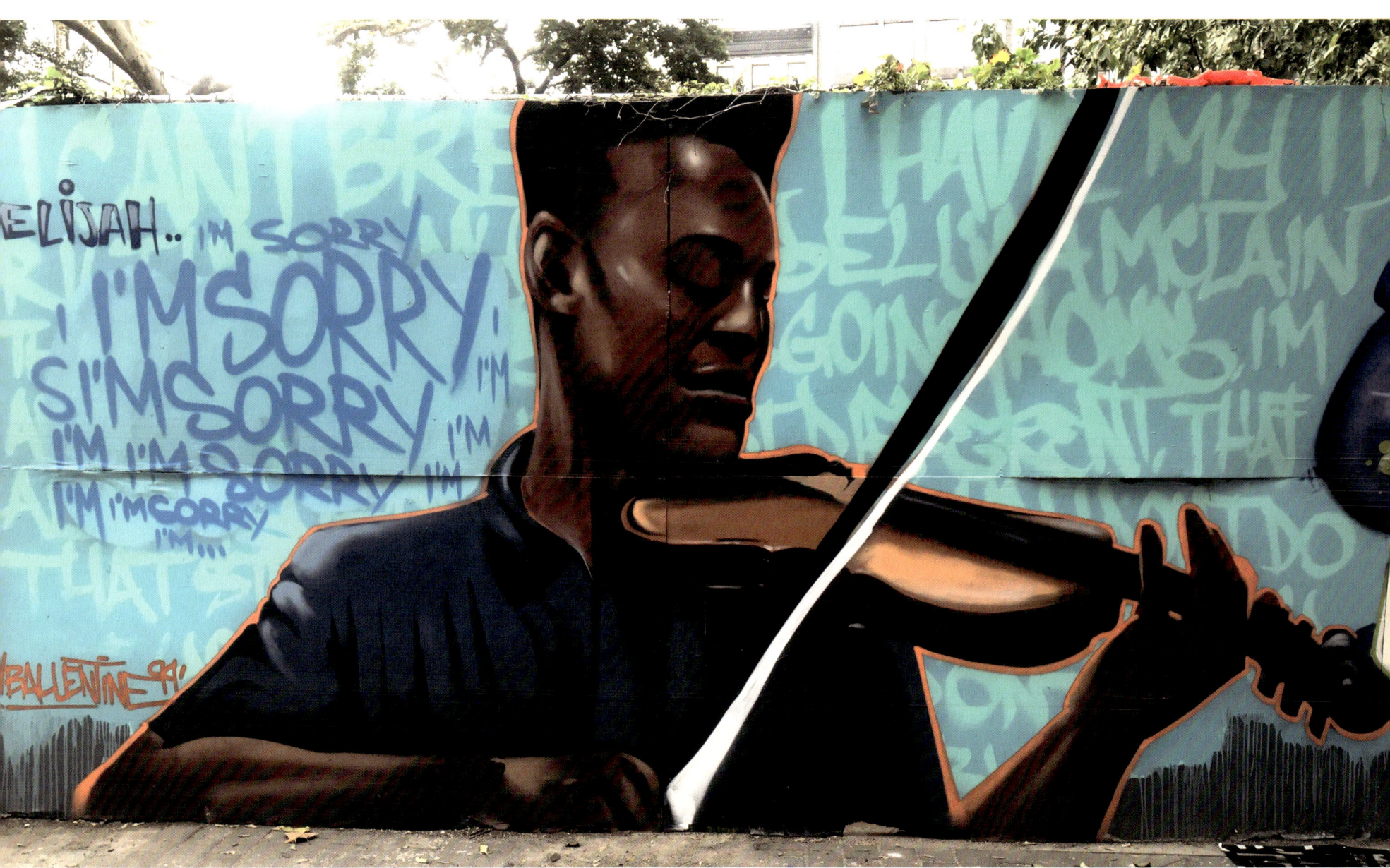

V BALLENTINE

Well-known New York City muralist V Ballentine painted a memorial tribute to Elijah McClain, killed by police brutality in Aurora, Colorado, in 2019.

FIRST STREET GREEN ART PARK, MANHATTAN, PHOTOGRAPHED IN 2020

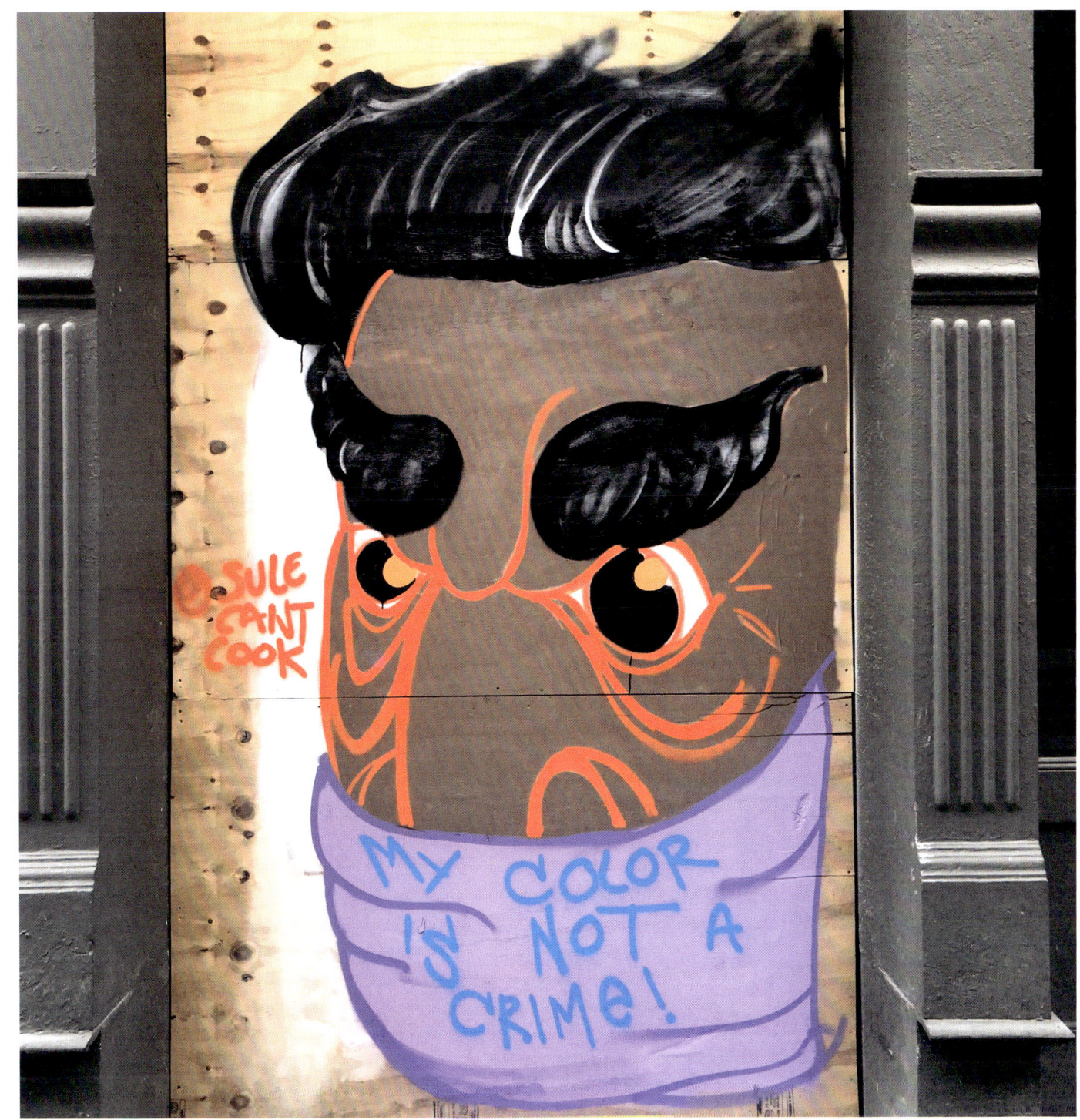

SULE

Street artist Sule Can't Cook painted this mural, *My Color Is Not a Crime*, during a Black Lives Matter protest in the Soho District. MANHATTAN, PHOTOGRAPHED IN 2020

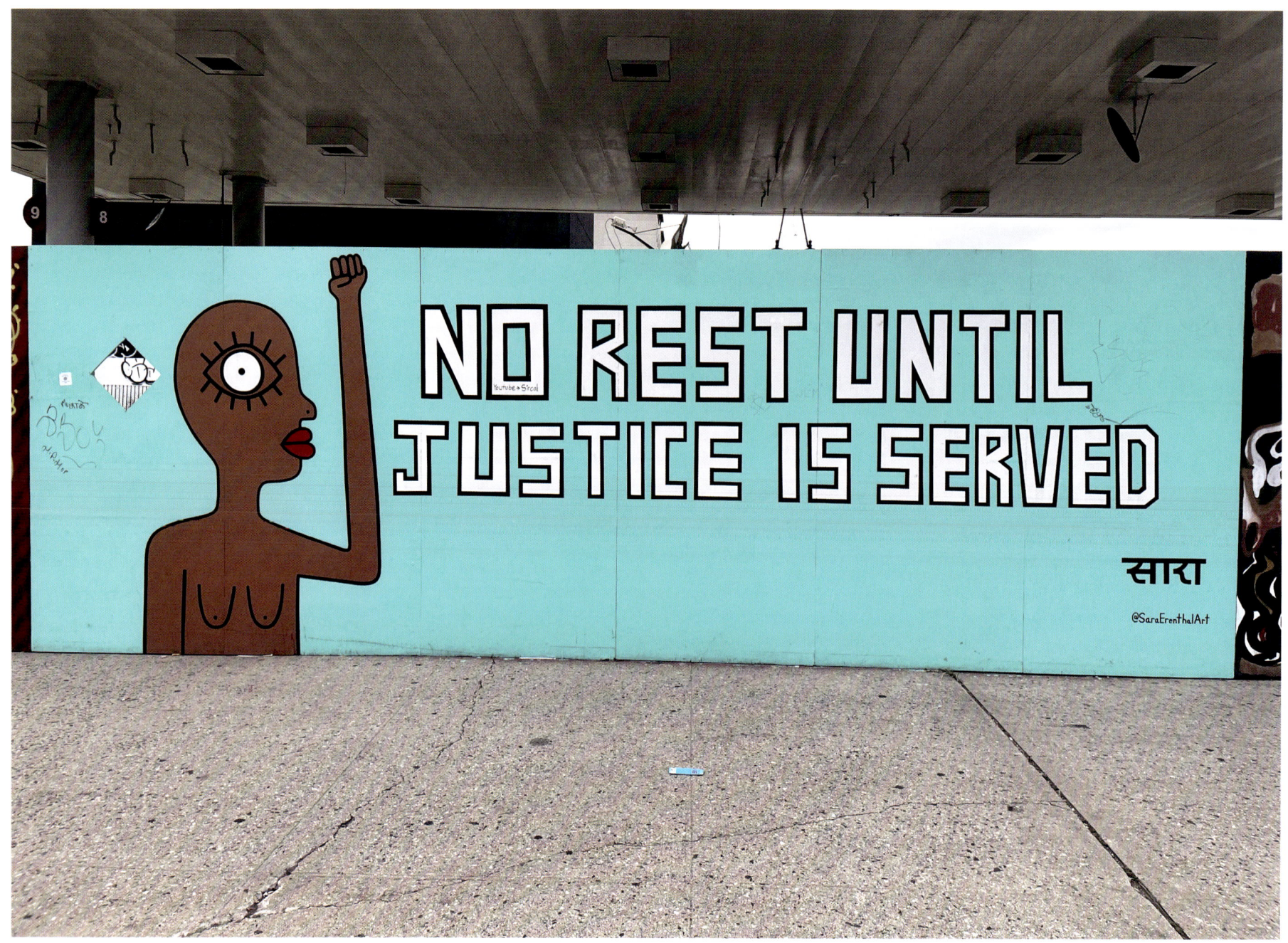

SARAH ERENTHAL
This is a great work by Sara Erenthal, a well-known social justice artist.
BROOKLYN, PHOTOGRAPHED IN 2021

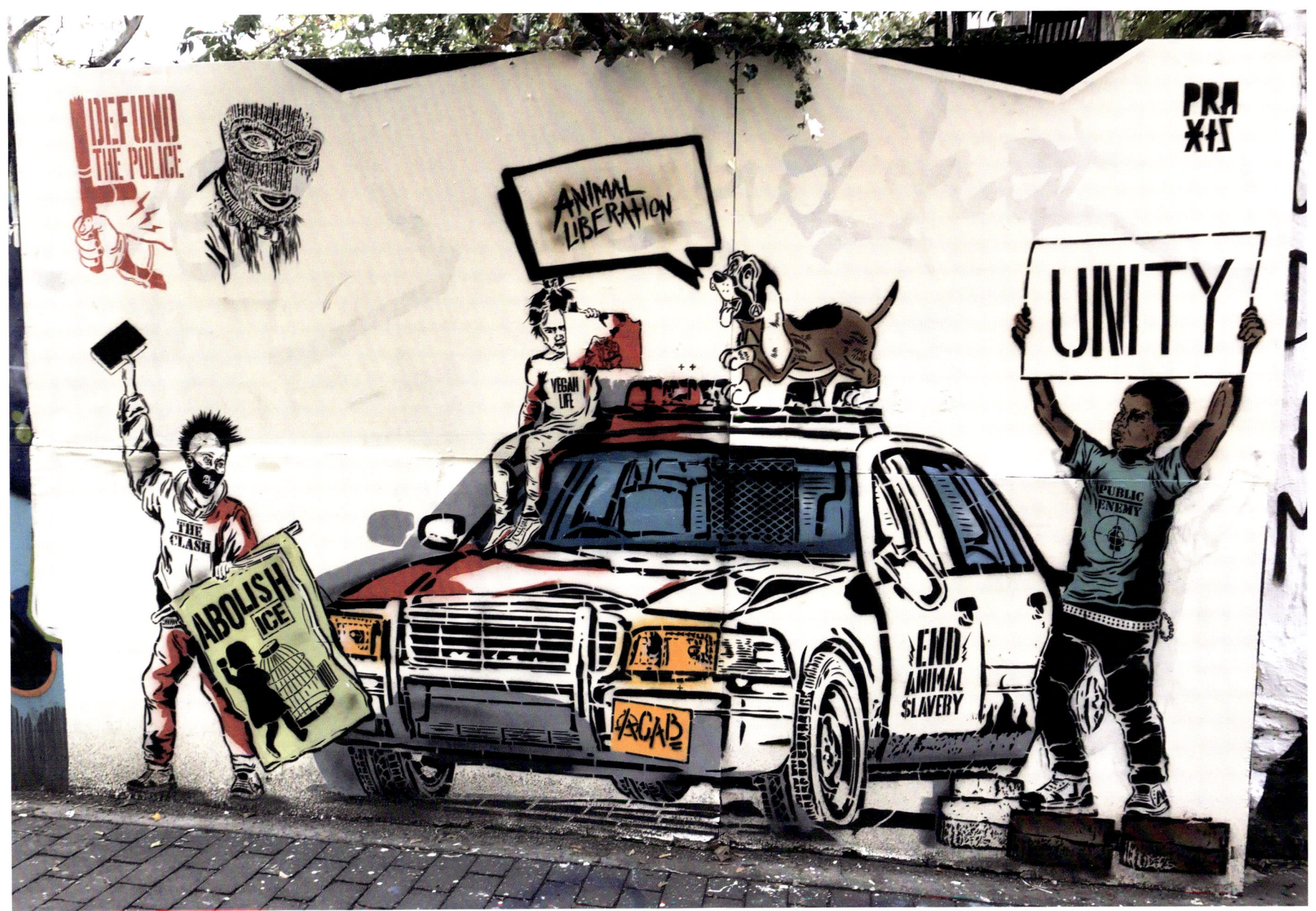

PRAXIS
FIRST STREET GREEN ART PARK, MANHATTAN, PHOTOGRAPHED IN 2020

ONE RAD LATINA
MANHATTAN,
PHOTOGRAPHED IN 2020

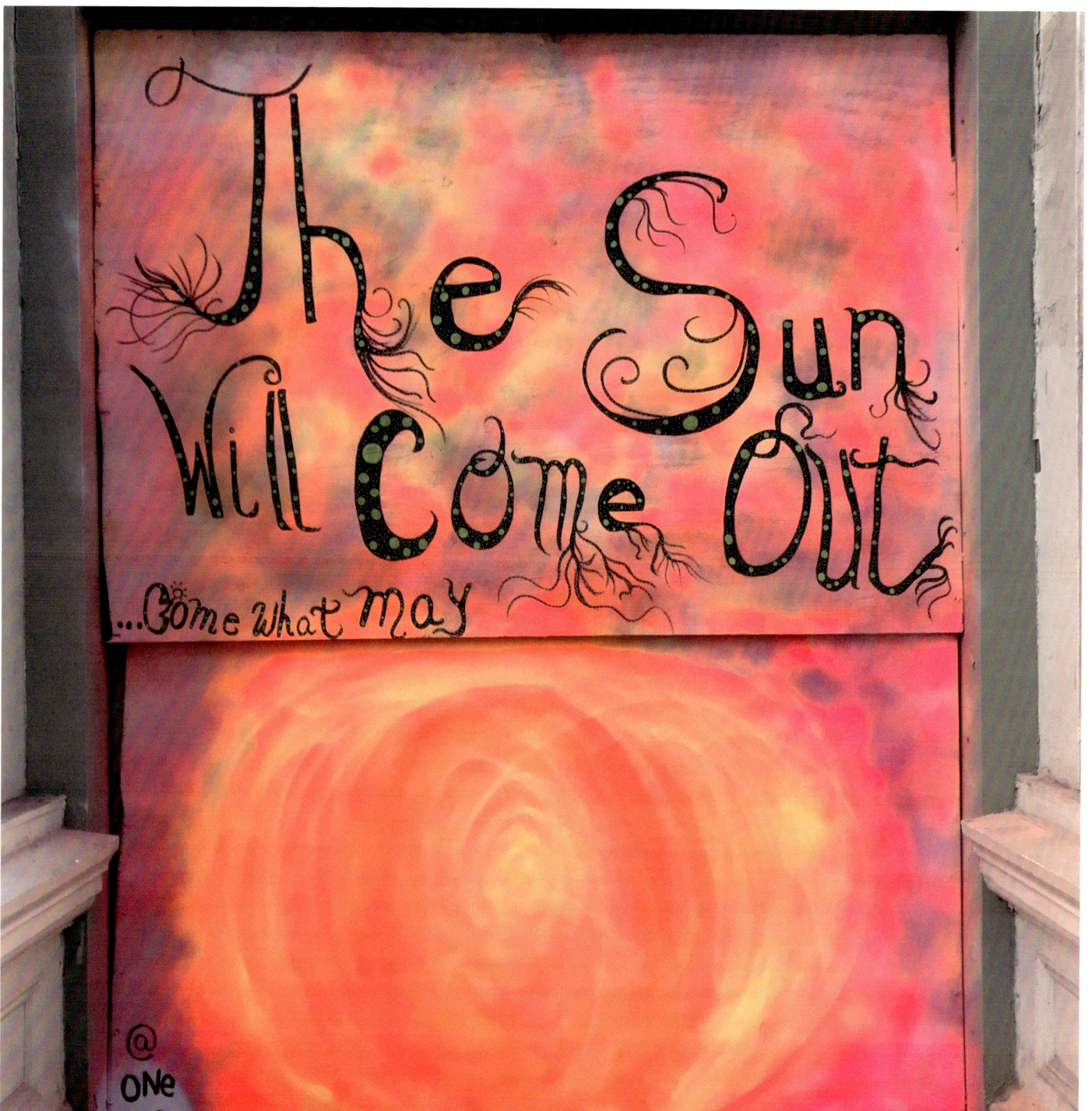

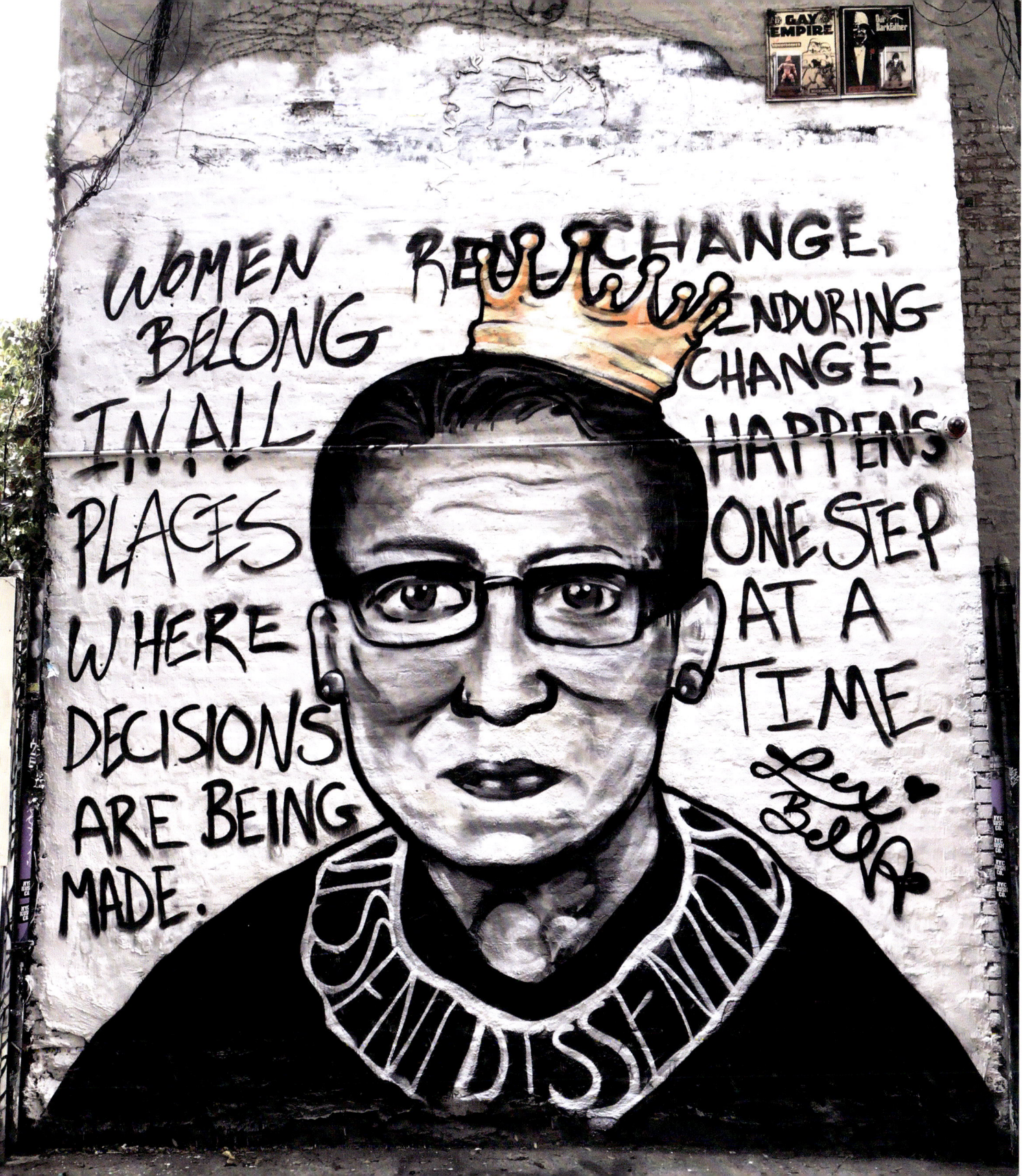

WOMEN BELONG IN ALL PLACES WHERE DECISIONS ARE BEING MADE.

REAL CHANGE, ENDURING CHANGE, HAPPENS ONE STEP AT A TIME.

I DISSENT

LEXI BELLA
FIRST STREET GREEN ART PARK, MANHATTAN, PHOTOGRAPHED IN 2020

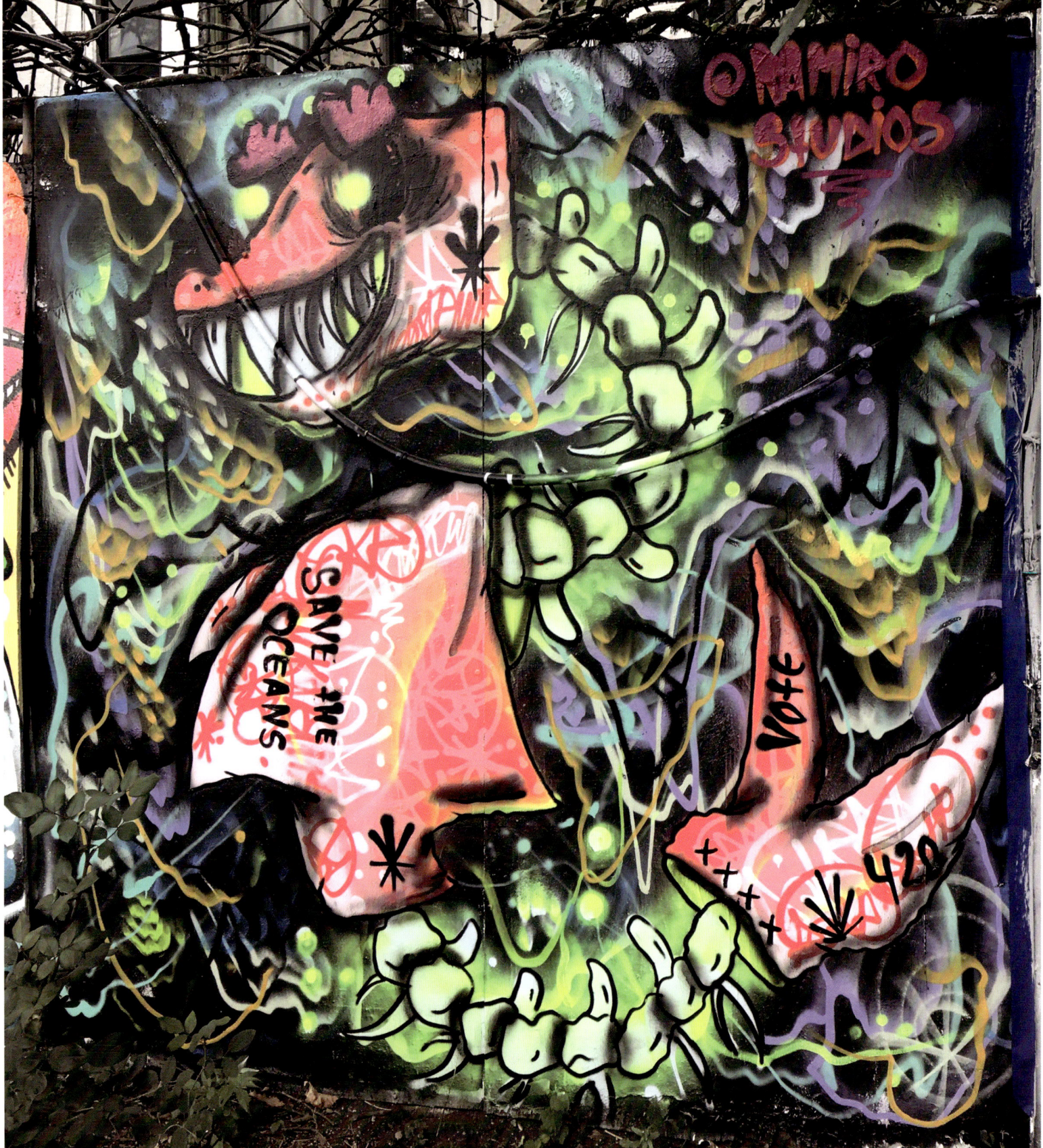

RAMIRO DAVARO COMAS
FIRST STREET GREEN ART PARK, MANHATTAN, PHOTOGRAPHED IN 2020

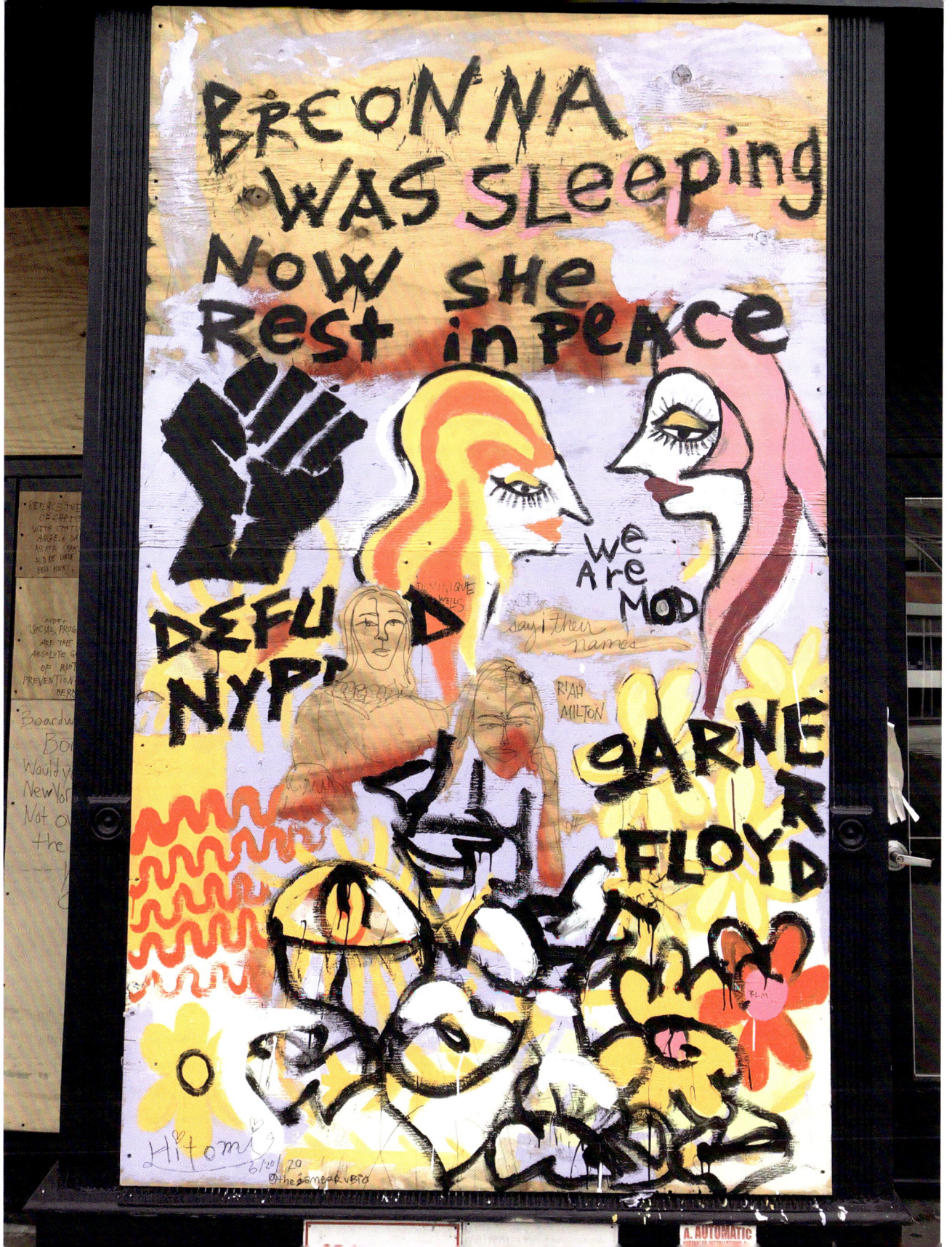

JAMES RUBIO, HITOMI
MANHATTAN, PHOTOGRAPHED IN 2020

MIKE 171, SJK 171
This social justice mural was painted by Mike 171 and SJK, two pioneering graffiti artists from Washington Heights and original members of UGA—United Graffiti Artists.
FIRST STREET GREEN ART PARK, MANHATTAN, PHOTOGRAPHED IN 2020

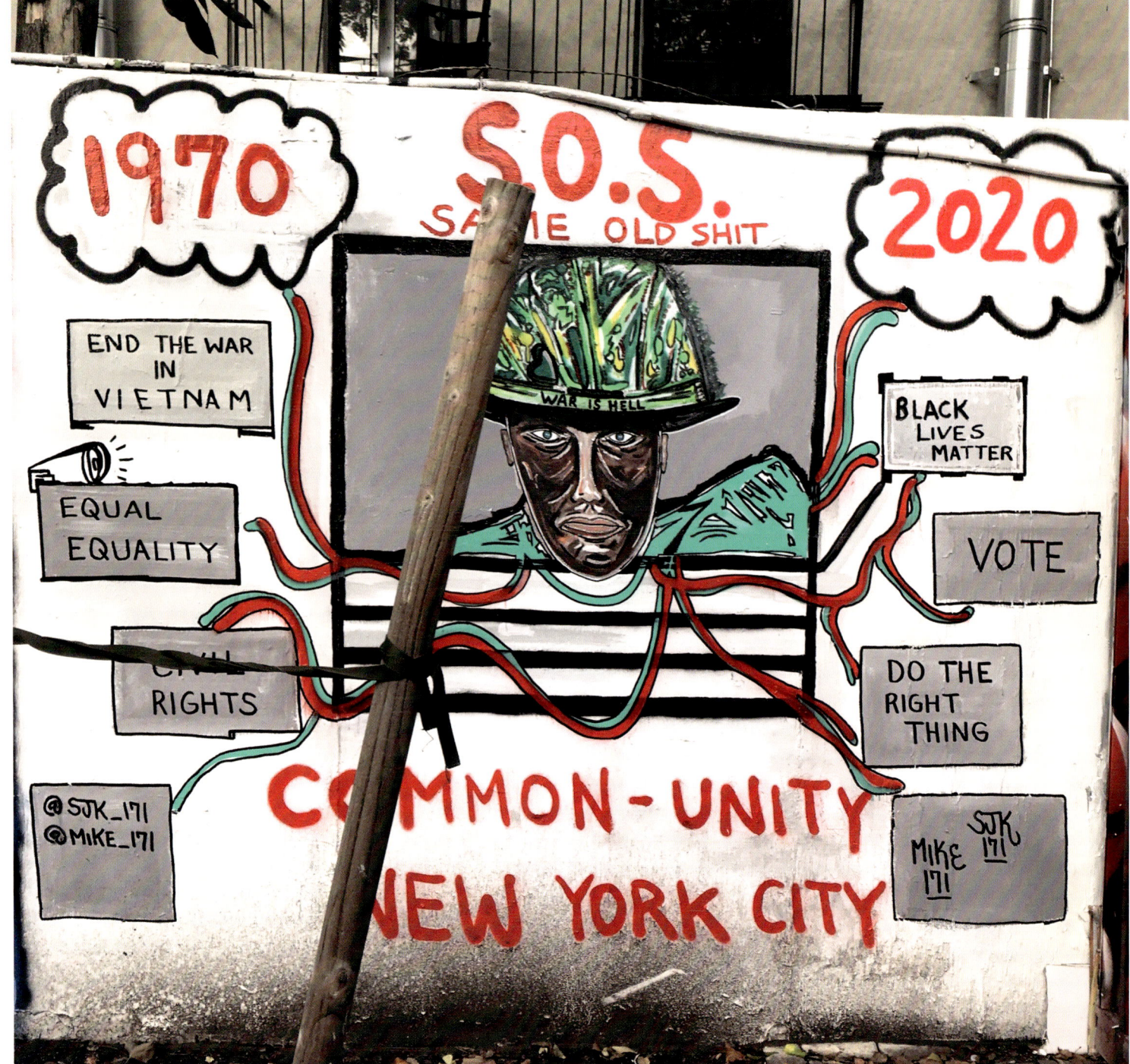

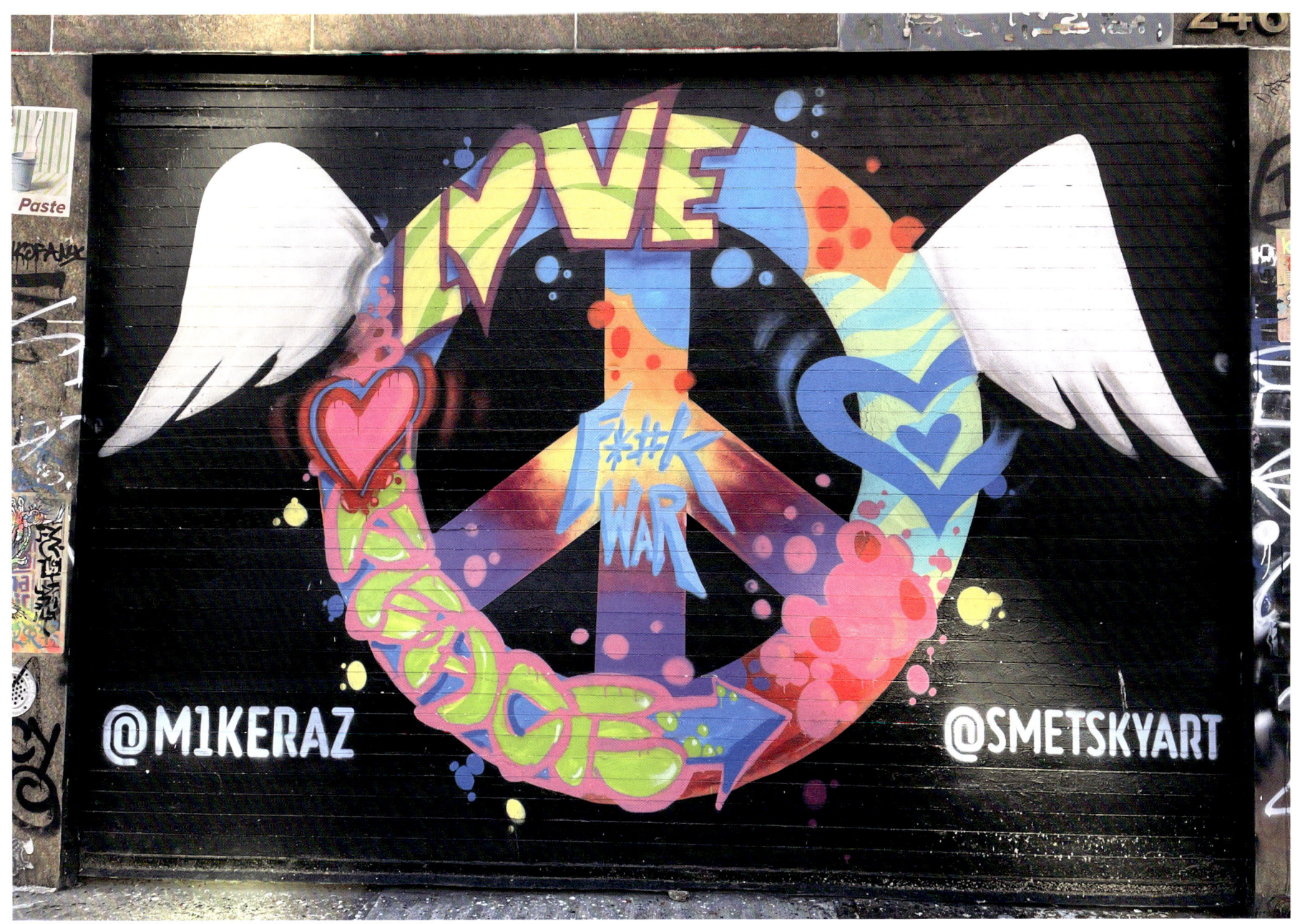

MIKE RAZ, SMETSKY ART

A beautiful mural by Mike Raz and Smetsky Art protesting military conflicts.
MANHATTAN, PHOTOGRAPHED IN 2023

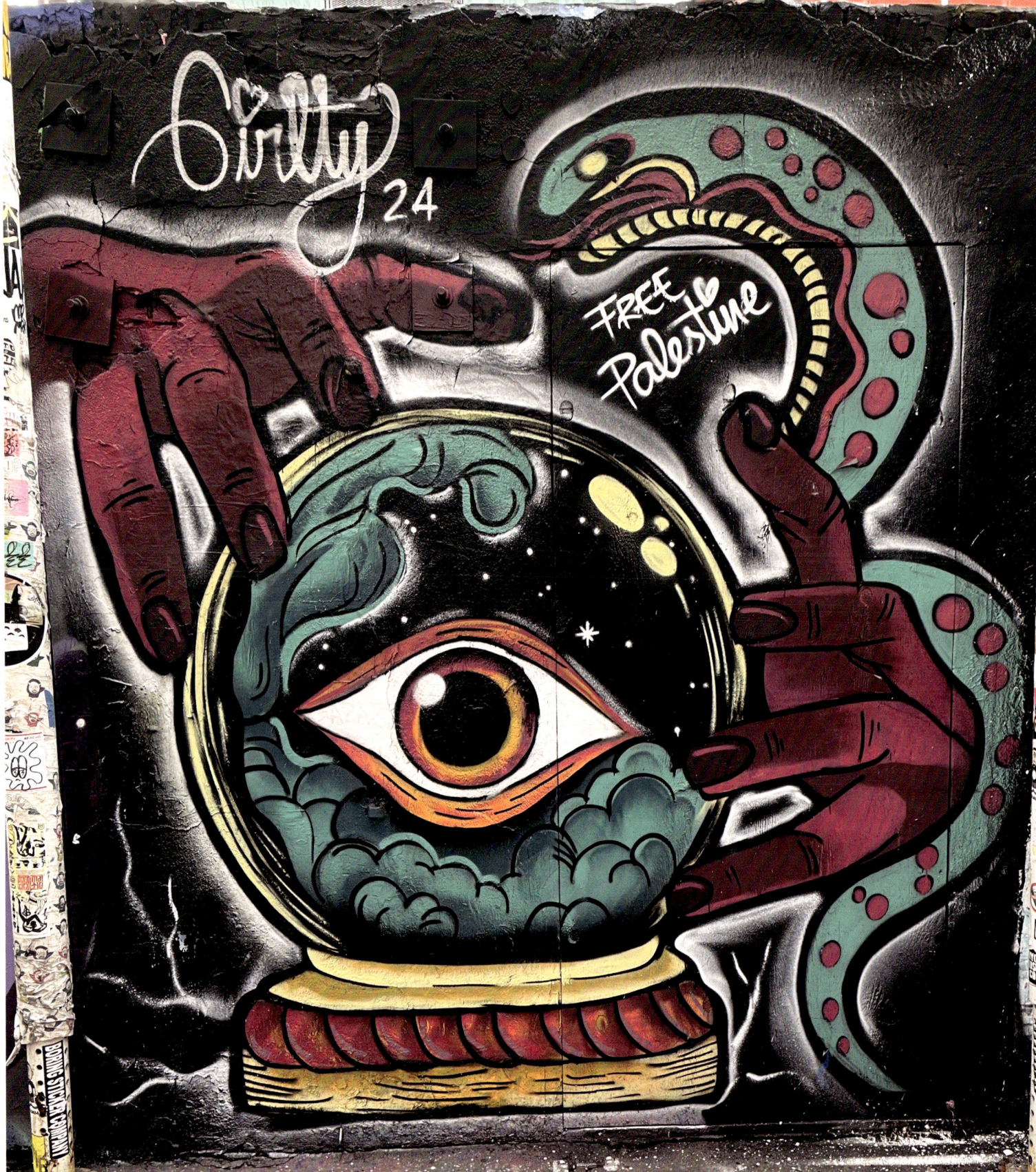

GIRLTY
Free Palestine mural by Girlty at Freeman Alley.
FREEMAN ALLEY, MANHATTAN, PHOTOGRAPHED IN 2024

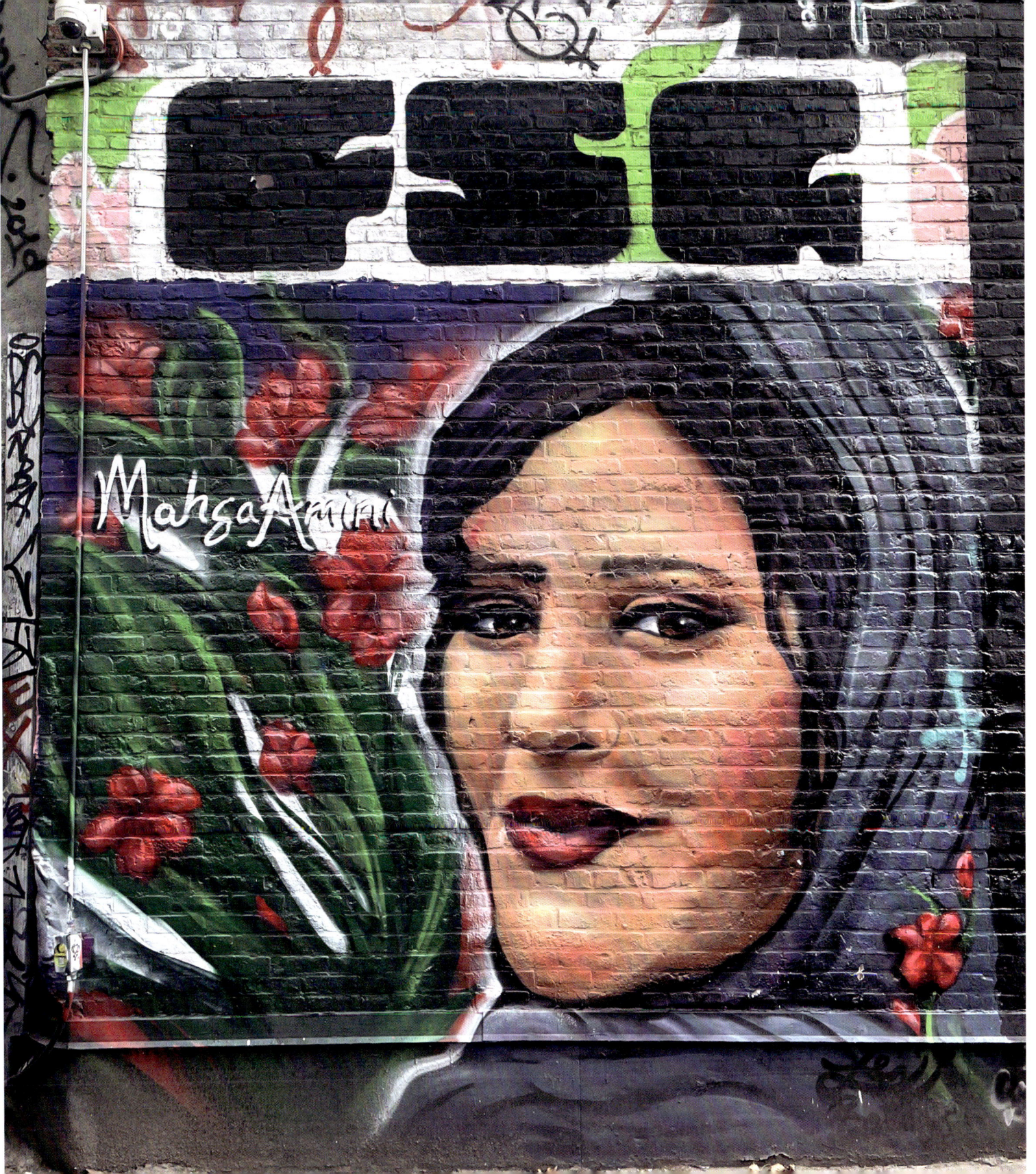

LEXI BELLA
FIRST STREET
GREEN ART PARK,
MANHATTAN,
PHOTOGRAPHED IN
2023

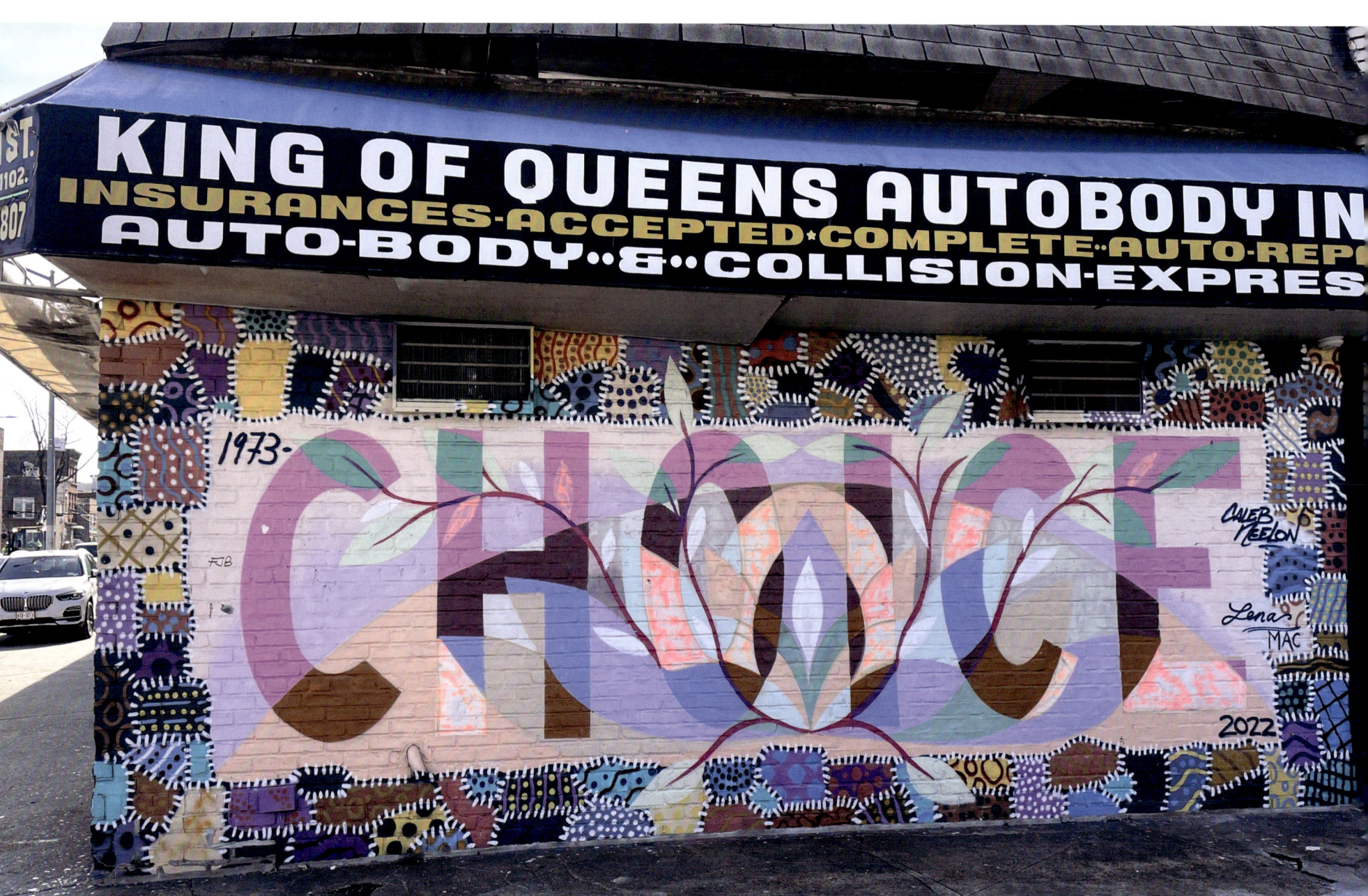

CALEB NEELON, LENA MAC
A colorful pro-choice mural by Caleb Neelon and Lena Mac.
WELLING COURT MURAL PROJECT, QUEENS, PHOTOGRAPHED IN 2024

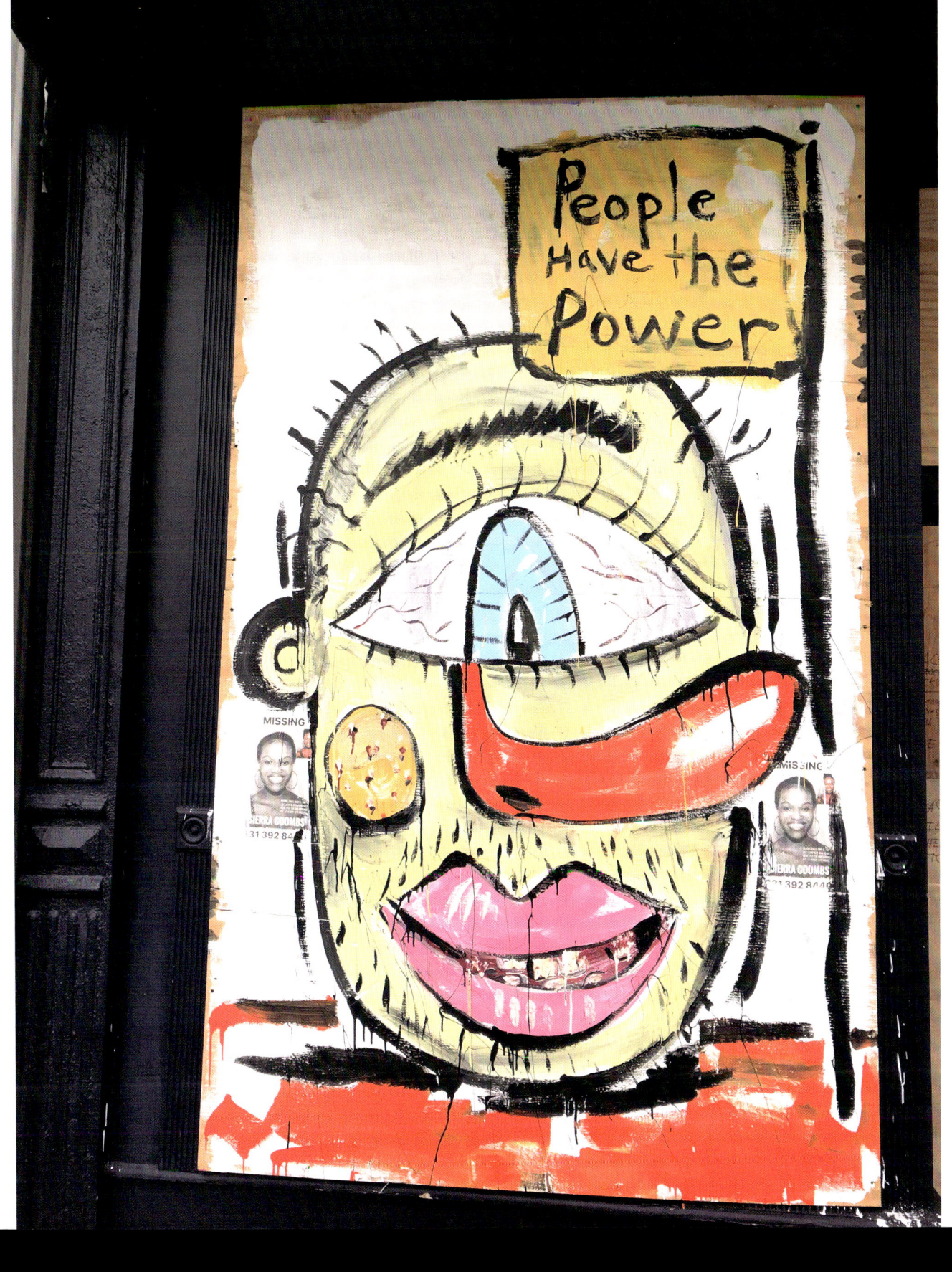

SCOOTER LAFORGE
Art made as a member of Bringing Back
the Bowery Artist Collective during a
Black Lives Matter protest in 2020 near
the Soho District.
MANHATTAN, PHOTOGRAPHED IN
2020

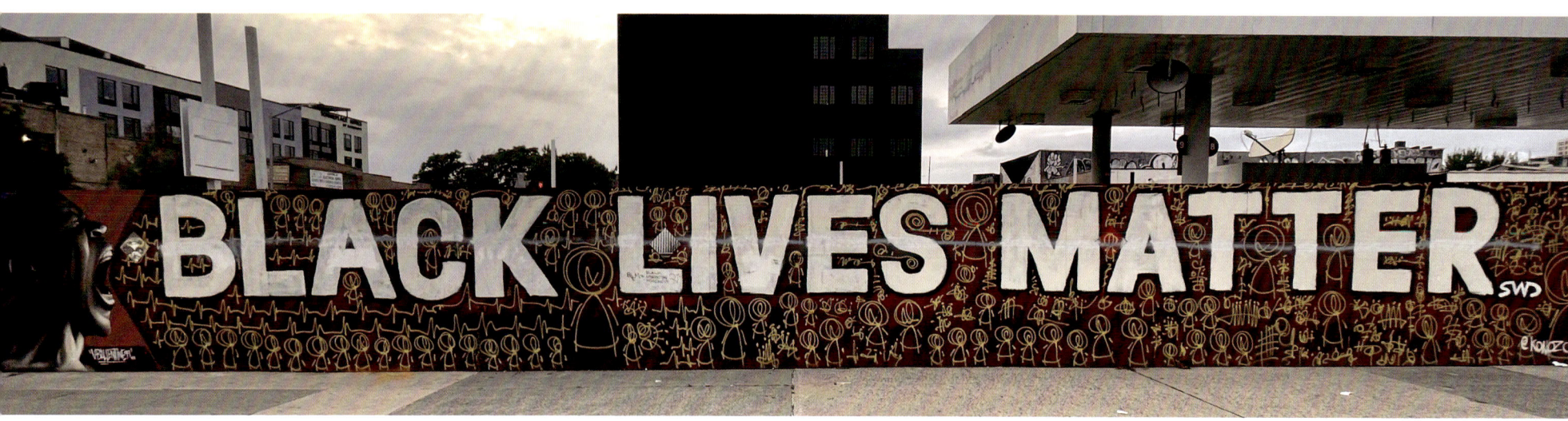

V BALLENTINE AND ESPARTACO ALBORNOZ ABREAU
BROOKLYN, PHOTOGRAPHED IN 2021

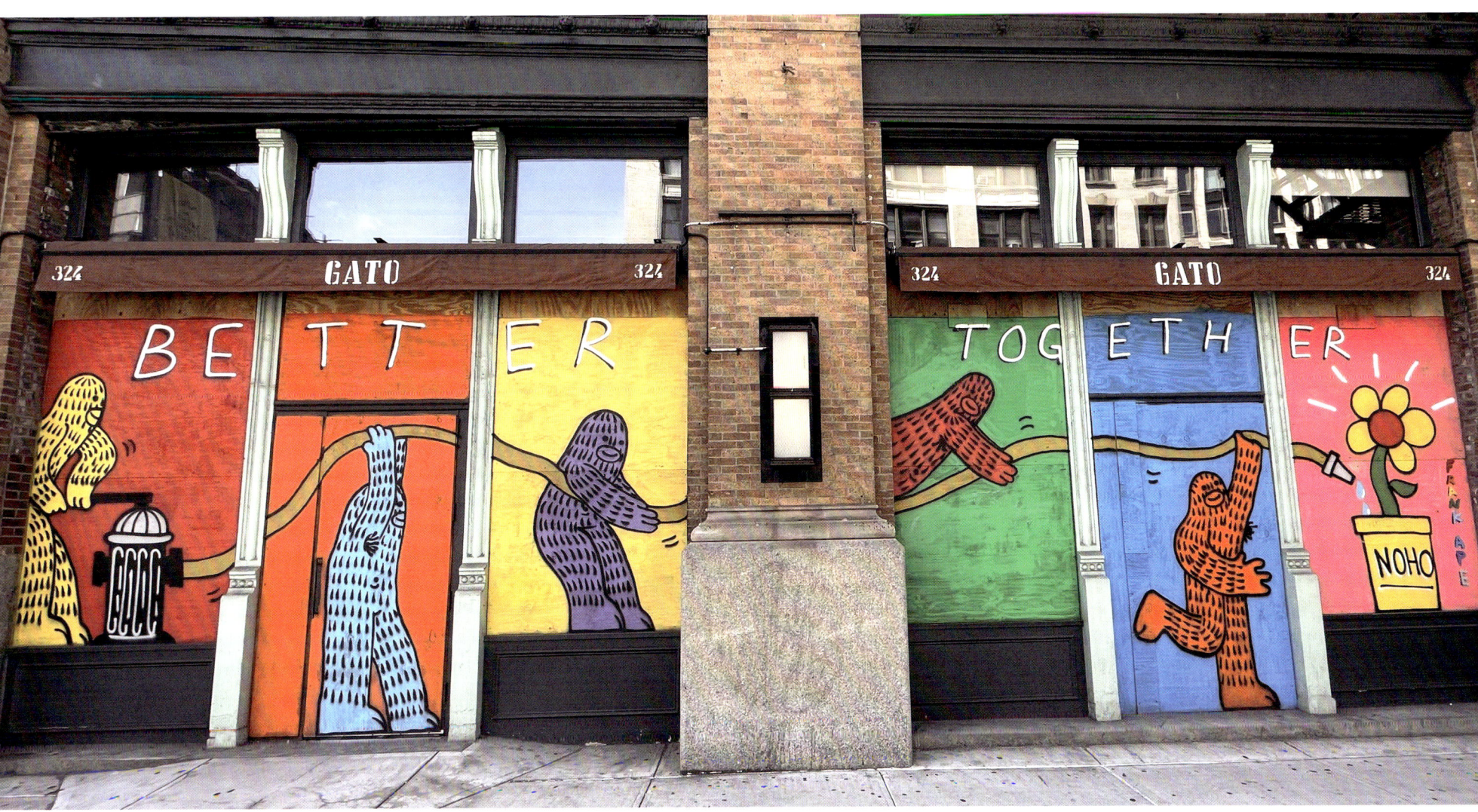

FRANK APE
Art made during a Black Lives Matter protest in 2020 in the Soho District.
MANHATTAN, PHOTOGRAPHED IN 2021

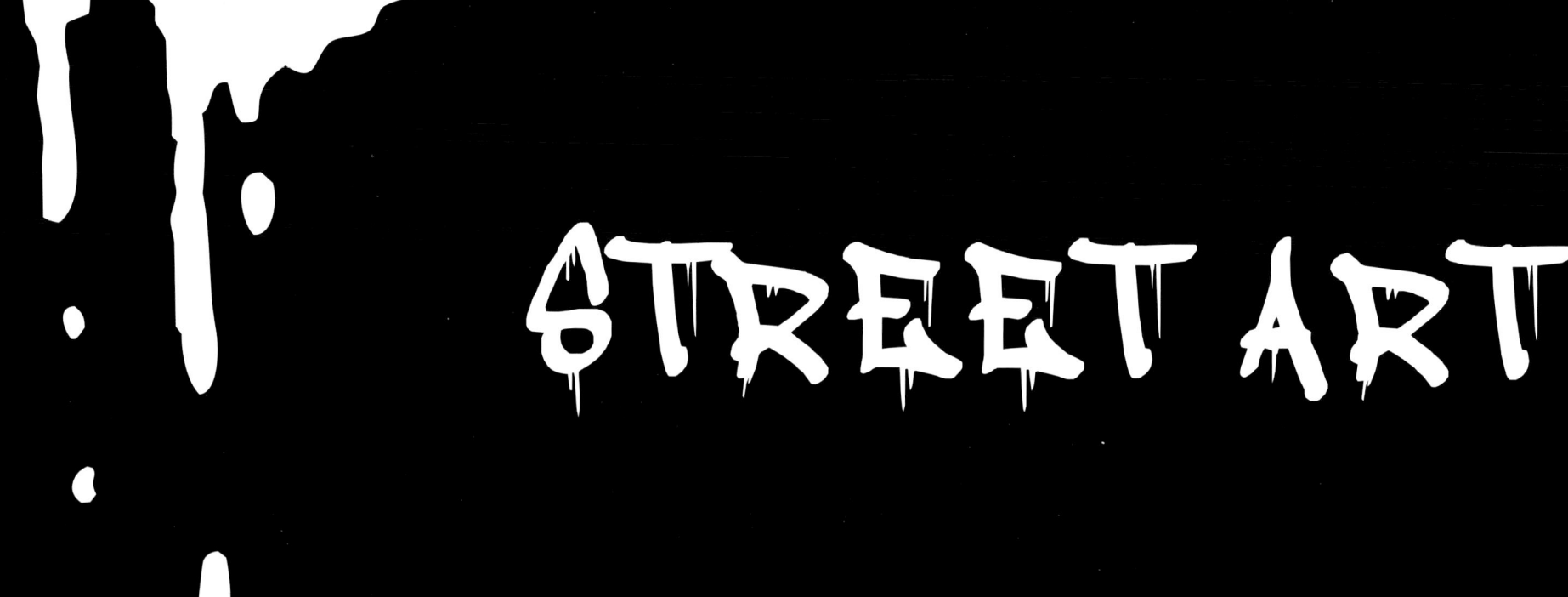

STREET ART

Street art can be used as a broad term to cover all public art. For this chapter, I selected photographs of artworks on walls and other outdoor surfaces that were eye catching and colorful. I photographed these works across the city in Brooklyn, Queens, Manhattan, and the Bronx. Some of the artworks are small as compared to a large-scale mural. I found these artworks to be the artist's vision and creativity for public artwork versus painting a themed work or a commission. Artists Spot, KMS Crew, Rath, COD, EL Souls, and TATS CRU, all of Boone Avenue Walls in the Bronx, and Shiro One of Graffiti Hall Of Fame are a few that stand out in New York City. Just the same, all the artists in this chapter are very creative in using spray paint to create their art. These photographs of street art show the skill level of the aerosol artist. In addition, the majority of the art in this chapter is no longer there and has been painted over for someone else to paint at that same location. Thus, the photograph becomes the document of the artwork. Though street art is ephemeral, the photos of the artwork make you wonder what these aerosol artists will paint next.

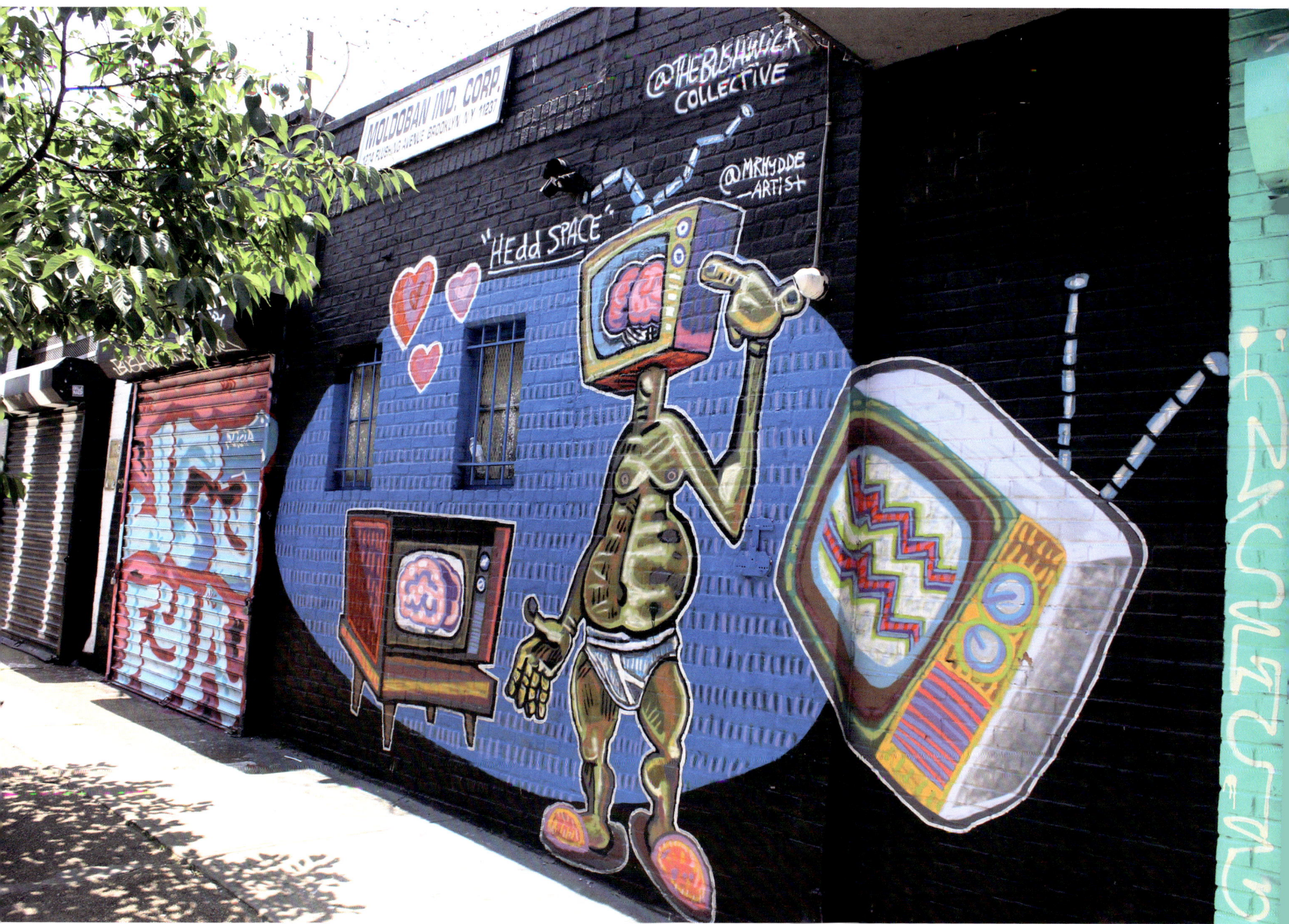

DARREN DEGENOVA
BUSHWICK COLLECTIVE, BROOKLYN, PHOTOGRAPHED IN 2023

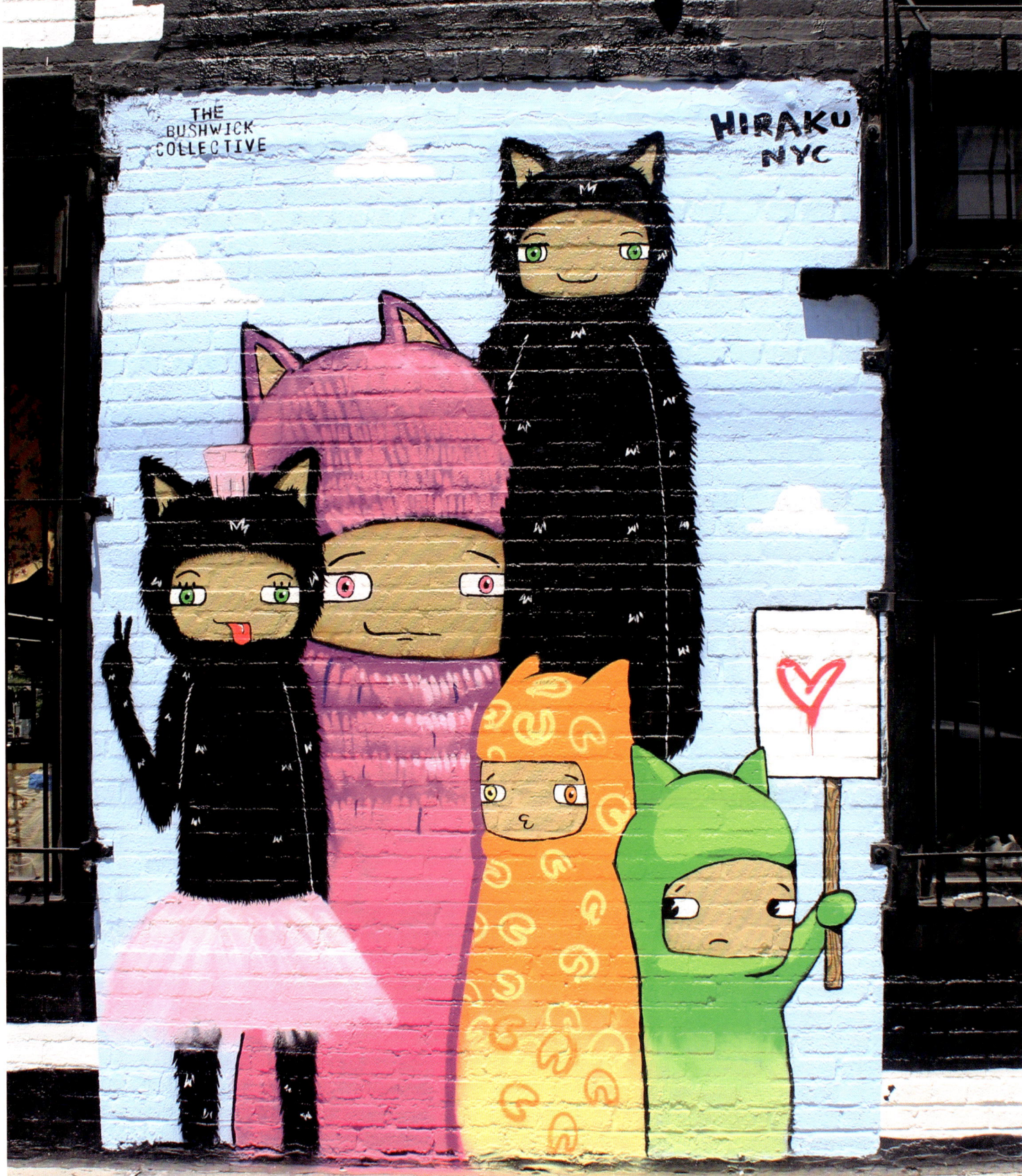

HIRAKU
BUSHWICK
COLLECTIVE,
BROOKLYN,
PHOTOGRAPHED IN
2023

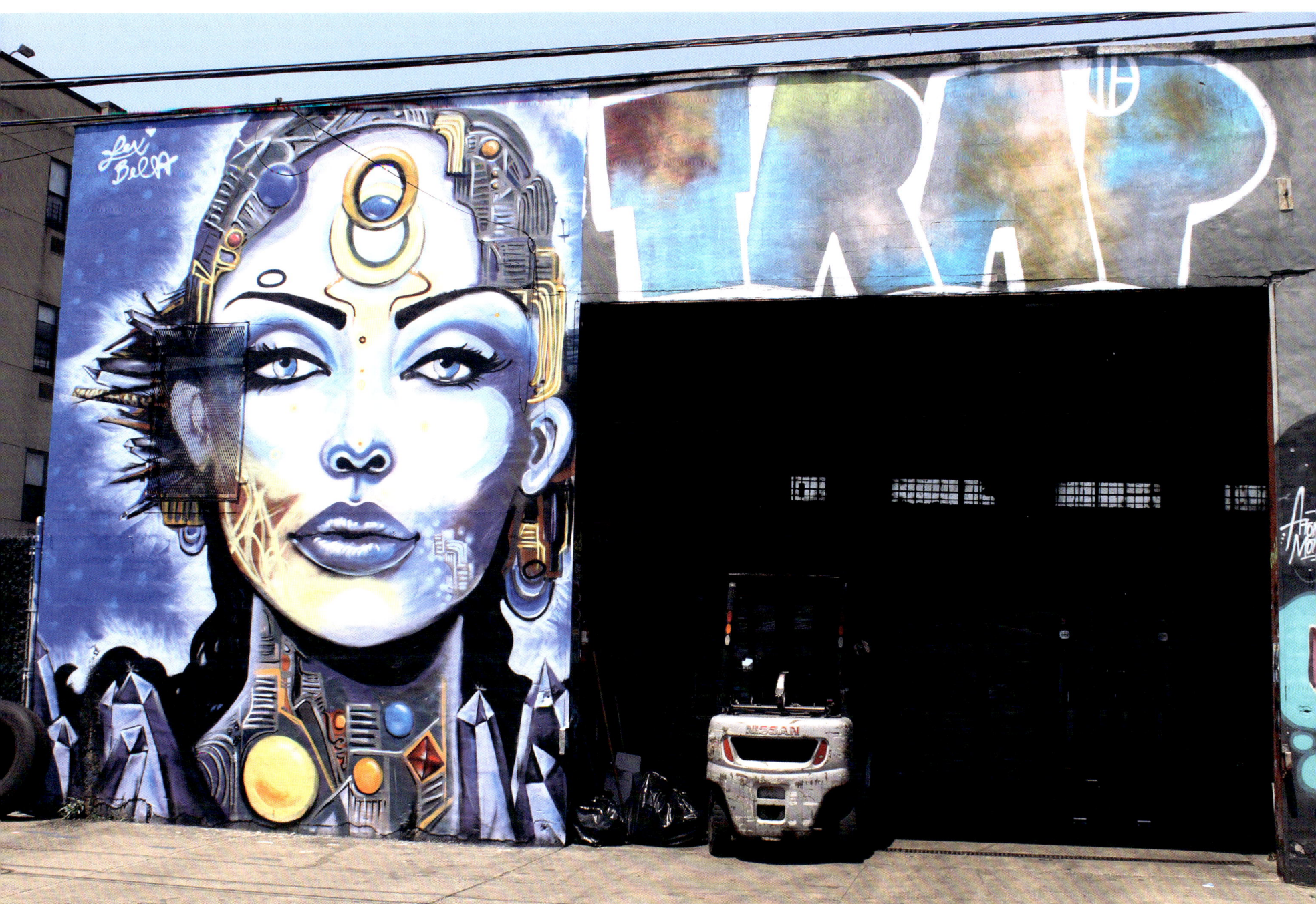

LEXI BELLA, TRAP
BUSHWICK COLLECTIVE, BROOKLYN, PHOTOGRAPHED IN 2023

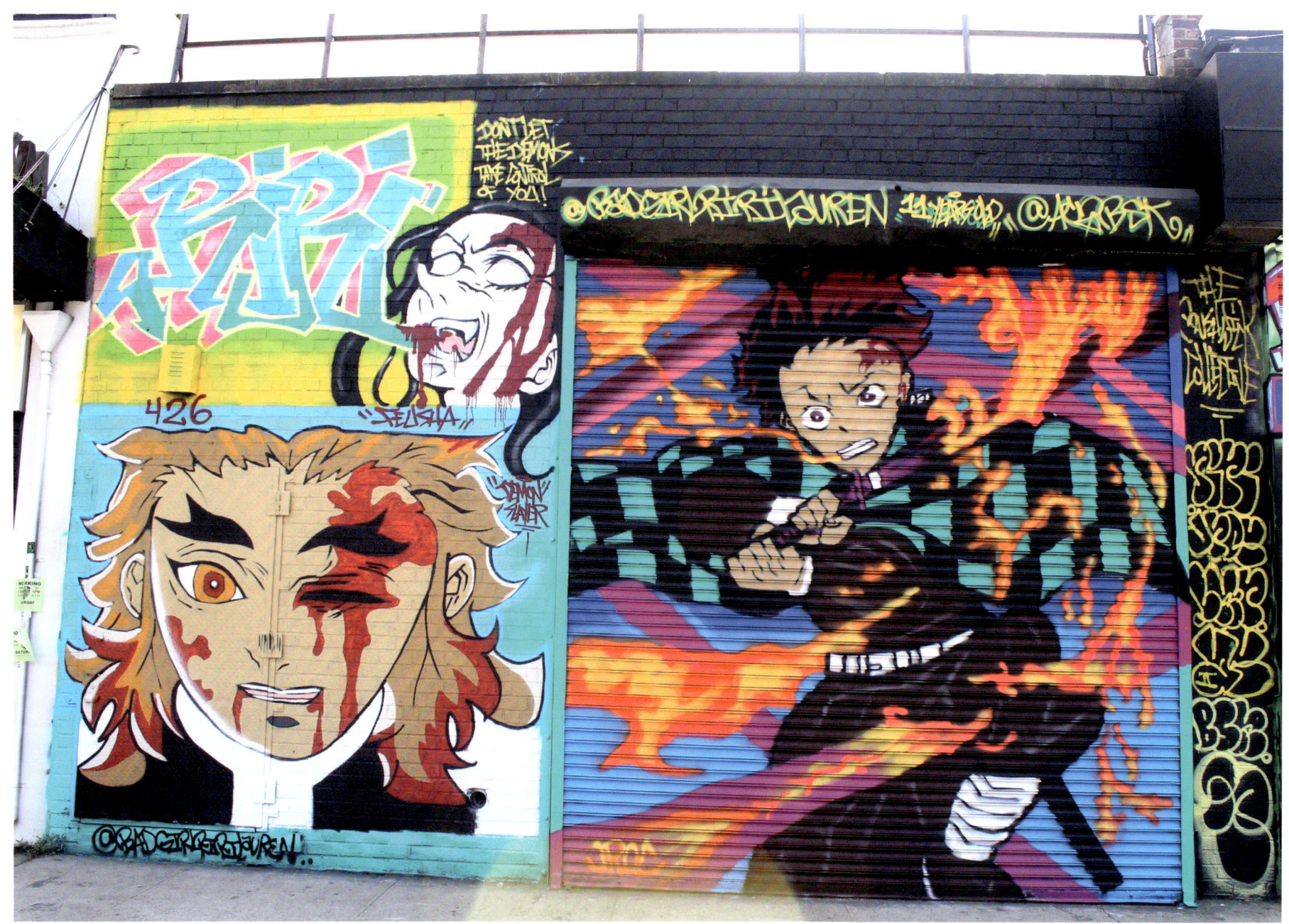

RIRILAUREN
BUSHWICK COLLECTIVE, BROOKLYN, PHOTOGRAPHED IN 2023

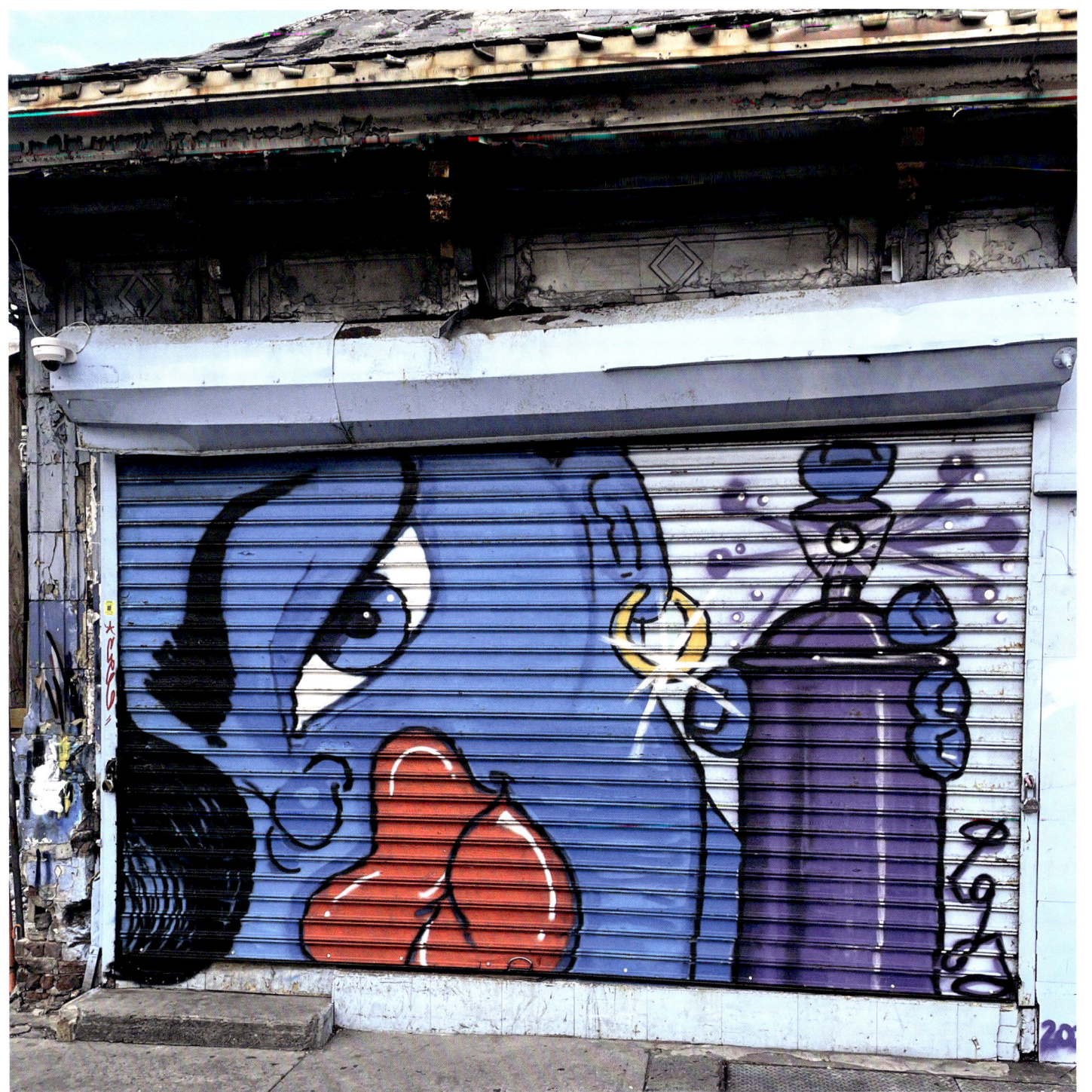

OLGA CORREA

Olga is a popular graffiti and street artist from the Bronx. BRONXLANDIA, THE BRONX, PHOTOGRAPHED IN 2023

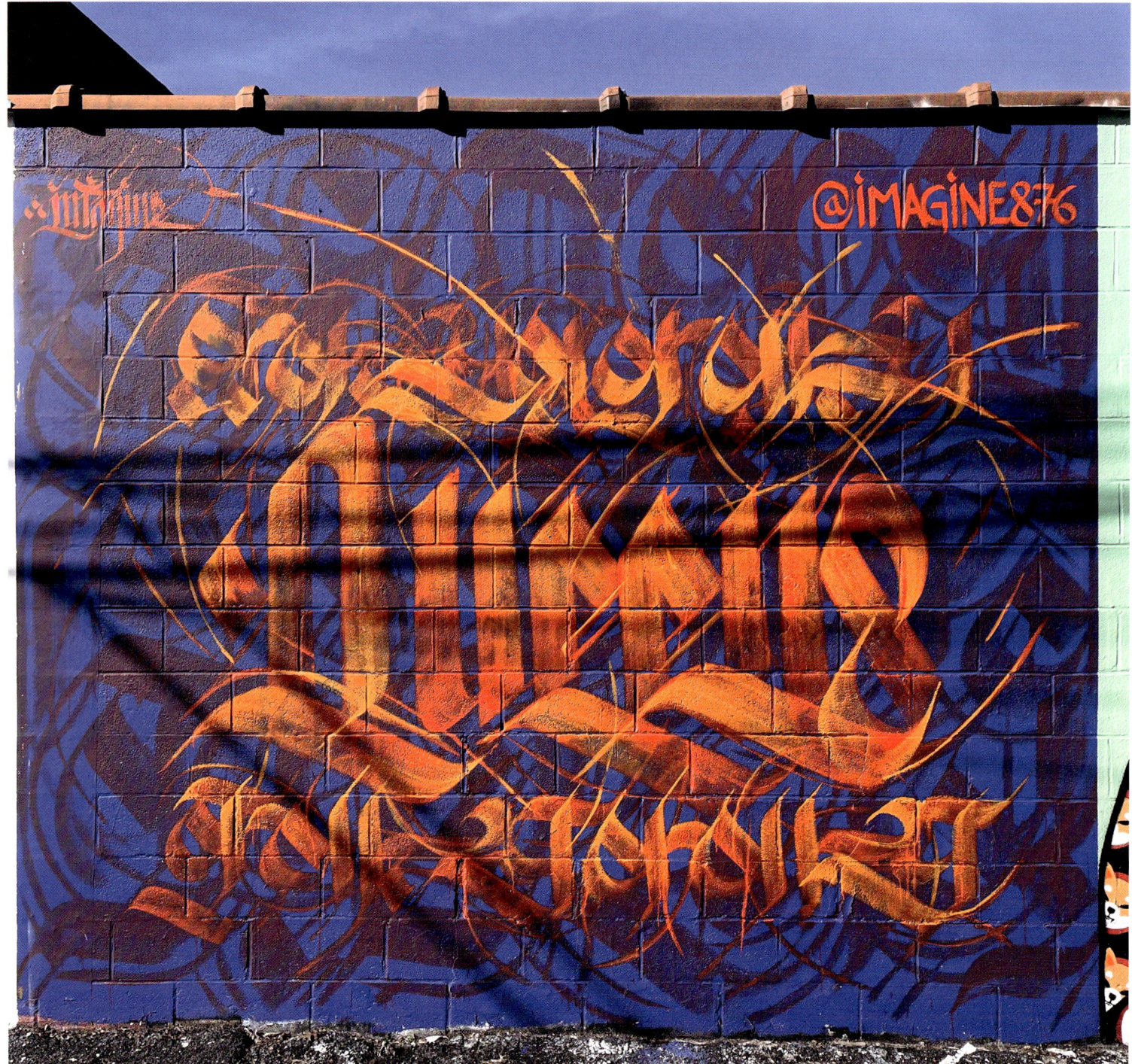

IMAGINE 876
Sneha Shrestha, from Nepal, whose street-art name is Imagine, often uses Nepali language lettering in her artwork.
WELLING COURT MURAL PROJECT, QUEENS, PHOTOGRAPHED IN 2024

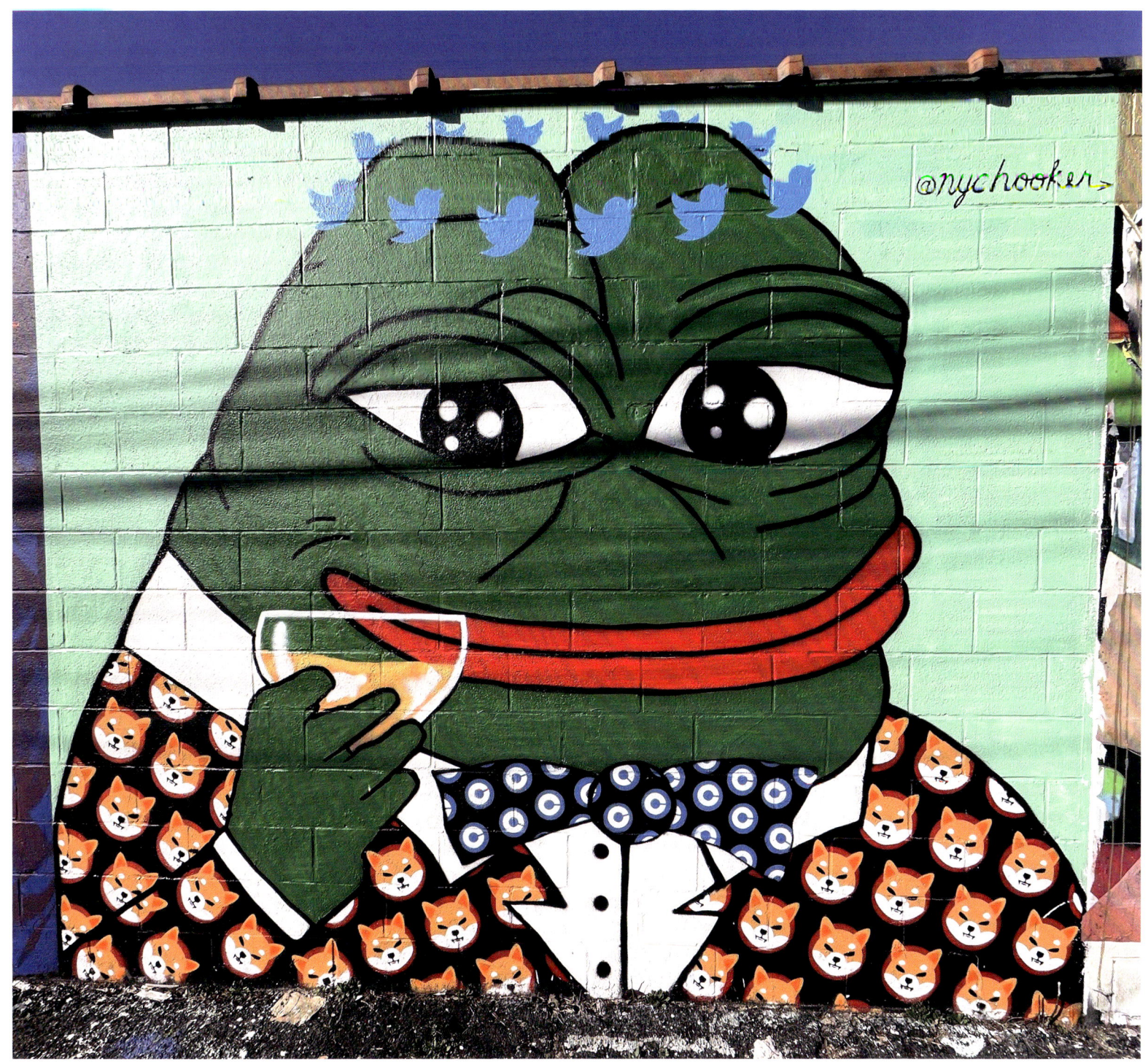

@nychooker

**CHRISTIAN
HOOKER**
WELLING
COURT MURAL
PROJECT,
QUEENS,
PHOTOGRAPHED
IN 2024

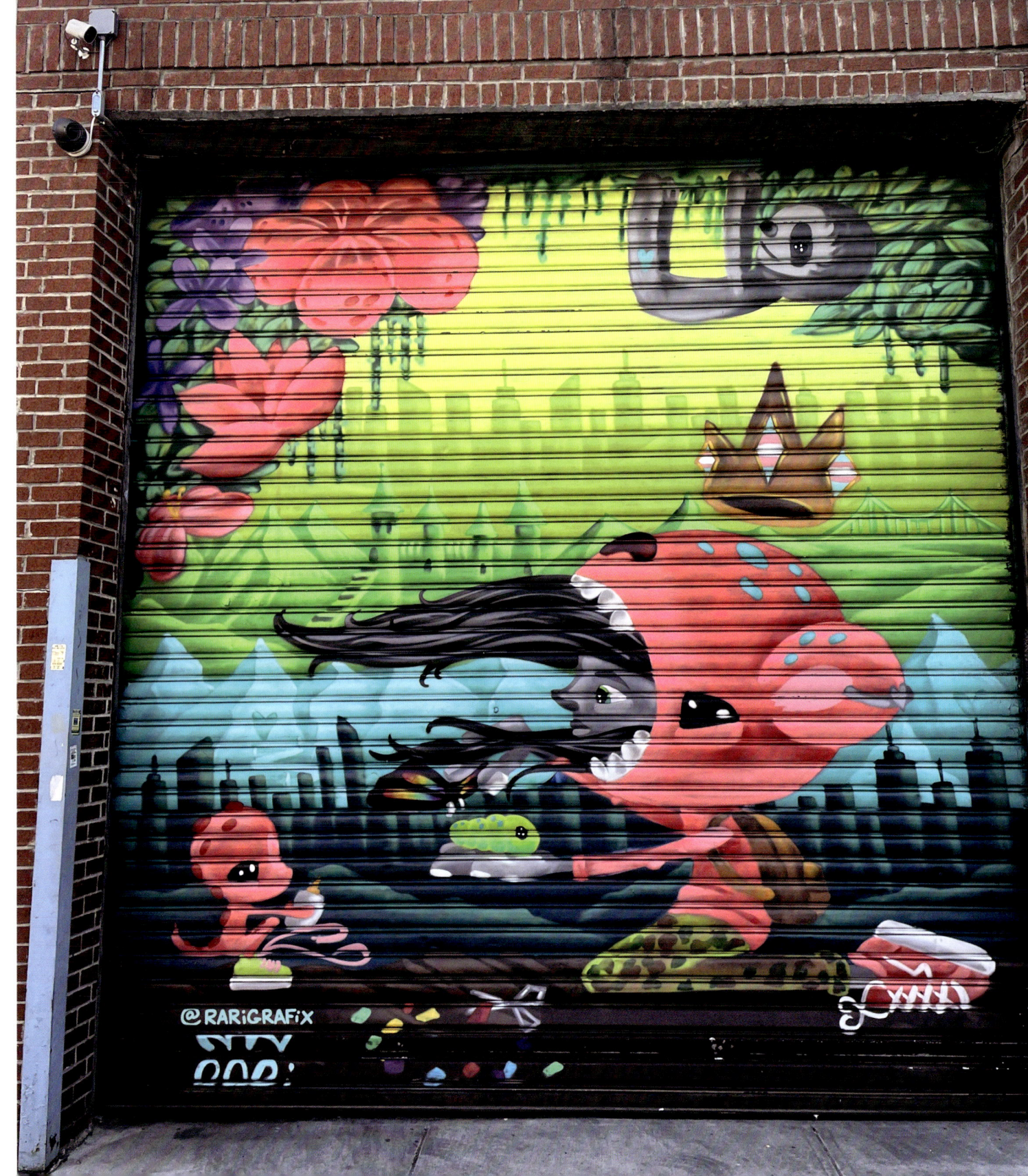

KATIE REIDY
WELLING COURT MURAL
PROJECT, QUEENS,
PHOTOGRAPHED IN 2024

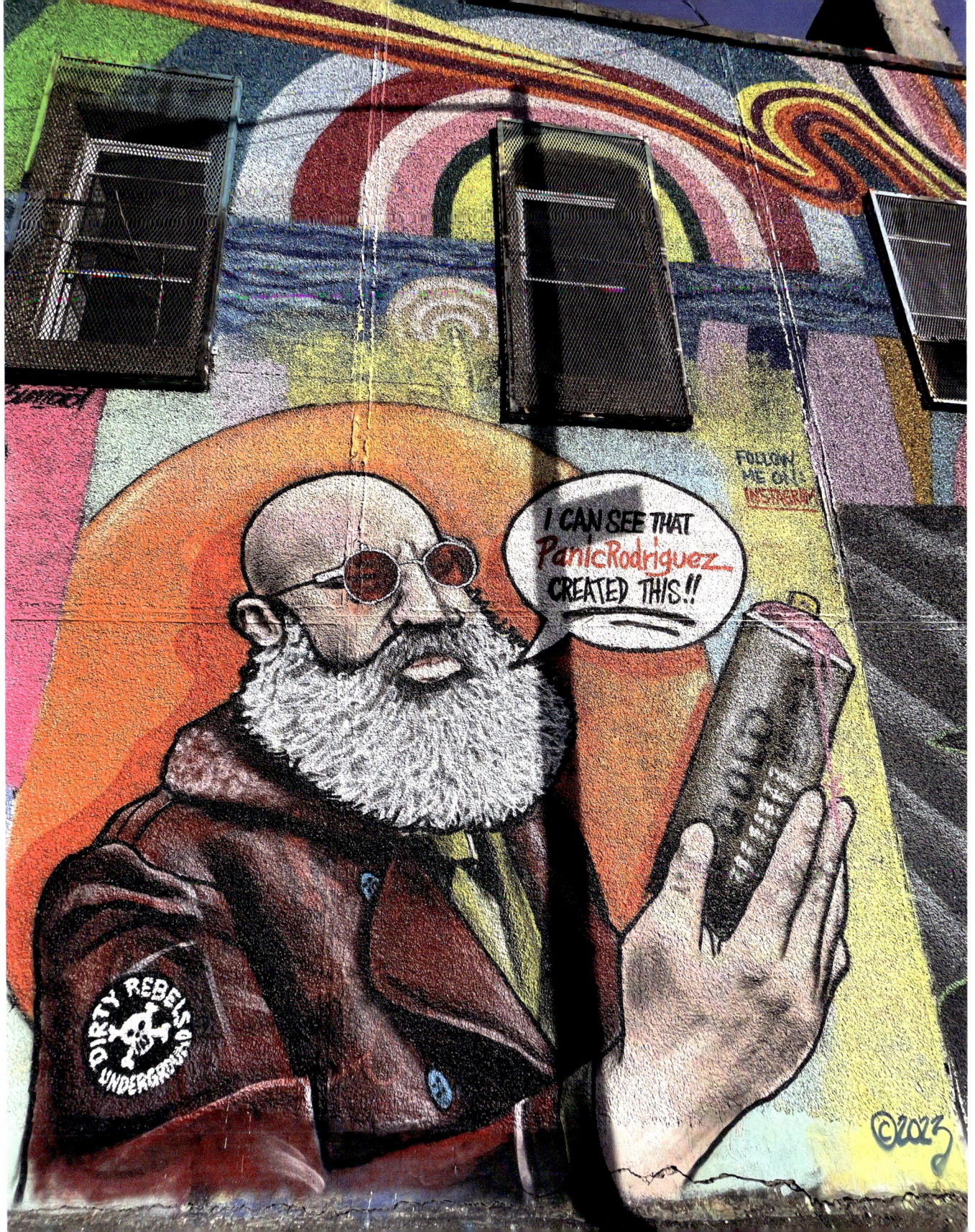

PANIC RODRIGUEZ
WELLING COURT MURAL
PROJECT, QUEENS,
PHOTOGRAPHED IN 2024

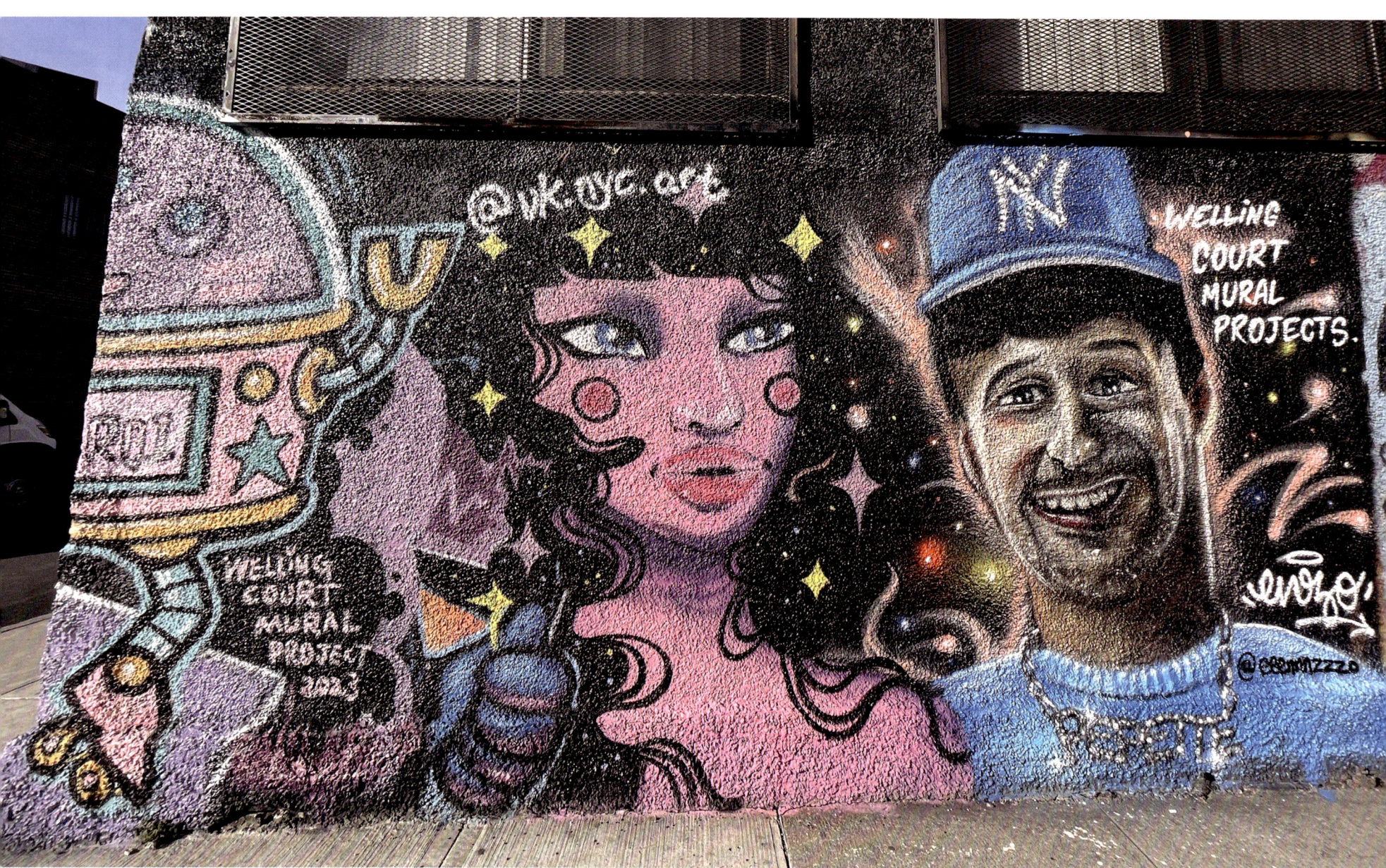

VANESSA KREYTAK, ENZO
WELLING COURT MURAL PROJECT, QUEENS, PHOTOGRAPHED IN 2024

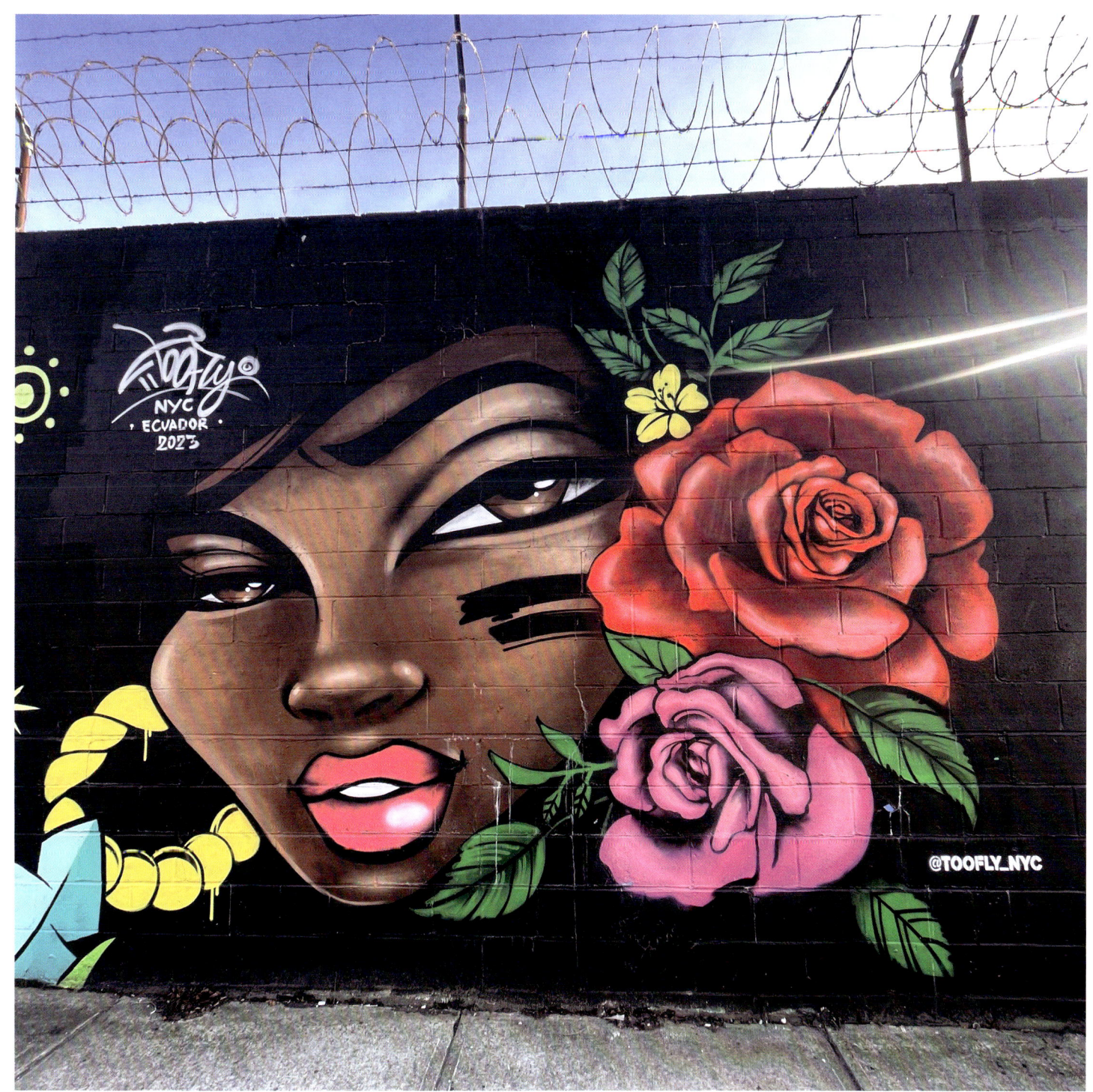

TOOFLY
WELLING COURT MURAL
PROJECT, QUEENS,
PHOTOGRAPHED IN 2024

@TOOFLY_NYC

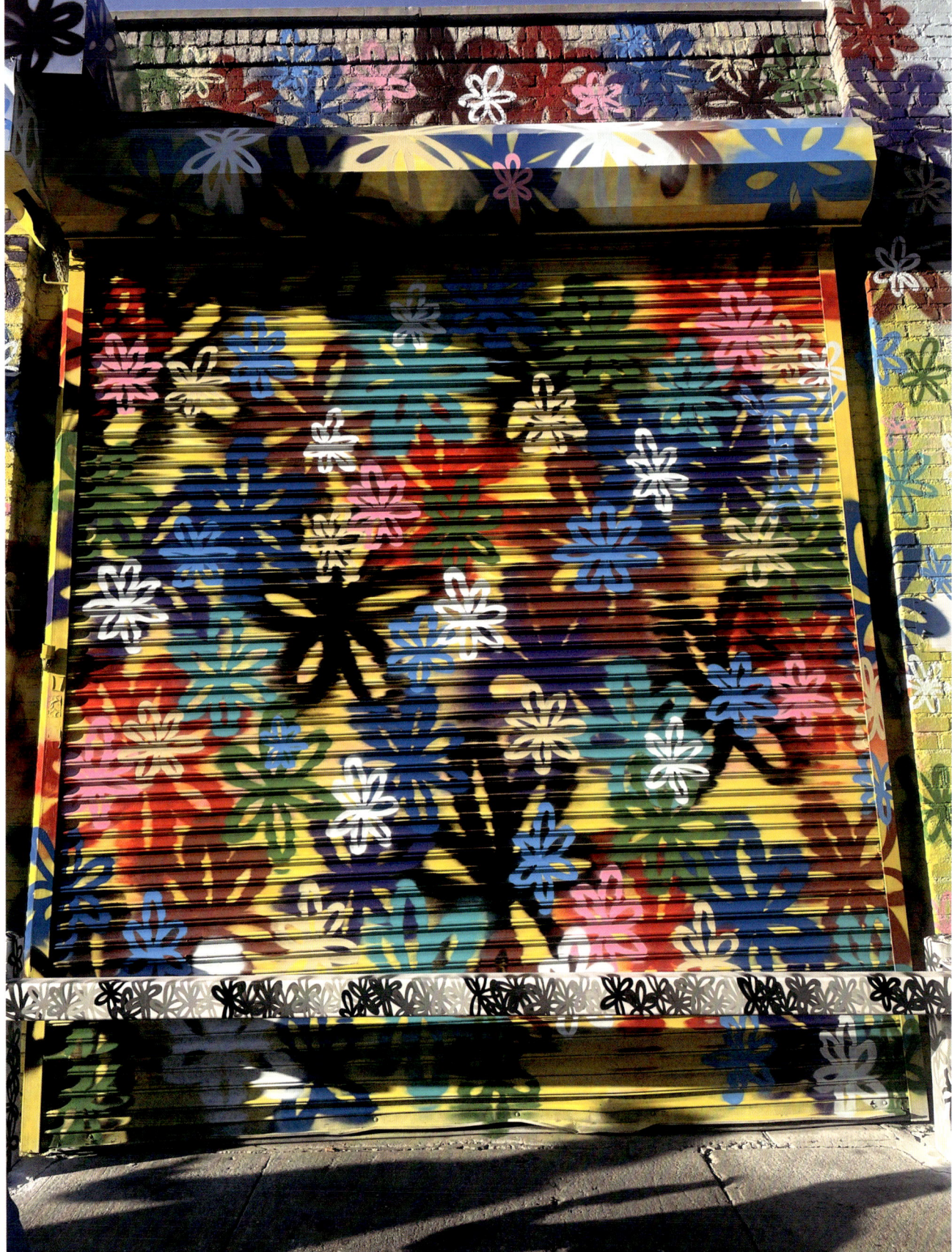

BC

BC is an early writer from the 1980s
subway graffiti era.
BED-STUY WALLS, BROOKLYN,
PHOTOGRAPHED IN 2022

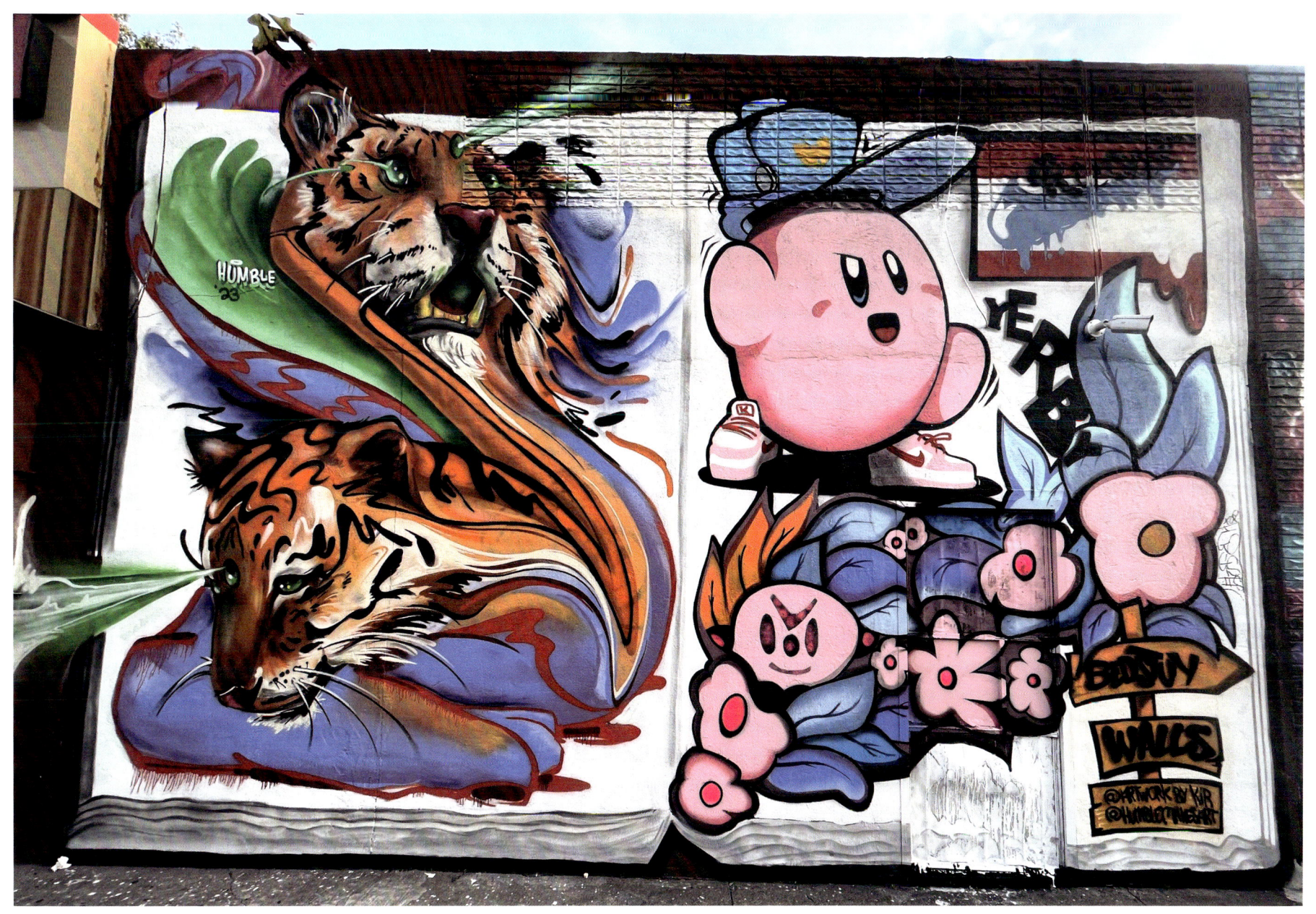

KIR, HUMBLE
BED-STUY WALLS, BROOKLYN, PHOTOGRAPHED IN 2023

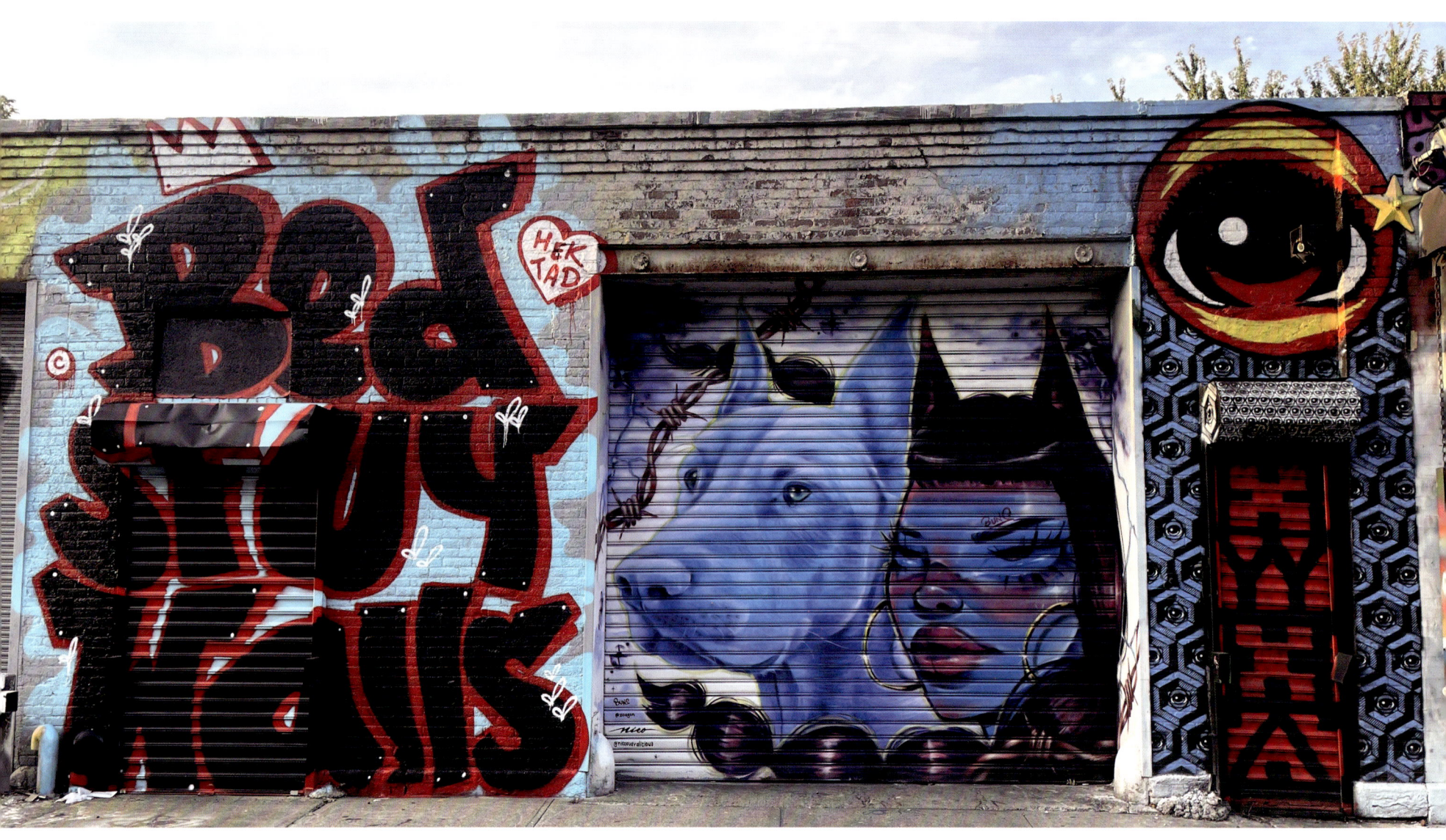

NICOSUAVALICIOUS, BUNS, PEAT EYEZ
BED-STUY WALLS, BROOKLYN, PHOTOGRAPHED IN 2024

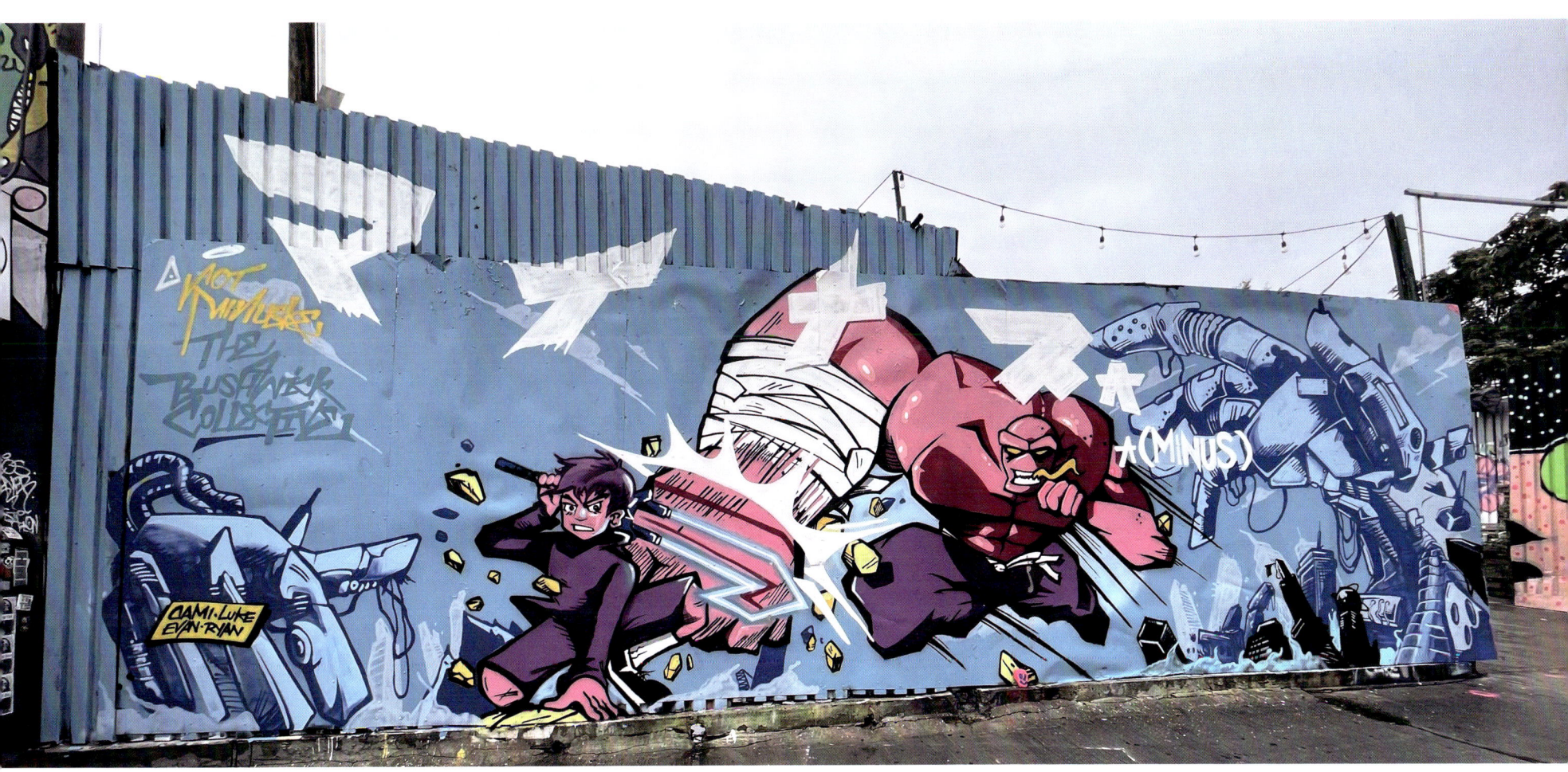

MINUS ONE
BUSHWICK COLLECTIVE, PHOTOGRAPHED IN 2024

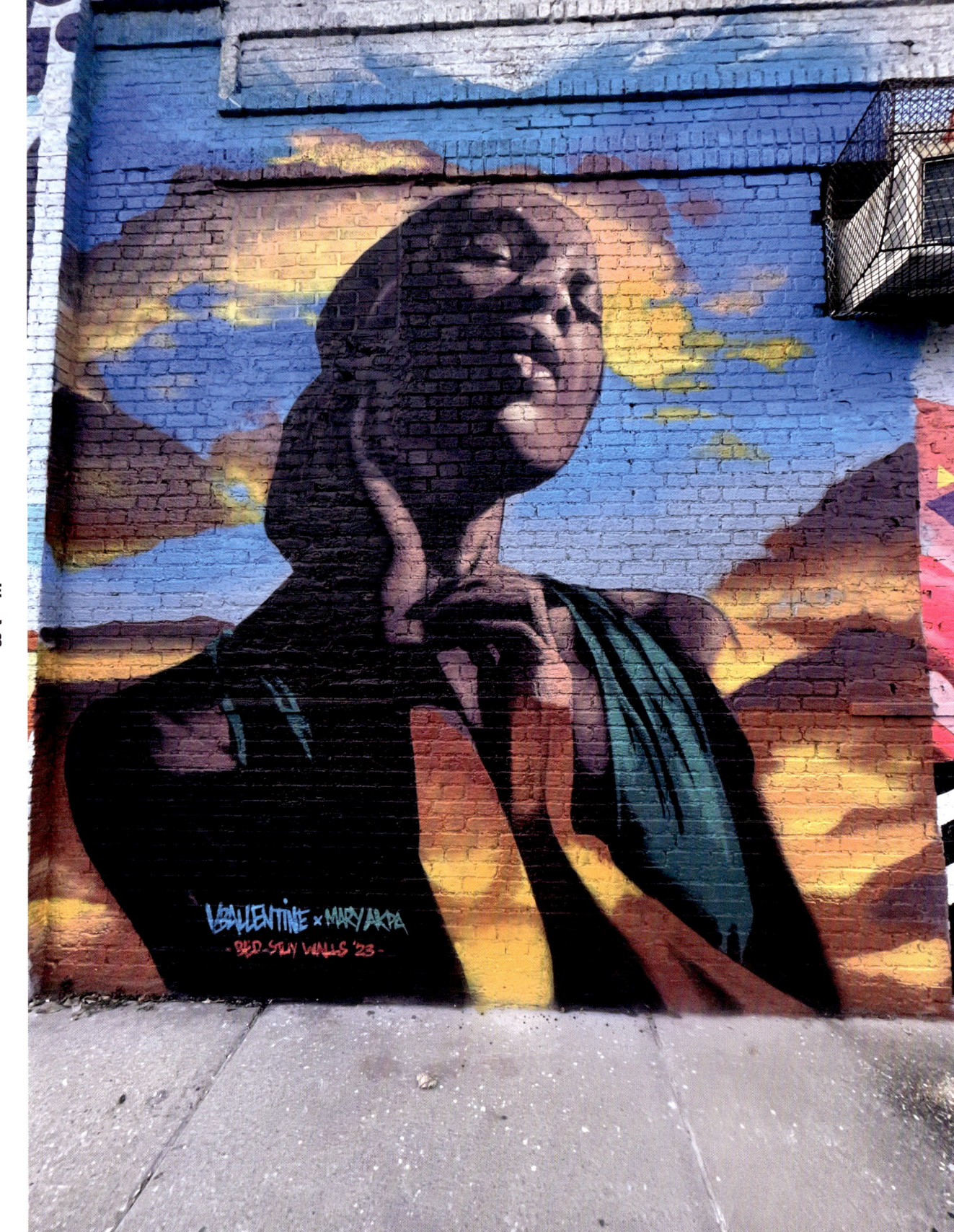

V BALLENTINE
BED-STUY WALLS, BROOKLYN,
PHOTOGRAPHED IN 2023

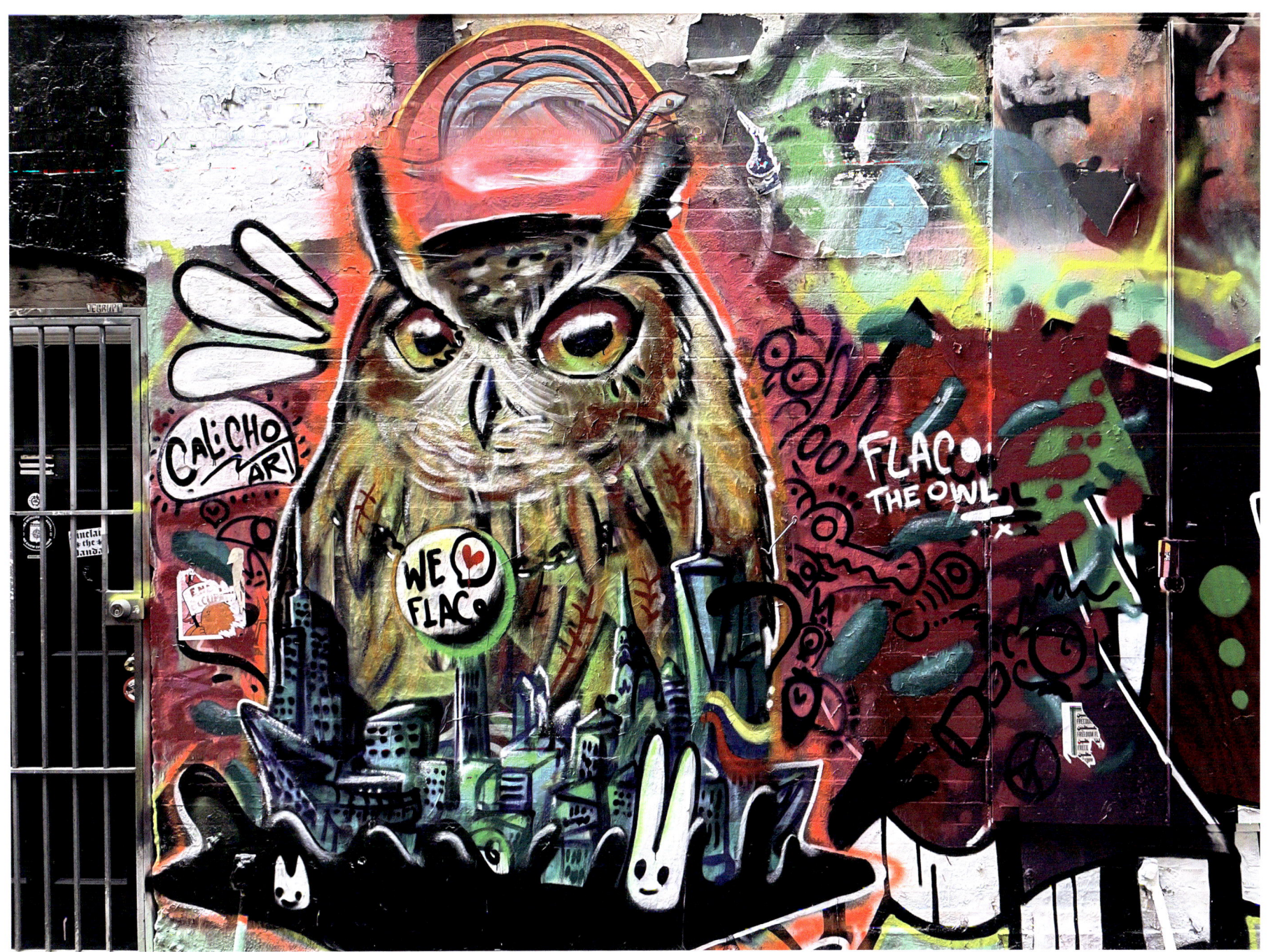

CALICHO ART
FREEMAN ALLEY, MANHATTAN, PHOTOGRAPHED IN 2024

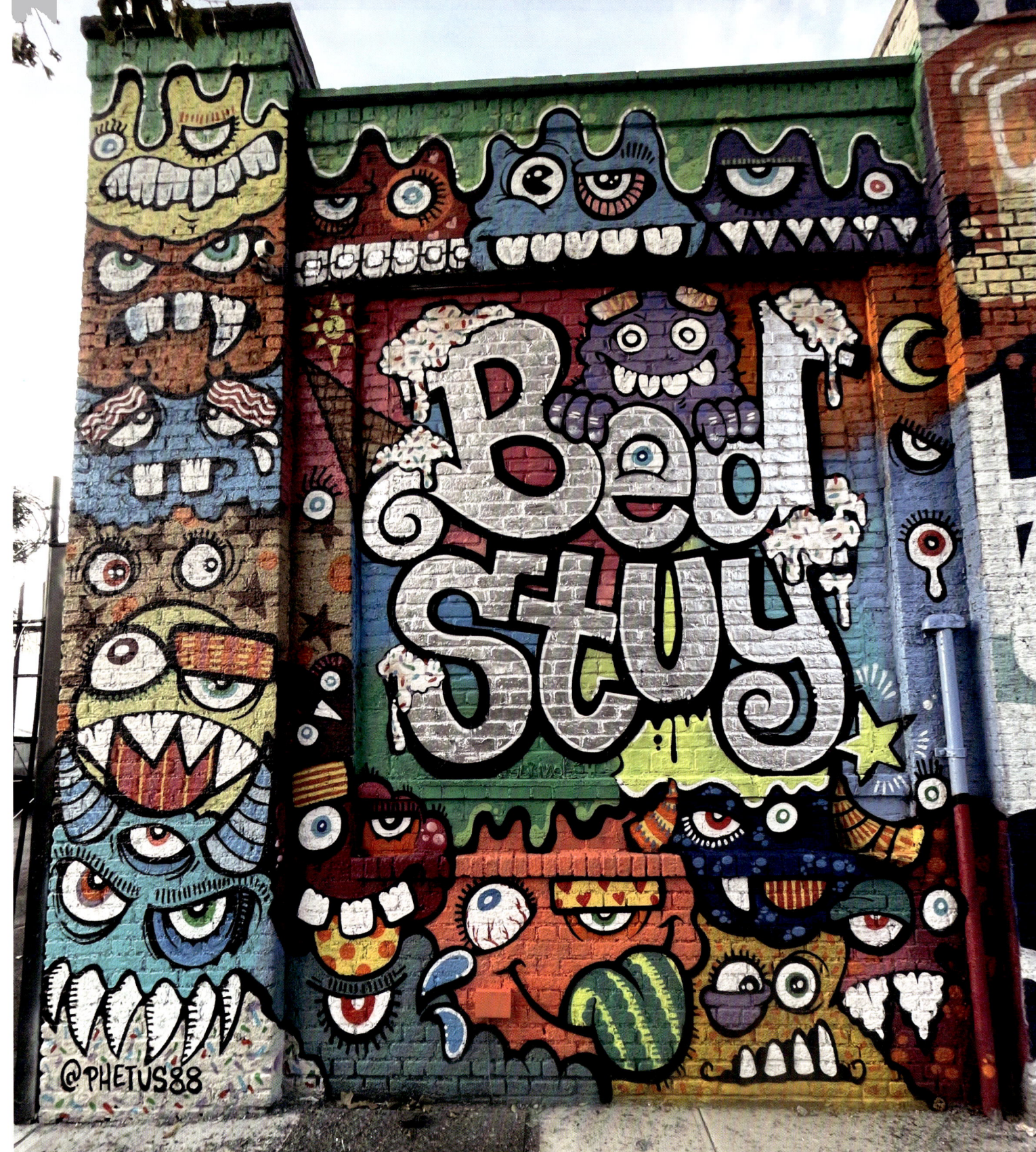

PHETUS

Phetus is a great artist and illustrator who has a long history in graffiti arts and hip-hop culture.
BED-STUY WALLS, BROOKLYN, PHOTOGRAPHED IN 2023

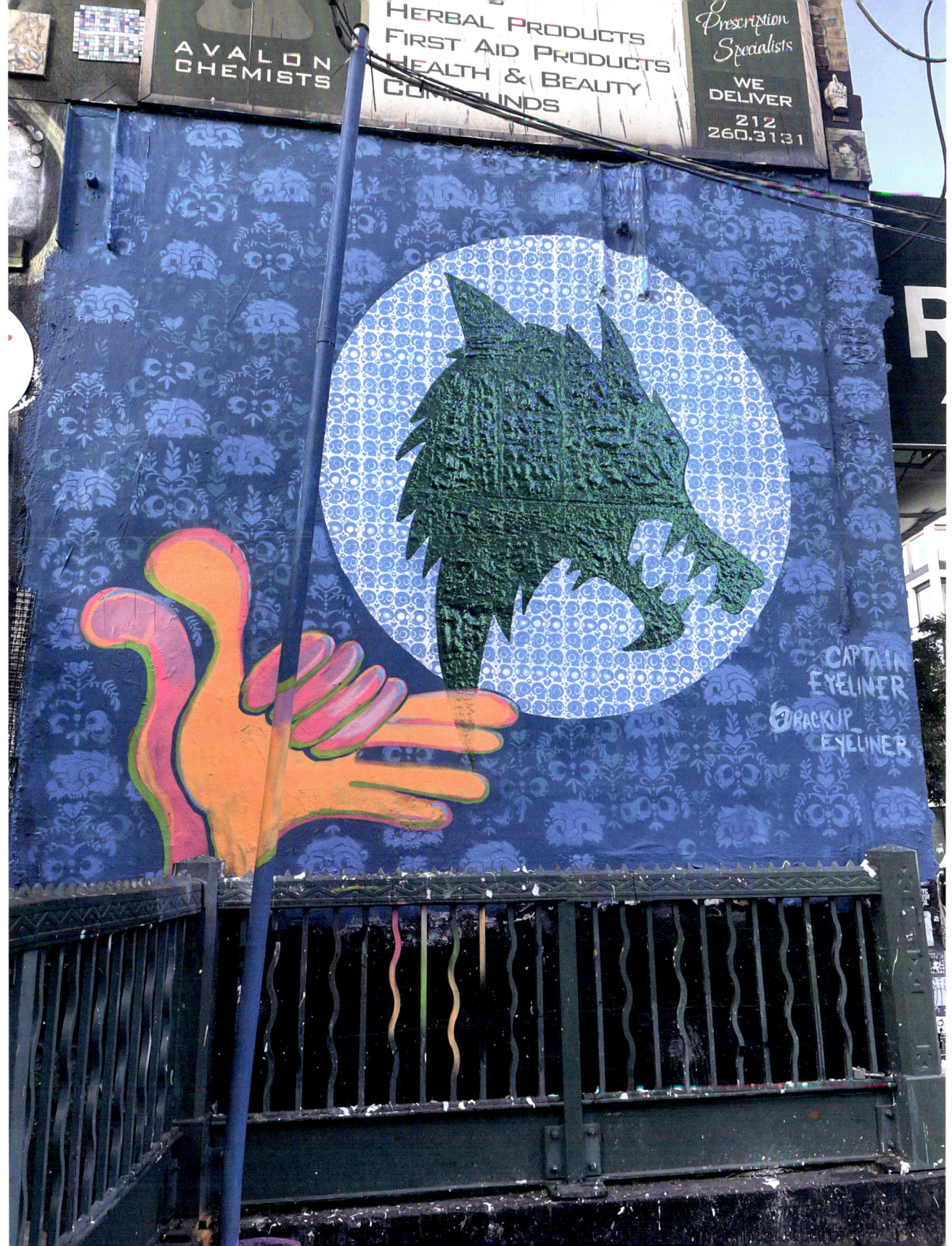

CAPTAIN EYELINER
MANHATTAN, PHOTOGRAPHED IN 2023

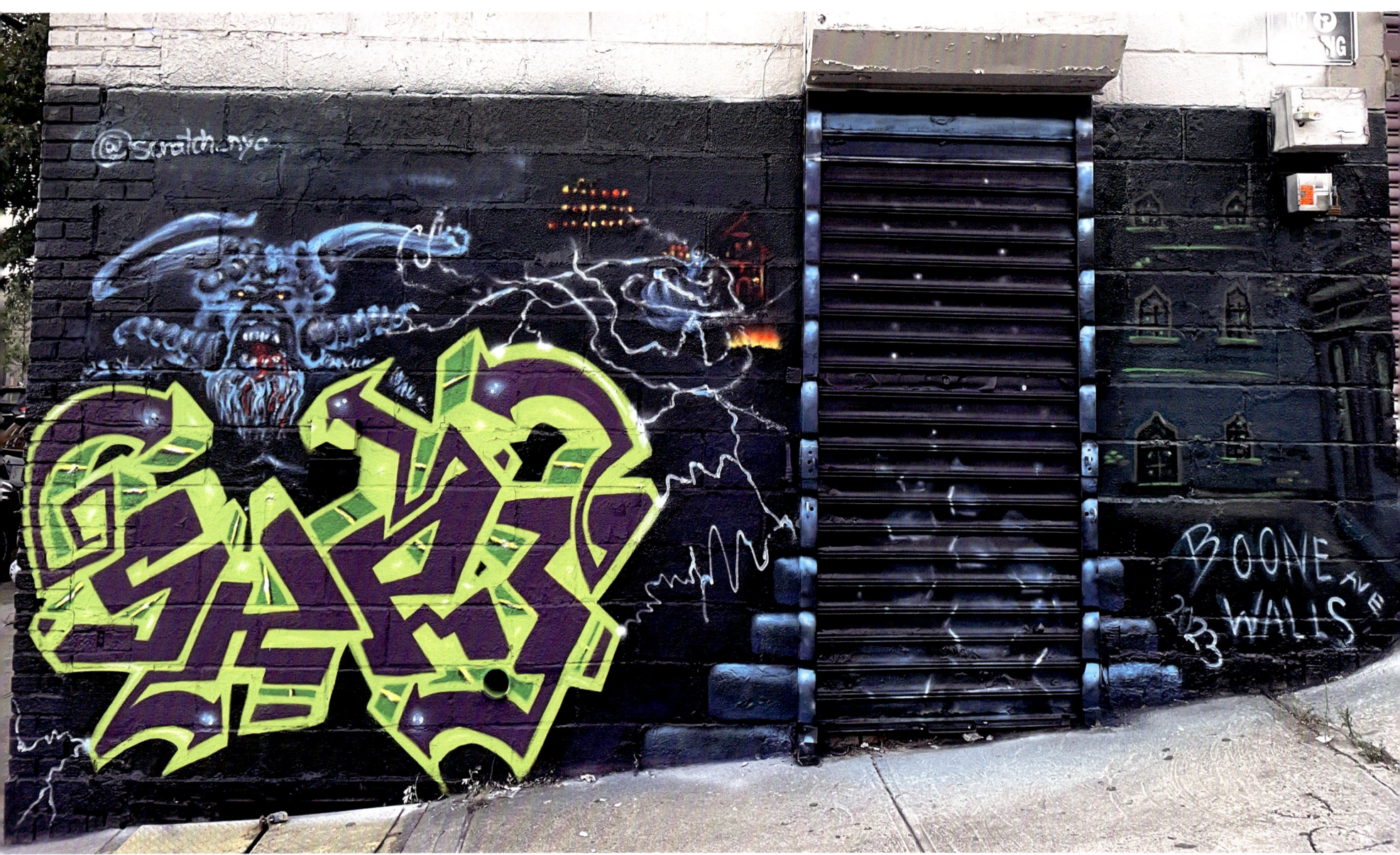

SCRATCH NYC

Scratch is a dynamic aerosol artist who uses many different styles in the creation of her murals.
BOONE AVENUE WALL, THE BRONX, PHOTOGRAPHED IN 2023

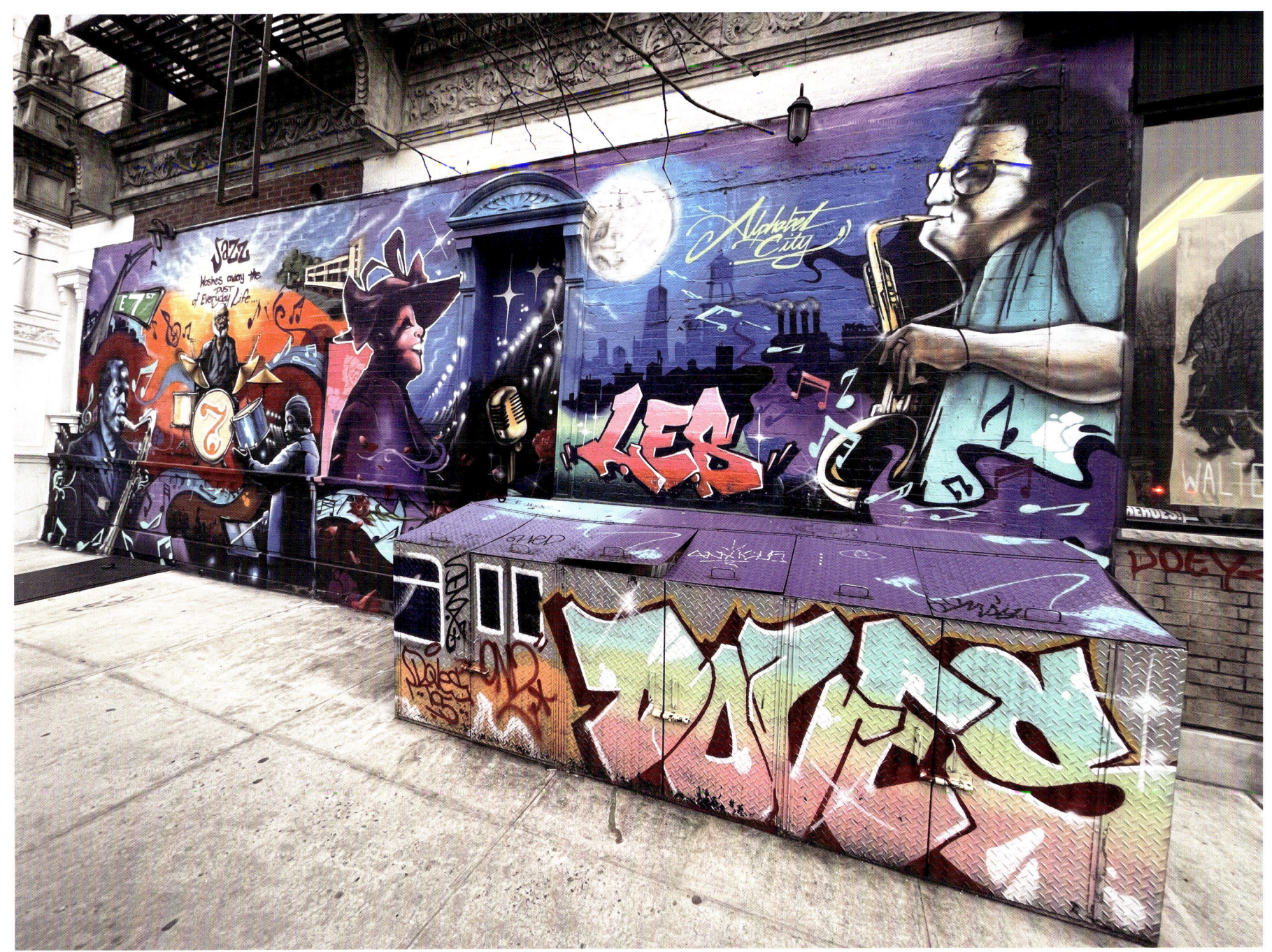

CHARLIE DOVE
MANHATTAN, PHOTOGRAPHED IN 2024

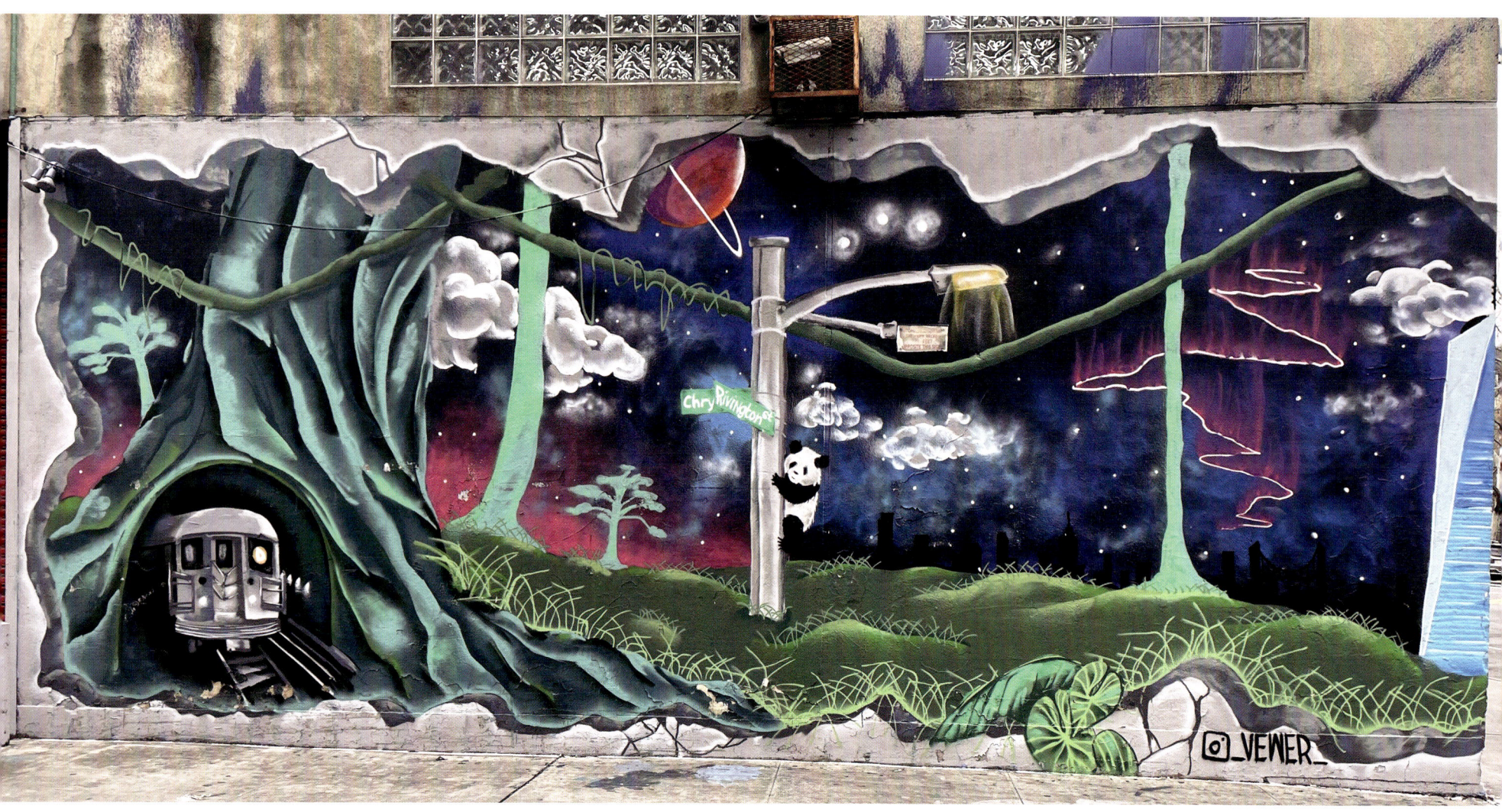

VEWER

Vewer is a talented street artist. In this piece, he shows his skill level and imagination when using a spray paint can.
MANHATTAN, PHOTOGRAPHED IN 2024

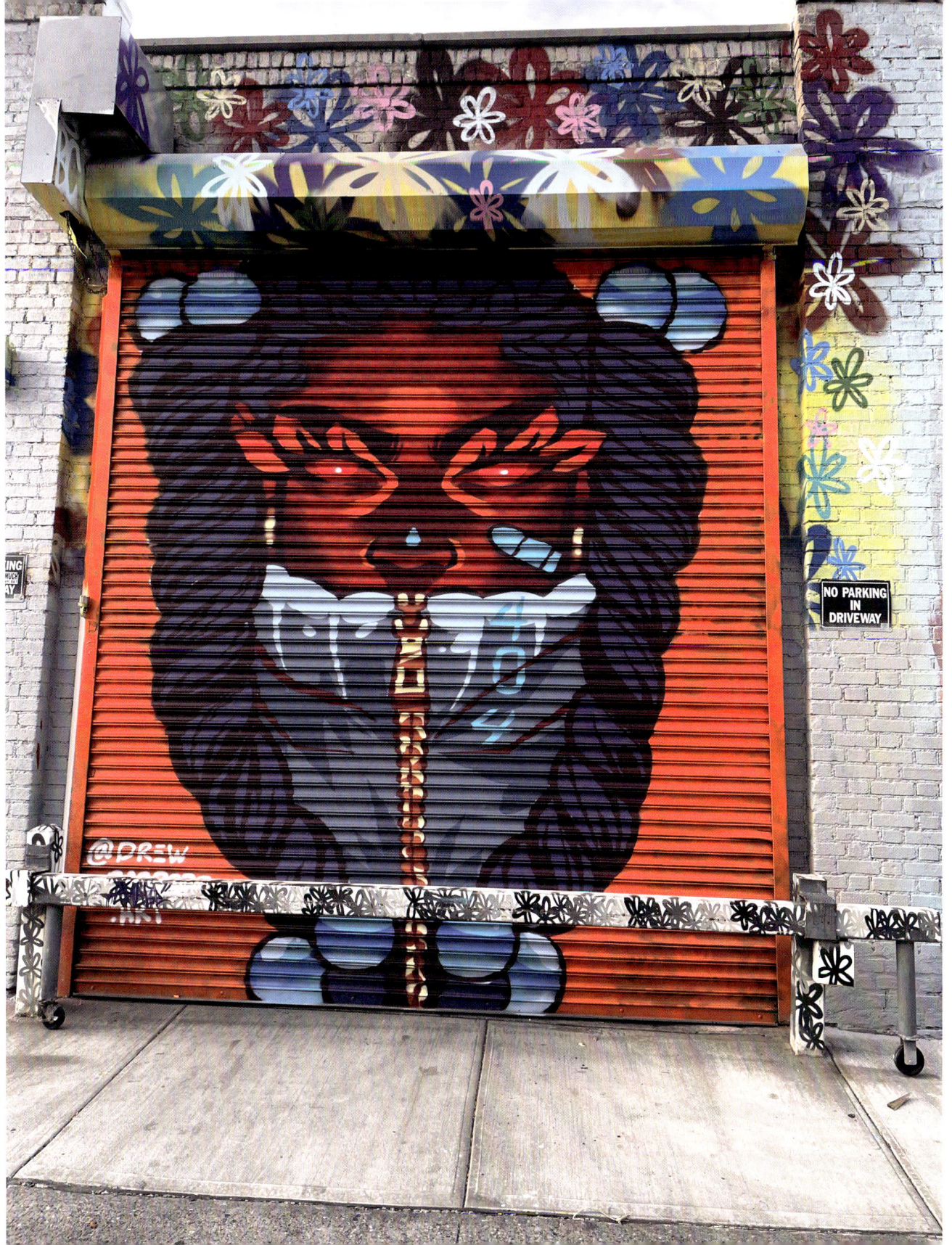

DREW BORDERS, BC
BED-STUY WALLS, BROOKLYN,
PHOTOGRAPHED IN 2023

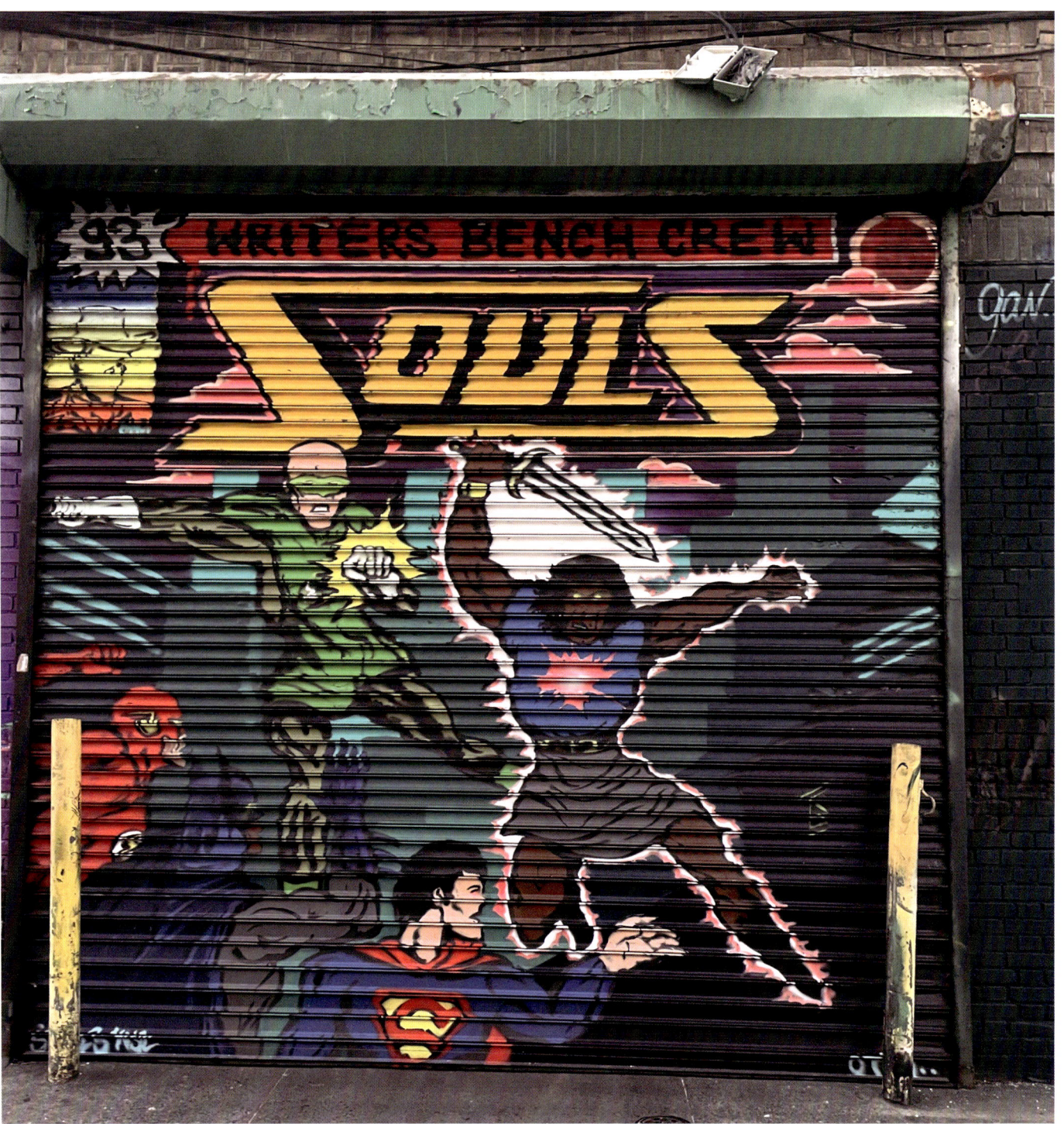

EL SOULS
BOONE AVENUE WALLS, THE
BRONX, PHOTOGRAPHED IN
2022

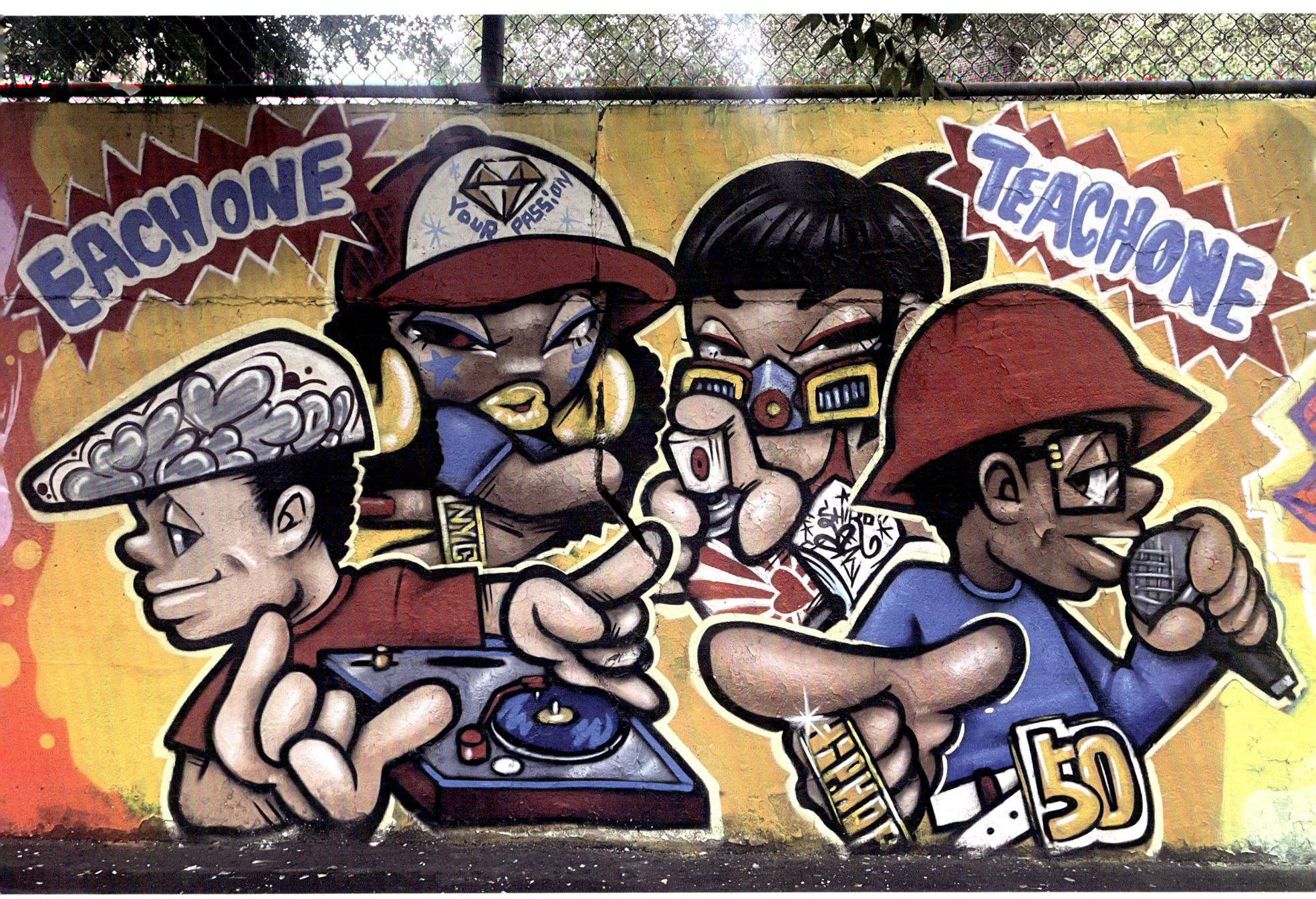

SHIRO ONE
GRAFFITI HALL OF FAME, MANHATTAN, PHOTOGRAPHED IN 2023

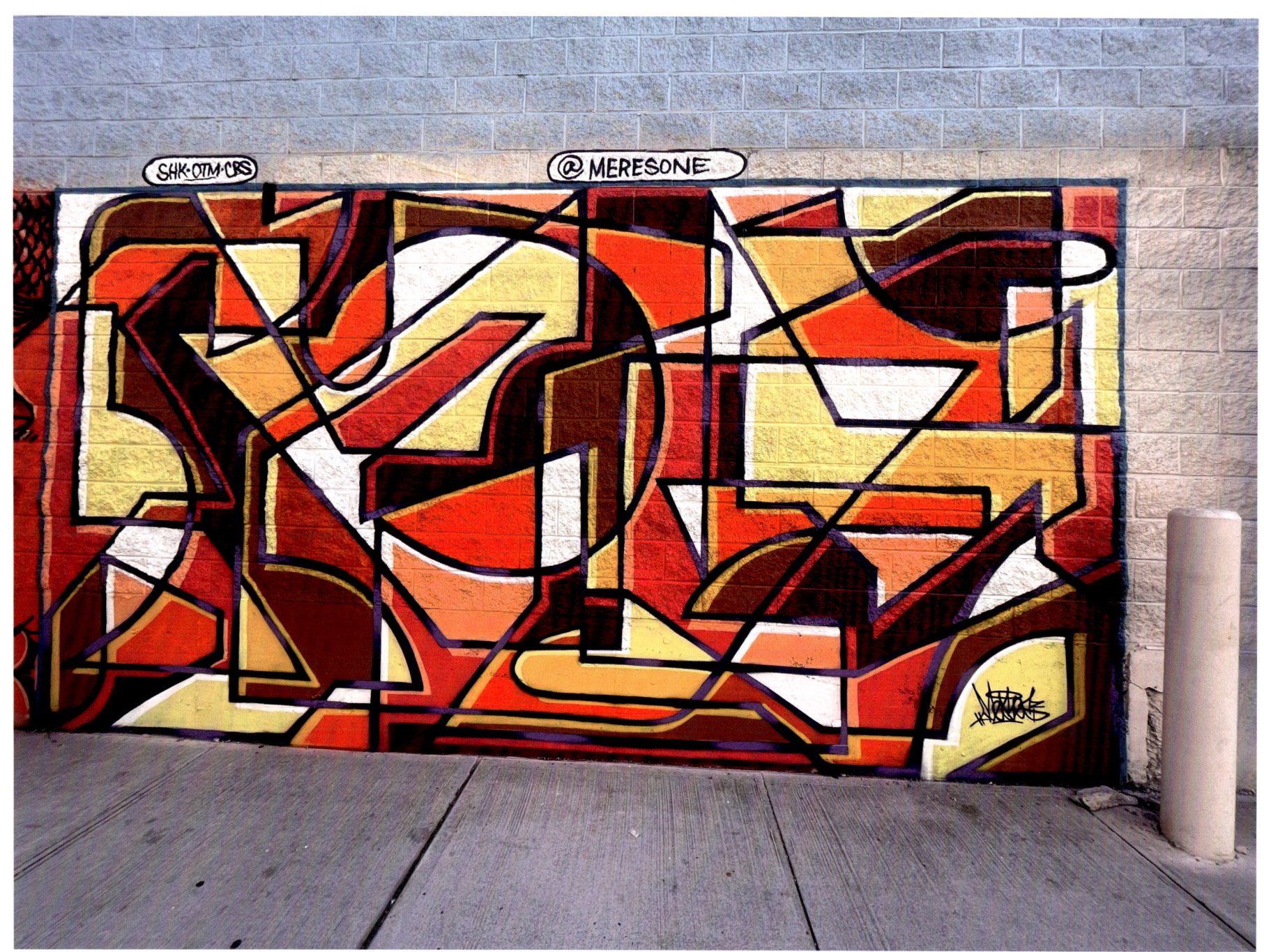

MERES ONE
BOONE AVENUE WALLS, THE BRONX, PHOTOGRAPHED IN 2023

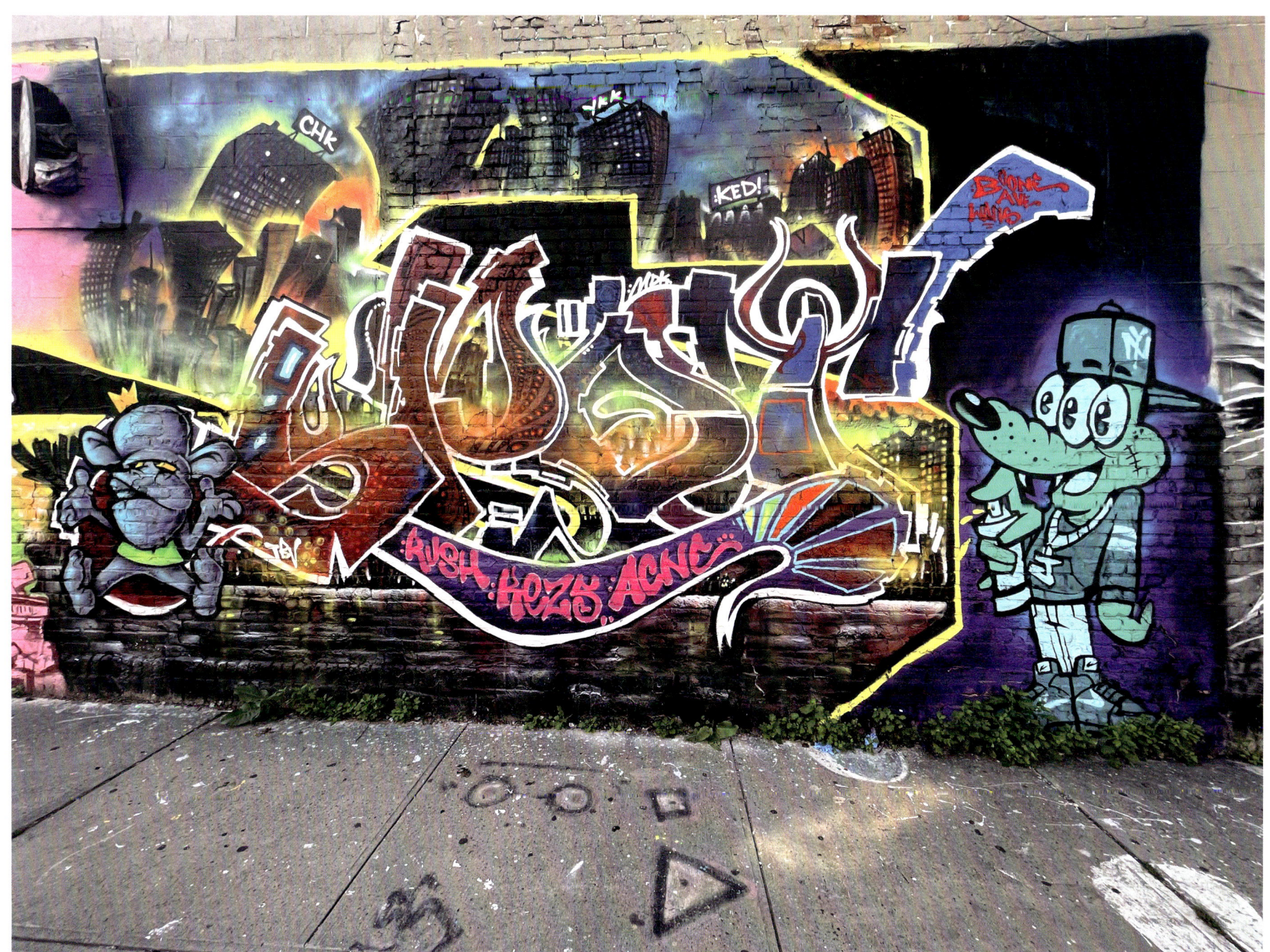

SPOT KMS CREW
BOONE AVENUE WALLS, THE BRONX, PHOTOGRAPHED IN 2023

137

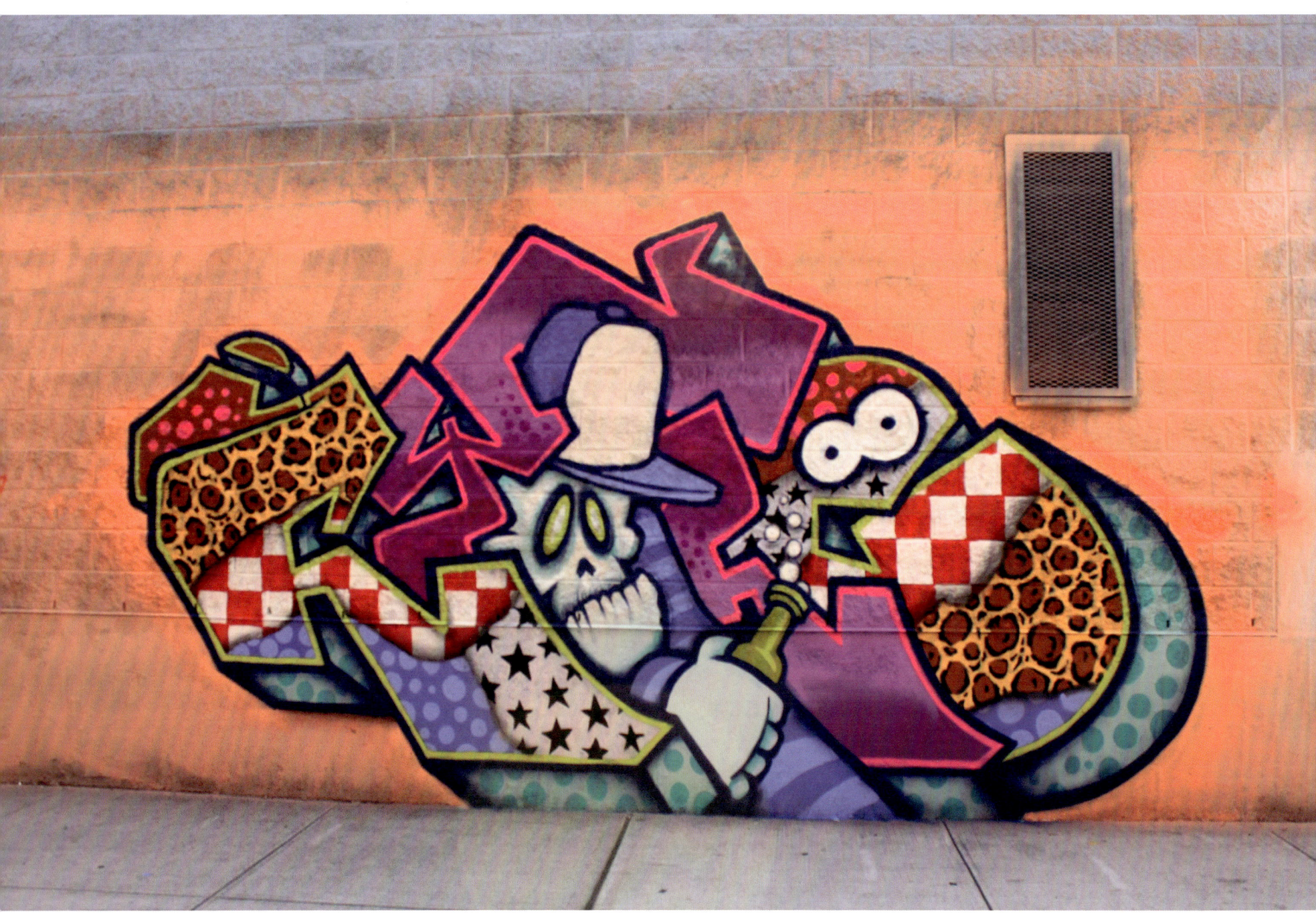

CYCLE IMOK
BOONE AVENUE WALLS, THE BRONX, PHOTOGRAPHED IN 2023

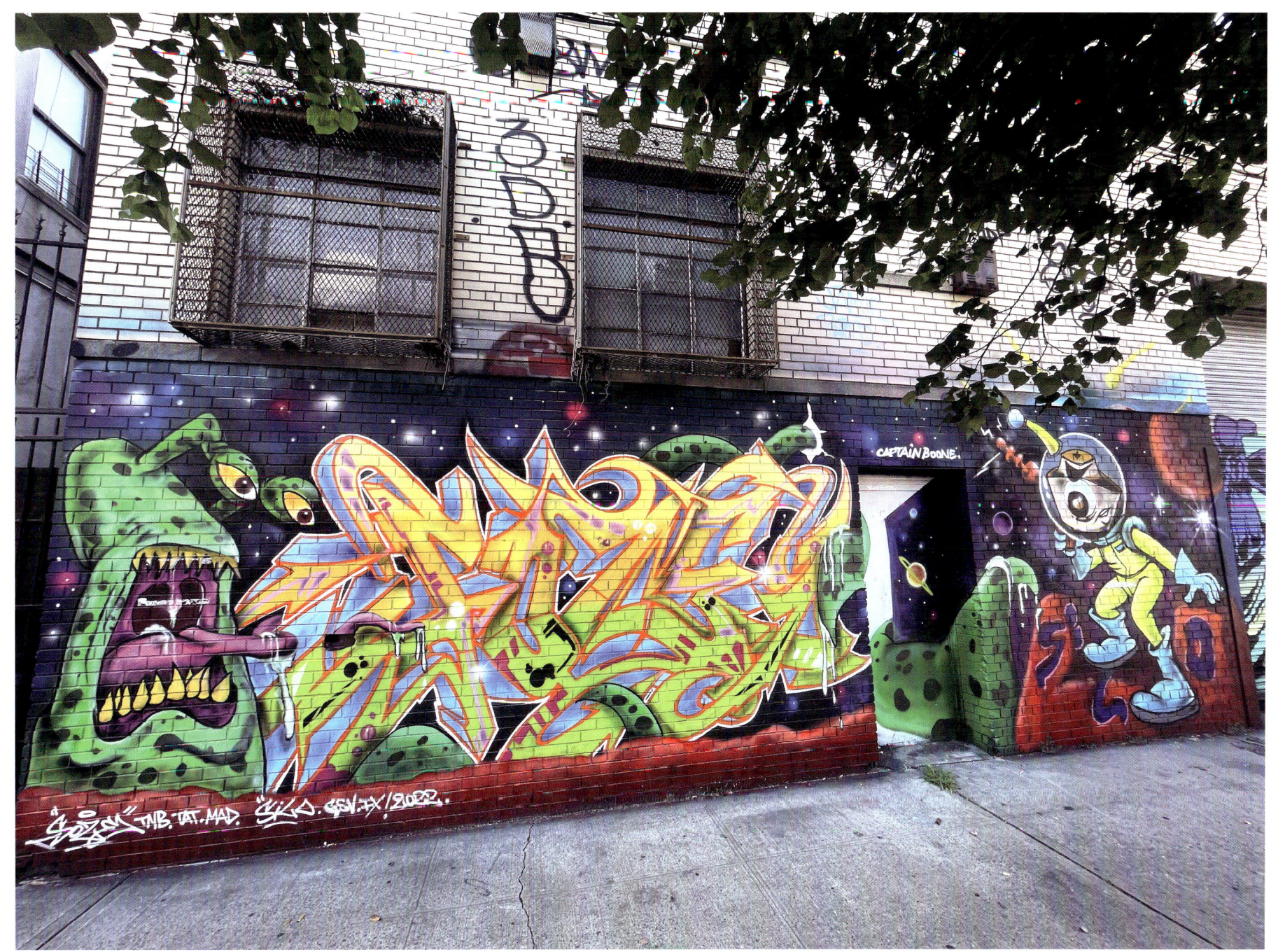

SOZE 527, SILO
BOONE AVENUE WALLS, THE BRONX, PHOTOGRAPHED IN 2023

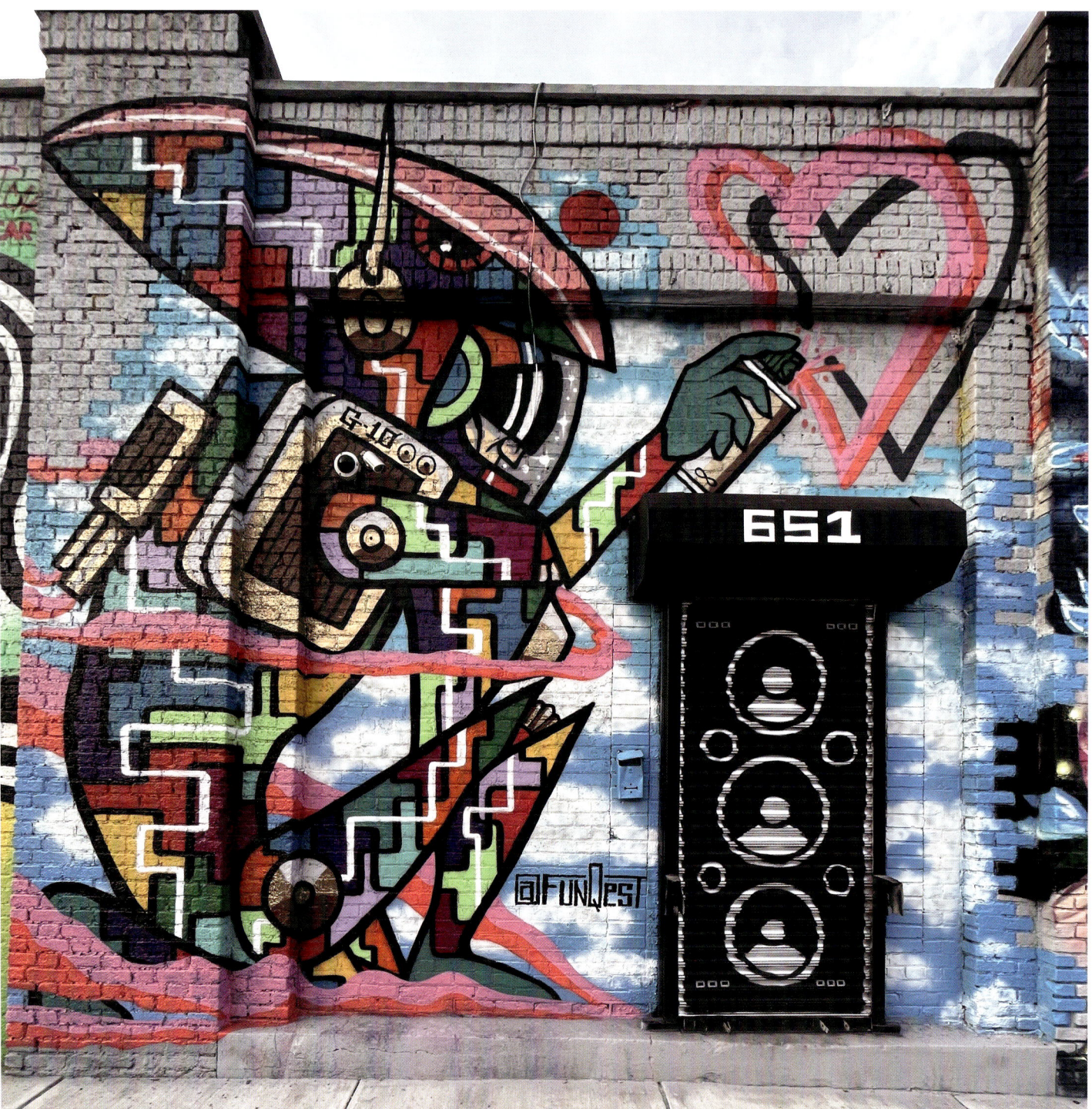

FUN QEST
BED-STUY WALLS,
PHOTOGRAPHED IN 2023

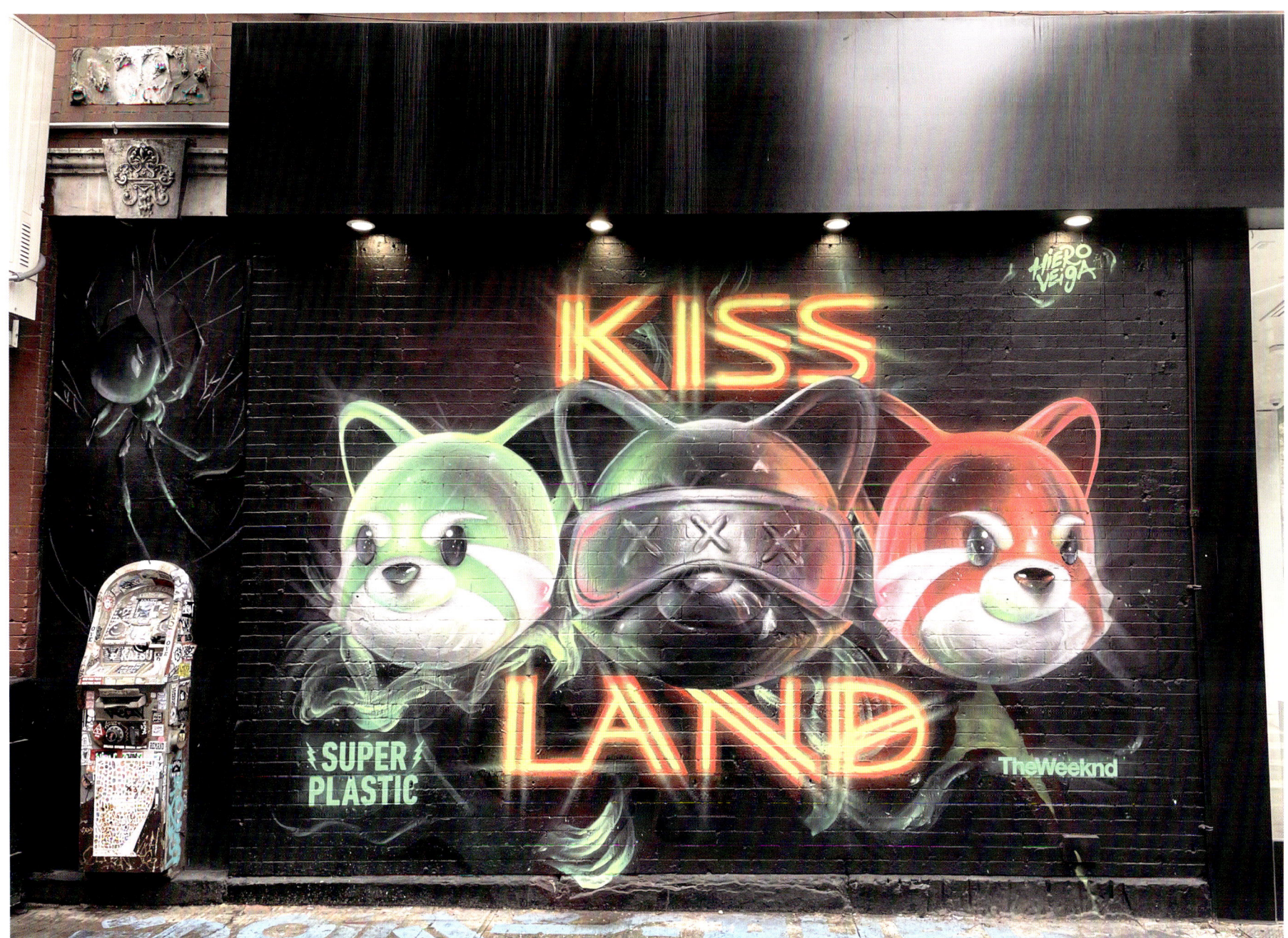

HIERO VEIGA

An internationally known muralist.
MANHATTAN, PHOTOGRAPHED IN 2024

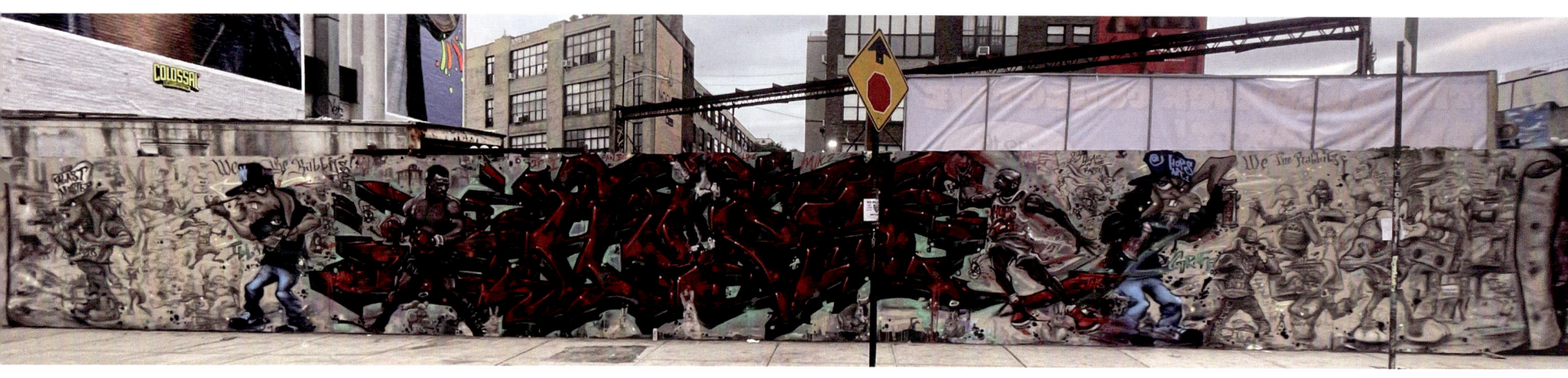

HOPS ART
BUSHWICH COLLECTIVE, BROOKLYN, PHOTOGRAPHED IN 2023

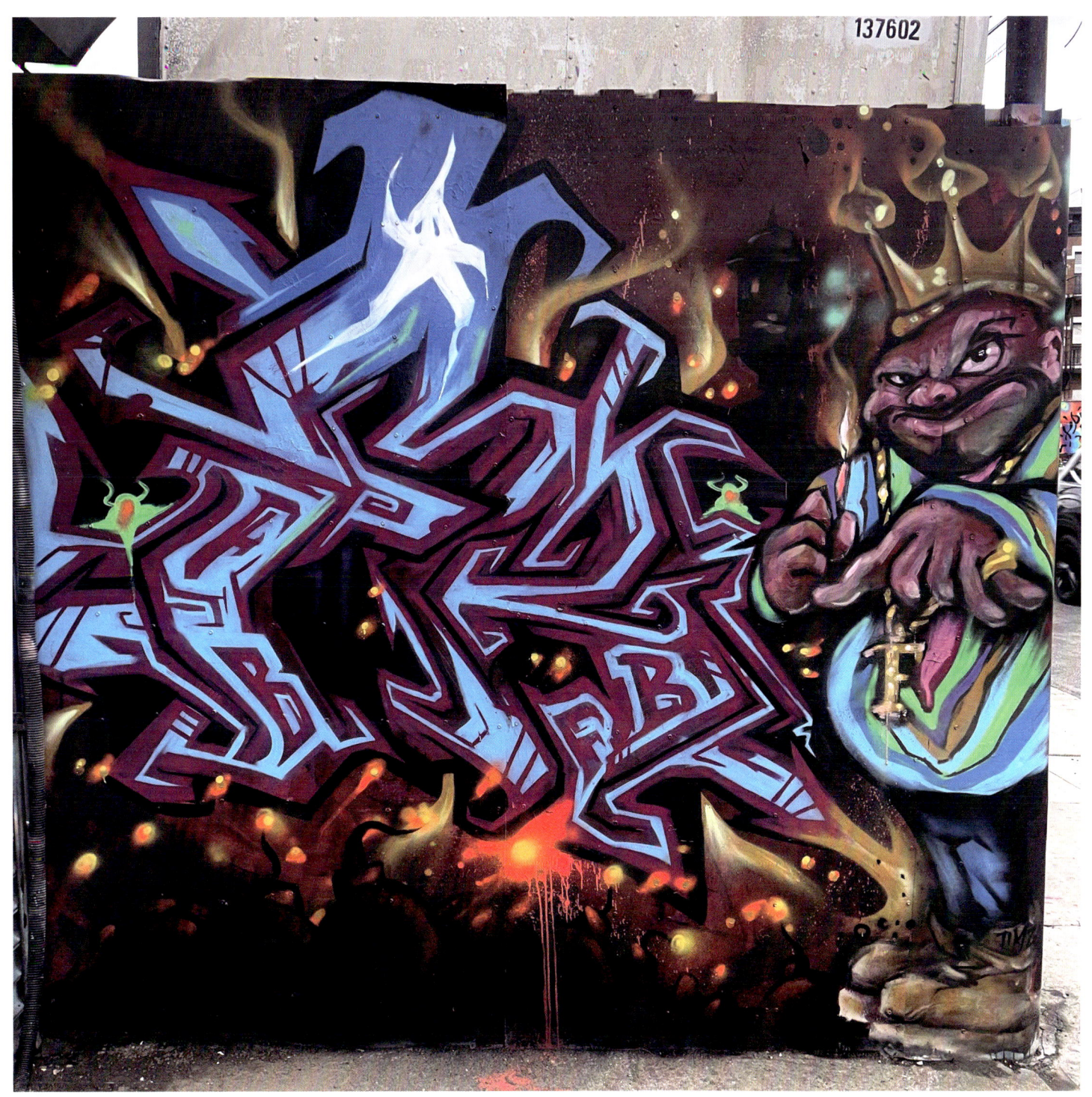

HOPS ART
BUSHWICK COLLECTIVE,
BROOKLYN,
PHOTOGRAPHED IN 2023

INDIE 184

Indie 184 is a well-known street artist
known for a feminist graffiti style.
MANHATTAN, PHOTOGRAPHED IN
2023

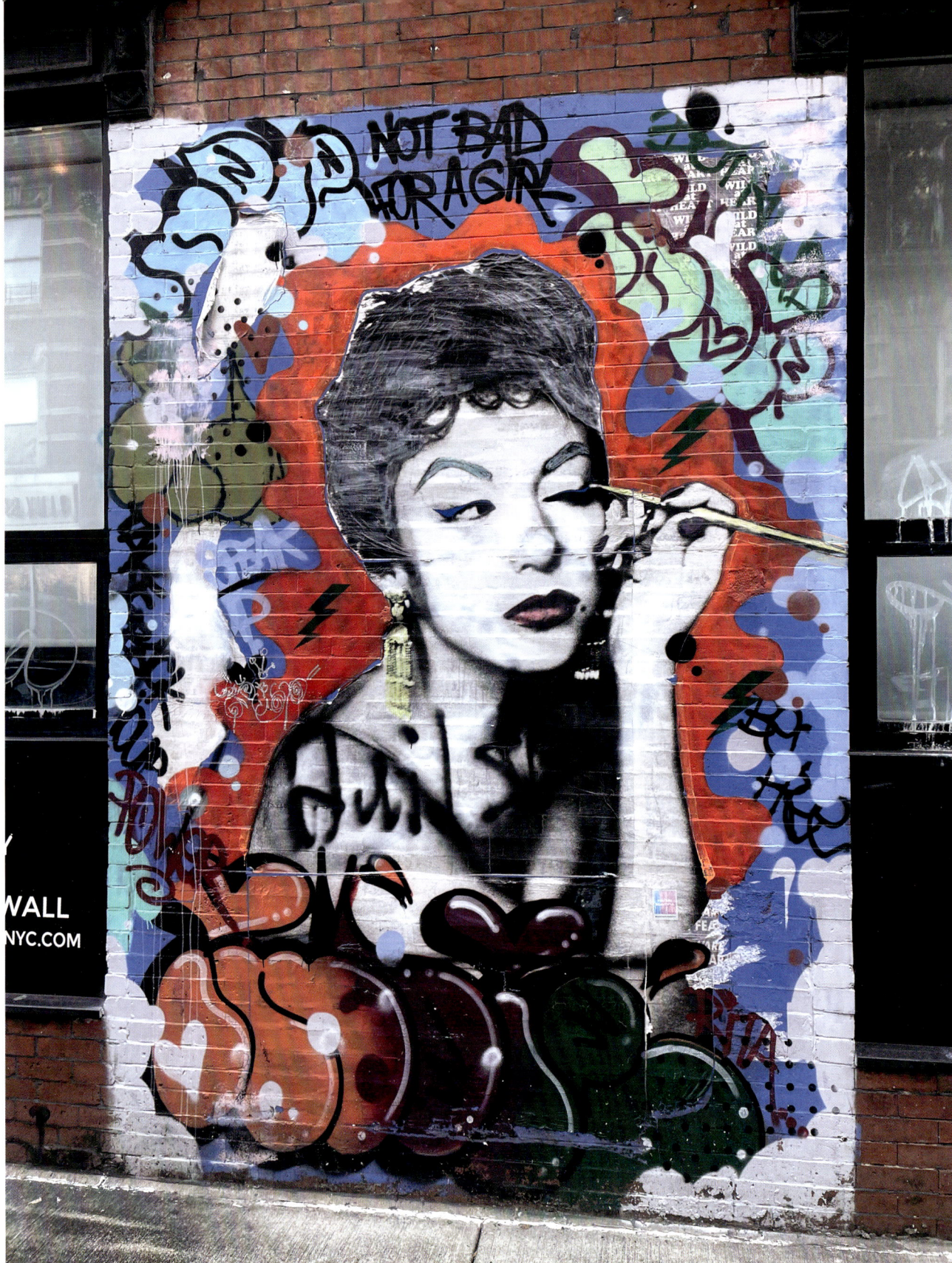

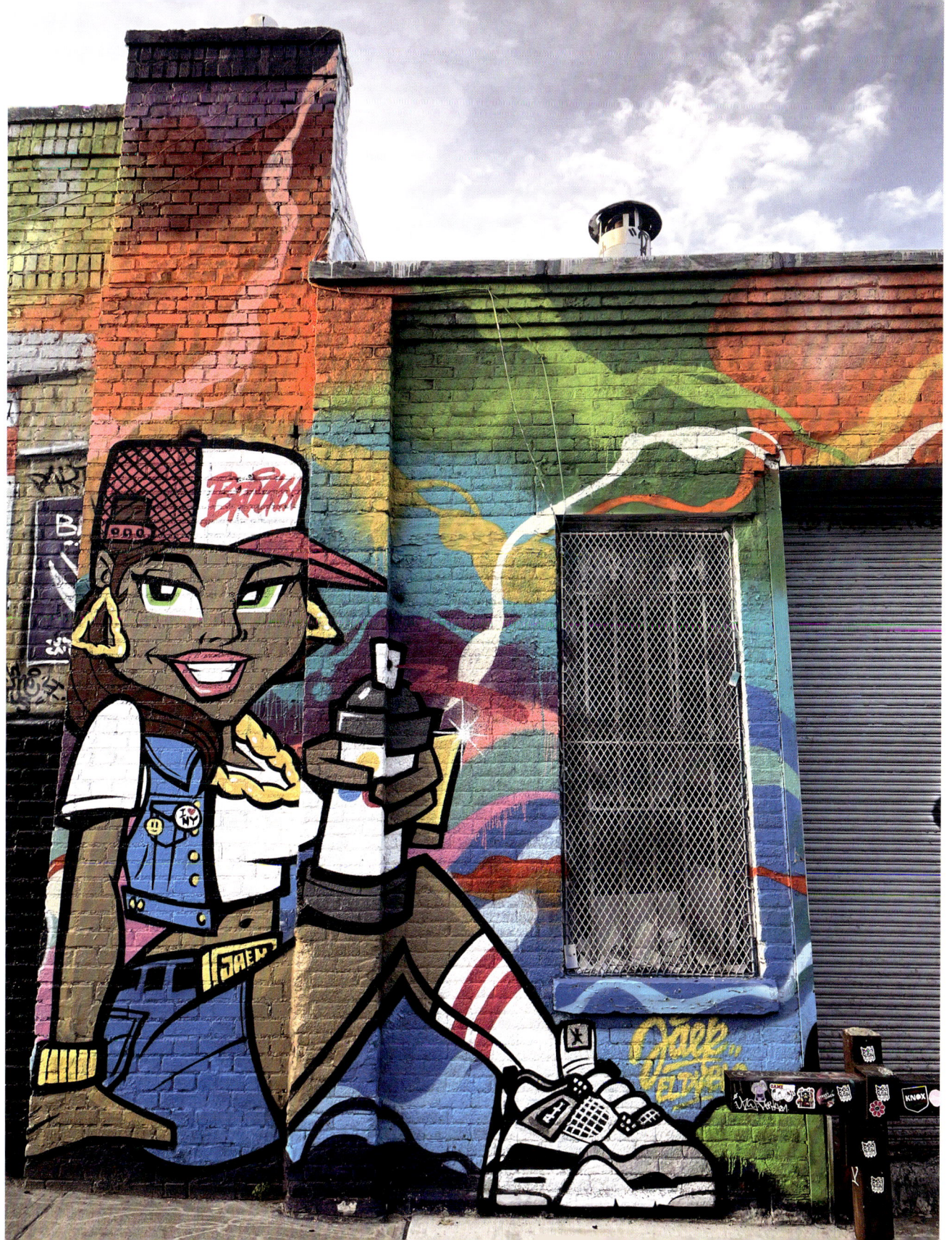

JAEK EL DIABLO
BED-STUY WALLS, BROOKLYN,
PHOTOGRAPHED IN 2023

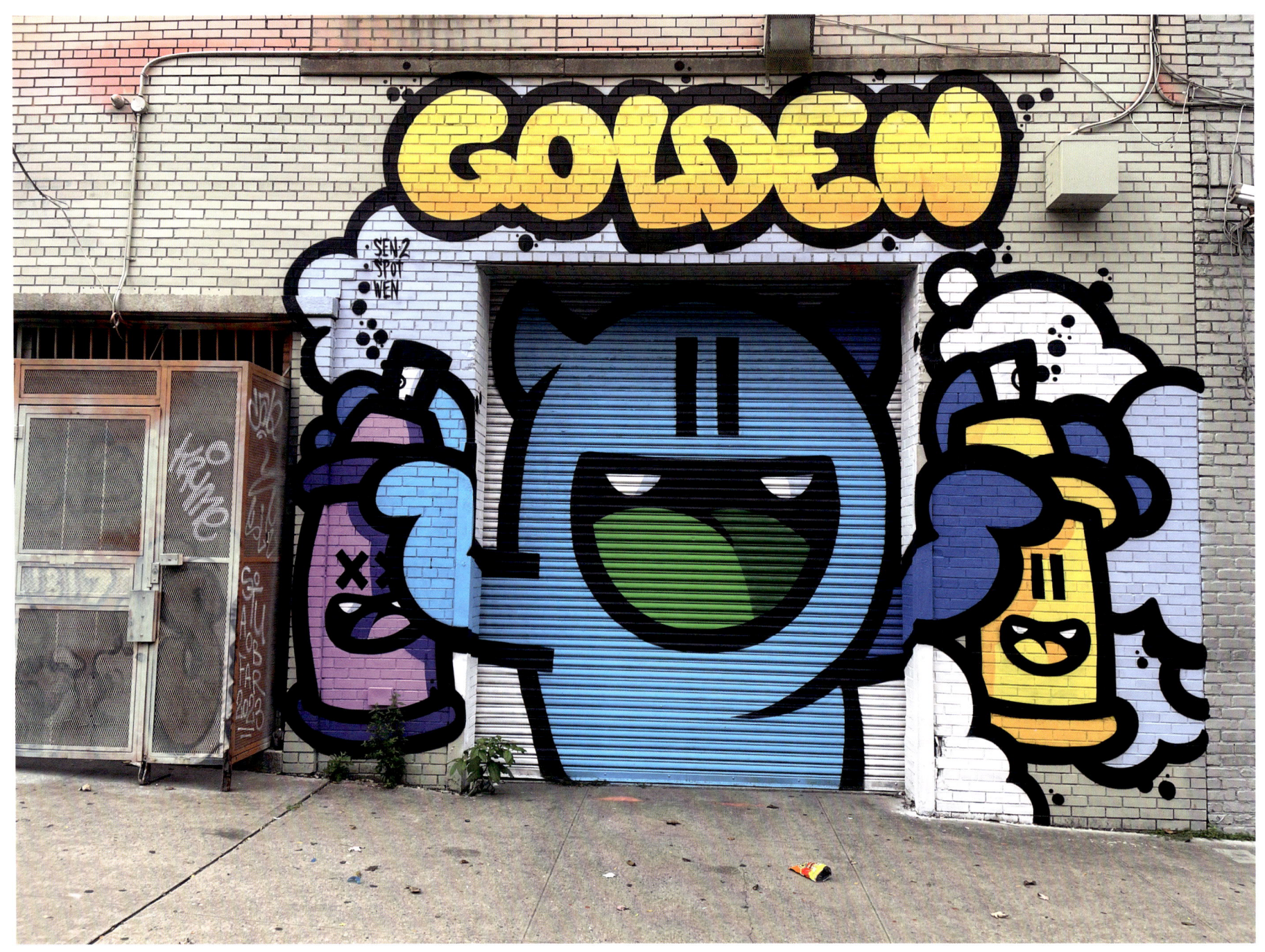

GOLDEN 305
BOONE AVENUE WALLS, THE BRONX, PHOTOGRAPHED IN 2023

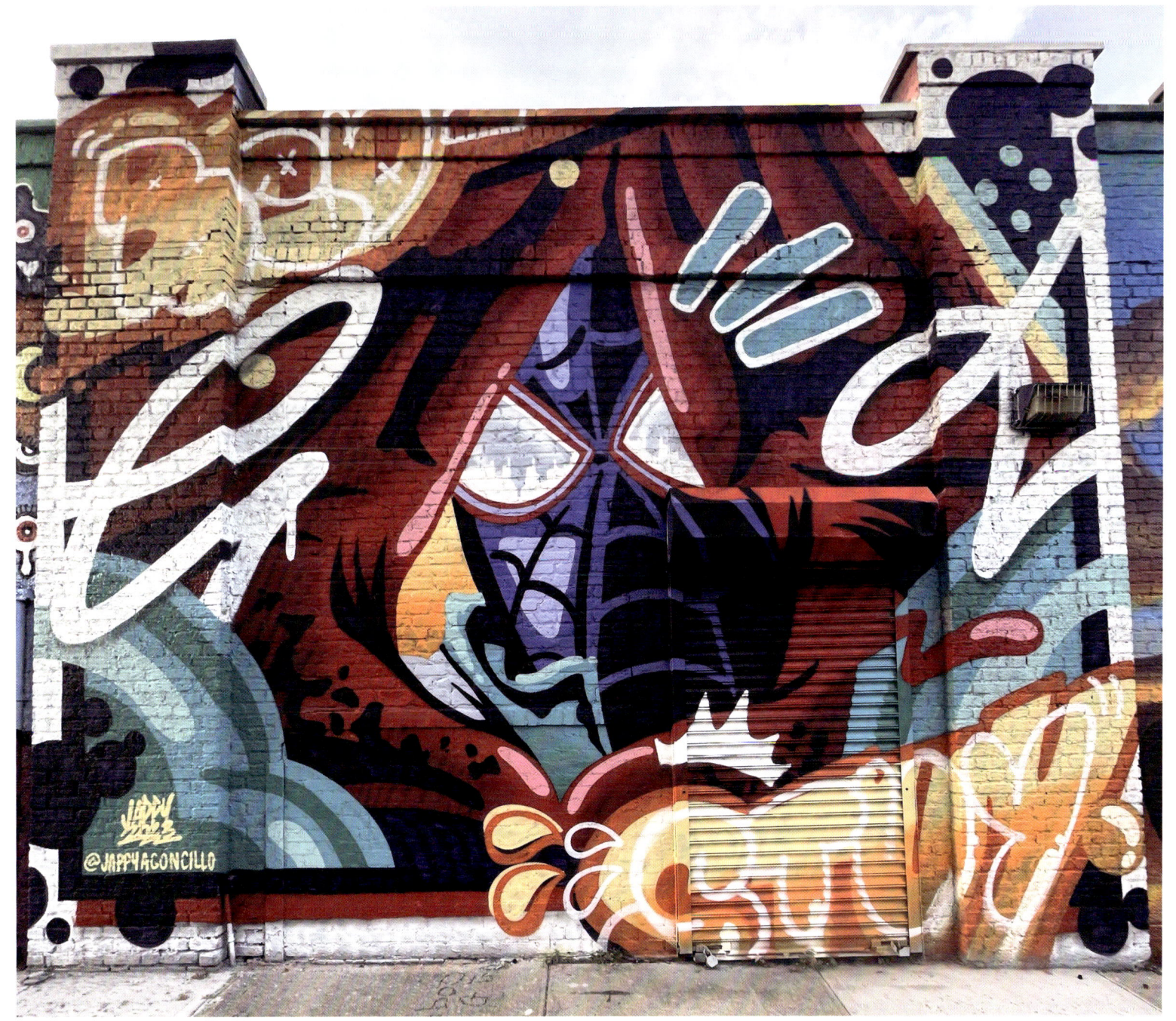

JAPPY AGONCILLO
BED-STUY WALLS, BROOKLYN, PHOTOGRAPHED IN 2023

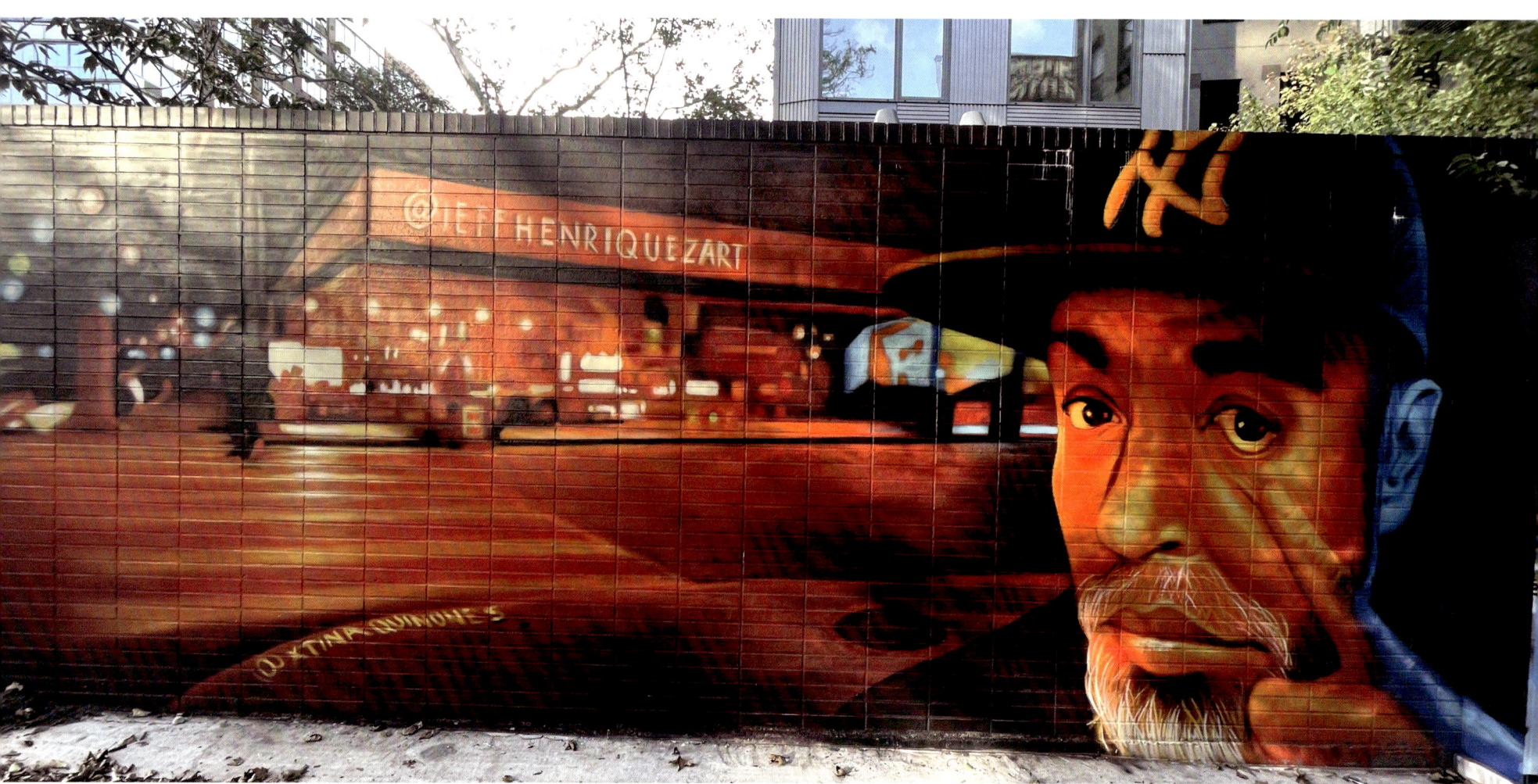

JEFF HENRIQUEZ
FIRST STREET GREEN ART PARK, MANHATTAN, PHOTOGRAPHED IN 2023

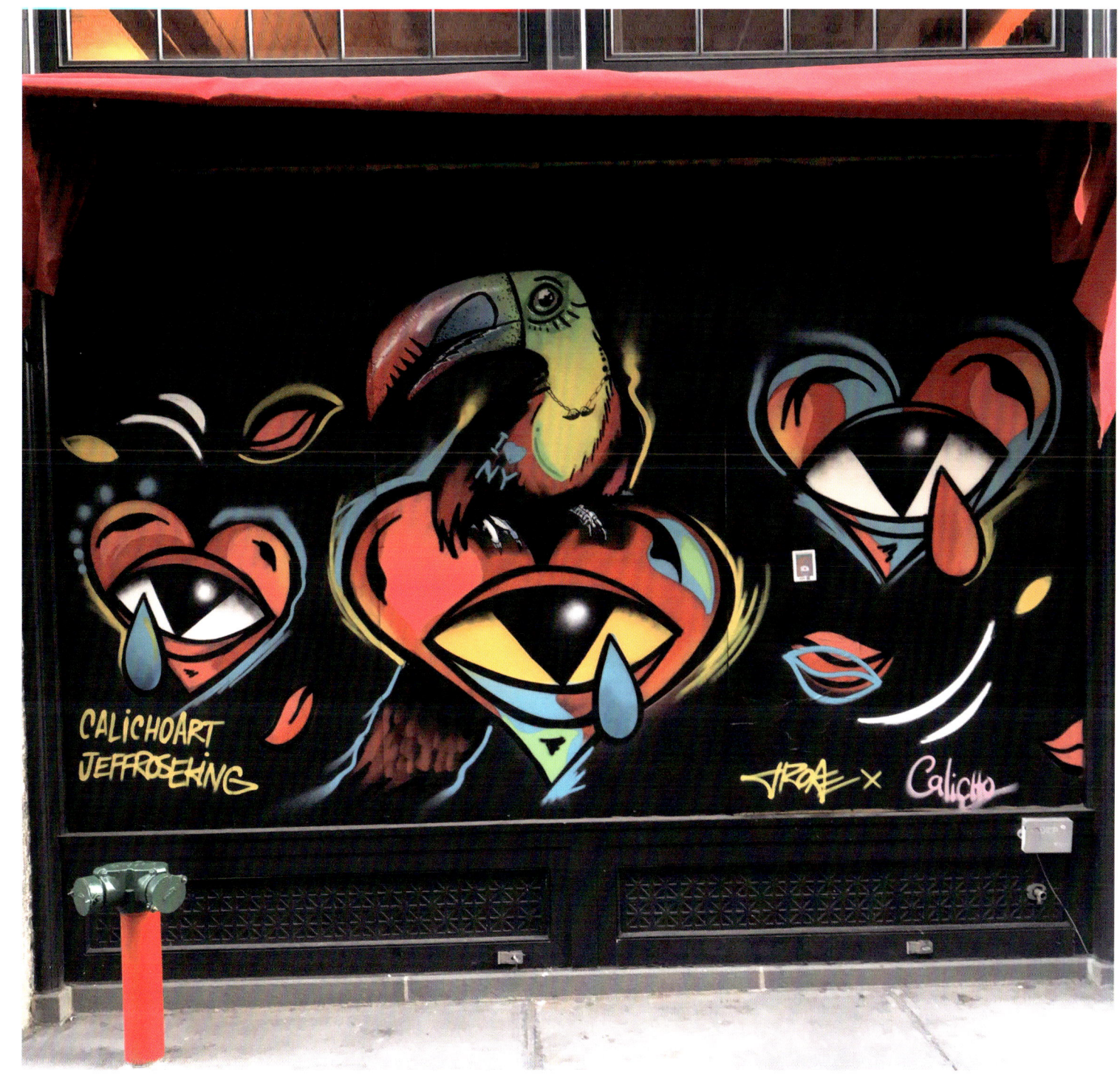

JEFF ROSE KING,
CALICHO ART,
MANHATTAN,
PHOTOGRAPHED IN
2020

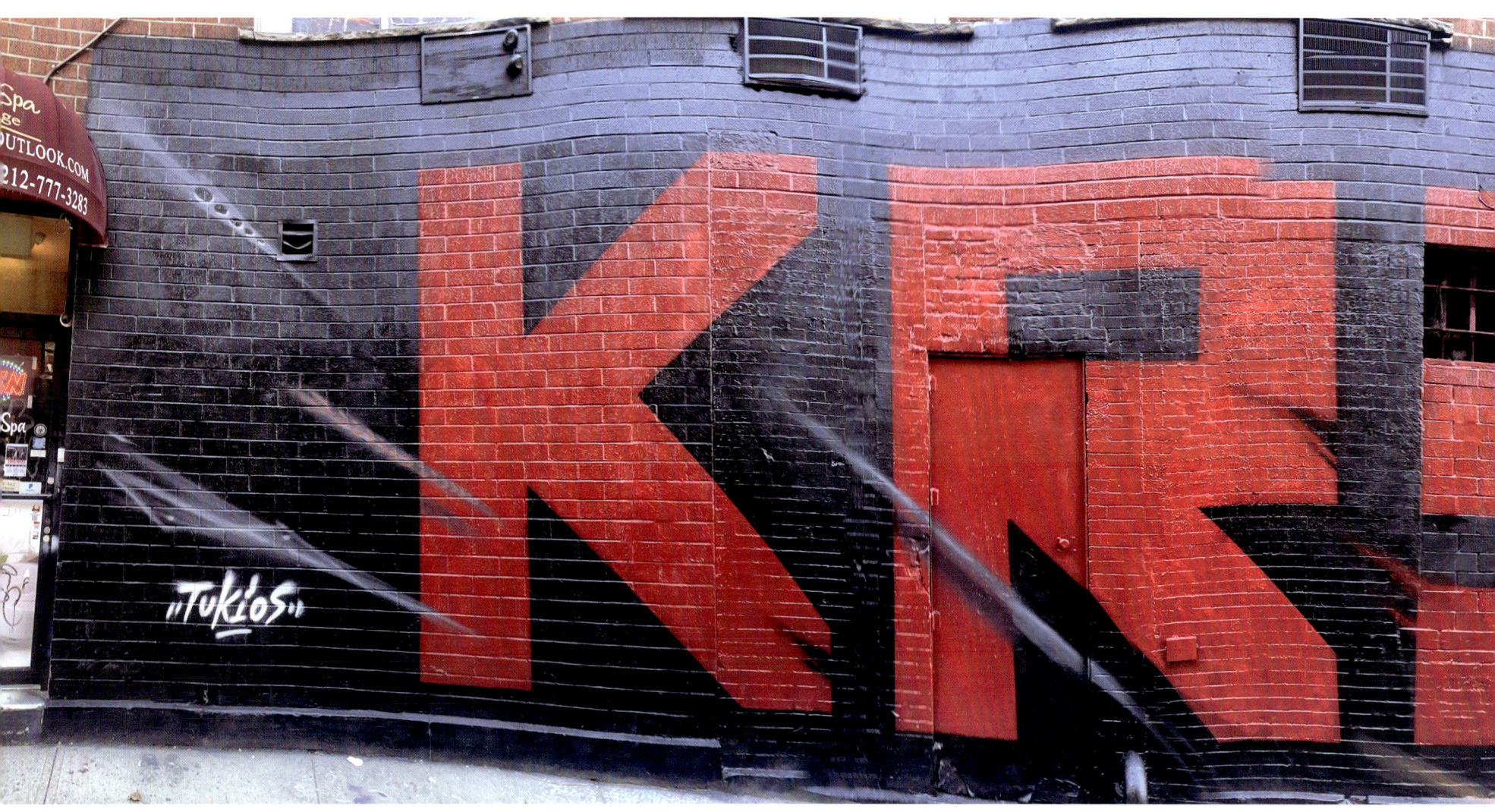

JORIT, TUKIOS
MANHATTAN, PHOTOGRAPHED IN 2023

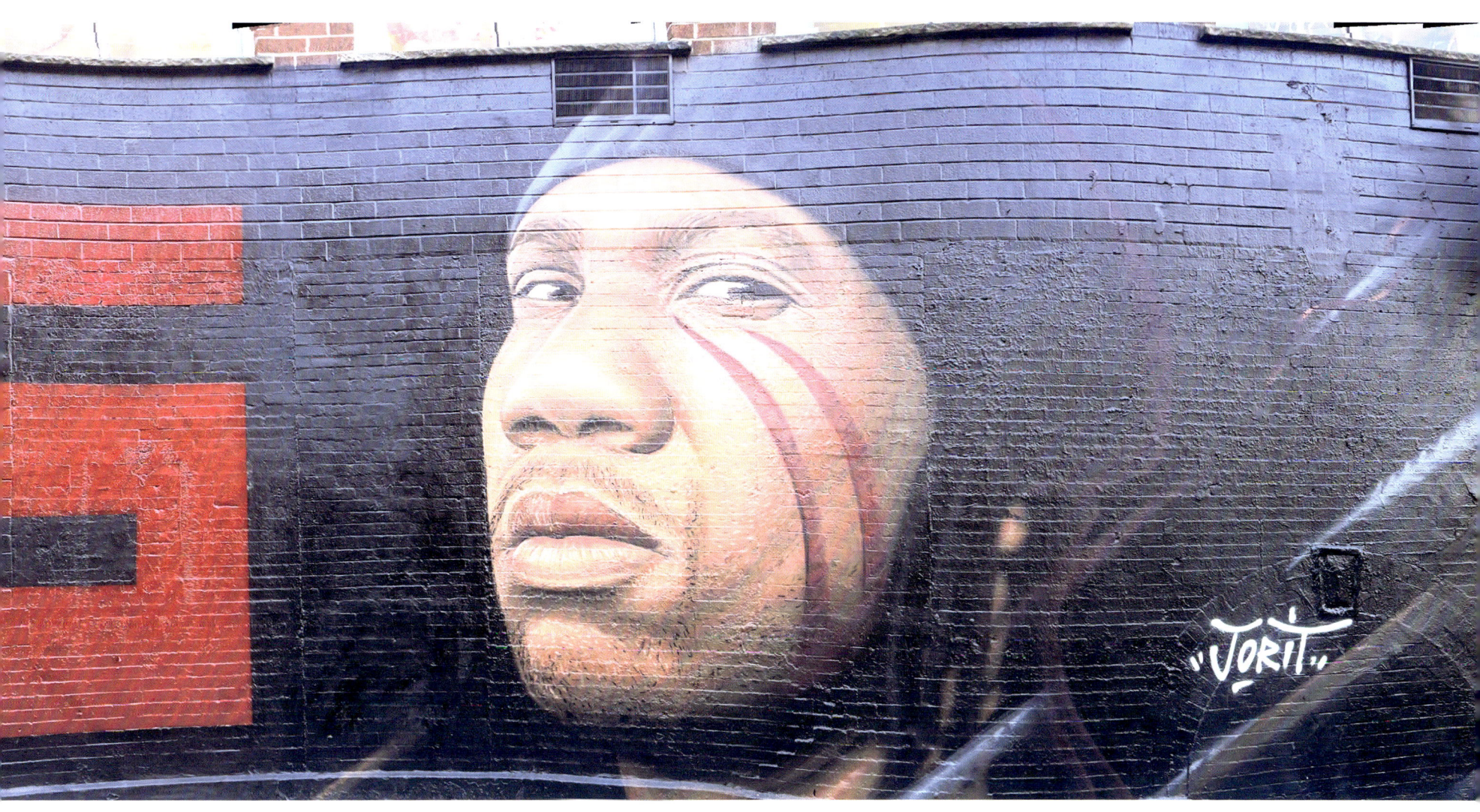

151

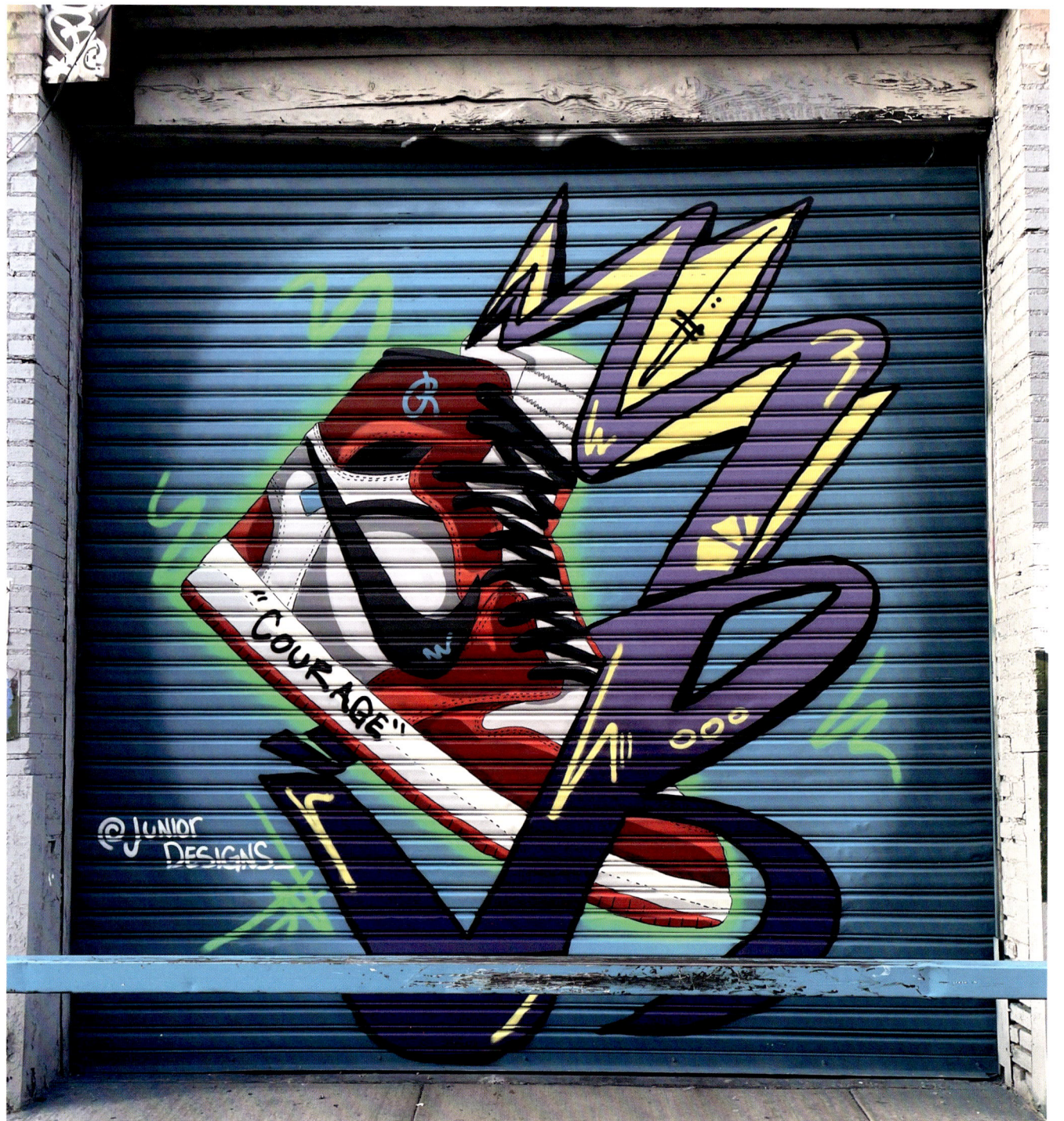

JUNIOR GOMEZ
BED-STUY WALLS, BROOKLYN,
PHOTOGRAPHED IN 2023

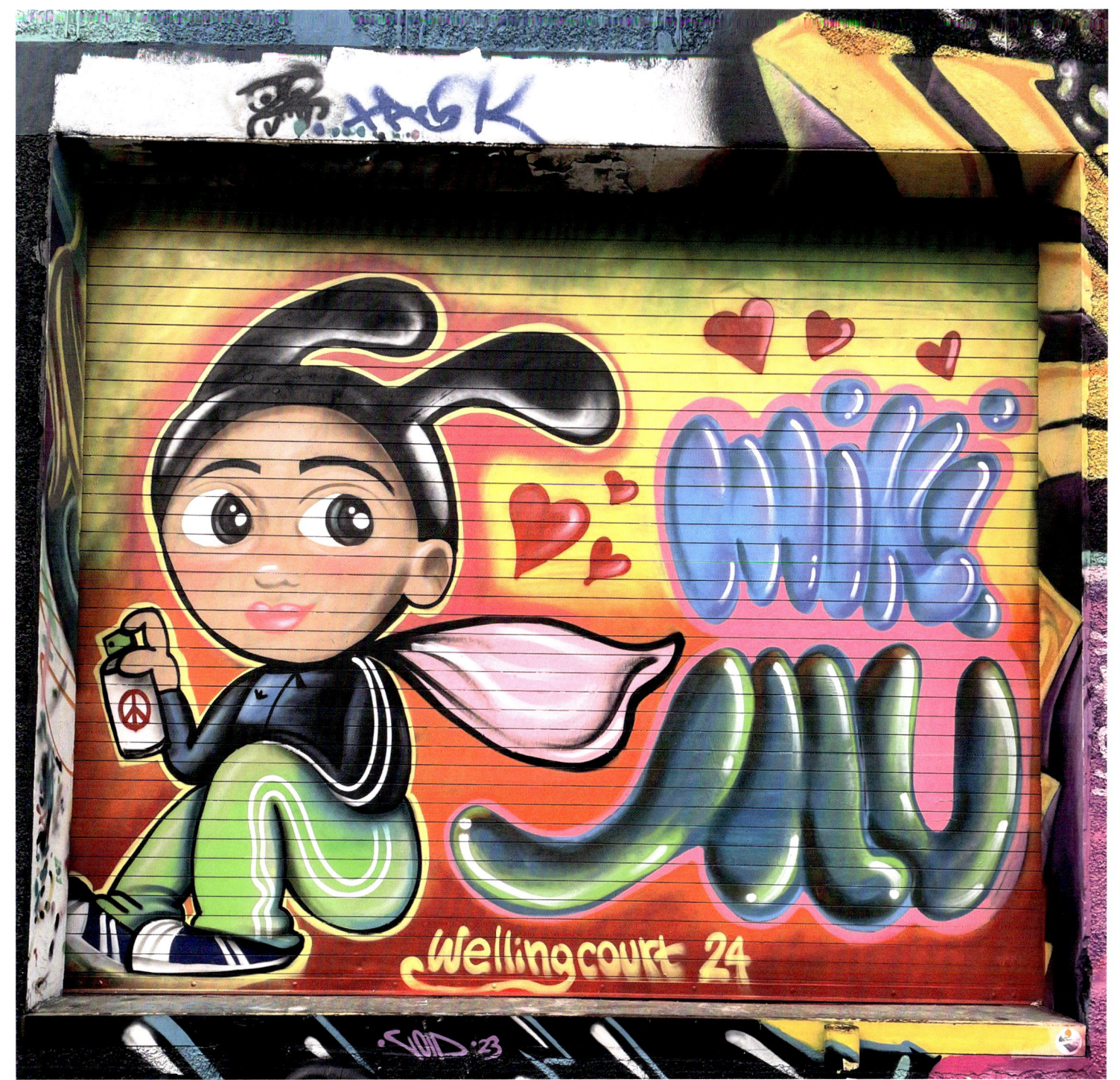

MIKI MU
Miki Mu is a rising star in aerosol art community.
WELLING COURT
MURAL PROJECT,
PHOTOGRAPHED IN
2024

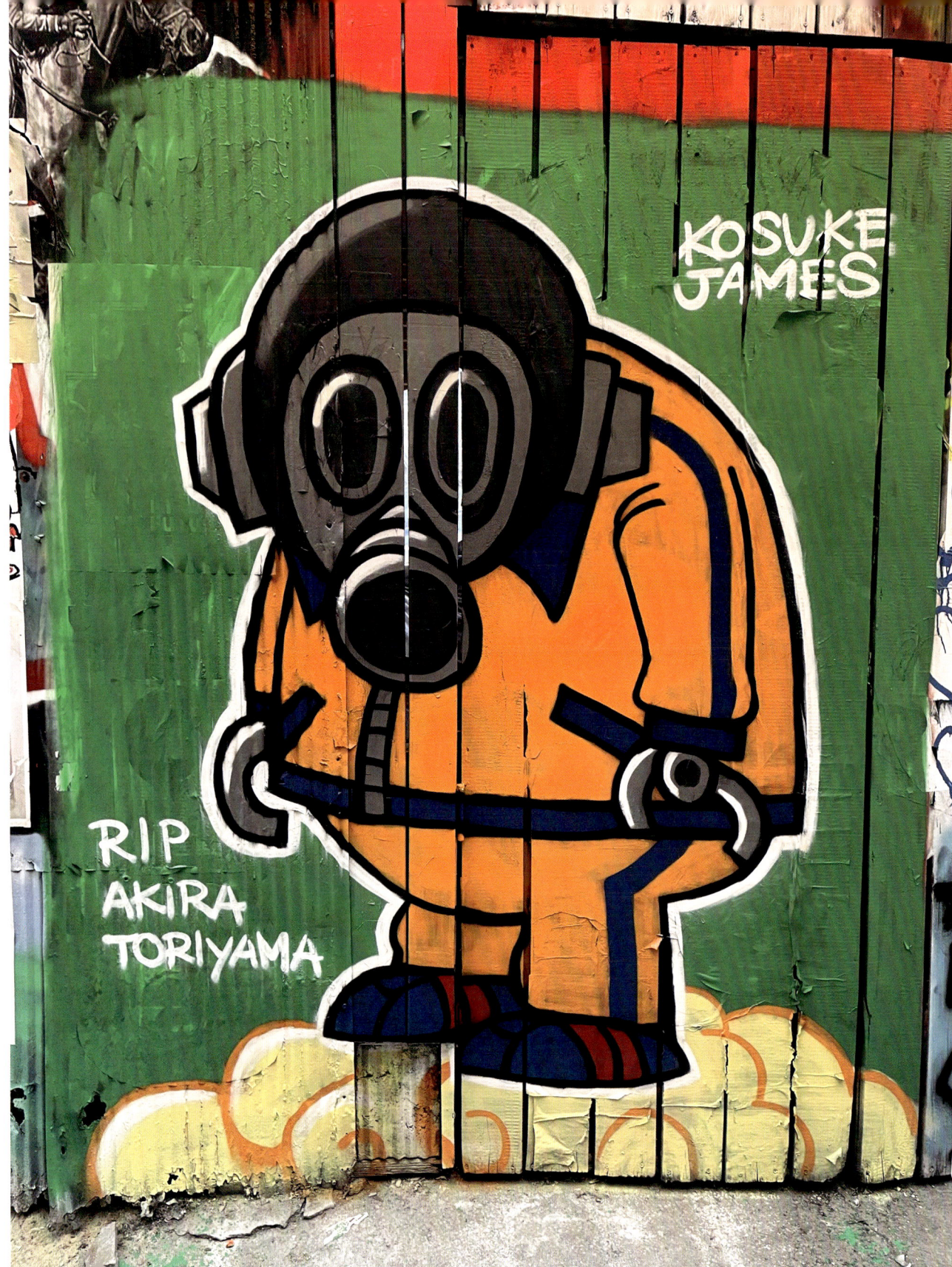

KOSUKE JAMES
Kosuke James is Japanese street artist
based in New York City.
FREEMAN ALLEY, MANHATTAN,
PHOTOGRAPHED IN 2024

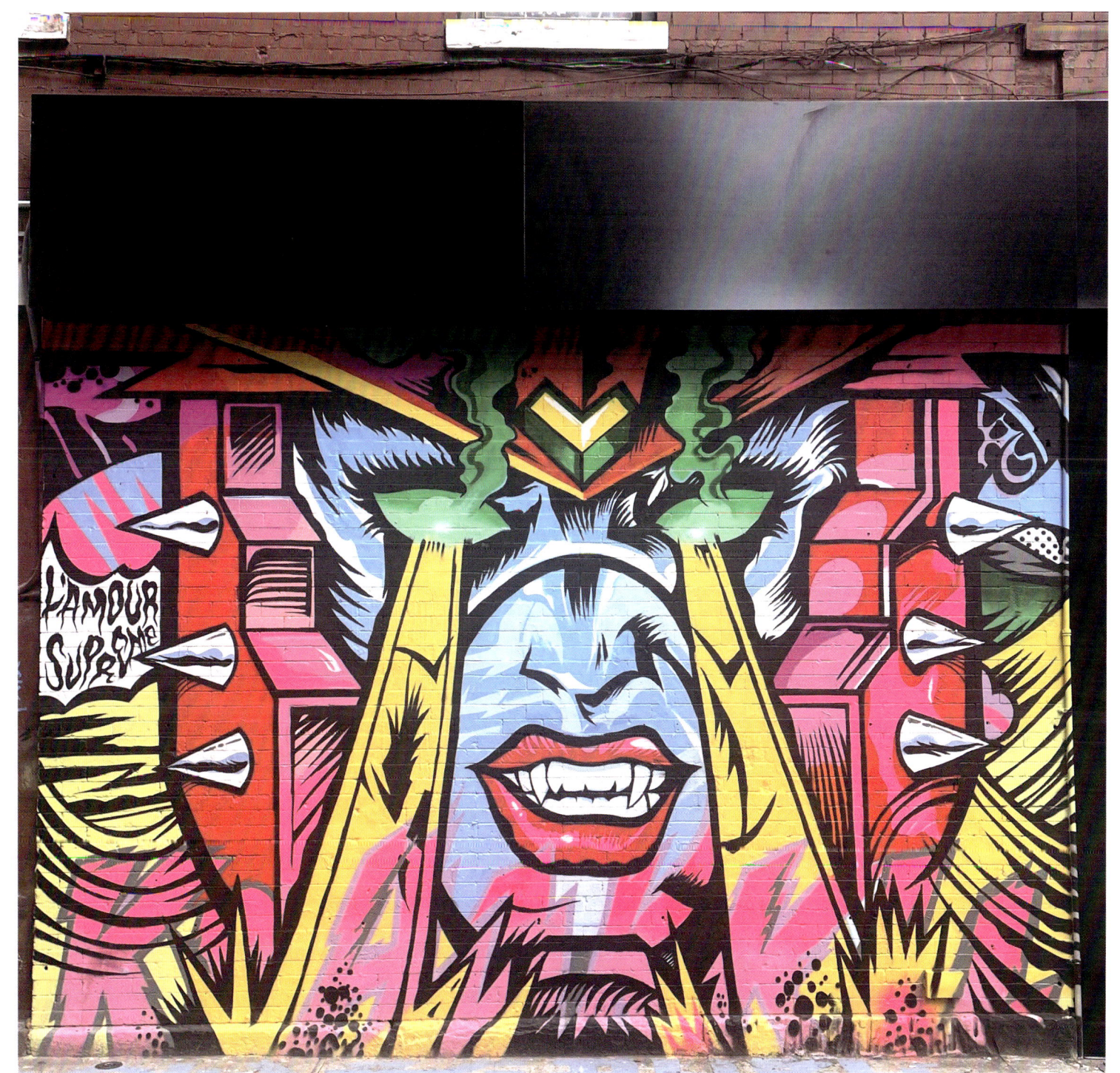

LA MOUR SUPREME
A popular muralist in New York City.
MANHATTAN, PHOTOGRAPHED IN 2022

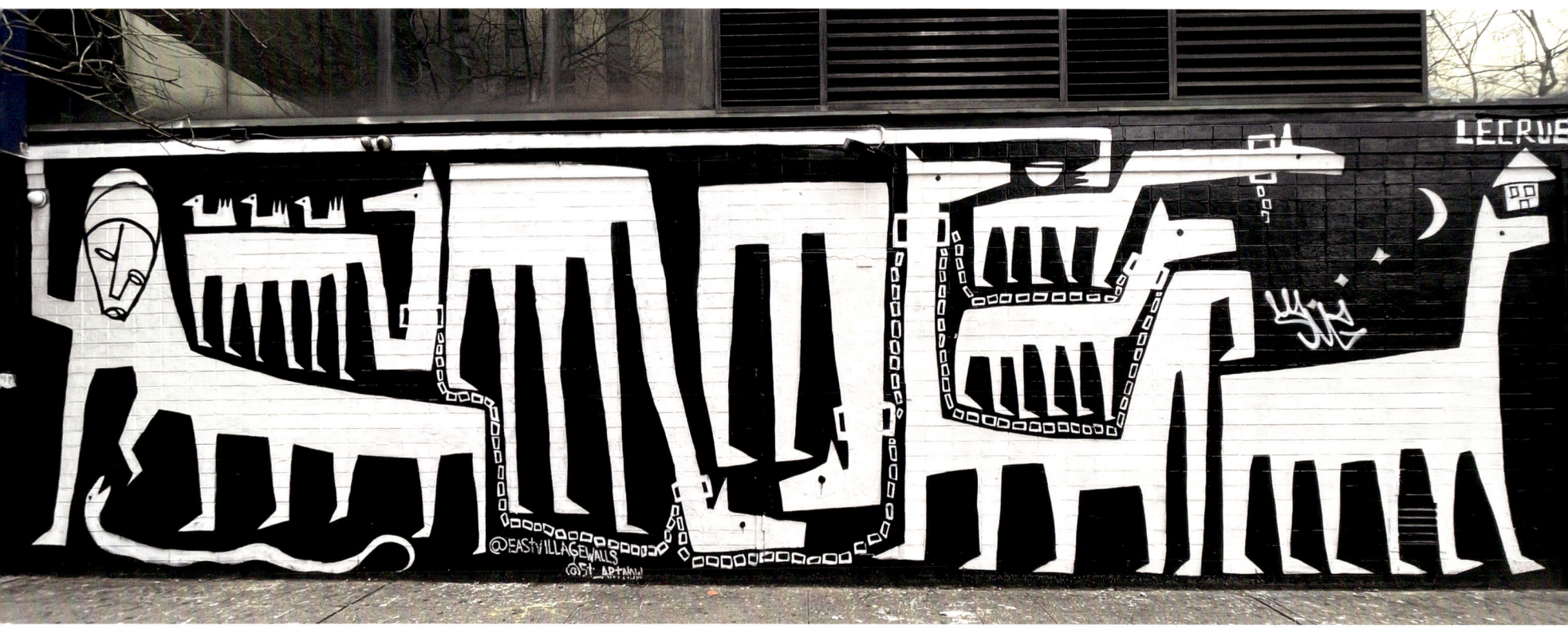

LECRUE
LeCrue is a street artist with a studio practice based in New York City.
MANHATTAN, PHOTOGRAPHED IN 2024

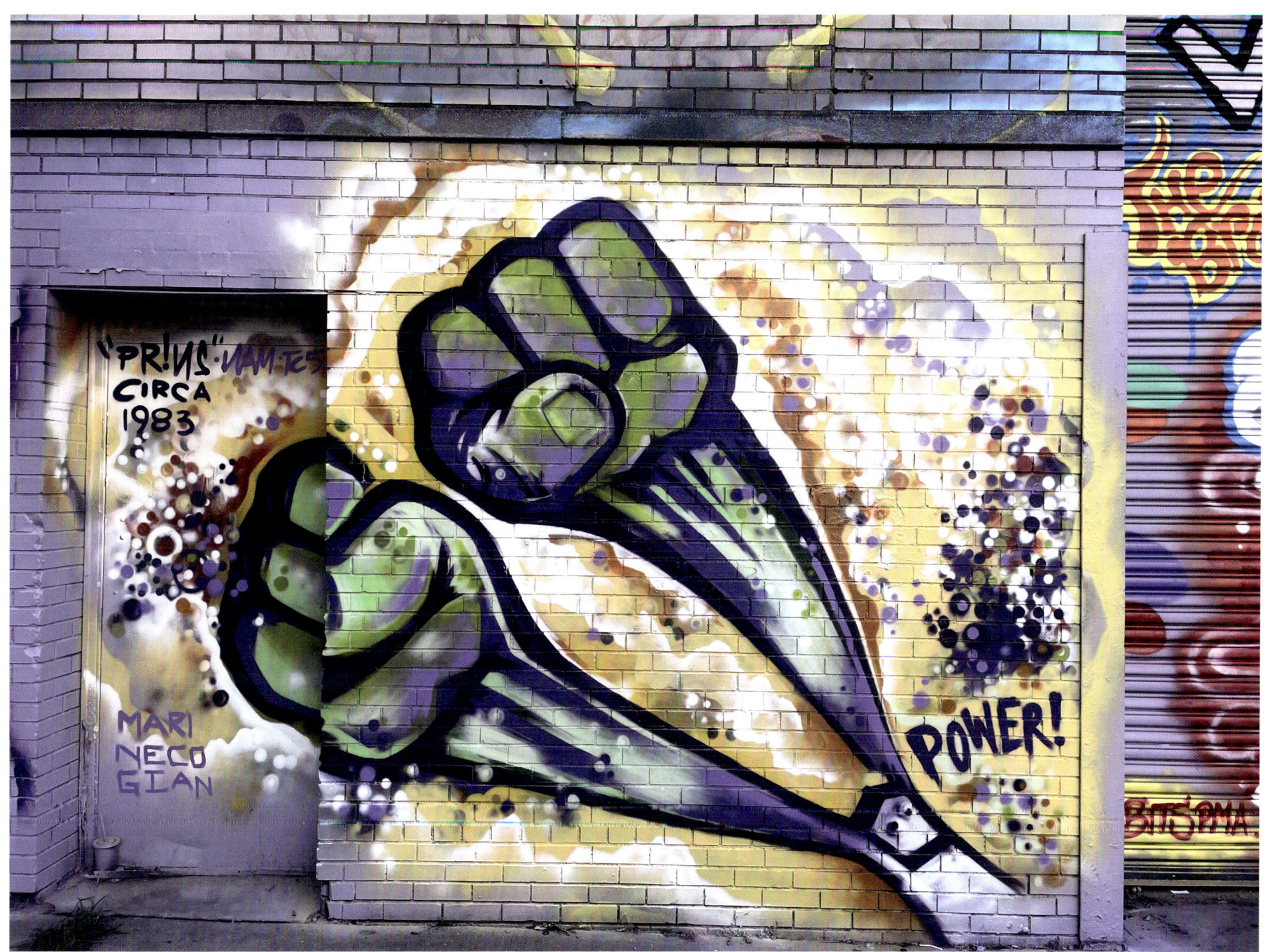

MANUEL ACEVEDO
BOONE AVENUE WALLS, PHOTOGRAPHED IN 2023

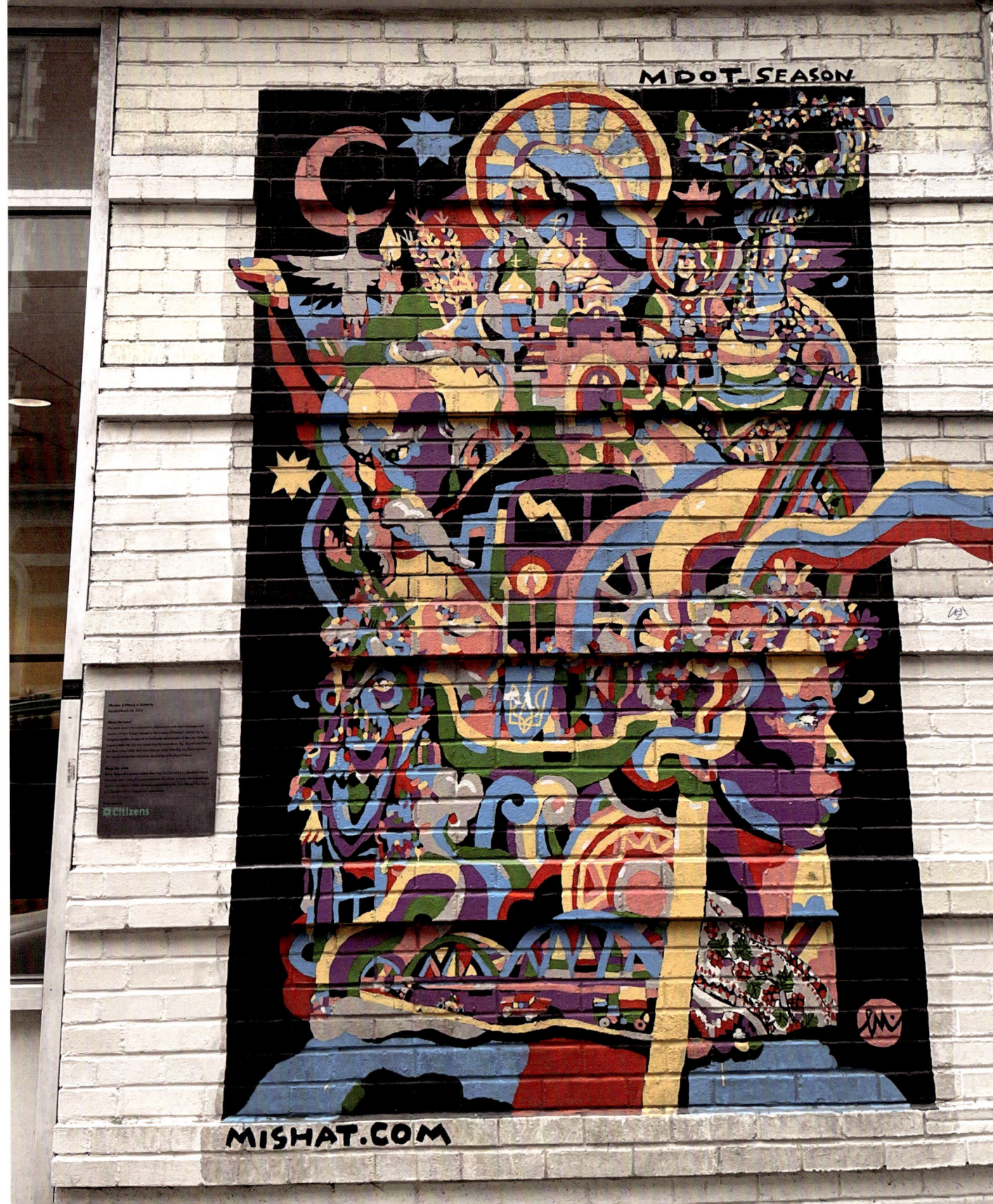

MISHA TYUTYUNIK
MANHATTAN,
PHOTOGRAPHED IN 2024

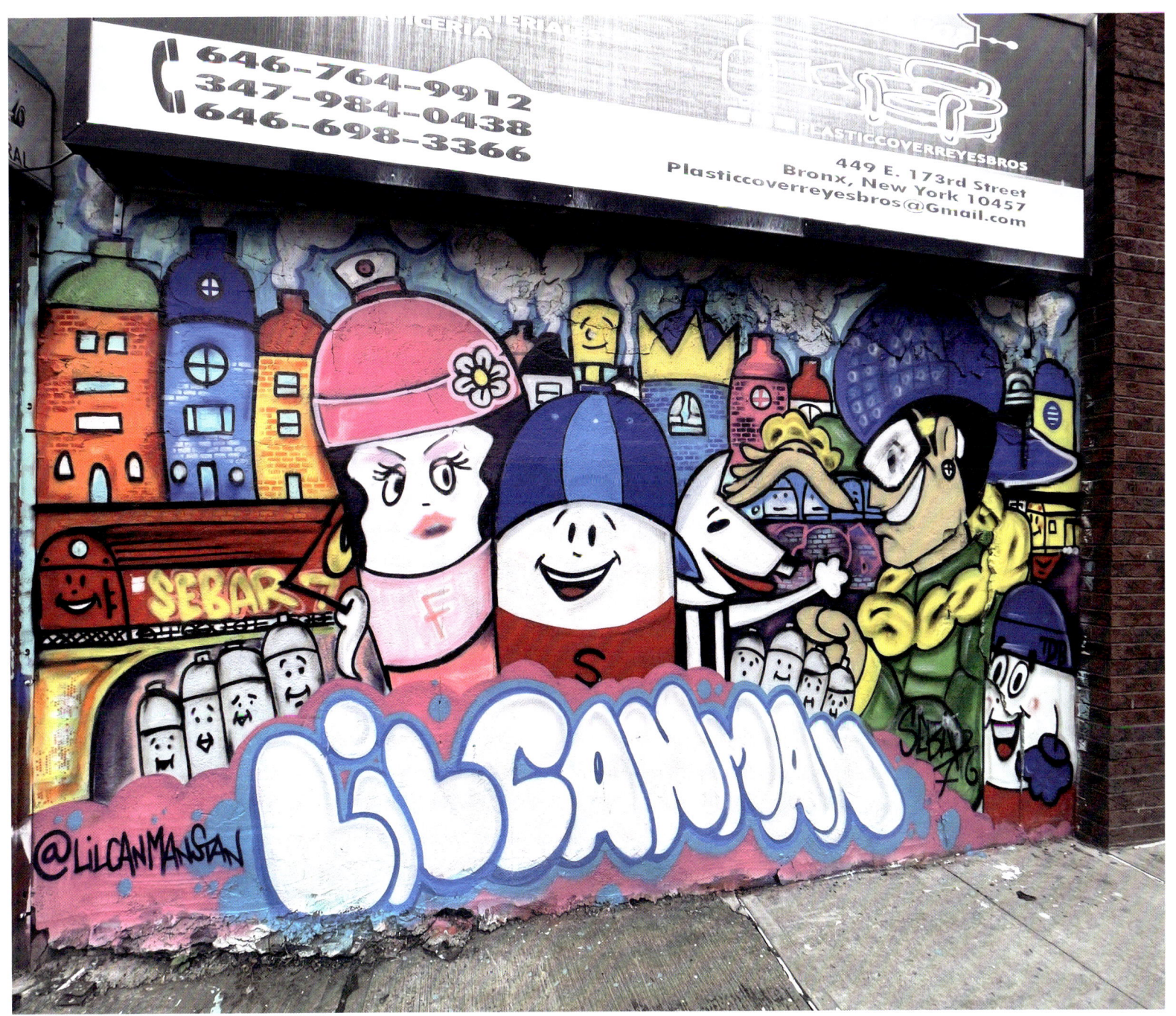

SEBAR
THE BRONX, PHOTOGRAPHED IN 2023

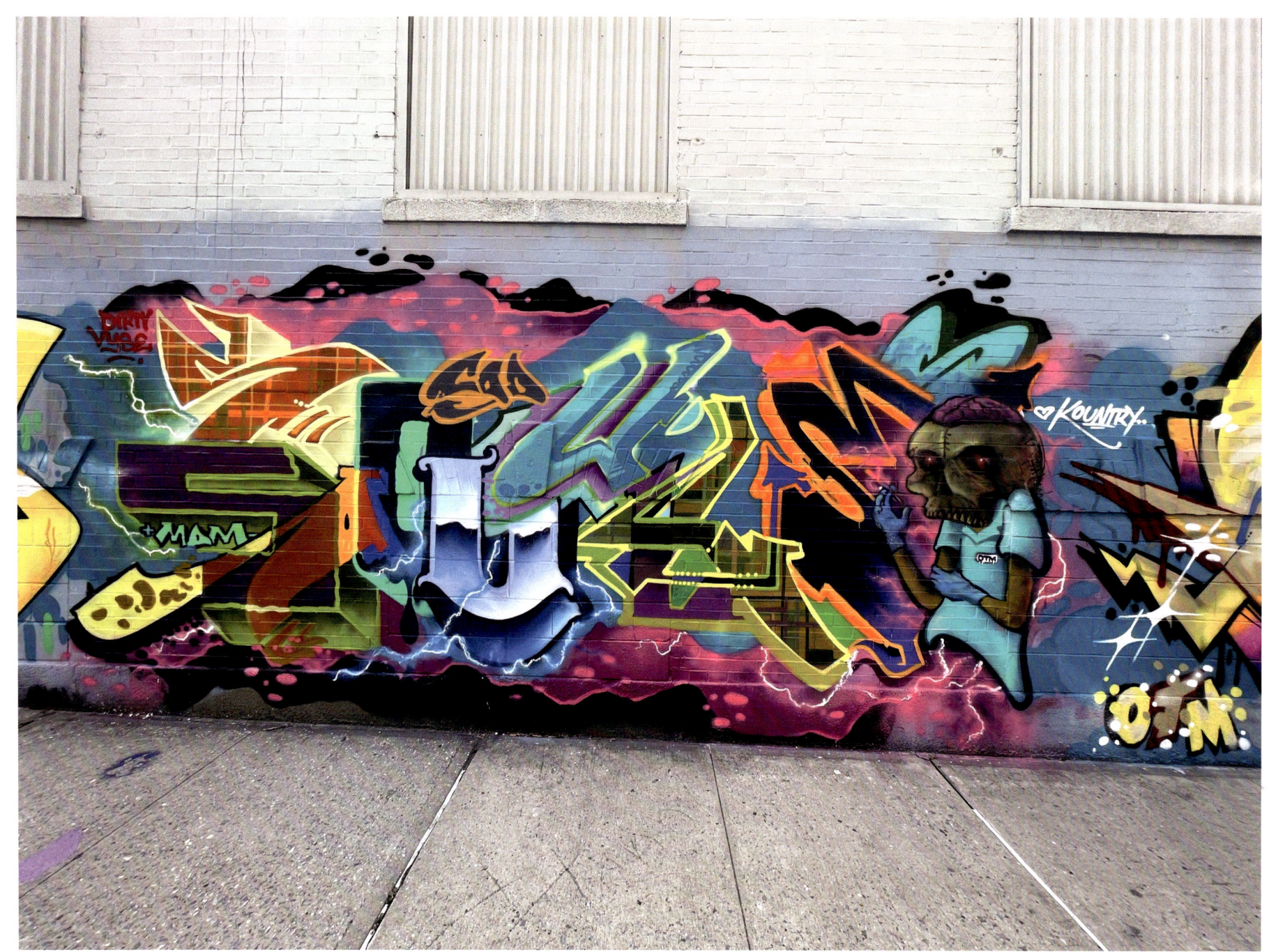

EL SOULS
BOONE AVENUE WALLS, THE BRONX, PHOTOGRAPHED IN 2024

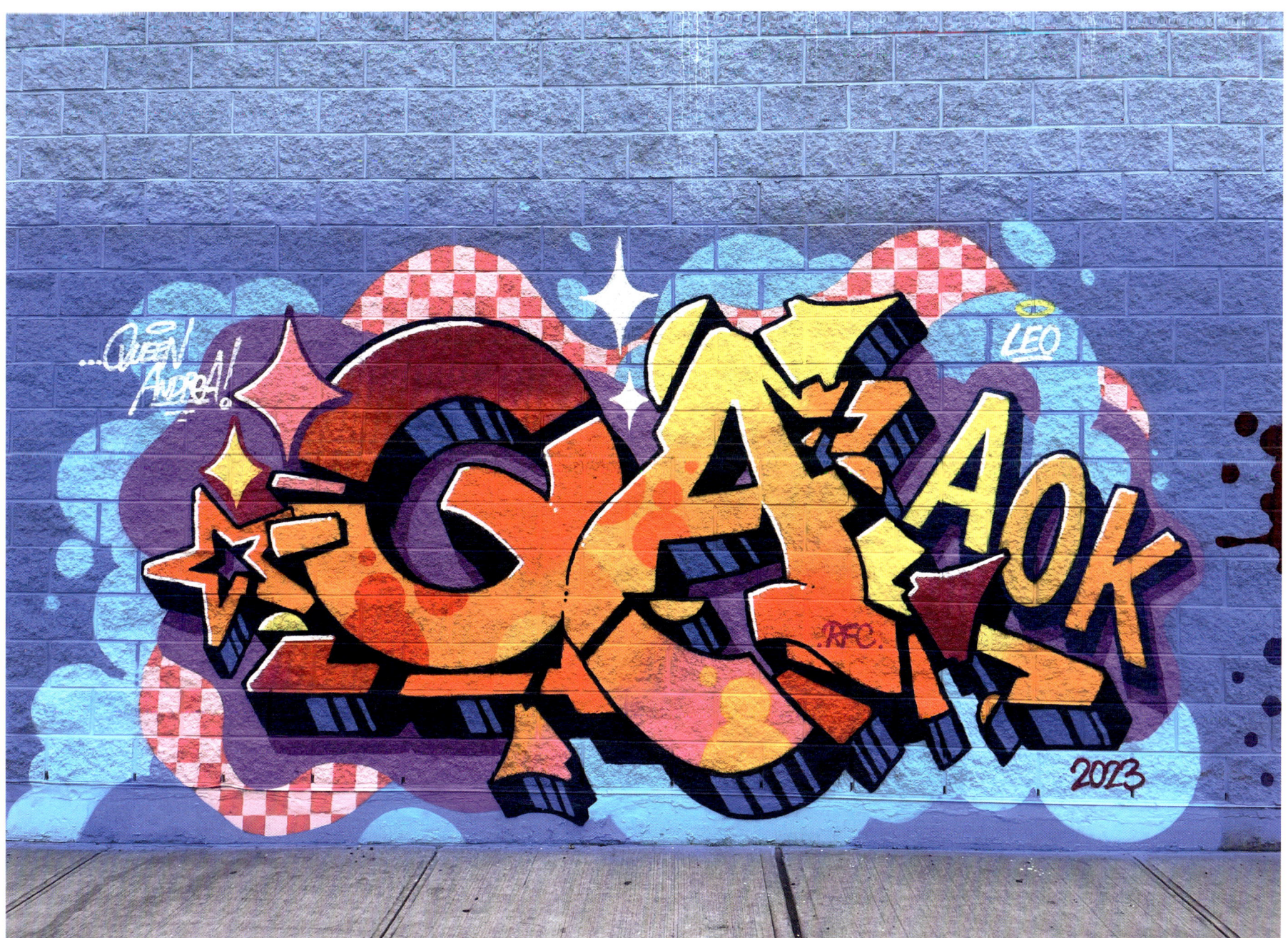

QUEEN ANDREA
Queen Andrea is a legend and is a pioneer in aerosol art culture. She has been active in the graffiti arts since the 1980s.
BOONE AVENUE WALLS, THE BRORNX, PHOTOGRAPHED IN 2023

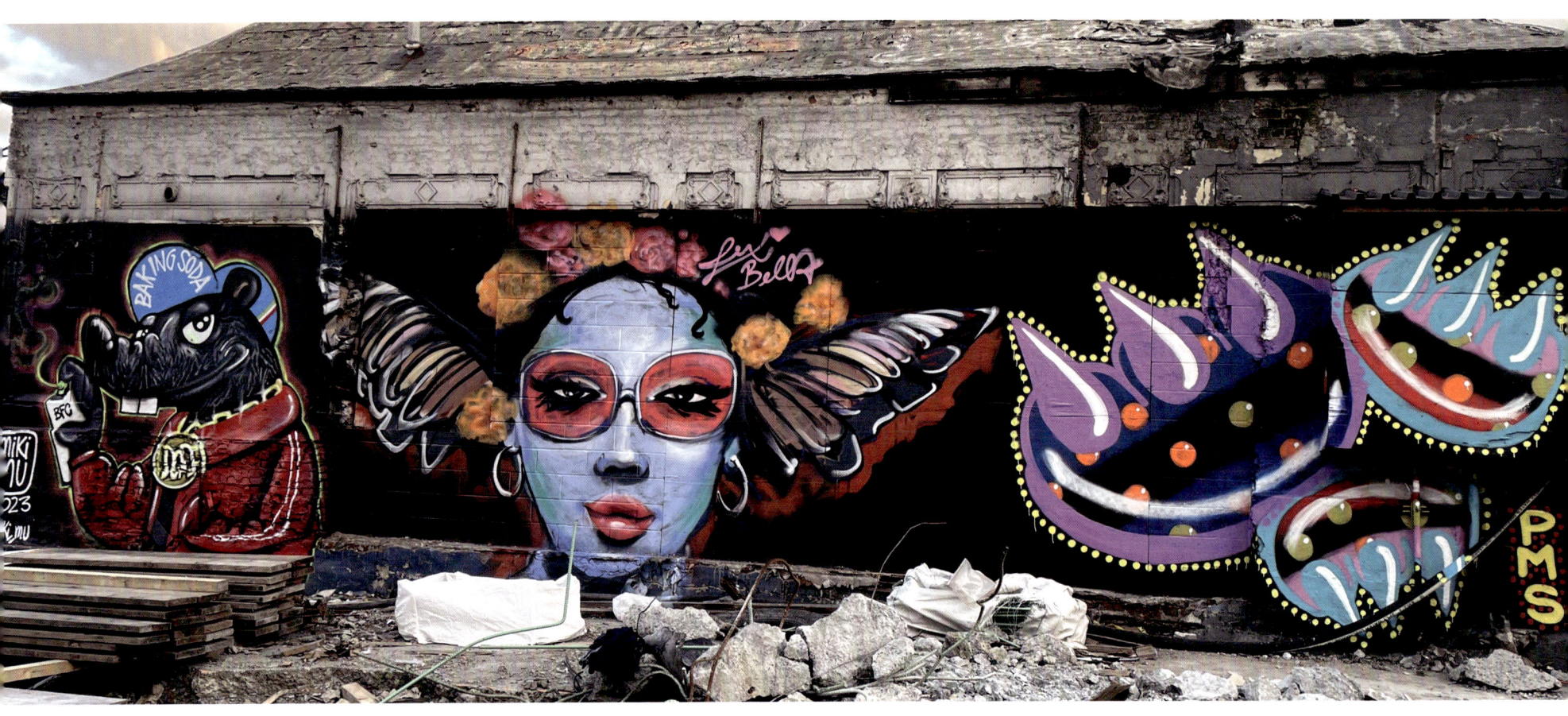

MIKI MU, LEXI BELLA, CLAW MONEY
BRONXLANDIA, THE BRONX, PHOTOGRAPHED IN 2023

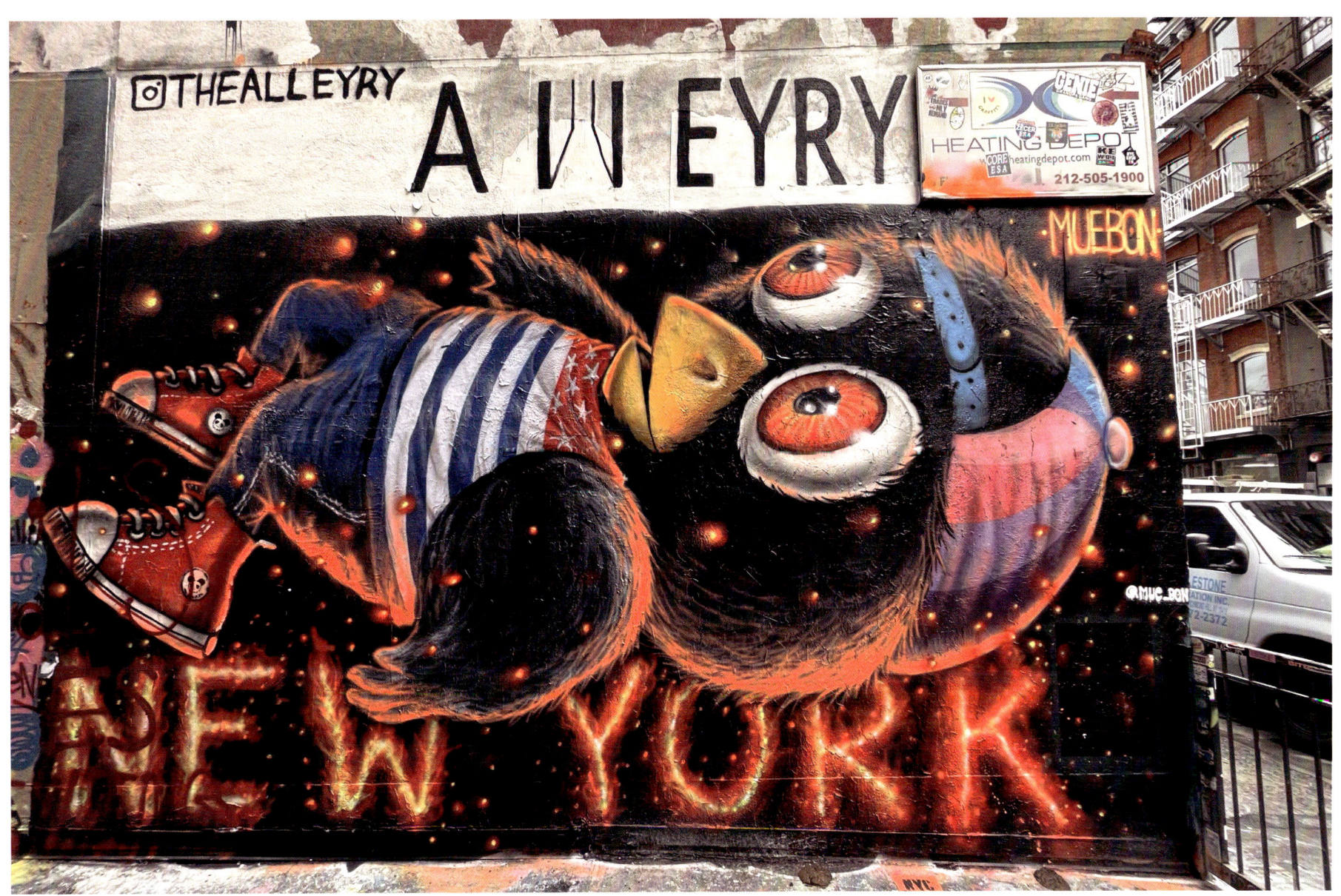

MUEBON

Muebon is an internationally known street artist from Thailand.
FREEMAN ALLEY, MANHATTAN, PHOTOGRAPHED IN 2024

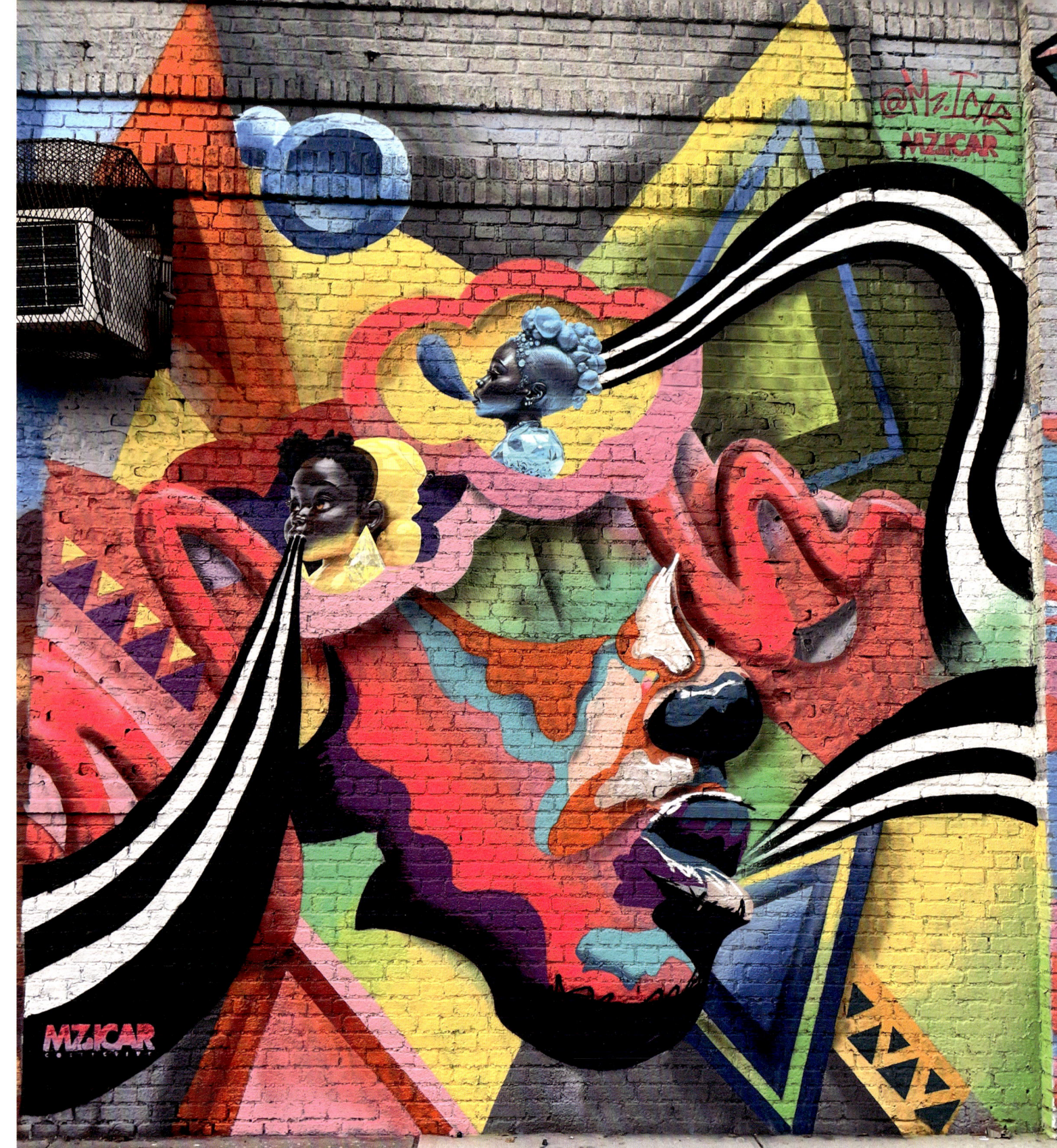

MZI CAR
BED-STUY
WALLS,
BROOKLYN,
PHOTOGRAPHED
IN 2023

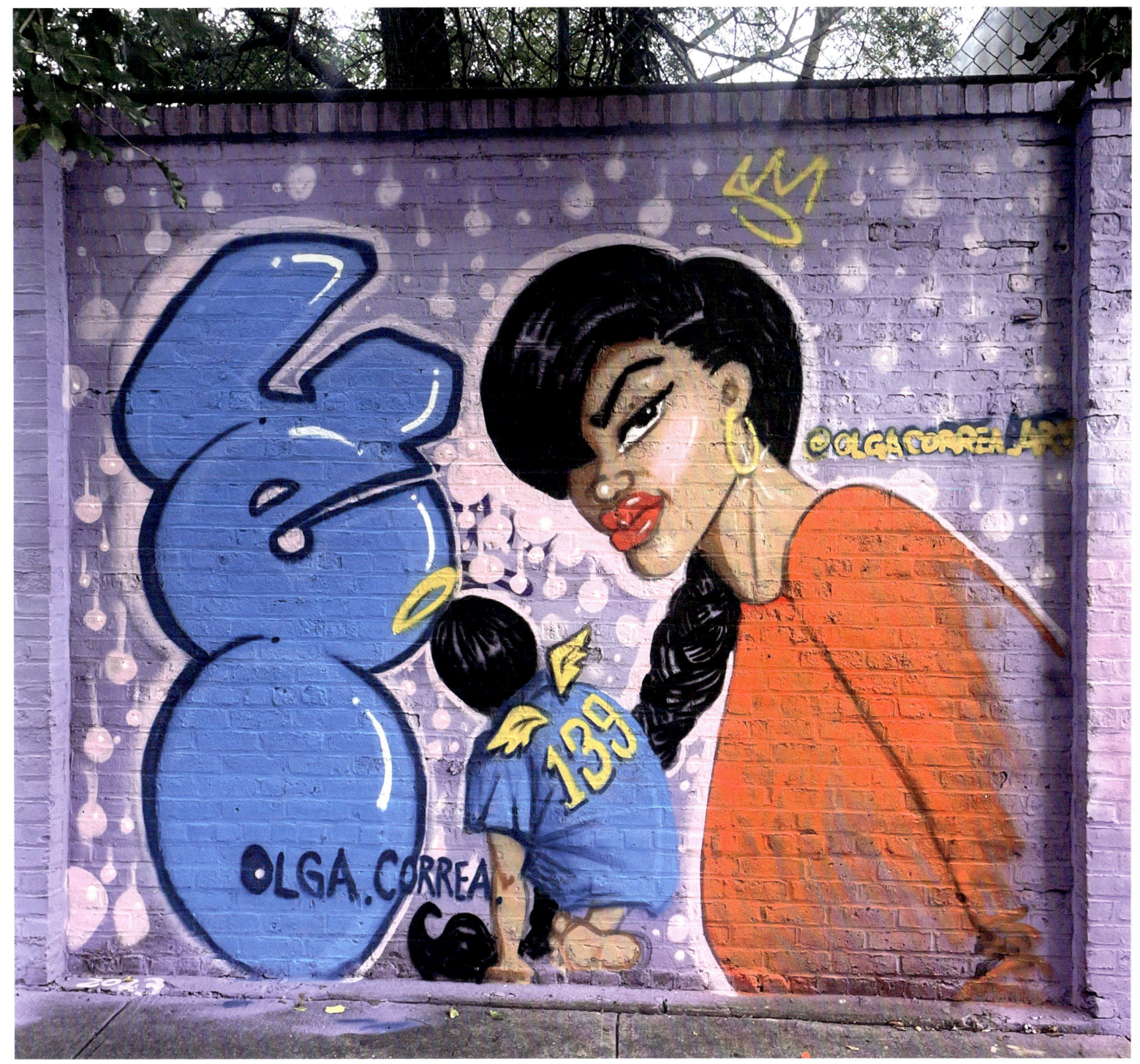

OLGA CORREA
BOONE AVENUE
WALLS, THE
BRONX,
PHOTOGRAPHED
IN 2023

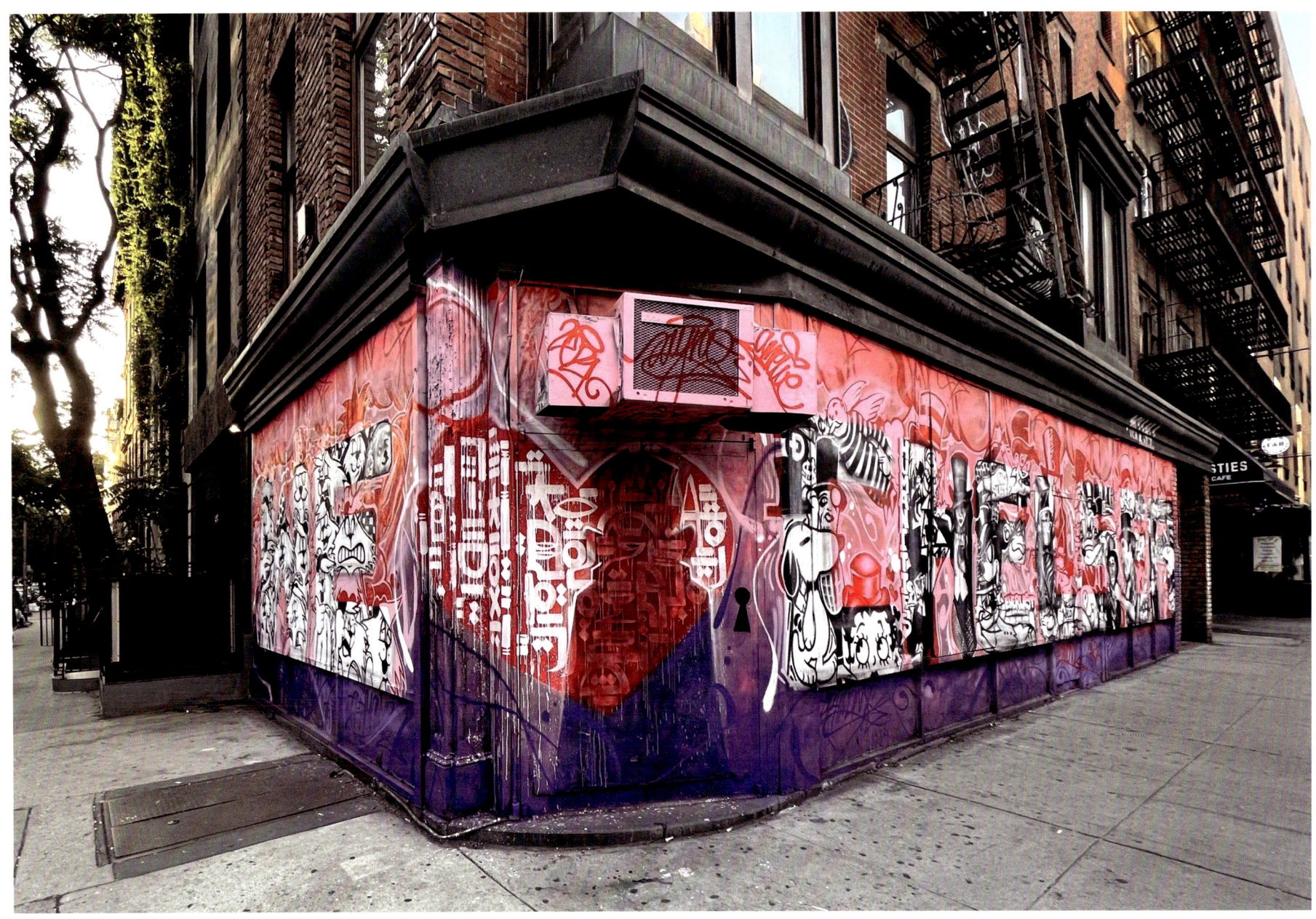

OPTIMO NYC

Optimo is prolific street artist. His artwork can be seen on buildings all across New York City.

MANHATTAN, PHOTOGRAPHED IN 2021

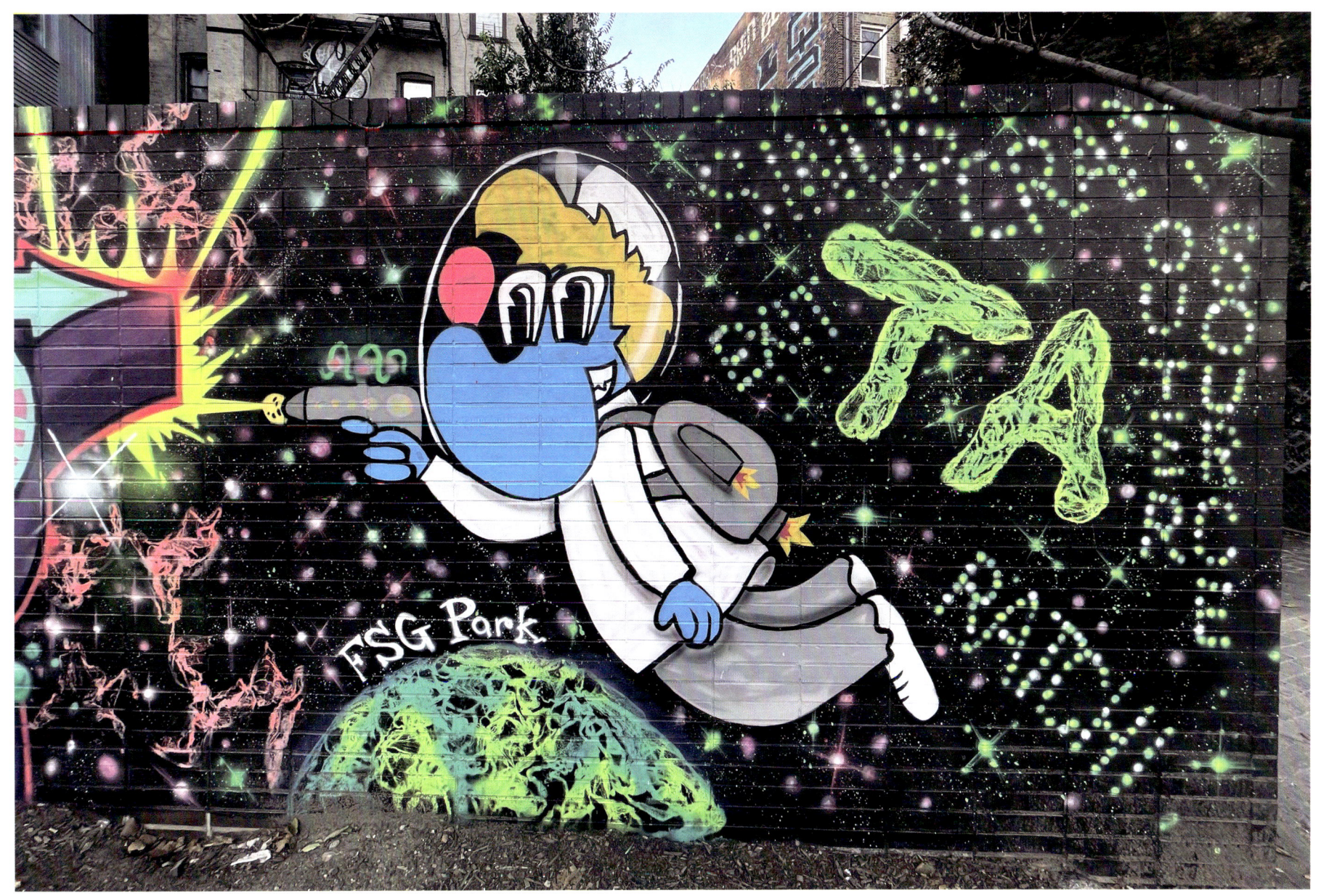

OUTER SOURCE, RATCHI
FIRST STREET GREEN ART PARK, MANHATTAN, PHOTOGRAPHED IN 2023

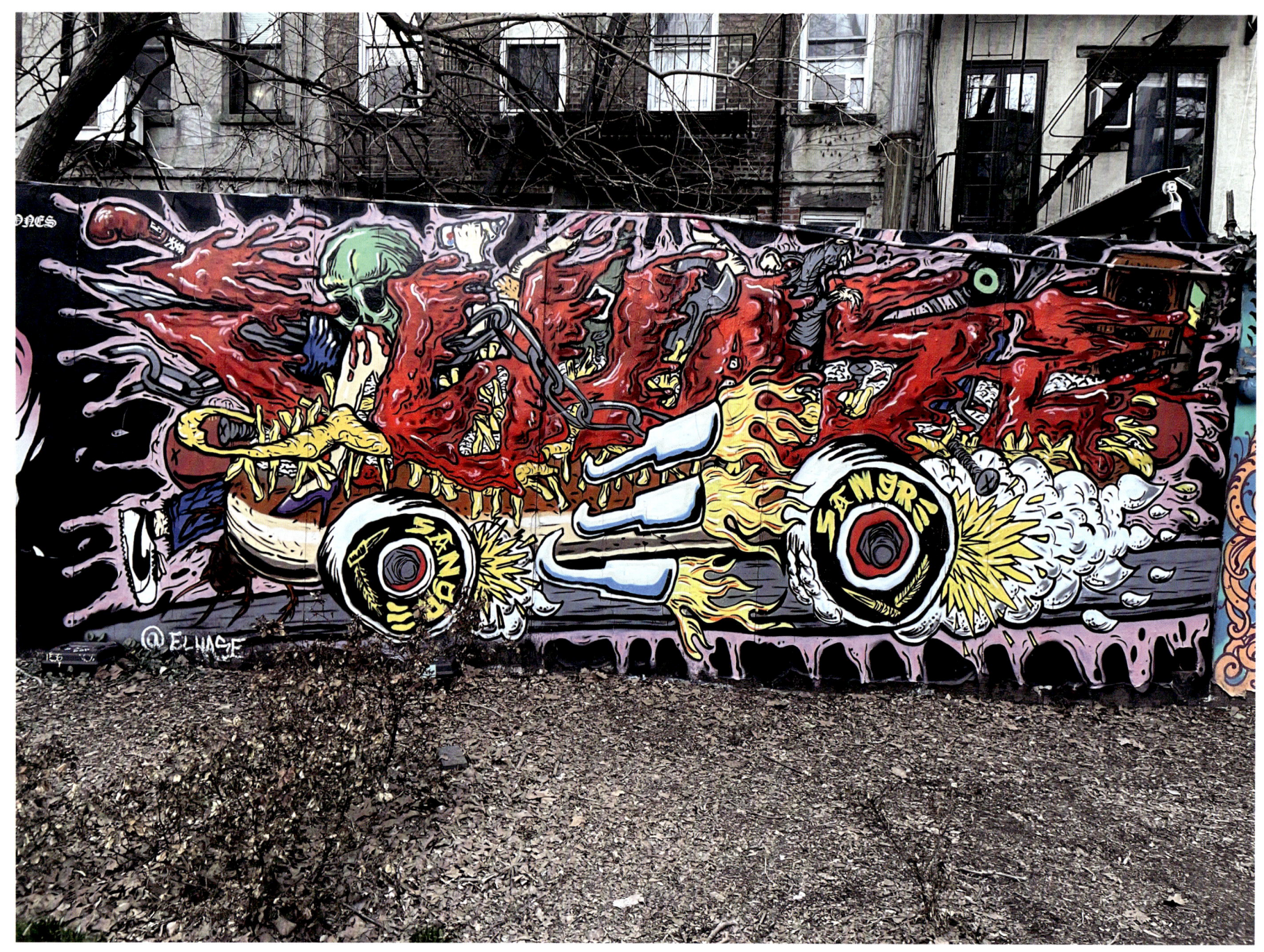

EL HASE
FIRST STREET GREEN ART PARK, MANHATTAN, PHOTOGRAPHED IN 2024

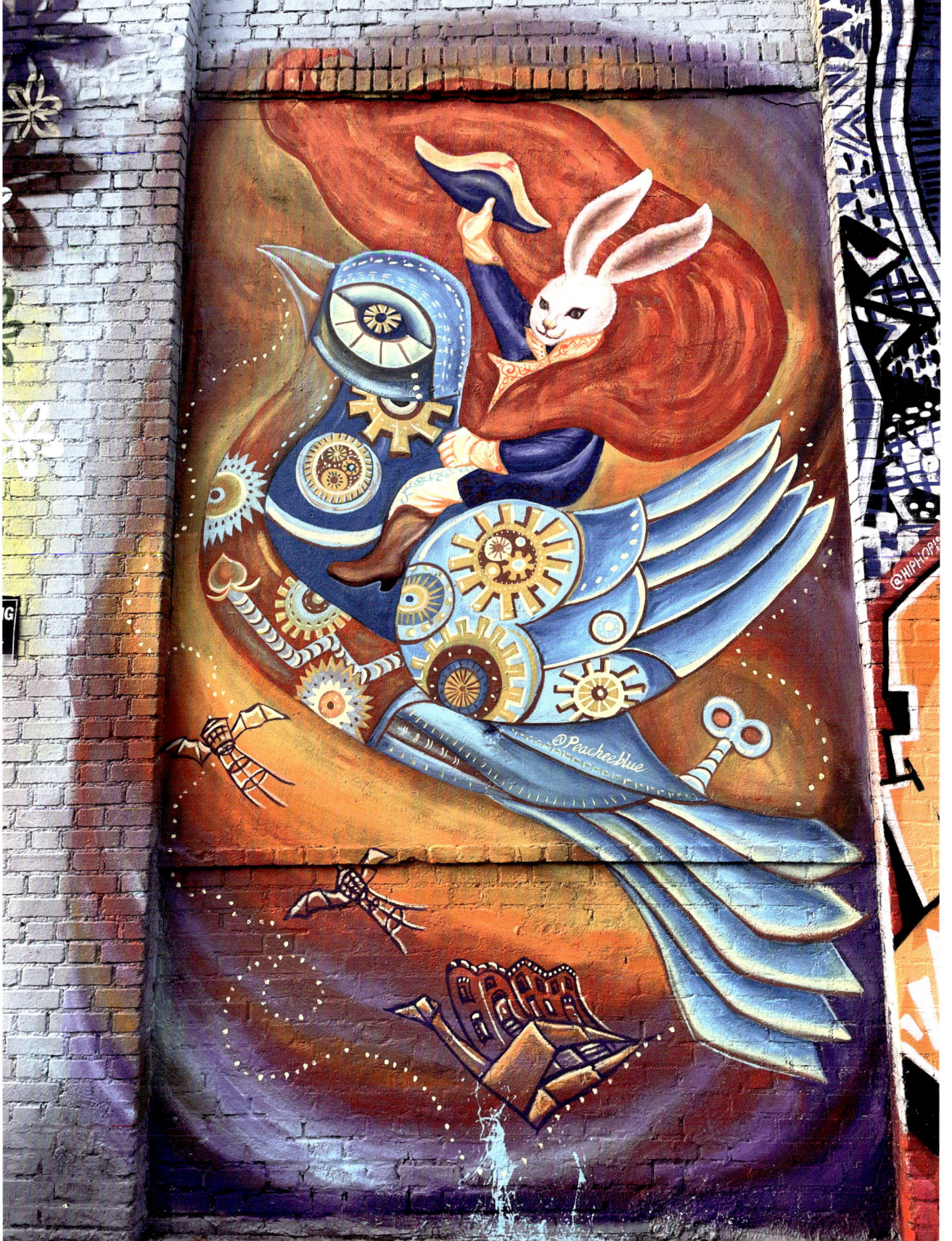

PEACH TAO
BED-STUY WALLS, BROOKLYN,
PHOTOGRAPHED IN 2023

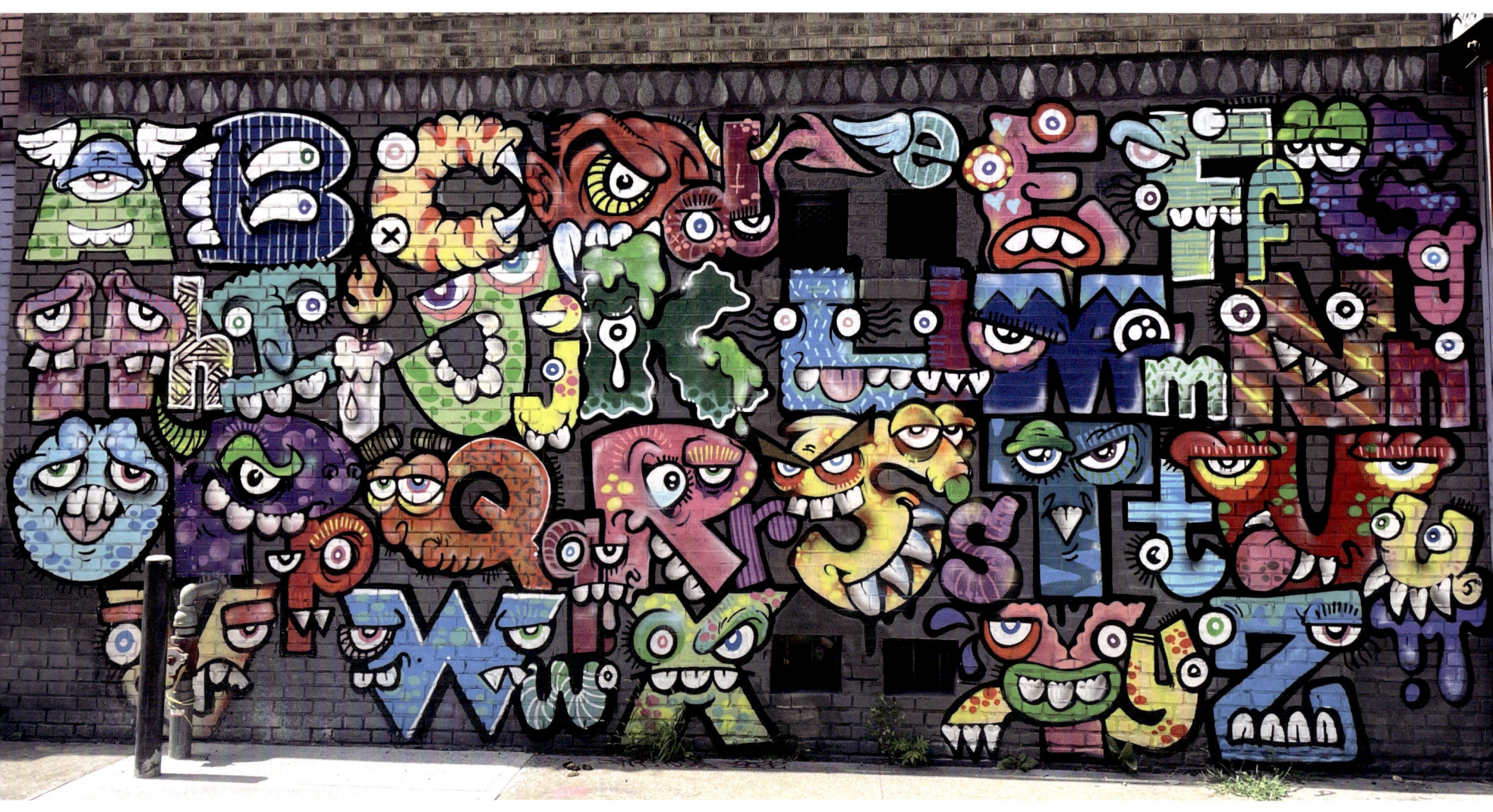

PHETUS
BOONE AVENUE WALLS, THE BRONX, PHOTOGRAPHED IN 2023

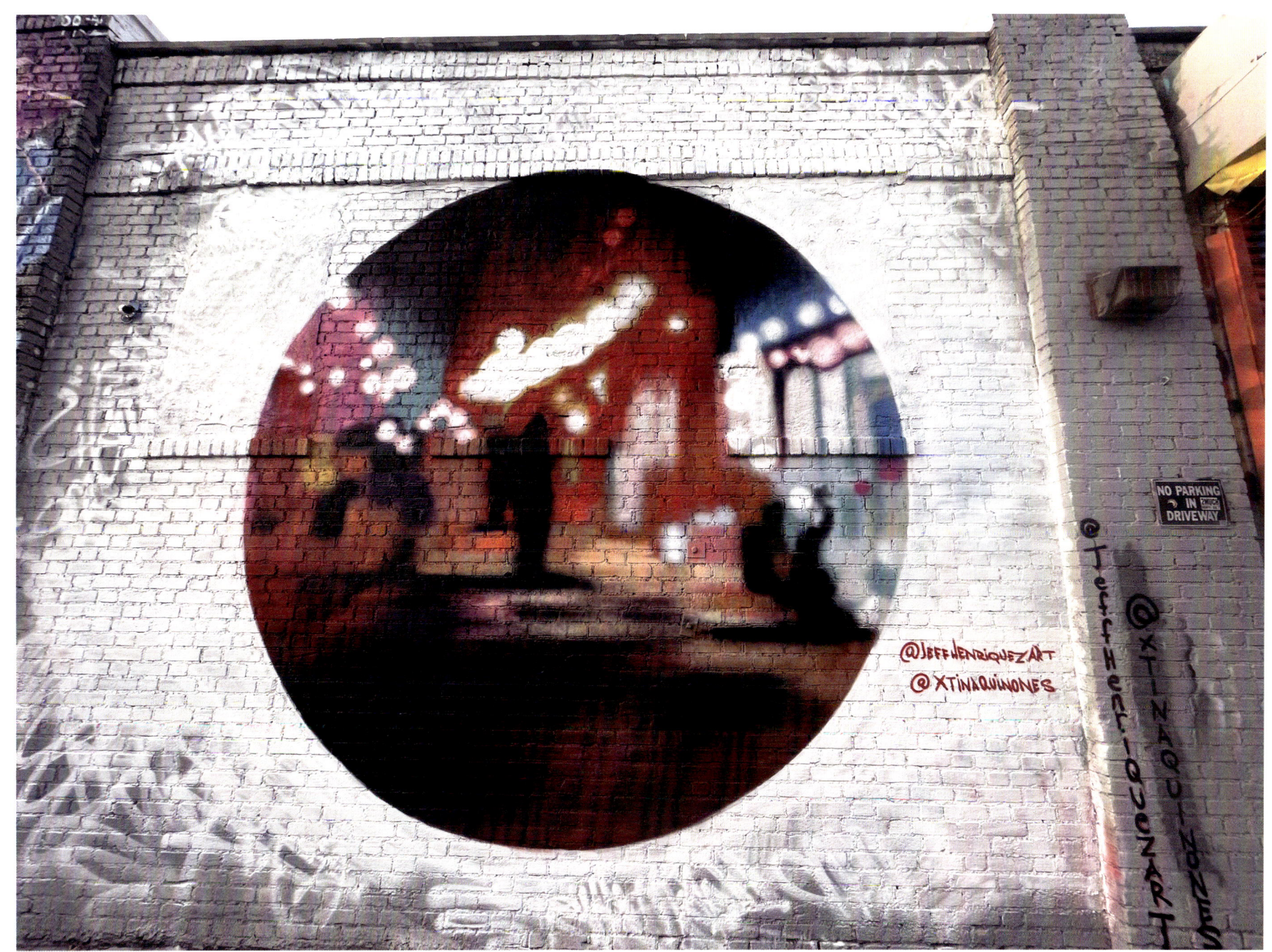

JEFF HENRIQUEZ, XTINA QUINONES
BED-STUY WALLS, BROOKLYN, PHOTOGRAPHED IN 2023

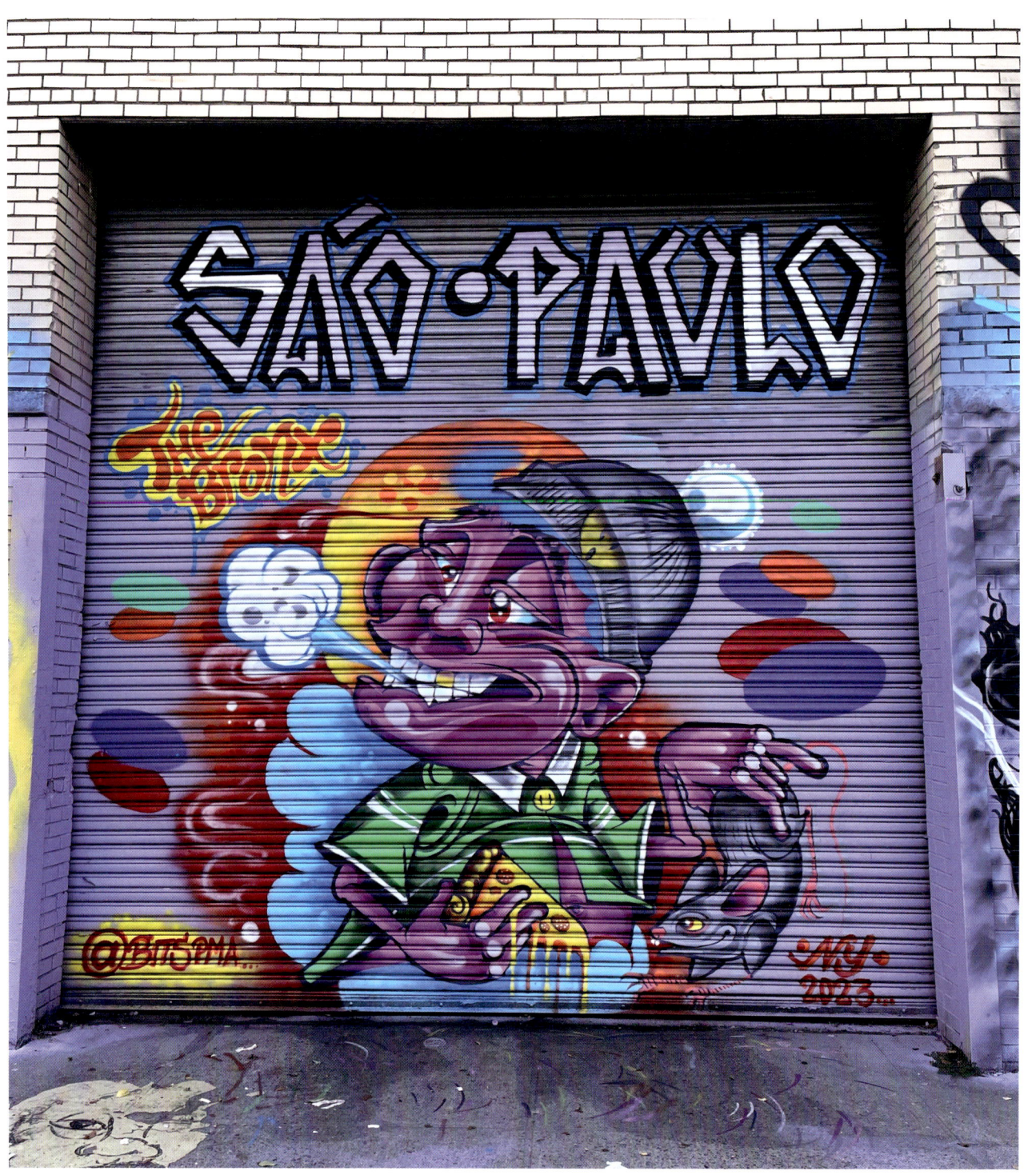

BITS
BOONE AVENUE WALLS, THE BRONX,
PHOTOGRAPHED IN 2023

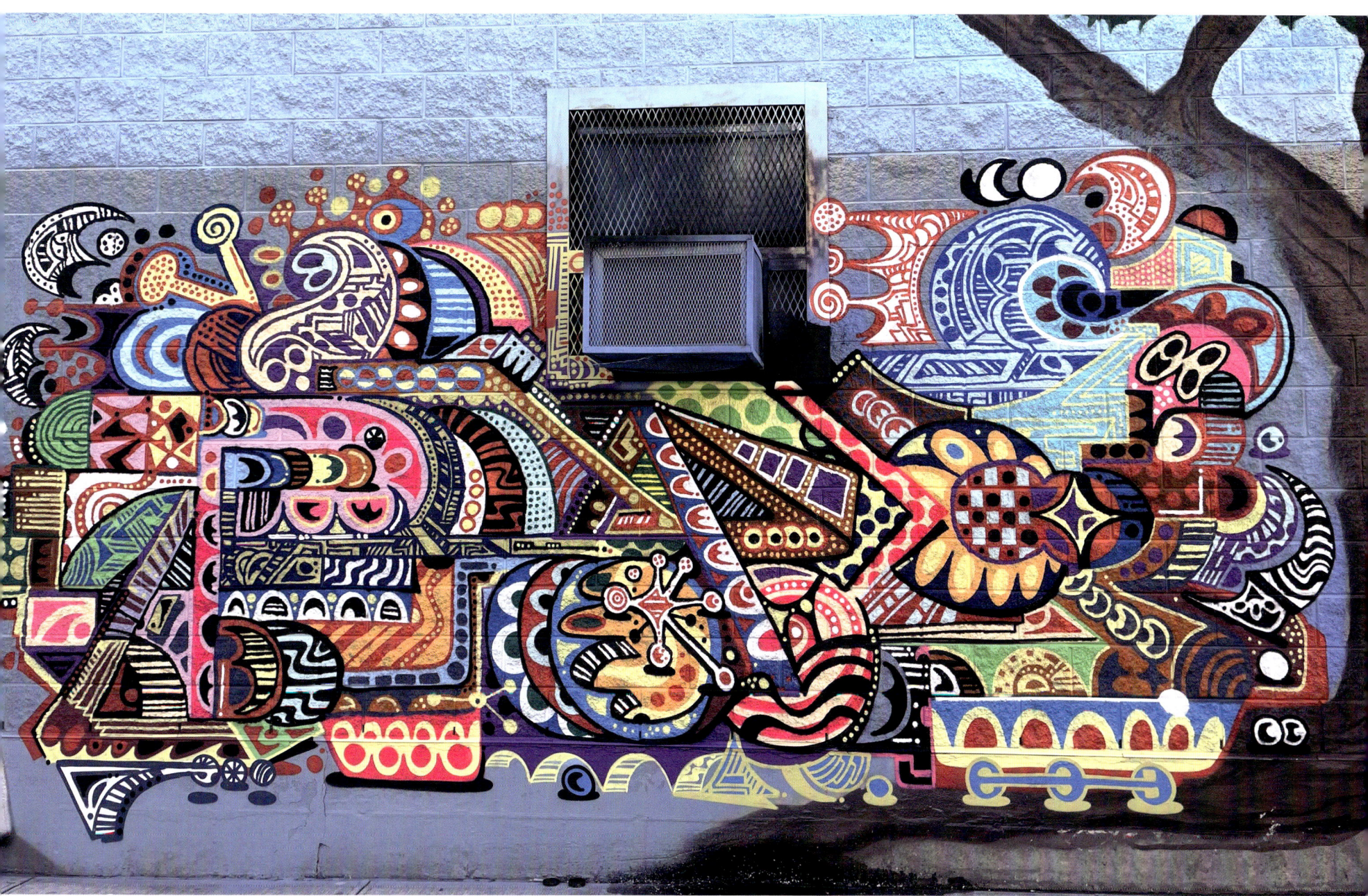

MUCHO
BOONE AVENUE WALLS, THE BRONX, PHOTOGRAPHED IN 2023

NAP DON'T SLEEP
BUSHWICK COLLECTIVE,
BROOKLYN, PHOTOGRAPHED IN
2024

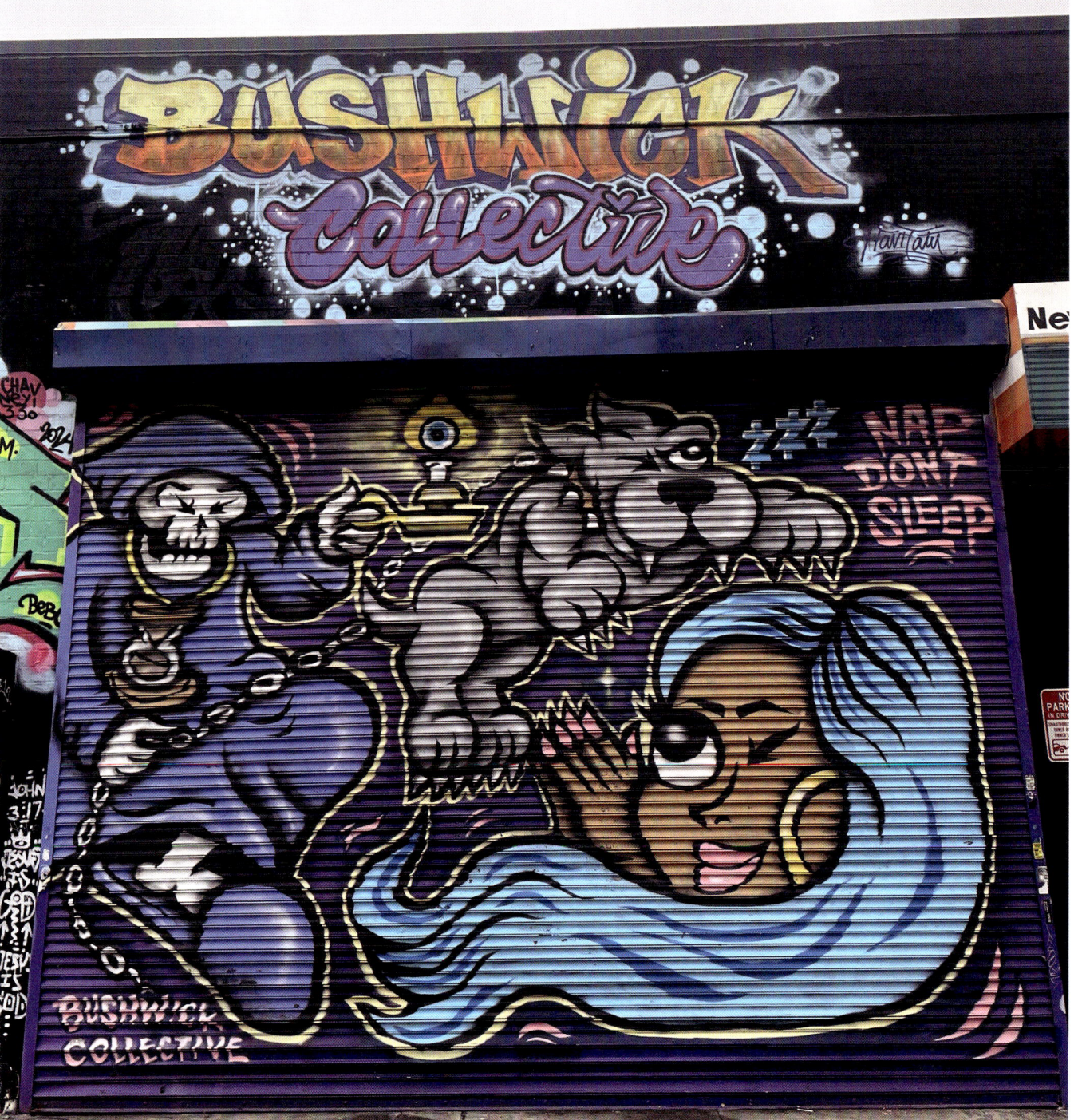

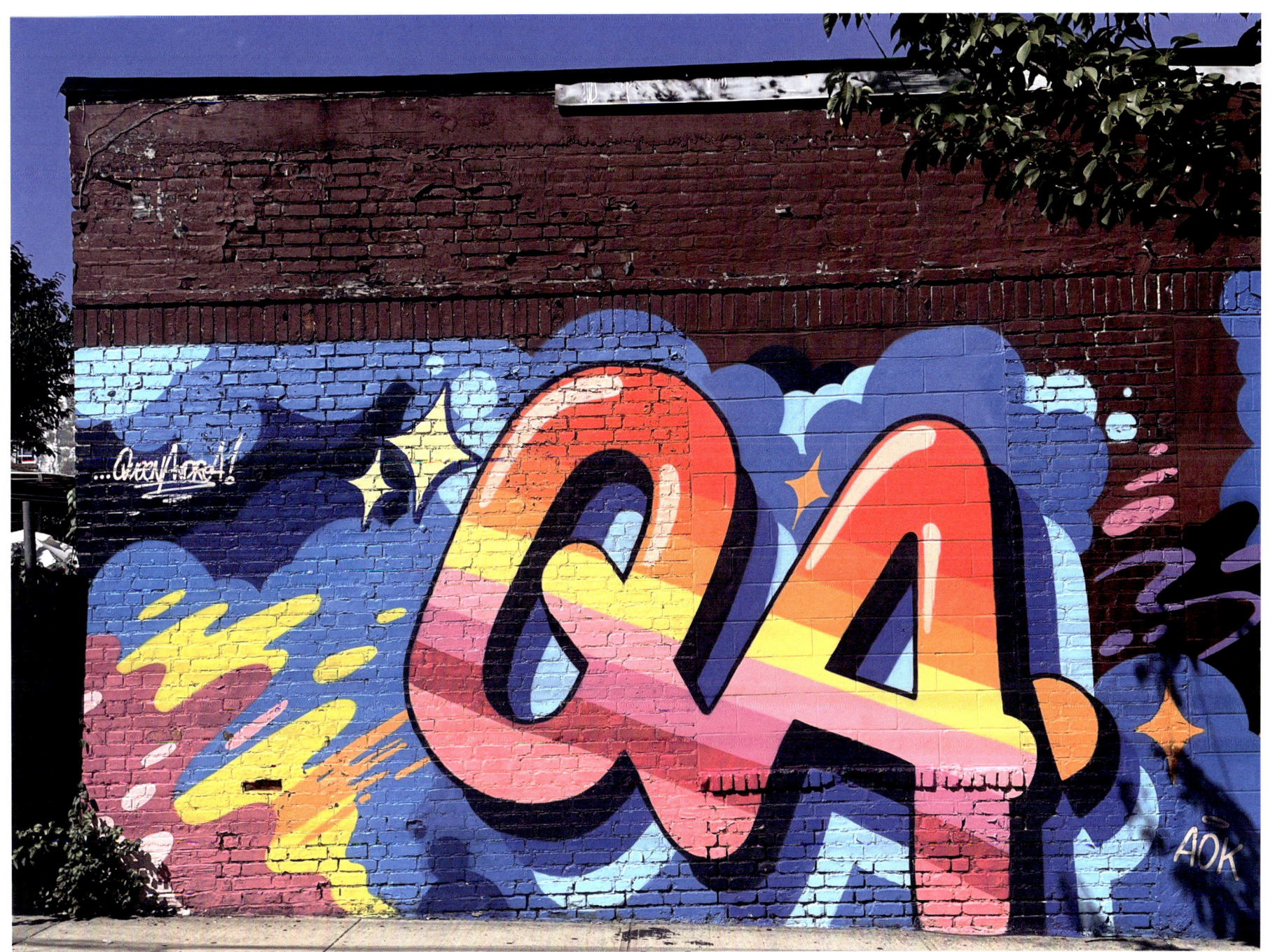

QUEEN ANDREA
BOONE AVENUE WALLS, THE BRONX, PHOTOGRAPHED IN 2024

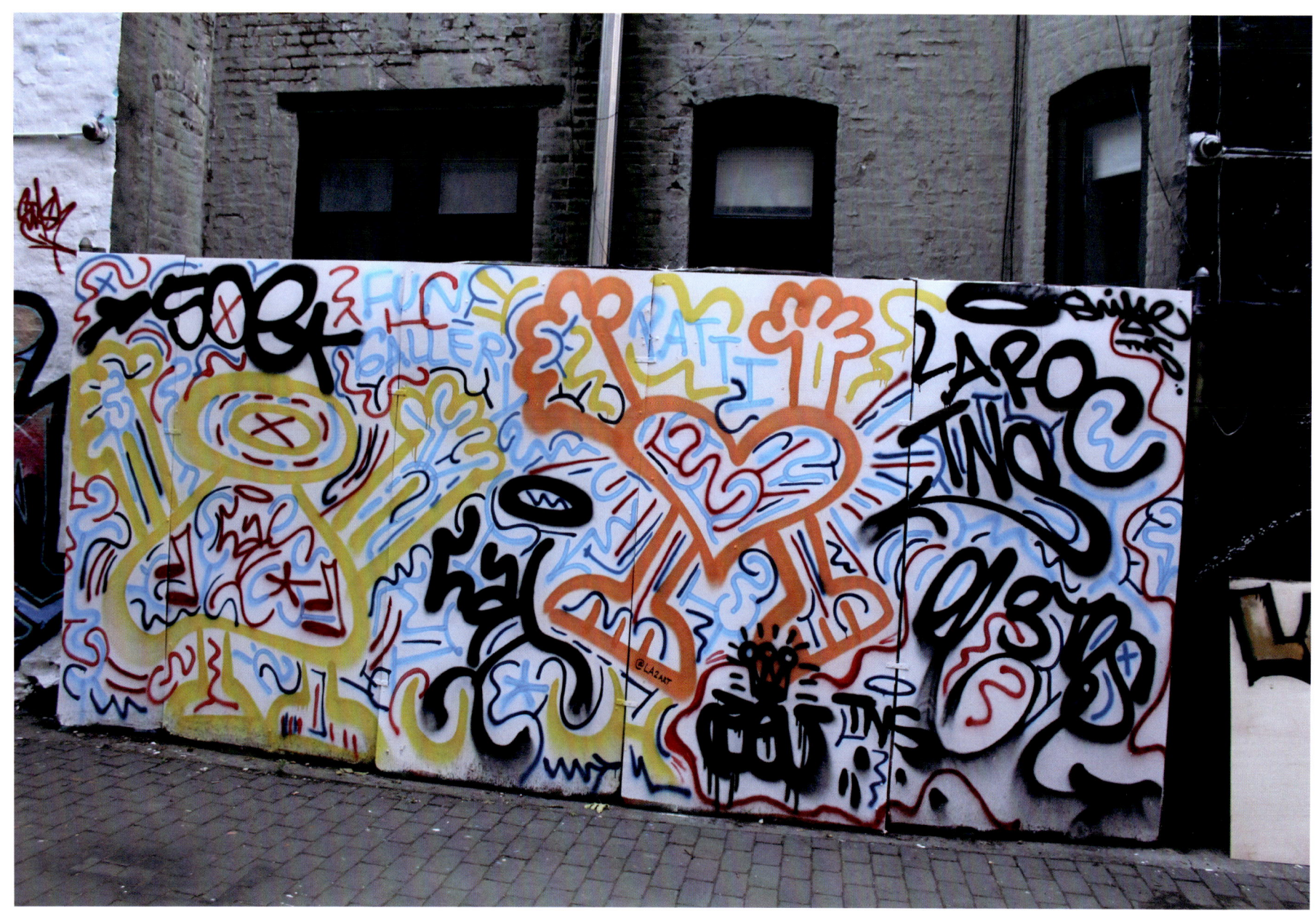

LA 2
Patti Astor tribute.
FIRST STREET GREEN ART PARK, MANHATTAN, PHOTOGRAPHED IN 2024

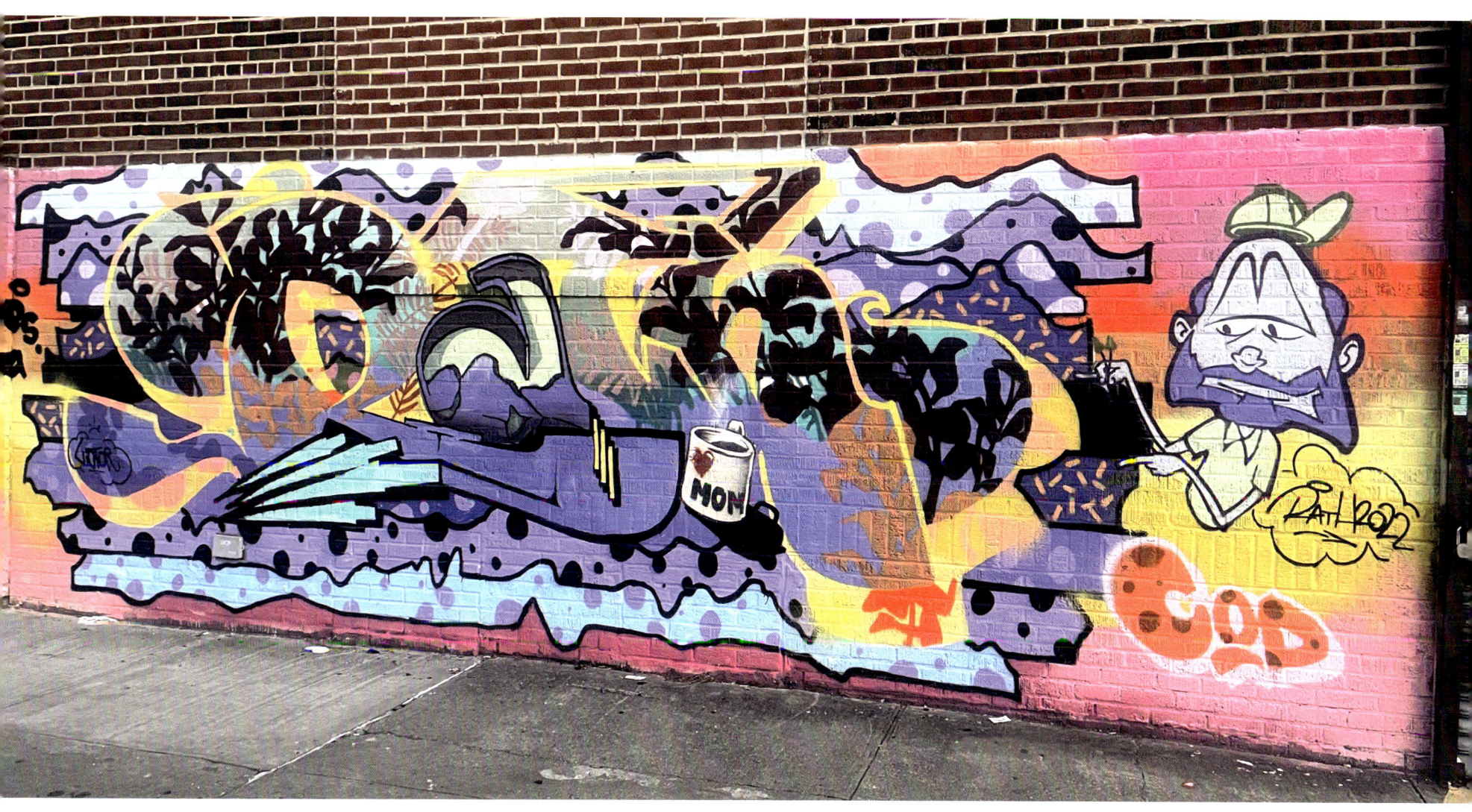

RATH COD
BOONE AVENUE WALLS, THE BRONX, PHOTOGRAPHED IN 2023

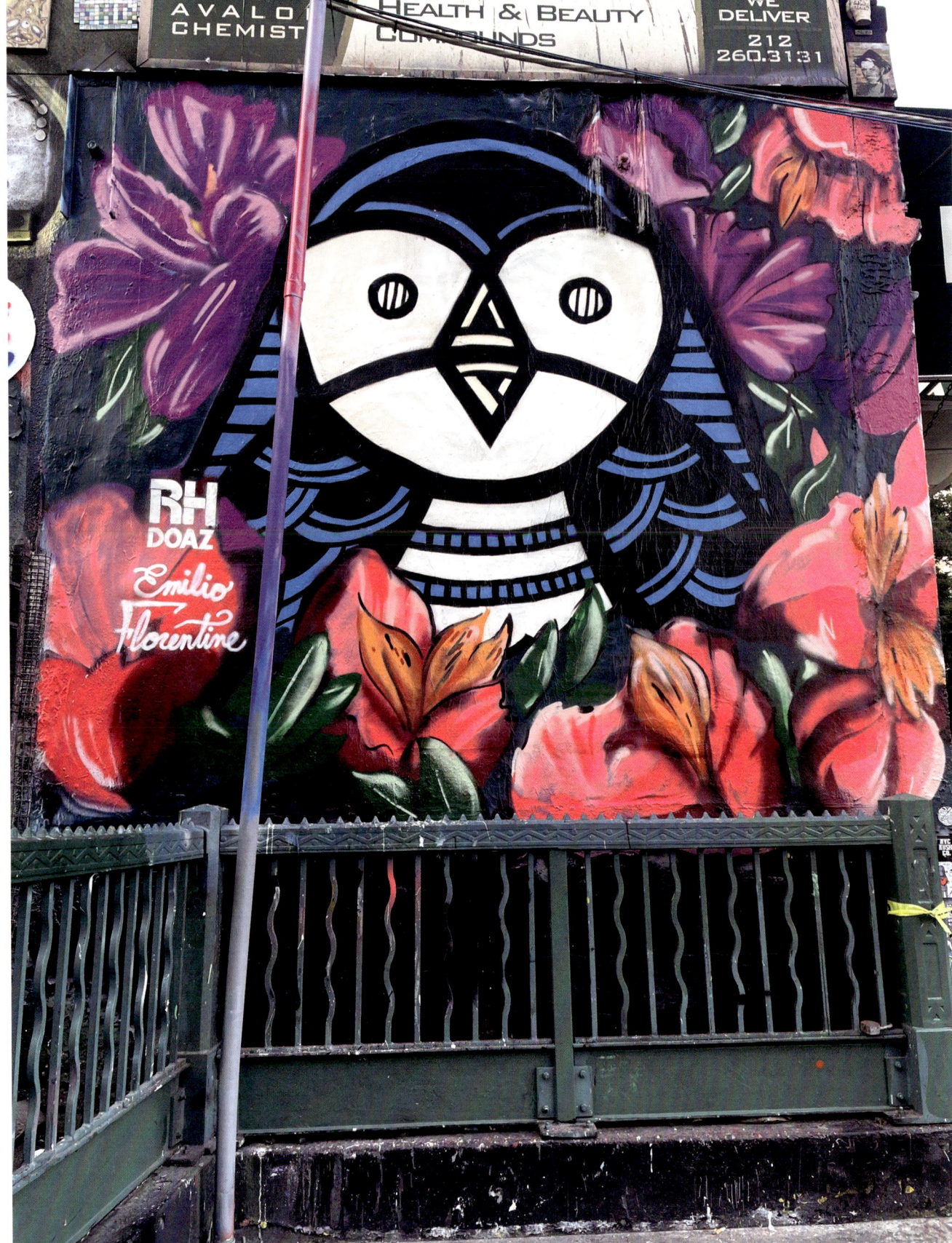

RH DOAZ

MANHATTAN, PHOTOGRAPHED IN 2023

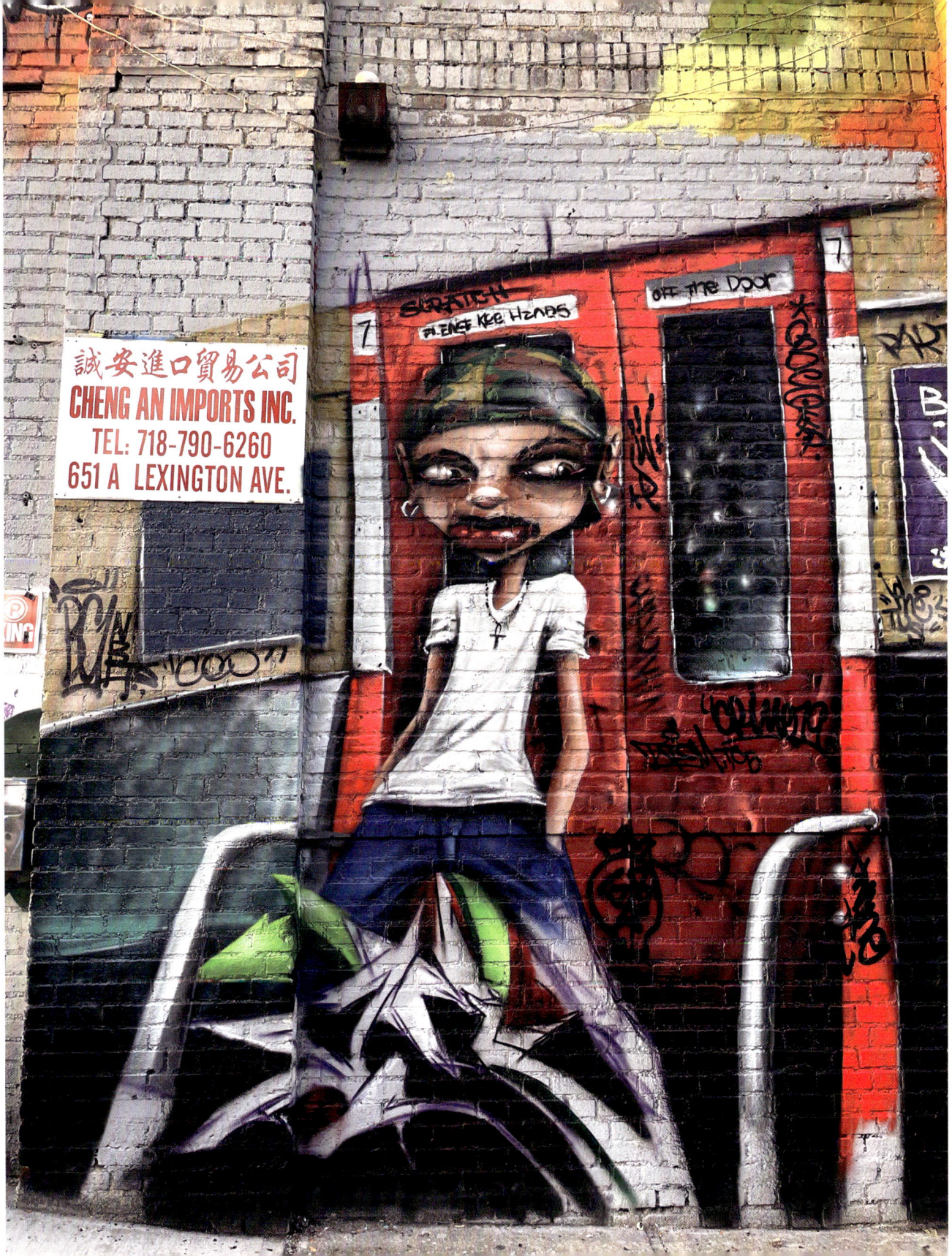

SCRATCH NYC
BED-STUY WALLS, BROOKLYN,
PHOTOGRAPHED IN 2023

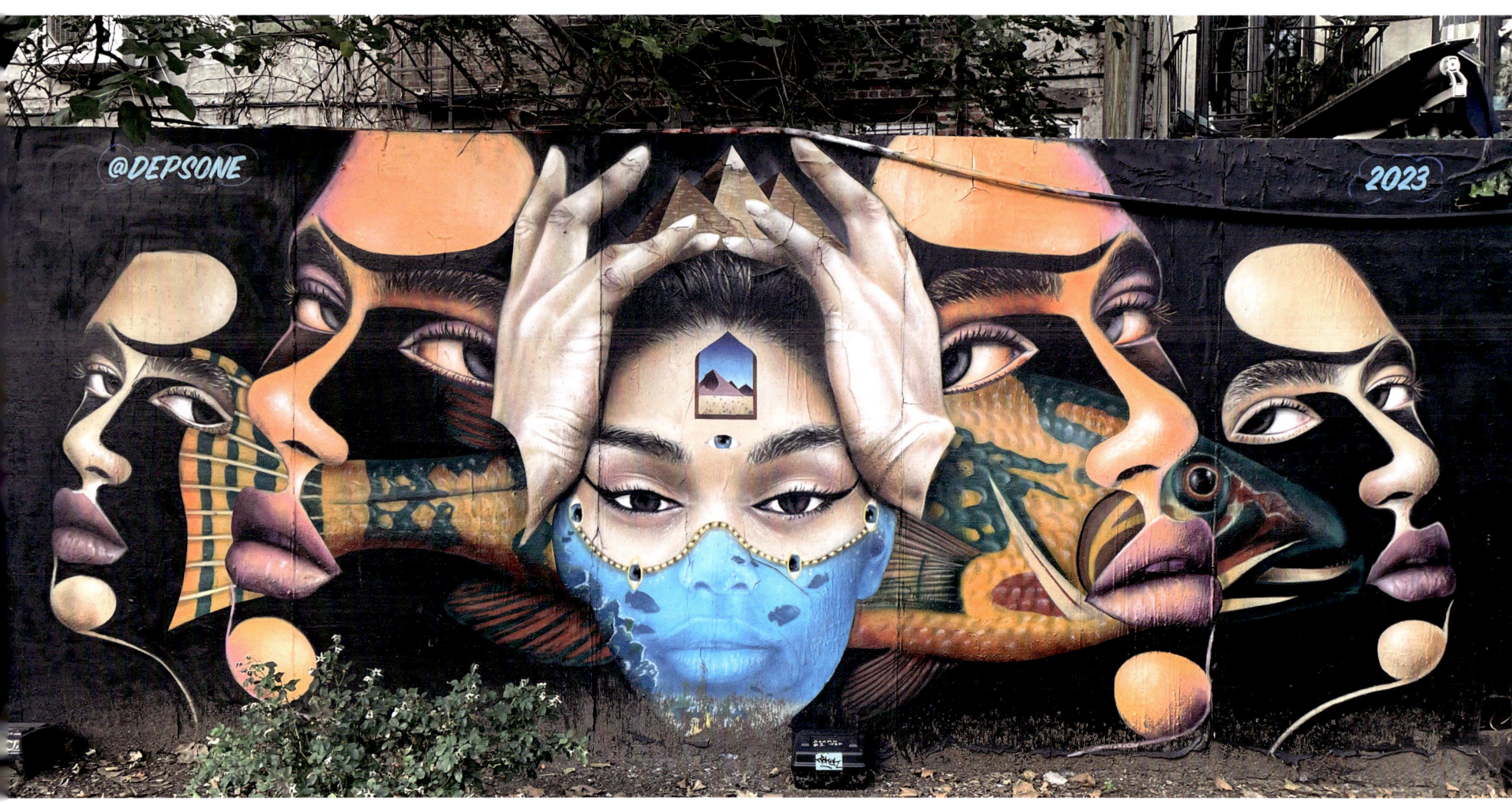

CARSON DEYOUNG
FIRST STREET GREEN ART PARK, MANHATTAN, PHOTOGRAPHED IN 2023

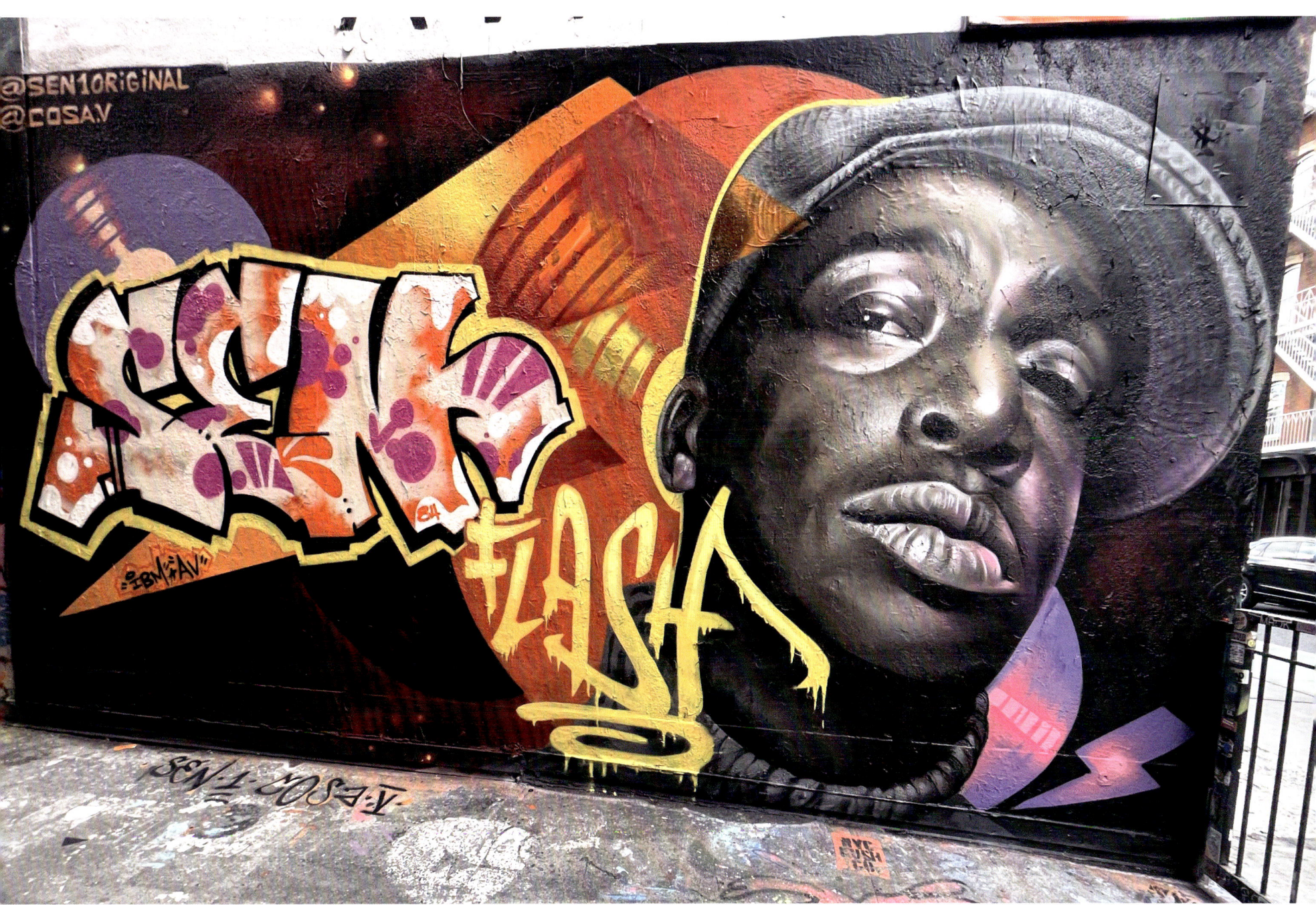

SEN 1, COSA
FREEMAN ALLEY, MANHATTAN, PHOTOGRAPHED IN 2024

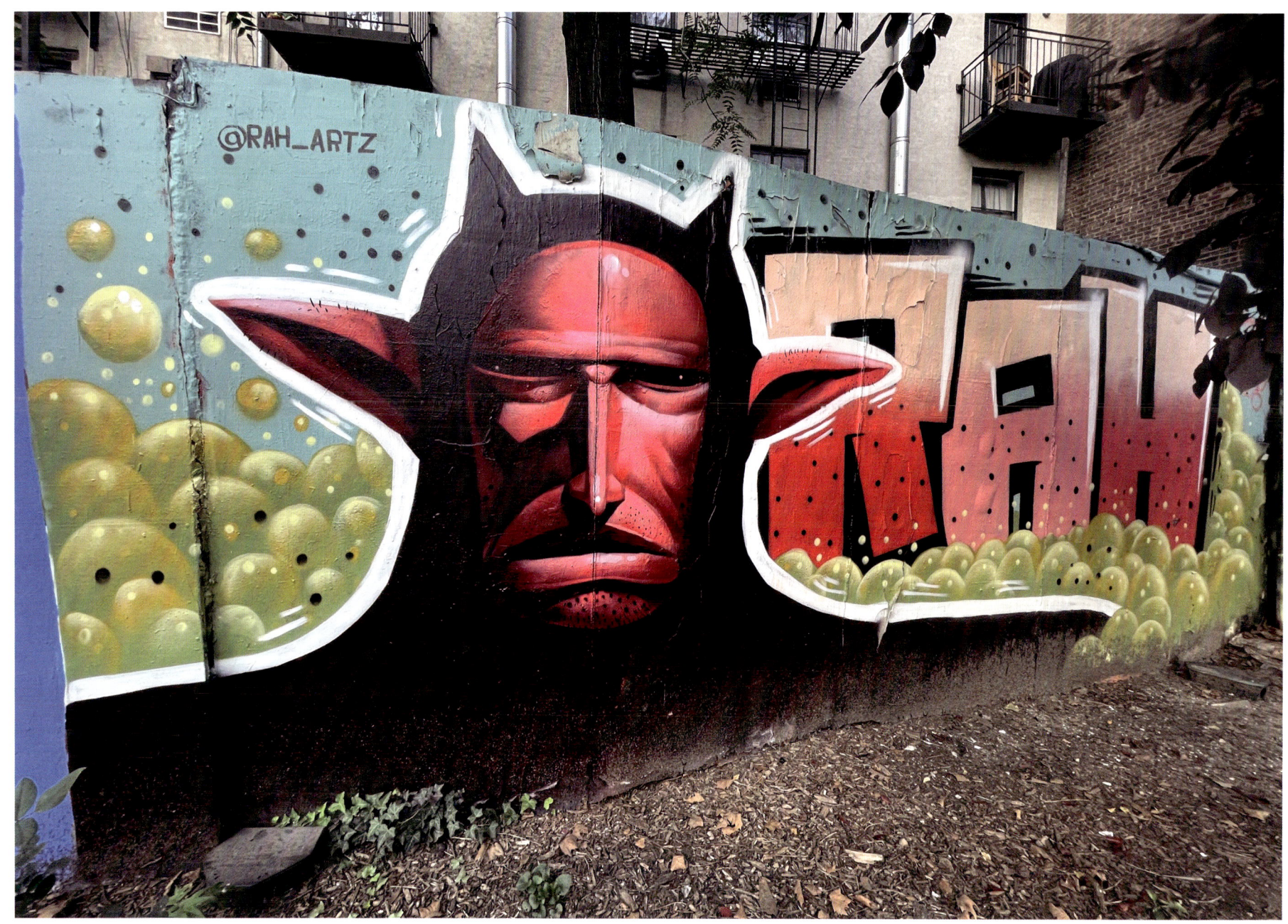

EZRA CUMBO
FIRST STREET GREEN ART PARK, MANHATTAN, PHOTOGRAPHED IN 2023

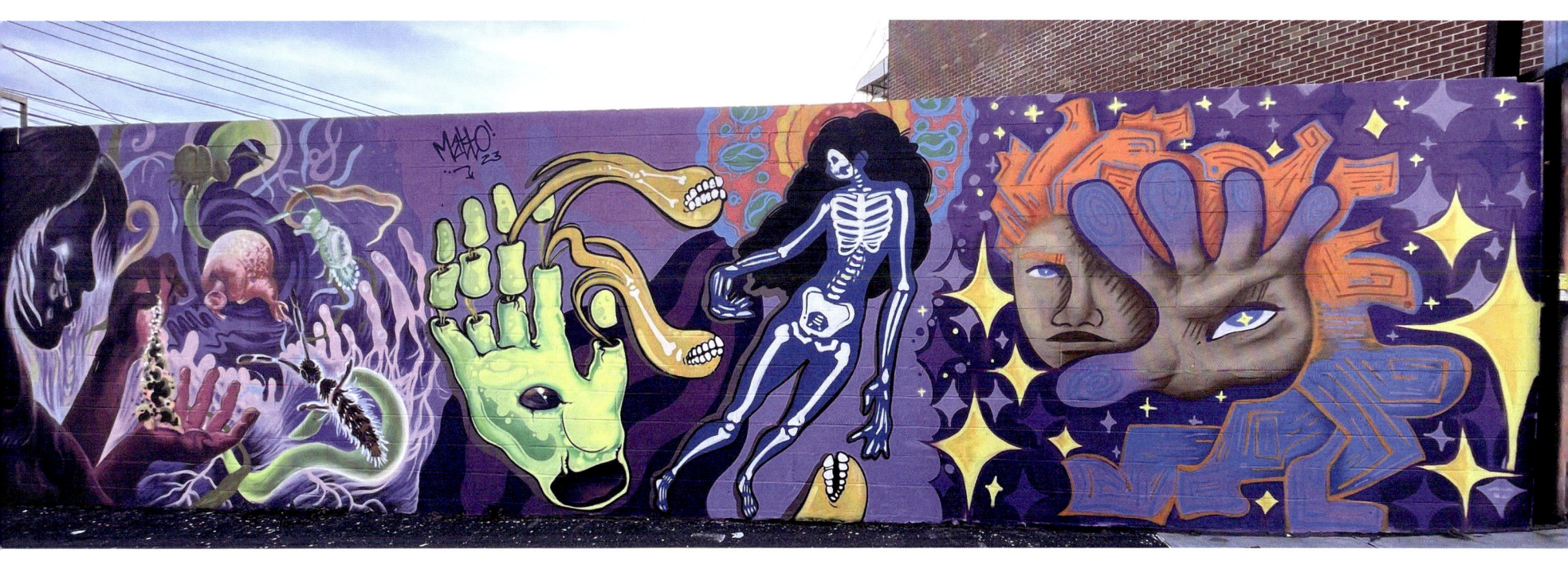

MATTO MATT.OCONNOR
WELLING COURT MURAL PROJECT, PHOTOGRAPHED IN 2024

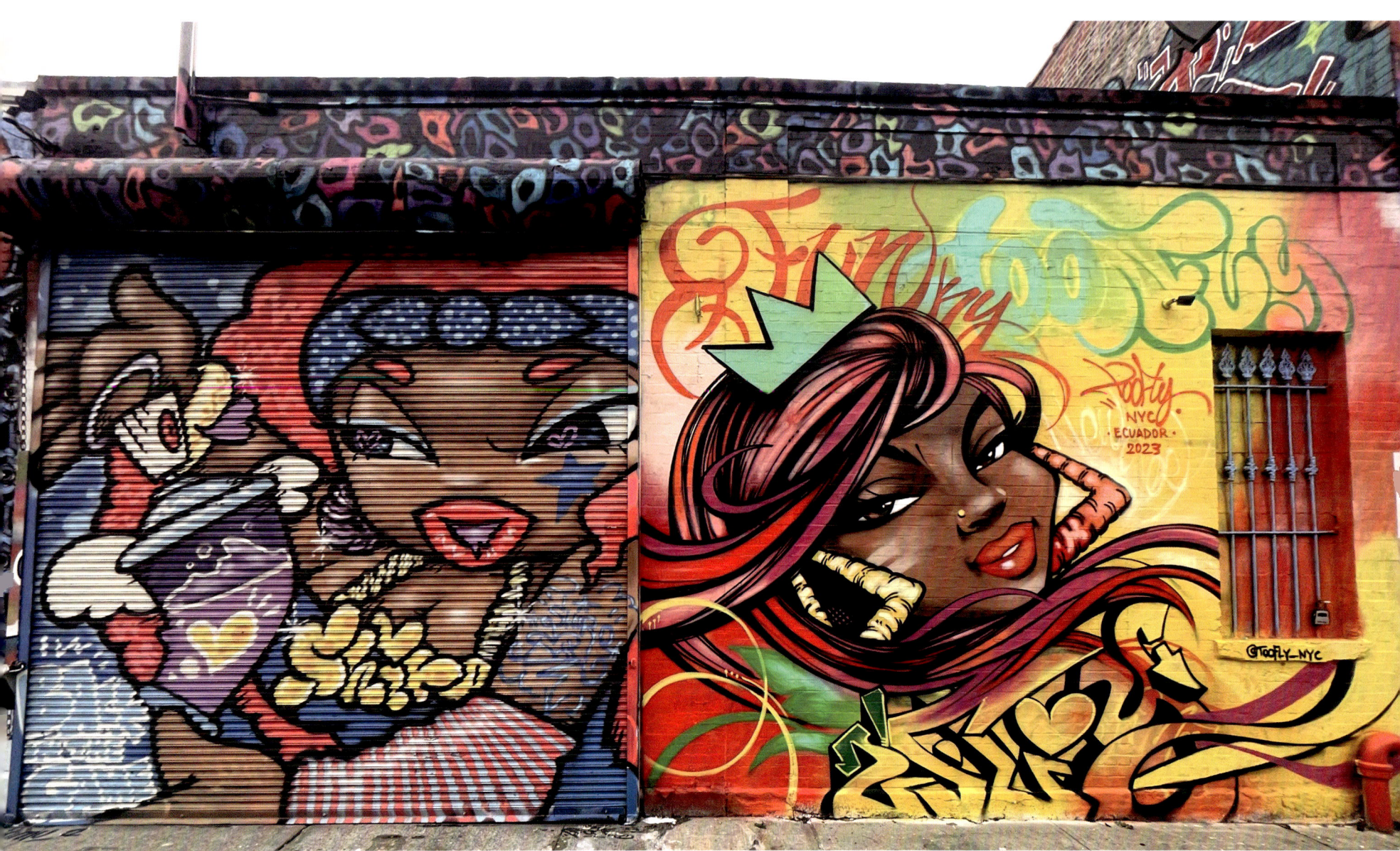

SHIRO ONE, TOOFLY
BED-STUY WALLS, BROOKLYN, PHOTOGRAPHED IN 2023

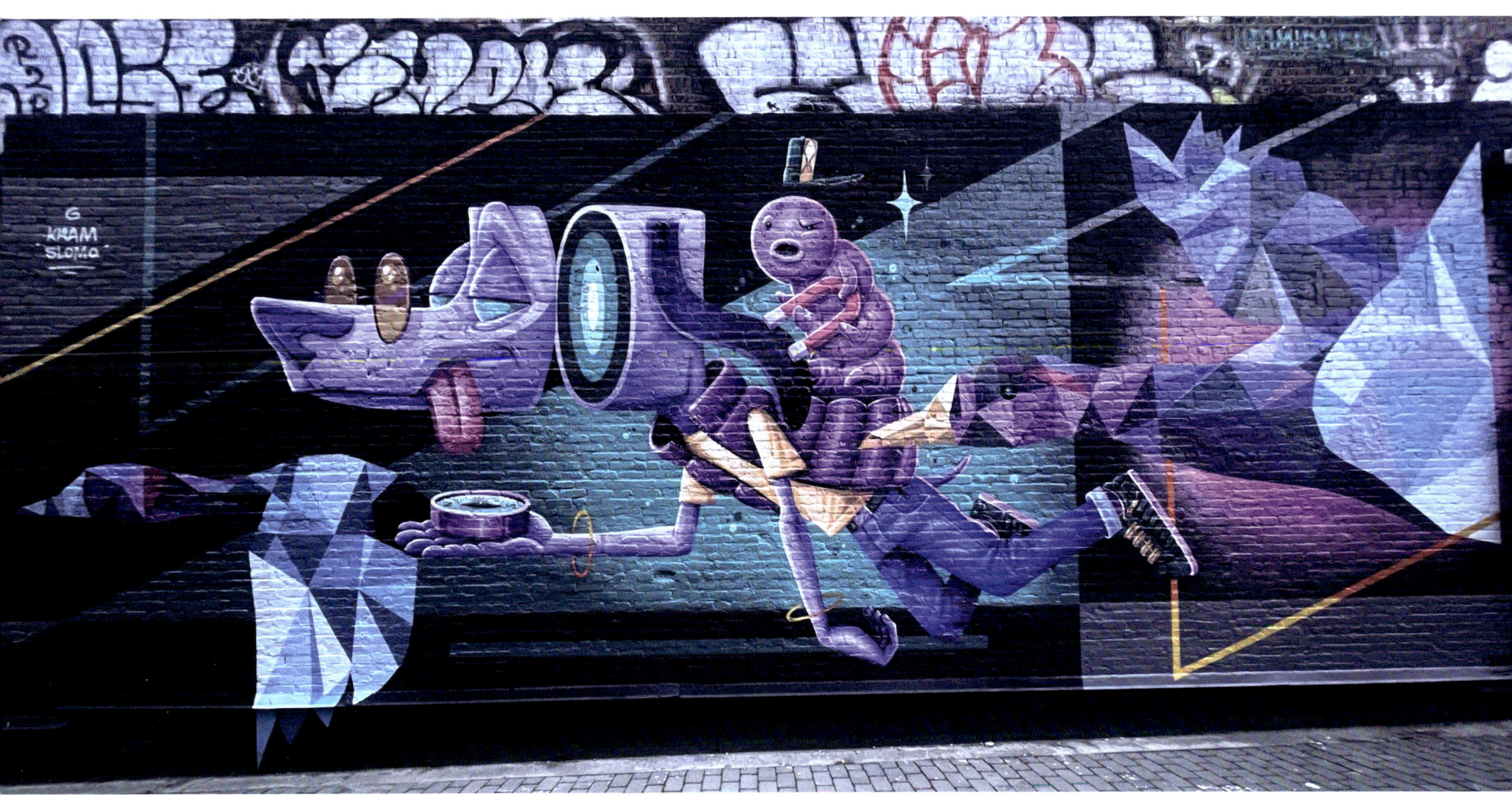

SLOMO, KRAM
FIRST STREET GREEN ART PARK, MANHATTAN, PHOTOGRAPHED IN 2024

EL SOULS
WELLING COURT MURAL PROJECT,
QUEENS, PHOTOGRAPHED IN 2024

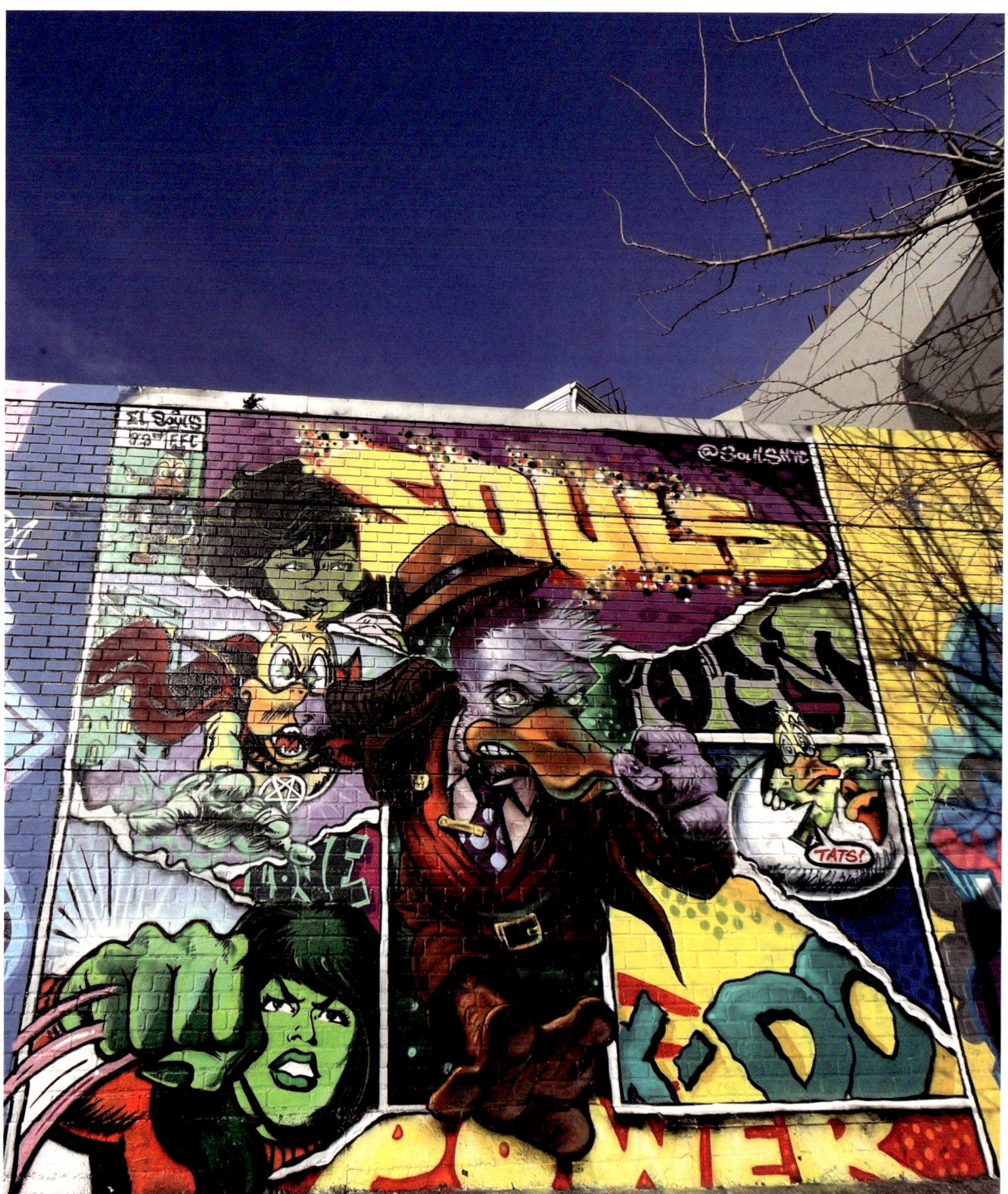

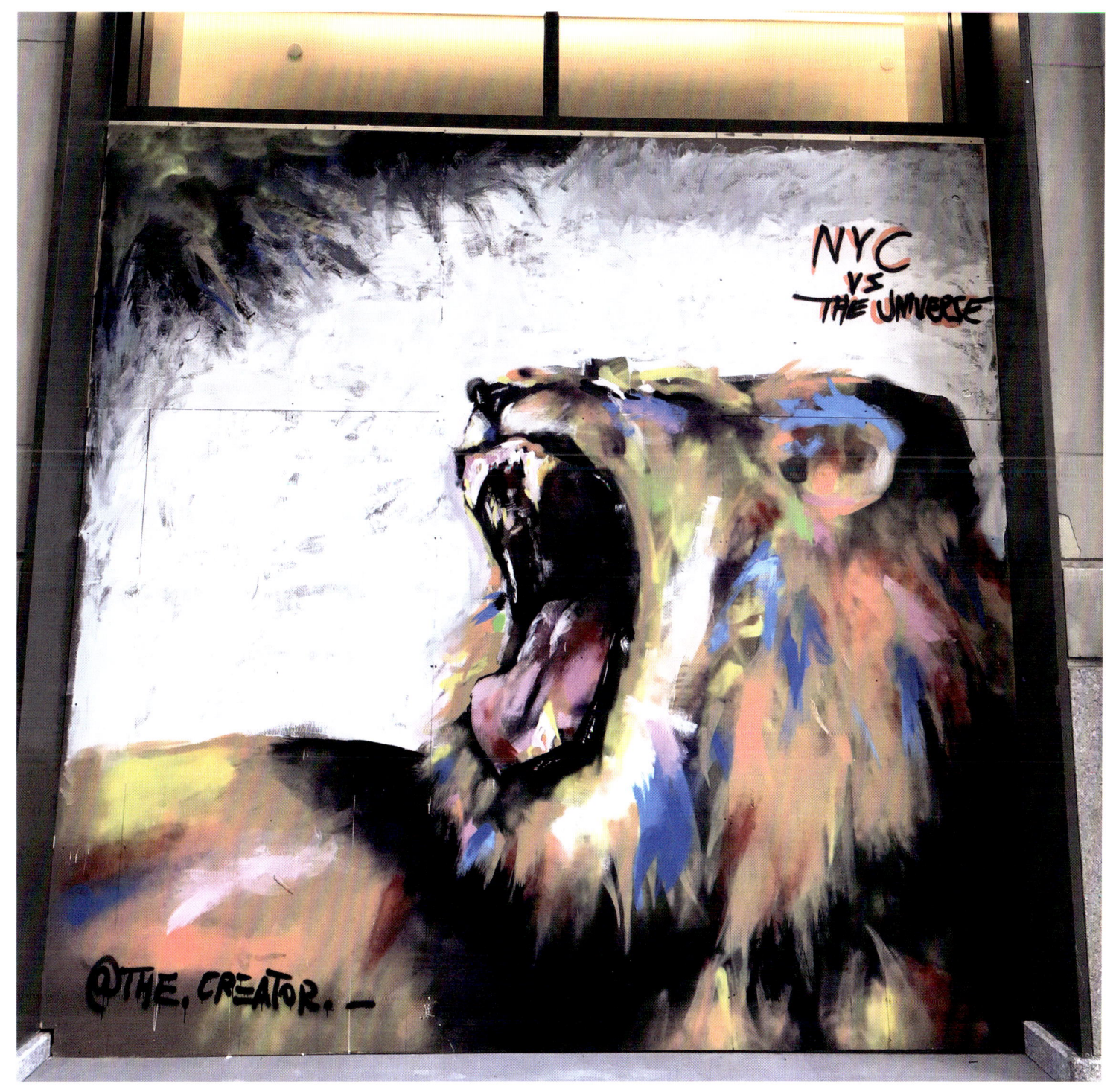

MANUEL "THE CREATOR" ALEJANDRO
Commissioned by New York Public Library
MANHATTAN, PHOTOGRAPHED IN 2020

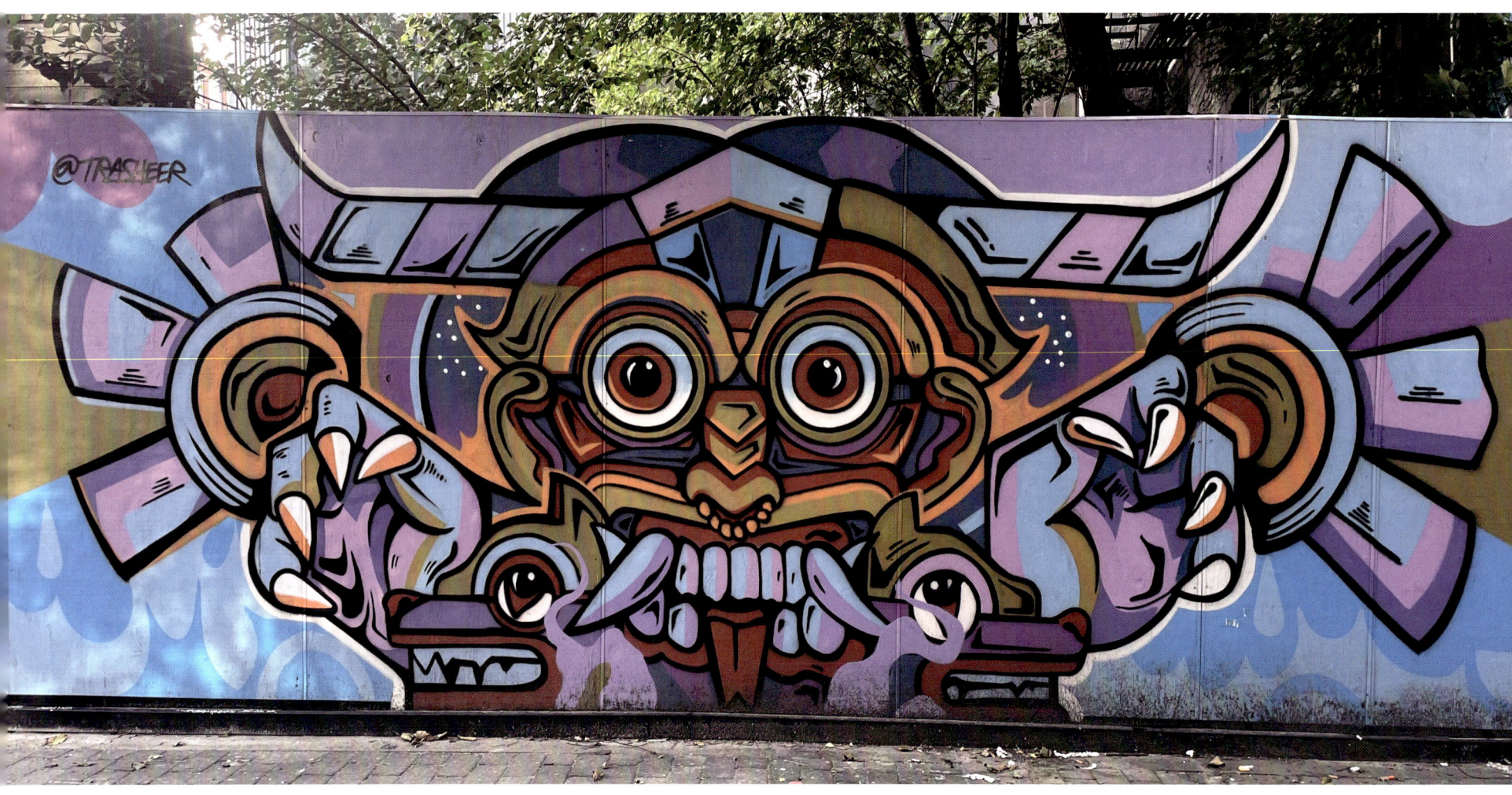

TRASHER
BROOKLYN, PHOTOGRAPHED IN 2023

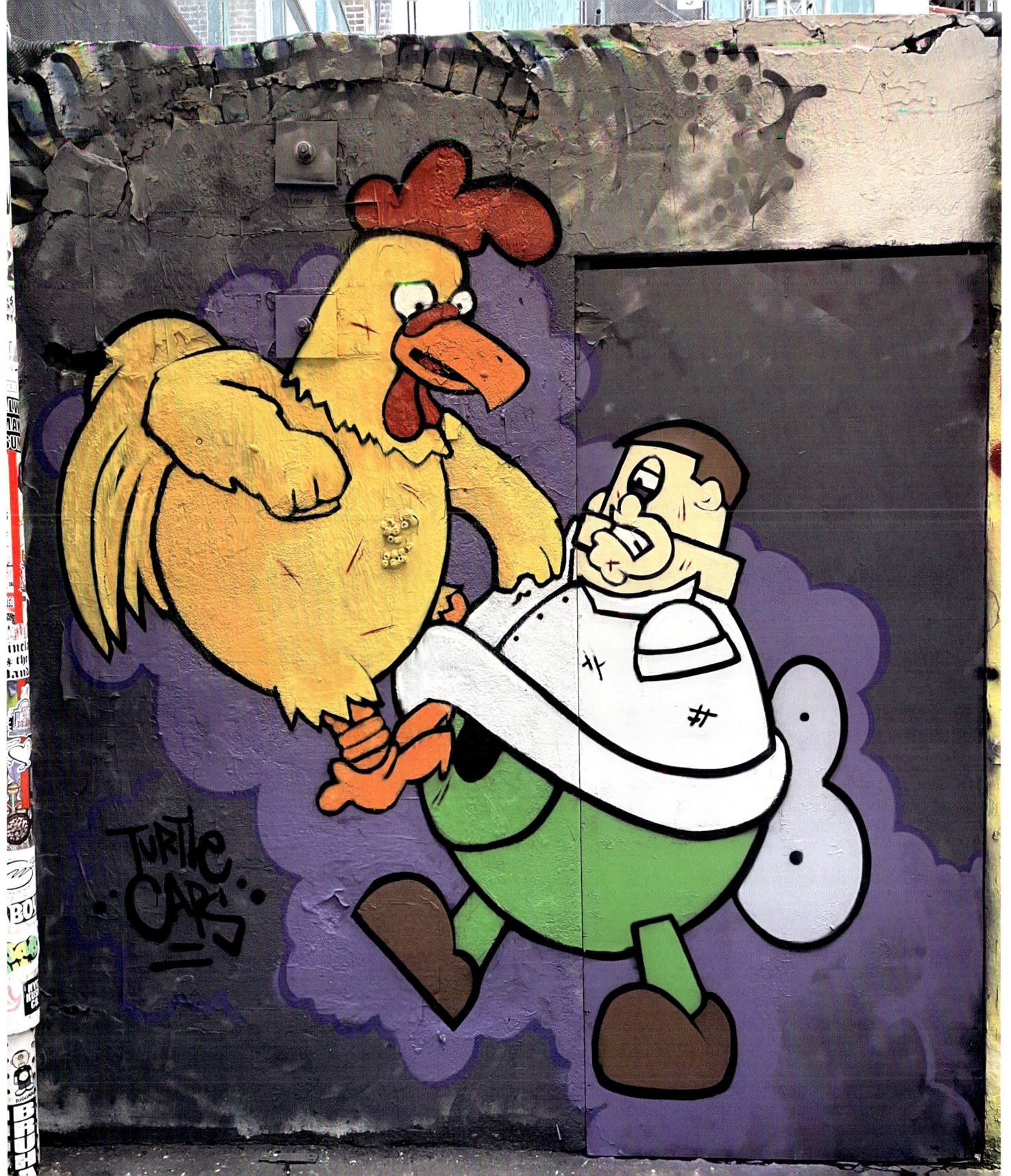

TURTLE CAP
FREEMAN ALLEY,
MANHATTAN,
PHOTOGRAPHED IN
2024

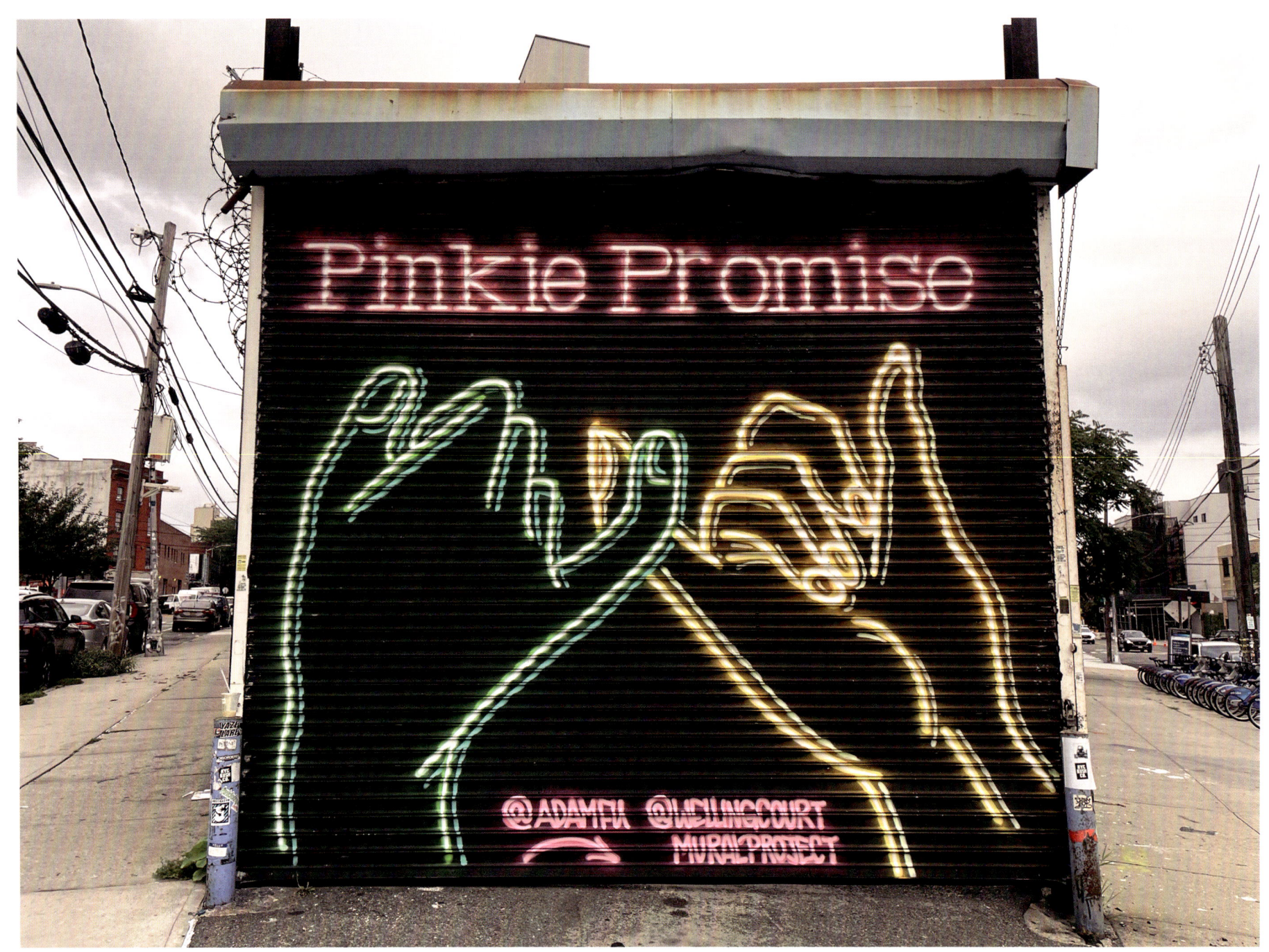

ADAM FU
WELLING COURT MURAL PROJECT, QUEENS, PHOTOGRAPHED IN 2024

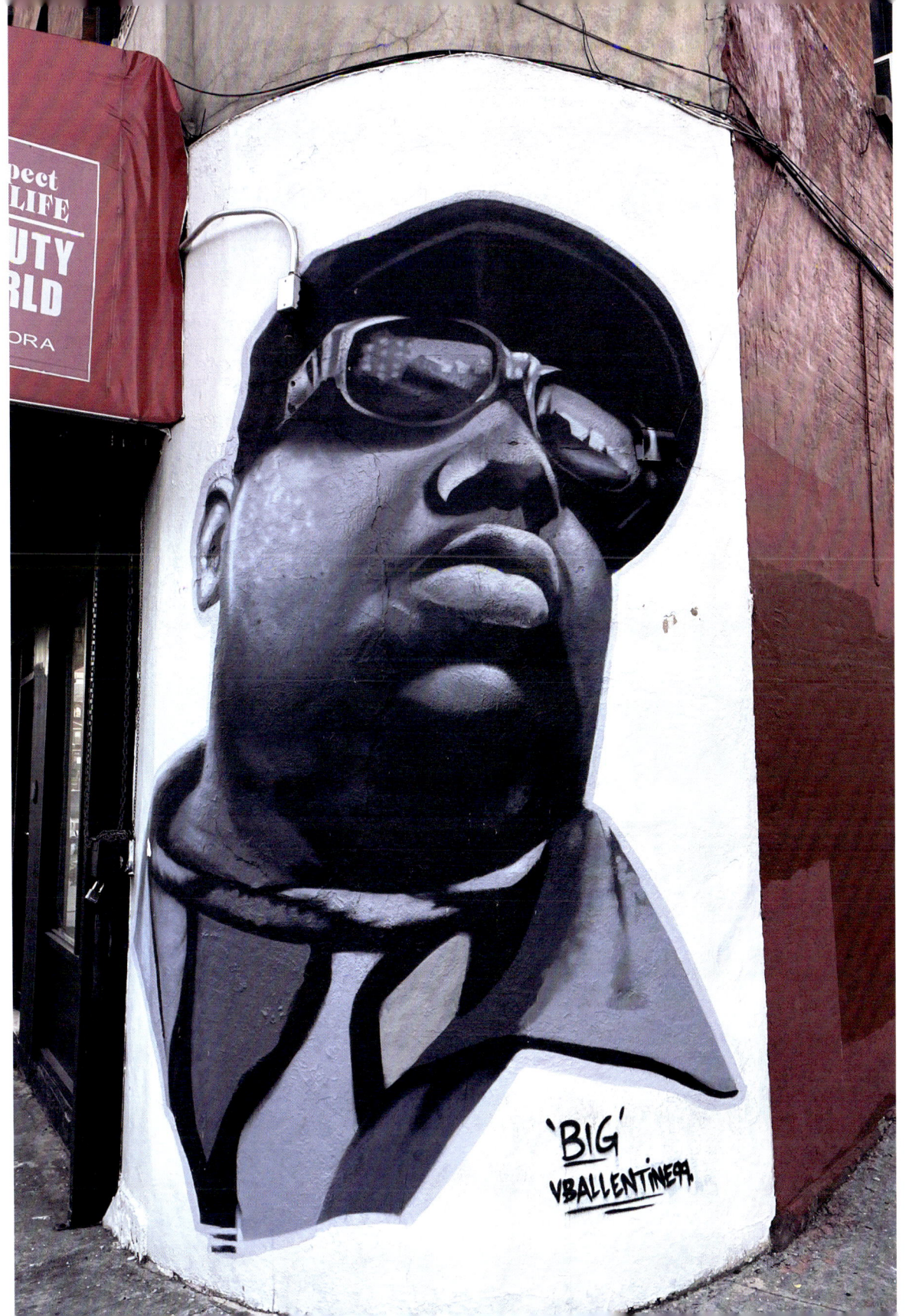

V BALLENTINE
BROOKLYN, PHOTOGRAPHED IN 2024

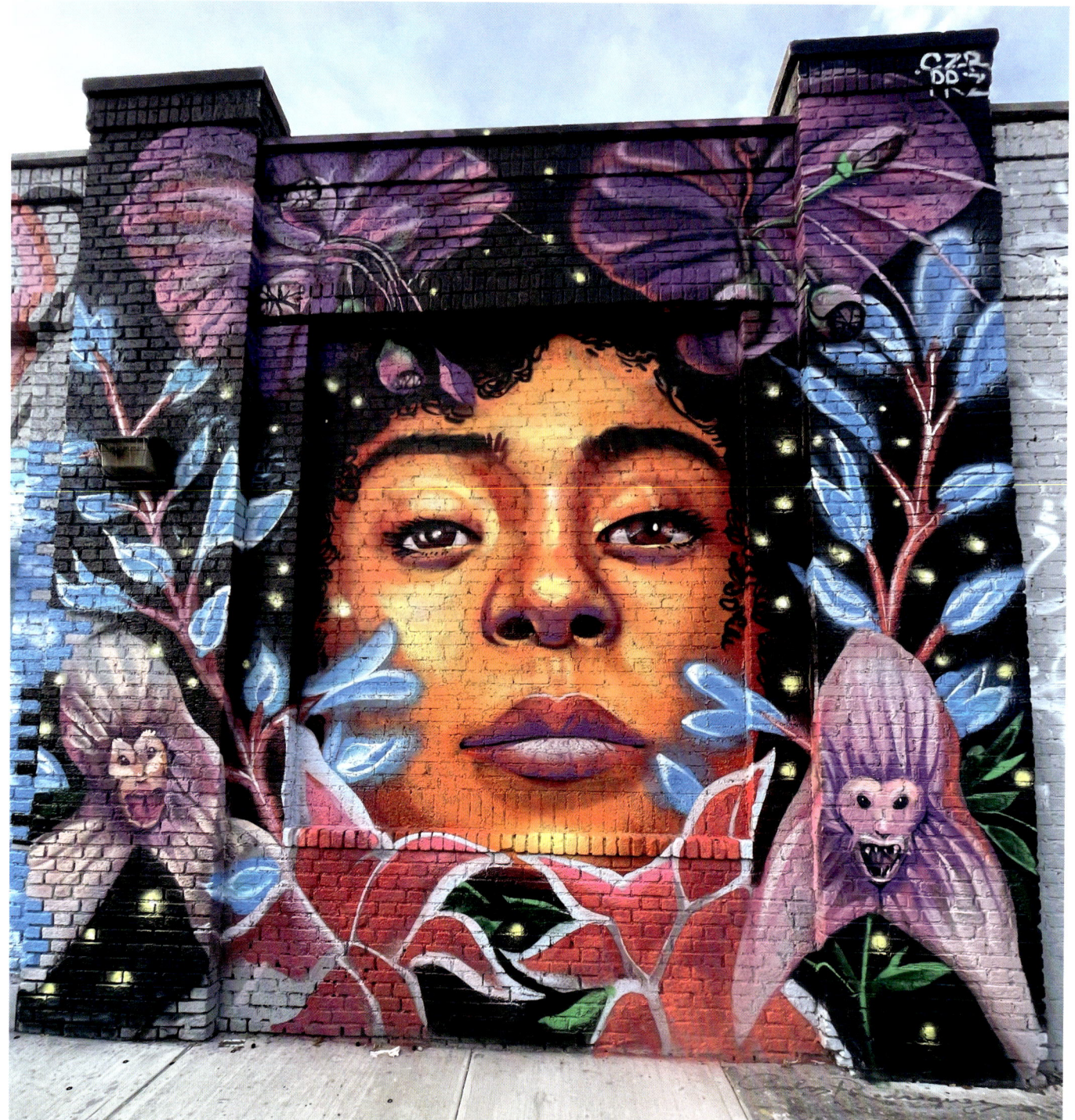

CAESAR PEREZ
BED-STUY WALLS,
PHOTOGRAPHED IN 2023

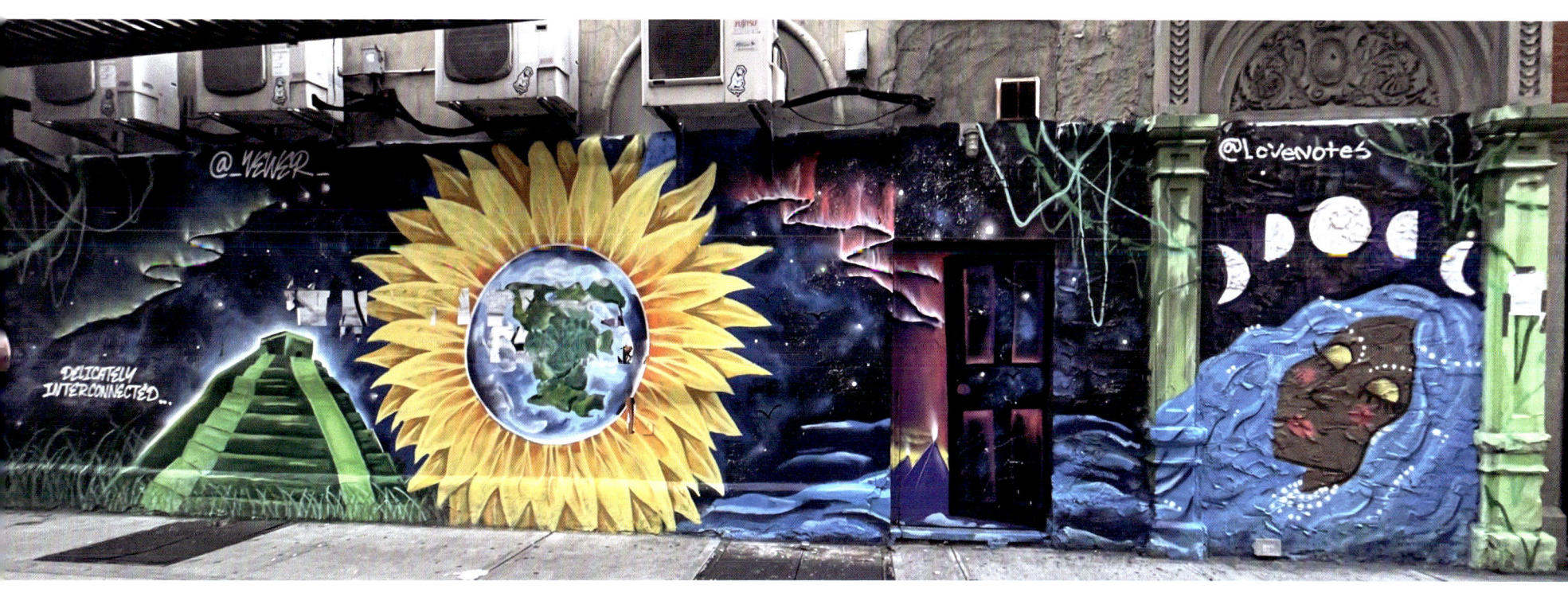

VEWER, LOVE NOTES
MANHATTAN, PHOTOGRAPHED IN 2023

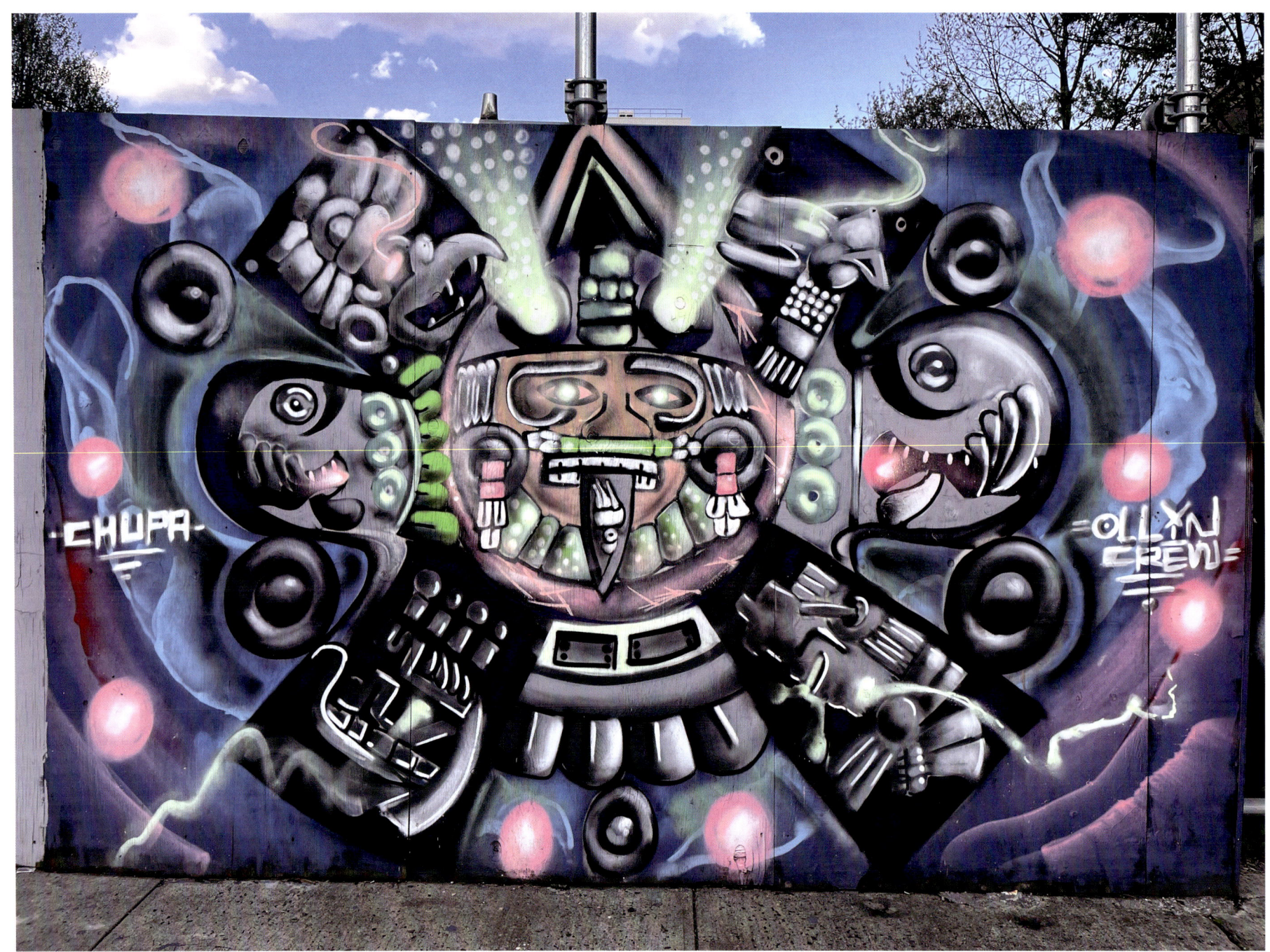

CHUPA OLLIN CREW
BROOKLYN, PHOTOGRAPHED IN 2024

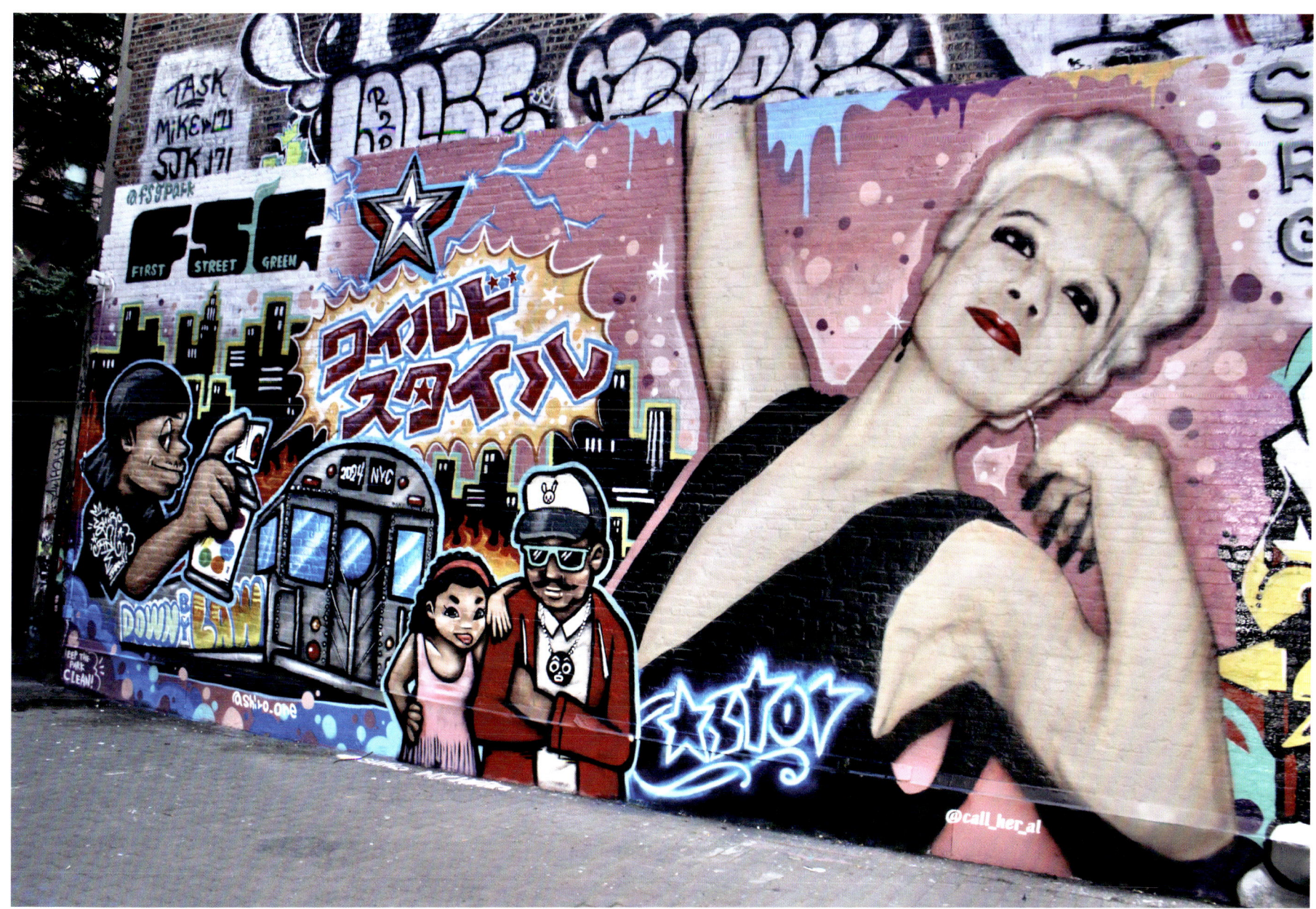

SHIRO ONE, AL RUIZ
Patti Astor tribute.
FIRST STREET GREEN ART PARK, PHOTOGRAPHED IN 2024

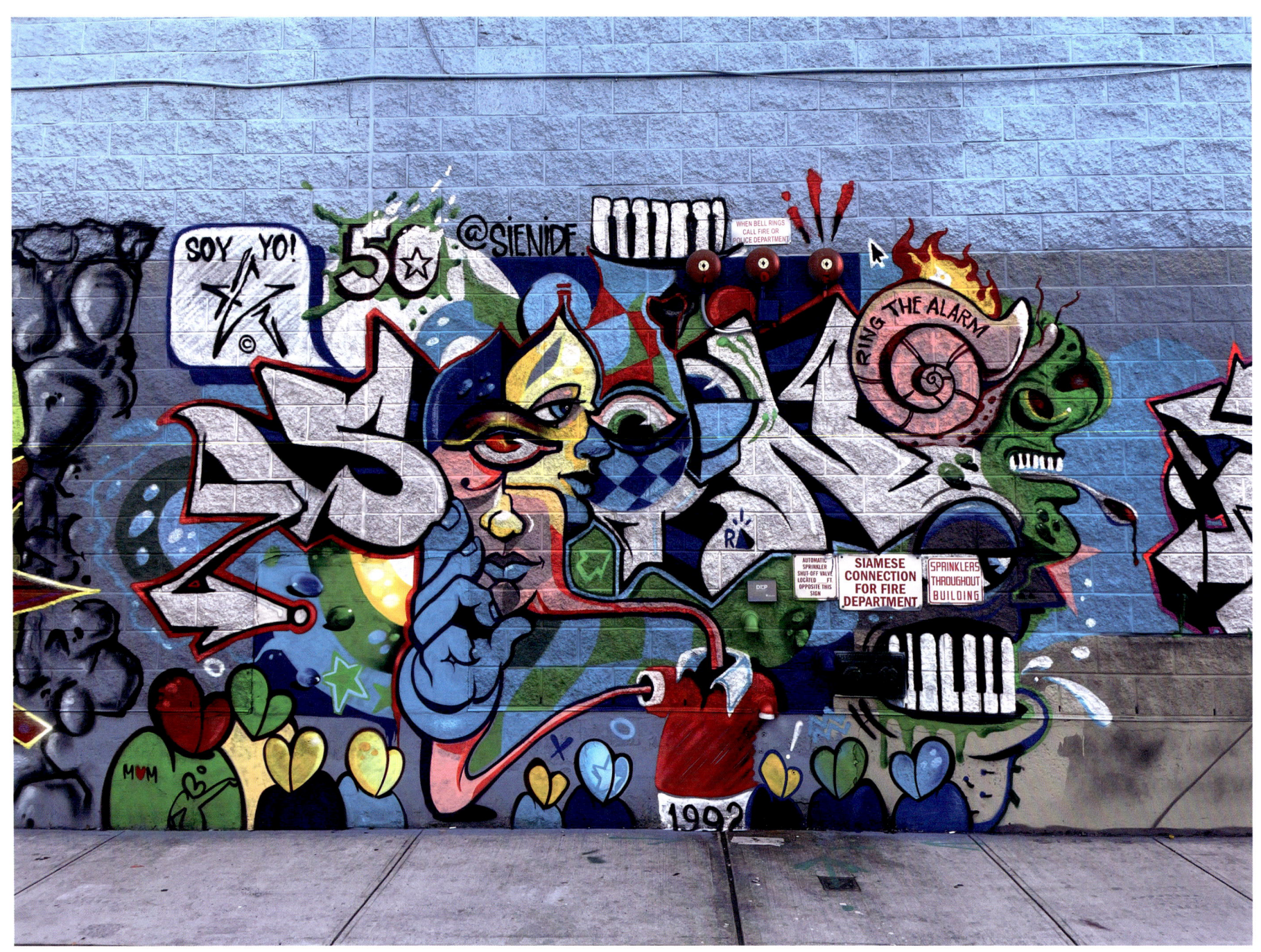

SIENIDE
BOONE AVENUE WALLS, THE BRONX, PHOTOGRAPHED IN 2023

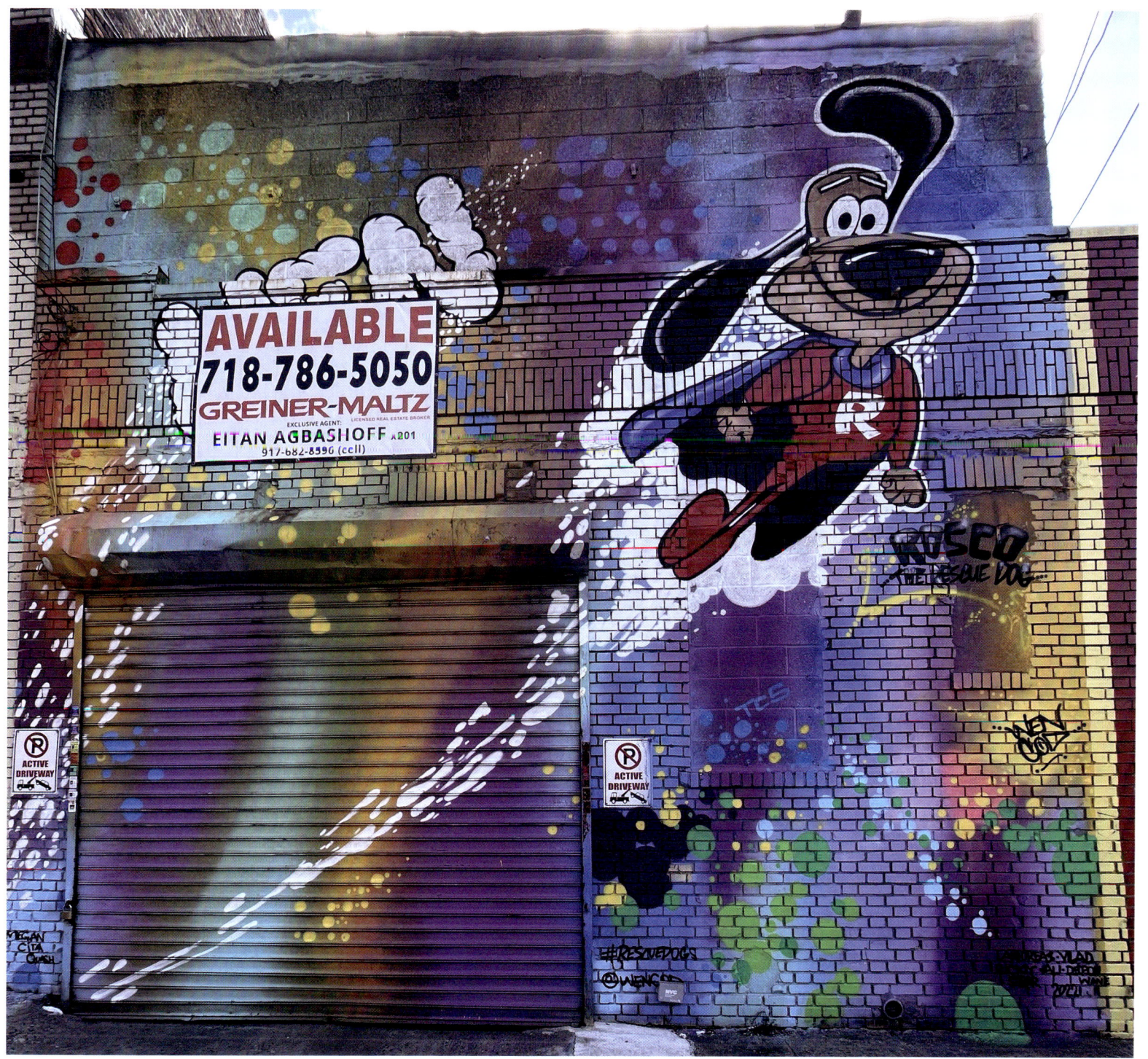

WEN COD

Wen Cod Is the founder of Boone Avenue Walls Foundation. This mural is a memorial to his dog.
THE BRONX, PHOTOGRAPHED IN 2024

WILL POWER, AL DIAZ
Will Power is a popular New York City street artist and renowned for hip-hop artist murals. Al Diaz is a world-famous street artist who is best known for his *SAMO* collaboration with Jean-Michel Basquiat.
BED-STUY WALLS, BROOKLYN, PHOTOGRAPHED IN 2023

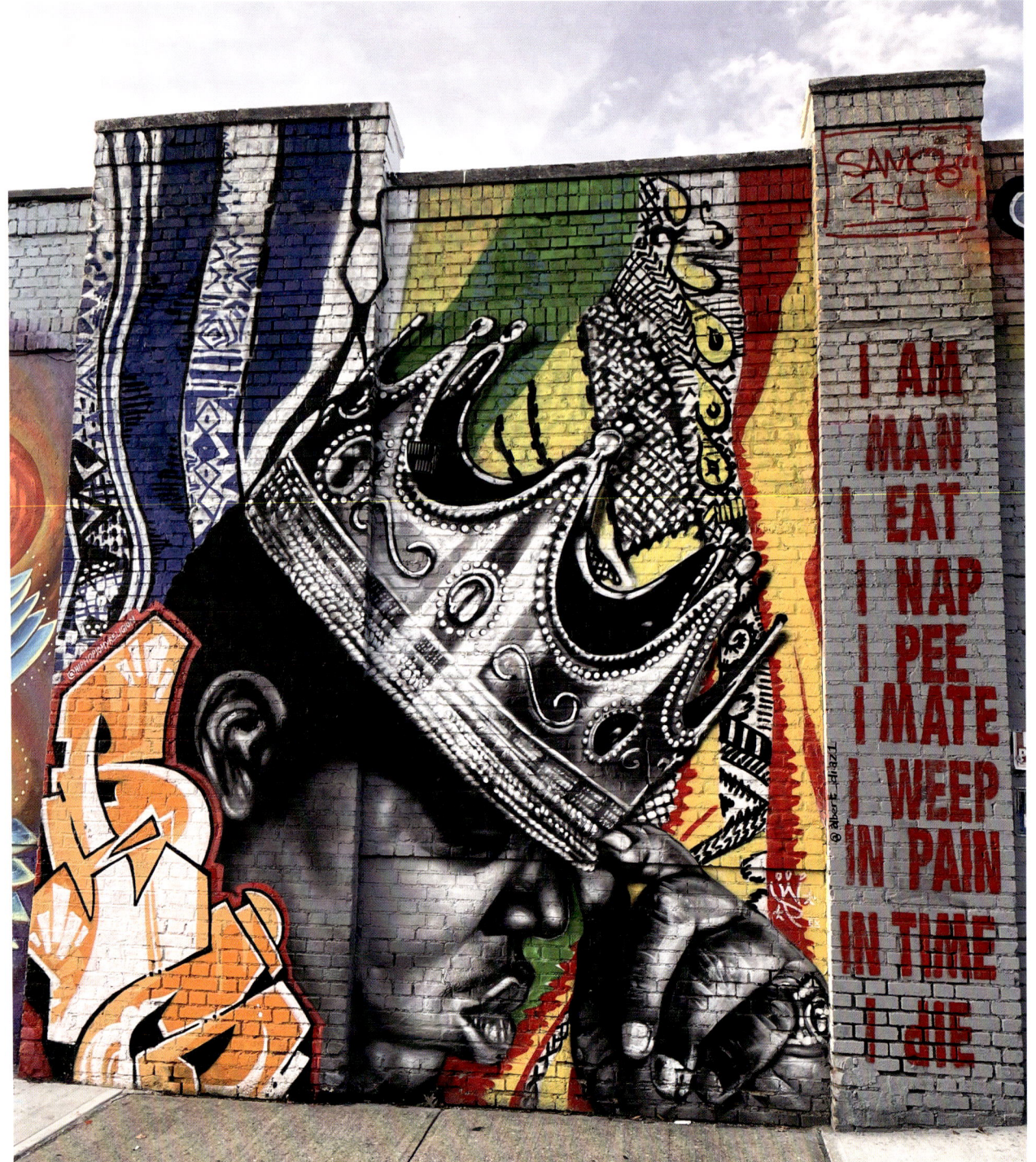

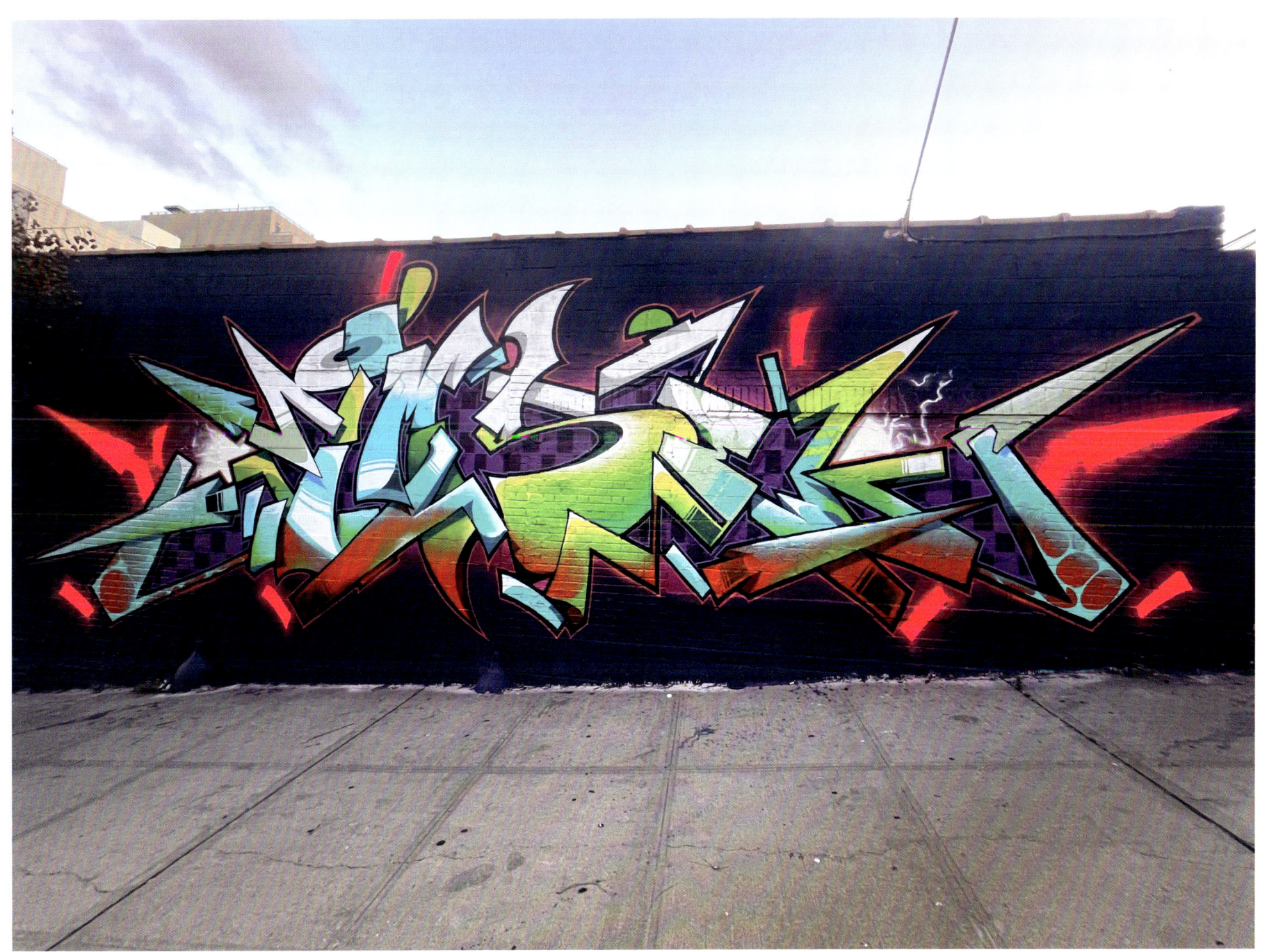

IMSE 704
BOONE AVENUE WALLS, THE BRONX, PHOTOGRAPHED IN 2023

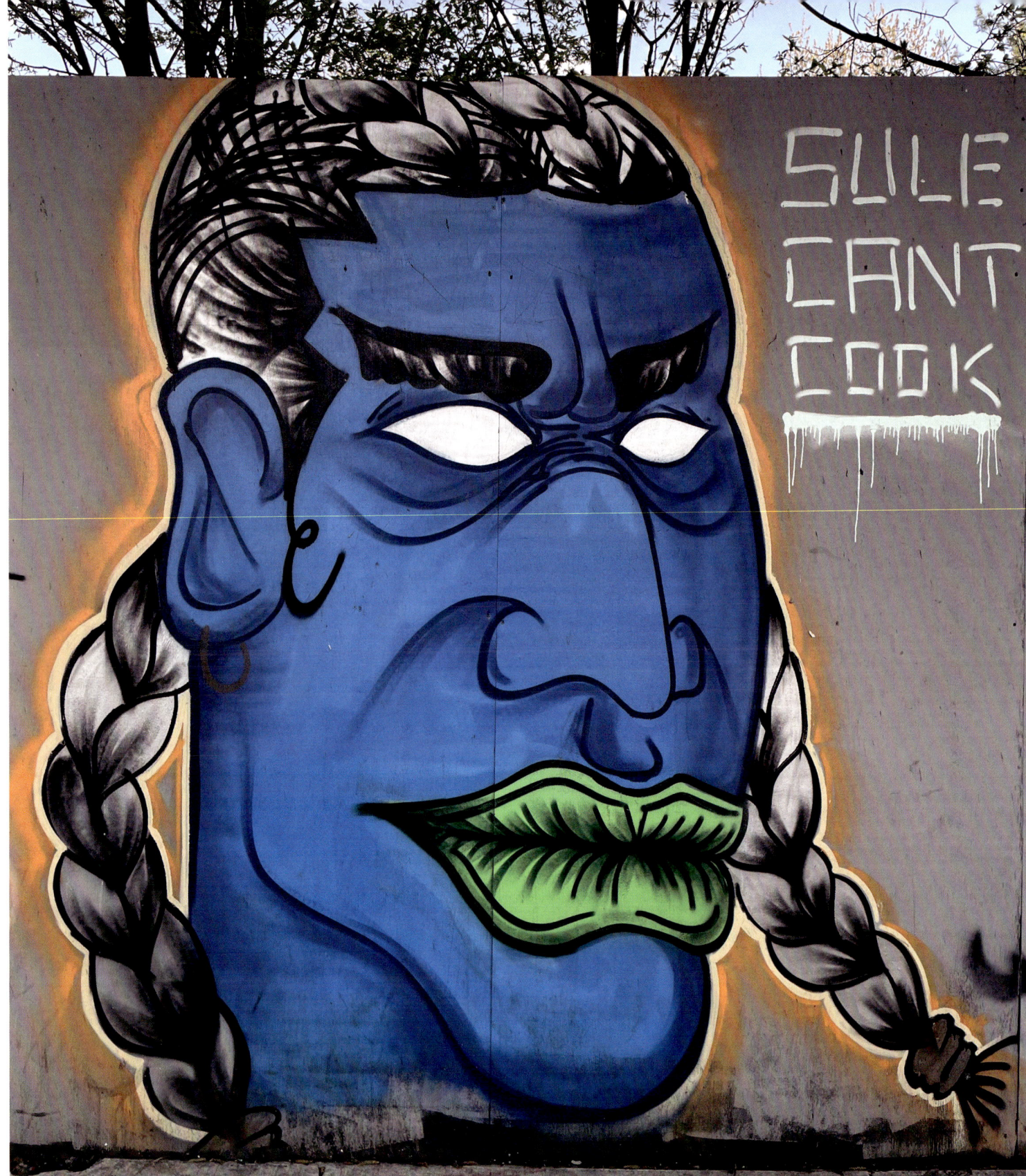

SULE
BROOKLYN,
PHOTOGRAPHED IN
2024

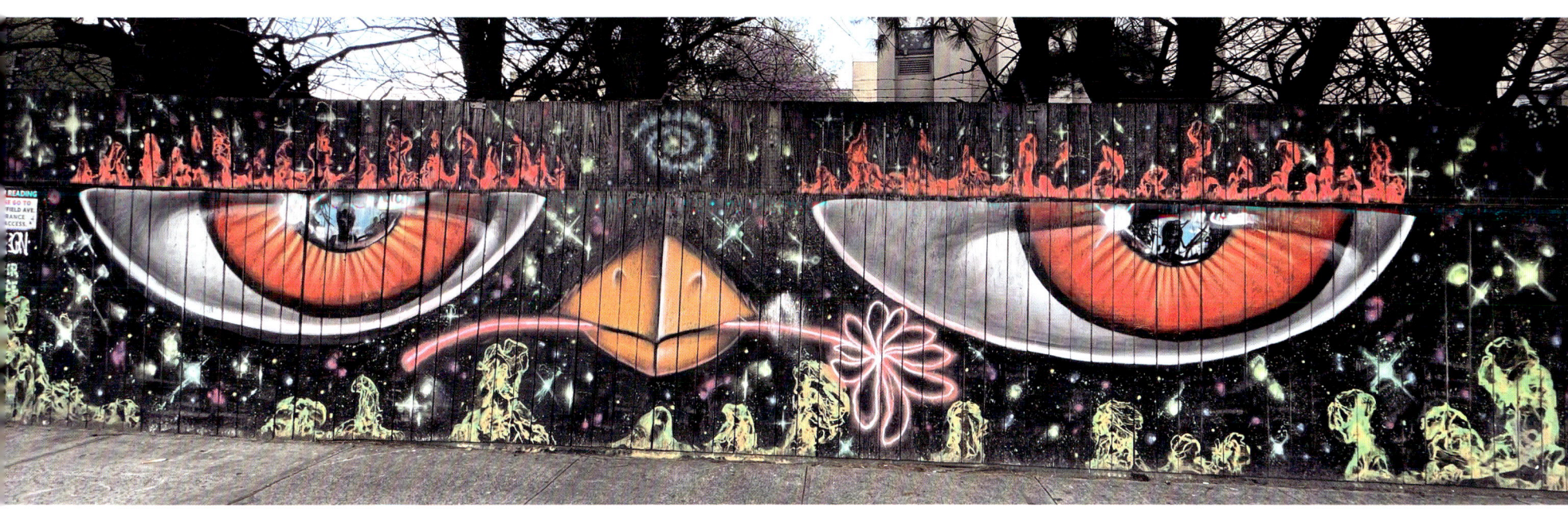

OUTERSOURCE, MUEBON
BROOKLYN, PHOTOGRAPHED IN 2024

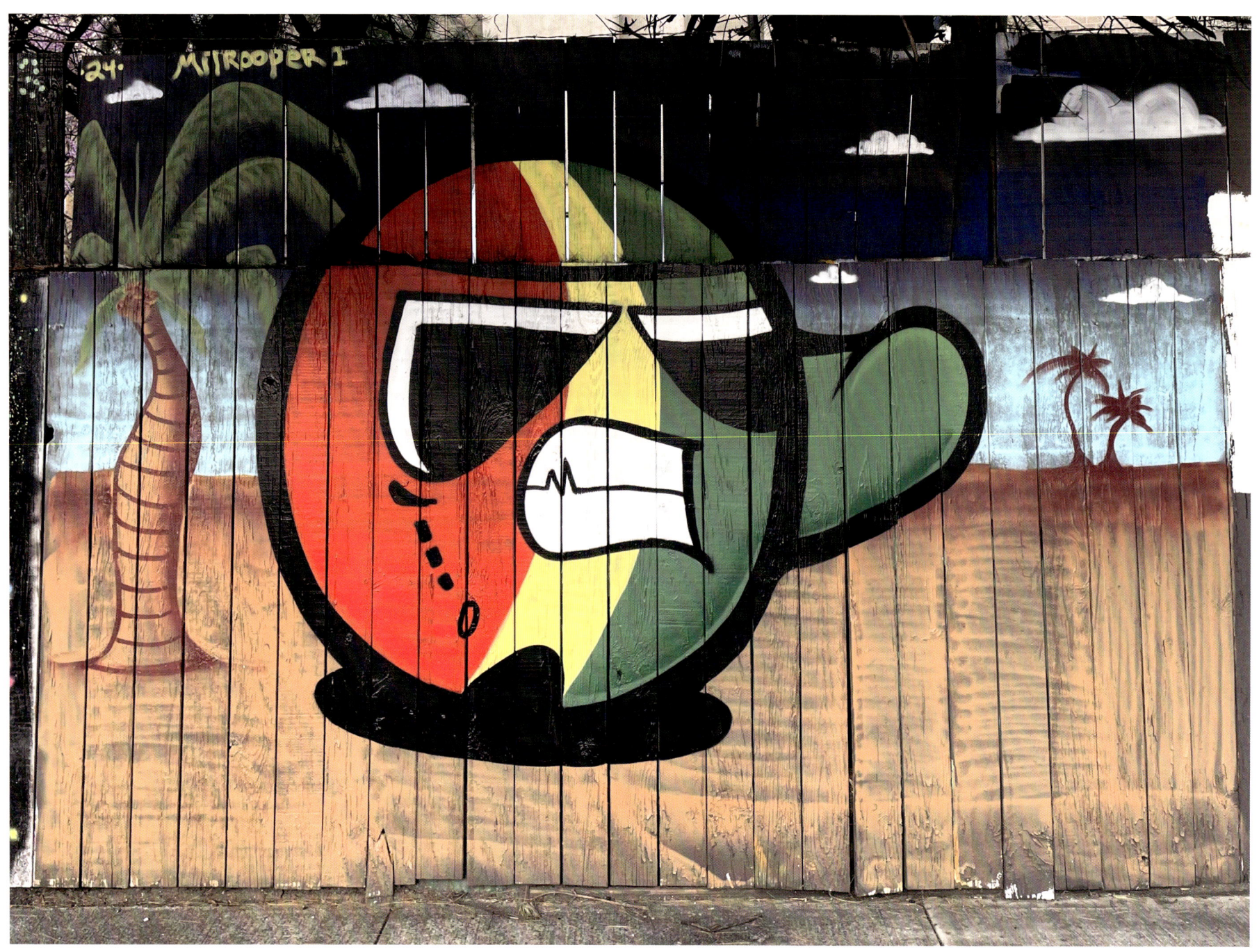

MITROOPER 1
BROOKLYN, PHOTOGRAPHED IN 2024

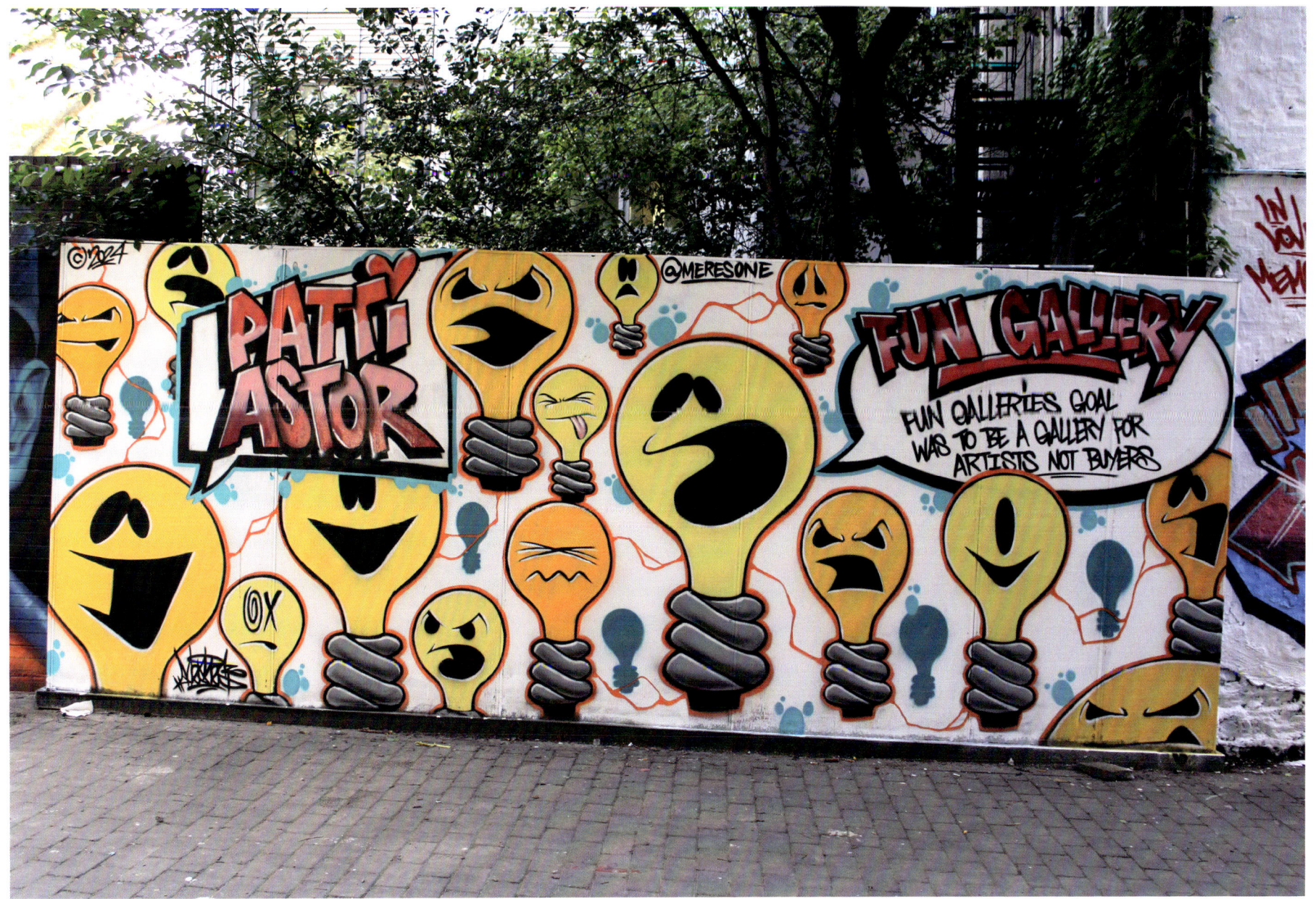

MERES ONE
Patti Astor tribute.
FIRST STREET GREEN ART PARK, MANHATTAN, PHOTOGRAPHED IN 2024

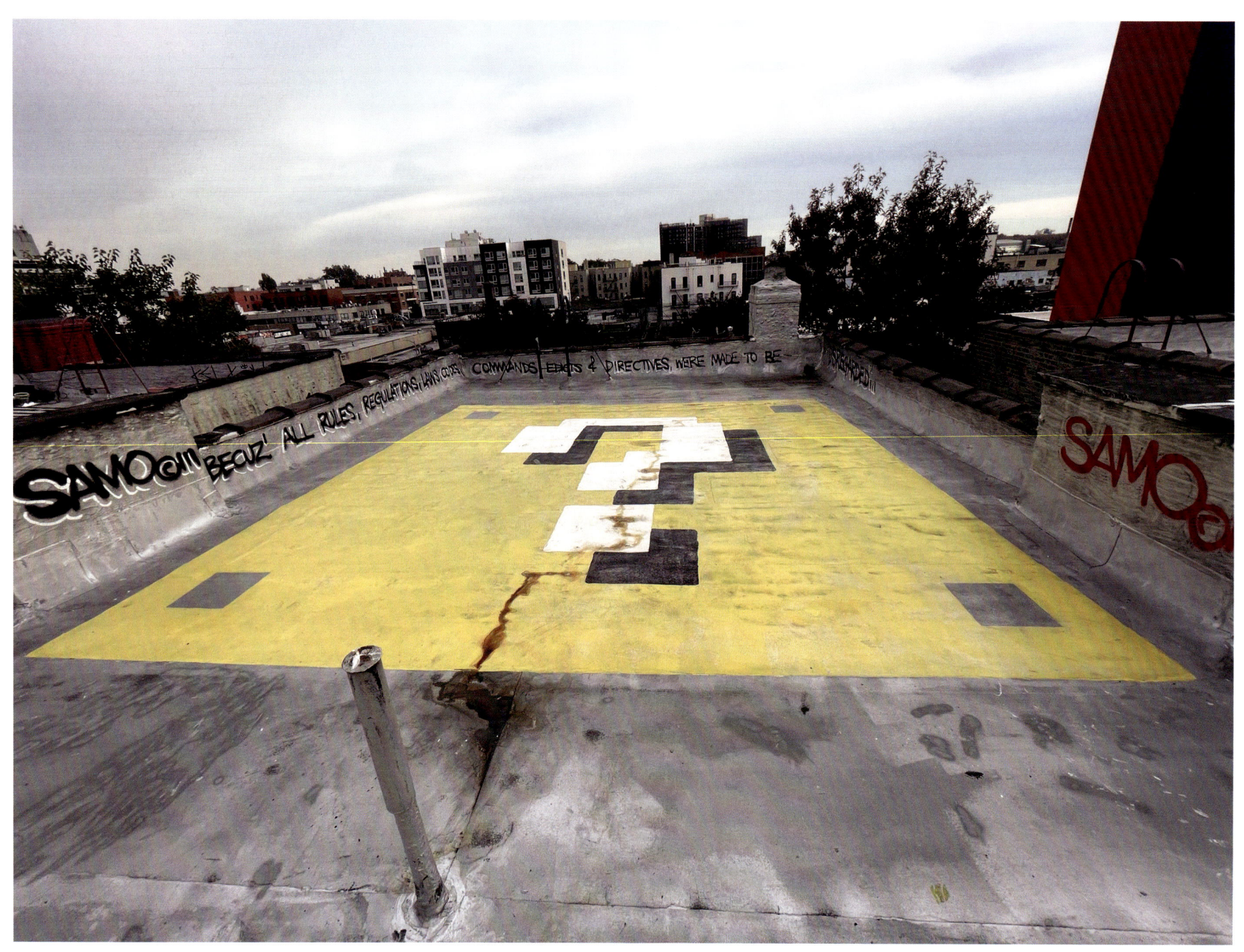

QUESTION MARKS, AL DIAZ
ROOFTOP GRAFFITITERIA, QUEENS, PHOTOGRAPHED IN 2023

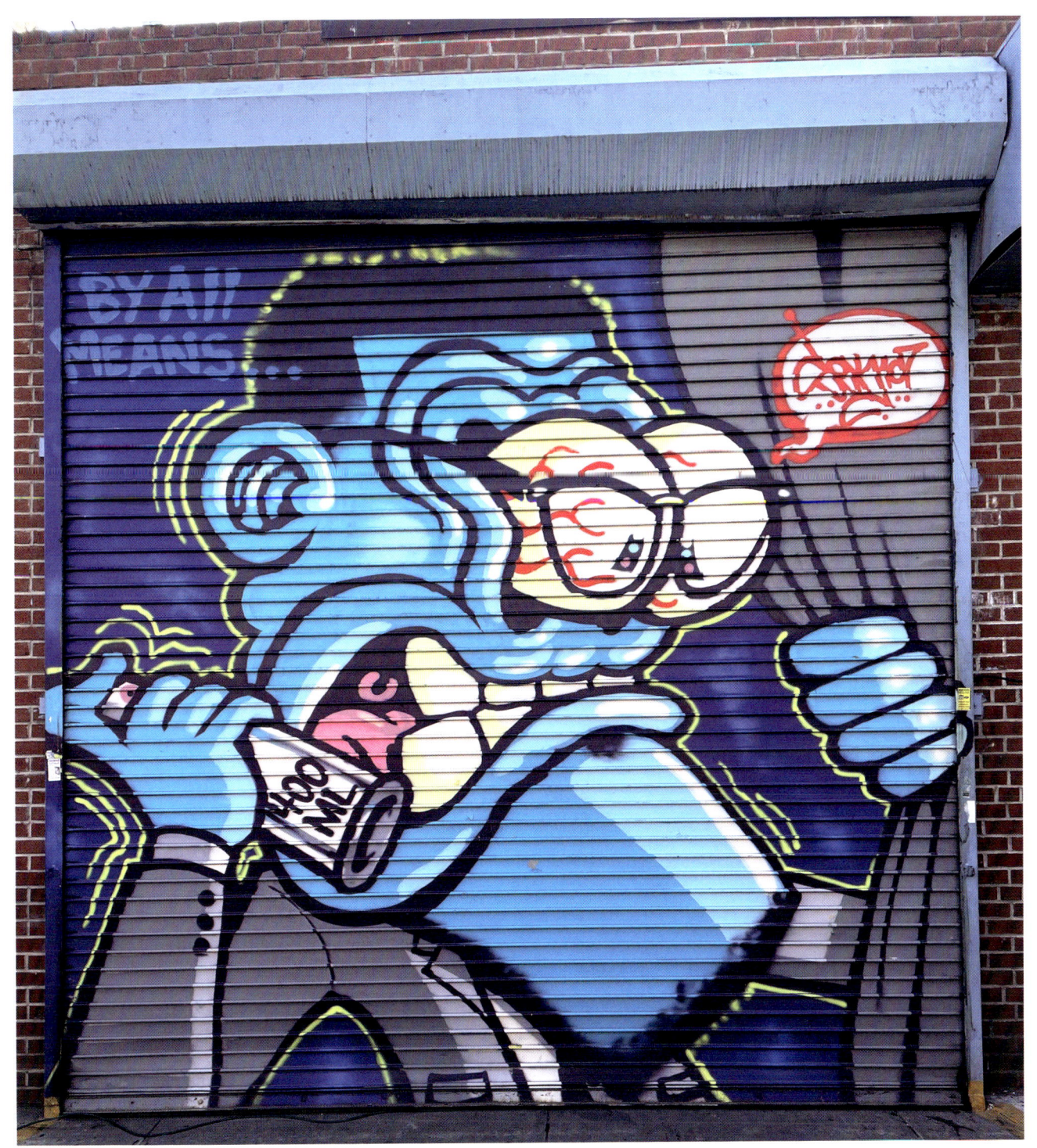

SEK FINK
WELLING COURT MURAL PROJECT,
QUEENS, PHOTOGRAPHED IN 2024

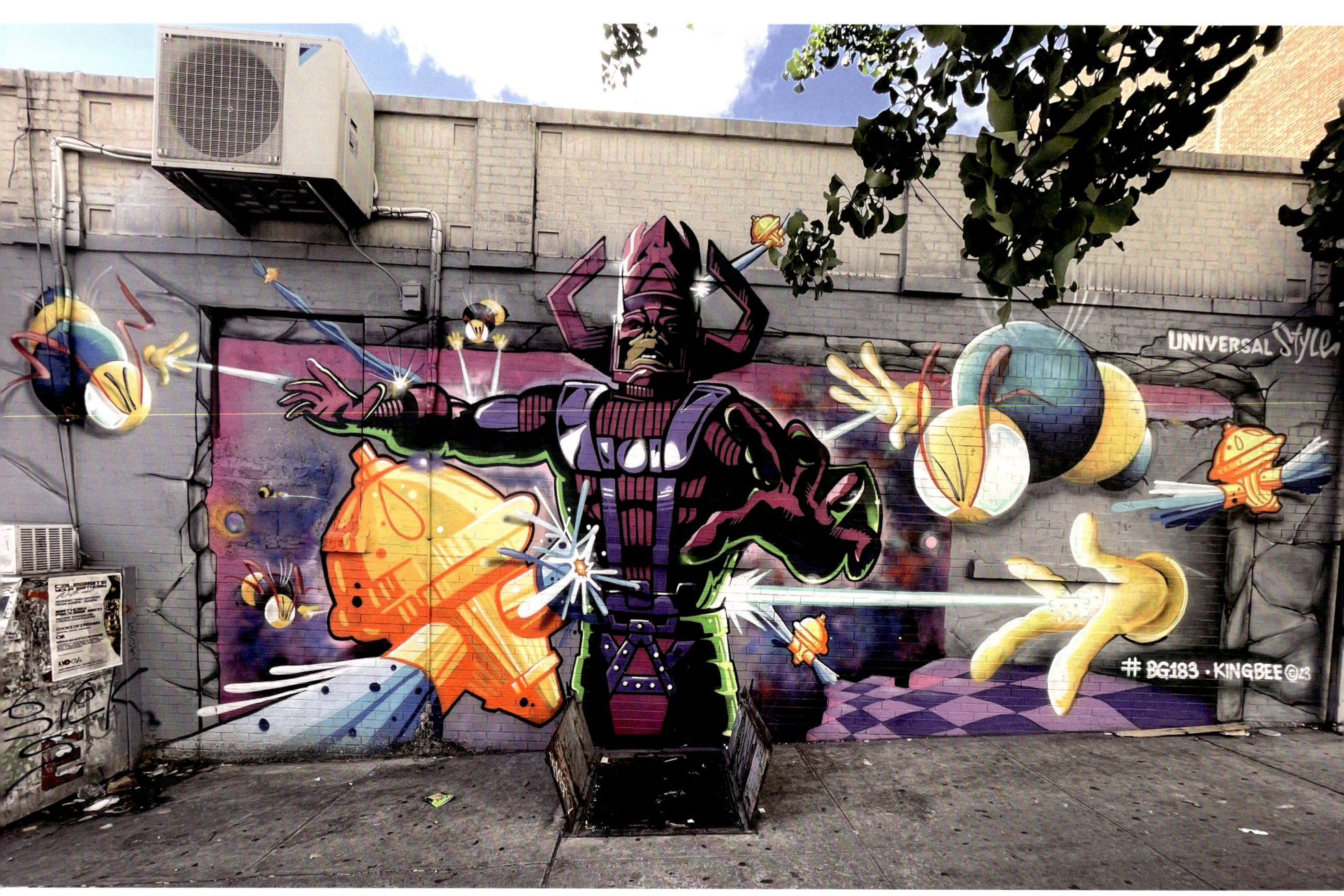

KING BEE, BG 183
THE BRONX, PHOTOGRAPHED IN 2024

MURALS

Some of the best aerosol artists in the world have painted murals in New York City. I found and photographed many of these murals by happenstance as I commuted around the city on the subway and walking around. Others I photographed as part of art festivals at Welling Court Mural Project, Bed-Stuy Walls, Boone Avenue Walls, Graffiti Hall of Fame, or the Bushwick Collective. In this chapter, you will see photos of murals by Kobra, Alec Monopoly, Danielle Mastrion, Tats Cru, and many other well-known aerosol artists. Murals are also ephemeral in street art culture and on the business side of doing murals for commercial brands or local businesses. Murals can last longer than one year before they are painted over, to make way for a new mural. The exterior walls of the Oculus at the World Trade Center have very large murals on them that are usually up longer than a year.

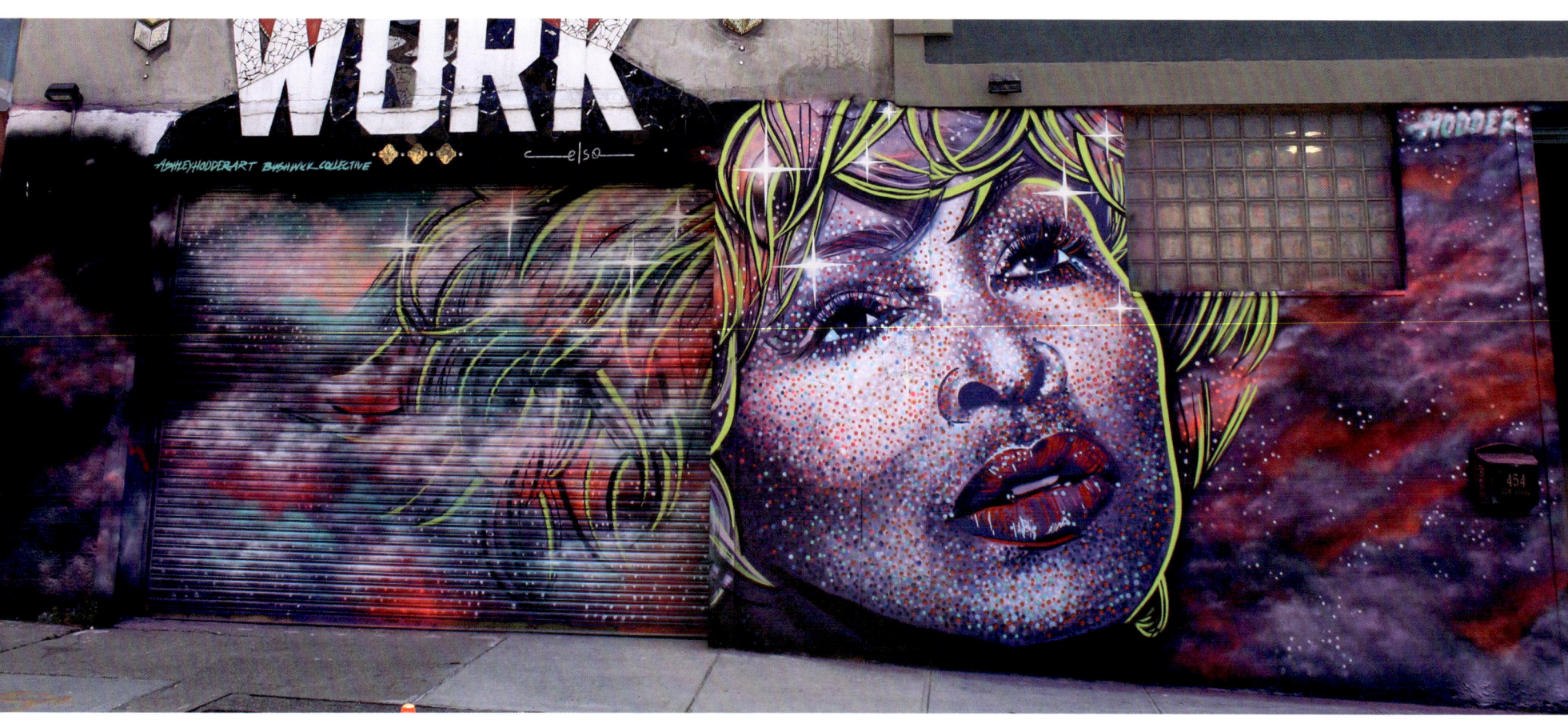

ASHLEY HODDER

Ashley Hodder is a popular aerosol artist based in Pittsburgh, Pennsylvania.
BUSHWICK COLLECTIVE, BROOKLYN, PHOTOGRAPHED IN 2023

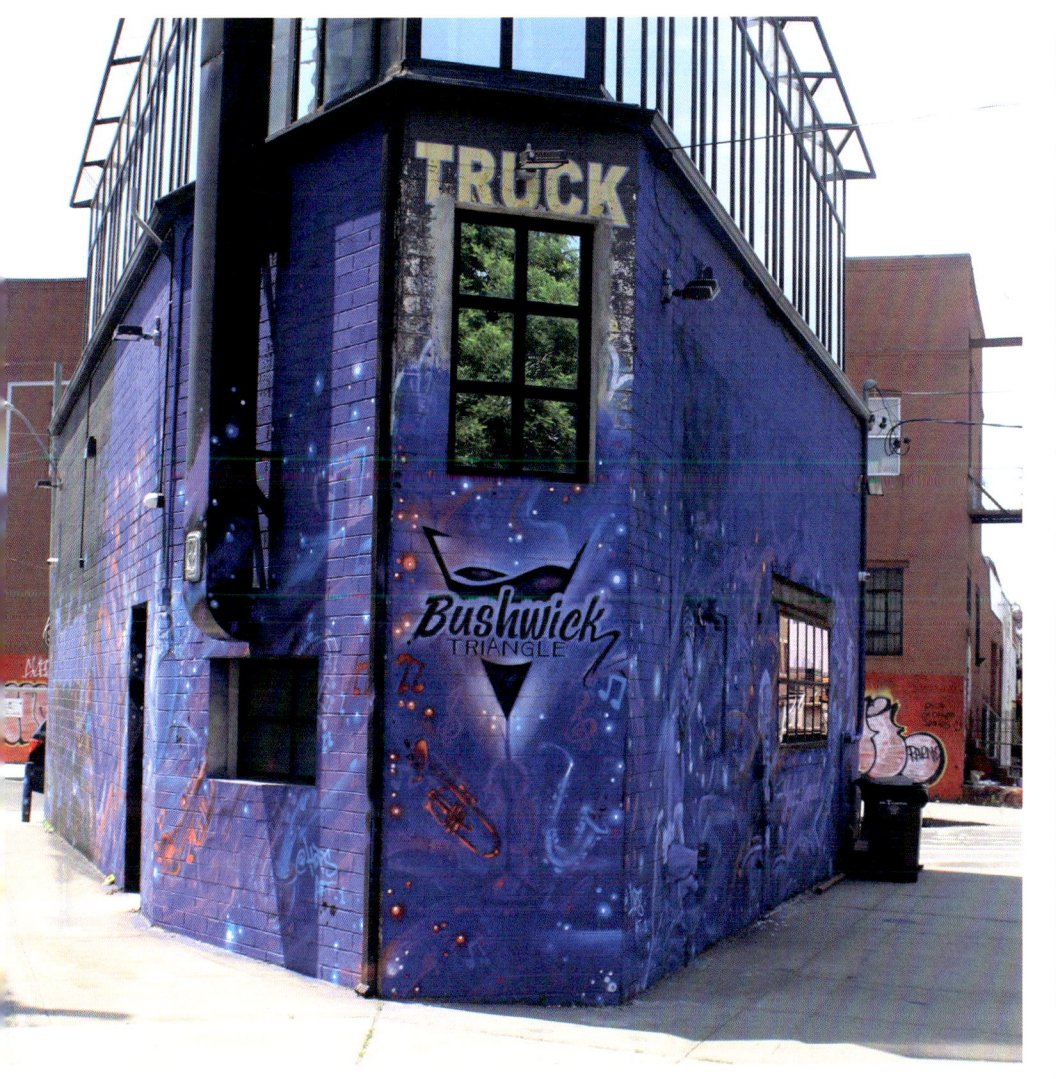

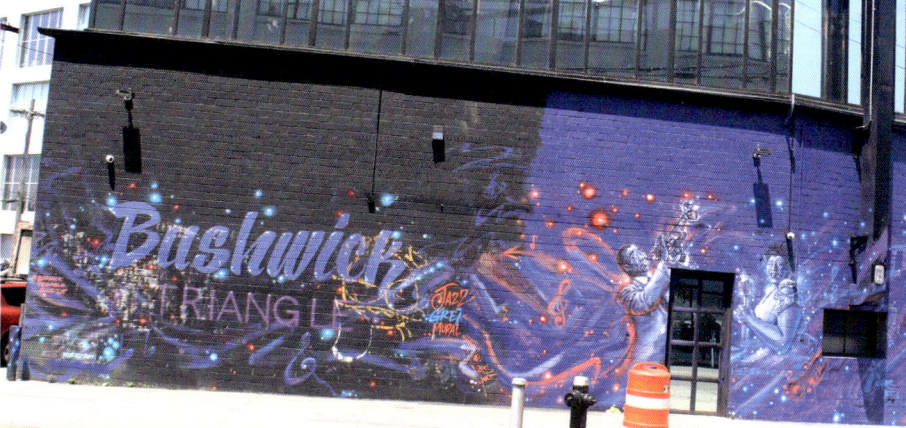

HOPS ART
BROOKLYN, PHOTOGRAPHED IN 2023.

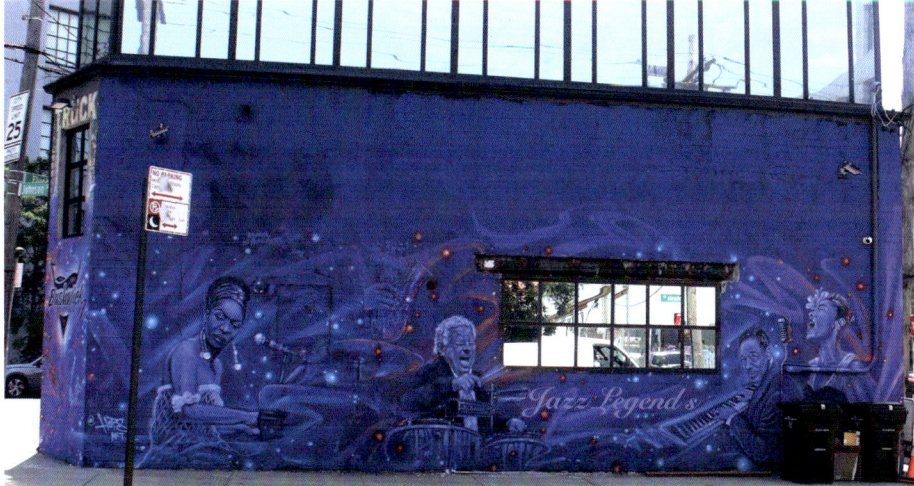

HOPS ART
Hops Art is a muralist, illustrator, and graffiti artist.
BROOKLYN, PHOTOGRAPHED IN 2023

HOPS ART
BROOKLYN, PHOTOGRAPHED IN 2023.

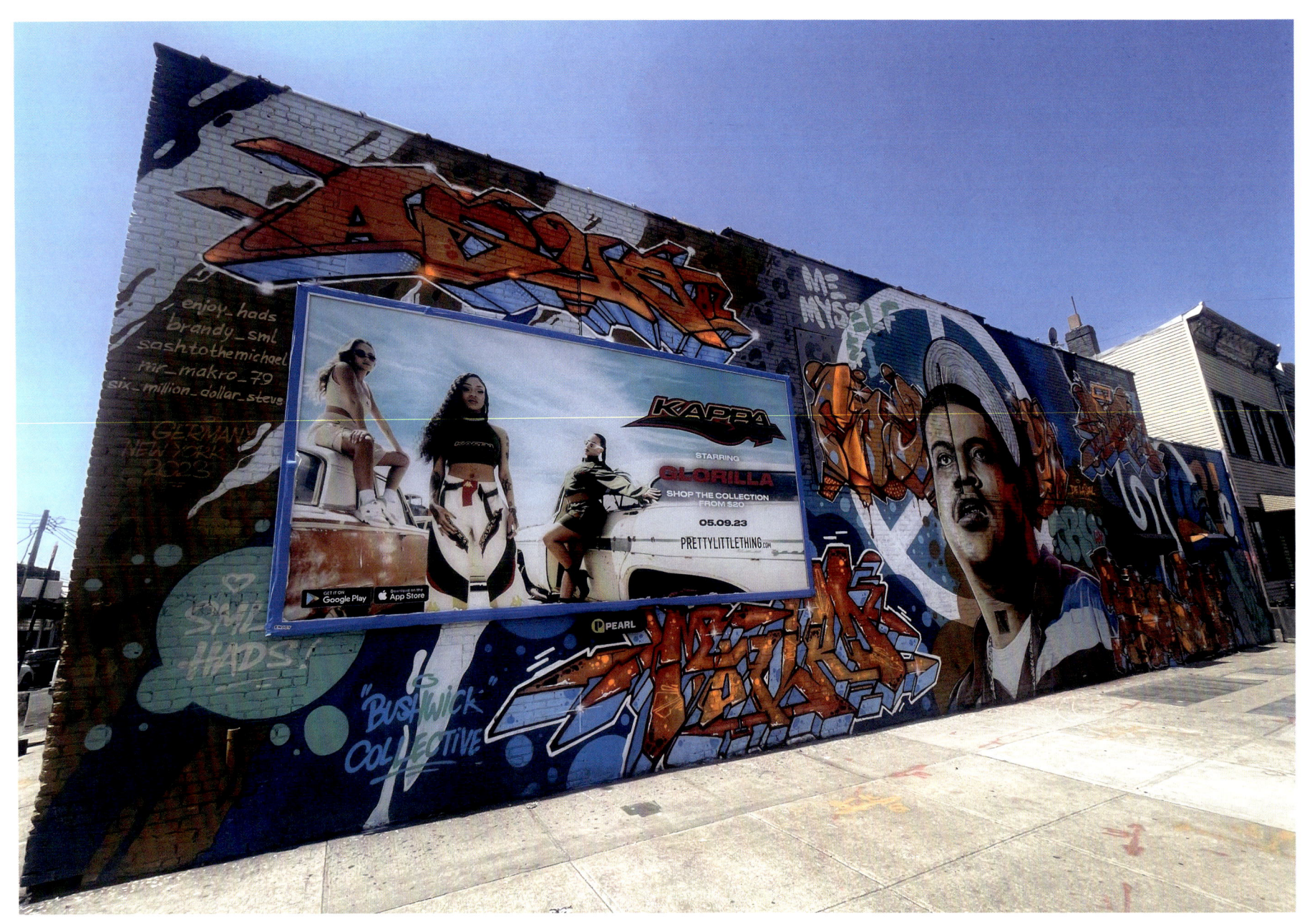

KRO 79, SURE 78, BRAND SML, SIX MILLION DOLLAR STEVE
BUSHWICK COLLECTIVE, BROOKLYN, PHOTOGRAPHED IN 2023

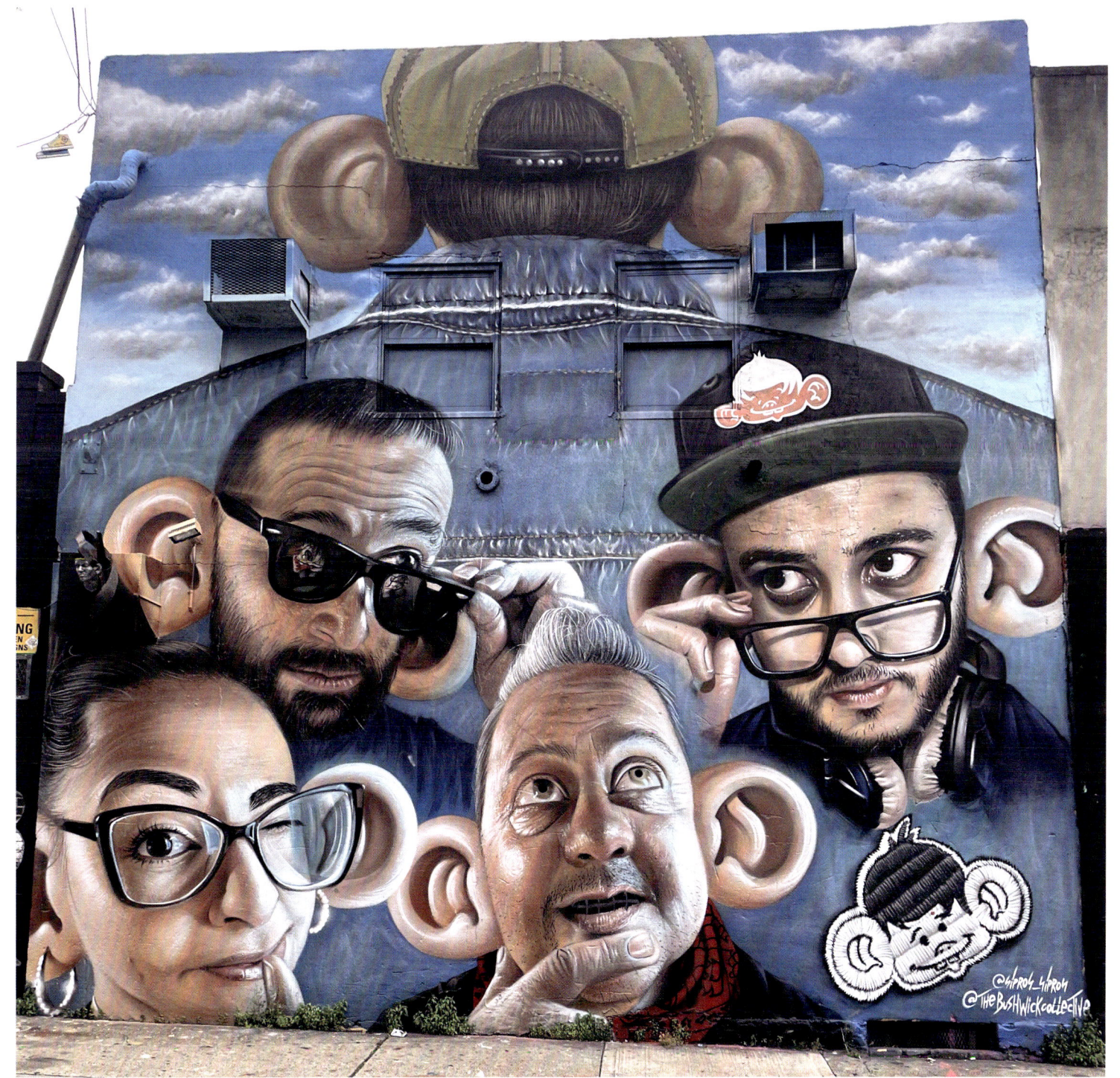

SIPROS

Sipros is an internationally recognized muralist and street artist. BUSHWICK COLLECTIVE, PHOTOGRAPHED IN 2024

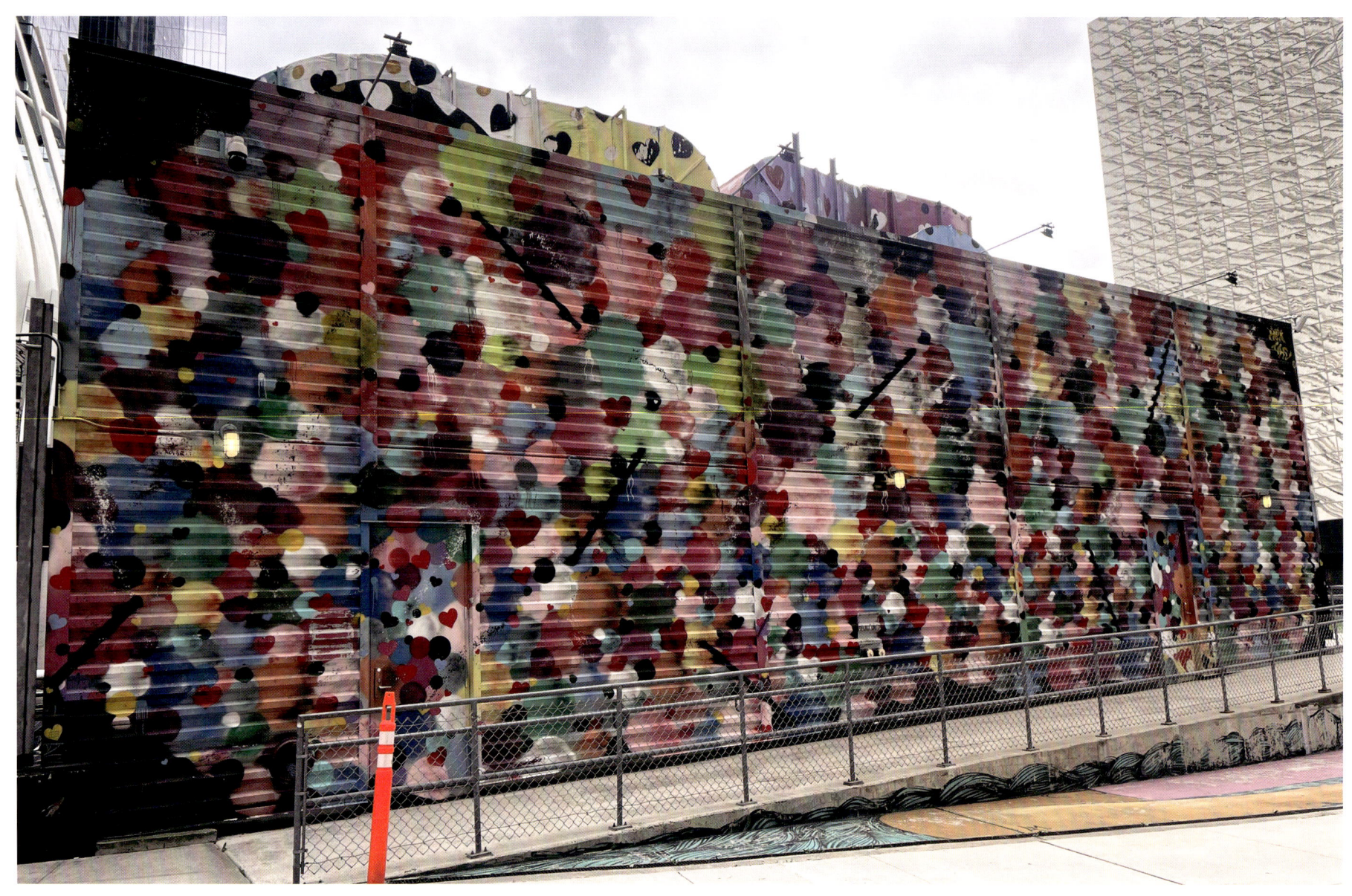

HEK TAD
MANHATTAN, PHOTOGRAPHED IN 2023

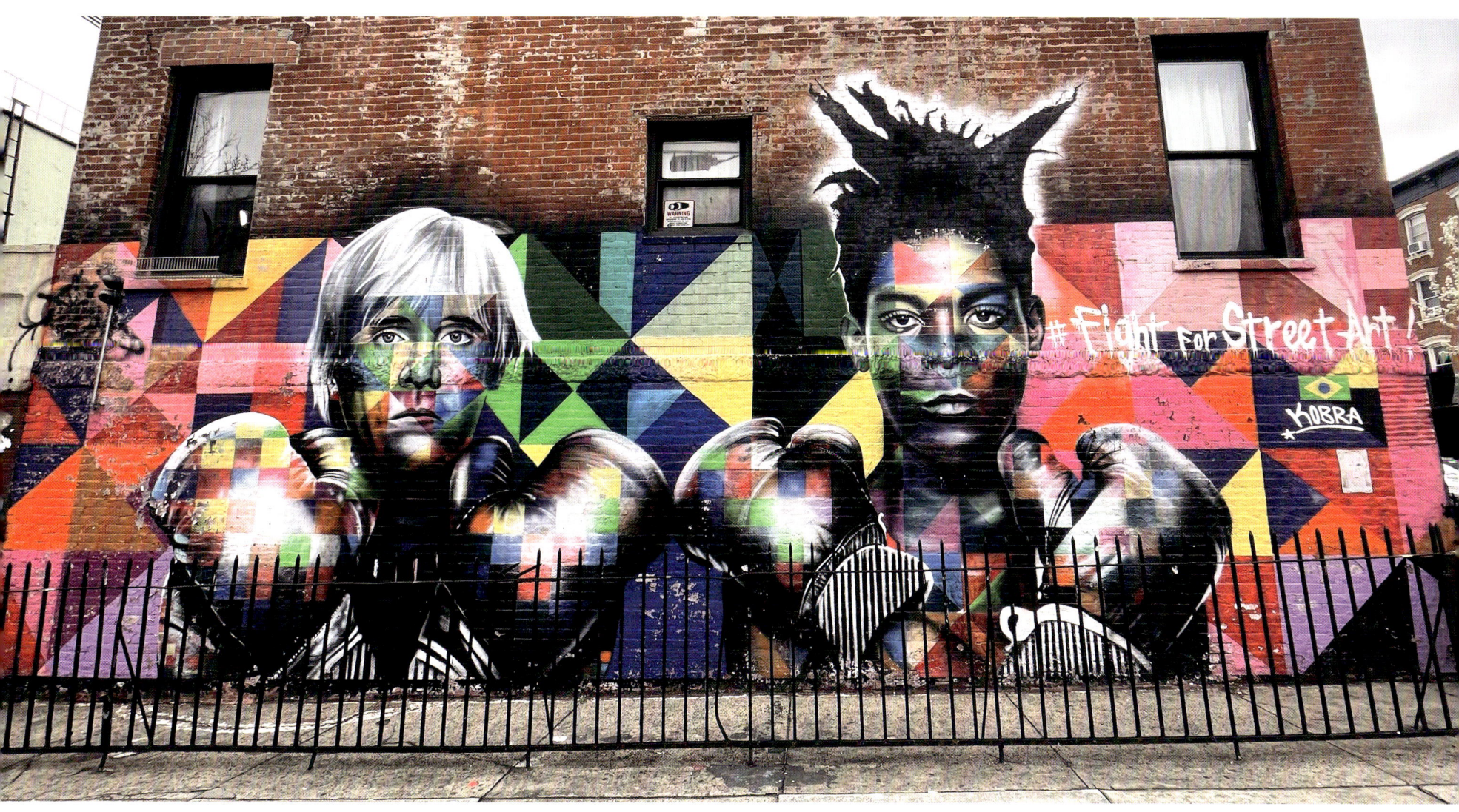

KOBRA
Kobra is an internationally acclaimed aerosol artist and muralist.
BROOKLYN, PHOTOGRAPHED IN 2022

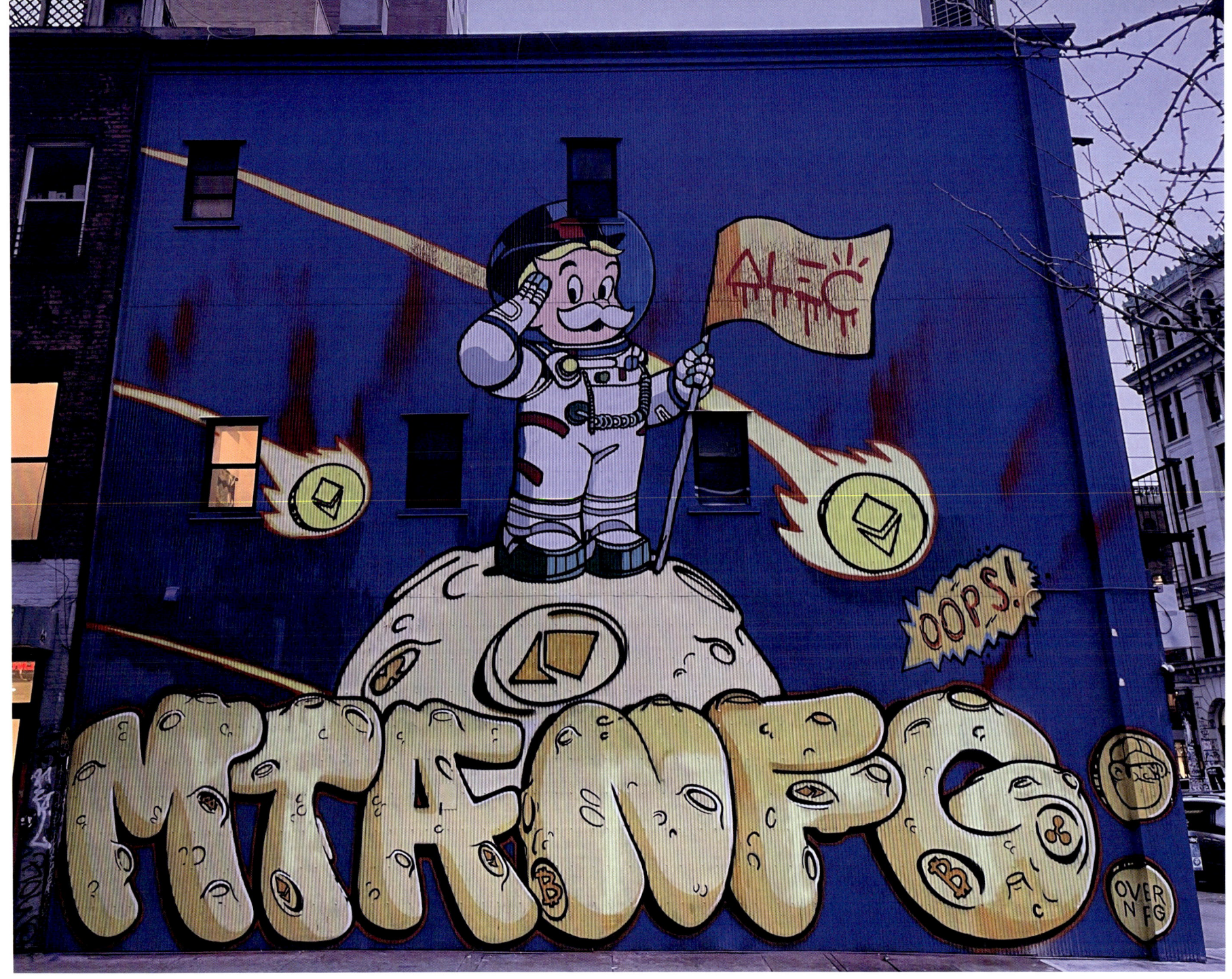

ALEC MONOPOLY

Alec Monopoly is an internationally acclaimed muralist.
MANHATTAN, PHOTOGRAPHED IN 2023

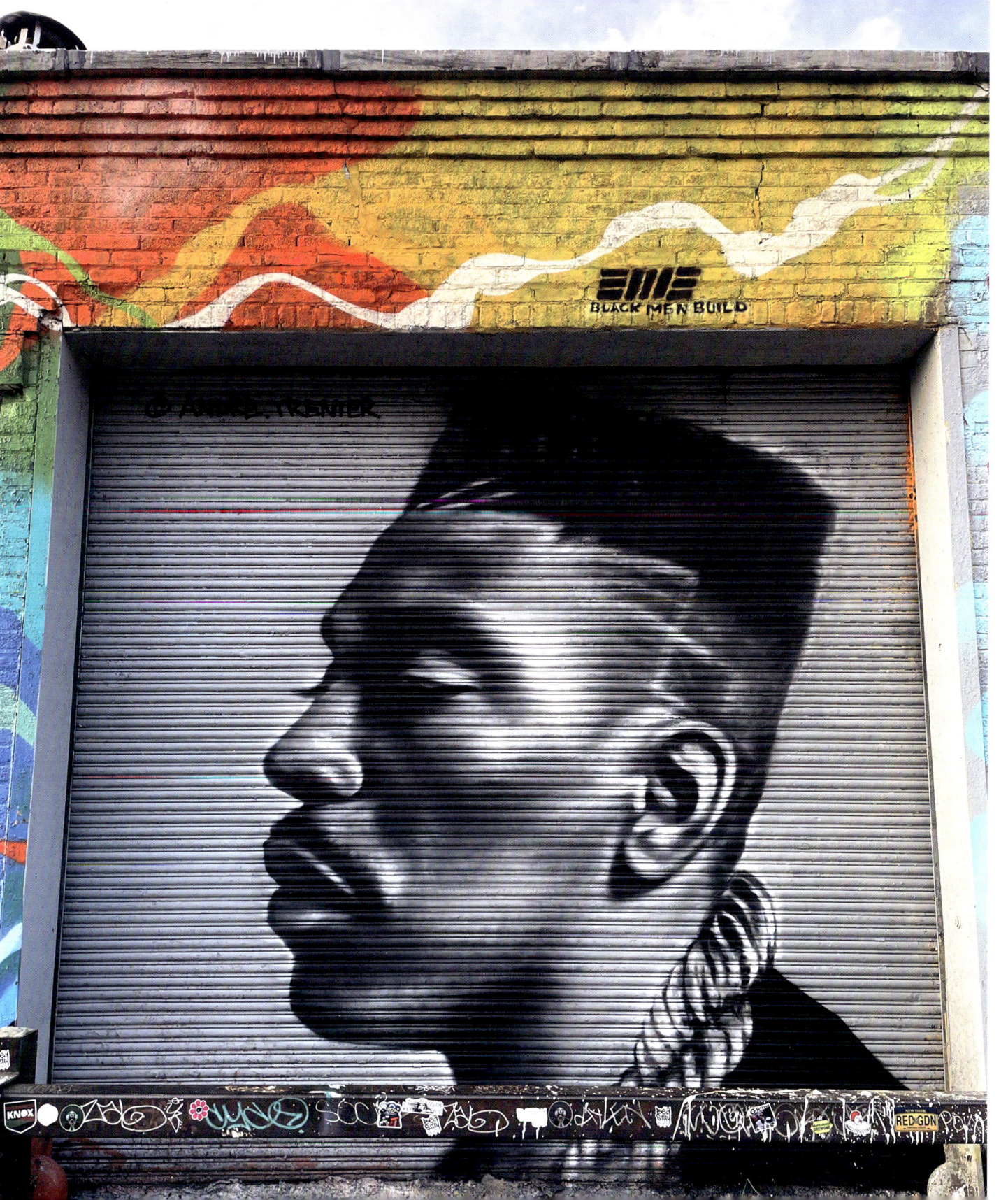

ANDRE TRENIER

Andre Trenier is a popular muralist in New York City. You can see many of his murals at Yankee Stadium.
BED-STUY WALLS, BROOKLYN, PHOTOGRAPHED IN 2023

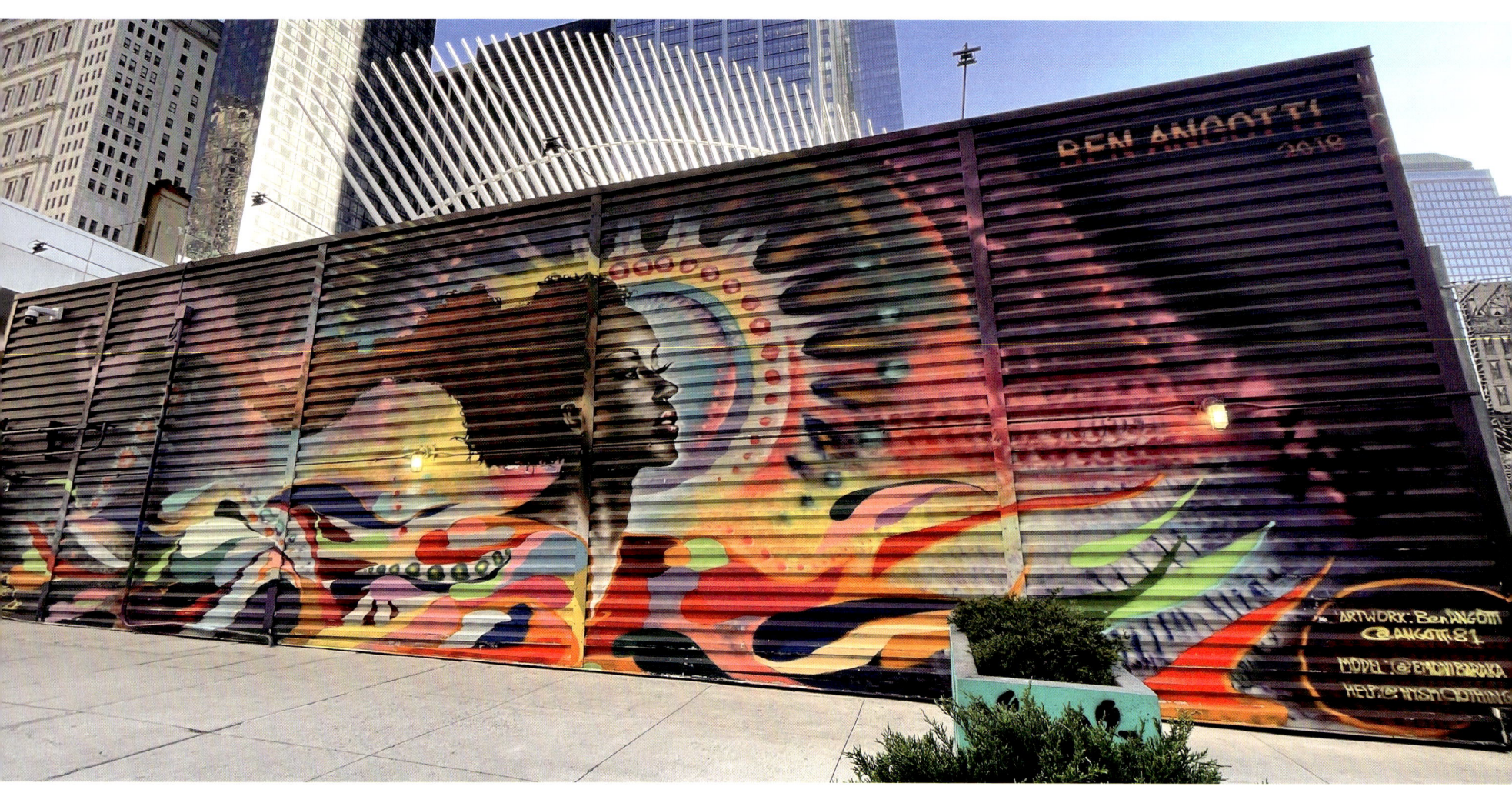

BEN ANGOTTI
MANHATTAN, PHOTOGRAPHED IN 2022

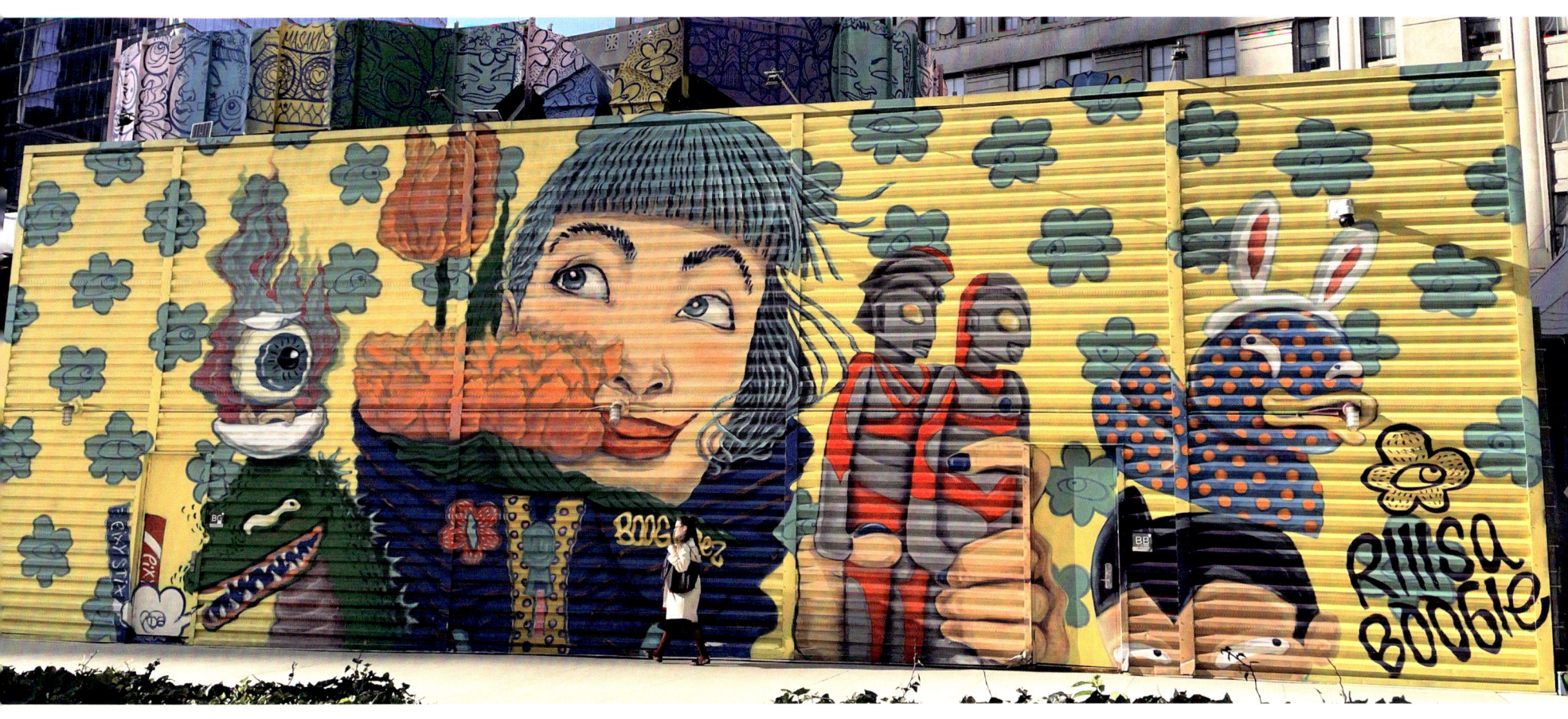

RIIISA BOOGIE

Riiisa Boogie is a popular muralist in New York City. You can see her work around the city.

MANHATTAN, PHOTOGRAPHED IN 2022

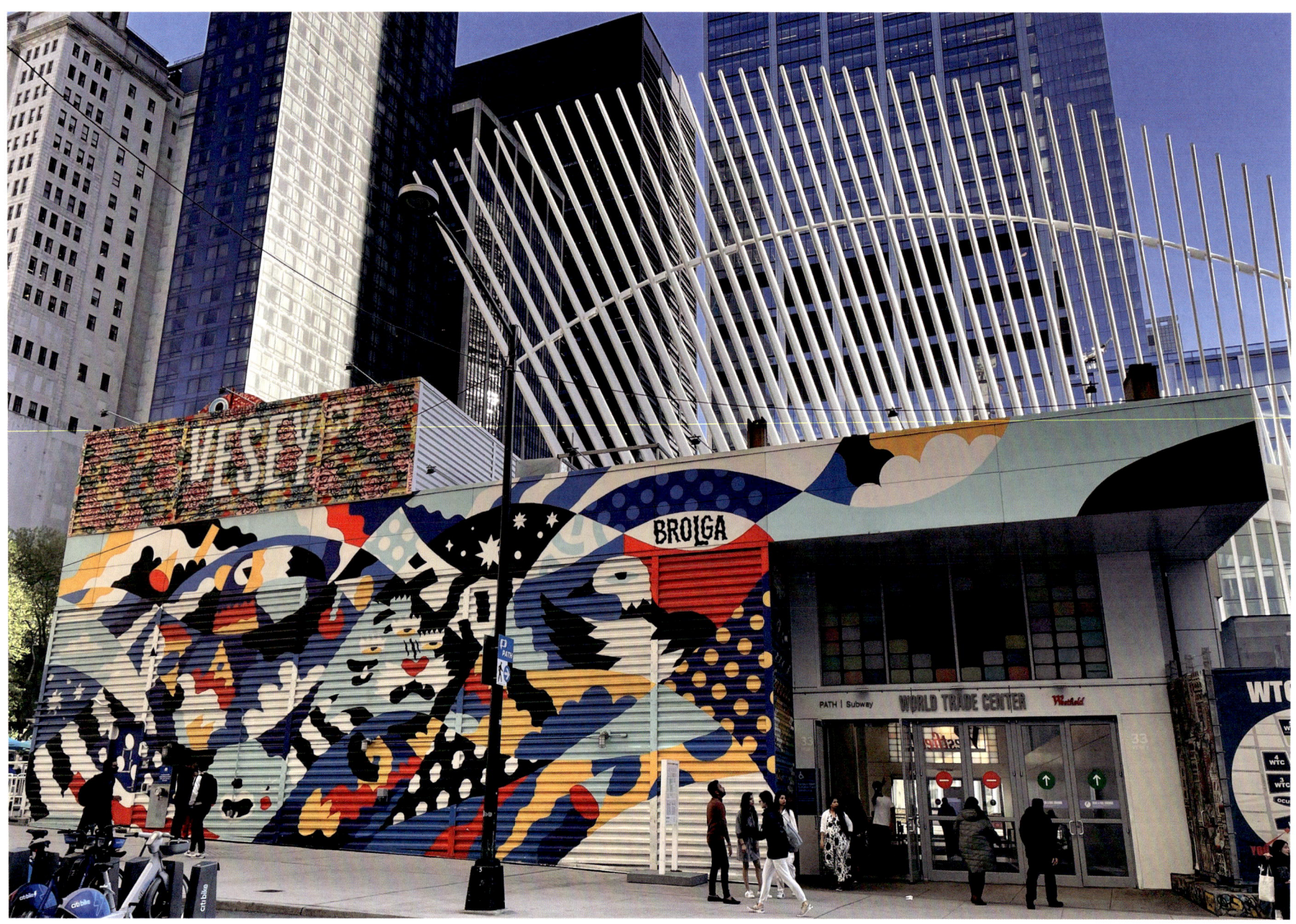

BROLGA

Brolga is an Australia-based muralist and illustrator.
MANHATTAN, PHOTOGRAPHED IN 2022

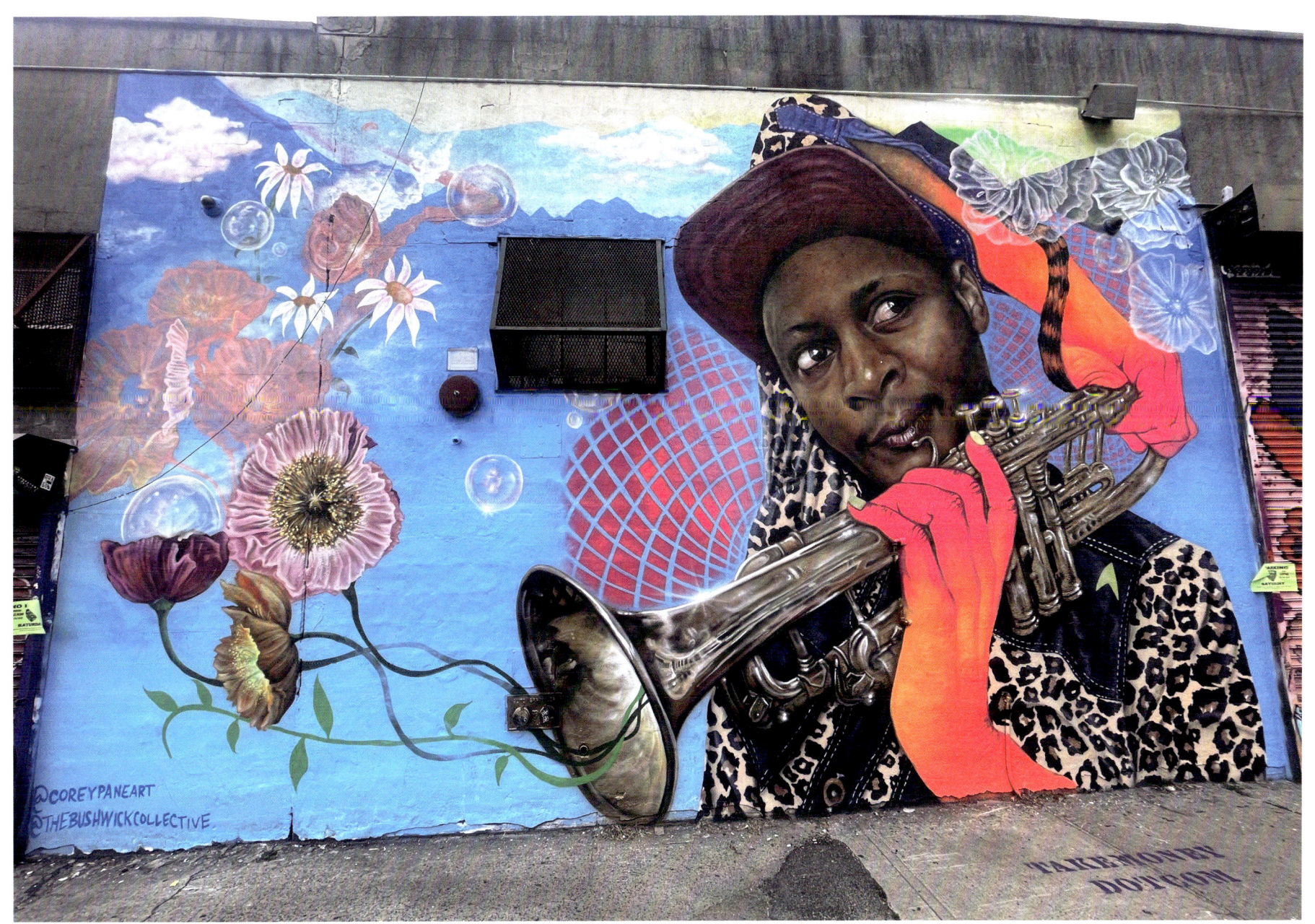

COREY PANE ART
BUSHWICK COLLECTIVE, BROOKLYN, PHOTOGRAPHED IN 2023

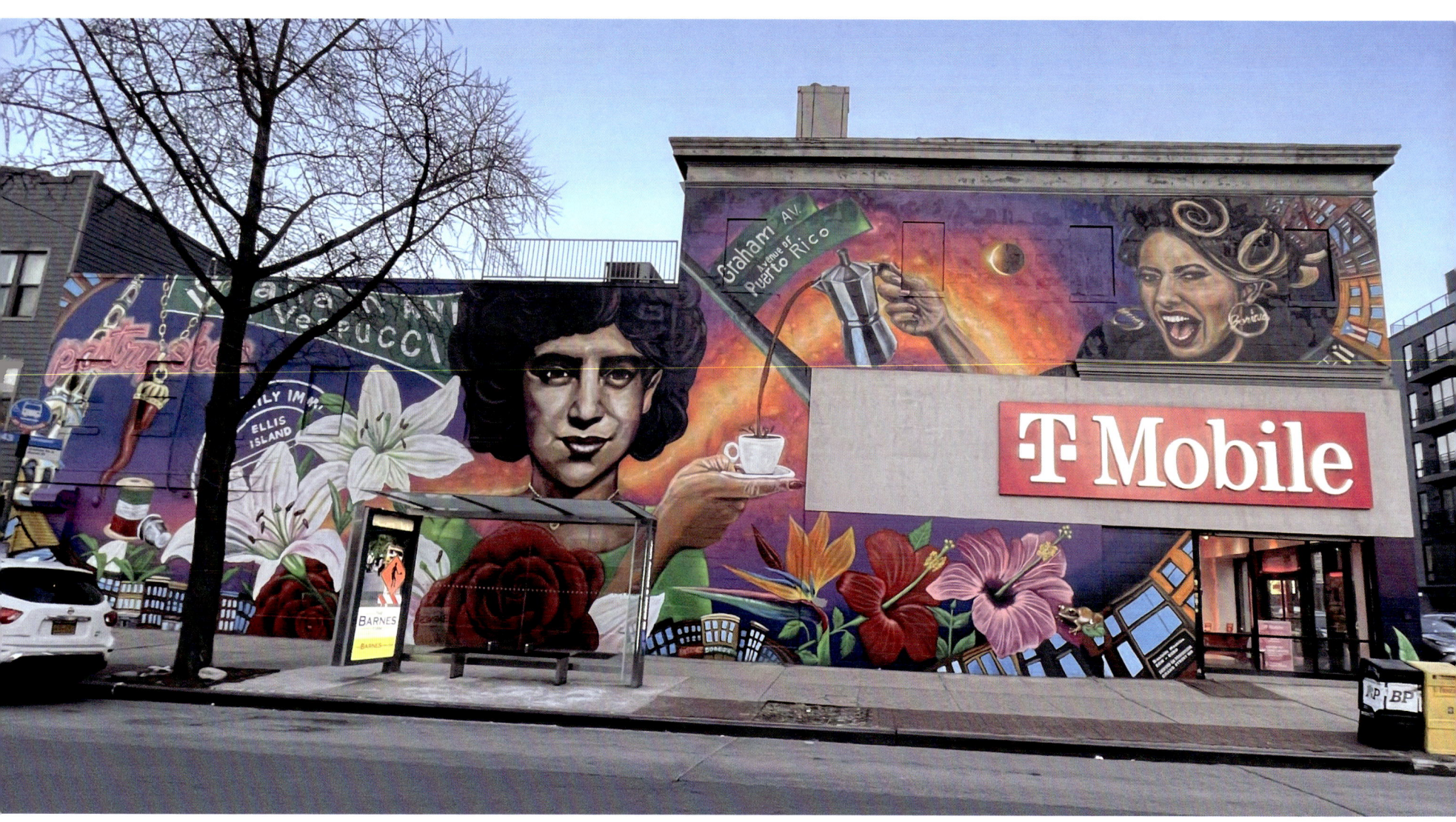

DANIELLE MASTRION
BROOKLYN, PHOTOGRAPHED IN 2024

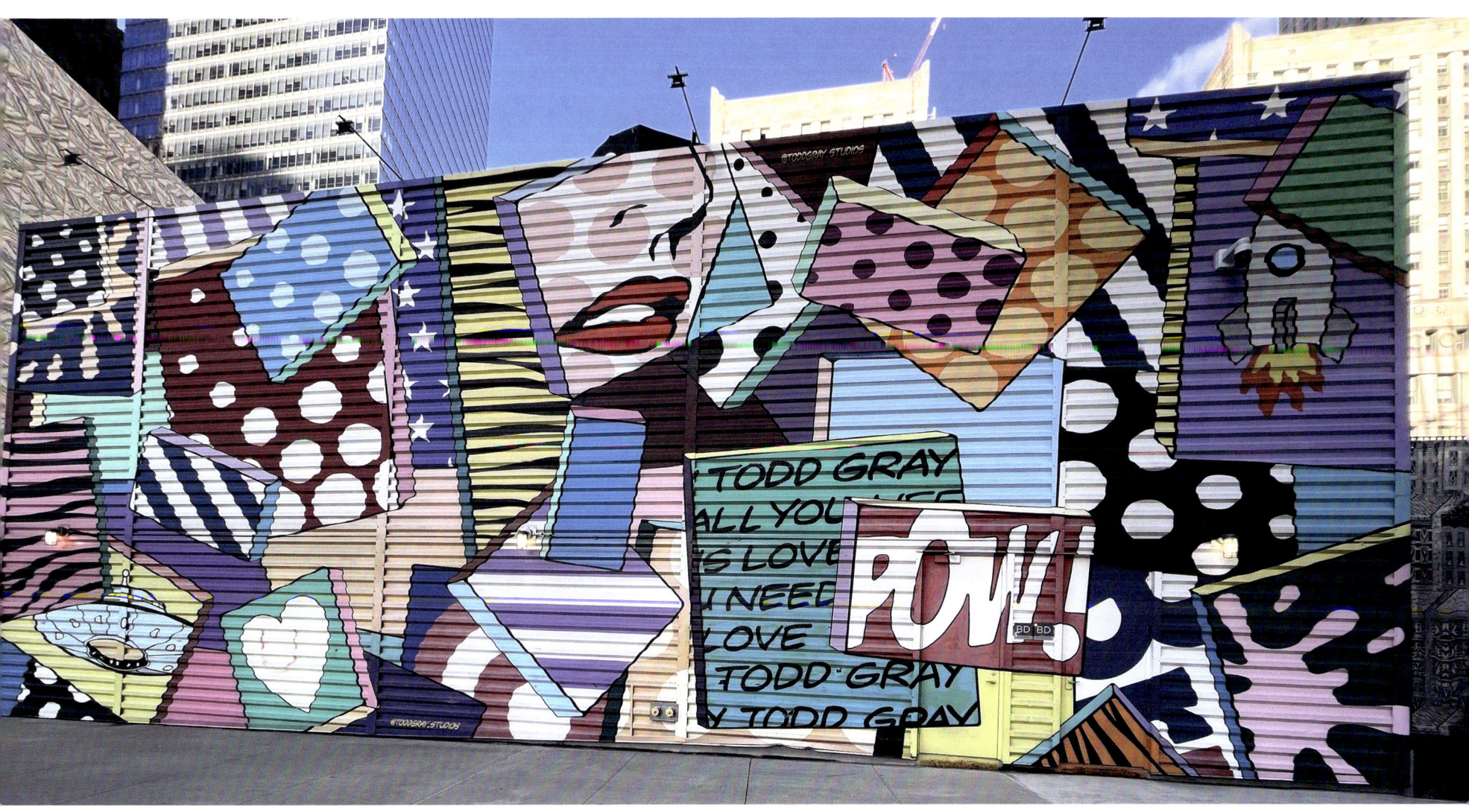

TODD GRAY
MANHATTAN, PHOTOGRAPHED IN 2024

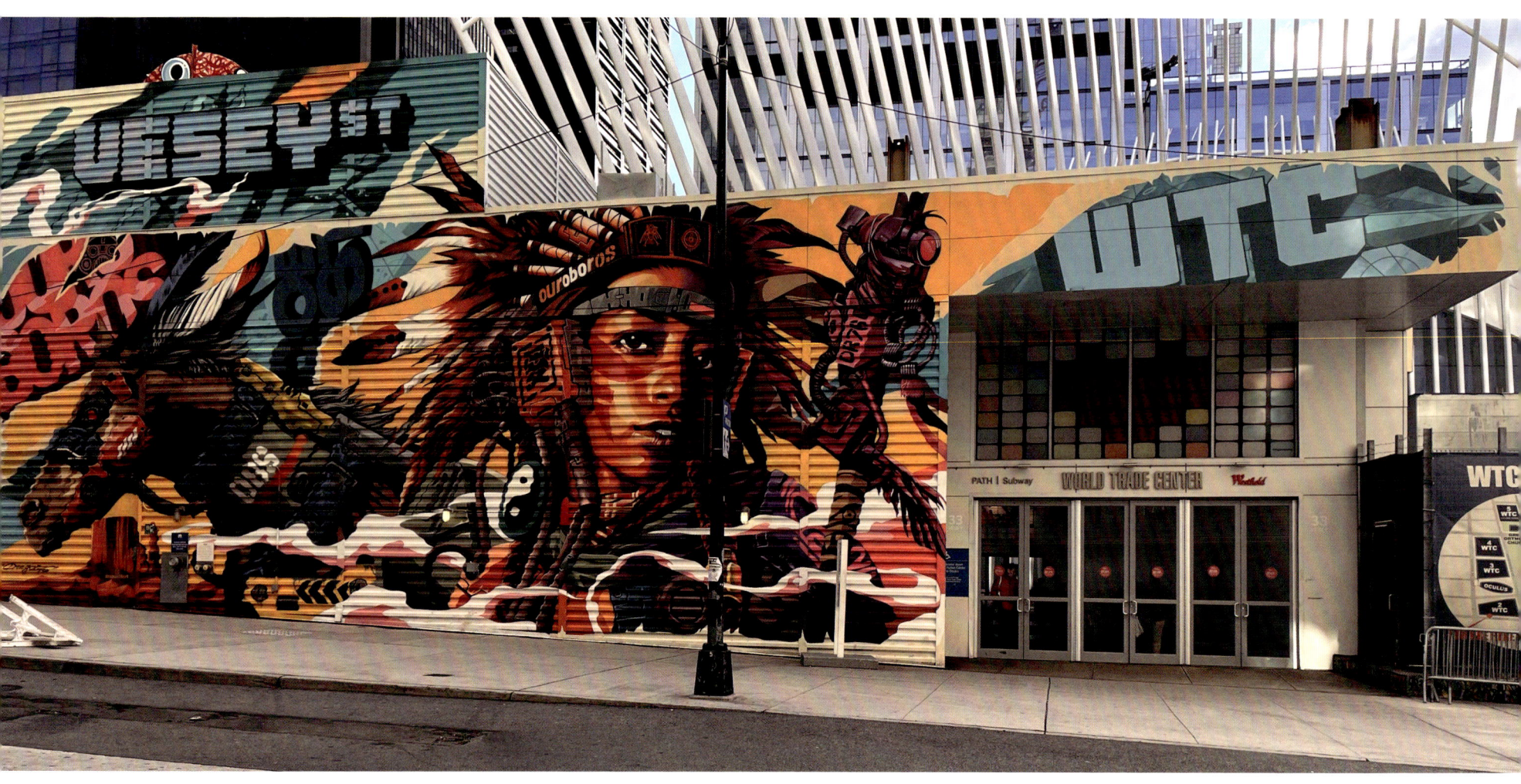

DRAGON 76
MANHATTAN, PHOTORAPHED IN 2024

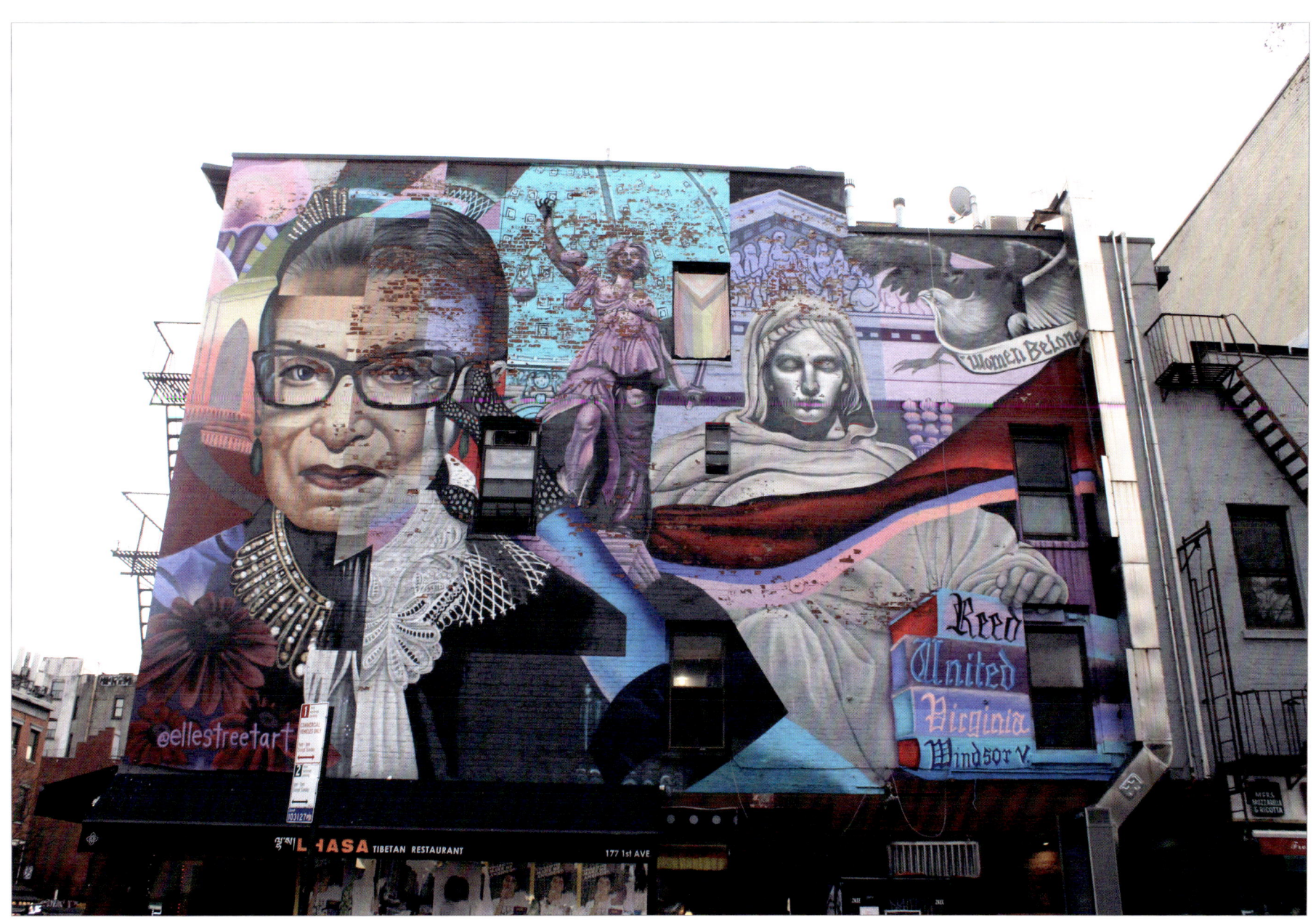

ELLE STREET ART
MANHATTAN, PHOTOGRAPHED IN 2024

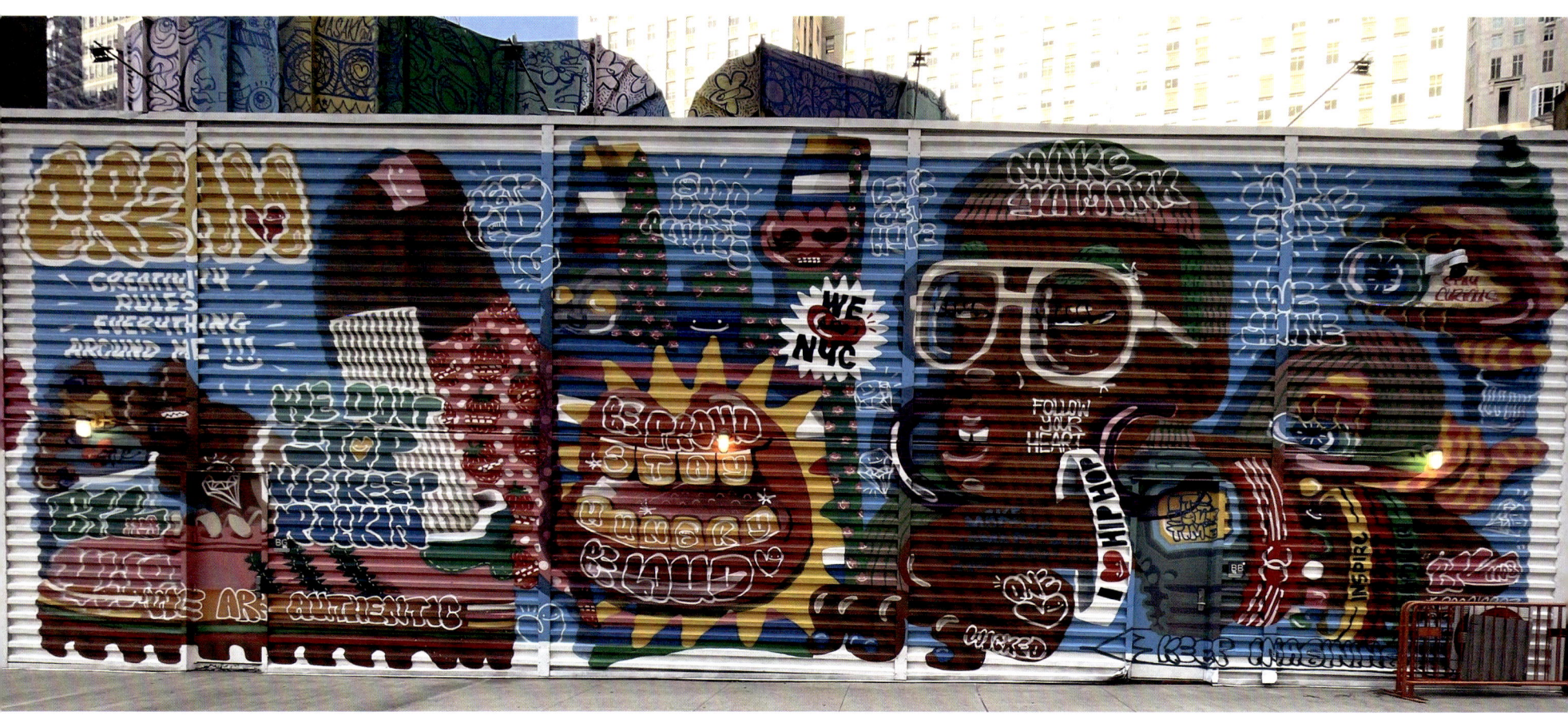

RIIISA BOOGIE
MANHATTAN, PHOTOGRAPHED IN 2024

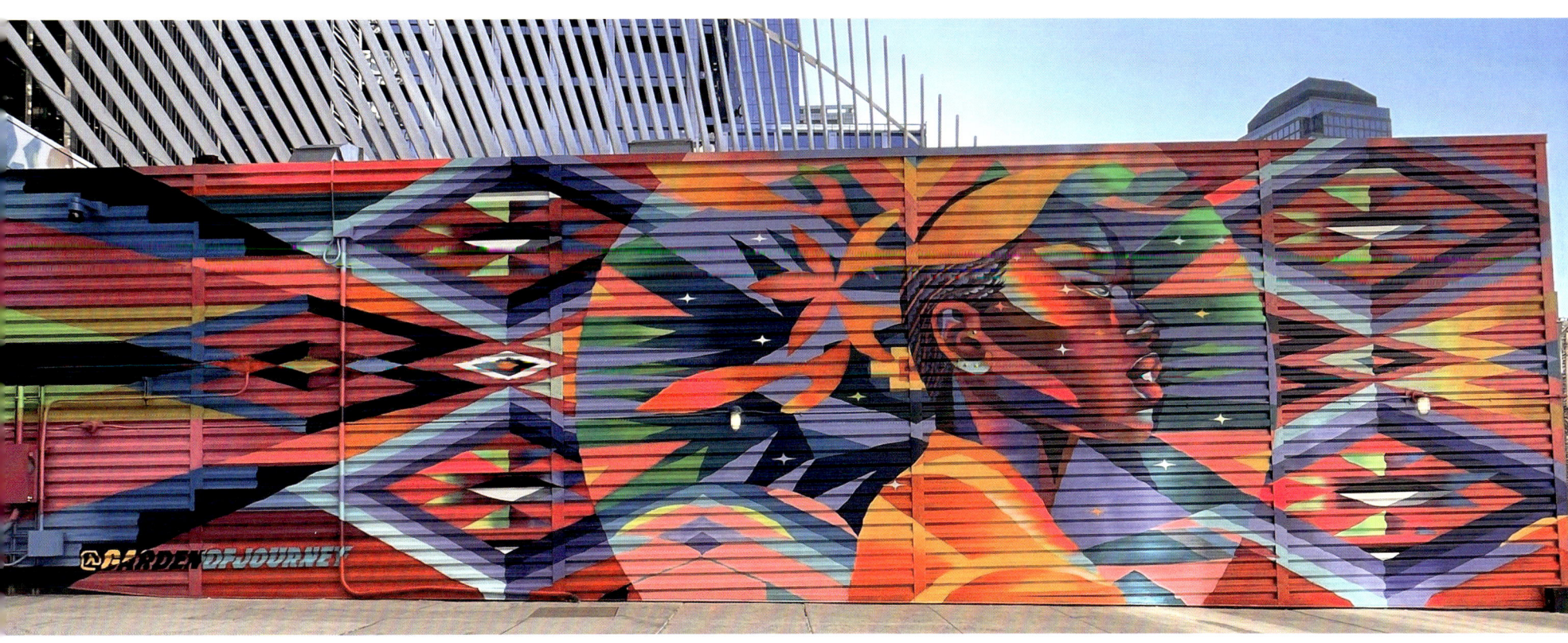

GARDEN OF JOURNEY
MANHATTAN, PHOTOGRAPHED IN 2023

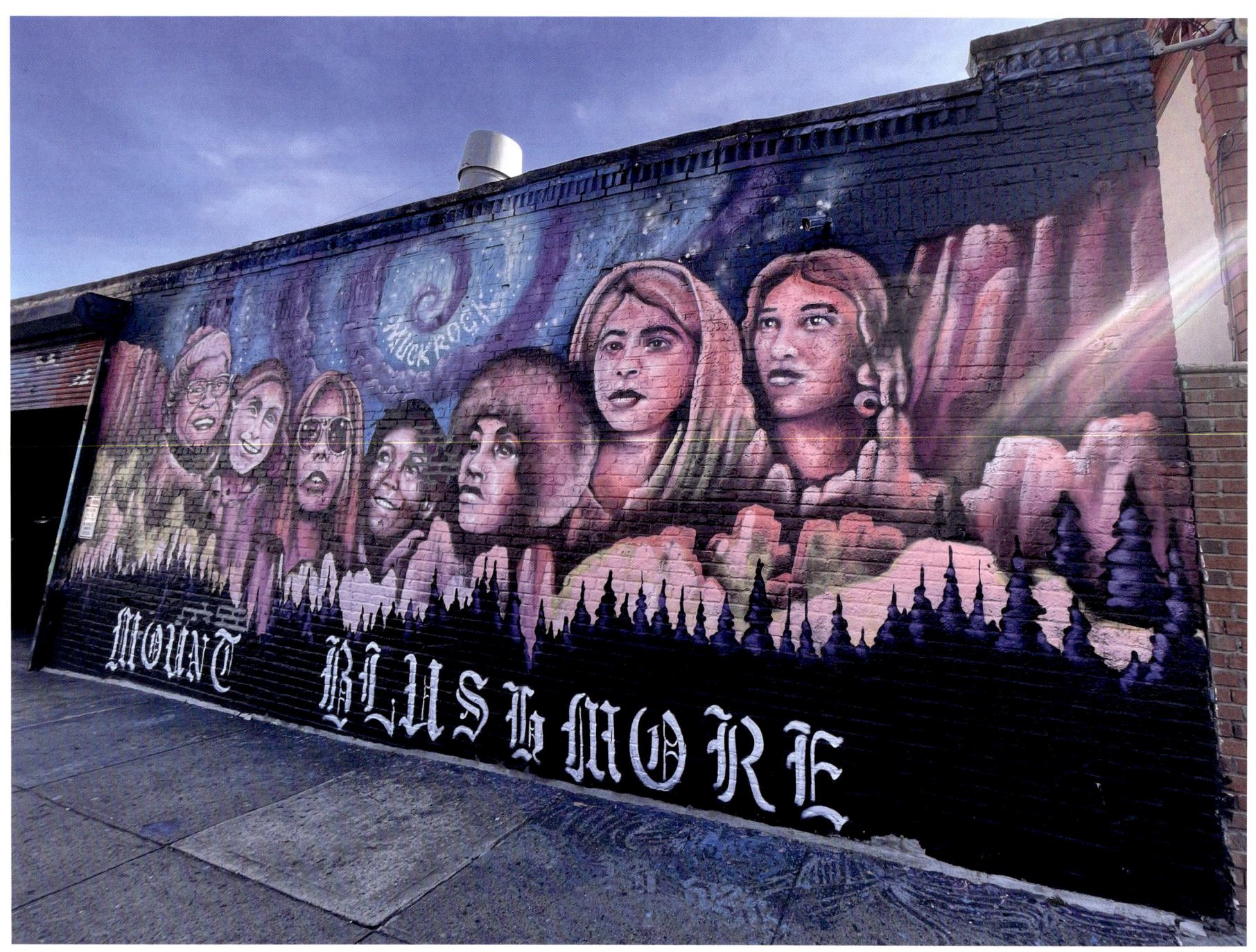

JULES MUCK
WELLING COURT MURAL PROJECT, QUEENS, PHOTOGRAPHED IN 2024

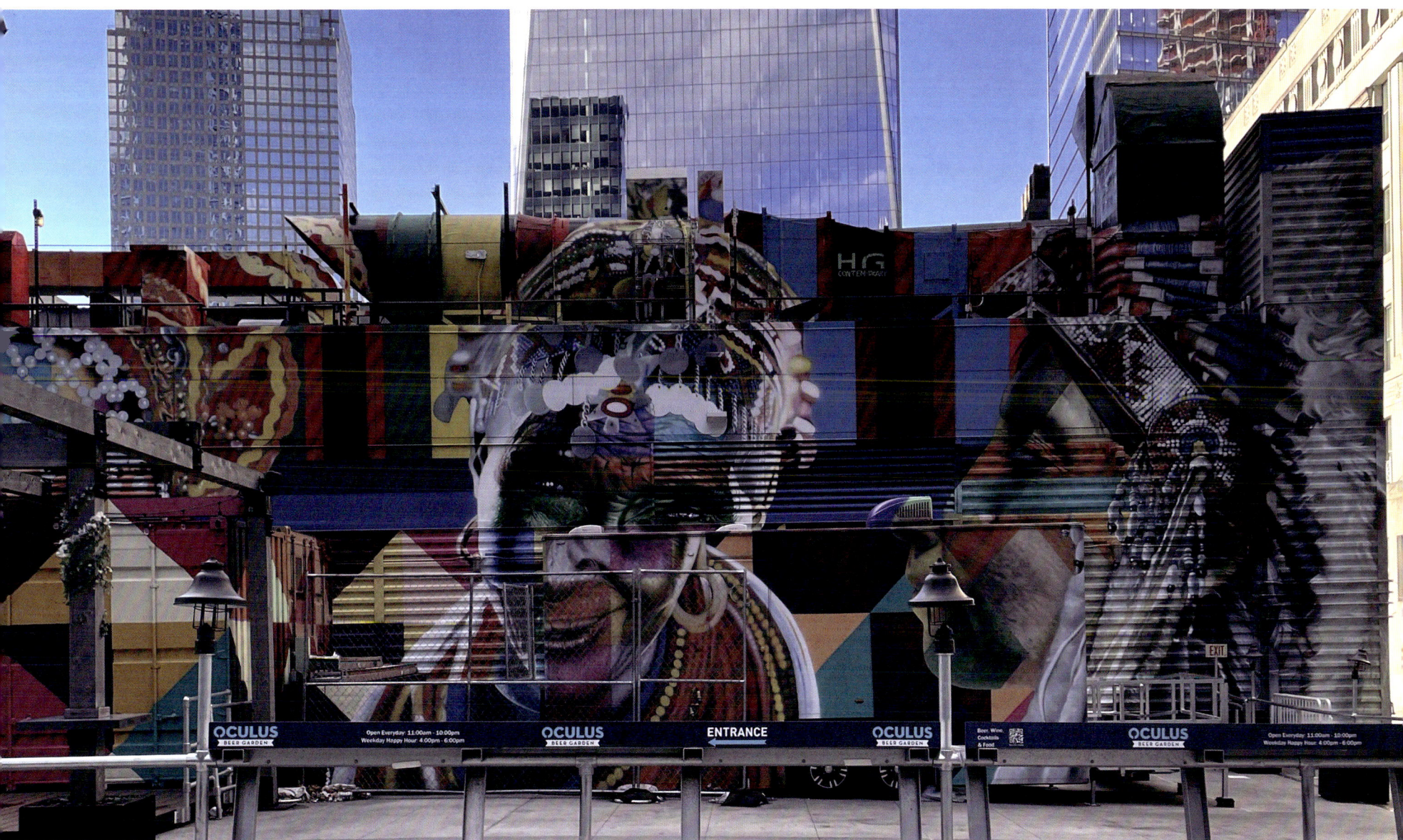

KOBRA
WORLD TRADE CENTER, MANHATTAN, PHOTOGRAPHED IN 2024

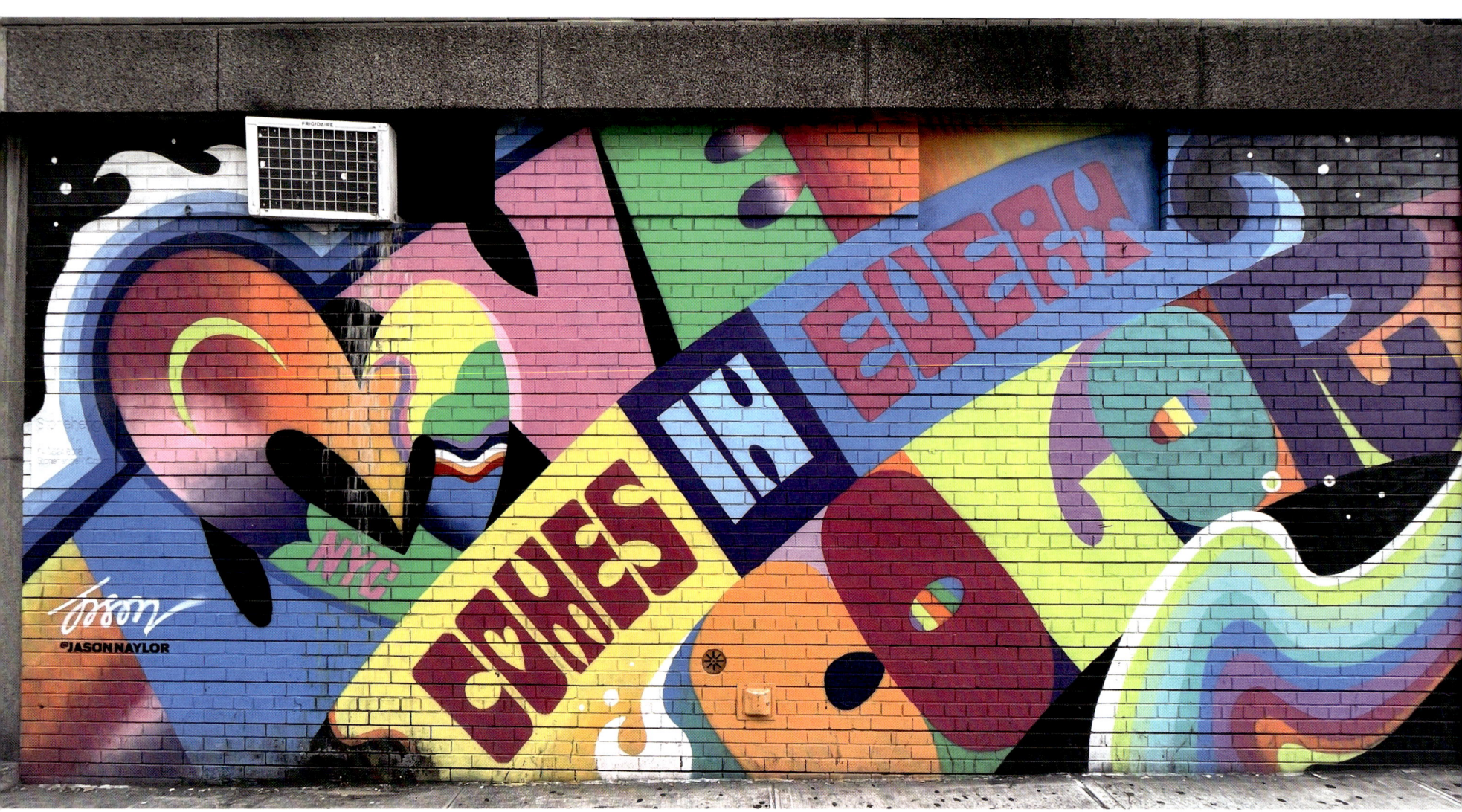

JASON NAYLOR
MANHATTAN, PHOTOGRAPHED IN 2023

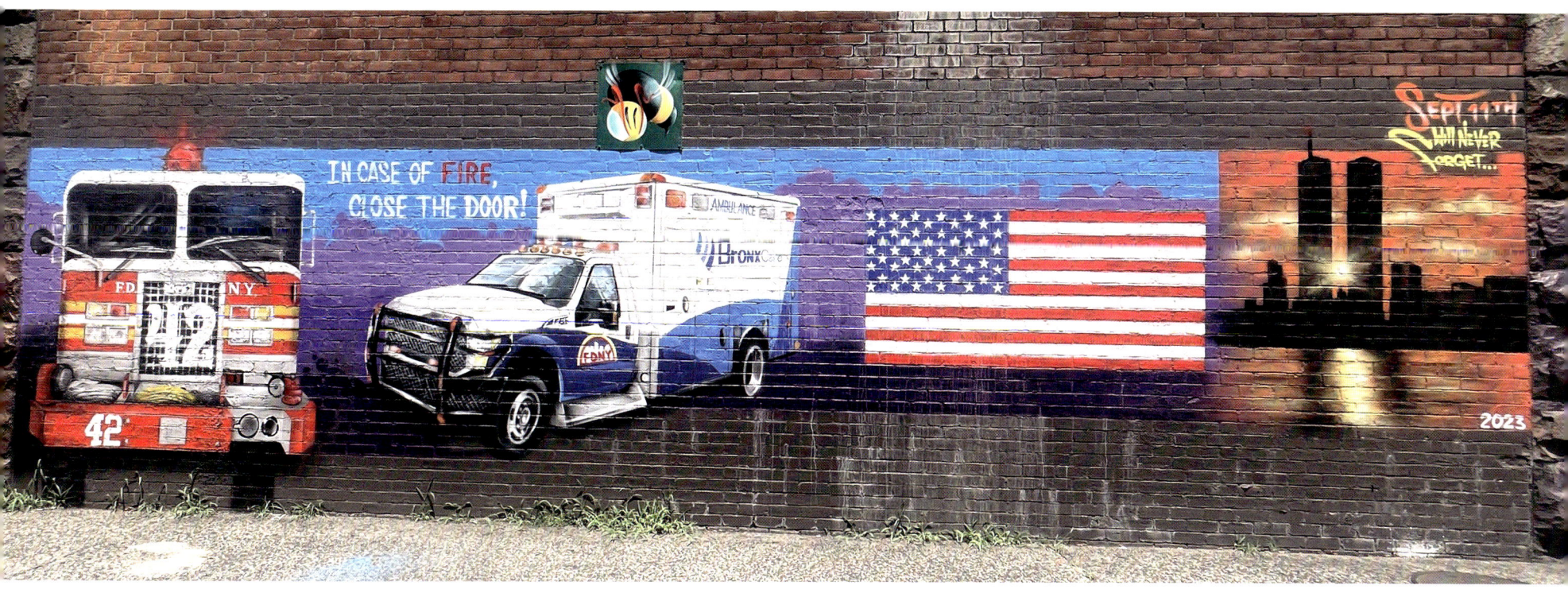

KING BEE UW
THE BRONX, PHOTOGRAPHED IN 2023

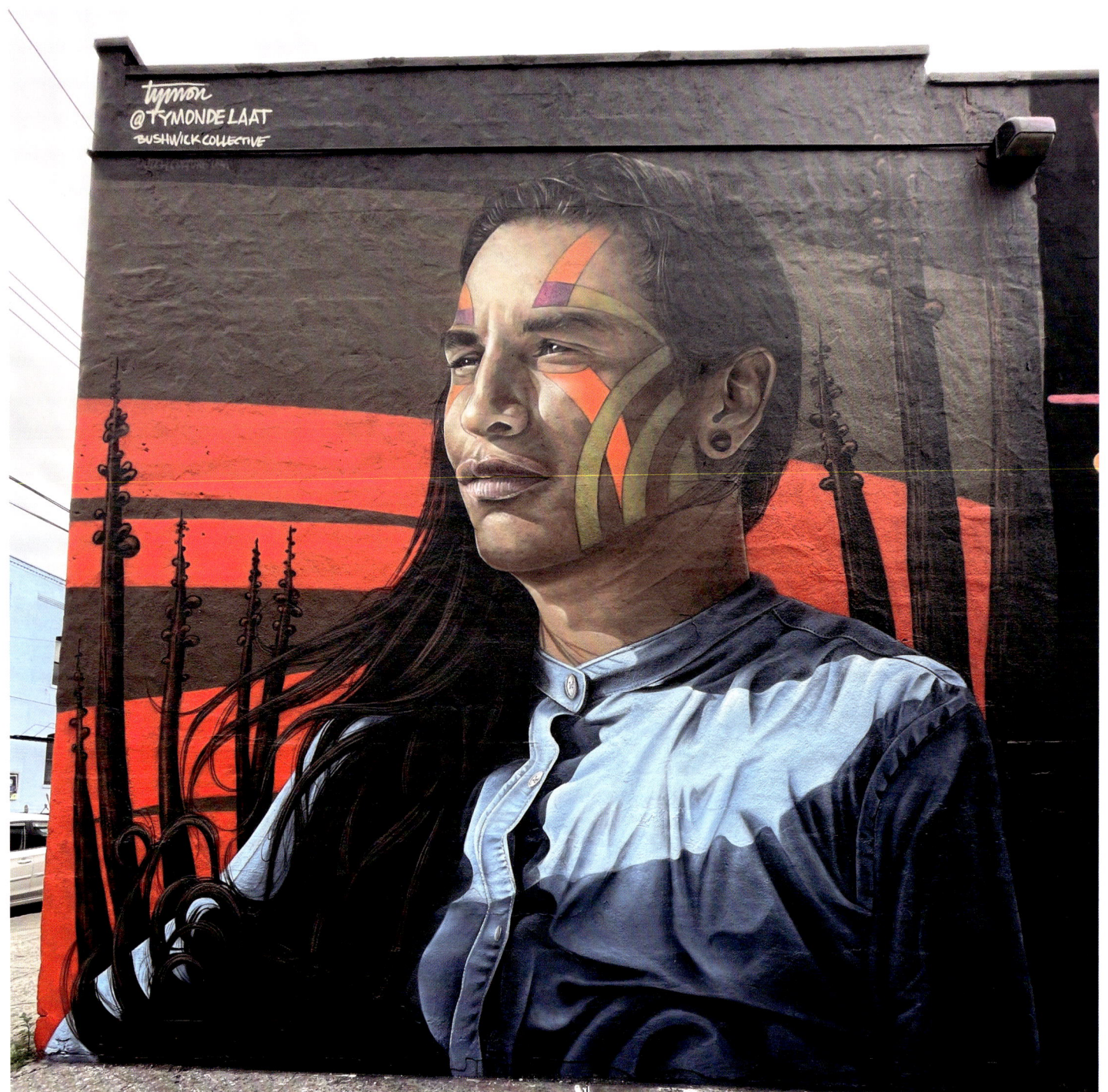

TYMON DE LAAT
BUSHWICK COLLECTIVE,
BROOKLYN,
PHOTOGRAPHED IN 2023

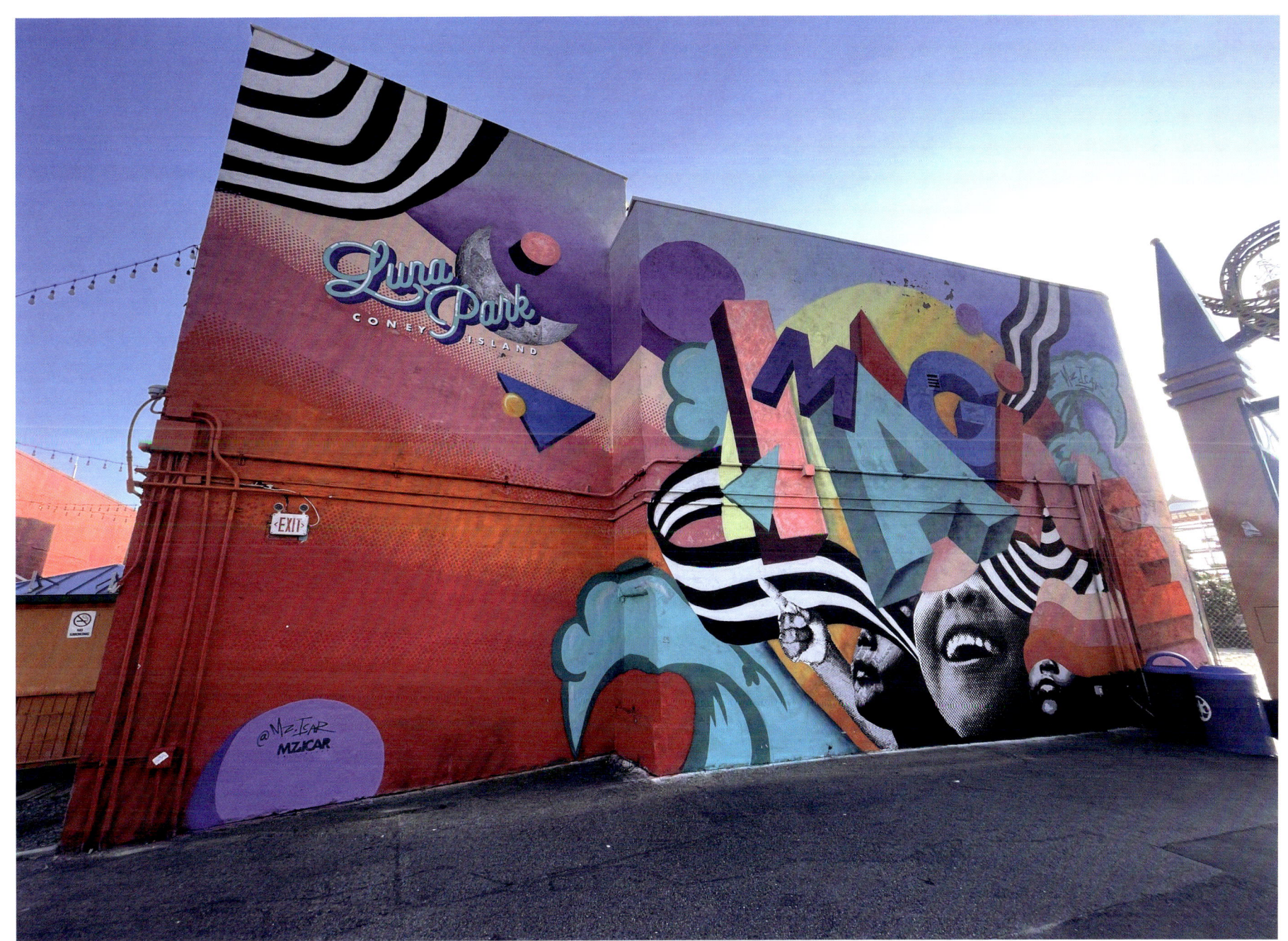

MZ ICAR
Coney Island.
BROOKLYN, PHOTOGRAPHED IN 2023

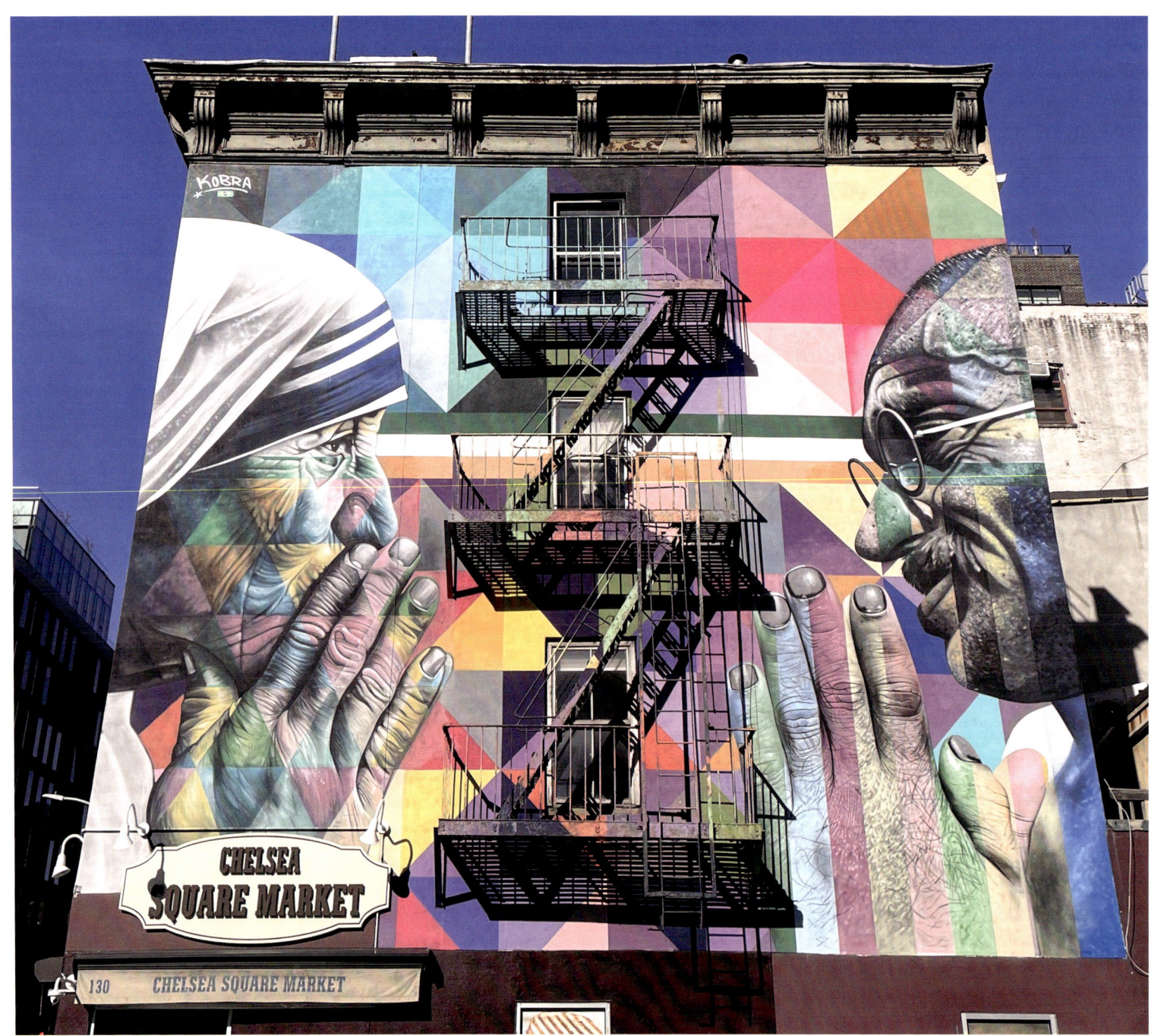

KOBRA
MANHATTAN, PHOTOGRAPHED IN 2024

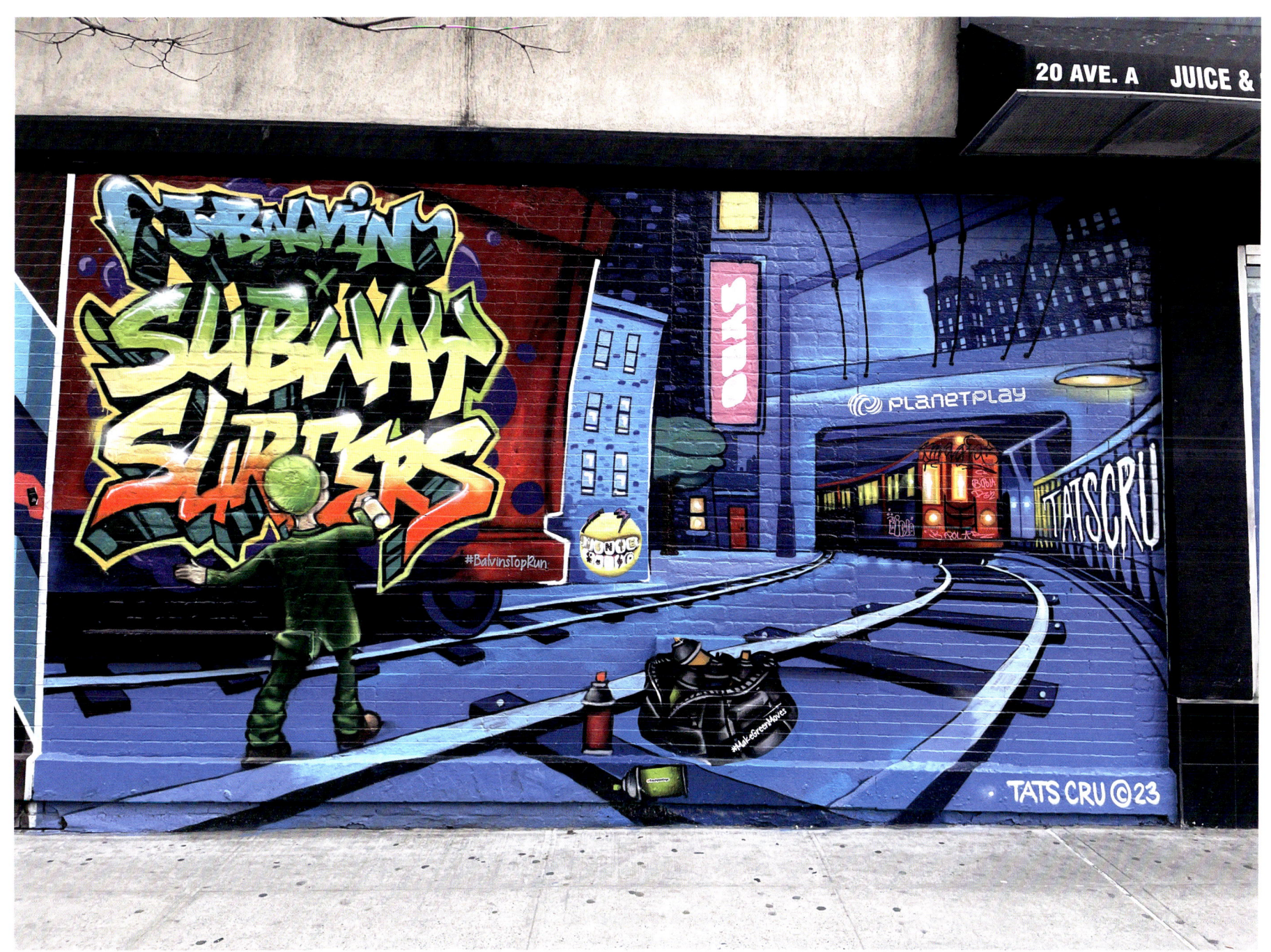

TATS CRU
MANHATTAN, PHOTOGRAPHED IN 2024

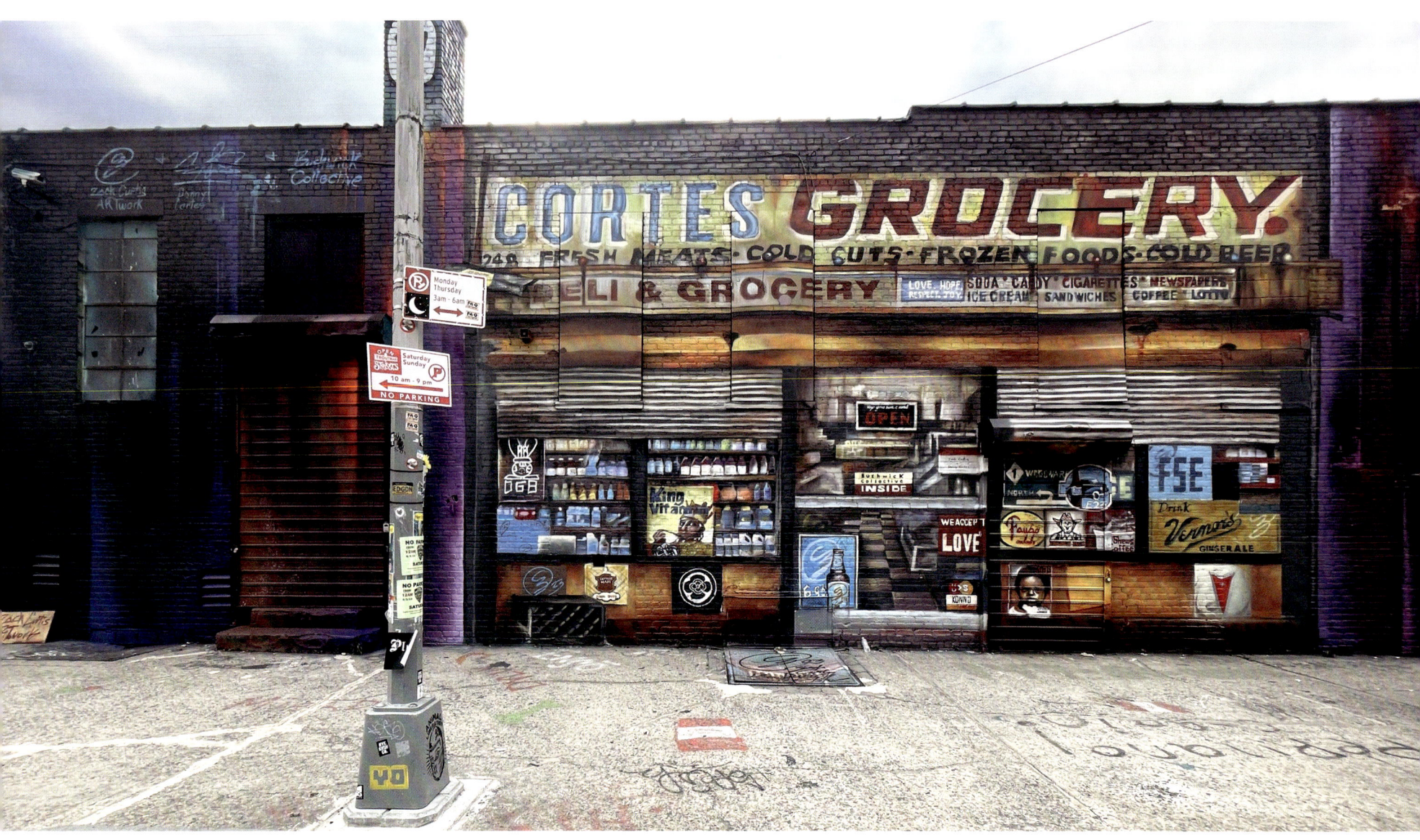

ZACH CURTIS, DANNY CORTES
BUSHWICK COLLECTIVE, BROOKLYN, PHOTOGRAPHED IN 2023

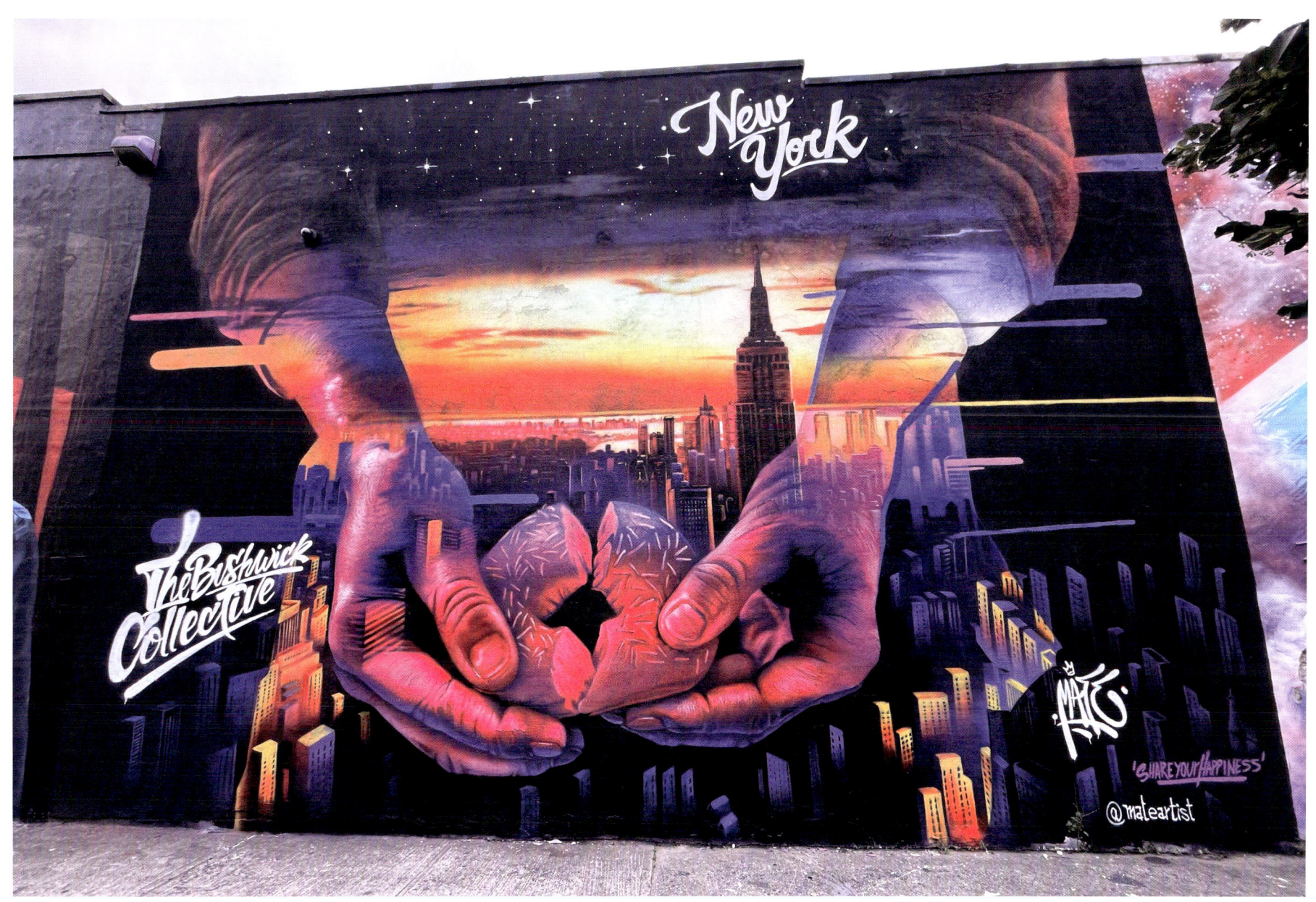

MATE ARTIST

Mate Artist is an international artist who painted this New York City masterpiece.
BUSHWICK COLLECTIVE, BROOKLYN, PHOTOGRAPHED IN 2023

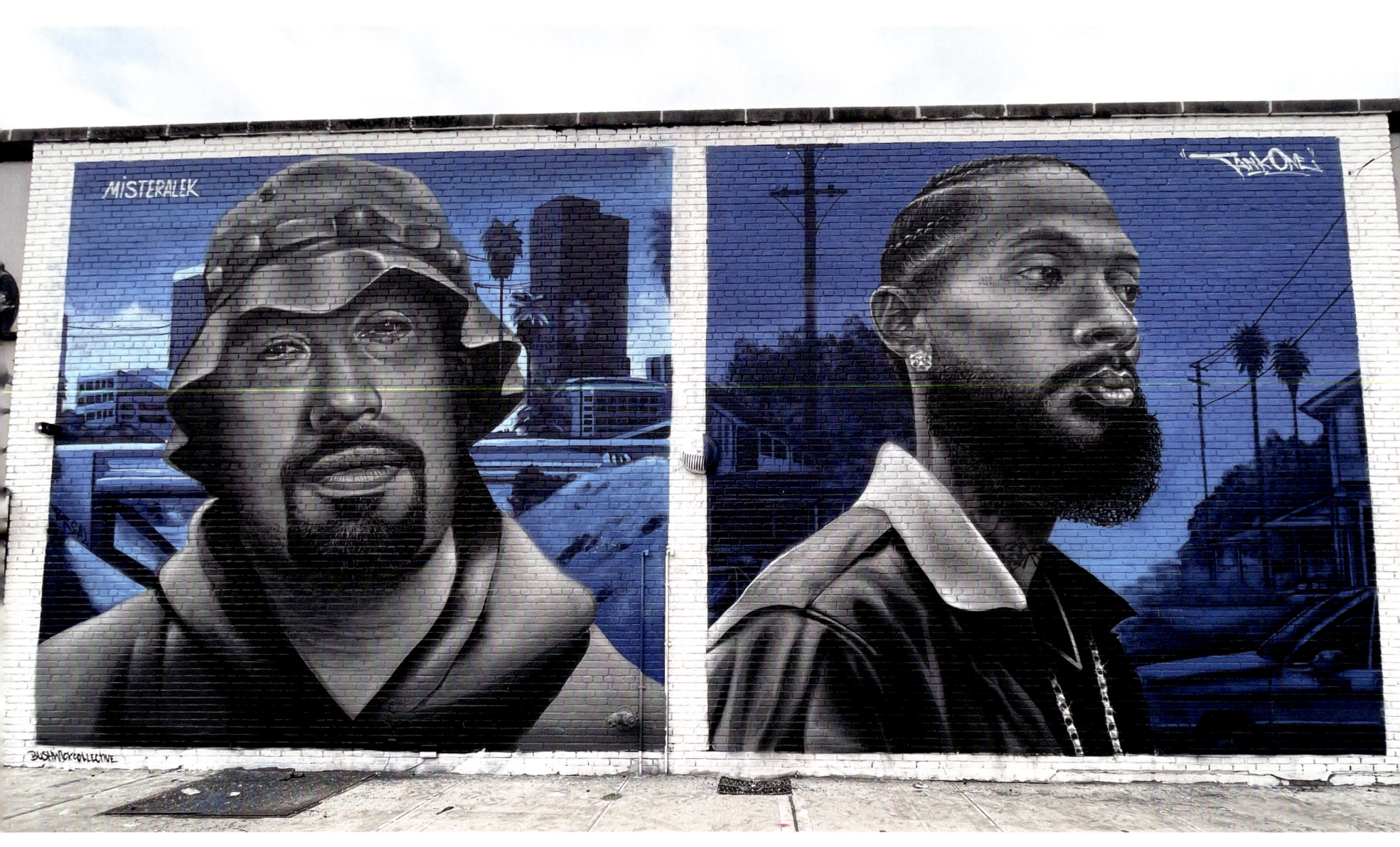

MISTERALEK, TANK ONE
BUSHWICK COLLECTIVE, BROOKLYN, PHOTOGRAPHED IN 2023

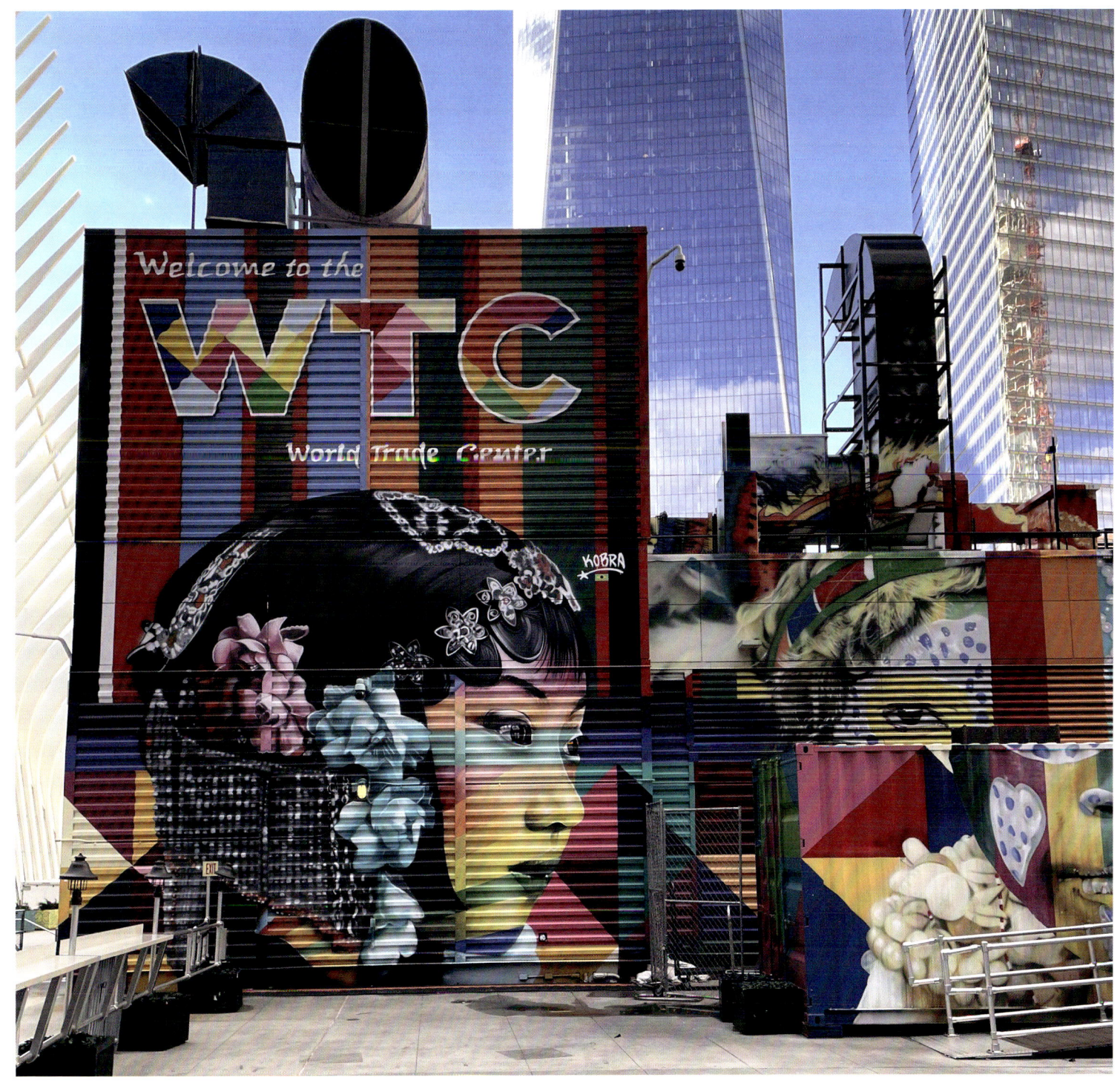

KOBRA
MANHATTAN,
PHOTOGRAPHED IN
2024

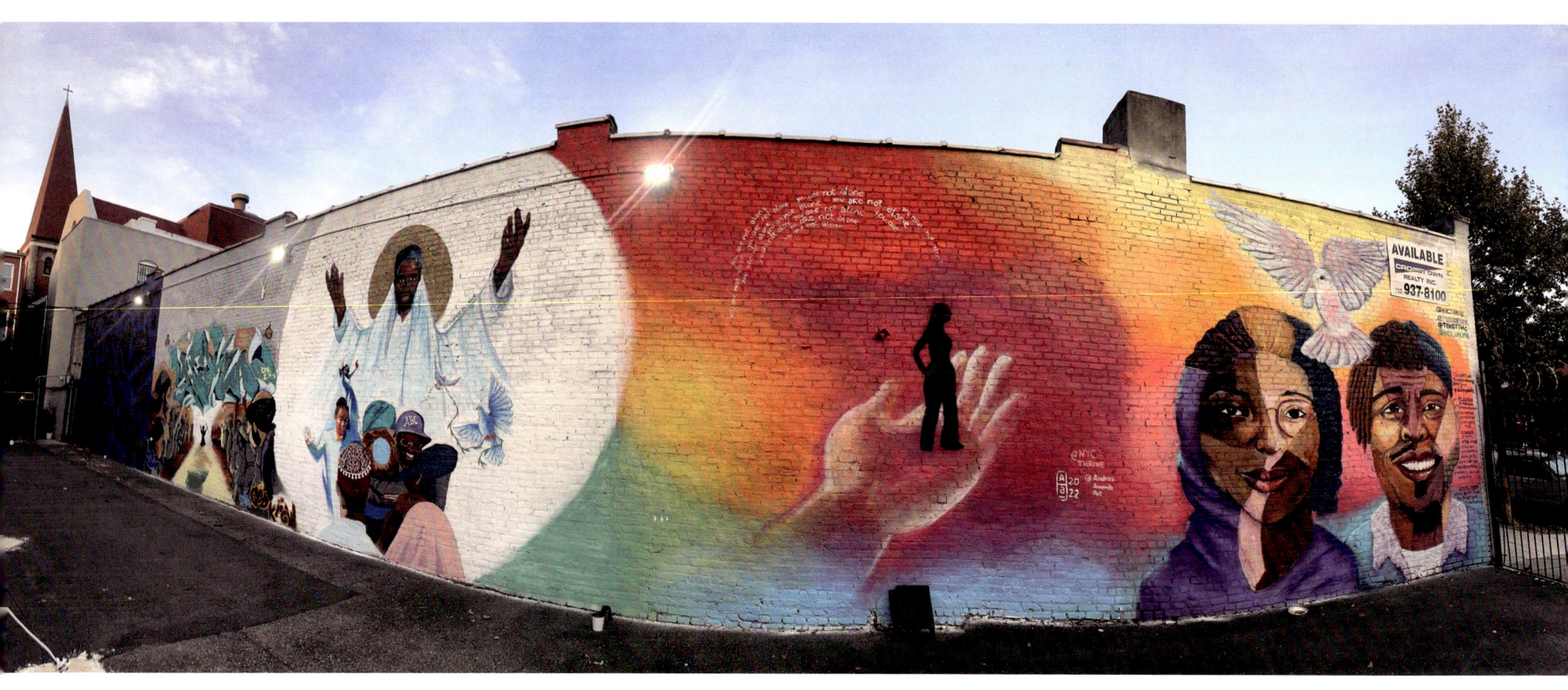

NYC THRIVE COLLECTIVE
BED-STUY WALLS, PHOTOGRAPHED IN 2023

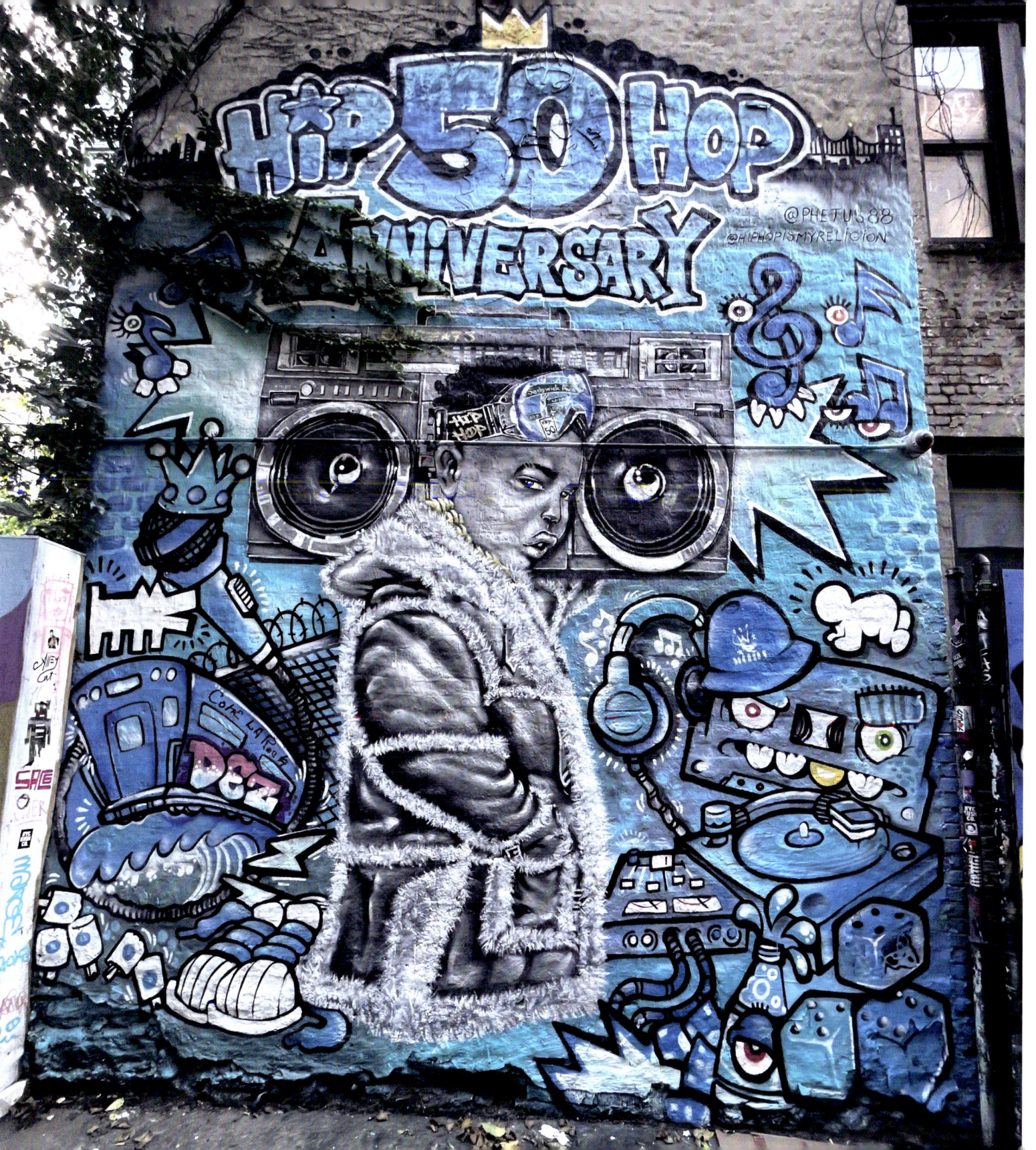

PHETUS
Hip-hop 50th-anniversary mural. FIRST STREET GREEN ART PARK, MANHATTAN, PHOTOGRAPHED IN 2023

BMIKE, MARTHA LICIA
MANHATTAN, PHOTOGRAPHED IN
2023

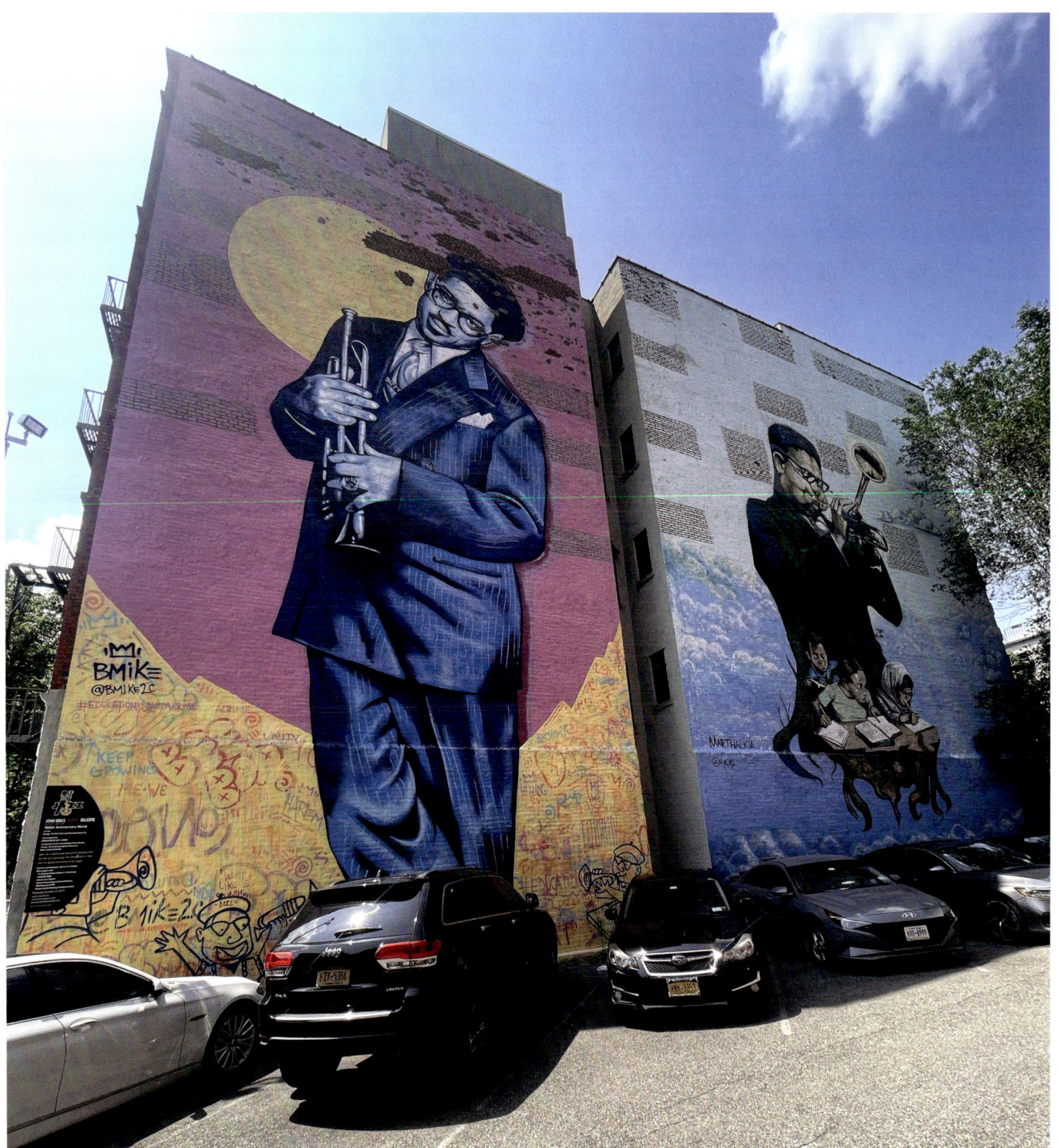

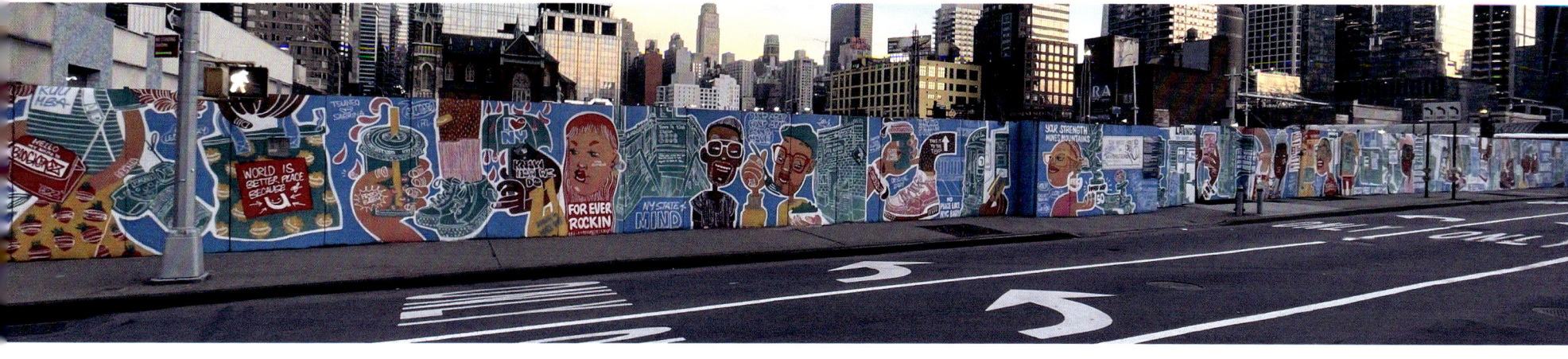

RIIISA BOOGIE
MANHATTAN, PHOTOGRAPHED IN 2024

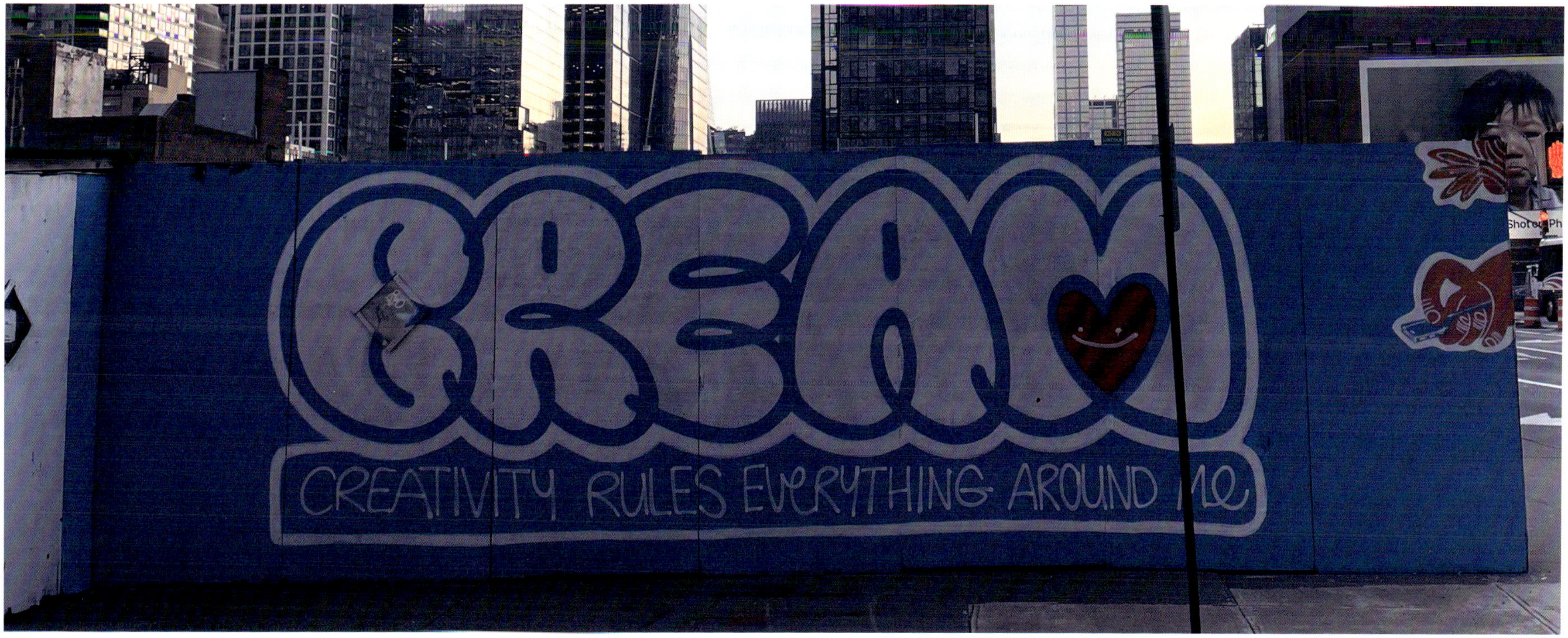

RIIISA BOOGIE
MANHATTAN, PHOTOGRAPHED IN 2024

OSGEMEOS

OSGEMEOS are famous twin brothers and aerosol artists from Brazil.
MANHATTAN, PHOTOGRAPHED IN 2023

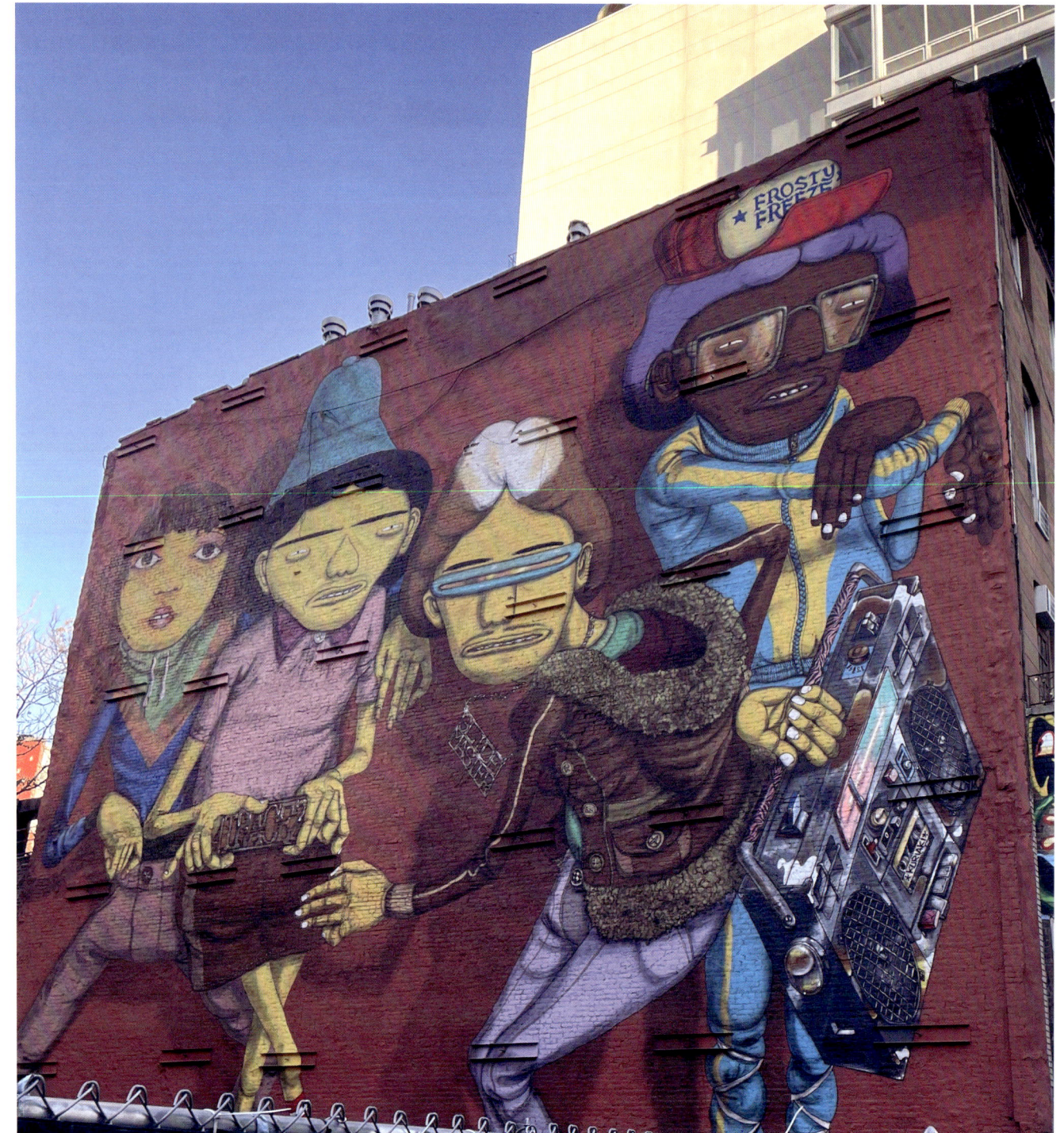

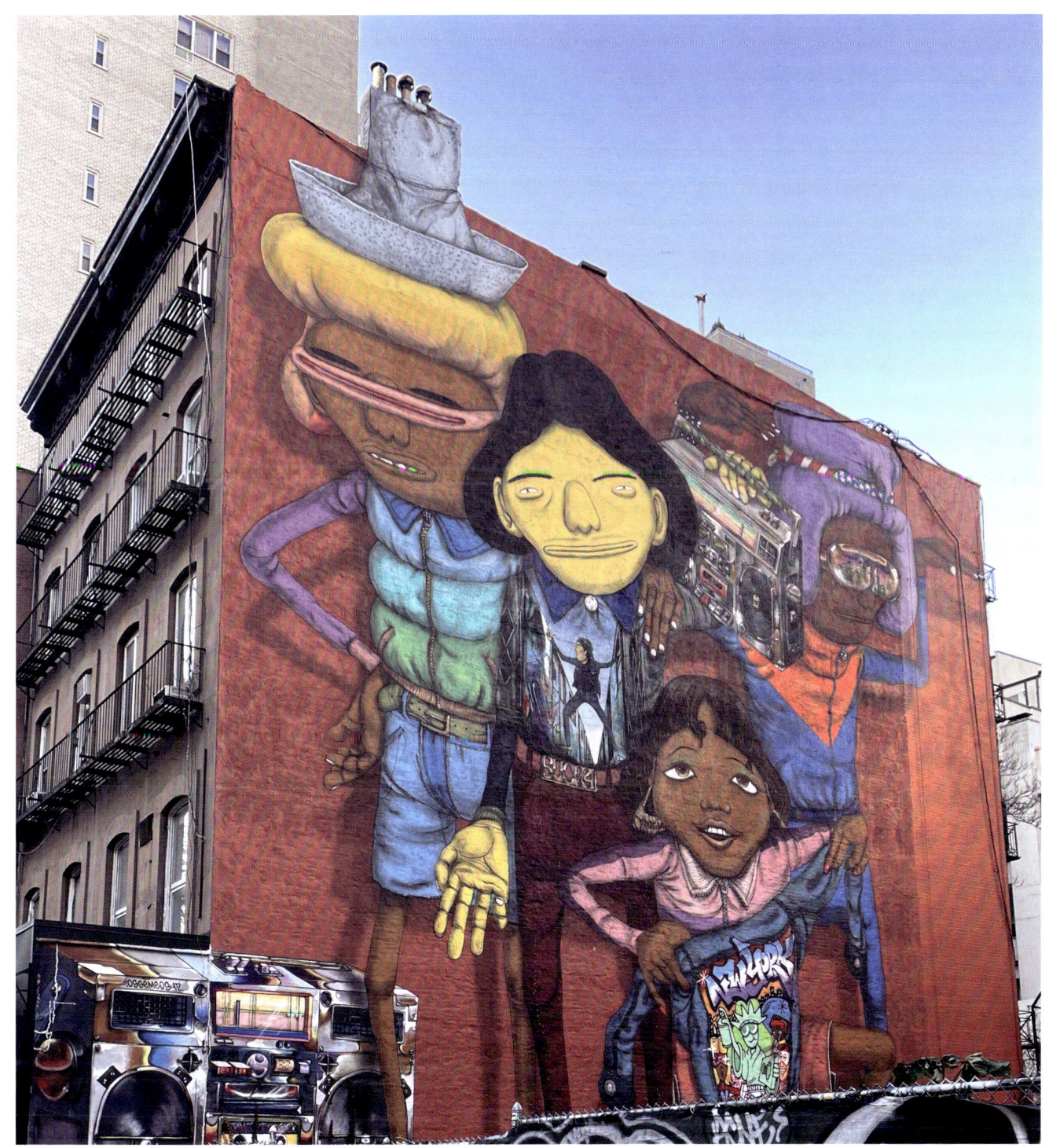

OSGEMEOS
MANHATTAN, PHOTOGRAPHED IN 2023

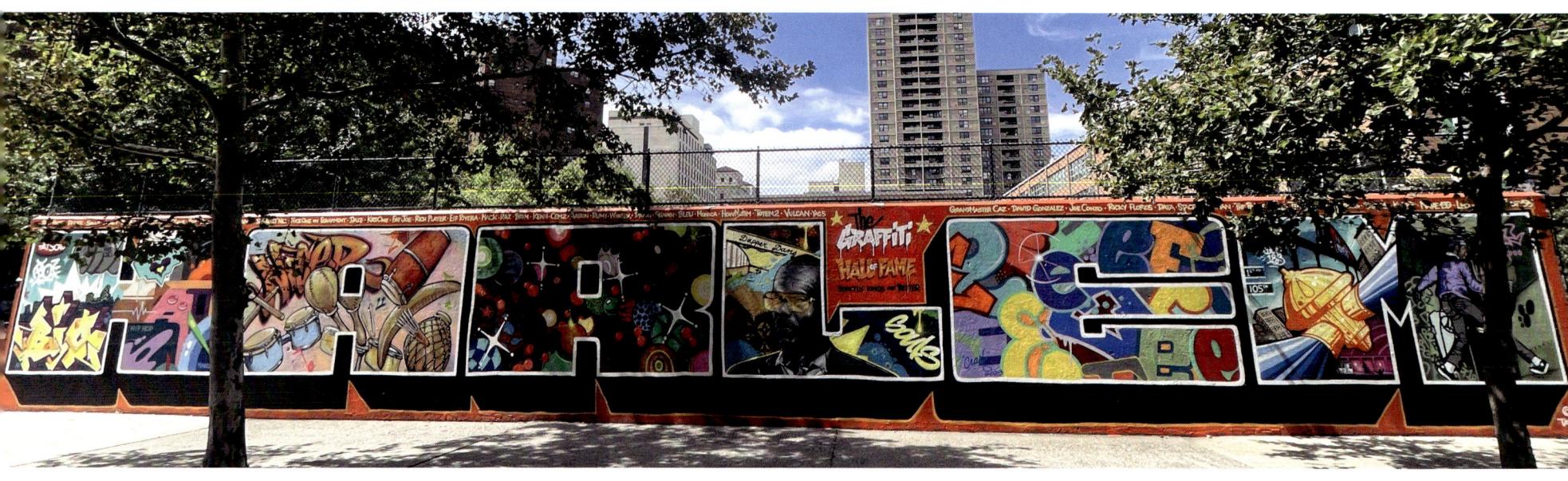

TATS CRU
GRAFFITI HALL OF FAME, MANHATTAN, PHOTOGRAPHED IN 2023

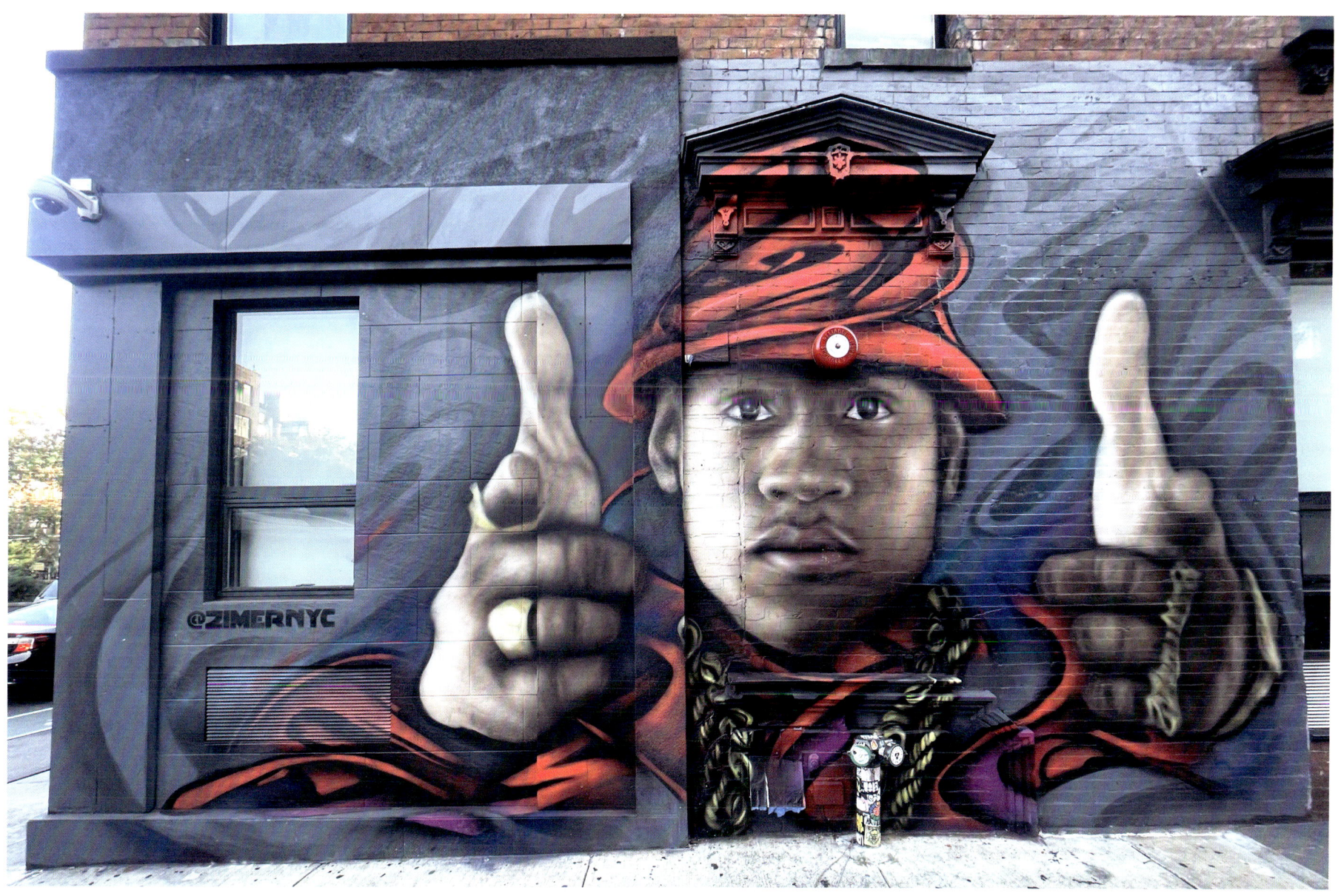

ZIMER
MANHATTAN, PHOTOGRAPHED IN 2023

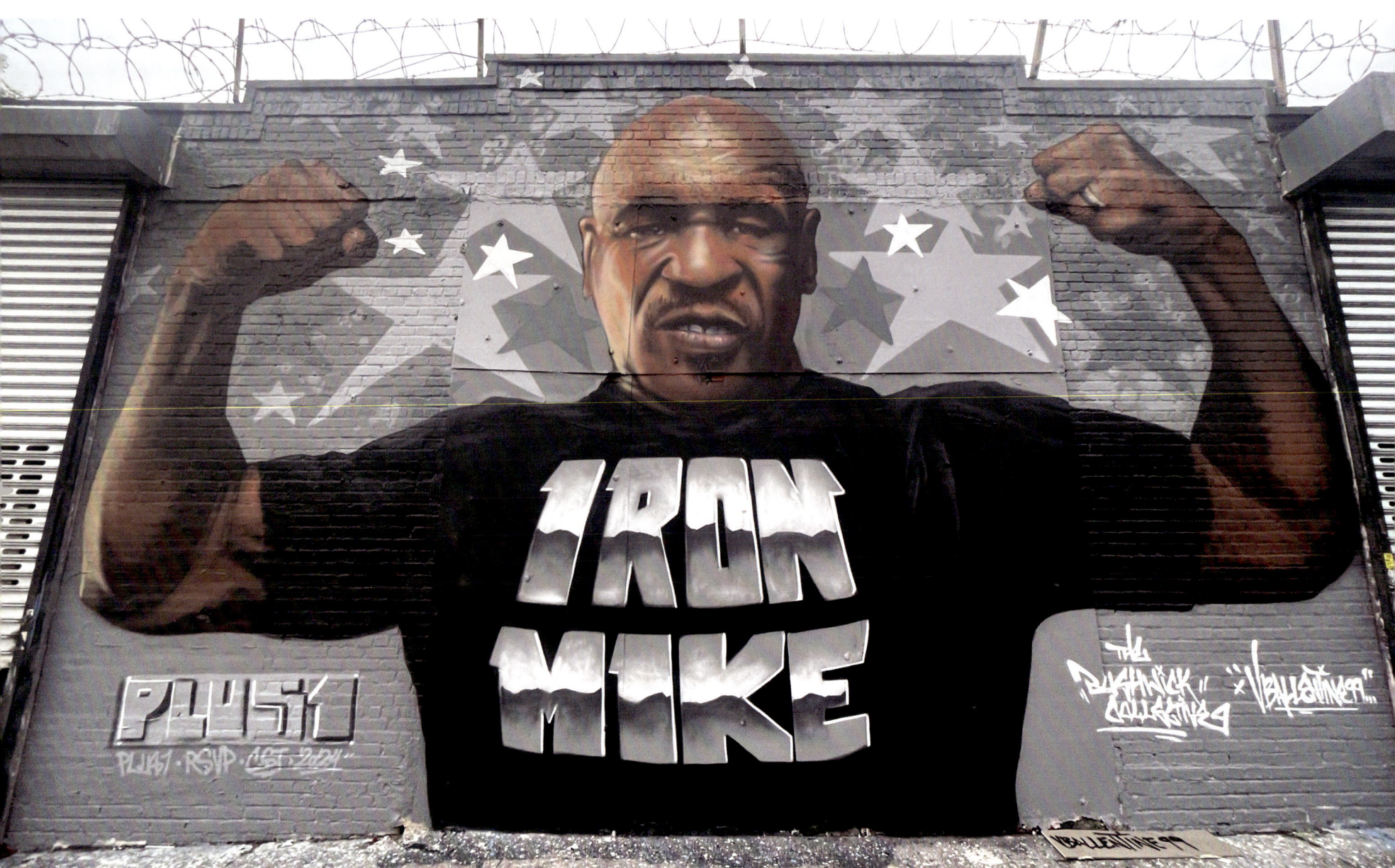

V BALLENTINE
BUSHWICK COLLECTIVE, PHOTOGRAPHED IN 2024

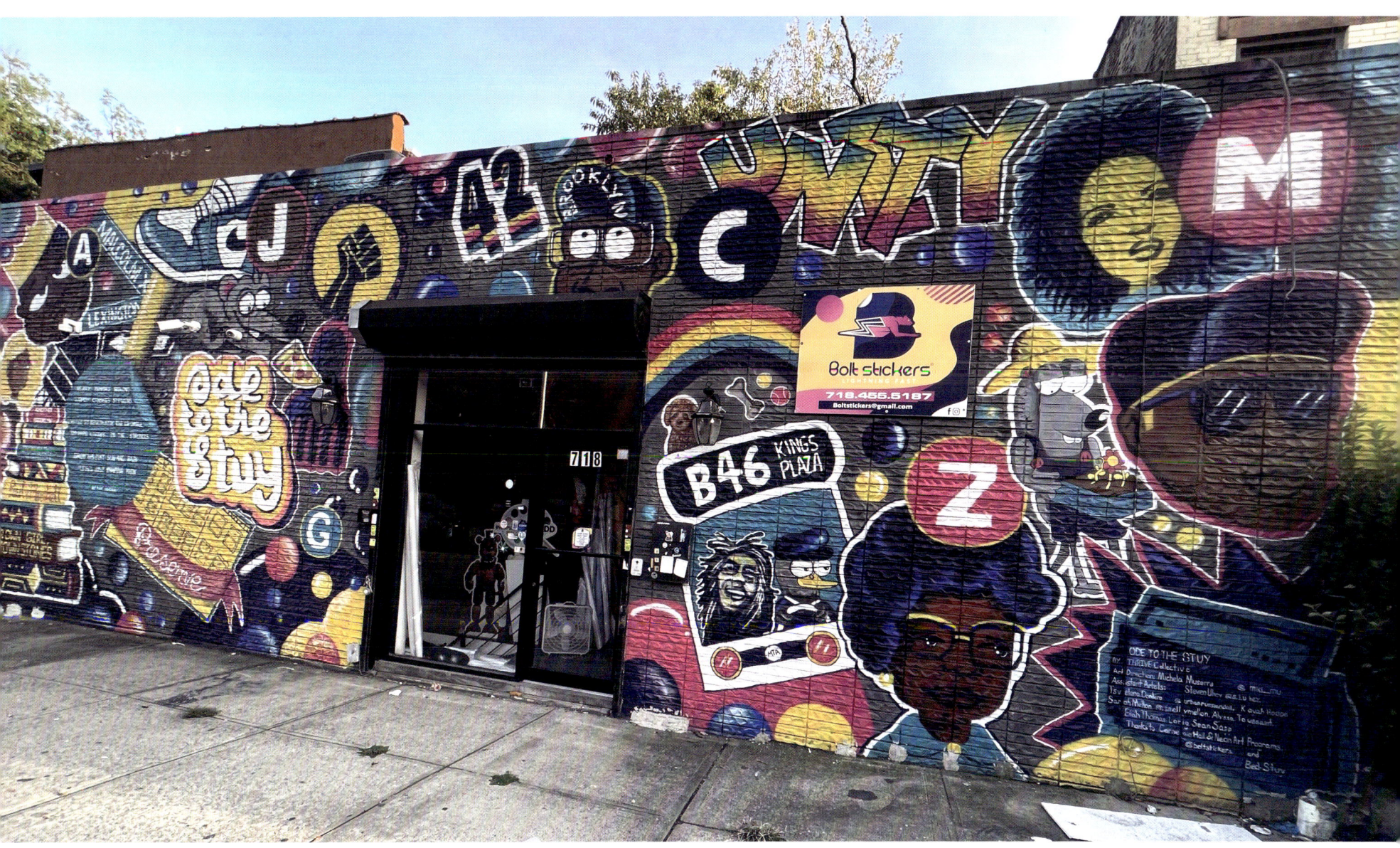

THRIVE COLLECTIVE
BED-STUY WALLS, BROOKLYN, PHOTOGRAPHED IN 2023

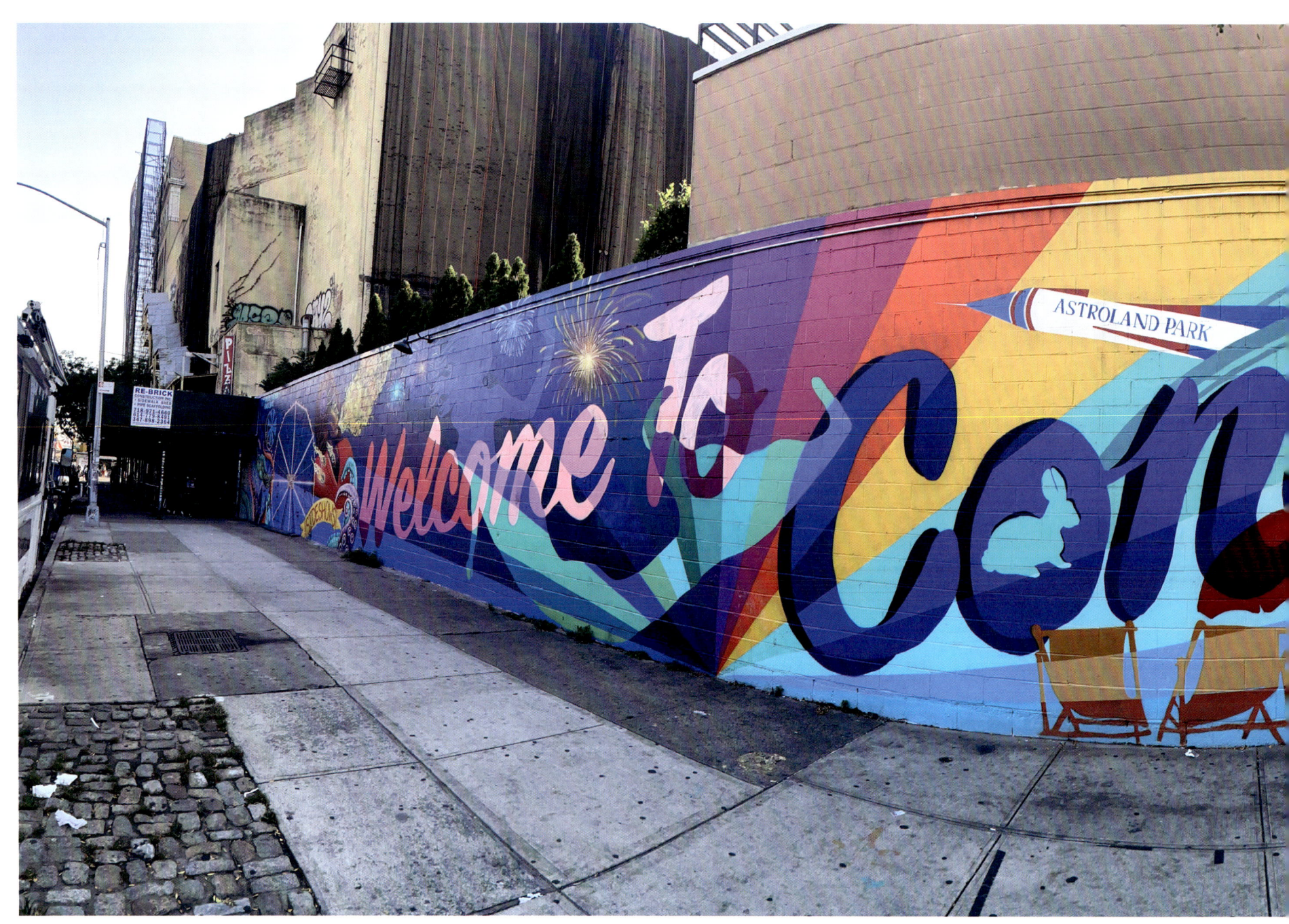

DANIELLE MASTRION
BROOKLYN, PHOTOGRAPHED IN 2023

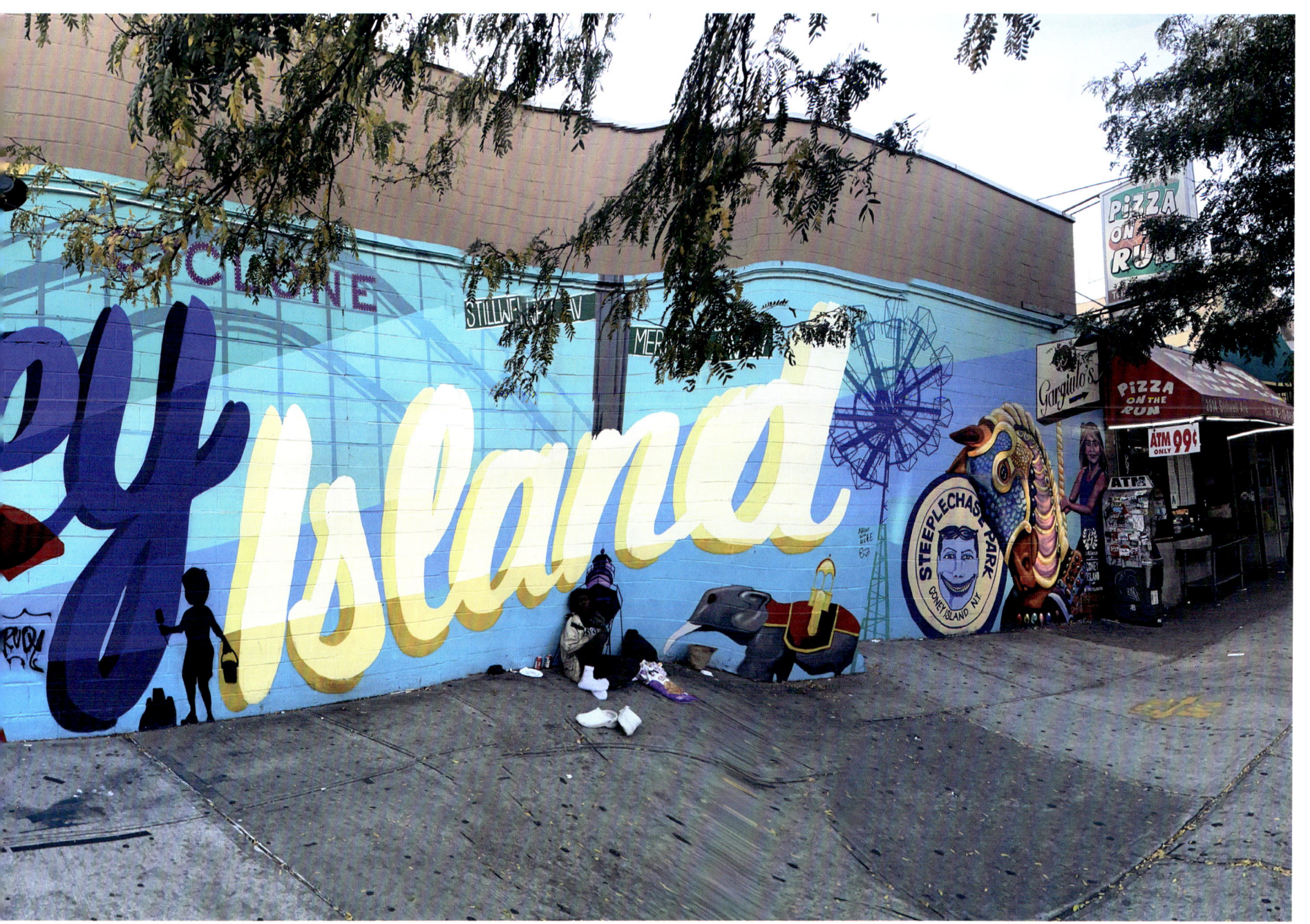

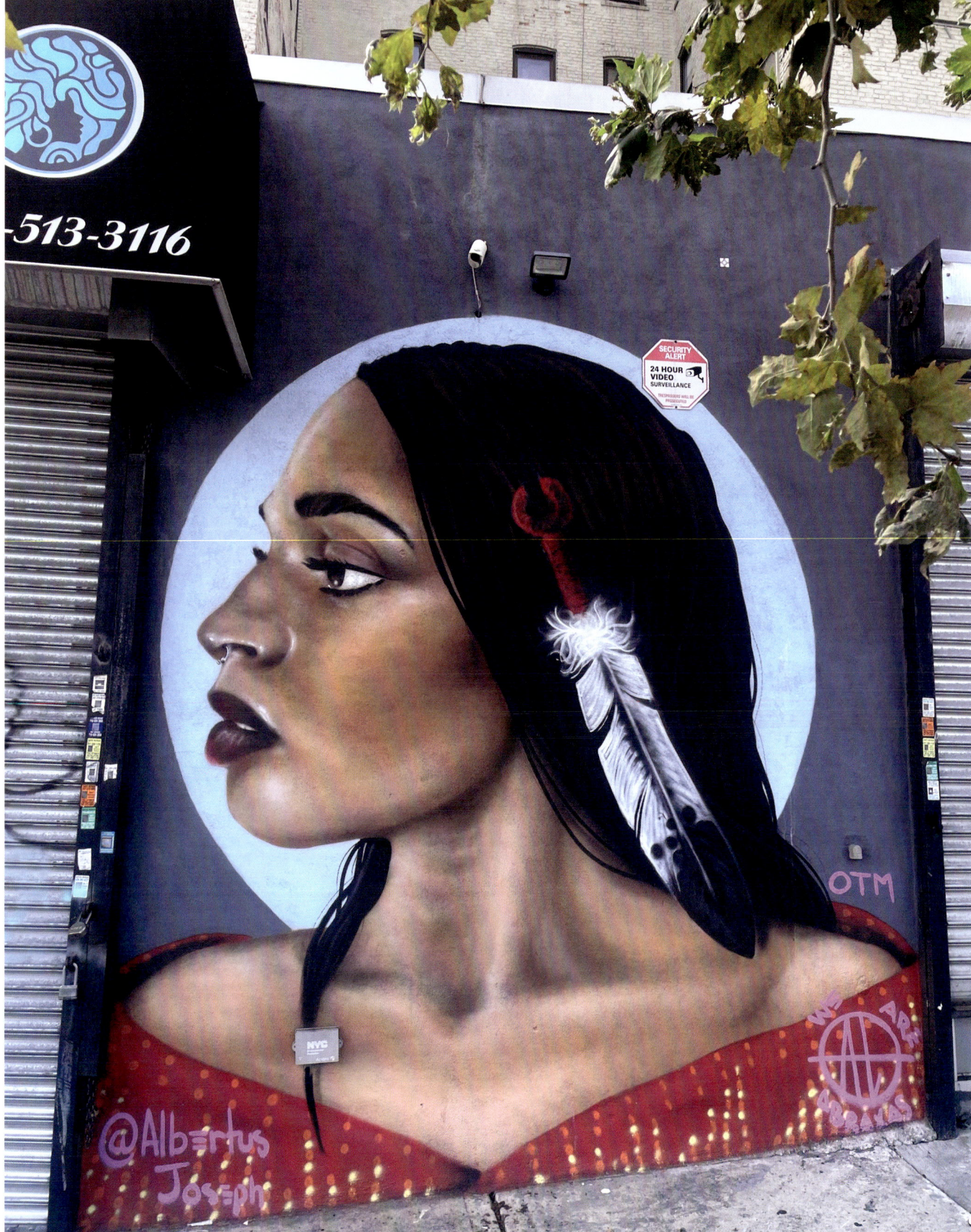

ALBERTUS JOSEPH
BOONE AVENUE WALLS, THE
BRONX, PHOTOGRAPHED IN
2023

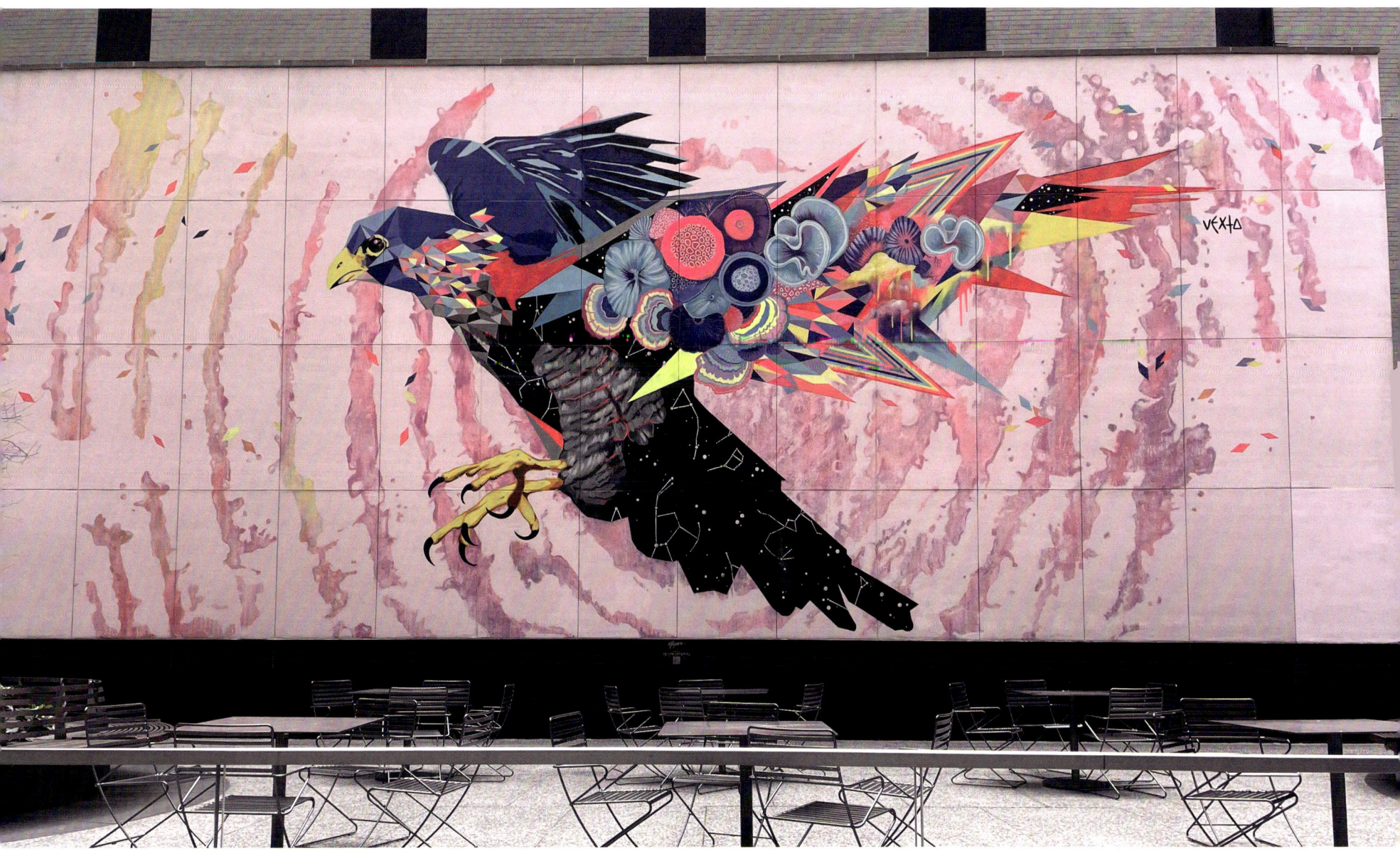

VEXTA
MANHATTAN, PHOTOGRAPHED IN 2024

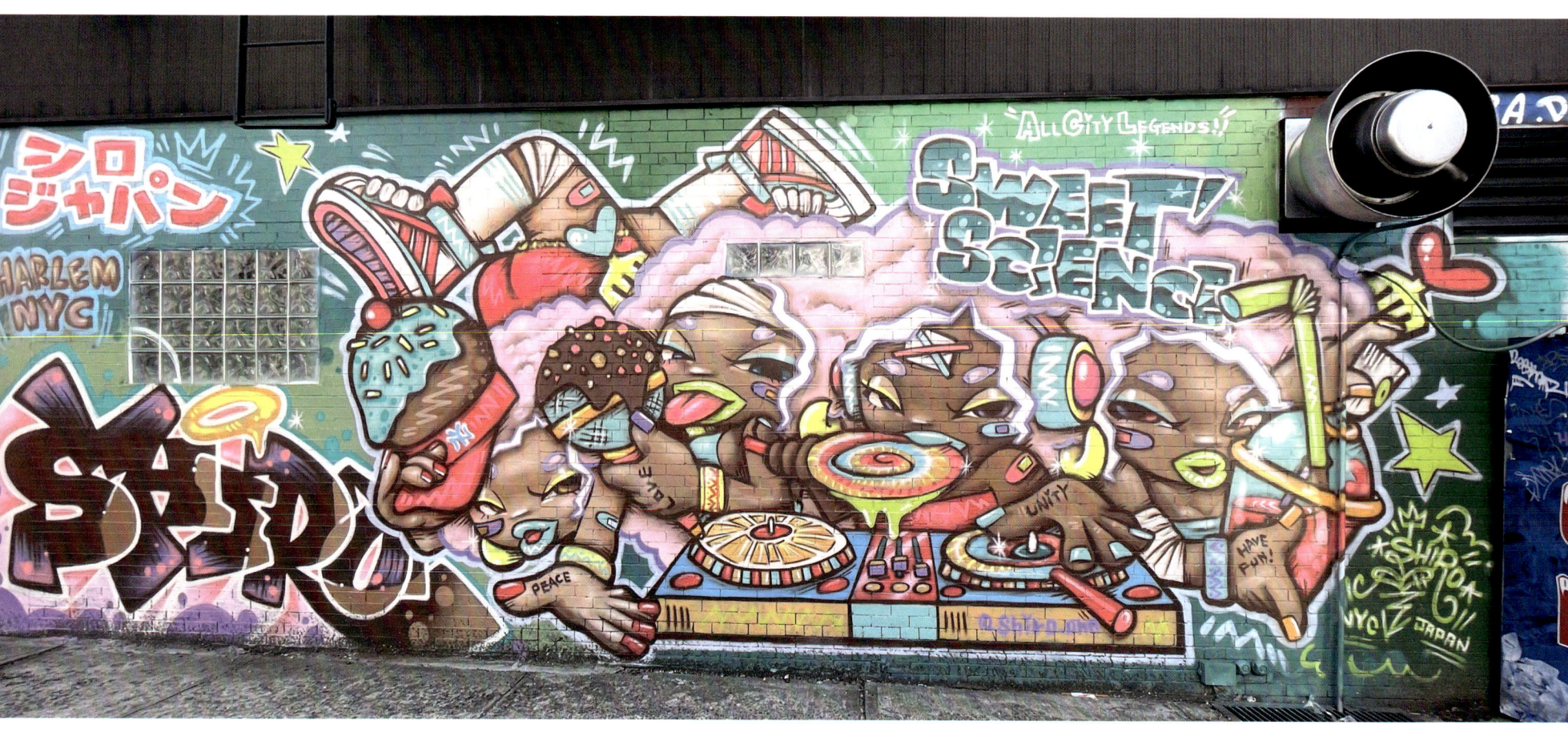

SHIRO ONE

Shiro One is a native of Japan. She is one of most popular street artists today in New York City and does fashion collaboration, exhibition, and commission jobs.
MANHATTAN, PHOTOGRAPHED IN 2024

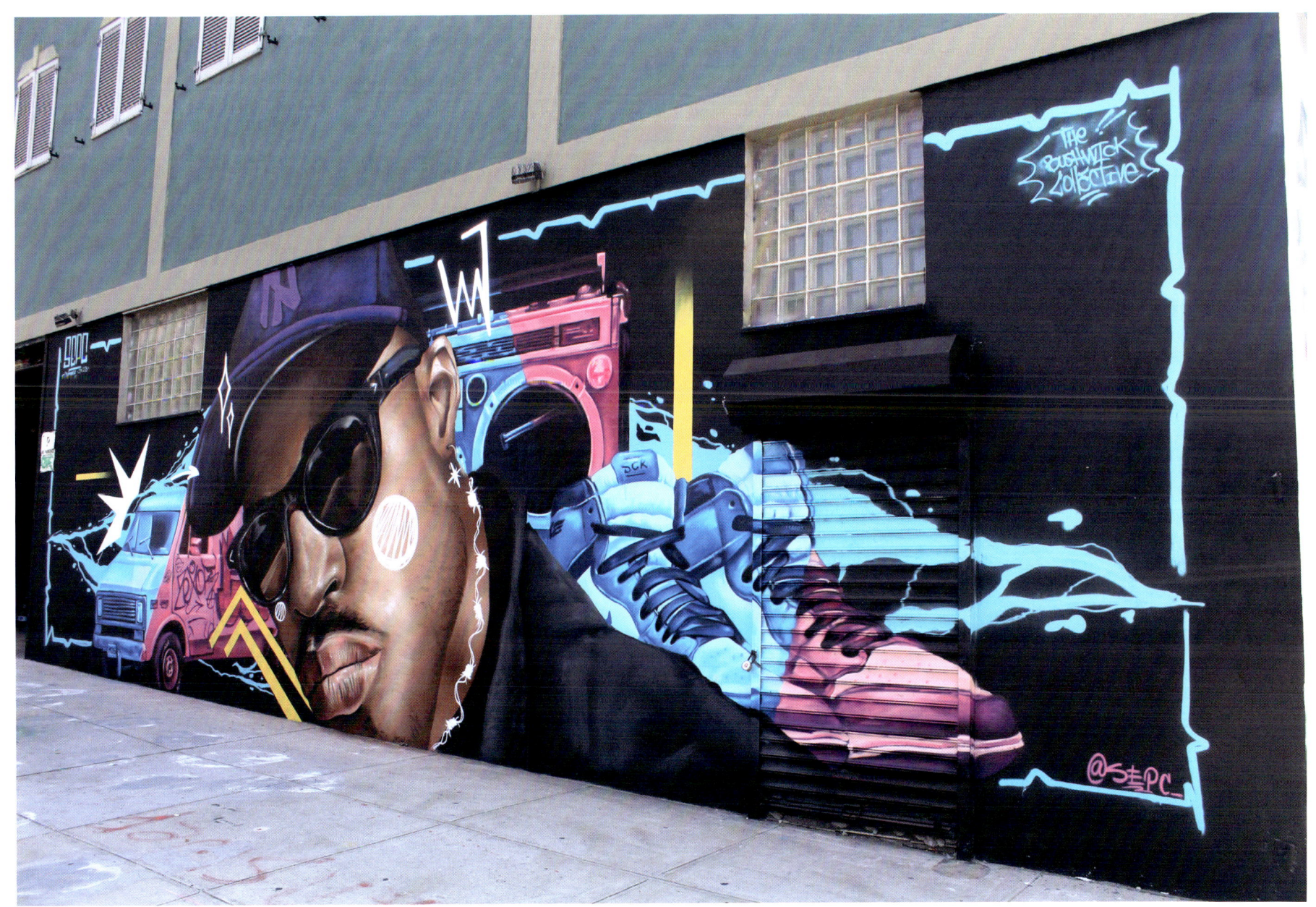

SEPC
BUSHWICK COLLECTIVE, BROOKLYN, PHOTOGRAPHED IN 2023

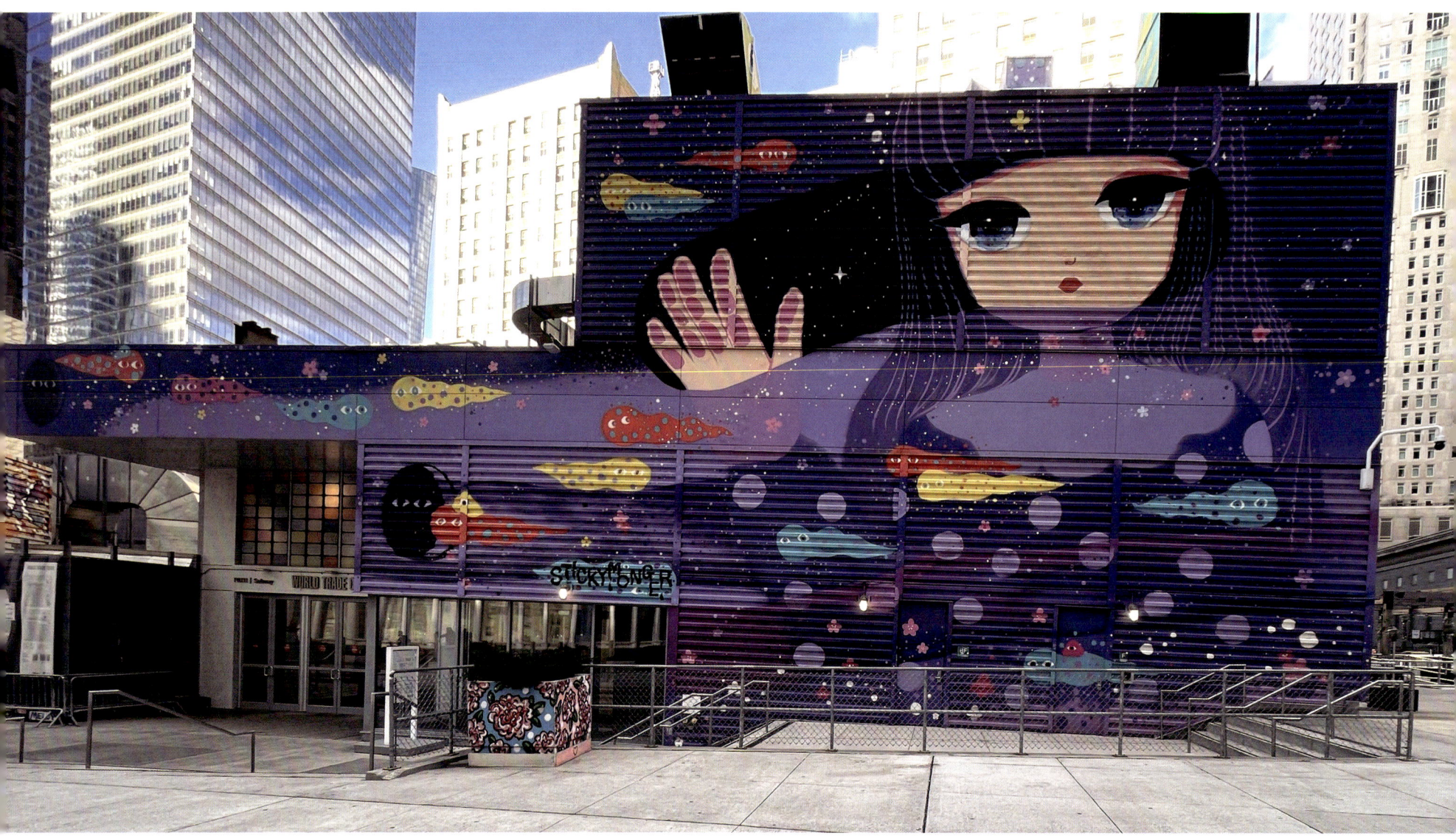

STICKY MONGER
MANHATTAN, PHOTOGRAPHED IN 2024

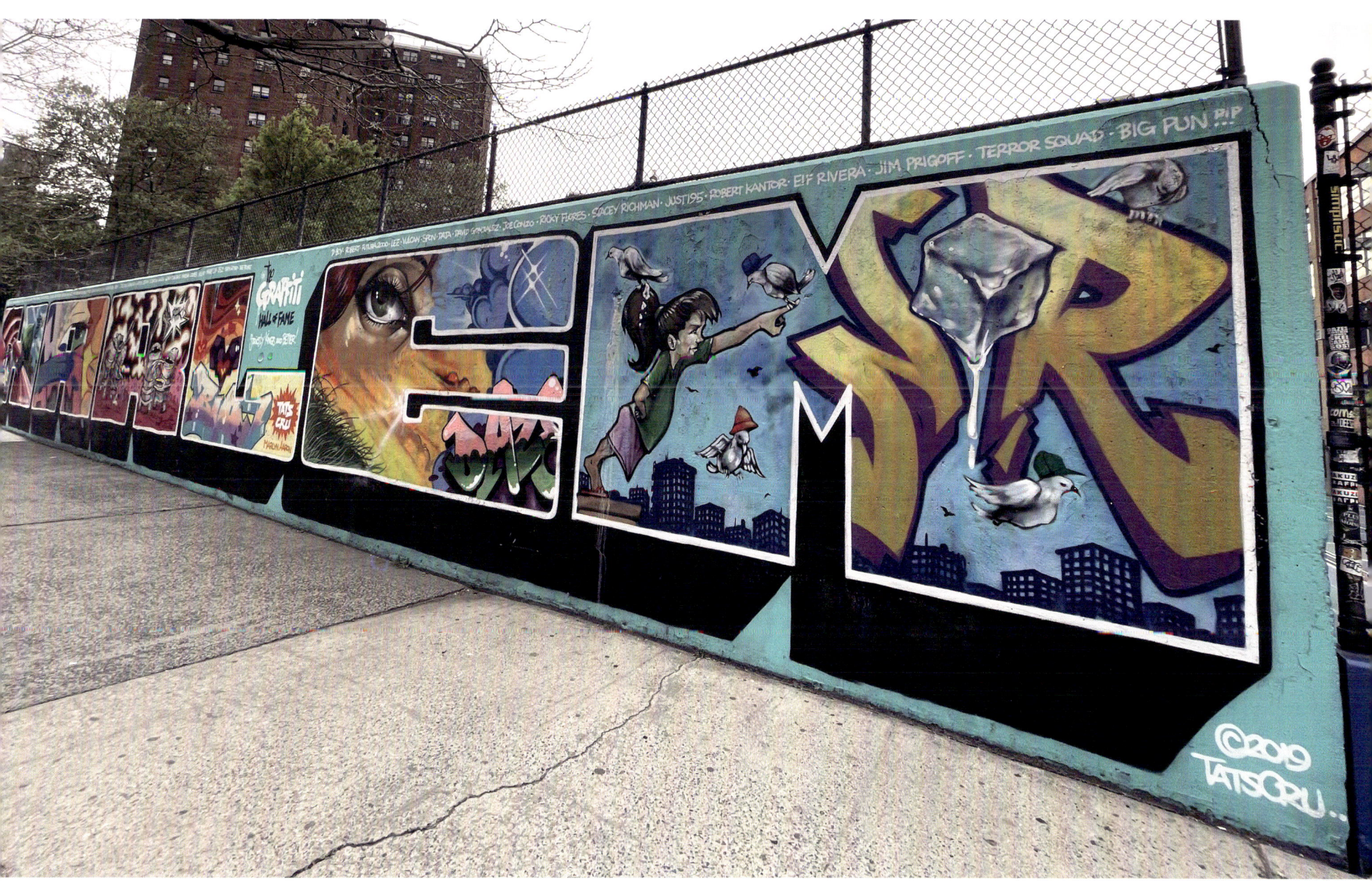

TATS CRU
GRAFFITI HALL OF FAME, MANHATTAN, PHOTOGRAPHED IN 2021

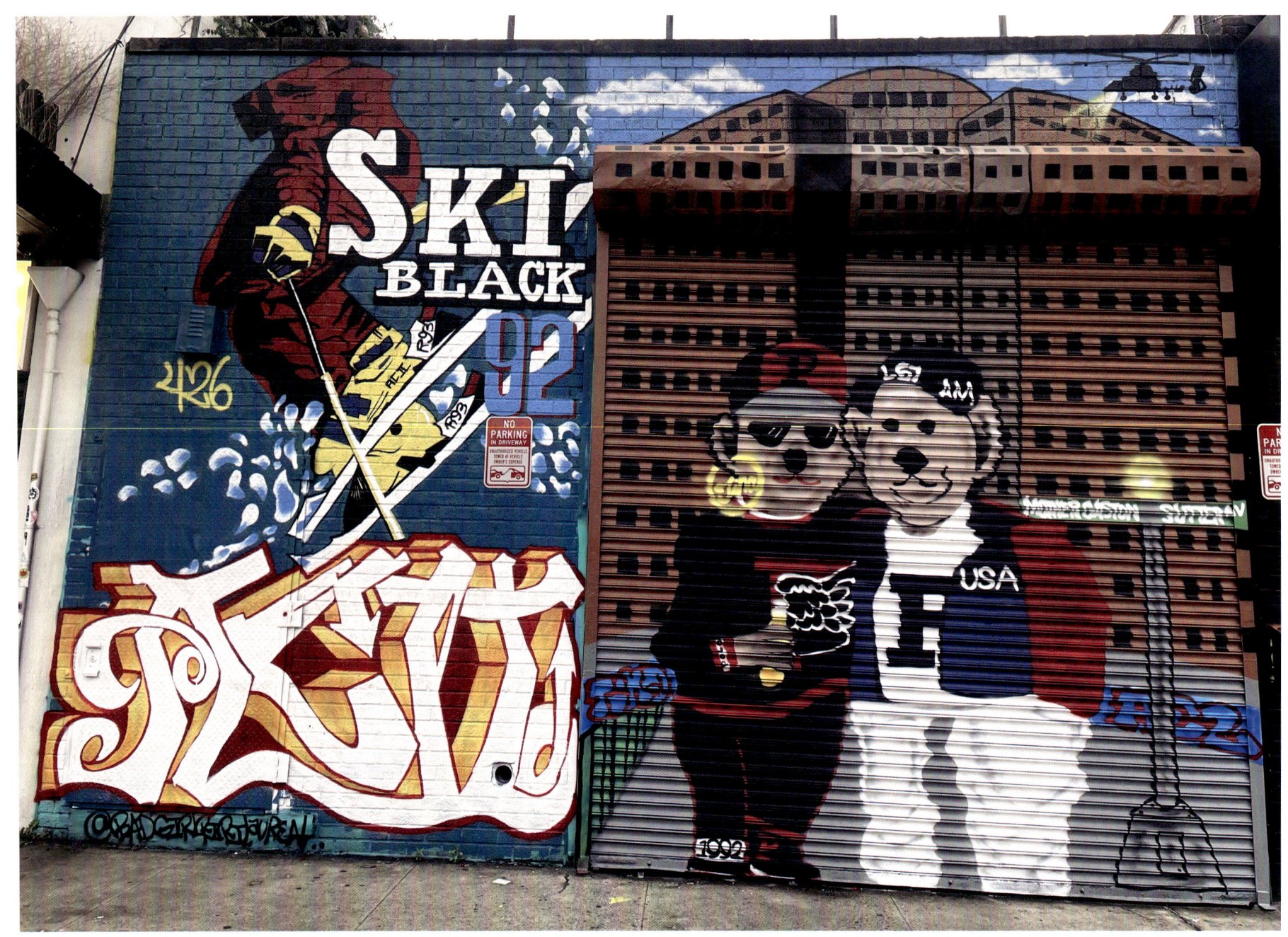

RIRI LAUREN
BUSHWICK COLLECTIVE, BROOKLYN, PHOTOGRAPHED IN 2024

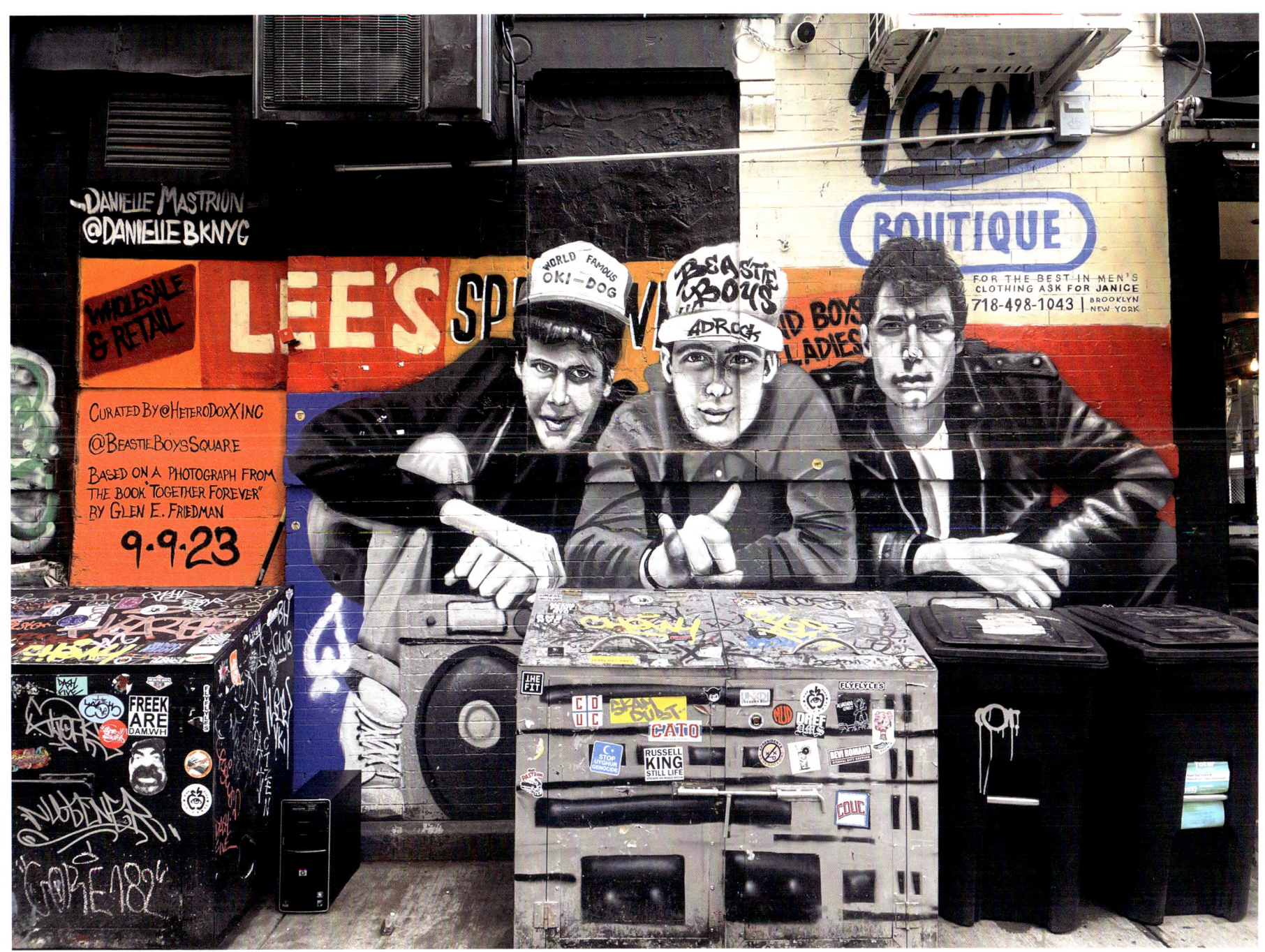

DANIELLE MASTRION
MANHATTAN, PHOTOGRAPHED IN 2024

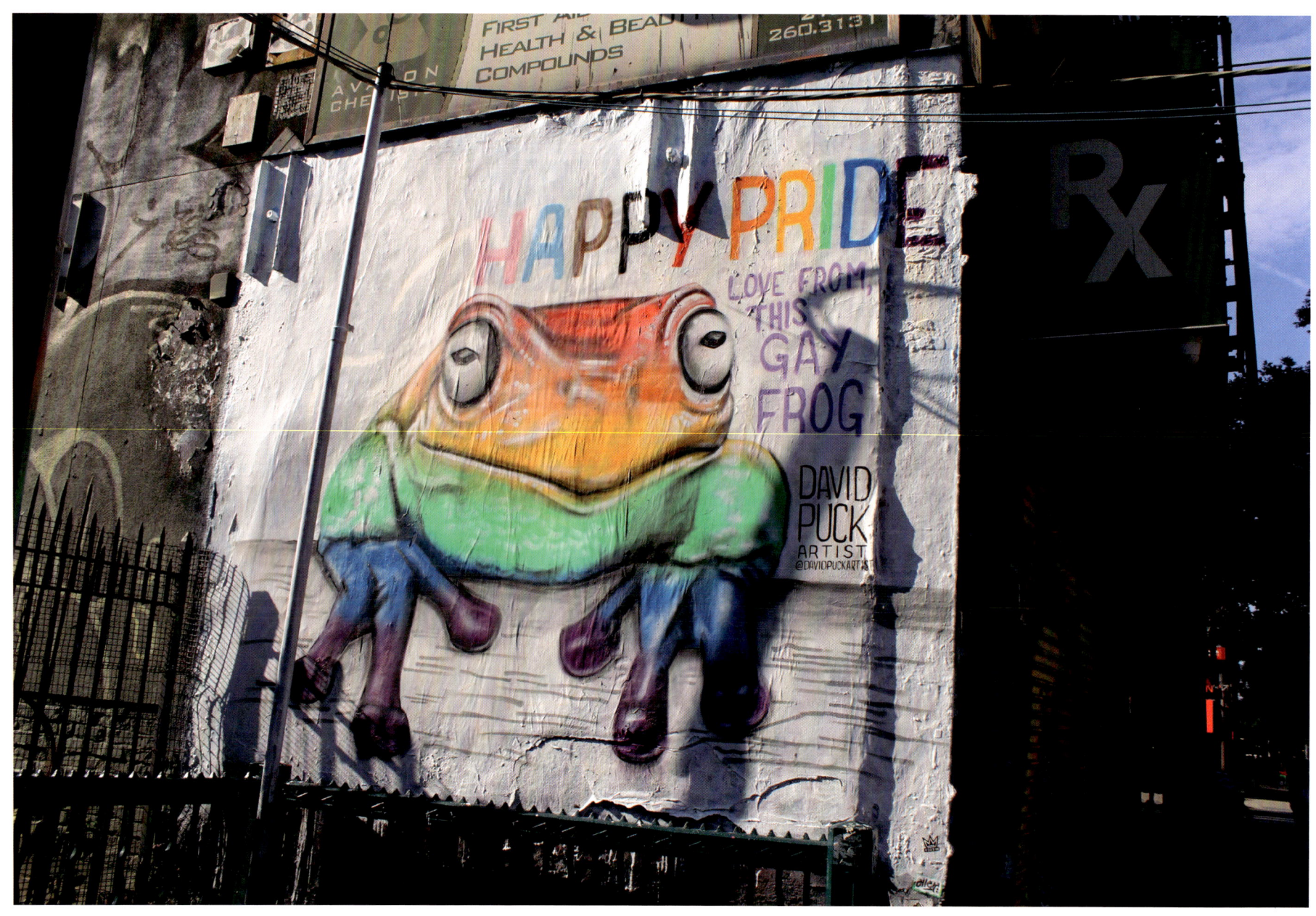

DAVID PUCK
MANHATTAN, PHOTOGRAPHED IN 2024

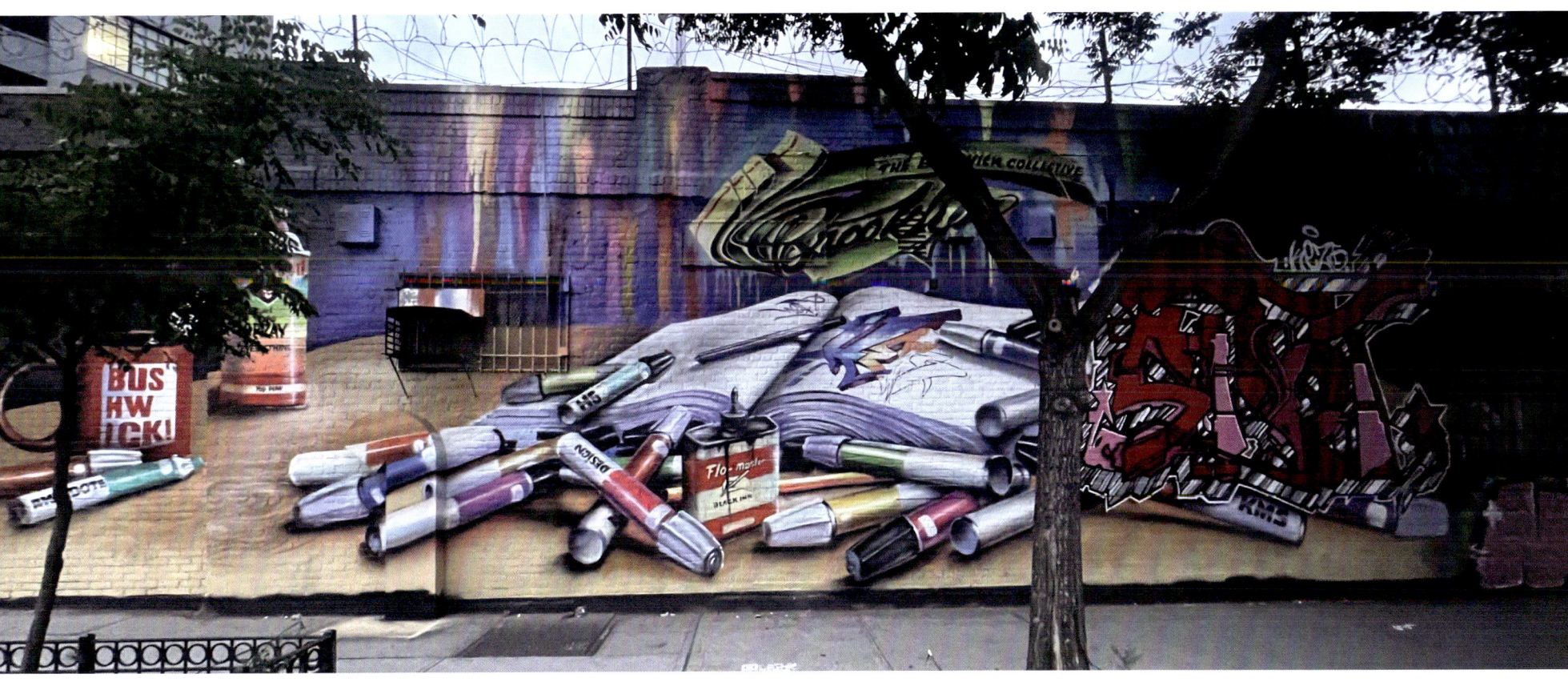

KMS CREW, KEZ5
BUSHWICK COLLECTIVE, BROOKLYN, PHOTOGRAPHED IN 2023

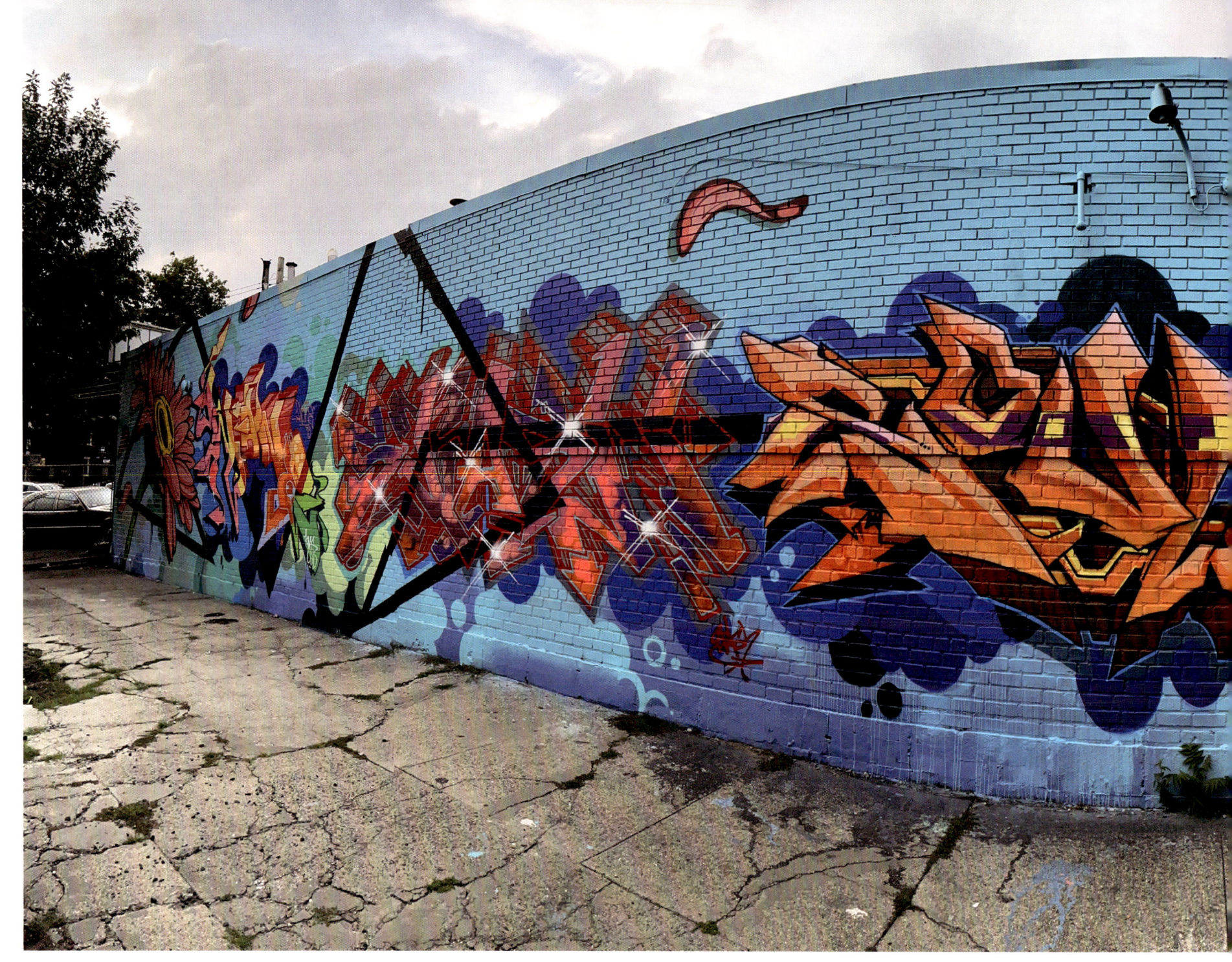

WANE COD, EL SOULS, STASH, DEPOH, EPIC UNO, CHRIS RWK
WELLING COURT MURAL PROJECT, QUEENS, PHOTOGRAPHED IN 2024

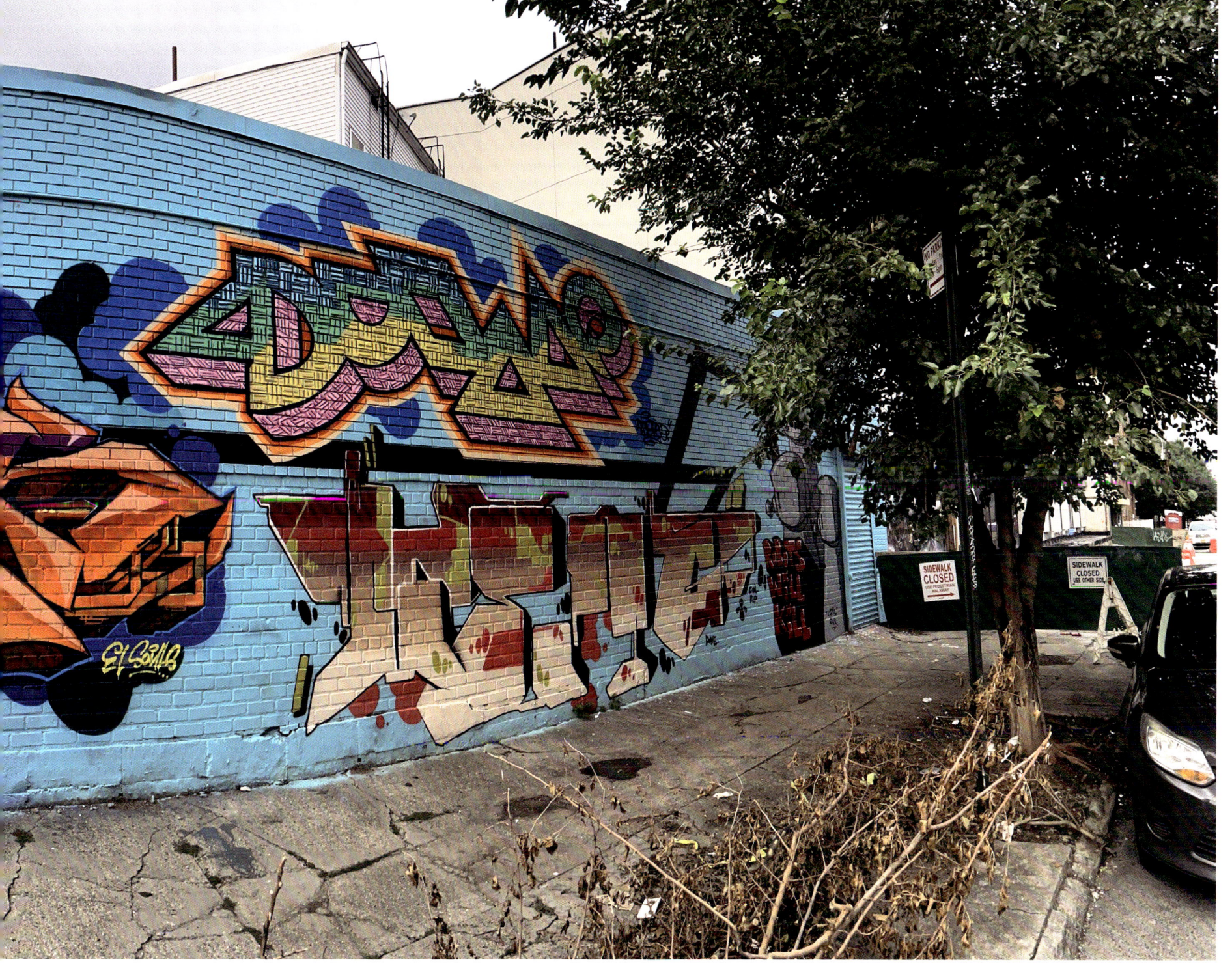

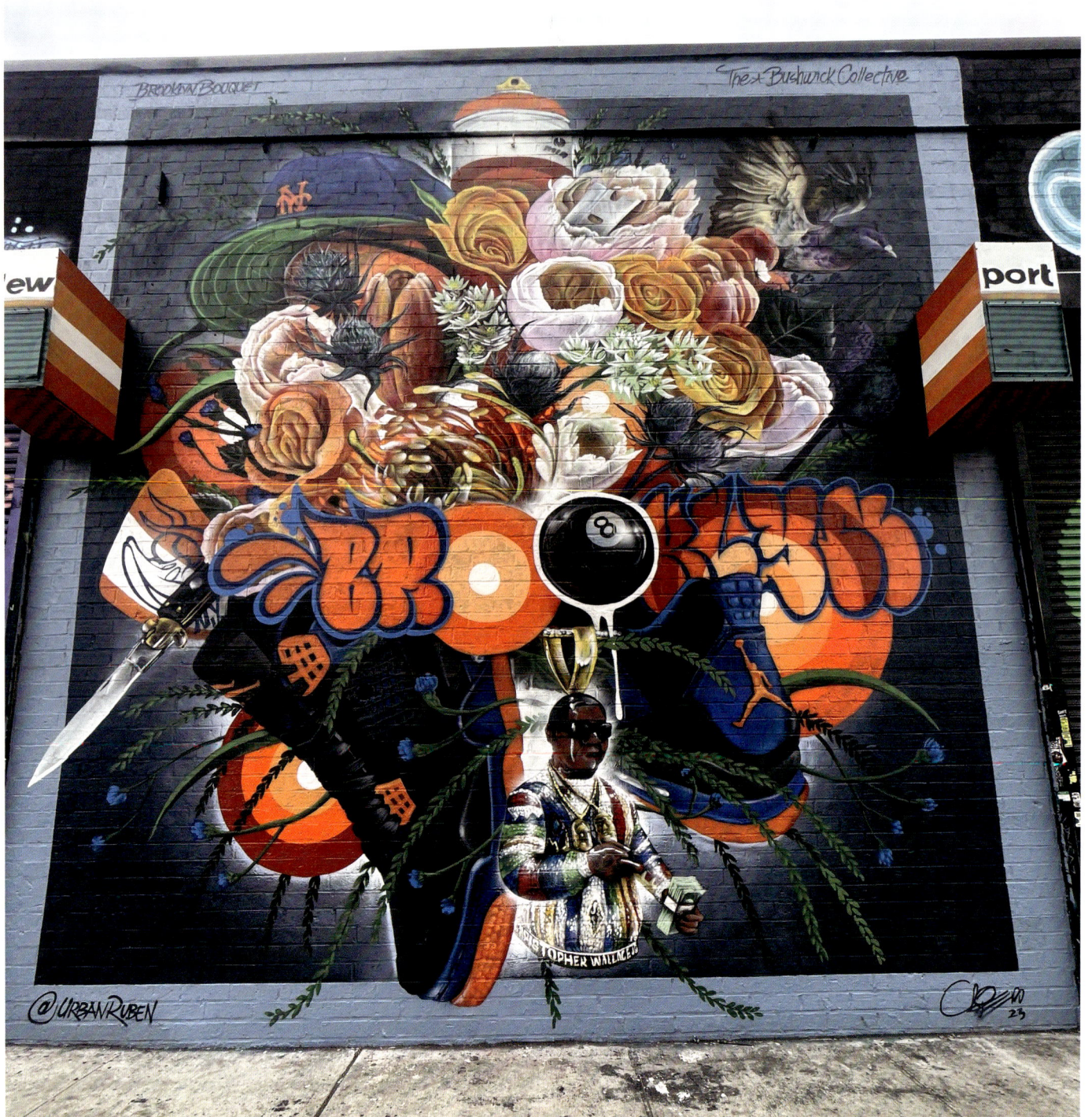

URBAN RUBEN
BUSHWICK COLLECTIVE,
BROOKLYN, PHOTOGRAPHED
IN 2023

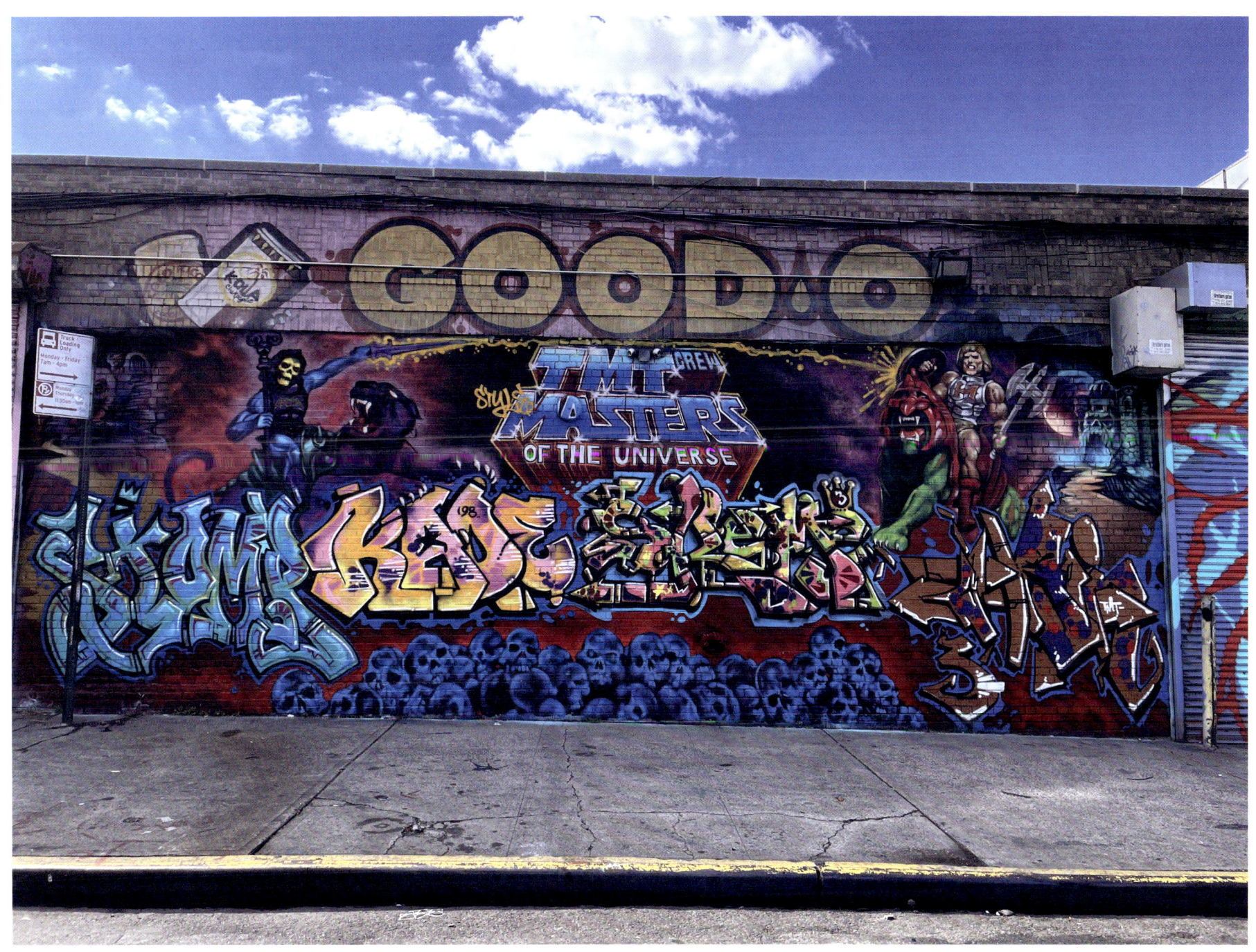

SKEME, ANDRE TRENIER, KADE, CHAIN 3
BOONE AVENUE WALLS, THE BRONX, PHOTOGRAPHED IN 2024

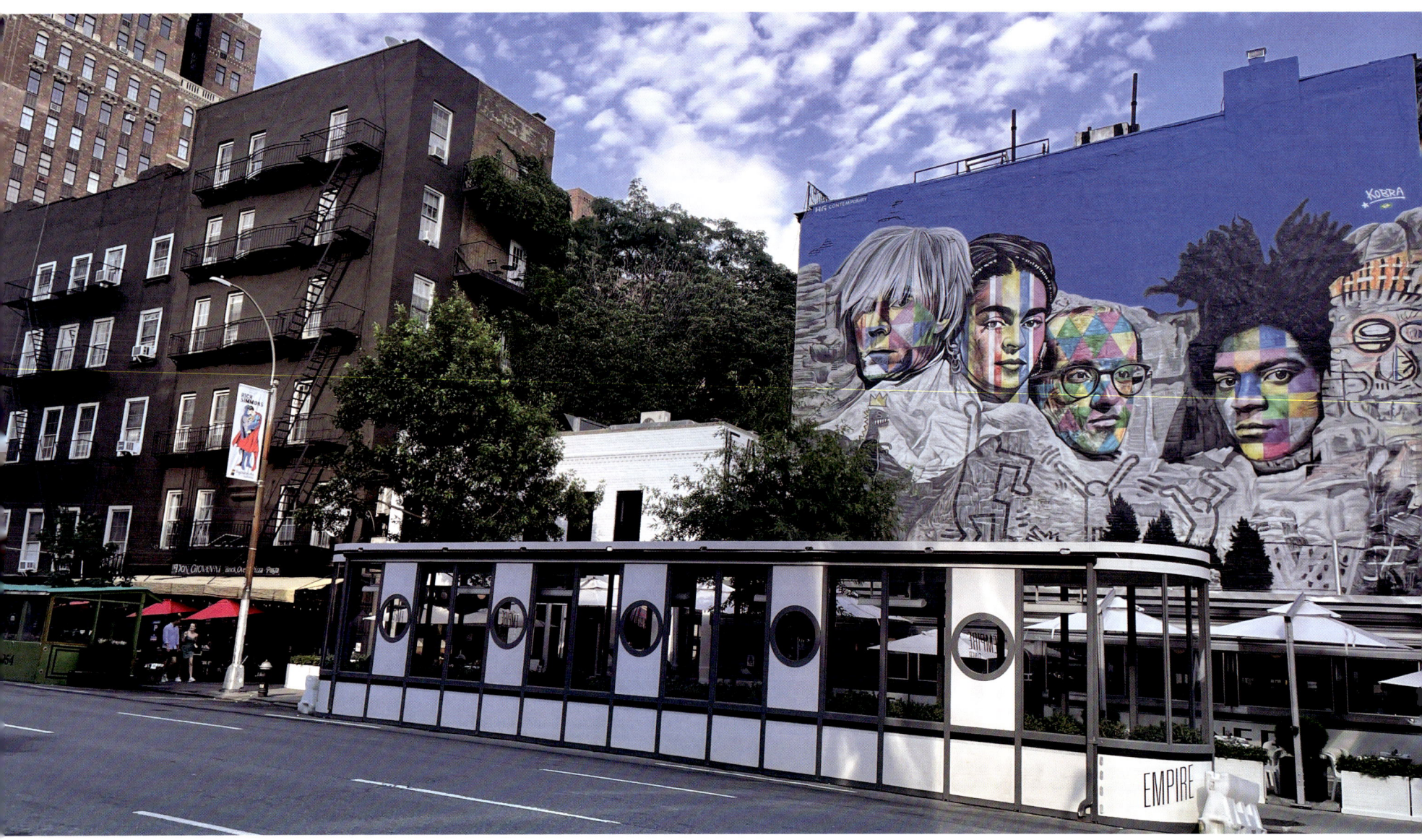

KOBRA
MANHATTAN, PHOTOGRAPHED IN 2022

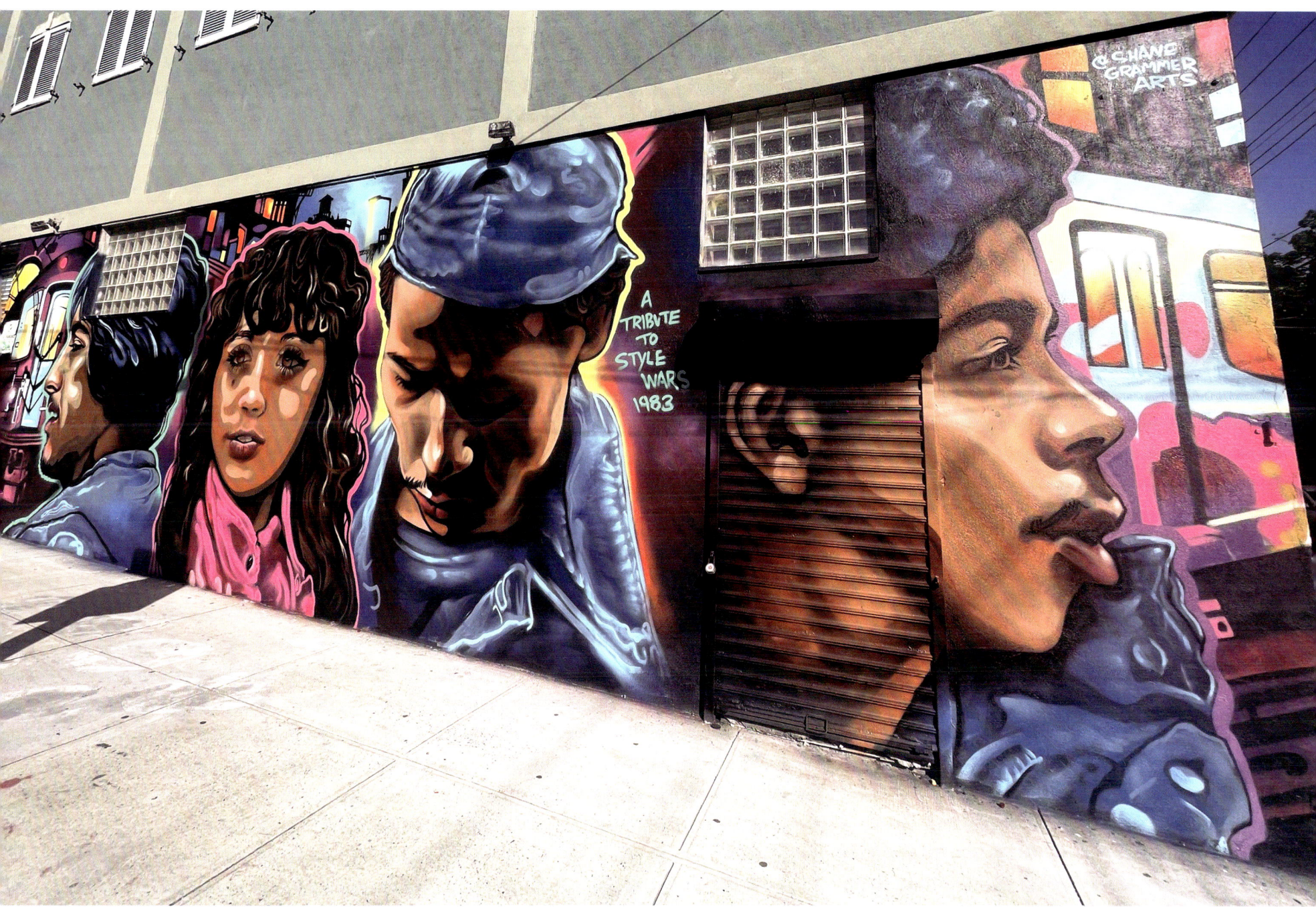

Text within mural: A TRIBUTE TO STYLE WARS 1983

Text within mural: @SHANE GRAMMER ARTS

SHANE GRAMMER
BUSHWICK COLLECTIVE, BROOKLYN, PHOTOGRAPHED IN 2024

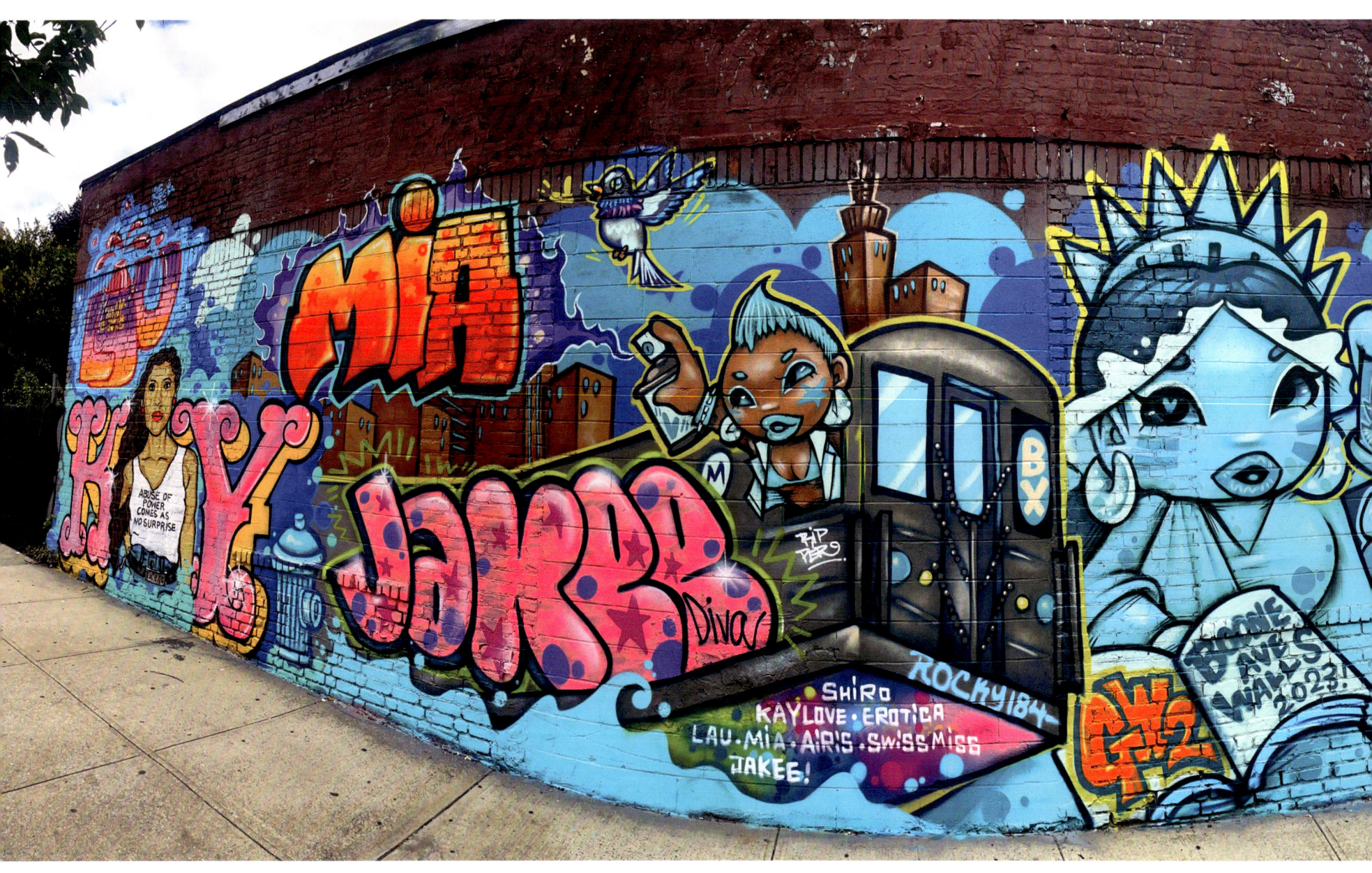

KAY LOVE, MIA, JAKEE AIRIS, EROTICA, LAU, SWISS MISS, SHIRO ONE
BOONE AVENUE WALL, THE BRONX, PHOTOGRAPHED IN 2023

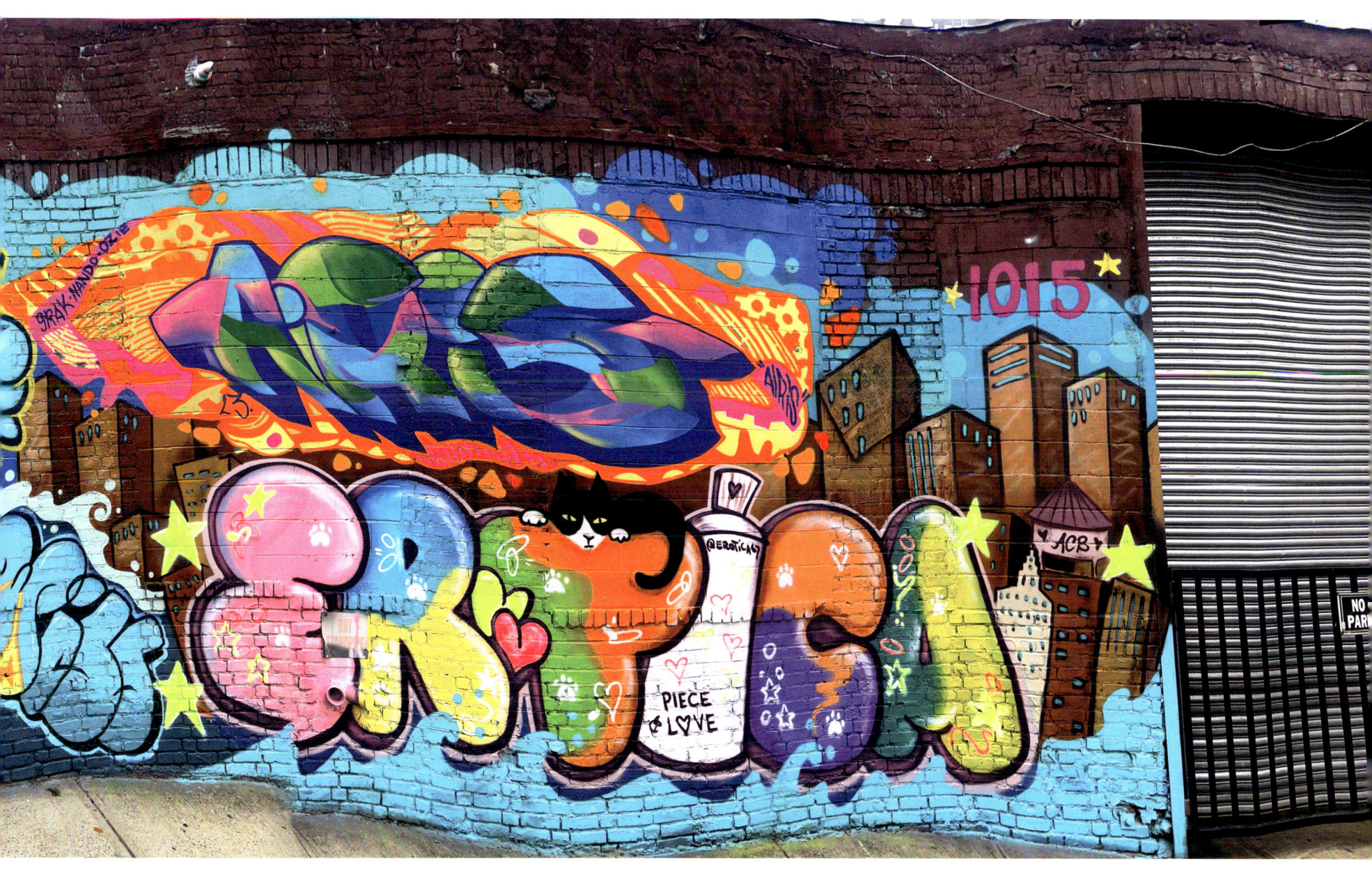

267

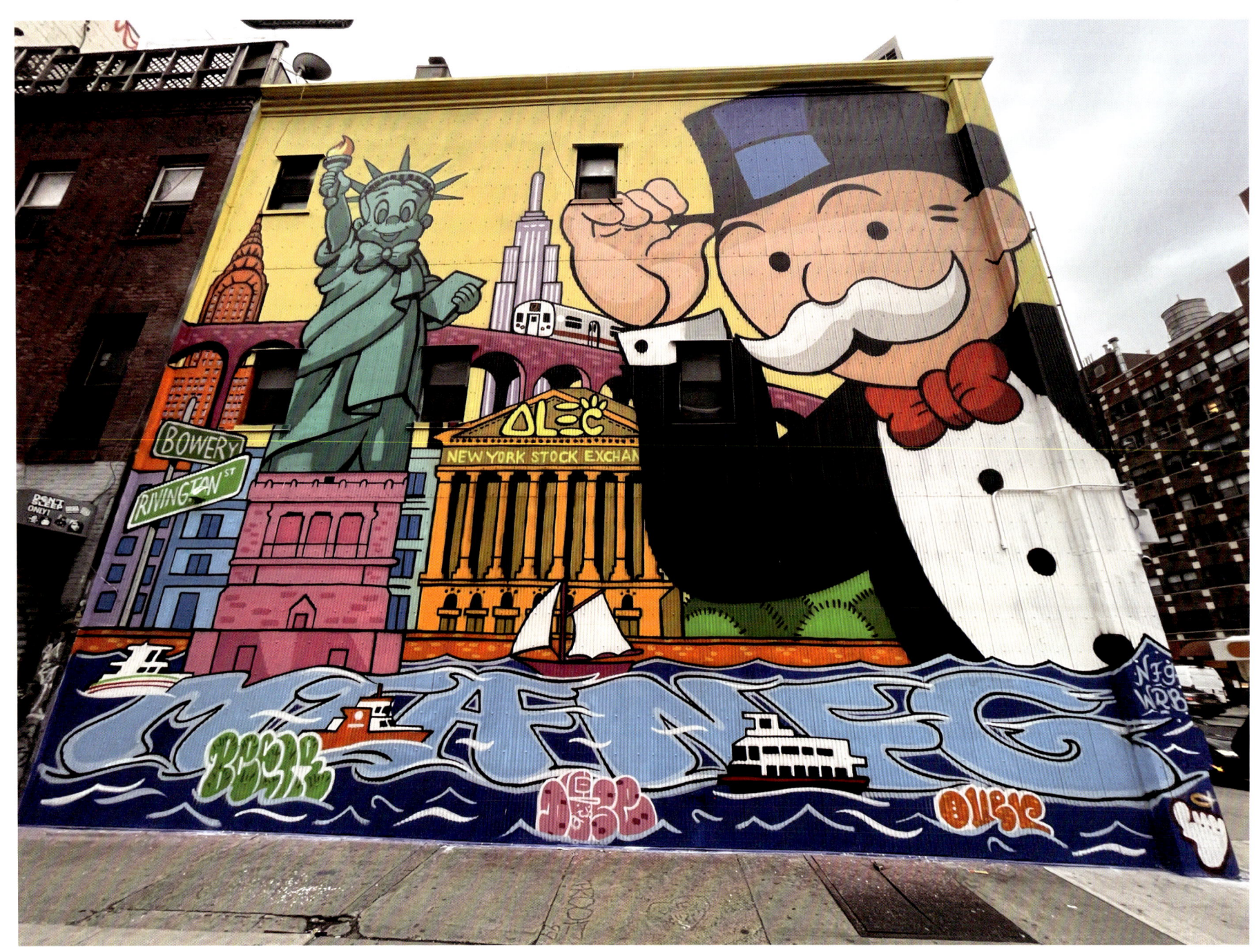

ALEC MONOPOLY
MANHATTAN, PHOTOGRAPHED IN 2024

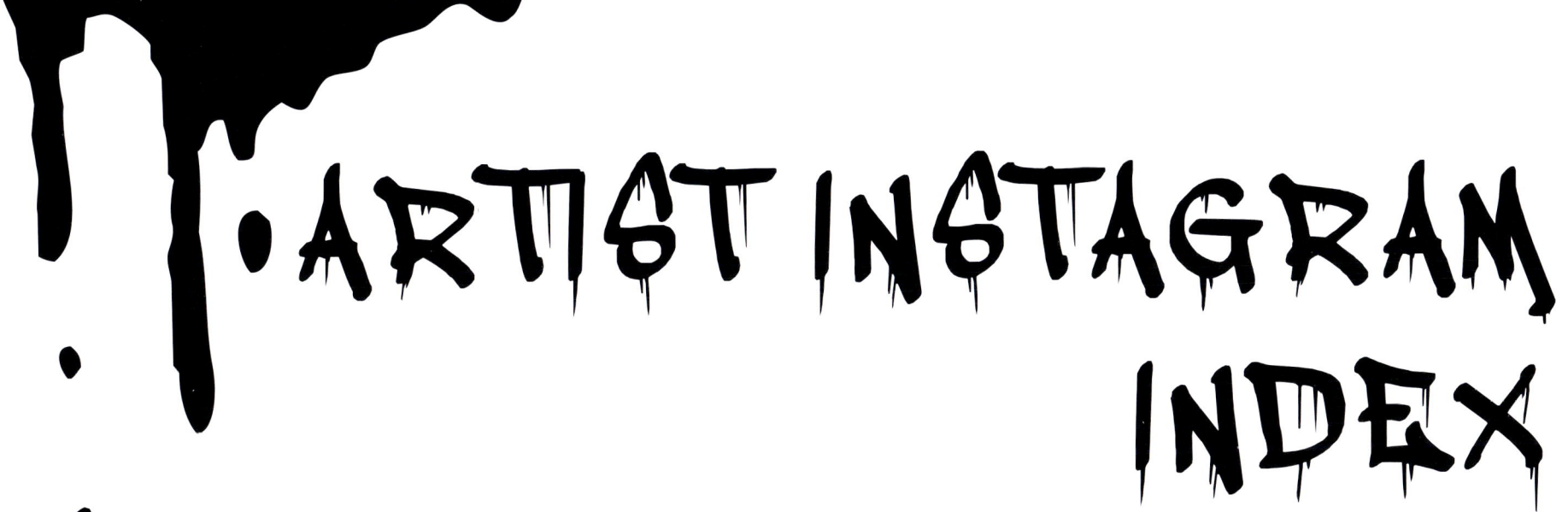

ARTIST INSTAGRAM INDEX

STREET AND GRAFFITI ARTS EVENTS AND LOCALES

Event/Locale	Event/Locale	Event/Locale
GRAFFITI HALL OF FAME	@GRAFFITIHALLOFFAMENYC	MANHATTAN
BED-STUY WALLS	@BEDSTUYWALLS	BROOKLYN
FIRST STREET GREEN ART PARK	@FSGPARK	MANHATTAN
FREEMAN ALLEY	@THEALLEYRY	MANHATTAN
BOONE AVENUE WALLS	@BOONEAVENUEWALLS	THE BRONX
WELLING COURT MURAL PROJECT	@WELLINGCOURTMURALPROJECT	QUEENS
BUSHWICK COLLECTIVE	@THEBUSHWICKCOLLECTIVE	BROOKLYN

"STYLE WRITING" CHAPTER
(LISTED IN CHAPTER 1 PHOTO ORDER)

Artist(s)	Instagram	Event/Location
CRASH	@CRASHONE	Boone Avenue Walls, THE BRONX
SKEME	@SKEMETHREEYARDKINGS	Graffiti Hall of Fame, MANHATTAN
BG 183	@BG183TATSCRU	Boone Avenue Walls, THE BRONX
SPOT KMS	@KMS_CREW	Boone Avenue Walls, THE BRONX
KING BEE	@KINGBEEUW	Graffiti Hall of Fame, MANHATTAN
WANE ONE	@WANEONECOD	Graffiti Hall of Fame, MANHATTAN
COES SNEAKERS	@COESSNEAKERS	Bushwick Collective, BROOKLYN
COPE 2	@MRCOPETWO	Graffiti Hall of Fame, MANHATTAN
WORE ONE	@WORE_ONE	Boone Avenue Walls, THE BRONX
CRAM CONCEPTS	@CRAMCEPTS	First Street Green Art Park, MANHATTAN
STASH	@MR_STASH	Boone Avenue Walls, THE BRONX
DAZE	@DAZEWORLDNYC	Boone Avenue Walls, THE BRONX
KING 157	@1984.YO	Boone Avenue Walls, THE BRONX
DELTA 2	@DELTA2NYC	Graffiti Hall of Fame, MANHATTAN

STASH	@MR_STASH	First Street Green Art Park, MANHATTAN
TKID	@TKID170	Graffiti Hall of Fame, MANHATTAN
EL SOULS	@SOULSNYC	Boone Avenue Walls, THE BRONX
DOVE ROC, ZORE 64, ADAM FU	@DOVEROC, @ZORE64, @ADAM	FU Boone Avenue Walls, BRONX
EPIC UNO	@EPICUNO	Graffiti Hall of Fame, MANHATTAN
MIKE 171, SJK 171, ALBERTUS JOSEPH	@MIKE_171, SJK_171, @ALBERTUSJOSEPH	QUEENS
SOZE	@SOZE527	Graffiti Hall of Fame, MANHATTAN
BIO TATS CRU	@BIOTATSCRU	Boone Avenue Walls, THE BRONX
KING 157, ROBERT NEXUS	@1984.YO, @OG_NEXUS_408	Bed-Stuy Walls, BROOKLYN
SCRATCH NYC	@SCRATCH_NYC	Graffiti Hall of Fame, MANHATTAN
DOME NYC	@DOMENEWYORKCITY	Graffiti Hall of Fame, MANHATTAN
BC	@BC_NBA	Graffiti Hall of Fame, MANHATTAN
JAEK EL DIABLO	@JAEKELDIABLO	Boone Avenue Walls, THE BRONX
BG 183	@BG183TATSCRU	Boone Avenue Walls, THE BRONX
YES ONE	@YESONE	Boone Avenue Walls, THE BRONX
MRSBX	@MRRS.BX	Boone Avenue Walls, THE BRONX
WEN, SPOT KMS	@WENCOD, @KMS_CREW	Boone Avenue Walls, THE BRONX

WILL POWER, BUTCH 2, BOT 707, DAC, OBE1	@HIPHOPISMYRELIGION, @COCOA_BUTTER_SUPREME	THE BRONX
REE2, CHAIN 3, WILL POWER	@REE_VILOMAR, @HIPHOPISMYRELIGION, @CHAIN3TMT	THE BRONX
MANUEL ACEVEDO	@698MANUELACEVEDO	Boone Avenue Walls, THE BRONX
TOPAZ, JERMS	@TOPAZFTR, @DJJS1	Boone Avenue Walls, THE BRONX
TKID	@TKID170	MANHATTAN
HOMESICK	@MAGICFOREVERLIVES	MANHATTAN
MIKE 171	@MIKE_171	QUEENS
STEFANO PHEN	@STEFAN0_PHEN	Graffiti Hall of Fame, MANHATTAN
BOONE AVENUE WALLS	@BOONEAVENUEWALLS	THE BRONX
SMART RIS	@SMART_RIS	MANHATTAN
RIME MSK	@RIME_MSK	Graffiti Hall of Fame, MANHATTAN
COPE 2	@MRCOPETWO	Graffiti Hall of Fame, MANHATTAN
SKEME	@SKEMETHREEYARDKING	Graffiti Hall of Fame, MANHATTAN
SAK	@SAK1_MBTEAM	Boone Avenue Walls, THE BRONX
CHAIN 3	@CHAIN3TMT	Graffiti Hall of Fame, MANHATTAN
RATH	@HEAVYLOX	Boone Avenue Walls, THE BRONX
PETER PAID	@PETERPAIDNYC	BROOKLYN

DE GRUPO	@DEGRUPO	BROOKLYN
OBE, KEOTOP	@COCOA_BUTTER_SUPREME, @THEEXVANDALS	Graffiti Hall of Fame, MANHATTAN
MERES ONE	@MERESONE	Graffiti Hall of Fame, MANHATTAN
NEV, KING BEE UW	@KINGBEEUW	Boone Avenue Walls, THE BRONX
SERVE, SAK, SHAME 125	@SAK1_MBTEAM, @SHAME_HARLEM125	Graffiti Hall of Fame, MANHATTAN
ROB CES PROVENZANO	@CES4WISH	Bushwick Collective, BROOKLYN
SOZE	@SOZE527	Graffiti Hall of Fame, MANHATTAN
SUCH RIS	@AKA_SUCH	BROOKLYN
GOOD TIMES CREW	@GOODTIMESCREW	BROOKLYN
DEZO	@DEZO_TC5_FC	Boone Avenue Walls, THE BRONX
SEN 2, HOACS, EPIC UNO	@SEN2FIGUEROA, HOACS, EPICUNO	Bushwick Collective, BROOKLYN
NWC CREW	@DGNWC1985	BROOKLYN
ZIM NWC	@DGNWC1985	BROOKLYN
THE LASH ONE, TOPAZ	@THE_LASH_ONE, @TOPAZFTR	BROOKLYN
BG 183 TATS CRU	@BG183TATSCRU	Boone Avenue Walls, THE BRONX

"SOCIAL JUSTICE" CHAPTER
(LISTED IN CHAPTER 2 PHOTO ORDER)

Artist(s)	Instagram	Event/Location
LEXI BELLA	@LEXIBELLAART	BROOKLYN
BIANCA ROMERO	@BIANCADOESNYC	First Street Green Art Park, MANHATTAN
AMIR DIOP	@DIOPSTUDIOS	MANHATTAN
LOUIS MICHEL	@LOUISMASAIMICHEL	First Street Green Art Park, MANHATTAN
DAVID HOLLIER	@DAVIDHOLLIERART	BROOKLYN
ONE RAD LATINA	@ONERADLATINA	MANHATTAN
PROJECT BARKADA, SAVIOR EL MUNDO LADY J DAY	@PROJECTBARKADA, @SAVIORELMUNDO, @LADYJDAY	MANAHATTAN
HEKTAD	@HEKTAD_OFFICIAL	MANHATTAN
KONSTANCE PATTON	@KENEEGOKESHEKSTUDIO	MANHATTAN
ZIMAD	@ZIMAD_ART	First Street Green Art Park, MANHATTAN
WORE ONE	@WORE_ONE	First Street Green Art Park, MANHATTAN
BUTTERFLY MUCH	@BUTTERFLYMUSH	First Street Green Art Park, MANHATTAN
AMIR DIOP	@DIOPSTUDIOS	MANHATTAN
CALICHO ART	@CALICHOART	First Street Green Art Park, MANHATTAN

V BALLENTINE	@VBALLENTINE99	First Street Green Art Park, MANHATTAN
SULE	@SULECANTCOOK	MANHATTAN
SARAH ERENTHAL	@SARAERENTHALART	MANHATTAN
PRAXIS	@PRAXIS_VGZ	First Street Green Art Park, MANHATTAN
ONE RAD LATINA	@ONERADLATINA	MANHATTAN
LEXI BELLA	@LEXIBELLAART	First Street Green Art Park, MANHATTAN
RAMIRO DAVARO COMAS	@RAMIROSTUDIOS	First Street Green Art Park, MANHATTAN
JAMES RUBIO AND HITOMI	@THEJAMESRUBIO, @HITOMIGIRLXYZ	MANHATTAN
MIKE 171 AND SJK 171	@MIKE_171, @SJK_171	First Street Green Art Park, MANHATTAN
MIKERAZ AND SMETSKYART	@MIKERAZ_, @SMETSKYART	MANHATTAN
GIRLTY	@ARTSY_GIRLTY	Freeman Alley, MANHATTAN
LEXI BELLA	@LEXIBELLAART	First Street Green Art Park, MANHATTAN
CALEB NEELON AND LENA MAC	@CALEBNEELONART, @_LENA_MAC_	Welling Court Mural Project, QUEENS
SCOOTER LA FORGE	@SCOOTERLAFORGE	MANHATTAN
V BALLENTINE, ESPARTACO ALBURNOZ ABREAU	@VBALLENTINE99, @KONOZCO	BROOKLYN
FRANK APE	@FRANK_APE	MANHATTAN

"STREET ART" CHAPTER
(LISTED IN CHAPTER 3 PHOTO ORDER)

Artist(s)	Instagram	Event/Location
DARREN DEGENOVA	@MRHYDDE_ARTIST	Bushwick Collective, BROOKLYN
HIRAKU	@HIRAKUNYC	Bushwick Collective, BROOKLYN
LEXI BELLA AND TRAP	@LEXIBELLAART, @TRAP.IF	Bushwick Collective, BROOKLYN
RIRI LAUREN	@BADGIRLRIRILAUREN	Bushwick Collective, BROOKLYN
OLGA	@OLGACORREA_ART	THE BRONX
IMAGINE	@IMAGINE876	Welling Court Mural Project, QUEENS
NYC HOOKER	@NYCHOOKER	Welling Court Mural Project, QUEENS
KATIE REIDY	@RARIGRAFIX	Welling Court Mural Project, QUEENS
PANIC RODRIGUEZ	@PANICRODRIGUEZ	Welling Court Mural Project, QUEENS
VANESSA KREYTAK AND ENZO	@VK.NYC.ART, @ENZOARTWORLD	Welling Court Mural Project, QUEENS
TOO FLY	@TOOFLY_NYC	Welling Court Mural Project, QUEENS
BC	@BC_NBA	Bed-Stuy Walls, BROOKLYN
ARTWORK BY KIR AND HUMBLE MAKES ART	@ARTWORK_BY_KIR	Bed-Stuy Walls, BROOKLYN
NICOSUAVALICIOUS, BUNS MSG, PEAT EYEZ, HEKTAD	@NICOSUAVALICIOUS, @ZOEGEN, @HEKTAD_OFFICIAL, @EYEZ	Bed-Stuy Walls, BROOKLYN

MINUS ONE	@MINVSKEI	Bushwick Collective, BROOKLYN
V BALLENTINE AND MARY AKPA	@VBALLENTINE99, @MARYAKPA	Bed-Stuy Walls, BROOKLYN
CALICHO ART	@CALICHOART	Freeman Alley, MANHATTAN
PHETUS	@PHETUS88	Bed-Stuy Walls, BROOKLYN
CAPTAIN EYELINER	@CAPTAIN_EYELINER	MANHATTAN
SCRATCH NYC	@SCRATCH_NYC	Boone Avenue Walls, THE BRONX
CHARLIE DOVE	@CHARLIEDOVESNYC	MANHATTAN
VEWER	@_VEWER_	MANHATTAN
DREW BORDERS AND BC	@DREWBORDERS.ART, @BC_NBA	Bed-Stuy Walls, BROOKLYN
EL SOULS	@SOULSNYC	Boone Avenue Walls, THE BRONX
SHIRO ONE	@SHIRO_ONE	Graffiti Hall Of Fame, MANHATTAN
MERES ONE	@MERESONE	Boone Avenue Walls, THE BRONX
SPOT KMS	@KMS_CREW	Boone Avenue Walls, THE BRONX
CYCLE IMOK	@CYCLE_IMOK	Boone Avenue Walls, THE BRONX
SOZE AND SILO	@SOZE527, @SILO_ONE	Boone Avenue Walls, THE BRONX
FUN QEST	@FUNQEST	Bed-Stuy Walls, BROOKLYN
HIERO VEIGA	@HIEROVEIGA	MANHATTAN

HOPS ART	@HOPSART_1	Bushwick Collective, BROOKLYN
HOPS ART	@HOPSART_1	Bushwick Collective, BROOKLYN
INDIE 184	@INDIE184	MANHATTAN
JACK EL DIABLO	@JAEKELDIABLO	Bed-Stuy Walls, BROOKLYN
GOLDEN 305	@GOLDEN305	Boone Avenue Walls, THE BRONX
JAPPY AGONCILLO	@JAPPYAGONCILLO	Bed-Stuy Walls, BROOKLYN
JEFF HENRIQUEZ	@JEFFHENRIQUEZART	First Street Green Art Park, MANHATTAN
CALICHO ART AND JEFF ROSE KING	@CALICHOART, @JEFFROSEKING	MANHATTAN
JORIT AND TUKIOS	@JORIT @TUKIOS_ART	MANHATTAN
JUNIOR GOMEZ	@JUNIORDESIGNS	Bed-Stuy Walls, BROOKLYN
MIKI MU	@MIKI_MU	Welling Court Mural Project, QUEENS
KOSUKE JAMES	@KOSUKEJAMES	Freeman Alley, MANHATTAN
LAMOUR SUPREME	@LAMOURSUPREME	MANHATTAN
LECRUE	@LECRUE_EYEBROWS	MANHATTAN
MANUEL ACEVEDO	@698MANUELACEVEDO	Boone Avenue Walls, THE BRONX
MISHA TYUTYUNIK	@MDOT_SEASON	MANHATTAN
SEBAR	@SEBAR7	THE BRONX

EL SOULS	@SOULSNYC	Boone Avenue Walls, THE BRONX
QUEEN ANDREA	@QUEENANDREAONE	Boone Avenue Walls, THE BRONX
MIKI MU, LEXI BELLA, CLAW MONEY	@MIKI_MU, @LEXIBELLAART, @CLAWMONEY	THE BRONX
MUEBON	@MUE_BON	FREEMAN ALLEY, MANHATTAN
MZ. ICAR	@MZ.ICAR	Bed-Stuy Walls, BROOKLYN
OLGA CORREA	@OLGACORREA_ART	Boone Avenue Walls, THE BRONX
OPTIMO NYC	@OPTIMONYC	MANHATTAN
OUTERSOURCE AND RATCHI	@OUTERSOURCE, @RATCHINYC	First Street Green Art Park, MANHATTAN
SERGIO BARRIOS	@ELHASE	First Street Green Art Park, MANHATTAN
PEACH TAO	@PEACHEEBLUE	Bed-Stuy Walls, BROOKLYN
PHETUS	@PHETUS88	Boone Avenue Walls, THE BRONX
JEFF HENRIQUEZ AND XTINA QUINONES	@JEFFHENRIQUEZART, @XTINAQUINONES	Bed-Stuy Walls, BROOKLYN
BITS	@BITS_PMA_ARTS	Boone Avenue Walls, THE BRONX
MUCHO	@PUNJABIKICHI	Boone Avenue Walls, THE BRONX
NAP DON'T SLEEP	@NAPDONTSLEEP	Bushwick Collective, BROOKLYN
QUEEN ANDREA	@QUEENANDREAONE	Boone Avenue Walls, THE BRONX
LA2	@LA2ART	First Street Green Art Park, MANHATTAN

RATH	@HEAVYLOX	Boone Avenue Walls, THE BRONX
RH DOAZ AND EMILIO FLORENTINE	@RHOAZ @EMILIOFLORENTINE	MANHATTAN
SCRATCH NYC	@SCRATCH_NYC	Bed-Stuy Walls, BROOKLYN
CARSON DE YOUNG	@DEPSONE	First Street Green Art Park, MANHATTAN
SEN 1 ORIGINAL AND COSA.V	@SEN1ORIGINAL, @COSA.V	Freeman Alley, MANHATTAN
EZRA CUMBO	@RAH_ARTZ	First Street Green Art Park, MANHATTAN
MATTO'	@MATT.OCONNER	Welling Court Mural Project, QUEENS
SHIRO ONE AND TOOFLY	@SHIRO_ONE, @TOOFLY_NYC_	Bed-Stuy Walls, BROOKLYN
SLOMO AND KRAM	@KRAM_BCN, @SLOMO29	First Street Green Art Park, MANHATTAN
EL SOULS	@SOULSNYC	Welling Court Mural Project, QUEENS
THE CREATOR	@MANUELALEJANDRO.NYC	MANHATTAN
TRASHER	@TRASHEER	BROOKLYN
TURTLE CAP	@TURTLECAPS	Freeman Alley, MANHATTAN
ADAM KIYOSHI FUJITA	@ADAMFU	Welling Court Mural Project, QUEENS
V BALLENTINE	@VBALLENTINE99	BROOKLYN
CAESAR PEREZ	@CZRPRZART	Bed-Stuy Walls, BROOKLYN
VEWER AND LOVE NOTES	@_VEWER_ , @LOVENOTES	MANHATTAN

CHUPA OLLIN CREW	@OLLIN_CREW_	BROOKLYN
SHIRO ONE AND AL RUIZ	@SHIRO_ONE, @CALL_HER_AL	First Street Green Art Park, MANHATTAN
SIENIDE	@SIENIDE	Boone Avenue Walls, THE BRONX
WEN COD	@WENCOD	THE BRONX
WILL POWER, AL DIAZ	@HIPHOPISMYRELIGION, @ALBERT_DIAZ1	Bed-Stuy Walls, BROOKLYN
IMSE 704	@IMSE704	Boone Avenue Walls, THE BRONX
SULE	@SULECANTCOOK	BROOKLYN
OUTERSOURCE AND MUEBON	@OUTERSOURCE, @MUEBON	BROOKLYN
CHY WALTON	@MITROOPER1	BROOKLYN
MERES ONE	@MERESONE	First Street Green Art Park, MANHATTAN
QUESTION MARKS AND AL DIAZ	@QUESTIONMARKS_OFFICIAL, @ALBERT_DIAZ1	Roof Top Graffiteria, QUEENS
SEK FINK	@SEKFINK	WELLING COURT MURAL PROJECT, QUEENS
KING BEE, BG183	@KINGBEEUW, @BG183TATSCRU	THE BRONX

"MURALS" CHAPTER
(LISTED IN CHAPTER 4 PHOTO ORDER)

Artist(s)	Instagram	Event/Location
ASHLEY HODDER	@ASHLEYHODDERART	Bushwick Collective, BROOKLYN
HOPS ART1	@HOPSART1	Bushwick Collective, BROOKLYN
HOPS ART1	@HOPSART1	Bushwick Collective, BROOKLYN
HOPS ART1	@HOPSART1	Bushwick Collective, BROOKLYN
KRO_79, ENJOY_HADS, SURE 78, BRANDY SML, SIX MILLION DOLLAR STEVE	@MR_MAKRO_79, @ENJOY_HADS, @SASHTOTHEMICHAEL, @BRANDY_SML	Bushwick Collective, BROOKLYN
SIPROS	@ENJOY_HADS, @SASHTOTHEMICHAEL, @BRANDY_SML	Bushwick Collective, BROOKLYN
HEKTAD	@HEKTAD_OFFICIAL	MANHATTAN
KOBRA	@KOBRASTREETART	BROOKLYN
ALEC MONOPLY	@ALECMONOPLY	MANHATTAN
ANDRE TRENIER	@ANDRE.TRENIER	Bed-Stuy Walls, BROOKLYN
BEN ANGOTTI	@ANGOTTI81	MANHATTAN
RIIISA BOOGIE	@RIIISABOOGIE	MANHATTAN

BROLGA	@BROLGA	MANHATTAN
COREY PAYNE	@COREYPANEART	Bushwick Collective, BROOKLYN
DANIELLE MASTRION	@DANIELLEBKNYC	BROOKLYN
TODD GRAY	@TODDGRAYSTUDIOS	MANHATTAN
DRAGON 76	@DRAGON76ART	MANHATTAN
ELLE STREET ART	@ELLESTREETART	MANHATTAN
RIIISA BOOGIE	@RIIISABOOGIE	MANHATTAN
GARDEN OF JOURNEY	@GARDENOFJOURNEY	MANHATTAN
JULES MUCK	@JULESMUCK	Welling Court Mural Project, QUEENS
KOBRA	@KOBRASTREETART	MANHATTAN
JASON NAYLOR	@JASONNAYLOR	MANHATTAN
KING BEE	@KINGBEEUW	THE BRONX
TYMON DE LAAT	@TYMONDELAAT	Bushwick Collective, BROOKLYN
MZ.ICAR	@MZ.ICAR	BROOKLYN

KOBRA	@KOBRASTREETART	MANHATTAN
TATS CRU	@TATSCRU	MANHATTAN
ZACH CURTIS AND DANNY CORTES	@ZACHCURTISARTWORK, @DANNYCORTESNYC	Bushwick Collective, BROOKLYN
MATE ARTIST	@MATEARTIST	Bushwick Collective, BROOKLYN
MISTERALEK AND TANK ONE	@MISTERALEK, @TANKONE	Bushwick Collective, BROOKLYN
KOBRA	@KOBRASTREETART	MANHATTAN
NYCTHRIVE GROUP	@NYCTHRIVE	Bed-Stuy Walls, BROOKLYN
PHETUS	@PHETUS88	First Street Green Art Park, MANHATTAN
BMIKE AND MARTHA LICIA	@BMIKE2C, @MARTHALICIA	MANHATTAN
RIIISA BOOGIE	@RIIISABOOGIE	MANHATTAN
RIIISA BOOGIE	@RIIISABOOGIE	MANHATTAN
OSGEMEOS	@OSGEMEOS	MANHATTAN
TATS CRU	@TATSCRU	Graffiti Hall Of Fame, MANHATTAN
ZIMER	@ZIMERNYC	MANHATTAN

V BALLENTINE	@VBALLENTINE99	Bushwick Collective, BROOKLYN
THRIVE COLLECTIVE	@NYCTHRIVE	BROOKLYN
DANIELLE MASTRION	@DANIELLEBKNYC	BROOKLYN
ALBERTUS JOSEPH	@ALBERTUSJOSEPH	Boone Avenue Walls, THE BRONX
VEXTA	@VEXTA	MANHATTAN
SHIRO ONE	@SHIRO_ONE	MANHATTAN
SEPC	@SPEC_	Bushwick Collective, BROOKLYN
STICKY MONGER	@STICKYMONGER	MANHATTAN
TATS CRU	@TATSCRU	Graffiti Hall Of Fame, MANHATTAN
BAD GIRL RIRI LAUREN	@BADGIRLRIRILAUREN	Bushwick Collective, BROOKLYN
DANIELLE MASTRION	@DANIELLEBKNYC	MANHATTAN
DAVID PUCK	@DAVIDPUCKARTIST	MANHATTAN
KMS CREW	@KMS_CREW	Bushwick Collective, BROOKLYN
WANE, EL SOUL, STASH, DEPOH, EPIC UNO, CHRIS RWK	@WANECOD, @SOULSNYC, @MR_STASH @DEPOH, @EPICUNO, @CHRISRWK	Welling Court Mural Project, QUEENS

URBAN RUBEN	@URBANRUBEN	Bushwick Collective, BROOKLYN
SKEME, ANDRE TRENIER, CHAIN 3, KADE	@SKEME3YARDKING, @KADETMT, @ANDRE.TRENIER, @CHAIN3TMT	Boone Avenue Walls, THE BRONX
KOBRA	@KOBRASTREETART	MANHATTAN
SHANE GRAMMER	@SHANEGRAMMERARTS	Bushwick Collective, BROOKLYN
SHIRO ONE, KAY LOVE, MIA, EROTICA, JAKEE, AIRIS	@SHIRO_ONE, @KAYLOVEBX, @MIA_UNKWN1, @EROTICA67, @AIRISUNIVERSE, @ALLCITY_LEGENDS	Boone Avenue Walls, THE BRONX
ALEC MONOPOLY	@ALECMONOPOLY	MANHATTAN

ABOUT THE AUTHOR

Kurt Boone, a New York–based writer, poet, and photographer, focuses on urban street cultures and has authored over 30 books, with works in prestigious collections like MoMA and the Schomburg Center. He's documented NYC street art since 2018, exhibited his photography, appeared on *PBS Metro Focus*, and contributes to *Up Magazine*. He lives in Newark, New Jersey. *Photograph courtesy of Ronald Herard*

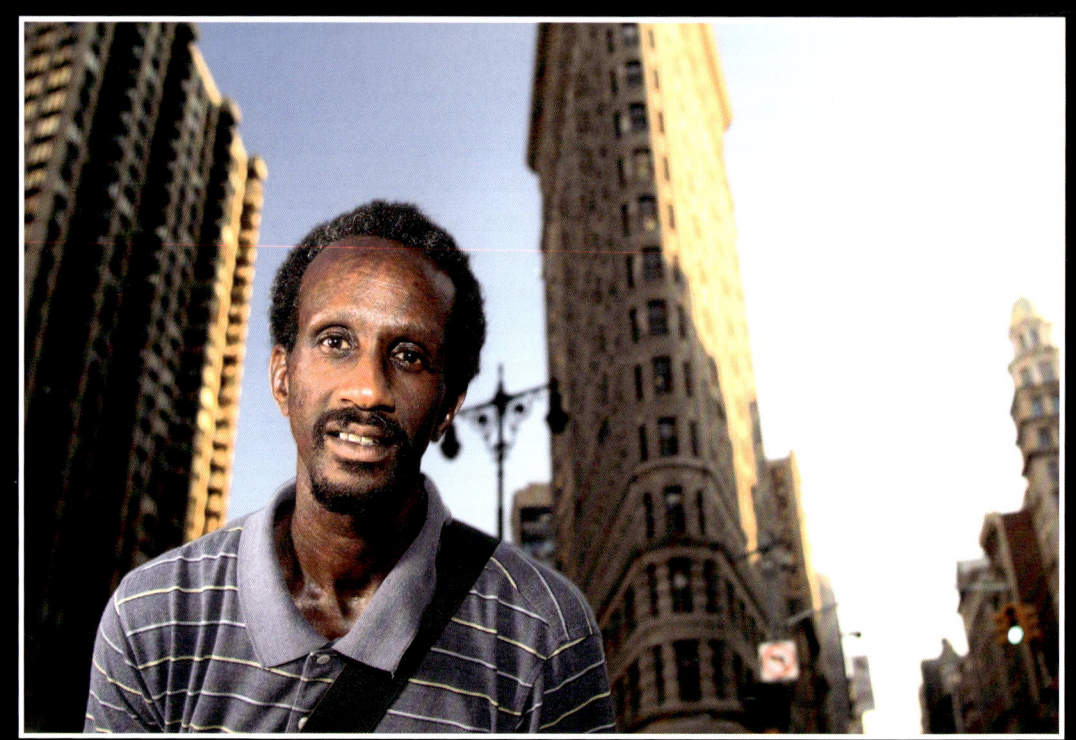

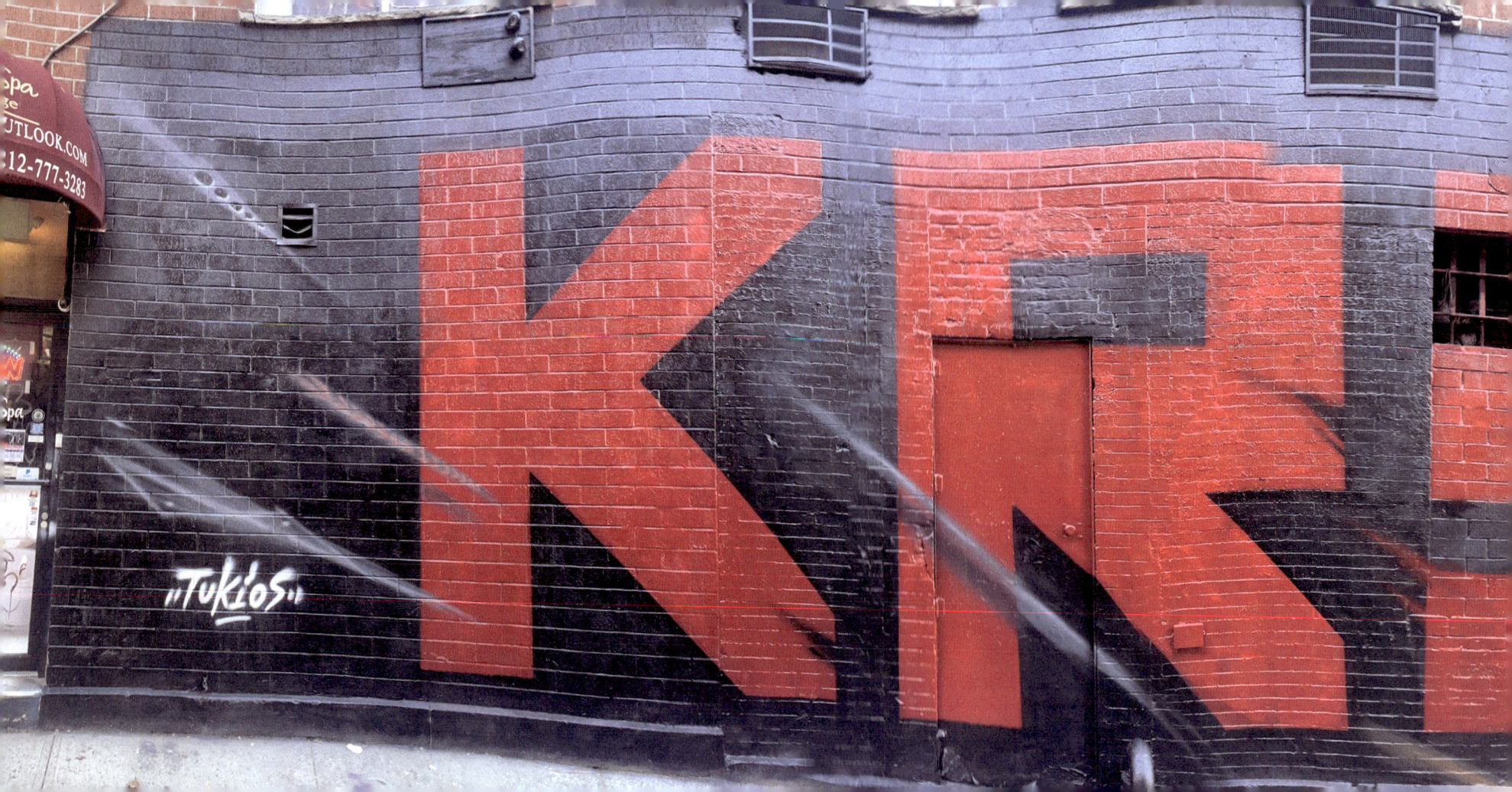